STEVIE RAY VAUGHAN

JOE NICK PATOSKI AND BILL CRAWFORD

STEVIE RAY VAUGHAN

caught in the crossfire

LITTLE, BROWN AND COMPANY

BOSTON NEW YORK TORONTO LONDON

FIRST PAPERBACK EDITION

Frontispiece photograph by W. A. Williams

Library of Congress Cataloging-in-Publication Data

Patoski, Joe Nick.
    Stevie Ray Vaughan : caught in the crossfire / by Joe Nick Patoski
and Bill Crawford.
        p.   cm.
    Includes index.
    ISBN 0-316-16068-7 (hc)
    ISBN 0-316-16069-5 (pb)
    1. Vaughan, Stevie Ray. 2. Rock musicians—United States—
Biography. I. Crawford, Bill. II. Title.
    ML419.V25P37 1993
    787.87'166'092—dc20
    [B]   92-38924

10 9 8 7 6 5 4 3 2 1

MV-NY

Designed by Barbara Werden

Published simultaneously in Canada by
Little, Brown & Company (Canada) Limited

PRINTED IN THE UNITED STATES OF AMERICA

contents

STEVIE RAY VAUGHAN

1

DON'T TOUCH MY GUITAR

Looking over his shoulder to make sure his big brother was gone, eleven-year-old Steve Vaughan stepped quietly toward the closet door of the bedroom he shared with his only sibling. As he reached for the doorknob, he paused for a moment, tingling with a guilty thrill for the pleasure he was about to experience. He opened the door and looked inside. There they were — the forbidden objects of pleasure — an electric guitar and an amplifier. Steve walked in, plugged the guitar into the amplifier, turned on the amp, and sat down. He felt the instrument come alive in his hands.

It was a forbidden thrill, all right. Nothing else came close. Rub and stroke the wood and wires just right, and every wish was at your command. Cradling the long skinny end in the palm of his left hand, he wrapped his fingers around the neck, pressed his fingertips on the thick strands of wire, grinding them against the thin metal fret bars. He ran the fingers of his right hand across the strings above the fat part of the hardwood body. After a little practice, the handiwork could coax sounds out of the instrument that transformed it into a transcendent spiritual machine, a vehicle that could transport him to strange and distant places far from this place called Oak Cliff, far from all the hassles, rules, frustrations that went with being a kid.

This guitar, it did things to his head. Made him forget about Mamma and Daddy, even made him forget about Jimmie, his big brother and the best guitar player in all of Dallas. Just blocked it all out. Steve didn't think about his friends down the block or his enemies, especially the mean kids who called him Tomato Nose. Picking out notes on the strings, singing the melodies under his breath to help figure out the tough parts, Steve worked so intensely that he forgot the teachers, the principal, church, the long, languid heat of the summer that seemed to go on forever, the smell of pork and beans from the Van Camp's plant around the corner, his little teeth, the mysterious sensation of feeling shy around people but still wanting to please them. Everything.

Hook the magic instrument up to an electric amplifier and the sounds not only got louder, they became fuzzier, gnarlier, weirder, wilder, and as strange and far out as you wanted to get, depending on what you knew and what you did with what you knew. Like that tune that went, "Get high, everybody, get high." It was on the record album by the Nightcaps that Jimmie used to play over and over all the time. They were Dallas boys who all wore fancy sparkling blue tuxedos on the album cover and played down-and-dirty blues. Or the new records Jimmie was bringing home by all those bands from England, or the latest LP by Jimmy Reed. Didn't matter what it was or whether Jimmie would let him even touch them. He couldn't stop Steve from hearing them so many times that he learned all the guitar sounds by heart. More than anything, he loved playing guitar. Almost as much as his big brother did. He told anyone who asked and many who didn't that someday he was going to play guitar in a band, too, just like Jimmie.

His meditation in the closet had taken him to some snow-capped mountains where the air was pure and the sound was crisp, when it was broken by the sound of the closet doorknob being turned. He had been in such a trance that he hadn't heard the slamming of the front door and the footsteps coming down the hall. Dang. He squinted at the light. It was Jimmie, with some friend of his. Jimmie looked pissed, as usual. The friend looked amused. Steve cowered, holding up his arms defensively, waiting for the hit.

WHOMP.

It was a hard right to his left shoulder, but it only hurt for a few seconds.

The words hurt worse.

"I told you, goddammit, don't touch my guitar."

The boy hesitated momentarily, then ran through the bedroom and into the kitchen. He waited until he heard footsteps again.

The front door slammed. Then he heard car doors open and shut and an engine rev up, followed by the squeal of tires on the pavement. He was safe now. He opened the door. He looked down the hall and peeked out the front window. The coast was clear. He tiptoed back into the bedroom and opened the closet door. The cord that connected the guitar to the amplifier was still plugged in. He reentered the closet, picked up the instrument, and once again made it sing.

You could say it was in his blood, stretching back half a century to the time when both sides of the boys' family first planted their roots in the black gumbo soil of northeast Texas. The music part was understandable. Someone or another in the family always had a guitar or some other instrument to play around the house. He'd heard the stories about Grandmother Laura Belle LaRue Vaughan and the player piano she had in her living room, and how her children gathered on warm nights and Sundays to sing church songs and popular standards of the day. The determination that was etched on young Steve's face when he tried to learn how to play guitar was a trait that could be traced back to Laura Belle's daddy, Robert Hodgen LaRue, a deeply spiritual man with an air of mysticism imparted by his long, flowing beard and his uncanny gift for grafting exotic plants. Relatives and neighbors still spoke in awe about the Japanese persimmon tree in his backyard that bore fruit as big as grapefruit. The old man, they marveled, had the touch.

Robert LaRue packed his family and their meager belongings in a covered wagon in 1890, moving them from Kentucky to Terrell, a small town in Rockwall County thirty-three miles due east of Dallas, in the heart of what was then the most productive cotton-growing region in the United States. That was about the same time James Robert and Sarah Catherine Vaughan arrived in the area after leaving their home in Fulton County, Arkansas, in search of opportunity. Their collective lives crossed when Robert's daughter Laura Belle LaRue and Vaughan's ruggedly handsome son, Thomas Lee, met, fell in love, and declared their devotion to God and each other by getting married. On July 13, 1902, they were wed by the pronouncement of I. N. Crutchfield, Ordained Minister of the Gospel.

The young couple moved onto a piece of land in southwestern Rockwall County known as the Griffith League. Like most other tillers on the blackland prairie, the Vaughans were sharecroppers, poor tenant farmers who paid their rent with "thirds and fourths" of the cotton and grain they raised, scraping by on whatever surplus remained. Laura Belle Vaughan bore her husband nine children, eight of whom survived infancy, including the twins, Jimmie Lee and Linnie Vee, who were born on September 6, 1921. Seven years later, their father, Thomas Lee, passed away from Bright's disease, an illness of the kidneys. He left his wife and eight children to earn their living from the soil at the onset of the Great Depression, when hard times got even harder.

Steve remembered his dad telling him about growing up on the farm, the agony of stooping over in the hot sun to pick cotton off the bolls all day long, helping his older brothers raise potatoes, pinto beans, and hogs for the family table. But Big Jim never did tell his boys much about what his brothers and sisters called his own natural ear for a melody, and how he could play "Tiger Rag" on the piano like no one else in the family.

Jimmie Lee Vaughan liked to talk about seeing the world in the Navy, and how proud he was to have served his country by enlisting at the onset of World War Two. The way he described it, dropping out of school at age sixteen seemed almost beside the point. A high school diploma didn't mean much on the front lines in the South Pacific, maybe just about as much as it meant to a future guitar man. The war actually turned out to be a character builder for Jimmie Lee. He returned a full-grown adult, ready to seek his own fortune in the bright lights of Dallas. He landed a job as one of the smiling, necktied attendants at a 7-Eleven, America's pioneer convenience-store chain, founded in the heart of Oak Cliff, right across the Trinity River from downtown Dallas, where the flying red neon horse atop the Mobil building ruled over the sprawling metropolis.

"We Gladly Give Curb Service" was the motto the creators of 7-Eleven had coined in the late forties. It was the motivating force behind Jim Vaughan's job. Whenever an automobile pulled up to the front of the building and honked its horn, Jim answered the call by racing outside and greeting the driver with a smile and a tip of his hat. He would take the order for bread, milk, eggs, ice, soft drinks, cigarettes, or beer, sprint inside to collect the requested items, and deliver them to the waiting motorist along with a bill. It was certainly a novel way of shopping. The job and the company had potential, Jim Vaughan was convinced, if only he could stick with it long enough.

His future climb up the 7-Eleven ladder, which could have eventually led all the way to the high-rise corporate towers of the Southland Corporation, one of Dallas's business giants before reckless expenditures made it an easy takeover by a Japanese holding company, was deterred by one Martha Jean Cook.

Martha was a particularly loyal customer of some means and independence. After all, Jim observed, she was driving her own car. And she was a looker to boot. Martha had a lot in common with Jim Vaughan. The families of both her father, Joseph Luther Cook, and her mother, Dora Ruth Deweese, farmed cotton in northeast Texas. Joe L. and Ruth were high school sweethearts who tied the knot shortly before Joe L. hired on with the Lone Star Gas Company in the boomtown of Eastland, 126 miles west of Dallas near the extremely productive Ranger oil field. In 1940, Joe L. was promoted to foreman and moved back to the Dallas area with his wife and five children. They settled down in Cockrell Hill, an incorporated community adjacent to the Oak Cliff part of Dallas. It was a good life. The family lived simply but comfortably. "My father was easygoin'," remembered Martha's brother, Joe Cook, known to the family as Joe Boy. "I never heard my mother and dad holler at each other."

Martha was the eldest of the Cook children. After graduating from Sunset High School and having her share of youthful romances, she worked as a secretary at the Grove Lumber Company in Oak Cliff. It was on her daily drive home that she fell into the habit of dropping by Jim Vaughan's 7-Eleven for an Eskimo Pie. Just as advertised, the store's location was certainly convenient. So was the store policy of serving customers from the comfort of their automobile. But truth be told, Martha wasn't really that big on 7-Eleven or Eskimo Pies. It was the man who brought the frozen confections to her that struck her fancy.

She needed to look no farther than his arms. They were as much an attraction as the sight of a well-turned ankle would be to a man. Jim Vaughan's massive, thick forearms and bulging biceps were nothing short of remarkable as far as Martha was concerned. Anyone could tell that they were strong enough to heave a hundred-pound block of ice, or lead a pretty young lady effortlessly across a crowded dance floor. When Jim was transferred to another store in Oak Cliff, Martha Jean changed the route she took driving home from work so those same strong arms would bring her more Eskimo Pies. Jim Vaughan took note of his loyal customer, her sweet smile, her engaging conversation. So he summoned up the courage and asked her out for a date.

Though their family backgrounds were similar, Jim Vaughan and Martha Cook quickly discovered their personalities were very different. He was gruff, temperamental, and physical (the arms should have been the tip-off). Sometimes, when he took to drinking at one of the lounges off Beckley Avenue, or at some of the shadier, rougher haunts along Industrial Boulevard across the Trinity, he'd get so worked up screaming and hollering that he'd lose his voice. Martha, on the other hand, was a proper woman, quiet and reserved.

They found common ground on the dance floor, where they spent many weekend nights, especially when one of their favorite swing or western bands was providing the entertainment at Pappy's Showland, the Winter Garden, the Longhorn, or any one of a dozen ballrooms in the area. Jim quickly learned how to get a rise out of Martha. Whenever her favorite western swing band, Hank Thompson and His Brazos Valley Boys, from Waco, were in town for an engagement, he'd gently poke her and ask, "You gonna go out and see your boyfriend tonight?" As long as those big strong arms were leading her around the wooden floor that was made smooth and slick with sawdust, Martha Cook would take all the ribbing that Jim cared to dish out.

The couple decided to make their relationship whole in the eyes of

God and his Son the Lord Jesus Christ and exchanged wedding vows on January 13, 1950. Burdened with new responsibilities, Jim opted to quit car-hopping at the 7-Eleven in favor of something more secure. With his older brother's help, he lined up a steady-paying job as a member of the Asbestos Workers Union Local 21 in Dallas. Union members worked construction projects building power plants, refineries, and office buildings across the South, insulating pipes and ducts with fiberglass and cork, troweling on a mixture of calcium silicate and ground asbestos known as "mud." At the time, neither Jim Vaughan nor his 250 union brothers gave a moment's thought to the potential health risks of working with ground asbestos, something that wouldn't become public knowledge for another thirty years. All he knew was that the job gave him the financial security he needed to raise a family.

His timing couldn't have been much better. On March 20, 1951, Martha Vaughan gave birth to her first child in the Florence Nightingale ward of the Baylor Medical Center. Even though he arrived two weeks past his due date, Jimmie Lawrence Vaughan was a tiny newborn who weighed only 5 pounds and measured 17½ inches in length. He was named for his father and the doctor who delivered him. Three and a half years later, on October 3, 1954, Jimmie's brother was born at Methodist Hospital. He, too, arrived two weeks late, and was even smaller than his brother, weighing a mere 3 pounds, 9¼ ounces, and measuring 17½ inches long. He was so tiny that he spent the first three weeks of his life in the hospital as a precautionary measure. Martha noticed that his coloring was different from Jimmie's. His light red hair came from her side of the family. Jim and Martha didn't decide on a name for their second son until it came time to fill out a birth certificate. She named the baby Stephen Ray Vaughan because she thought it sounded nice.

Early on, the boys lived like gypsies. Jim followed construction jobs across Texas, Arkansas, Louisiana, and Mississippi, bringing his family with him. "Stevie and I grew up all over the South," Jimmie later recalled with little fondness. "I mean we lived in thirty houses when we were growing up, or more." The unsettled lifestyle was particularly hard on his little brother. After one stretch on the road that lasted several months, Steve spied his uncle Joe Boy Cook standing in the driveway, ready to welcome him back home with a big hug. The first words that tumbled out of his mouth said it all: "I don't like the country."

Jim Vaughan eventually was able to work jobs closer to Dallas, and the family purchased a small, neat frame house on Glenfield Street in Oak Cliff. It was a modest home, but a decided improvement on Jim's boyhood home. Installing asbestos was demanding, physical labor that left Jim drained and spent when the five-o'clock whistle blew. To relax, he drank. Sometimes he drank too much. And when he drank too much, he turned into a real bear capable of terrorizing his wife, his boys, his friends, anyone within shouting range of his voice. Martha tried to shield the children from her husband's volatile temper, but his outbursts helped feed young Steve's insecurities. He was deathly afraid to be left alone.

Uncle Joe Boy Cook realized this when Martha asked him to look after her boy in the grocery store. "Just don't let that kid get out of your sight," she warned. "He just goes crazy."

Joe's curiosity got the best of him. Would Steve really go crazy or was that just his mama talking?

"He was going along and I got to the end of the aisle. I jumped around the corner to where he couldn't see me and I was peeking around. He looked this way and looked that way and screamed. And I thought, 'Darn, she's right.' And I felt real bad for playing that trick on him."

Being scared was bad enough. Steve realized early on what it was like to be an ugly duckling. His big brother had jet black hair, a pug nose, and a cute smile. All the kinfolk called him handsome. Steve was all legs and arms, had a scrawny physique and a face dominated by a mashed nose, never mind the smile that revealed tiny teeth and big gums. The nose was courtesy of a surgeon who performed a rhinoplasty operation on the six-year-old boy to relieve a painful sinus condition that sometimes made it difficult for Steve to breathe.

"The old guy didn't believe in straightening out your nose," said Uncle Joe Boy Cook, who underwent a similar surgical procedure. "He went up there and reamed it out, you know. He went on a theory that you cut it out like a horse, because a horse was made to run." Years after Steve "had the gravel removed from his driveway," as his doctor described the operation, his speech still sounded labored, as if he was holding his nose. It did little to help his self-confidence.

The only time Steve seemed to be really comfortable was when he was around music. He enjoyed going over to visit his redheaded cousin Connie Trent and laughed as she tried to learn dance steps from his uncle Preston. Oftentimes, Jim and Martha had company over for an evening social. Friends, relatives, and Jim's fellow asbestos workers would come over to play forty-two, eighty-four, Nello, and Lowboy and other domino games. The loud clacks of the ivories slapped on the table were accompanied by music coming from the record player or strummed on a guitar that someone had brought along. The Vaughan family loved music. A distant relative, Charles LaRue, blew trombone with the Tommy Dorsey Band. The boys' older cousins, Sammy and J. L. "Red" Klutts, played drums and guitar and bass in several western bands in the Dallas area. Martha's brothers, Joe and Jerrel Cook, were partial to picking out songs by Hank Williams and Merle Travis on guitar.

For all the melodic sounds constantly swirling around them, the

Vaughan boys discovered music by accident. Jimmie loved to show off his flattop haircut to neighborhood kids while riding around on his bicycle, listening to the radio he'd rigged on the handlebars. But he didn't contemplate playing music instead of just listening to it until he broke his collarbone trying to play football. While laid up at home, a friend of Jim's named Steve Stevenson, who was the father of a rock-and-roll musician named Robert Louis Stevenson, gave Jimmie a guitar with three strings.

"Play this," he said jokingly. "It won't hurt you."

"I was at home for about a month and I just started farting around with it," Jimmie would later explain. "Just one thing led to another."

From the first notes he plunked out, it was clear that Jimmie wasn't just gifted, he was a certified prodigy. "He made up three songs the first day," his little brother later recalled proudly. "He didn't have to try. It just came out."

When Steve Stevenson dropped by the Vaughans' a few days later, Jimmie showed him what he'd learned. Stevenson was so impressed that he took back the guitar, had it repaired and restrung, and presented it to the twelve-year-old. Jimmie held it in his hands and proceeded from there. No one, not even his mother, could get him to put down the instrument. "It was just like he played it all his life," Martha Vaughan marveled. "He picked it up and he started playing."

This development did not go unnoticed by young Steve Vaughan. It was the classic big brother/little brother symbiosis, or, as Stevie Ray later described it, the "Wow, me too!" syndrome. Once, after he'd seen Jimmie try to play a neighbor's drums, he fashioned a set of his own out of shoe boxes and pie pans, banging on them with clothes hangers for drumsticks. When Jimmie dabbled with a saxophone, Steve grabbed it when he wasn't looking and tried to play it, though he couldn't coax more than a few squeaks out of it. The guitar, though, was easier to figure out. All he had to do was watch Jimmie. "Just the thought of him playing made me want to jump up and play," he recalled.

For Christmas, Martha and Jim bought their youngest son a toy guitar, a Masonite model from Sears decorated with cowboys, horses, and other Wild West decals. The boys looked so cute with their pint-sized instruments that Martha and Jim photographed them standing in front of the family's Airline stereo speakers pretending that they were prepubescent music stars.

The boys, though, didn't think they were pretending at all. Steve was stubborn in his determination to get music out of his instrument, which he didn't regard as a toy at all. "It wouldn't tune," he said. "So we took half the strings off and struck it like a bass, tuning it down."

Martha and Jim encouraged their little guitar pickers, egging them on to play at family reunions and in front of guests at house parties.

Jimmie was the focus of the family pride. He was older and had quickly shown promise with an uncanny ability to hear a tune and pick it out himself, sounding just like the original. The tagalong little brother, stumbling after his sibling like an eager puppy dog, went largely unnoticed by the eyes and ears riveted on Jimmie. But everything Jimmie was absorbing, Steve was absorbing, too. In fact, he had a decided edge, though no one knew it at the time. Jimmie didn't have the instructional side benefit of a prodigy to emulate. Steve did. "We didn't pay much attention to him," Martha Vaughan said with candor. "Then all of a sudden he was playing, too. After he started playing, he just never quit."

Steve made do with Jimmie's hand-me-downs, gifts he received whenever Jim and Martha bought Jimmie a new guitar. When Jimmie graduated to a Gibson ES-300, Steve finally got to hold Jimmie's first electric guitar, a three-quarter-scale Gibson Messenger ES-125T, without fear of getting pounded. Both Gibsons were major investments. The Vaughans had enough money to live on, what with Martha supplementing Jim's income by doing clerical work. That afforded them a house, a car, and a pickup but theirs was by no means a lavish lifestyle. Daddy didn't need to lecture them about treating the guitars as more than playthings.

Whatever their shortcomings as parents might have been, Jim and Martha understood music and the powerful effect it worked on people. Singalongs were among their respective family traditions. Dancing to music, especially live music, remained an inexhaustible fount of pleasure, one of the reasons Jim and Martha stayed in love. It didn't take a rocket scientist to recognize their boys had a way with music, what with the way they could play them ol' guitars. If they wanted to live it, breathe it, wallow in it day and night, hide in their bedroom all day and night listening to records and trying to imitate what they were hearing, let them. It was damn sure a better way of making a living than sweating in a damp crawl space that's 120 degrees in the middle of August, slapping asbestos mud on any surface that would hold it.

Many nights Martha Vaughan would crack the door of their bedroom and see her two boys fast asleep, their instruments cradled in their arms. If the boys could make others feel as good as Hank Thompson and His Brazos Valley Boys made Jim and Martha feel, it was only right to help out as much as possible.

In his dreams, preferably with a guitar in his hands, ten-year-old Steve forgot about sibling rivalry, temper tantrums, fits of rage, and feeling ugly. In his dreams, his world was populated by characters with exotic names like Howlin' Wolf, Muddy Waters, Johnny Ace, and Bobby "Blue" Bland who wove magical musical fairy tales by conjuring images like he'd never heard before.

Smokestack lightning. Got my mojo working. Meet me in the bottoms. Turn on your lovelight.

Maybe he couldn't see them, but the language, the stories that they wove, the raw sounds that drove these bizarre tellings of lowdown lust, bravado, bad luck, and pain were so direct, so sharp in image and detail, that comic books seemed tame. Even color television could not compare to the exotic music these personalities manufactured.

The sounds entered his consciousness through the small white earplug of a transistor radio hidden under his pillow. This simple amusement accessory, one of the first electronic consumer items imported in mass quantity at a ridiculously cheap price from Japan to the United States following World War Two, introduced Steve Vaughan to the forbidden world of the Big Beat: an enticing mixed bag of rhythm and blues and rock and roll that crisscrossed the skies and filled the Texas ether in the early sixties.

Between the records, there were disc jockeys, as colorful and cryptic as the musical artists they featured. "Owwwwwwww," howled Wolfman Jack from XERF as he hustled baby chicks, pep-up pills, and rhythm-and-blues records. There was Art Roberts on WLS in Chicago, a low-key hipster who spun all the latest Top 40 releases. John R and Hoss Allen, on Nashville's WLAC, delved in a darker shade of music and sales pitch, spinning and hawking the latest B. B. King and Jimmy Reed records, available by mail order from Randy's Record Shop in Gallatin, Tennessee.

The local Dallas equivalents were even more influential on the kids from Oak Cliff. John R had nothing on Jim Lowe, the mellifluous-voiced host of Kats Karavan, a nightly rhythm-and-blues program that first aired in April 1954 on WRR, a station owned by the city of Dallas. The color of the announcer's skin was the only thing white about Kats Karavan, who kicked off every show with the rousing "All Nite Long" by the Rusty Bryant Band, frequently followed by the careening instrumental guitar masterwork "Okie Dokie Stomp" by a Texas native who went by the colorful name of Clarence "Gatemouth" Brown. Typical Kats Karavan fare included doo-wop songs by the Drifters, the Clovers, and the Spaniels, the familiar midnight moan of Jimmy Reed and his slow-and-sweet-as-molasses harmonica, the unfathomable musings of Sam "Lightnin' " Hopkins from Houston, and the cool finger-popping swing sounds of Johnny "Guitar" Watson, also out of Houston, Ted Taylor, and Roscoe Gordon.

During daylight hours, Steve Vaughan could eavesdrop on a purer version of the black experience on KNOK. Rhyming, jiving disc jockeys like the Mad Lad appealed specifically to black listeners in Elizabeth Chapel, Fair Park, the Bottoms, Stop Six, Como, and other ethnic communities in north central Texas who woke up each morning to a cover version of Sonny Boy Williamson's "Wake Up, Baby" by a local white boy named Delbert McClinton.

Then there was KLIF, the Mighty Eleven Ninety, Dallas's most popular radio station. Most of the records KLIF played were of a rock-and-roll nature, but given the huge popularity of black rhythm and blues and soul music among north Texas whites, it was not unusual to hear a KLIF double play of Bill Doggett's "Honky Tonk" followed by Slim Harpo's "Scratch My Back," or "Linda Lu," the timeless shuffle by Fort Worth's Ray Sharpe segued into Tommy Tucker's deep-slurred reading of "High Heel Sneakers." It all sounded both fitting and logical, since it was a time when a radio station like KLIF tried to be all things to all people rather than appealing to a particular demographic niche. When the British rock invasion introduced bands like the Rolling Stones, Cream, and the Yardbirds who were doing jumped-up, electrified cover versions of American blues music, KLIF stayed in the forefront with personalities like Jimmy Rabbit, a hep cat so in tune with the latest trends that he drew his own crowds of rabid teens whenever he made a personal appearance.

Radio was more than a cue, an audio finger pointing Steve Vaughan toward the musical moon. It was a siren's call that transcended restrooms and drinking-water fountains labeled WHITES ONLY or COLORED. It busted the line of segregation that stated Negroes must live in their own neighborhoods and attend their own schools. The cross burnings in Oak Cliff, the bombings of black families in South Dallas, the nigger jokes that his family members told could not counterbalance what Steve heard on the radio. Feelings cut across color lines. The Beatles were a pretty good band. But hey, "nigger music," as white Oak Cliff kids called it, made the Beatles sound like shit.

The radio was just the start of the learning process. In order to learn how to play guitar, in order to transport himself more easily into his own personal, private guitar heaven, Steve needed something more, something that he could sit with and study. When Uncle Joe Boy Cook gave Jimmie his first amplifier, a Silvertone model with a ten-inch speaker, Steve noticed that Joe Boy threw in a Chet Atkins guitar book. He heard him tell his brother he better look over the book good.

"If you don't learn this finger-picking style, you ain't gonna amount to a hill of beans," Joe Boy told Jimmie.

Steve watched closely while his older brother tried to follow his uncle's advice. He never got farther than two pages into the book. Learning from the printed page was too slow, he said. Steve knew exactly what Jimmie was talking about. He liked Jimmie's improvised system better. Saturdays, Jimmie headed down to the Top Ten Record Shop on Jefferson, where he purchased his version of study books, the latest 45 RPM records for ninety-eight cents apiece. Back home, Steve watched Jimmie slap the little record with the big hole on the turntable, playing it over and over and over again, slowing down the speed of the record until he could make out every single note. Jimmie tried to repeat what he heard on his guitar, fumbling around with his fingers, searching for the right note on the fretboard. He was oblivious to his kid brother standing right beside him, pestering him to show him what he had just learned. If he felt kindly toward him, Jimmie would pause to demonstrate a chord or a note. But Steve bugged him. He just got in the way. If the little squirt wanted to learn how to play guitar, he'd just have to pick it up himself.

"He taught me how to teach myself," remembered Stevie. "And that's the right way."

Just look at the Nightcaps. They were one of dozens of neighborhood teen bands surfacing around Dallas at the time. They may have been white, but they all dug R&B and picked up a lot of tricks from a flashy black guitarist named Royal Earl. With a little practice and a lot of balls, the Nightcaps made a whole album of the music they liked, not just a 45 single. In the process they irrevocably altered the lives of thousands of impressionable Texas teens, among them two boys named Steve Miller and Boz Scaggs who attended the elite St. Marks prep school in North Dallas and who founded a popular band called the Marksmen.

The Nightcaps' title tune, lifted from an old blues chant by a veteran Dallas blues performer named Li'l Son Jackson, celebrated drinking — at school, even — in a way that no one before had articulated, galvanizing a generation bent on wallowing in forbidden thoughts and unspoken sins long before sex and drugs became accepted integral elements of the culture fostered by rock and roll. "Wine, Wine, Wine" was so with it that old Jim Lowe, the Kats Karavan disc jockey, broke the color barrier and made the Nightcaps the first local white act he'd ever featured on his show.

For Steve and his big brother, the Nightcaps were the entrance exam that got them into blues school. Once they learned the repertoire that included blues-inflected songs like "Thunderbird," "I Got My Mojo Working," "24 Hours," and "Sweet Little Angel" — songs that turned teens on to forbidden black rhythms in a way Bill Haley, Paul Anka, Pat Boone, and other interpreters could never do — there was no turning back.

"I learned how to play lead, rhythm, bass, and drums, all off that one album, just trying to copy them," Jimmie said. Steve became so smitten with the song "Thunderbird" — the one where the singer, Billy Joe Shine, calls out to "all you kids in Texas, you grow so big and tall" — that he set up the record-player speakers on the front porch and stood in front of them with his guitar, using a coat hanger for a microphone. When his girlfriend came walking by, he started mouthing Billy Joe's vocals.

"Get high, everybody, get high/Have you heard?/What's the word?/ Thunderbird!"

She was not impressed.

"Take that record off the stereo," she scolded. "And stop acting like a fool!"

The boys' record library grew steadily by the week. Jimmie did most of the buying, investing his allowance money in works by B. B. King; "Red River Rock" by Johnny and the Hurricanes; "The Worm" by Kenny Burrell and Jimmy McGriff, the quintessential soul-influenced jazz guitar and organ duo; "Wipeout" by the Ventures; Santo and Johnny's reflective "Sleepwalk"; the wild surf instrumentals of Dick Dale and the Del Tones; Chuck Berry; Muddy Waters; T-Bone Walker; Lightnin' Hopkins; the Johnny Burnette Trio; Howlin' Wolf; Littles Walter and Richard; Slim Harpo; Brother Jack McDuff; Larry Williams; and Buddy Guy. If there was guitar on it, he scarfed it up.

Steve heard it all, too. He'd listen to anything, and if it gave him goose bumps, he'd learn it. He worked his way through the Nightcaps and Jimmy Reed to the surf guitar and twang instrumentals in Jimmie's collection. His friend Roddy Colonna lent him an album by Albert King. This guy, who held a weird-looking guitar shaped like a V on the cover of his record album, he stood out like a sore thumb. Whenever Steve looked at the album cover, he thought about a rocket ship about to take off. Which is exactly what the record sounded like on the turntable.

Fighting over baseball cards or betting who could run faster was stupid. Steve wanted to play guitar like Jimmie did, making his instrument sound exactly the way it sounded on the record. Neither brother knew it, but they were accumulating an encyclopedic knowledge of styles, riffs, plucks, and licks that weren't found in a Chet Atkins or Mel Bay instructional book. And Steve could hold his own. OK, maybe Jimmie could beat him at playing the stinging sharp notes that B. B. King could pull off without a sweat and the frantic attacks of Buddy Guy. Steve concentrated on imitating Albert King's muscular tone, something that Jimmie thought was impossible. Placing the phonograph needle on the lead break time and again paid off. Shoot, he wasn't even technically a teenager yet and he could do Albert King like Albert King.

"That's how people learn," he concluded with a shrug, not knowing any better.

There was one record, "Wham" by Lonnie Mack, that was so thrilling Steve lifted it from Jimmie and claimed it as his own, although some years later Jimmie set the record straight with the statement, "That was my record, the way I remember it." Whether it was the maniacal, out-of-control attack, the raunchy, fuzzed-out distortion, or the lightning speed with which it was played, Mack's 1963 instrumental did a number on Steve. He played "Wham" over and over and over until the grooves began to wear off the 45. He slowed it down to 33⅓ RPM to decipher the notes that blurred past at the speed of sound and the tricky turnarounds. When his fingers could not comprehend the lines, he hummed along with the melody to unlock the mysterious passage. When he didn't think the record sounded loud enough anymore, he borrowed a friend's Shure Vocal Master public-address microphone and placed it in front of the stereo speakers and cranked up the volume.

His single-minded determination not only annoyed his elder brother, it drove his father nuts. After hearing the song for what must have been the 726th time, Big Jim Vaughan burst into Steve's room, yanked the record off the turntable, and smashed it to bits. Undeterred, Steve simply went out and bought another copy.

Though he was cranky when he was angry or had had one too many, Big Jim mostly supported his boys' musical interest. Most other kids' parents gave their kids hell for listening to rock and roll. Jim willingly shuttled his boys around in his pickup truck so they could play music with friends. Steve was almost as excited as Jimmie when Jimmie's friend Ronnie Sterling got a set of drums in 1964 and the two boys formed a band called the Swinging Pendulums with a bass player named Phil Campbell. Big Jim Vaughan even let the trio practice in the garage. He and Phil's and Ronnie's fathers actually enjoyed visiting with each other over a few beers while their boys practiced being rock stars. "At first we played dime dances for students before school, talent shows, at each other's house," Jimmie said. When the Swinging Pendulums learned enough songs to perform in public and get paid for their efforts, Big Jim gladly loaded up their equipment and drove the boys to wherever they were booked to play. If Steve was lucky, Jim would take him along, too, to places where boys, much less teens, were normally not allowed.

Jimmie's first professional engagement was at the Hob Nob Lounge, where the Swinging Pendulums played six nights a week. It wasn't exactly the big time. Lacking a PA system, they sang through the club's jukebox and played their guitars through their Silvertone amps, while a go-go girl danced on a nearby platform. The fathers took turns chaperoning their underage sons, who each took home fifty dollars for the week. "We'd get paid for playing and get to stare at the go-go girl," Jimmie said with awe. "Shoot, I was on top of the world."

The Swinging Pendulums were good enough to get gigs all over the city, at places like the Beachcomber, the Fog Club, Surfers-A-Go-Go, the Funky Monkey, and the Loser's Club, a joint in a strip shopping center where Billy Joel once served a stint as the happy-hour piano man. The dim, neon-lit world of a Dallas bar was pure adventure for Steve. By the time he had turned twelve, he had become good enough on guitar to sit in for a song with his brother's band, his courage fortified by snitching a few sips of his father's beer when no one was looking. This was better than home. There was music all the time in these places, along with dancing, laughing, and clapping. This was where people could appreciate who he was and what he could do with a guitar.

Even if it hadn't been in their blood, the guitar came naturally enough to the Vaughan boys. Music was the one popular art form indigenous to Dallas and the state of Texas, and guitar was typically the force that drove it. The Texas guitar sound is almost as legendary as the Alamo, reflecting the vast wealth of jazz, cowboy tunes, blues, swing, and rock and roll that native musicians created. The guitar's portability gave it a home on the range, favored by Anglo cowboys and Mexican vaqueros for campfire storytelling and romantic serenades. It was an entertainment fixture in lumber camps, church sing-alongs, and anywhere more than three people gathered to make music. The guitar built bridges between races, cultures, and languages.

In the twenties and thirties, guitars were fixtures in the speakeasies, saloons, and whorehouses clustered along Upper Elm Street east of downtown Dallas. The area, known as Deep Ellum, was first settled by ex-slaves freed in the aftermath of the Civil War. By the advent of the jazz age, Ellum had evolved into Dallas's version of Harlem, a wide-open black neighborhood immortalized in the much-covered song "Deep Ellum Blues," a ditty that warned visitors to "put your money in your shoes." Blind Lemon Jefferson, one of the first black musicians to make an electronic recording of a song, worked the streets of Deep Ellum, singing "Black Snake Moan" and other songs from his repertoire for tips as he was led around by a younger man named Huddie Ledbetter, who later achieved fame as Leadbelly. But of all the guitar-toting characters who frequented Deep Ellum, no one made quite the same impact as a youngster from Oak Cliff named Aaron Thibeault Walker.

T-Bone, as his mother called him, grew up in the black neighborhood surrounding the Elizabeth Chapel, just a few miles east of the Vaughan house. T-Bone was a consummate entertainer who defined the electric blues guitar sound in the thirties and forties while astounding audiences by hoisting his instrument behind his head and doing splits without missing a lick. Walker plugged the electric guitar straight into the blues, creating trademark shuffles, boogies, and linear runs that have been studied and reinterpreted by rock and blues guitarists ever since.

In his younger days, T-Bone had picked up a few pointers hanging out with another Dallas-born guitarist named Charlie Christian. Both Christian and Walker liked to swap licks with Chuck Richardson, an

Oklahoma City guitar man who showed them how to play their axes like horns, engaging vocalists in intimate musical conversations. These two Texas guitarists came of age at the dawn of the amplification era, a technological breakthrough that brought the guitar out of the shadows of the rhythm section and into the lead spotlight. While T-Bone continued to perform until he passed away in 1975, Charlie Christian managed to change the sound of jazz guitar in the short three years he played with the Benny Goodman Quintet, before his untimely death at the age of twenty-three in 1942.

On the heels of Christian and Walker were two other black Texans, the Moore Brothers, Oscar and Johnny, who reigned as the undisputed masters of the electric guitar in the forties and early fifties. Older brother Johnny headed up his own jumping unit, the Three Blazers, one of the first and smokingest rock-and-roll bands to break out of Los Angeles, where both Moores had relocated. The Three Blazers featured a warbling vocalist who hailed from Beaumont, Texas, named Charles Brown. Younger brother Oscar signed on as the string man for the King Cole Trio, led by smooth piano operator named Nat "King" Cole, and proceeded to put a varnish of sophistication and savoir faire over the forlorn wisdom of old blues, musically embodying the bronze ideal of tuxedos, expensive jewelry, evening dresses, and processed 'dos. In 1947, Oscar left Cole to become the fourth member of Johnny Moore's Three Blazers.

Growing up in Dallas, in T-Bone Walker's part of town, no less, vested Steve and Jimmie Vaughan with a guitar-playing pedigree, which complemented their unique physical attributes. The massive forearms each had inherited from their father allowed them to bend strings with startling ease. Steve in particular possessed huge hands, a trait the Cooks claimed came from their side of the family, and that made it all the easier to wrap his thumb all the way around the back of the neck to play bar chords.

That they were white boys enraptured with the music of black artists mattered little. Music was the one arena of race mixing that was tolerated in the South and practically venerated in pockets of Texas. In that respect, the Vaughans were part of a tradition established by Bob Wills, Milton Brown, Elvis Presley, Johnny Horton, Webb Pierce, and local heroes Ronnie Dawson and Groovy Joe Poovey, who graced the stage of the Big D Jamboree, a variety show held through the fifties and sixties at the Sportatorium wrestling arena on Industrial Boulevard, just across the viaduct from Oak Cliff. They all may have been white, but their music was inspired by blacks.

The Vaughan brothers were also products of their time. Neither Jimmie nor Steve knew it, but as kids playing electric guitars, they were not only part of a Texas musical legacy, they were on the cutting edge of a worldwide movement that promised liberation through music to an entire generation of young people. The Beatles were proof that music wasn't just a tremendous form of expression, but a great financial opportunity too, the same kind of opportunity that sports promised. Teenagers from all across Dallas began to drag their parents downtown to McCord's music store in the belief that a guitar or a drum set would be their ticket to fame and fortune. Jim and Martha Vaughan understood that if their kids worked hard to develop their talents, they had a shot at something better, even if it was a long shot.

No one epitomized this new breed of Dallas musician better than Doyle Bramhall, a boy from the Dallas suburb of Irving who would become the most significant influence on Stevie Ray Vaughan's singing style as well as his closest music-writing collaborator. In 1964, Doyle Bramhall convinced his father to buy a drum set for fifty dollars. Though it was a third of what he earned every week at the cement plant where he worked, Doyle's father agreed to do it and helped his son turn the family garage into a practice room. There Doyle jammed with his twin brother, Dale, and other neighborhood kids, including Frank Beard and Dusty Hill, who would later make up two thirds of the band ZZ Top. Listening to records by Sonny Boy Williamson, Muddy Waters, and other rhythm-and-blues artists in his elder brother Ronnie's record collection, Doyle learned to do a shuffle, the foundation of all danceable blues. But his voice was the real showstopper. He had an emotional tenor that made him sound three times his actual age. Depending on his mood, Doyle could prompt comparisons to the angelic delivery of Stevie Winwood, the kid who fronted the Spencer Davis Group from England, or the groans and screams of James Brown, aka Soul Brother Number One.

Doyle came out of his garage to join an established fraternity band from North Texas State College in Denton, thirty miles north of Dallas. They were called the Chessmen and worked an extensive circuit that took them to Lubbock, to Little Rock, and to Austin, the home of the University of Texas. Though Beatles music was their bread and butter, their Vox Grenadier cabinets and Fender echo units hummed with a mixed bag of other rock and blues standards ranging from "Gloria" by Them, "Satisfaction" by the Rolling Stones, and "For Your Love" by the Yardbirds to Bo Diddley's jungle chants and the entire catalog of Chuck Berry. Doyle's cover of Ray Charles's "Georgia on My Mind" was guaranteed to moisten more than a few panties in the audience. Their reputation solidified when the Chessmen recorded and released a single, "I Need You There," that received extensive airplay on both KLIF and KBOX, Dallas's other Top 40 radio station.

The Chessmen were so successful that Doyle was soon earning more money than his father. The old man was so supportive of his son that he handled the boy's finances. The conservative Dallas Independent School District was not quite so impressed. School administrators didn't care much for the music, and they were really concerned about all the new ideas that the culture this music spawned was putting into the heads of Dallas youth. Beatles haircuts and wide-lapel Carnaby Street jackets from London — they were just the tip of the iceberg. If kids didn't straighten up and start getting some discipline, they'd be quoting Karl Marx, carrying around Mao's little red book, and mixing with coloreds before you knew it.

Doyle Bramhall's father realized he wasn't dealing with rational minds when he attempted to speak in front of the school board. This wasn't about rock and roll or the way someone dressed at school. This was about money. "He's not gonna get a haircut just because you got a rule and throw away five hundred dollars a week," the elder Bramhall explained to the administrators who were threatening to throw his kid out of school for wearing his hair long. "That's stupid."

His pleas fell on deaf ears. He enrolled Doyle at Oak Cliff Christian Academy, a private school that attracted reprobates from throughout the Dallas school system. The preacher and his wife who operated the school were tolerant to the point of laxity. Classes were scheduled from eight to two. Tuesdays and Thursdays were designated study days, with no formal instruction. "It was a joke," said Alex Napier, one of the longhairs who attended the school. "You paid your seven hundred dollars a year and got your diploma."

The Chessmen almost fell apart when Robert Patton, the band's Paul McCartney look-alike, tragically drowned in a late-night boating accident on White Rock Lake, east of downtown. Band members were shocked at losing their friend, but they couldn't afford to spend too much time grieving. Their booking agent had lined up a full schedule of gigs, and they needed to find a replacement, fast. Doyle suggested a guitarist from Oak Cliff he had heard about named Jimmie Vaughan.

Doyle and his brother Dale drove over to the Vaughan's house in Oak Cliff to talk with Jimmie and his parents about joining the band. "It was a lot like selling vacuum cleaners," remembered Dale, who worked as the informal manager for the Chessmen. "Mr. and Mrs. Vaughan must have thought I was crazy at first, a fifteen-year-old kid in the music business. But after I explained to them how many gigs we had lined up, and how much money Jimmie would make, they were convinced."

It was Jimmie who hesitated. He didn't want to abandon his partners in the Swinging Pendulums. Besides, he didn't much care for Beatles music. But he finally gave in to Dale's persuasive arguments, and signed on with his first real rock band.

In a matter of months, Jimmie became a bona fide teenage rock star.

He affected a cockney accent, pulled down more coin than his old man was making, and was initiated to the shadowland of booze, illicit drugs, and willing girls who swooned whenever he shook his thick, dark mane. Having female fans pursue him relentlessly was better than listening to the old-bag teachers prattle on at school. Steve was the one who often answered the calls from his brother's admirers. "Another one?" he would sigh with his nasal inflection as he went to fetch his big brother to talk with yet another adoring Lolita. He just wished that sometimes the calls were for him.

Steve idolized his big brother. He was a star. He was good-looking. And he could sure play that guitar. Steve figured he would never be as handsome or as popular as Jimmie, but at least he knew he could keep up with him on guitar. He proved it whenever Jimmie went out of the house and left his equipment behind. To hell with the hand-me-downs, he thought. He could handle whatever Jimmie was playing. He just didn't want to get caught.

"Jimmie, you left the radio on," Dale Bramhall told Jimmie once when they were leaving the house. Dale swore he was hearing music from the boys' bedroom.

"That's not the radio," Jimmie grumbled, turning back toward the front door. "That's my little brother. I told him not to play that fuckin' guitar. He's playing that Silvertone amp, and it's got two blown speakers. I told him not to do that. He's got his own shit in there."

Dale trailed Jimmie into the bedroom. They opened the closet door and found Steve sitting on top of the 610 amp, playing big brother's guitar. Steve looked up sheepishly and said, "I thought you guys already left." Jimmie proceeded to pound him physically and verbally.

"Goddam," swore Dale, shaking his head. "How old are you?"

" 'leven," Steve mumbled shyly.

"Goddam," said Dale. "You're a motherfucker."

Doyle Bramhall made the same discovery a few days later, when he came over to the house looking for Jimmie. Instead, he found Steve working out on "Jeff's Boogie," the signature tune of English guitarist Jeff Beck, note for note in his bedroom. When he saw Doyle, Steve started to take the strap off Jimmie's guitar. Doyle raised his hand to stop him.

"No, no," he said. "Please play some more." As Steve began to play again, a huge smile of approval crossed Doyle's face. Another Vaughan who played guitar. It must be in the genes. Steve never forgot Bramhall's patient appreciation. "He was the first one who told me I was good," he later explained.

The guitar got his big brother respect and admiration from his mom and dad. Slowly, however, Steve watched that respect change to hostility.

Jim and Martha had gone along with Jimmie's decision to drop out of T. W. Browne Junior High School to attend Oak Cliff Christian so he could keep his hair long. Jim still drove Jimmie to gigs when he didn't have a ride. And they brought members of the family to see the Chessmen play, like the time they won the Battle of the Bands at the Yelo Belly Drag Strip.

But as they heard rumors of drinking, drugs, and girls, and saw their son stagger into their home at all hours, they began to think differently of the music business. Steve felt the tension, which often led to violent outbursts. Jimmie was like his father, tough, abrasive, with a clenched jaw and a bullheaded mind of his own. Steve favored his mother. He was a shy, sensitive kid. As the situation between Jimmie and his parents worsened, it made him want to withdraw even more into himself and into the world of his music. Finally, things got to be too much for both Jimmie and his father. Jimmie moved out of the house in 1967 and into an apartment complex in North Dallas where the other Chessmen were living. He was a sixteen-year-old rock-and-roll star who convinced himself he had it made, with or without his parents' support or blessings. "Me and my dad had a falling out, and I ran off," Jimmie explained curtly in an interview twenty years later. "And that's the end of the story."

Jimmie may have given him a hard time at home, but with him gone, life was even harder on Steve. Guitars reminded Jim and Martha of Jimmie, and that was not a memory they treasured anymore. Their stares and sharp comments told Steve all he needed to know. It was all right if he rode his bike to play under the bois d'arc trees at Kiest Park or hung out with his friends at Page's Drugstore in the Westmoreland Heights shopping center, but one kid in the family with a guitar in hand and a Beatle haircut on his head was enough. They weren't going to lose their Steve without a fight.

On the other hand, Jimmie's departure did force his little brother to learn how to assert himself more confidently. He didn't have much choice. He hadn't been the brainiest kid at Lenore Kirk Hall Elementary School, and he certainly wasn't destined to make the honor roll at L. V. Stockard Junior High. But what did those kids know? They could talk all they wanted about careers. If they wanted to be businessmen, lawyers, nurses, or teachers, that was their business. He was going to play guitar for a living. He didn't need school. At least he tried to show his folks that he could be responsible. After class, he delivered newspapers, but managed to lose two different routes. His folks were thrilled when he took a job for seventy cents an hour at the Dairy Mart, a nearby hamburger stand across Westmoreland Street from the Dairy Queen. Steve's detail included dumping the trash into bins out back, a tricky task that required traipsing over vats of used grease that were covered by wooden lids.

One day, while cleaning out the trash bin, he slipped on a lid and nearly immersed himself in grease. It was a turning point in his life. He knew what he wanted and it sure wasn't doing shitwork at a burger joint. All he wanted to do was play guitar, and nobody, not even the people he loved the most, was going to tell him any different.

2

FUCKHEAD

His fingers knew where to press the strings on the frets when his ears processed the sounds from the records, but pieces of vinyl weren't enough to satisfy Steve Vaughan's passion for music. Seeing musicians play live, that could teach you twenty times more than any record. But for a twelve-year-old white boy growing up in Dallas, there were precious few places to see and hear the black sound Steve dug. The significant exception was the State Fair of Texas.

The October event was, and still is, one of the largest annual exhibitions in the world, a combination trade exposition, car show, carnival, sports extravaganza, and agricultural meeting that attracts millions of Texans to Fair Park, an impressive collection of art deco buildings two miles east of downtown Dallas. Jim Lowe, the Kats Karavan disc jockey, provided the drawling voice of the fair's giant mascot, Big Tex ("Howdy, y'all. Welcome to the State Fair of Texas"), an invitation that Dallas teens readily accepted on the Friday they were let out of school specifically to attend the event. The kids typically bypassed the demonstrations showing off the latest developments in cow-milking technology in favor of the Midway, a garish strip of thrill rides, bizarre attractions, greasy food (the corn dog was invented here), and games of chance. On the Midway, you could play tic-tac-toe with a chicken, cheer on dogs ridden by monkey jockeys, or watch a man hammer a nail into his nose, as long as you had money in your pocket. You could also get a glimpse of the strange, alluring world of Negro entertainment that beckoned behind a canvas tent advertising the Cotton Club for the price of a few quarters.

For a Dallas teenager, even one whose brother was a notorious guitar player, there were not many opportunities to witness music being played live and in person, especially the kind of music that intrigued Jimmie and Steve most — music performed by black folks. One of the best opportunities was in the Cotton Club at the State Fair.

Blacks may have been banned for many years from riding the "Dodge 'Em Scooter" or entering the "Laff in the Dark" attraction, but everyone was always welcome at the Cotton Club, an all-black revue featuring blues and soul singers and musicians, tap dancers, suggestive go-go girls, and bawdy comedians, interspersed with various hustles, cons, and come-ons intended to persuade the audience to part with a little bit more of their hard-earned cash. Buy a box of peppermint candies for the exorbitant price of one dollar and — who knows? — you might find an imitation gold watch or a genuine, simulated-diamond ring enclosed. The performers were a cut below what older people paid good money to see at real black venues in Dallas like the Ascot Club or the Guthrie Club, but the Cotton Club Revue was nonetheless an educational introduction to night life on the forbidden side of town.

Steve was thrilled to see and hear the Cotton Club spectacle, but it was a black teenager playing on the stage at the Students' Day talent show who made an even stronger impression. He was the lead singer of a young band called the Misters from North Dallas High, and he was even more of an eye-catcher than the foxy cheerleaders who were waving their pompons around him. Those old-timers at the Cotton Club had nothing on this singer, especially the way he growled, howled, and shouted his way recklessly through Roy Head's big soul hit "Treat Her Right." If he had the talent to sing and dance like the guy gyrating in front of him, Steve mused, he wouldn't even mess around with a guitar. He wasn't the least bit surprised when the judges awarded the Misters first prize in the talent show. He made a mental note to remember the singer's name: Christian Plicque.

Stockard Junior High had a reputation as a tough school, a reputation that was justified in comparison to Brown Junior High, the other school that fed students into Justin F. Kimball High School. The boy with reddish hair and the round, green John Lennon sunglasses looked and acted weird enough to get punched out by bullies on several occasions just for being different. He wasn't particularly interested in his studies, but he wasn't a hood either. He just couldn't get into schoolwork like he got into playing the guitar. Even the desk-football games, flicking triangular pieces of folded paper across the large wooden tables in Mr. Keebler's homeroom, seemed boring.

One of the few activities at Stockard that got Steve really excited was the school talent show. It presented the perfect opportunity to show off his ambitions. Following the Spanish Club's performance of the Mexican Hat Dance, he took the stage with some of his friends. The group played "Swing, Swing, Swing," the jumping Benny Goodman jazz standard from the thirties. The whole band was good enough to get a rousing round of applause from the assembly. But the guitar player outshined them all. "You could tell that he was going to keep on playing after he left junior high," said Richard Goodwin, who played trumpet for the performance.

A few months later, Steve took the bus downtown to look up Christian Plicque, that black vocalist who impressed him at the State Fair. He found him at Neiman-Marcus, the classiest, most extravagant and outrageously expensive department store in the Southwest, if not the world. Christian's grandparents had worked as the butler and cook for store president Stanley Marcus. In return for their years of loyal service, Marcus had taken their grandson under his wing and set him up as a junior trainee sales clerk in the toy department. When Steve approached him, Christian thought the timid, rail-thin waif in blue jeans was just another customer.

"Can I help you with anything?" Christian inquired politely.

"I saw you play at the talent show at the State Fair," Steve said. "I'm forming a band and I'm looking for a singer. A black singer."

"I'm not really interested," Christian replied formally, thanking him for asking nonetheless.

"Here's my phone number, just in case you change your mind," Steve said. He may have looked like he just fell off the turnip truck, but Christian admired the boy's bold forthrightness.

Civic boosters liked to brag that Dallas was the city that worked, a modern, growing can-do metropolis brimming with business opportunities at every corner. Beneath the surface of shiny new skyscrapers and modern freeways, though, was another Dallas, a repressed city that still hadn't shaken the vestiges of a Southern cracker town. The white leadership treated the city's colored people kindly so long as they kept their place. They expected that civility to be returned in kind. Typical of the de facto segregation that still existed in the late sixties in Dallas was the Longhorn Ballroom. Six days of the week, the Longhorn featured country and western music. Monday nights were Soul Nights at the Longhorn, the one evening of the week when B. B. King, Little Milton, and other black chitlin-circuit acts performed for black audiences. Even so, a small roped-off area was reserved to accommodate whites who wanted to see the show. That same method of accommodating the minorities was reversed when it came to habitation. Coloreds should have their own neighborhoods, civic leaders believed. And those neighborhoods, they agreed, included Oak Cliff.

Though Oak Cliff was technically part of the city of Dallas, the geographical boundaries defined by the Trinity River to the north and east established it as a community unto itself, a community separate from the high-priced developments that were sprawling pell-mell across the flat farmland stretching to the north. At various times in Oak Cliff's history, visionaries, promoters, and land speculators had attempted to transform the hilly landscape into a socialist utopia, a college town, and a world-class amusement park. The area once heralded as "the Brooklyn of the South" had grappled with an image problem for decades in spite of the fact there were pockets of wealth. Though the community had voted itself dry in the mid-fifties, banning all alcohol sales, it was regarded by folks living on the other side of the Trinity River as a dangerous place. The sixties did nothing to dispel that negative notion. Lee Harvey Oswald, the alleged assassin who gunned down President John F. Kennedy in broad daylight in downtown Dallas on November 22, 1963, lived in a boarding house on Oak Cliff's Beckley Avenue with his Russian-born wife, Marina. Jack Ruby, the two-bit mobster and strip-joint owner who shot Oswald in the basement of the Dallas Police Department in front of a live national television audience, lived just around the corner from Oswald. The Kennedy assassination earned Dallas a worldwide reputation as the City of Hate. And the City of Hate hated Oak Cliff.

"You had more to prove, being from Oak Cliff," said Mike Rhyner, a classmate of Steve Vaughan's who auditioned Steve for his band, Freestone, but ultimately rejected him because he didn't know any Beatles songs. "You definitely had a chip on your shoulder, you rode into town carrying baggage. Whenever you have a depressed or repressed situation like that — an outlet for that depression comes through the creative process."

While upscale white neighborhoods mushroomed all over North Dallas, area realtors quietly schemed to keep minorities south in Oak Cliff. The practice of red-lining, in which financial leaders refused to loan money for housing in "bad" neighborhoods, was technically illegal. But anyone looking for a home in Oak Cliff knew where the red line began and ended. Classified real estate advertisements that read "east of Beckley" meant black. Ads that specified a location as "west of Beckley" meant white.

White homeowners in Oak Cliff were in mortal fear of minority encroachment, so much so that in 1966 a group called the Oak Cliff Council charged that real estate developers were trying to turn Oak Cliff into "an all-Negro ghetto." Many white families moved south of Oak Cliff to suburbs like Duncanville, De Soto, Lancaster, and Cedar Hill. As property values declined, the Vaughans and other Oak Cliff families who could not afford to move felt besieged by a racial tide they could not stop.

The Vaughan boys did not share the racial prejudices of their parents' generation — most of the records they bought were by black people — but they were all too aware of Oak Cliff's bad reputation. Other high schools in Dallas had social drinking clubs patterned after college fraternities. Oak Cliff had clubs for fighting, like the legendary Dirty Thirty, nicknamed the D.T.E.P., as in Dirty Thirty Eat Pussy. Oak Cliff kids were considered badasses. Fun was going downtown on Friday nights to beat up homosexuals, a practice that ended when one well-known hood was blown away by his intended victim. Everyone who grew up in Oak Cliff was familiar with the Oak Cliff Oh syndrome. Whenever Oak Cliff kids told kids from other parts of Dallas where they were from, the response was always a pregnant pause, followed by "Oak Cliff? Ohhhhhhhhh . . ."

Christian Plicque knew about Oak Cliff, too, but from a distant perspective. Still, he was intrigued by the invitation from the skinny boy who visited him at Neiman-Marcus. On a whim, he gave Steve a call and agreed to come over to his house. Christian knew his own background was unusual. His father was a successful businessman and one of the first blacks to live in Highland Park, the poshest neighborhood in all of Dallas. But this Oak Cliff fellow he was going to see didn't strike him as typical either.

"Stevie was like a black person who was poor and had nothing, and I was like a white person who had everything," Christian remembered. "The colors were just different."

The house that Christian drove up to was nowhere near as fancy as his own home. The man sitting on the porch with the rolled-up sleeves was a marked contrast to the well-heeled, manicured individuals his parents usually associated with. Steve had warned him about Big Jim Vaughan in advance. He could be rude and surly, depending on his mood.

Steve introduced his father to Christian.

"Nice to meet you, Mr. Vaughan," Christian said.

Jim Vaughan glared at his son's black friend.

"You know," he drawled, "there's only one thing a nigger can do for me."

Steve furrowed his brow at Christian, who looked back at him with a slight, knowing smile.

"What's that, Mr. Vaughan?" he politely responded.

"You see these shoes?" Big Jim said, pointing down.

"Yes, sir," replied Christian.

"That's what a nigger can do for me. Shine my shoes."

Steve quickly ushered his new friend inside and apologized. For Big Jim, calling someone a nigger was an insult. For Steve, being called a nigger would become the highest compliment.

Despite Big Jim's brusque welcome, Christian and Steve discovered they shared many of the same interests, particularly the kind of music they liked. The Oak Cliff kid was a hell of a guitar player, Christian figured, and when it got down to the nitty-gritty, even old Jim was a decent fellow. "Over a period of time, he began to see that I was a person like he was," he observed.

By the time Steve entered Justin F. Kimball High School, he had quite a résumé as a musician. With his buddy Billy Knight on drums and Steve Lowery pumping a Farfisa organ, Steve performed at Lee Park, the open space in Dallas where all the hippies congregated on Sunday afternoons. The band wasn't exactly welcomed with open arms — "We played inside the mansion until they kicked us out," recalled Billy Knight, "then we played on the front porch until they cut the electricity off, then we got ourselves a generator" — but at least they had a Ripple-wine drinking, pot-smoking, braless audience that appreciated the renditions of "Rollin' and Tumblin'," "Big Boss Man," "Crossroads," and "Jeff's Boogie" blasting out from beneath the park's statue of Robert E. Lee.

They were good enough for Billy Knight to hustle a gig at a hip local nightspot known as the End of Cole. When they arrived at the club, the manager asked, "Who's gonna play guitar?"

Billy pointed proudly at Steve. "That little buck-toothed motherfucker right there." He might not have been much to look at, but when he plugged in his instrument, the manager was not disappointed.

The band names and the personnel changed by the week — the Chantones, the Epileptic Marshmallows, the Southern Distributors, the Brooklyn Underground, and Lincoln. None of them were remotely considered equals of established bands like Jimmie Vaughan's band, the Chessmen, but anyone who heard them could tell that Steve Vaughan had something that the other kids did not.

"I knew this kid is either gonna become a multimillionaire, or he's gonna starve in the pits," remembered Christian Plicque. "He wasn't that smart intellectually, but when it came to music, that guitar was his whole life."

While Steve was struggling to get a band together, a slightly older musician was revolutionizing the world of rock. His name was Jimi Hendrix. Like Steve, Hendrix was a shy young man who became obsessed with the guitar, learning his first licks from the radio and records in the sanctuary of his bedroom, where he slept with his instrument. After leaving the army in 1962, Hendrix freelanced as a rhythm-and-blues sideman with Little Richard, the Isley Brothers, King Curtis, and young John Hammond, among others. His big break came when he traveled to England in 1966 under the managerial wing of Chas Chandler, a founding member of the popular British rock group the Animals. His audacious stage flamboyance and inconceivable guitar sound blew away critics and musicians alike. When the Jimi Hendrix Experience stormed onto the American airwaves in 1967 with the album *Are You Experienced?* and the single "Purple Haze," the guitarist from Seattle confounded everyone's preconceptions about rock and roll.

Whether it was a demographic quirk or a storm warning on the horizon, Dallas-area record stores reportedly sold more units of Hendrix product than any other region in the United States. Steve Vaughan, once again, had a front-row seat to this phenomenon, courtesy of his older brother. Jimmie Vaughan learned about Hendrix when the Chessmen made an appearance on the local teen-dance television program "Sumpin' Else," hosted by KLIF disc jockey Ron Chapman. He found a promotional 45 of "Purple Haze" in a trash can and, having vaguely recalled reading about the band in a magazine, took it home, put it on the turntable, and blew his mind.

"It sounded like Muddy Waters to me, only wilder," he said.

The music was light years beyond the single-string speed riffs of the surf bands. It was the blues on acid, a total sensual experience that involved the fingers, the brain, the entire body, and all the electronic frequencies that had never before been stimulated by the nerve center of the electric guitar.

Jimmie went out, bought the album, and learned it forward and backward, flamboyant excesses and all. Like Jimi, he learned to play his guitar behind his back, with his teeth, and occasionally lit his instrument on fire. He copped Hendrix's clothing style, donning satin pants and high-heeled shoes. "It's hard to imagine Jimmie like that," recalled Christian Plicque, "before he got into that really blues niggery thing."

When the Jimi Hendrix Experience played dates in Dallas and Houston, the Chessmen were hired to open the concerts. In deference to the headliner, Jimmie Vaughan's band shelved their own cover versions of Jimi Hendrix in favor of playing songs by Cream, the three-piece band of blues-rock pile drivers from England led by Eric Clapton, formerly of the Yardbirds. "They were amused," Jimmie said of the Experience's experience. Amused and so impressed by the tone and control Jimmie had over his guitar that after the show, Jimi Hendrix gave Jimmie Vaughan forty dollars and his wah-wah pedal in exchange for Jimmie's Vox wah-wah.

Steve did not get as close to Hendrix as Jimmie did, but he was no less enraptured by the music. He'd never heard anything like it before. Hendrix could coerce sonic rumbles out of an electric guitar that no one, not even Jimmie, could duplicate from his records. If Steve tried to absorb every nuance of Hendrix, getting big goose bumps on his arms whenever he visited Electric Ladyland, he was not alone. "Fuckin' Hendrix, man" became the new catch phrase of the incipient rock-and-roll generation, a mass obsession that would forever alter the electric guitar's place in popular music.

For all his interest in Jimi, Steve had more immediate concerns. It was hell trying to find the right guys to play with, especially when it seemed like the old man would get pissed off anytime he mentioned anything to do with music. Worse, his number one role model, his brother, wasn't handling his own success too well. For all the money they were pulling down, the Chessmen were a classic case of Too Much, Too Soon. They played hard and partied hard, chugging everything from Romilar to Swiss Up, smoking whatever was passed around, gobbling tabs and pills, and swapping needles to shoot up speed, the hippest drug in Dallas at the time. Doyle Bramhall contracted hepatitis and got so sick he was confined to bed for several months. The bass player also succumbed to what musicians referred to as "hippy titus" and moved back to Midland in west Texas to become a Jesus freak. The band fell apart.

Jimmie didn't seem too upset about the demise of the Chessmen. Or at least that's what he told his little brother. He was sick of playing Top 40 cover tunes and wanted to play that Dirty Leg music from the wrong side of town. When Doyle recovered, the two formed a new band called Texas Storm, with a song list that blew off the Beatles in favor of soulmen like Eddie Floyd and Sam and Dave. The gum-chewing pretty boy with the black Les Paul and the Vox amp wasn't just fucking around anymore. He was serious, a bona fide guitarslinger who liked nothing better than to engage in cutting contests with crosstown rivals like Bugs Henderson, the lead player with the Dream, or Seib Meador, the wild axeman with the spiked hair who would go on to lead a mildly successful glam-rock band known as the Werewolves.

Jimmie's badass reputation grew at the expense of his income. Texas Storm didn't play the kind of music that fraternities or Dallas bar owners wanted to hear. The band had to scrounge for every gig. When their bass player was thrown in jail, Jimmie asked his kid brother if he would help out.

Would he sit in with Jimmie's band? It didn't take Steve two seconds to reply. He borrowed his big brother's Barney Kessel guitar, tuned it down slack enough to sound like a bass, and became one half of Texas Storm's rhythm section.

After trying to keep up with his hero for most of his life, he was a peer, an equal — or at least good enough to play bass. With his place in the band came a new name as other musicians began to refer to Jimmie's kid brother as Stevie. It sounded cool.

Texas Storm was Stevie's introduction to Austin, the state capital and home of more college students than anywhere else in the Southwest. The band had a booking at the Vulcan Gas Company, a loosely run music club that was the most notorious hippie hangout in Texas. Texas Storm was cobilled at the Vulcan with Sunnyland Special, another blues-rock band. Keith Ferguson, the bass player for Sunnyland Special, had seen Jimmie and the Chessmen open for the Jimi Hendrix Experience in Houston the year before and came away thinking he was one of the most gifted guitarists he'd ever heard. Ferguson was surprised to see how the mighty had fallen in such a short period of time.

"They looked so bad that I went to Galloway's next door and got them five hamburgers for a dollar and fed the band," he said.

> Stevie was laying on a car hood, throwing up on Congress Avenue 'cause he was trying to keep with the rest of the band and Phil Campbell, the drummer, was drinking Gypsy Rose wine. They were all like speed freaks. Nobody knew that Stevie played anything, he was just this punk kid. And they blew us out of the building. They were astonishing. Phil Campbell was playing killer drums and at the last note of the last song of the set, he fell off of the drums and rolled down this ramp and came to a stop unconscious. It was scary.

For the brief spell that Stevie filled in on bass for Texas Storm, Jimmie pushed him harder than ever. "I was a little brother, especially then," Stevie shrugged. "What happened was that he was moving ahead a little faster than me and I guess I was dragging him down a bit, so that didn't work out too well. But I think with any brothers there's just a period of time when the little brother gets in the way. That's just brother to brother shit."

The "brother to brother shit" was good enough to carry the band through several dates at Candy's Flare, Oak Cliff's rock-and-roll showcase. The Flare was run by Mr. and Mrs. M. L. King and named for their coquettish blond-haired daughter, Candy. The Kings started out promoting weekly teen dances at the Glendale Village Presbyterian Church, where the response was so great that they moved the shows to the Redbird National Guard Armory and expanded bookings to two nights a week.

Candy's Flare was as close to the Vulcan as it got in Oak Cliff, and it only cost a buck to get in. A neon sign above the door welcomed kids into a cavernous hall about half the size of a football field, with bandstands set up on either end. As far as the Oak Cliff in-crowd was concerned, Candy's was like one of those love fests they'd heard about in San Francisco, a free-for-all zone where they could drink sodas, eat popcorn, and listen to well-known Dallas bands with hit records like the Five Americans ("I See the Light," "Zip Code," "Western Union"), the Southwest FOB ("The Smell of Incense"), Kenny and the Kasuals ("Journey to Time"), and the Felicity, a Denton college band led by a singing drummer named Don Henley.

Thrill seekers could purchase marijuana cigarettes and dollar hits of LSD in the parking lot outside. If someone didn't want to free their mind with some righteous blotter or purple double-dome, they could always get their kicks staring at the White Trash Light Company's multimedia light show flashing on the walls or checking out chicks' bras under the black lights, which made them look really far-out.

One of those Oak Cliff hippies who saw Texas Storm with young Stevie Vaughan on bass was Robert Brandenburg, a burly, gregarious longhair a few years older than Stevie, who had been afflicted with polio as a child. Cutter, as he was called, really dug the band, even after two of the band members were hauled off by the cops for getting into a drunken brawl. But he was most impressed by the little-bitty kid with the giant guitar who was knocking out killer bass lines with his thumb.

"Even then Stevie had a presence about him," Cutter related. "He made me watch him and feel him and — boom! — instantly something changed and told me this is what I want to do. I met Stevie that night and the next thing I knew, he called me."

The two hit it off royally. Cutter was cool. He'd grown up in Oak Cliff, but he'd just gotten back from Cali-fuckin-fornia, the promised land of sunshine, surfer chicks, free love, and psychedelia. Even better, Cutter had wheels, a bitchin' Volkswagen Beetle with California license plates no less. If Cutter wanted to be his friend, Stevie was into it. Cutter thought it was neat hanging out with a musician, especially someone with real talent. His outgoing personality, which enabled him to "cut through the bullshit," as he liked to describe it, pulled Stevie out of the shell of shyness he often crawled into when he was around strangers. Between the car, the guitar, and their respective personalities, the two became dedicated soldiers in a rock-and-roll army, constantly on the prowl for gigs, glory, and girls.

Stevie attempted to dress the part of a rocker, wearing mismatched combinations of paisley shirts left over from the British invasion, bell-bottoms, fringed-leather jackets, fringed-leather boots, and gaudy sashes around his waist. He might have possessed an ugly mug compared to his brother's matinee-idol looks, but he shared his single-minded devotion to his instrument.

"He was taxing. Good god, the world is not a guitar!" Cutter recalled with exasperation. "He could take anything to extreme. He could
take a barbecue sandwich to extreme. But nothing to extreme like his
guitar. And that would drive you nuts. I never met a musician in my life
who was more dedicated to his craft."

Every Saturday morning Cutter, Roddy Colonna, and other friends
tried to duck him, knowing he'd badger them to give him a lift out to
Loop 12 to the Arnold and Morgan music store, where Stevie would test
out every guitar and amplifier in the store while fending off the sales-
clerks by politely mumbling, "I'm just lookin'."

When Texas Storm found a permanent bass player for the band,
Stevie found himself on his own again. This time, though, he vowed to
get really serious and stop messing around. He took his Telecaster, the
one with "Jimbo" scratched on the back and teethmarks on the edge from
an encounter Stevie had with some rednecks at a drive-in, and showed up
to audition for any band that was looking for new blood.

Scott Phares was familiar with Stevie Vaughan. He'd seen him in
the hallways at Kimball High and recognized him as a diehard rock and
roller by the way he dressed and the people he hung out with between
classes. But Phares had no idea exactly how good he was until Stevie
showed up at his house to try out for the bass player's position in his
band. Liberation, as they called themselves, was an eleven-piece, horn-
driven ensemble with a jazz-rock sound in the style of the hugely popular
Blood, Sweat and Tears and the Chicago Transit Authority. Phares could
immediately tell that the guy had a solid command of the bass. He probably could fit in just fine. Then Stevie suggested they switch off instruments for a minute while they were fooling around. When Scott heard
Stevie run off a series of blues riffs, his jaw dropped. He wasn't just good.
He was great. Two songs convinced Scott that he was playing the wrong
instrument. Stevie Vaughan should be Liberation's guitarist. He would
gladly step aside and play bass himself.

Cutter Brandenburg came along as part of the package. He took on
the backbreaking task of roadie, helping the band set up and tear down
equipment before and after a show, while making sure the instruments,
amplifiers, microphones, and sound effects were working properly when
the band was onstage. In exchange for his services, Cutter received whatever compensation he could hustle, maybe a drink or a few bucks here
and there. It didn't matter. He was happy to be hanging out with Stevie
and being around music. Wherever Stevie was headed, Cutter wanted to
go there with him. "Stevie used to look at me and say, 'I'm gonna play on
the moon,' " Cutter said. "And I thought, if anybody could play on the
moon, Stevie could do it. If anybody deserved to play on the moon, Stevie
deserved it."

Liberation reunited Stevie with Christian Plicque, the black singer from North Dallas, who had joined the band as one of the two lead vocalists. Scott and Stevie got Liberation plenty of exposure at Kimball sock hops, club fund-raisers, and student assemblies. The older, college-aged members of the band hustled up paying gigs in area clubs like the Blackout, the Town Pump, and the Fog Club.

It was at the Fog where two big-time musicians named Tommy Shannon and "Uncle" John Turner, fresh off the road with Johnny Winter's band, happened to stroll in one night. "I heard this guitar player inside and I went, 'Who's that?,' " Tommy remembered years later. "I went inside and there was this little kid in there looking up at all the big guys around him." Stevie knew both musicians by reputation and thought they were some of the toughest players around — after all, Johnny Winter was proving to the whole world that a white guy, a *really* white guy who was in fact an albino, really could play blues guitar. Although he was the youngest player in the band, Stevie felt confident enough to ask Tommy and Unk if they wanted to jam. Unk declined as a matter of course — hey, he was rock royalty — but Tommy said he was ready to go. Stevie was impressed. He wasn't some stuck-up asshole, but a down-to-earth cat. "Tommy was the only guy in the band that would talk to me. Everybody was too hip. I don't know . . . I was a fourteen-year-old fart."

Though the band didn't last but a few months, they did manage to secure a full week's engagement at Arthur's, a swanky club in the historic Adolphus Hotel downtown. On Friday night, three guys in their early twenties walked in and introduced themselves. They were a new group that would be releasing their first album in a couple of months. The manager of Arthur's owed their manager a favor, they said. Would it be all right if they could play during one of Liberation's breaks? No one in Liberation objected. Between sets, the trio took their places on the band-stand and introduced themselves to a thoroughly disinterested audience.

"Hey, everybody," the guitar player spoke into the microphone. "We're a little ol' band from Texas called ZZ Top."

Stevie recognized bass player Dusty Hill and drummer Frank Beard. They had grown up down the block from the Bramhall family in Irving and already achieved a certain amount of success with their band, American Blues, famous for their blue hairdos. Hill and Beard had gotten together with an extremely talented Houston guitarist named Billy Gibbons, whose band, the Moving Sidewalks, were statewide rivals with Jimmie Vaughan's Chessmen. Manager Bill Ham hooked the three together shortly after Rocky Hill, Dusty's brother and the lead guitarist of American Blues, dropped some acid one night and missed a gig as he ran around naked all over downtown Dallas searching, he said, for the Yellow Submarine.

ZZ Top proceeded to wake up the audience at Arthur's with a dazzling demonstration of Texas-boogie rock. Stevie, who was decked out in a spangled jacket with ostrich feathers, a gift from Jimi Hendrix that Jimmie passed along to his little brother, was so smitten with Gibbons's fiery chops, he asked the sit-ins if he could sit in with them. Gibbons was game.

"Whaddaya wanna play?" he asked.

Stevie suggested his favorite Nightcaps song, "Thunderbird." The band launched into a catchy little shuffle as Stevie sang the lyrics he'd been rehearsing since he was ten.

"Get high, everybody, get high/Have you heard?/What's the word?/Thunderbird!"

The swinging groove provided the perfect setting for the flurry of sharp, stinging riffs that Stevie and Billy Gibbons were trading. Gibbons might have been the Big Daddy guitar player in Houston, but Stevie could hold his own, matching Gibbons note for note and tossing in an extra trick of his own for good measure. Even Liberation's old-fart horn players, the guys working on their degrees in music theory who usually regarded Stevie as little more than a blues nut, took note and paid attention.

The encounter was one of the last times Billy Gibbons jammed with another guitarist in public. Manager Bill Ham felt his boys had nothing to gain by engaging in such impromptu battles, although they were as much a Texas tradition as electric guitars and the boogie beat. "Thunderbird," the song Stevie suggested, eventually became a staple of ZZ Top's live performances.

Liberation earned $660 for the week at Arthur's, which broke down to sixty bucks a man. It was, everyone agreed, an exceptional week. More typical were charity gigs or the time when members of the band had to wear funny-looking outfits for a party at a roller rink. It was enough to make Stevie, Christian, and Cutter all decide to quit. For a while Stevie played in a band called the Cornerstones with drummer Roddy Colonna. His instrument was an Epiphone that he got cheap because the sun had bleached the red color off the front. But looks didn't matter to Stevie. He played his guitar so hard at gigs the band scrounged in Dallas and Austin that he regularly broke the bridge off his instrument.

In the summer of 1970, Stevie and Roddy drifted back together with Christian Plicque in a band called Blackbird. Finally, Stevie had a band where he could play the way he wanted. He blasted Hendrix's "Red House" through twin Marshall amplifiers set to ten, often as not frying the equipment in the process. For other Hendrix tunes like "Purple Haze," Stevie would play Hendrix's guitar parts while Christian Plicque aped his vocals. On Cream's manic arrangement of "Crossroads," Stevie not only played an extended solo on guitar but felt comfortable enough to sing the Robert Johnson composition. At the same time, the band was just as likely to turn around and do a rave-up of Otis Redding's "Mr. Pitiful." Acid rock and Southern-fried soul were like peaches and cream to a Texas rock and roller.

Christian was the perfect band mate. Stevie thought he was a trip and a half, the way he liked to shock people. Both of his ears were pierced, he dyed his hair blond, and he loved to sashay across the dance floor in flowing African robes wearing nothing underneath.

The psychedelic era arrived in Dallas belatedly, but with a vengeance. Even Gordon McLendon, the radio station owner who introduced Top 40 radio to the world via KLIF, got on the bandwagon, introducing underground, or progressive, radio to the north Texas market on KNUS-FM. The FM band heretofore had been a graveyard dominated by classical and easy-listening music formats. McLendon borrowed a popular concept from KMPX-FM and KSAN-FM in San Francisco based on playing selections from albums by popular rock artists instead of just the hit single. Though the format was eventually co-opted and narrowly defined as AOR, or album-oriented rock, it brought a sense of freedom to the airwaves that reflected the libertine attitudes of its core audience.

It was in the midst of this craziness that Blackbird came into their own. Their regular haunt was a club called the Cellar. Located downtown at 2125 Commerce Street across the street from the KLIF and KNUS studios, the Dallas Cellar was part of a small chain of clubs that began in Fort Worth in 1959 and included locations in Houston and San Antonio. Owner Pat Kirkwood, a gambler and son of a gambler, had a beatnik coffeehouse in mind when he conceived the Cellar as a place where customers would come to sit on mattresses and pillows strewn on the floor, contemplate the messages painted on the walls and ceilings ("EVIL Spelled Backwards Is LIVE," "You Must Be Weird Or You Wouldn't Be Here"), and listen to cool jazz and poetry. The times and Texas dictated otherwise.

Instead of beatniks, the Cellars in the late sixties became a magnet for a strange blue-collar mix of Damon Runyan characters trapped in the Wild West — bikers, thugs, teenyboppers, horny business executives, and the oddball hippie or two. Even the owner's mother, Faye Kirkwood, a former rodeo cowgirl who had seen it all, thought the club was wonderfully disgusting, saying the Fort Worth location resembled "a Chinese dope fiend place."

The main attractions were rock bands that played constantly between 6 P.M. and 6 A.M., fake alcoholic drinks that somehow convinced minors they were drunk, and scantily clad waitresses who would perform impromptu stripteases when the mood struck them. An aura of forbidden pleasure surrounded the Cellars, epitomized by the bells that rang and the blue lights that flashed whenever a police raid was imminent, which was not infrequently.

"We had strange rules," Kirkwood told *Fort Worth Star Telegram* reporter Christopher Evans. "We'd give [real] drinks to doctors, lawyers, politicians, stag girls, policemen, anybody we thought we might need if something broke out." One of the strangest rules was in keeping with the prejudice that prevailed in Texas in the sixties: blacks were not admitted, performers excepted.

"If you were black and tried to get in, they'd ask for a reservation," Stevie explained. "If your name just happened to be on this fake list they had, they'd ask for a hundred-dollar cover. And if you handed them a hundred you'd damn sure get rolled before you got very far into the club."

Christian Plicque, the privileged youth who had given up his career at Neiman-Marcus to play with Blackbird, feared for his safety on many occasions. "I never got hit," he said. "But I got called names a few times."

Racist, sexist, seedy, dark, sleazy, riddled with drugs, guns, prostitution, knives, stinking of ammonia and urine, the Cellars were the biggest subterranean circuses going in Texas. The music, which fueled the Anything Goes attitude, was booked by Johnny Carroll, a onetime rockabilly performer who recorded the semi-hit "Wild, Wild Women" for Decca in the fifties. Carroll was regarded as a mean, pistol-wielding, Benzedrine-addled son of a bitch. But unlike any other club manager in town, he didn't give a shit what the bands played, as long as they showed up on time.

Carroll's attitude was responsible for the wild variety of blues, space rock, psychojazz, and the outer musical limits that graced the Cellars' stages: Cannibal Jones (aka Bongo Joe and George Coleman), a black man who pounded out street poetry on his own customized oil drums; a blond-haired folk musician named John Deutschendorf, who later achieved a modicum of success under the stage name of John Denver; Jimmie Vaughan and Doyle Bramhall's Texas Storm; the Winter Brothers, Edgar and Johnny; the Cellar Dwellers, a three-piece band that did nothing but Beatles covers; and the comedy duo of Jack Burns and George Carlin.

"That was the only place that let me do what I wanted to do because nobody cared about shit there," remembered Stevie, who was often accompanied by his girlfriend Glenda Maples, who danced seductively next to him on the pieced-together plywood stage while he played. But at least it was work that paid money, even though the long hours and the surly staff made that a risky proposition. "A couple of times, people would get pissed and start shooting at the stage. You ducked and kept playing," he laughed. Sometimes Blackbird worked two Cellars in one night, playing two forty-five-minute sets in Fort Worth, then driving thirty miles back to Dallas to do two more sets, pocketing ninety dollars apiece for their efforts. When they weren't at the Cellar all night, Stevie and drummer Roddy Colonna often headed over to Hall Street to sit in with black acts at the Ascot Club, a stone blues club where they were often the only white faces in the house. Their musical endeavors didn't leave much time for sleep, day jobs, or school. The answer to the riddle of how to play all night and stay up all day was simple: speed.

"Speed had this big mystique. Because of the hours you had to play, you had to do it," said Mike Rhyner, whose bands frequently worked the Dallas Cellar. "The hours were the popular excuse. The real reason was because it was hip."

Ups, bennies, black mollies, road aspirin, white crosses, footballs, LA turnarounds — no matter what it was called or what form it came in, speed, the catchphrase for amphetamines, methamphetamines, and related stimulants, was practically an American tradition. For decades, it had been favored by musicians, housewives, truck drivers, and working stiffs who used it to stay awake, keep slim, or feel perky. Speed labs had been part of the landscape of the rural Southwest since the fifties. The acceptance of illicit drugs that came with the hippie phenomenon only enhanced speed's appeal. In the late sixties, speed had replaced acid as the drug of choice in the Haight-Ashbury section of San Francisco, the birthplace of the hippie peace and love ethic. In Texas, it was already the traditional white-trash drug of choice, manufactured by so many north Texas "cooks" that Dallas came to be known as "Speed City." Bad speed, commonly known as brown biker speed, looked like chunks of sulphur, and smelled like old socks. Righteous speed, or crank, was an odorless, white crystalline powder.

The good shit, which went for a standard twenty-five dollars for a quarter gram, could be either snorted or injected with a needle. The preferred type of speed for certain patrons at the Cellar was known as dexies, little yellow pills that were soaked down before injected. The initial rush from the needle was orgasmic. The resulting high was pure, uncut Keystone Cops. Speed inspired users to perform the same physical activity again and again and again. An abuser could spend all night happily shuffling cards, shining shoes, or washing a car. One group of Texas bikers was busted after they drove around the same block two hundred times. For the Cellar crowd, the most popular physical activities were playing music and sex.

"Everybody was making crank back then," remembered Fredde Pharoah, a Dallas drummer who was introduced to the drug at the Cellar.

"Some girl come up to me and said, 'You ever do this? Come on.' I went and did it and got a blow job and I been doin' it ever since." Hepatitis, the dirty-needle disease that had ruined the Chessmen, was rarely discussed at the time. "It was wide open," Pharoah said. "If you got too drunk, you did a snort of crank. If you got too cranked up you did some heroin. If you didn't like heroin, you did some downers, Quaaludes, or reds. Then you drank more." Pharoah finally gave up speed after doing a stretch in jail for that vice.

Like everyone else in the Cellar crowd, Stevie played music, messed around with chicks, and did speed, exquisite kicks for a mere lad of sixteen. He did his best to keep his parents from discovering his bad habits. Whenever he had a gig, he'd tell them he was spending the night with a friend, or he'd sneak out with someone like Cutter. It was the only way he knew how to avoid them hassling him. In a strange way, he understood why they were so down on him. "When my brother left home, my folks were afraid of losing me, too," he said. "They saw me going in the same direction and they were scared about that. The first time I split, I tried to run away and be a man. You know how that is. We ran off and tried to become men when we were still boys." No matter what he was, he wasn't going to let the folks stop him from doing what he wanted to do.

Exhausted from playing music all night, hung over, still buzzing from the residual effects of whatever he'd smoked, popped, shot, or snorted, Stevie could do little more in the classroom at Kimball High School than sit quietly at his desk in the back of class and doze off. His grades reflected his lack of interest.

Typical was music theory. As much as it was a subject he was interested in, he managed to flunk all but one six-week period over the course of a year. "The teacher would sit down and hit a ten-fingered chord on the piano and you had to write all the notes down in about ten seconds," he later explained. "I just couldn't do it. It was more like math to me." He had once expressed a desire to join the Knight Beats, the Kimball stage band. But band members had to read music, something that Stevie Vaughan never learned to do.

Kimball High was hardly the kind of learning institution that nurtured the creative individual. W. P. Durrett, who'd been the principal since the school opened in 1958, was a former coach who ran the all-white educational institution like a giant athletic team. The strict disciplinarian quoted Vince Lombardi for inspiration and confronted troublemakers with the threat that he would turn their files over to J. Edgar Hoover for further investigation by the Federal Bureau of Investigation. He was a hard-liner who opposed busing and enforced the school dress code with religious zeal, going so far as to successfully defend it in court. "I had no problem with long hair," he explained. "Because the students knew I wouldn't stand for it."

Stevie Vaughan fit into the troublemaker category, though he was more a well-intentioned misfit than a rebel. To the kids from Brown Junior High, the cheerleaders, the football players, and the "hi-lifers," Stevie was Stockard Scum, a kid from Stockard Junior High — the wrong side of the tracks.

"Your status, what you were, and what you would be was predetermined by the time you got to Kimball. Stockard kids were blue-collar," explained Mike Rhyner. Stevie looked strange, too, with a big flat nose, a cadaverous physique, and his offbeat rock-and-roll couture. "They called me Stevie Wonder while they beat me up," he bitterly recalled.

"Everybody knew that this guy was weird," said classmate Joe Dishner. "But lots of students liked him because he knew what he wanted to do." One admirer even sneaked an amplifier out of the band room so Stevie could plug in and whip through a version of "Jeff's Boogie" during speech class. When Stephen Tobolowsky, a National Honor Society student who would go on to a successful career as an actor-director, wanted to record a couple of his songs for his band, the Cast of Thousands, he enlisted Stevie to play lead guitar. Sitting down on a chair, his legs crossed and his head bowed over his guitar, Stevie added some tasty licks to the two tracks the band contributed to the Dallas garage-band compilation album *A New Hi*. Though the album, like the band, quickly disappeared from public view, it marked Stevie's first studio experience.

One of the few disciplines he excelled in besides guitar playing was art. Stevie could draw well enough to have some of his cartoons published in the Kimball school newspaper. His art teacher, Elizabeth Knodle, encouraged him to pursue a career in the graphic arts. His most positive school experience came in the tenth grade when he was given a half scholarship to attend an experimental art class at Southern Methodist University. Stevie thought it was a course for gifted students, only to learn that it was a program designed to train art teachers by having them work with underachievers. He quickly got over his disappointment and blossomed in the free-form classroom environment, which was the polar opposite of the rigid disciplinarian approach stressed by Kimball principal Durrett. "It was completely wide open," he enthused. "We brought records and talked and worked. If you were working on a piece of sculpture and you decided to come and smash it, you did it. If you wanted to look at it, you did that. The class was great. . . . I learned a lot from it."

The founder of the program, Ann McGee-Cooper, urged students to critique one another's works in whatever medium they chose. It was the first time Stevie had been actually encouraged to experiment with his creativity and the first time his teachers actually approved of his unconventional artistry. Unfortunately, the evening class conflicted with other more important demands on his time. "It was on the nights when I was supposed to be rehearsing."

Juggling music at night and school during the day, he developed what a counselor would describe as an attitude problem. "I just began to realize that the schools I was going to cared more about how I looked and the way my hair grew. They weren't interested in teaching me anything. I had already learned on my own."

Jim and Martha did not appreciate that line of reasoning, to say the least. Even Jimmie, who had left home long ago, could see that. "My parents got a little mad, and they took it out on him," he said. "You know, they said stuff like, 'You can't play guitar' and 'You can't do nothin' except go to school.' " Music wasn't a path to a well-paying career. It was a waste of time.

When things at home got real bad, Stevie relied on Cutter to fetch him and get him away from his old man. "Dad's going crazy," he would say over the phone. "Come get me."

But there were times he couldn't get away fast enough. "I'd have the record player up so loud that I wouldn't hear my dad come in," Stevie said years later. "He'd kick me across the room and tell me — excuse the terminology — to 'take them fuckin' nigger clothes off!' "

He loved his parents dearly and put up with his father's drinking, his racist attitudes, and his outbursts. But even his friends at school could tell life at home was not very happy. A classmate, Allen Stovall, noticed a bandage on Stevie's ear one day while he prepared to play guitar for an assembly.

"What happened to you?" Stovall asked.

"Oh, my dad boxed my ear," Stevie answered.

"Shit, do you mean that?"

"Yeah," Stevie continued. "He told me he didn't want me to turn out like Jimmie."

Stovall was an outsider, too, a talented artist who had earned the grudging admiration of the Kimball "hi-lifers." He liked to hang out with Stevie on the blacktop outside, where they would smoke a cigarette or walk out beyond the athletic fields to pass around the occasional joint. One day, Allen, Stevie, and another friend, Greg Lowry, were approached by three of the school's physical education coaches who doubled as Kimball's enforcers of discipline. One of the coaches fixed his bulldog glare on Stevie.

"What's your name, fuckhead?" he barked.

Stevie mumbled his name, and the coaches turned to walk away.

"You better watch what you say," Greg Lowry defiantly yelled at the coach. "Someday your daughter's going to be paying money to stand in line to see him play."

"Thanks, man," Stevie mumbled appreciatively. He'd show them all someday.

3

LOST IN AUSTIN

Everyone, it seemed, was down on his case. If he stuck it out at Kimball for four more months, he'd graduate with a high school degree. Big goddamn deal. A club owner wasn't going to book him just because he had a piece of paper with fancy writing on it. Besides, he'd seen what the guitar did to people, how the girls went crazy when Jimmie made his instrument talk, how people like Cutter wanted to be his friend just because he knew where to put his fingers on a fretboard. It was a force too powerful to deny. Following the 1971 Christmas holidays, Stevie made up his mind. He wasn't going back for the spring semester.

Martha and Jim weren't happy about the decision. Stevie certainly didn't want to hurt the folks, especially after all the anguish that Jimmie had caused them. But he was seventeen now and had convinced himself that school was only getting in the way. He had already dedicated his life to mastering the guitar. The time had come to get down to business. And to do that, he had to get the hell out of Dodge.

When it came to making music, he had finally concluded, Dallas was a city with no soul, a Top 40 garbage dump. Everyone who ever played in a band knew that. If you didn't copy all the hits that were on the radio, you weren't going to survive very long. Stevie and the other members of Blackbird knew it didn't have to be that way. For the better part of a year, they had been shuttling in and out of Austin, where hippies, misfits, and outcasts formed the nucleus of a counterculture community exploding on the fringes of the University of Texas campus. Every time Blackbird came to town for a gig, they came back swearing on a stack of Bibles they had to move to Austin. Why put up with insults and hassles from rednecks and bulletheads when there's a place where everyone else is like you are? The Interstate 35 shuttle between Dallas and Austin ended when Roddy Colonna, one of their drummers, got married and declared he and his wife were splitting Big D for good. Since Roddy was the only band member with a van, the rest of Blackbird readily went with him.

The whole crew — Stevie, Roddy, second guitarist Kim Davis, the other drummer, John Huff, organist Noel Deis, bassist David Frame, singer Christian Plicque, Cutter in his support/sidekick role — fell right into the scene. They signed with Charlie Hatchett, a lawyer and agent who controlled bookings at most local clubs and the lucrative University of Texas fraternity-party circuit. Before each public gig, Cutter, Roddy, and Stevie jumped into the VW van and tore around the university area with a big staple gun, plastering every telephone pole, tree, and wooden fence with Blackbird posters.

Home base was the Rolling Hills Country Club, a ramshackle roadhouse run by Alex Napier, another hippie refugee from Oak Cliff Christian Academy who used to do the light show at Candy's Flare and once managed a head shop. The Rolling Hills was hidden away in the rural suburbs of town, located far enough off Bee Caves Road that Stevie, his band mates, and half the audience could get a good buzz on in the parking lot between sets with absolutely no fear of getting busted.

For a Dallas kid bound and determined to play guitar for a living, moving to Austin was better than dying and going to heaven. The whole city was a little San Francisco. If he was barely scraping by, so was just about everyone else in his circle of friends. Longhairs and chicks without bras were the norm in Austin, not the exception. San Antonio musician Doug Sahm dubbed it groover's paradise, a place where no one gave a shit about careers, financial planning, or security. Pursuing your art was the name of the game. For once, no one questioned Stevie or looked at him like he was crazy when he told them he was a guitar man.

In Austin, Stevie could practice playing his instrument all day, gig in clubs all night, make time with good-looking chicks who actually wanted to talk to him (as long as Glenda Maples, his main squeeze, wasn't around), get higher than a Georgia pine whenever he pleased, crash on the nearest sofa when sleep finally caught up with him, only to start all over when he woke up. No parents nagging at him, no principals, teach-

ers, or coaches leaning on him about rules or responsibility, no assholes
lurking in the shadows waiting to beat the crap out of him just because he
was different. Music, drugs, and women — that's what seventeen-year-
old Stevie Vaughan wanted and that's what Austin had to offer.

"It was like a circus," Stevie said. "I couldn't believe it. There were
real, full-blown hippies. I was trying to figure out, hey, what's happening
here? How are these people getting away with all this? This is the capital.
Where are the police?"

The police were there, it's just that they had their hands full keeping
track of some 40,000 students, an equal number of dropouts, and the
several hundred hell-raisers who were better known as the Texas state
legislators. Referred to at various times as skunks, buzzards, termites,
grub worms, and human ants, Texas politicians were a breed unto themselves, notorious for their love of the Three B's — beef, bourbon, and
blondes. History had recorded this motley crew of elected officials attempting to shoplift the state's archives, holding the governor hostage on
the second floor of the capitol building, inviting a group of cheerleaders
to protest legislative reform by sticking their butts out from the balcony
of the House of Representatives, and punching one another out to the
tune of "I Had a Dream, Dear" sung in barbershop-quartet harmony.

Such chicanery made buzzed-out flower children with a couple of
marijuana cigarettes small change as far as the Austin cops were concerned, a startling contrast to Dallas and Houston, where being caught
with one or two reefers often meant a heavy prison sentence.

With the prospect of that kind of heat off his back, Stevie could
concentrate on getting his music right, which he focused on to the exclusion of everything else, his girlfriend Glenda Maples excepted. He
didn't have any money — what little he earned was spent before he could
count it, much less save it. He didn't have a ride. But he had plenty of
work. Blackbird was becoming a regular attraction at the Rolling Hills
and rock-and-roll rooms like the Waterloo Social Club, the Black Queen,
the Back Door, and Mother Earth, notorious for their blisteringly loud
sets that covered the Allman Brothers (like the Allmans, Blackbird em-
ployed a twin–lead guitar, twin-drum lineup), Cream, and Jimi Hendrix.

"Stevie couldn't sing," Plicque said. "Back in those days he was
very shy and the guitar was the only thing he held on to. When he had his
guitar, he owned the world. So together, we made Jimi Hendrix. I was
the voice. He was the guitar."

Stevie quickly served notice he was one of the more talented young
guitarists in Austin, even though he wasn't legally old enough to buy a
drink at the bar. Playing through Marshall amps cranked up to ten, his
brute, muscular approach defined a hard-edged tone, which sounded
even harder with the thick fat strings he favored. "They were like fucking

telephone wires," Cutter remembered. "Just a little bit bigger piece of wood and you'd have a fuckin' piano."

Clapton Is God graffiti was everywhere. And nobody took the message to heart like Stevie. When he lit into Clapton's version of "Crossroads" during the second of the band's two ninety-minute sets, he made the rest of the band seem like a mere supporting cast. "Stevie never got better than he was then," Cutter claimed. "He just got more intense."

With a few dollars in his pocket after playing a gig, Stevie had no problem finding drugs, a party, and a place to crash. Pot was ten dollars a lid and rents were seventy-five dollars a month — real cheap when it was split three or four ways. Stevie didn't own much besides his guitar and, after he split with girlfriend Glenda, made do living on the couch circuit. Finally, he thought, he'd found a place where he had a chance to do his own thing. And he still had the best role model in the world to follow. Jimmie Vaughan, his idol of a big brother, had moved to Austin the year before, along with a whole crowd of music-playing reprobates from Dallas including Doyle Bramhall, whom Stevie thought was as fine a singer as Jimmie was a guitar player. How could Austin not be a cool place to be?

People had been coming to this part of central Texas to do their thing ever since Jacob Harrell settled on the north bank of the Colorado River in 1835. In the next three years he was joined by others who designated their community as Waterloo. In 1839, Mirabeau B. Lamar, the learned president of the new Republic of Texas, suggested locating the capital at Waterloo in a rush of poetic inspiration after shooting a buffalo. The community was renamed in honor of Stephen F. Austin, the first Anglo-American real estate developer in the region, who is widely acknowledged as the Father of Texas.

Located on the eastern edge of the Hill Country, the site was one of breathtaking natural beauty that featured dramatic limestone outcroppings covered with cedars and oaks, rife with clear-flowing artesian springs, creeks, and streams. Those attributes made Austin one of the few places in Texas that could actually be called picturesque. The establishment of the University of Texas in the sleepy little burg in 1883 attracted a community of writers, thinkers, and intellectual desperadoes, including William Henry Porter, who started writing short stories while incarcerated in the Austin city jail. Porter, who eventually published a periodical called *The Rolling Stone*, achieved world renown as a pundit using the nom de plume of O. Henry. He was followed some twenty-five years later by a group of University of Texas scholars that included John Lomax, Walter Prescott Webb, William Owens, Roy Bedichek, and J. Frank Dobie, an English professor who derisively referred to the Tower, the University's predominant architectural landmark, as "the last erection of an impotent administration."

The legacy of harboring cantankerous wits continued into modern times. In the fifties, Ronnie Dugger chose Austin as the place to publish the *Texas Observer*, the only openly liberal publication in the state. Lyndon B. Johnson's impact on Austin was chronicled in the book *The Gay Place* by Billy Lee Brammer, an Oak Cliff native whose speed habit led to an untimely death. John Henry Faulk, the CBS radio and television humorist who made his fight against the broadcasting industry's anticommunist blacklisting a lifelong crusade, was an Austin resident, although he kept a farm near Madisonville, 136 miles to the northeast. Faulk began his career as a folklorist and disciple of both Dobie and Lomax, recording the sermons and music of black churches, and his work mirrored the respect people in Austin had for roots traditions and peculiarities, the most important and evocative of which was music.

Songs of cowboys and vaqueros, the work hymns of black slaves and prisoners laboring in the fields, as well as the popular strains of hillbilly, western, blues, boogie, rock and roll, Cajun, and conjunto, were understood, scrutinized, and appreciated by music lovers and scholars in Austin like nowhere else in the Southwest. John Lomax established music as an integral part of American folklore by traveling more than 200,000 miles across the country to make field recordings, financed in part by grants from Harvard University and the Library of Congress. His first collection, *Cowboy Songs and Frontier Ballads*, was instrumental in preserving songs like "The Old Chisholm Trail," "Git Along Little Doggies," and "Home on the Range" as national treasures. He later convinced the governor of Louisiana to pardon one musically gifted black convict, Huddie Ledbetter, or Leadbelly. Alan Lomax, John Lomax's son, continued his father's work and in 1941 made the first field recordings of a twenty-four-year-old primitive blues guitarist from the Mississippi Delta named McKinley Morganfield, who became known throughout the world as Muddy Waters.

For all the academic scholarship in the folk and ethnic music idioms, Austin's own musical heritage was rather spotty. Legend has it that the turn of the century children's song "Wait for the Wagon" was inspired by a Sunday outing to Mount Bonnell, which overlooks the city from the west. History was defined largely by those who were just passing through. Fiddler Harry Choates, the performer who popularized the Cajun classic "Jole Blon," died under somewhat mysterious circumstances in the Travis County jail in 1951 after an extended drunk. The Skyline Club, a honky-tonk on the old Georgetown highway north of town, laid claim to being the site of the last performances of country singers Hank Williams and Johnny Horton.

From the end of World War Two to the mid-sixties, the Austin music scene was largely defined by a handful of heel-kicking western bands like Dolores and the Bluebonnet Boys, a doo-wop group known as the Slades who had a minor national hit with the song "You Cheated," and a rockabilly cat named Ray Campi who was trying mightily to follow in the footsteps of Elvis. Two local boys, Sammy Allred and Dwayne "Son" Smith, collectively known as the Geezinslaw Brothers, entertained the whole country with corn-pone humor and accomplished musicianship when they landed a regular spot on Arthur Godfrey's weekly variety show broadcast on CBS television.

Meanwhile, across the informal color line marked by Interstate 35, the successful musicians — bass player Gene Ramey, pianist Teddy Wilson, guitarist Pee Wee Crayton — were the ones who had split town. The black entertainment strip along Eleventh and Twelfth streets once had the reputation of Little Harlem, but by the mid-sixties integration of clubs west of the old Interregional Expressway had helped devolve the area into a crumbling row of boarded and shuttered buildings. Black road shows that regularly brought chitlin-circuit stars to Johnny Holmes' Victory Grill and the Doris Miller Auditorium had largely become a thing of the past while clubs like the IL Club, La Cucaracha, and Charlie's Playhouse, which formerly roared into the wee hours, tottered on their last legs.

The only reliable standbys left were Ernie's Chicken Shack, out on Webberville Road, where a half-pint and a craps game were always easy to come by, the Sunday afternoon jam at Marie's Tea Room Number Two, and rural joints like Alexander's south of town and, to the east, the Kung Fu Club in Elgin, where Hosea Hargrove, a primitive disciple of the Guitar Slim school of extroverted twang, held forth. Most of the better-known veterans were either retired — as was the case with Snuff Johnson, Erbie Bowser, T. D. Bell, Jean and the Rollettes, and The Grey Ghost — dead, or gone, although a few survivors like Robert Shaw, one of the great pre–World War Two Texas barrelhouse pianists, still played the occasional bar date after shutting down his barbecue pit on Manor Road.

The man most responsible for creating the vibrant Austin music scene that Stevie Vaughan walked into was a portly, white-haired gentleman named Kenneth Threadgill. In 1932 he opened a little combination beer joint and gas station on North Lamar Boulevard, the first establishment to secure a license to sell beer following the repeal of Prohibition. Threadgill's joint did a nice business, but the proprietor wasn't all that keen to be peddling longneck bottles of beer for a living. His real passion was hosting hootenannies once a week in his place, informal picking and singing sessions that drew a sizable contingent of musicians, bohemians, and other music lovers from the university.

The Threadgill's hoots were casual affairs: the stage was a table set up in the middle of the room that pickers would sit around, passing a microphone among themselves. If he was loosened up with enough bottles of Pearl and Lone Star, Kenneth Threadgill would frequently take the stage himself to warble a few blue yodels made famous by his hero, Jimmie Rodgers, one of the most popular singers in history, who sold a phenomenal 20 million records from the start of his brief recording career in 1927 until his death from tuberculosis in 1933. It was no fluke that much of Rodgers's appeal stemmed from his ability to wail the blues like a black man despite his white skin.

Threadgill's beer joint developed the reputation as the epicenter of Austin music. Regulars in the early and mid-sixties included Bill Neely, an elderly country gentleman from the blackland prairie east of Texas who, like Threadgill, was a Jimmie Rodgers devotee, as well as a guitarist who finger-picked his acoustic instrument just like the onetime sharecropper and black blues legend Mance Lipscomb; John Clay, a surly UT graduate student who was regarded as the godfather of the local folk music community; Powell St. John, a young virtuoso harmonica, mandolin, and guitar player; Lanny Wiggins, another accomplished guitarist who came from Port Arthur to study at the university along with a versatile singer named Janis Joplin. St. John, Wiggins, and Joplin joined forces as the Waller Creek Boys, a folk group that indulged in blues, jug band music, bluegrass, and old-timey country.

At the same time the Threadgill's hoots were going full blast, two clubs on Red River Street south of the UT campus — the Jade Room and the Old New Orleans House — started presenting live bands as the featured entertainment. Although these rooms initially booked frat cover bands, they began bringing in groups that appealed to the local hippie culture, which for all its California influences had taken on some peculiar provincial traits.

Texas hippies prided themselves as being different from other hippies. It might have been nothing but peace, love, and flowers in your hair out in Haight-Ashbury, but longhairs in Texas had to deal with the whole other reality of a society defined by macho, beer-tanked yahoos barely removed from the wild, Wild West. Their lifestyle wasn't a fashion statement but a badge of courage. Texas hippies got their heads bashed in for looking different. They had to fight a little bit harder for what they believed in. In that respect, Austin was a free space, a safe haven in a hostile, varmint-infested world, the only place between New Orleans and the Pacific Ocean where freaks could walk down the street without getting their ass kicked.

Although Austin's hippie community was considerably smaller and less notorious than San Francisco's, it had its charms. Peyote, a hallucinogenic cactus native to south Texas, was legally available in local garden stores until the state legislature outlawed its sale in 1965. True to the native proclivity to overreach, Texas hippies were even more over-the-top than their West Coast brethren. They didn't just drop acid, they scarfed it down like buttered popcorn, chasing it with Lone Star or Ripple and a post-prandial joint or three. Joplin, many of her musical cohorts, and a group of underground artists and illustrators headed by Gilbert Shelton, creator of the Fabulous Furry Freak Brothers underground comic strip, all congregated at the Ghetto, a small, low-rent pocket in the neighborhood west of the University of Texas campus and within walking distance of landmarks like Dirty's Hamburgers and Oat Willie's head shop, whose company motto, "Onward Through the Fog," was as much a hippie rallying cry as "Remember the Alamo" was for Texas patriots. There was even a community voice in the form of the underground newspaper known as *The Rag*, which served as a guide to the growing number of kids arriving from Slidell and Las Cruces and Ponca City who'd heard that Austin was the hassle-free place to be.

The Vulcan Gas Company, located at 400 Congress Avenue, just ten blocks down from the State Capital, was Austin's first music hangout for hippies. Founded in 1967 by Houston White and Sandy Lockett, the Vulcan presented a mixed bag of music on its small stage, embellishing the sounds with the first and most creative light show in the state. To avoid friction from the local police and the notorious Texas Liquor Control Board agents, the Vulcan sold neither beer nor wine, preferring to let imbibing customers bring in their own libations in a brown bag or a garbage can. Most of the clientele, however, preferred to get more bang for the buck with LSD, which at times sold for the low, low price of eight hits for a dollar.

Music, not booze, not dope, not money, was the motivating force behind the Vulcan. It was a radical concept that ran counter to the way other clubs in Austin operated, one that quickly caught the attention of the new generation of rock bands who were hitting the road. Groundbreaking acts like the Velvet Underground, Moby Grape, and the Fugs would have bypassed the entire state of Texas if not for the Vulcan.

On the local level, the Vulcan was instrumental in breaking down the color barrier between black and white Austin by introducing major blues performers to a student-hippie crowd. Among the marquee attractions the Vulcan brought to town were boogieman John Lee Hooker; Freddie King, who was still working black joints like the Chicken in the Basket back in Dallas; Big Mama Thornton; Jimmy Reed; Sleepy John Estes, who had a large following among the folk blues purists; and Lightnin' Hopkins, the consummate Texas electric blues guitarist who was already considered an idol by many young whites infatuated with the blues. By simply showing up at the Vulcan, all of them demonstrated to the young white musicians that there was a precedent for their experimental inclinations. When it came to understanding what it was like being outcasts, outlaws, and misfits, the hippies didn't have a leg up on black folks, whom they referred to as "spades." Out of this merging of old black and young white sensibilities came a sound that was wholly unique.

The best example in Austin was the Thirteenth Floor Elevators, a thoroughly deranged, totally inspired group that was led by a screeching banshee of a vocalist named Roky Erickson and powered by the electrified jug rhythms played by his collaborator, Tommy Hall. The Elevators used blues as a musical foundation, and with the help of LSD, took it into the great beyond, and even onto the Top 40 charts with the hit single "You're Gonna Miss Me," before seeking greener pastures in California. Meanwhile, the Vulcan became home to a growing community of like-minded groups like Shiva's Headband, the Conqueroo, Sunnyland Special, and Mother Earth, all of whom shuttled out to San Francisco at one time or another, joining influential Texas expatriates like Chet Helms, the proprietor of the Family Dog concert-promotion group who hitchhiked to California with his paramour Janis Joplin, and Bob Simmons, the program director of the free-form radio station KSAN-FM, who were creating the cultural revolution as they went along.

Of all the acts who appeared on the Vulcan stage, no single artist so thoroughly blew minds as did Johnny Winter, the albino guitarist from Beaumont. Members of the Conqueroo, one of the Vulcan's house bands, returned from a tour in Colorado raving about Winter. He might have been a whiter shade of pale, they said, but he played guitar like he was the ace of spades. They persuaded Houston White to take a chance on the guy, even though he'd never played Austin before for anything more than spare change. Winter was booked in early 1968 as the backup act for Muddy Waters, the reigning king of Chicago blues who had packed the house at the Vulcan a few months earlier after driving his band from the Windy City in a broken-down station wagon.

Each band played two sets. Winter's first set was witnessed by a crowd of twenty since most people were waiting for Muddy to start before they showed up. But the headliner could hear the opening act loud and clear from his dressing room. When Muddy Waters took the stage in front of a jam-packed room, he played like it was a matter of life and death. No punk hippie white boy was going to show him up. When it was Winter's turn again, the entire Muddy Waters band was seated near the front of the stage, making sure they were seeing what they had been hearing.

Winter's prowess as both a lead and rhythm player was so exceptional he needed nothing more than a bass and set of drums to propel his sound. He would fill in all the empty spaces himself. His drummer was Uncle John Turner, a big-boned running buddy who'd grown up down the road from Winter in Port Arthur. His bass player was Tommy Shannon, aka the Slut, a tall, gawky ding-dong daddy from Dumas, an isolated cowtown in the Texas panhandle. Winter had knocked around the club circuit between Houston and Louisiana for years working with his brother Edgar under a variety of guises — independent record producer Huey P. Meaux put out records by the Winters under the name the Great Believers, intentionally keeping them out of the public eye because, he said, "Every time people would see them, record sales would just stop because they were so freaky lookin'."

The appearance with Muddy Waters changed all that. Two local sound engineers named Bill Josey and Rim Kelley who had a small record label called Sonobeat used the Vulcan as a studio to record Winter's band. The tapes were so exceptional that Imperial Records leased the tapes and released them in 1969 as the record album *Progressive Blues Experiment*, a wild, rocked-up blues explosion that included classics like Waters's "Rollin' and Tumblin'," Howlin' Wolf's "Forty Four," Slim Harpo's "Got Love If You Want It," and originals such as "Mean Town Blues" and "Tribute to Muddy." The album, which was released on the heels of Winter signing a fat six-figure contract with Columbia Records, announced the arrival of a new guitar hero. He was the first white American player this side of the Butterfield Blues Band to attack electric blues music with as much feeling, heart, and soul as the elders he quoted from, though it was far from perfect, as evidenced by Winter's admonition to his bassist on the album, "Don't blow it, Slut, and I won't either."

Not only was the cutting edge of blues, which had been co-opted by British rock bands like Cream, the Yardbirds, and John Mayall's Bluesbreakers, back in the USA, but Winter's contract with Columbia signaled the beginning of a signing frenzy of new acts by record-company talent scouts eager to cash in on the burgeoning music scene being spun from the hippie movement.

Winter wasn't the only white-boy guitarist who fell under the spell of Muddy Waters. Waters's influence was indirectly responsible for Stevie's brother, Jimmie, quitting rock in order to devote his life to playing the blues. After Jimmie's band Texas Storm had backed up Big Brother and the Holding Company in Dallas in 1968, he hit it off with Big Brother's star vocalist, Janis Joplin, who took an immediate shine to the young Jimmie. The two partied hard and went nightclubbing until dawn. Janis told Jimmie she could get his band a record deal if he came out to California to showcase his band. In 1969, Texas Storm arrived in the Bay Area ready to be discovered. Instead, they discovered more high-quality speed than they had ever bargained for, as well as every other kind of pharmaceutical kick that was available for street consumption. By the time D.J. Jimmy Rabbit and manager Tom Ayers arranged for Texas Storm to play a showcase gig at the Whisky-A-Go-Go on the Sunset Strip in Los Angeles, opening for Junior Walker in August, they were all too far gone to realize what was at stake. Whether it was fear of success, too much speed, inexperience, or plain old stage fright, Jimmie and his band played so lamely that the visions of a big-time recording contract vanished before the first few songs were over. Big brother Jimmie screwed up big time.

Eighteen-year-old Jimmie Vaughan high-tailed it back to north Texas with his pregnant wife, Donna, settling down with a real job, hauling garbage for the City of Irving Department of Sanitation. Moving trash by day, drinking with the Bramhall boys while digging blues records by night, Jimmie had plenty of time to contemplate what had gone down. What was success anyway? Was it money? A nice apartment? Better equipment? More electronic gadgets? Trendier clothes? Cooler haircuts? Free drinks? Righteous dope? All the pussy in the world?

The truth came from watching Muddy Waters perform one night in Dallas. *He* certainly wasn't rich or famous, Jimmie realized, but he was most definitely the real thing. Muddy had the mojo and no record company dickhead could persuade him to give it up. All these other pretenders were a load of crap. Jimmie decided right then and there what he wanted to do. Fuck the Hollywood star trip. Fuck the record-company assholes in tight pants. Fuck the hippie peace and love rap. Fuck Janis's bullshit, Beatle haircuts, and flared bell-bottoms from Carnaby Street. Fuck the managers. Fuck the promoters. Fuck the booking agents. Fuck all the other sleazebags with their promises. All he was going to do forevermore was play the blues.

He knew Dallas, the City of Hate, was no place to do it. The memory of a pack of hoods rolling him at a Krystal hamburger joint just for having long hair was still fresh. As good as the Chessmen had been, they were still nothing more than a glorified cover band. Texas Storm had been on the right track, but California was a crock. The idea of going back to work the same joints both bands had worked made him sick to his stomach. His marriage was falling apart. He'd met a new girl named Connie Crouch, a junior high school friend of Stevie's. Stevie was one of the Oak Cliff kids who made Connie's room above the garage their unofficial clubhouse, gathering to drink on the sly, smoke pot, and listen to her brand-new eight-track tape player with the humongous speakers, entering and leaving through a window in the back where her father conveniently left a ladder. When Stevie brought along his big brother one day, Connie was infatuated. So was Jimmie, who found the pretty girl with the slight, delicate features irresistible. She had it all: good looks, a new purple Dodge Charger, credit cards, and parents willing to indulge her every whim. Connie's parents would even finance Jimmie's first single, which was released on the Connie label.

Jimmie knew if he was going to be a bluesman, Austin was the place to do it. He'd played the party circuit and clubs there long enough to know about Johnny Winter and the small, knowledgeable crowd of young blues freaks who were congregating there. Besides, there were also about a zillion hippie chicks on the loose in Austin, enough to take his mind off Connie Crouch, if only for a minute or two. Jimmie and Doyle Bramhall split Dallas for Austin in May of 1970, followed by Denny Freeman and Texas Storm vets Jamie Bassett and Paul Ray.

Most of the Dallas expatriates settled in small, bungalow rent houses in South Austin, a part of town that bore a striking resemblance to Oak Cliff. South Austin was on the wrong side of the Colorado River, a veritable Bubbaland of pickup trucks parked on the front lawn and backyard metal sheds. It had a mildly derelict charm, but it wasn't the hills or the old, twisted oaks that appealed to the new arrivals so much as the cheap rents. Starving musicians not only fit in among the poor and middle-class whites and Hispanics, it was about the only place in town that they could actually afford.

The trendy restaurants, the fashionable shops, the most palatial mansions were all north of the river, just like North Dallas. South Austin's leading merchants were the owners of auto parts stores, honkytonks, hamburger stands, twenty-four-hour cafés, and western hatters. The neighborhoods where the musicians settled were mostly within walking distance of bars and music halls like the Armadillo World Headquarters, which had replaced the Vulcan as Hippie Central when it opened in 1970 within weeks of the Vulcan's closing, and the Split Rail, a no-cover beer joint with live music seven nights a week.

Although the prevailing attitude was to sleep all day and party all night, Jimmie Vaughan joined Doyle Bramhall and Denny Freeman, who was known as the Professor for his encyclopedic knowledge of guitar stylings as well as his proclivity for holding down day jobs, as a construction worker. Not only did the work pay their bills, it was their ticket to the small time. One night they were gigging with Jamie Bassett, another survivor of the Texas Storm Whisky-A-Go-Go debacle, at the IL Club when a very excited, animated black man accosted them between sets. He was Tony Christian, their construction foreman, who happened to harbor ambitions of being a music promoter. He liked what he had just seen.

"You guys gonna be eatin' steaks next week," he promised them excitedly. He bought them all what he thought were sharp outfits and booked them into several small black nightclubs in the nearby small towns of Bastrop and Elgin, billing Jimmie as Freddie King, Jr. The initial reaction was predictable. One look at Jimmie Vaughan and the audience knew he was no son of Freddie King. But as soon as they heard him pick out the signature notes to the instrumental "Hideaway," they began to wonder. The arrangement lasted only a few days. The boys' brief encounter convinced them to concentrate on their own gig, not somebody else's.

There was a whole pecking order to the Austin blues scene: Jimmie and Denny and another ex-Dallasite named Derek O'Brien were cast as the young turks of the guitar, trying to follow in the footsteps of wildman Bill Campbell, who was generally regarded as Austin's first and best white blues guitarist and who was an ardent disciple of Albert Collins, Houston's answer to Freddie King. Paul Ray, Jamie Bassett, and Alex Napier all gravitated to the bass, along with a flamboyantly dressed character from Houston obsessed with Mexican conjunto music named Keith Ferguson. Lewis Cowdrey, an immigrant from Lubbock, earned the reputation as the most serious harmonica man around. Doyle, Dallas shuffle master Fredde Pharoah, the muscle-bound Rodney Craig, and Otis Lewis, a black man actually raised in Austin, were the drummers in most demand. The queen of the scene was Angela Strehli, the one contemporary, male or female, whose quiet intelligence and experiences in southside Chicago and California lent her all the credibility she needed. W. C. Clark, whose agility on bass as well as guitar and considerable road experience backing soul artists like Joe Tex provided the vital link to the black East Austin scene where he was raised.

Like most of the new blues boys in Austin, Jimmie relished his outsider's role, operating in a vacuum light years removed from acid rock and the hippie country movement that was beginning to infatuate Austin and the rest of Texas. "It just wasn't very popular, what we was doin'," he told critic Ed Ward. "It's just what we liked. We didn't care. I didn't think about career or money or what I was going to be later. I was just playing Lazy Lester songs and having a good time."

It didn't take long for Denny Freeman to figure out that Jimmie's approach to the music was different from everyone else's. "He really turned my head around that somebody could be this serious about playing hard-core blues, not just an assortment of R&B songs," he noted years later. One of his most important contributions was teaching others that feeling, not perfection, was the key to understanding the music. If a song fell apart, Jimmie would smile approvingly. "That was perfect. Don't you get it?" Blues wasn't supposed to be flawless, it was supposed to be dirty, low-down, greasy. Anything but perfect.

Jimmie's greatest contribution was putting the guitar back in its rightful place as an ensemble piece, a discovery that would still reverberate in music circles twenty years later. The average pimple-pocked American male teenager still believed that Jimmy Page and Eric Clapton invented the blues. It was time to educate them that the guitar was more than a big dick in the hand of an Englishman with a shag haircut. Jimmie had already mastered all the tricks of excess at the age of fifteen, doing all the "frentafrentafrentas" and all the "hiddleyhiddleyhiddleys" as fast as his fingers would allow. His blind date with Destiny and the music biz at the Whisky convinced him once and for all what he *didn't* want to be. "After I figured out that [stuff] was just sort of jerking off, it wasn't important to me," he said. "I think you can say more with a couple of notes than you can with fifteen, if the feeling's there."

Jimmie understood the value of holding back and saying only what you needed to say with your instrument. By doing so, he single-handedly deconstructed the modern electric guitar sound and refocused attention on its power as a rhythm instrument. It would be another ten years before anyone other than those rabid believers resting their elbows on the bars of the IL, the One Knite, and La Cucaracha would realize the significance of what was going down.

Jimmie didn't just play cool, he looked cool, rarely letting emotion show in his boyish face. He hardly moved from his spot onstage, but he oozed a coarse sexuality that drew fawning female admirers to every gig. "I was soaking up more than just his playing," gushed Kathy Valentine, a young guitarist who later had her moment in the spotlight as the bassist for the all-girl band the Go-Gos. "It was his attitude. He was so cool. To me, it was a whole persona, and he really had it."

Becky Crabtree, another Oak Cliff native, saw it, too. She was sixteen when she saw Jimmie playing onstage at the Rolling Hills Country Club outside of Austin, which her sister ran with Alex Napier. "He had a charisma that would knock any woman off her feet," she vividly recalled. "The way he looked, the way he talked, the way he played. He was magical." Becky fell in love with the guitar player, even though he was rebounding from his divorce from Donna and living with Connie Crouch, who had followed him to Austin. As a result of a drunken tryst, Becky became pregnant and bore a child whom she named Tyrone Vaughan, after soul singer Tyrone Davis and the man she said was the child's father. Jimmie wasn't so sure. Everybody in the blues tribe had fucked everyone else at one time or another. Who could tell?

Jimmie Vaughan's monastic approach onstage made a disciple out of his little brother. Stevie went to see Jimmie perform every chance he could. He stood up on chairs and hollered at the end of each song, and pestered Jimmie between sets to teach him new guitar tricks.

"It didn't seem like he was doing it to get out there and make money," observed Stevie. "It has more to do with what he really liked and what he really cared about, and that to me meant listening to your heart. When you listen to your heart it seems like you got something to say, whether it be through music or through whatever, 'cause it's not all in your head. It's got more to do with living it. I don't mean just tearing yourself down 'cause that's what you got to do. That's just the myth part."

Jimmie regarded Stevie as a pain in the ass, but there was no way he could ignore his fawning sibling. If he saw Stevie in the crowd and found the opportunity, he called him up to sit in, a courtesy he rarely extended to other guitarists.

"Stevie, who's the better guitar player, you or Jimmie?" Shirley Dimmick Ratisseau, an older blues aficionado would frequently tease whenever she saw Stevie show up to jam with his brother.

"Jimmie," he replied automatically. "He's the greatest."

"Stevie idolized his brother, he worshiped him," said Christian Plicque. "It almost made me sick."

Jimmie returned the compliment begrudgingly. Whenever he went out to hear Blackbird, his standard comment was, "You guys ain't no goddamn good." Stevie's band mates thought Jimmie treated their lead guitarist like shit. Still, he couldn't help but be impressed with the progress his little brother had made since he moved to Austin. "He was a motherfucker," Jimmie recalled. "He worked twice as hard as I did because he was trying to beat me." Jimmie even relented and once played a double bill with Stevie at the South Door club off East Riverside Drive in the middle of a student ghetto known as Apartment City in 1972. Anyone who came to the show anticipating a Vaughan cutting contest left disappointed, though. The boys may have been ruthless with other musicians, but they avoided slicing each other up onstage.

A burst of creativity struck eighteen-year-old Stevie Vaughan like a ballpeen hammer. The same code of conduct that was observed elsewhere was in effect here: the bands that filled the seats and sold the most beer got the sweetest, best-paying gigs. But instead of playing cover songs all night long, audiences actually encouraged performers to show them something new and completely different. The sense of artistic freedom that prevailed in Austin music circles was unlike anything any Texas boy or girl had experienced before. The only price was the absence of all the material trappings associated with success.

"It has always been an anti-commercial scene," explained artist Jim Franklin. "Most of the people are content to play the same clubs and just get by and smoke their dope and drink their beer. How do you take an atmosphere that's suspicious of capitalism and heavily anti-commercial and market it?"

Though there were hundreds of bands swarming around town, you could count the total population of managers, accountants, and other professionals typically associated with the business of music on two hands. When musicians talked about business, they were referring to how much they made off the door or by passing the hat. Nobody much cared whether or not the most successful talent in town made it big in Nashville or Hollywood. As long as they could do their own thing, Austin would do just fine. It was no way to get rich, but you sure could have one hell of a good time.

The guitar had already done more for Stevie than he ever dreamed. It liberated him from a bad situation at home. It got him to Austin. It introduced him to some mighty fine women who didn't care what he looked like or what kind of clothes he wore. He was going to enjoy this line of work, he thought to himself.

4

CRAWLIN' TO LA

Nothing else mattered except guitars. When Stevie was onstage, his head bowed, working his way through a tight, improvisational passage, his amps cranked up to ten, he felt like he'd left the material world. Offstage, he scrounged around music stores and pawnshops, looking at the new arrivals and testing out the merchandise. Even when he lived on the couch circuit, he always made sure to bring along his axe, his portable stereo, and his favorite records so he could practice playing along with Albert King, Muddy Waters, B. B. King, Eric Clapton, and Jimi Hendrix. Even without an instrument in his hands, his fingers were always moving, working the strings and frets of an imaginary air guitar as he waited in line at a 7-Eleven or a Mexican restaurant.

In his mind, it was all part of the discipline, the kind that they didn't teach in school. But from the perspective of the circle of friends he ran with, Stevie's tunnel vision sometimes made him a real pain in the ass. When he needed something to eat, when the rent money was due, or when he blew up his equipment, which happened more often than it should have, he relied on his pals for assistance. Cutter Brandenburg was always there for Stevie, doing what he could, even going so far as to scour the streets, alleys, and trash bins to collect aluminum cans to keep Stevie going. Music, that was always the top priority, they both agreed. "We weren't even thinking food," Cutter insisted. "Fuck food. We needed to get Stevie some strings."

Stevie's girlfriend Glenda Maples helped out, too. The chicks, the old ladies, and the female fans were the great unsung saviors of the music scene. Musicians pursued their art. Their squeezes held down the regular jobs. The men postured like a bunch of macho baboons, but it was in fact an odd matriarchy in which the men provided the thrills and the women provided the bucks.

Stevie was devoted to Glenda, but the way he saw it, sex was part of his job. He couldn't help it if his guitar got women all hot and bothered, and he couldn't tell a fan to go away, not when she looked like a stone fox. Glenda begged to differ, which was the basis for constant fights. When Stevie and Glenda were sharing a house with Christian Plicque, the couple got into a particularly nasty knock-down-and-drag-out that climaxed with Glenda splitting the premises. A few minutes later, Christian peeked in to see how his partner was handling it. Stevie was in bed fast asleep, cradling his guitar.

Blackbird fell apart less than a year after the band moved to Austin. Toward the end, the tension was visible onstage. Christian was singing like a wimp as far as Stevie was concerned. If he couldn't be heard when Stevie cranked up the guitar volume, that was his problem. Besides, he had grown tired of the band's revolving door of support players and the material they were playing. A young black guy prancing around stage like a pansy didn't fit in with a blues band, even if he had the right skin color. A cat like Doyle knew more about blues than Christian ever would. "You'll never be black," Stevie jeered.

It was time for a change. Christian Plicque eventually left town with a pile of unpaid debts in his wake and settled first in France, then in Finland, where he made a name for himself as a gospel singer. Stevie jumped out of Blackbird and into the unknown.

Austin's blues scene was like a swap meet. Musicians jammed with one another constantly, breaking off and reforming into different combinations like blobs in a lava lamp. "Every month there was somebody new in the band," Stevie said of Blackbird. "I learned how to play with someone until the energy was gone and before it was really a deadbeat kind of thing. It was a real neat growing experience." While this may have been an essential part of the learning process, it didn't generate much cash. Cutter was so broke that he left Stevie to work for one of the few bands in town that was making a decent living, a band called Krackerjack. From almost the minute he hit town, Stevie gravitated to the big two-story house on Sixteenth Street where the band lived.

Krackerjack was considered a rock-and-roll band, though with a definite affinity for blues. Every gig was a full-blown production from start to finish, which impressed their sizable following and pleased club owners who considered bar receipts the ultimate arbiter of a band's success or failure. Krackerjack's drummer, Uncle John Turner, and bassist, Tommy Shannon, had already achieved legendary status by virtue of their association with Johnny Winter, a wild limo ride that began at the old Vulcan Gas Company and cruised through Woodstock before spinning out in early 1970 when Winter fired them after a disastrous European tour marked by drug busts and confiscated equipment.

There was more to Krackerjack than just Unk and Slut, though. Guitarist Jesse Taylor, a Lubbock native who'd already tried the star trip in Los Angeles, was a pretty fair guitarslinger in his own right. Lead singer Bruce Bowland, another Dallas product, possessed an exceptionally histrionic voice and stage presence that could hold any crowd's attention from the moment he first wailed into the microphone. Mike Kindred, another Oak Cliff escapee, had a facile touch improvising lead lines on the keyboards while adding rhythm fills.

Unk, a burly figure who kept his receding hairline covered with a scarf, was the brains behind the operation. He was just about the only player even vaguely associated with the Austin blues scene who had any head for the business part of music. In some respects he was too smart for his own good, often scaring off talent scouts by voicing his opinions on artistic control and cover art long before negotiations got under way.

Shortly after Jesse Taylor left the band, Stevie was recruited as his replacement. His buddy Roddy Colonna joined the band as well, and the two moved into the Krackerjack house along with their women. It was a startling introduction to playing in a real band. Playing your instrument well was only a small part of the job, Unk stressed. You couldn't just show up and plug in, you had to approach every single hour-and-twenty-five-minute set like it was a concert, down to the boxes of Crackerjack candy you threw out to the audience before the encore. Stevie thought it was kind of jive, but he respected Unk as a showman and as a front man who gave club owners and agents like Charlie Hatchett fits, especially when he injected "hippie talk" into the conversation. One of the tricks of the trade Turner passed on to Cutter was how to book a gig. There were three crucial dates a band should be working every month, Turner told him: the first and fifteenth, which were the days that state employees received their paychecks, and full-moon nights, when the crowds were the rowdiest.

Cutter's loyalty was beyond question. He and his dog moved into the mini–storage warehouse where Krackerjack kept their equipment, just to be sure that they didn't get ripped off. His bed was a piece of foam rubber that was used during gigs to baffle the bass drum. His bathroom was the men's room at the Pizza Hut down the block. "The cops would come by and bring me coffee," he recalled. "They kind of liked it 'cause I kept an eye on things."

One of the clubs on Krackerjack's regular circuit was the Abraxis, in Waco, ninety miles north of Austin. The money was good at the Abraxis, but the management's willingness to provide band members with all the booze and drugs they could consume before, during, and after the show was even better. As the kid in the band, Stevie looked out for others. Memories of being left out of the party were still fresh on his mind. After one Abraxis gig, he approached his old Oak Cliff pal Billy Knight, who was working as a roadie, hauling Krackerjack's equipment.

"Hey, Billy, I just had some great cocaine!" Stevie exclaimed excitedly.

"Great, man," said Knight, who was packing up the amplifiers and guitar cases. "How come I didn't get any?"

"I'll get you some, Billy, don't worry," Stevie said apologetically.

Minutes later a burly fellow materialized in front of Knight with a plastic bag full of sparkling white powder. Knight shovelled the coke into his nose with a guitar pick, packed up the car, rounded up Stevie, and hit the road. "All the way back to Austin, Stevie was playing riffs with the neck of his guitar pressed up against my neck," Knight said. "We were both high as motherfuckers. It was a feeling I'll never forget."

The stint with Krackerjack only lasted a few weeks. Roddy got a case of hepatitis and had to drop out. Unk was convinced that the band had to start wearing makeup like Dallas's Werewolves, the New York Dolls, and other glam-rock bands. Stevie was not into it at all. Two Dallas musicians, Gary Myrick and Mark Stinson, came down to audition for Unk and Tommy, and Stevie got the boot. He didn't miss much. Soon after he was fired from the band, Krackerjack self-destructed in a mushroom cloud of speed, heroin, acid, and reds. In July of 1973, Cutter, Tommy, and Bruce Bowland were busted for drug possession along with future *Playboy* magazine Playmate Janet Quist, one of the band's most avid groupies. Tommy was the only one actually taken into custody by police, his thousand-dollar bail posted by booking agent Charlie Hatchett. Six months later Thomas L. Smedley, aka Tommy Shannon, pleaded guilty to possession of LSD and served two years' probation. One of the conditions of his probation was that he "cease employment with his present band, the Krackerjacks [sic]."

Though Stevie wasn't busted, his moorings were coming unraveled. He began shooting speed to the point that friends voiced their concern and his relationship with Glenda cratered. He didn't give a shit. As long as he could play — and he could play, all right — it was his business if he wanted to get high. Cutter for all his loyalty didn't like what he was seeing and decided to get out of Austin, signing on with the touring rock band Jo Jo Gunne and eventually seeing the world as part of pop star Andy Gibb's road crew. "Before I left, I saw Stevie and he looked pretty bad," he admitted. "I was worried about him. I knew I couldn't do anything for him at that point. He was real excited by the possibility of this deal with Marc Benno."

And why shouldn't he be? Marc Benno was a curly haired waif of a songwriter, guitarist, and pianist from East Dallas. Benno couldn't play half as well as Stevie, but nonetheless he managed to hit it big in Hollywood after falling in with a well-connected, multitalented pianist from Oklahoma named Leon Russell. The two collaborated as the Asylum Choir, a band they dreamed up in Russell's home studio in North Hollywood in the late sixties that yielded two mildly successful albums shortly before Russell took off as a solo act in 1970.

The Leon connection scored Benno a substantial contract of his own with A&M Records, who released albums under Benno's name while he was also conducting a crack Memphis band called the Dixie Flyers, the support group for a saucy chick singer named Rita Coolidge. Coolidge liked Benno's songs and covered several of them on her albums, two of which, "Nice Feelin' " and "Second Story Window," garnered a smattering of radio airplay.

Benno's MO in making his first three albums, *Marc Benno, Minnows,* and *Ambush,* and the much later released *Lost in Austin,* was to assemble all-star lineups of studio musicians. Over the course of those records his supporting cast included the soul singer Bobby Womack, guitarists Jesse Ed Davis, Albert Lee, Ry Cooder, and Eric Clapton, bassists Carl Radle and Ray Brown, drummer Jim Keltner, pianist Mike Utley, and sax player Bobby Keys. Then again, Benno himself was a distinguished studio cat of sorts, having achieved some renown when he answered Jim Morrison's call for a Texas guitar player who could play a big-legged kind of guitar lead for a song his band the Doors was cutting called "L.A. Woman."

Despite his extensive ties to the Hollywood music scene and all the visible trappings of wealth and success, Benno was bummed out with his station in life. He wasn't comfortable with the privileged and handsomely underwritten life of a rock star. He wanted to yowl like a colored man and make the notes on a battered acoustic sing and sting like only those lean, old-man fingers could do. He set out on a personal quest, pointing his Porsche east toward Texas, to the front porch of country blues legend Mance Lipscomb, who lived in the small Brazos Valley town of Navasota. "I was going through a lot of changes which unfortunately I had to go through in front of the entire audience including the record company," Benno said. "I'd never made a record that sounded like me."

As the white boy from Hollywood traded licks with the elderly Negro bluesman, he swore to himself that his next album had to be a Texas album. Back in LA, he convinced the generous and groovy executives who held the purse strings at A&M Records to finance his dream. In the late fall of 1972, with company running change in his pocket, Benno aimed the Porsche back to Texas, this time to Austin to create his fourth album.

Benno sent word to Memphis for bassist Tommy McClure, his old buddy from the Dixie Flyers, to join him. In mid-January, they persuaded Charlie Freeman, the Dixie Flyers' guitarist, to come on down to hang, play, and get loaded. Freeman, a wildman's wildman, was at the end of his string. He'd spent most of the previous year hanging out all around the country with other musicians, looking for work and getting way too high by ingesting anything he could get his hands on. He arrived to find Benno and McClure in similarly tore-down states of mind. The three proceeded to tear things down even further. After four days and four nights of trying to find inspiration via any means possible, Freeman passed out and didn't get up. He had overdosed on heroin and was pronounced dead at Brackenridge Hospital on the last day of the first month of 1973.

Benno was not to be denied. He tracked down Jimmie Vaughan, whose "high-powered, high-volume" sound had impressed him ever since the days when he'd drop in to watch the Chessmen at the Studio Club back in Dallas. "I remember thinking his stuff was better than Hendrix, better than Clapton," Benno mused. Now Jimmie was doing exactly what Benno wished he could be doing — blues with no compromise — which was exactly the sound he was looking to get on his next album. But Jimmie made it plain he was not interested, no matter how much money was in the deal. Benno was no blues cat.

"No, I can't do it," he told him. "I'm into the blues only. I'm not gonna play any of that other stuff. But my brother, man, you oughta hear him. He can do it."

Benno vaguely remembered Stevie Vaughan's no-holds-barred approach when he saw him sitting in with Jimmie's band, Texas Storm, at the End of Cole Club in Dallas in 1969. He followed up Jimmie's recommendation and went to see Stevie going through the motions at Mother Earth. Sure enough, Stevie played blues guitar like a rockin' mother with the flame on, down to the purple velvet jacket he wore.

Stevie was thrilled and a little intimidated when Jimmie introduced him to Benno. Hey, this guy was a genuine major-league rocker. Jimmie told him Benno was the real thing, no shit. "This guy's going to Hollywood. He's got a happening deal," he said.

"You think I oughta go with him?" Stevie asked his brother.

"You oughta go," nodded Jimmie.

Just when he needed a break, a change of scenery, something, anything, salvation arrived in the form of this gnome in a Porsche. Then it got even better. Benno approached Doyle Bramhall, who he thought was "the best white singer in the whole world," and a tough drummer, too, and Doyle said yes and left Jimmie Vaughan's band the Storm. So did Billy Etheridge, another Chessmen vet who had just come off a stretch with Krackerjack, as well as bassist Tommy McClure. It wasn't exactly Mance Lipscomb or Lightnin' Hopkins, but it was close enough for Benno. "These guys were the bad boys and I had them in my band."

It was easy for Stevie to buy in. Shit, just working with Doyle was an accomplishment. He was a hero, someone he'd always looked up to. Doyle had the blackest voice of any white boy he'd ever heard, and he had heard a lot. The others were no slouches either. These cats were his brother's equals. And now they were his equals, too. And together, they would all get the full-blown, deluxe rock-star treatment they only read about in magazines. A&M supplied the band with new gear and gave them a salary and per diems while they rehearsed and played warm-up gigs at small clubs like the Flight 505 in Austin.

Stevie was rich, or as he and his friends put it, "nigger rich." For the first time in his life, he could actually afford to buy all the packs of cigarettes he wanted, a big bottle of liquor on the side, all the dope he wanted. He lived like there was no tomorrow while putting some songs together.

Suitably jacked up and in tune, the band, dubbed Marc Benno & the Nightcrawlers, did the recording trip first-class. With A&M's cash and stroke, they went on the road for a handful of arena concert dates opening for Humble Pie and the J. Geils Band. Mega-manager Dee Anthony, who handled both headline acts, agreed to add the Nightcrawlers to the tour to see if they were worth managing, but Anthony didn't take the bait. In fact he dumped Humble Pie during the tour. But at least the concerts gave the Nightcrawlers a chance to road-test their material. Benno and the band were then flown to Hollywood and housed at the Sunset Marquis while producer David Anderle blocked out most of April at Sunset Sound. Through it all, Stevie kept practicing.

"We were way over our heads. We thought we were stars," Benno laughed. "Plus we were completely out of control. We were doing things the Rolling Stones didn't do until no one was looking. We were ripping and running pretty hard. We were all into our diseases pretty bad. We could care less what people thought."

Anderle was a seasoned pro, having produced the Beach Boys and Eric Clapton with Delaney and Bonnie and Friends, among others, and he knew practically every competent session player in LA. But the teen-aged Texan Benno had brought along could play guitar like no one he'd seen. He played with the touch and experience of someone three times his age. Anderle saw potential in the quiet kid with the serious look and the massive forearms. He could be another Clapton, Anderle mused. He was sufficiently intrigued to loan Stevie a white Fender Stratocaster that had belonged to the recently departed Charlie Freeman.

The gesture floored Stevie. The Strat was the finest guitar he'd ever caressed. It made the Barney Kessel he was playing seem obsolete. He felt blessed. Just because he could play and wanted to play, just because he had talent, people were willing to drop gifts on him like the Strat. He was residing in the lap of luxury with a swimming pool and maid service and someone to drive him around wherever he needed to go. "Man, I'm standing here on the corner in LA and there goes Chuck Berry," Stevie screamed over a pay phone to a friend in Seattle. "God! I can't believe it."

Every day he was meeting some heavy dude or another, someone like Jim Keltner and Lee Sklar, the best rhythm section in the business, cats who weren't too high and mighty to throw a few compliments his way, especially the way he picked out his beloved blues. "You don't sound like a white boy," they'd say. "You play like you were born black." Yeah, the Hollywood star trip was OK by him.

Anderle recorded eight tracks by the Nightcrawlers: "Dirty Pool," a wickedly wretched dirge written and sung by Doyle; a rambling ode to caffeine called "Coffee Cup"; "Take Me Down Easy," a Benno original that could have just as well been a page torn out of Leon Russell's songbook; "Love Is Turning Green," in which Stevie came closest to hitting his signature Albert King tone; three fairly forgettable tracks — "Hot Shoe Blues," "Mellow Monday," "Crawlin' " — and "Last Train," which eventually turned up on Benno's *Lost in Austin* album, with Eric Clapton doing the honors on lead guitar. On this earlier version, though, the solo was Stevie's. Benno was a fair picker himself, but just as he let Doyle do most of the singing, he wisely deferred to Stevie when it came to the guitar parts. Still, Stevie was young and impressionable enough to let Benno's and Anderle's LA dynamics rub off. Instead of a dirty, fat tone, his leads evoked the laid-back, mildly funky sound that was currently in vogue in recording circles.

"At that time, I was trying to get him to play some sweet licks," Benno said, referring to the kind of clean single notes that Clapton was turning out for Delaney and Bonnie Bramlett, whose epochal *On Tour* album opened the floodgates for the progressive-blues revival collectively known as Southern rock. "Stevie was doing some colorful, beautiful work with lightning speed," Benno observed. To round out the proceedings, Anderle brought in saxophonist Plas Johnson, who once contributed the honks and bleats behind rock-and-roll trailblazer Little Richard.

A&M president Jerry Moss hated the record. "Marc," he said, after listening to the reference tape that Benno brought him. "This doesn't sound *anything* like you. This is not what I'm looking for." The album was too greasy, Moss complained, a reflection of the spiritual pits the band had sunk to after too many days of doing too much of everything. "Where is Marc Benno?" Moss wanted to know.

Benno was dumbfounded. He thought he had made the kind of Texas record everyone had agreed he should make. He told Moss he respected Doyle's singing so much, he let him do the vocals.

"I've already got Joe Cocker," Moss replied. "What do you want me to do with this?"

A&M rejected the album and Anderle instructed Benno to get back to the drawing board.

Stevie was shocked when Benno broke the news to him. He had been celebrating completion of the project and entertaining visions of arenas full of screaming fans, piles of money, even bigger piles of dope, and all the chicks he could handle. All of a sudden, the dreams vanished. It couldn't be true. He didn't know who to blame — the suits at the record company, Benno, the band, or all of them.

Benno knew it was either his ass or the band's. If it didn't work out, he chalked it up to the vagaries of the music business. He didn't have much choice. "When I had to go tell these guys, they hated my guts," Benno said. "I told them I wanted it to work, but it was over. We had touched the platinum success, riding in limos and everything. Our feet never touched the street."

Stevie was pissed off, all right. The rock-and-roll star trip was kaput. Suddenly, he was back in Austin, broke and broken-spirited. He moved in next door to Doyle, his wife, Linda, and their two children, Doyle, Jr., and Georgia. For a few months, Becky Crabtree, Jimmie's onetime paramour, and her son, Tyrone, moved in to share Stevie's part of the house. Using persistence and guilt-tripping, Becky persuaded Stevie to put down his guitar long enough to baby-sit Tyrone now and then. If Becky was telling the truth, if Tyrone really was Jimmie's son, that made Stevie Tyrone's uncle. And an uncle had to look after his nephew. It was only right. But it sure wasn't easy, doing all the things you were supposed to do for a baby. "What Stevie dug the most was feeding him," remembered Becky, who was struggling to raise her son with welfare checks and odd jobs. "I'd come home and there'd be peas and carrots and spinach all over his face and I would say, 'Well, did any make it through his mouth?' "

Benno stayed behind in Los Angeles, trying to salvage his record deal. Back in Austin, Stevie, Doyle, and Billy Etheridge decided to keep the Nightcrawlers together. They didn't need a front man anyway. Tommy McClure fell out and was replaced by Keith Ferguson, the Houston bass player who quit Jimmie Vaughan's band to sign on, much to Jimmie's vociferous displeasure. Then they added Drew Pennington, a handsome young man who could blow a serviceable harmonica. The reborn Night-crawlers slithered into the regular Tuesday-night slot at the One Knite, the bar that had become the unofficial home of the blues in Austin.

The One Knite Dive and Tavern, as it was formally known, was a dark, dank, wonderfully forbidden place. Patrons entered the old stone building at the corner of Eighth and Red River, just around the corner from the police station, by walking through the frame of an upright coffin. Once inside, the smell of stale beer, yesterday's smoke, and puke immediately filled the nostrils. The cluttered *objets de junque* hanging from the ceiling — old kitchen sinks, bicycle tires, mangled appliances — sent up warning flags that this was not a joint for the meek or faint of heart. To the musicians working the cramped stage for whatever money the customers happened to drop in the hat that was passed around, the One Knite was purgatory, if not exactly paradise, a somewhat reputable establishment where young white boys smitten with the blues could in-dulge themselves to their hearts' content without some uptight bar owner telling them to "stop playing that damned nigger music."

The One Knite's peculiar stench was worth enduring almost any night of the week. Mondays belonged to Jimmie Vaughan's band, the Storm, a group that had evolved from the old Texas Storm. Tuesdays were the Nightcrawlers. Southern Feeling with Angela Strehli, W. C. Clark, and Derek O'Brien provided the entertainment on Wednesday, and Otis Lewis and the Cotton Kings held down the Thursday slot, with folk and country-rock bands on the weekend.

Of all those bands, the Nightcrawlers were easily the motliest. The pain Doyle Bramhall sang about did not seem secondhand when he growled through Little Willie John's "Grits Ain't Groceries" or Little Walter's "Boom Boom, Out Go the Lights." Billy Etheridge pounded on the keys like he was still playing to 18,000 screaming fans at Cobo Hall in Detroit with Marc Benno instead of two dozen patrons who were dis-tracted by the nasty broads in short shorts who just walked in the door. Keith Ferguson cut a dashing, somewhat inscrutable figure with his lay-ered rock-star haircut and colored scarves providing an intriguing con-trast to his gold-capped teeth and tattoos.

But it was the skinny runt with the flat, wide nose who stood out the most. Older men on the same stage physically grimaced whenever they took their turns trying to squeeze emotion out of every pluck of the guitar strings. The kid did it effortlessly like he'd been born into the role. When it came his time to take a lead, he meekly stepped forward, his head bent over his instrument, and cut loose with a barrage of notes and grinding chords channeled through a wall of distortion. Sometimes, he'd get so into manipulating the strings, he'd leave the band behind, launching out into renditions of songs like Stevie Wonder's "Superstition" that no one else knew. Every once in a while, he'd do the same thing with Hendrix material. The audience loved it. The band hated it.

"Hey, man, cool it," one of his band mates would yell over his solo. "We don't do that song, Stevie. Savvy?"

The kid's gift did not go unnoticed. Hell, it would have been impossible for anyone to ignore him.

"Who is *that?*" asked a guy with an oval patch that read "Evan" on his gas station shirt, who had interrupted his game of nine ball to check out what was happening on the minuscule stage.

"Little Stevie Vaughan," replied a bearded fat man wearing a sleeveless denim jacket and lining up a shot. "He's Jimmie's little bro'. He's gonna be big someday, man. He may be even better than Jimmie."

Evan laughed derisively, flicking his cigarette on the floor and chalking up his cue stick. "He's hot shit, all right. But better than Jimmie? Kiss my ass."

Evan might not have bought in, not just yet, anyway. But two North Austin fifteen-year-olds who knew Billy Etheridge immediately saw the light. Eddie Stout had a motor scooter and a bass guitar and his friend David Murray was a guitar fanatic. At Etheridge's suggestion, they sneaked into the One Knite to check out his band. Eddie and David were impressed with the Nightcrawlers, all right, but they were floored by the guy with the Barney Kessel. The other guys were old enough to be called men. But the guitar player, he was like they were, a mere kid of eighteen who looked even younger than his years. The boys couldn't help but compare Stevie to his big brother using sexual metaphors. "Jimmie makes love to you the way he plays," Eddie would say, only to have David counter, "Yeah, Stevie just throws you down and rapes you."

Eddie and David would absorb the music, then hop on Eddie's motor scooter and go back home to try and replicate what they'd just heard. It was an imprecise method of learning, but it worked. By his sixteenth birthday, David Murray wheedled his way onto the One Knite stage. His playing might have been a bit tentative, but he'd studied his mentor well.

It didn't take long for Stevie to notice Eddie and David sneaking into the club, hanging out at rehearsals at Billy Etheridge's, or coming over to Denny Freeman's house on Wilson Street, trying to get him to show them a few chords. Wherever Stevie went, they always seemed to turn up, peeking around corners to check him out. Stevie took a shine to both boys. He saw more than a little of himself in them. It wasn't that long ago that he was sneaking into joints to watch the older guys run through their paces. Given David's interest in guitar, he took him under his wing and treated him like the kid brother he never had.

One night after the Nightcrawlers finished their last set at the One Knite, Stevie walked off the stage and made a beeline straight to Murray. He extended his hand and gave him a bone-crushing shake.

"Man, I want to get with you and work together every chance we get." David winced and grinned at the same time. "I almost fainted," he said. "It was like Jesus coming to a disciple. I was just charged."

David wanted to learn. Stevie had plenty of chops to show him, but didn't have a driver's license, much less a car. David drove a red '64 Pontiac Tempest. The two became fast friends. David listened to what Stevie had to say and went to extremes to get it right. He bought a Strat, just like the kind Stevie had just traded for. He bought the same kind of amp. And although he wasn't born with his mentor's hands and forearms, David learned to play heavy-gauge strings, just like Stevie.

"That's the only way your hands will ever get strong," Stevie'd tell him. "The rock guys, they try to get their tone with a Les Paul and a Marshall," Stevie said. "That's the pussy way. You gotta get it with your fingers. Skinny strings won't stay in tune. They won't get a tone. There's nothing there to express yourself."

When he wasn't showing him licks and riffs, he liked to play David his favorite records. It was all about soul, he'd tell him.

"Listen!" he'd instruct David, jabbing him to make sure he heard all the important parts, repeating passages over and over until he was sure David understood. It was the way Jimmie taught him to play. Now it was his turn to be the teacher.

"Listen to the way B. B. King does it. He can say more with one note than other guys can with twenty. Just make sure it comes from your heart. You gotta connect with what's inside you."

Stevie would also show him what not to do. The cardinal sin of all white boys, he believed, was the stupid little trill they'd put on the end of a riff, lingering on the last note as long as their wiggling fingers could coax a sound from the fretboard. "That is the absolute worst, that is the whitest trick of them all."

Stevie opened doors for David, whom he started calling Little Brother. He introduced him to musicians and friends, put him on the guest list for gigs, and convinced David he could be doing the same thing he was doing if only he'd practice and stay focused. He even stood up for David when club owners caught him and threw him out for being underage. He understood. He'd been there.

Mostly they played guitar, working on their instruments through the night until the sun came up. Denny used to give Stevie shit about it, saying, "Hell, Stevie, you'd set up and play in a 7-Eleven if they'd let you." As far as he was concerned, Denny couldn't have paid a bigger compliment.

True to many peoples' instinctive desire to identify themselves individually and collectively with markings, Stevie decided to certify his dedication to blues, the guitar, and the musician's life. He wanted a tattoo. Blues buddy Mark Pollock had already pierced one of his ears, using a diaper pin borrowed from Doyle Bramhall's baby. But a tattoo was something else. It couldn't be any tattoo, either. It had to be something unique that would stand out even around someone like Keith Ferguson, who was the closest thing to the Illustrated Man that Stevie knew.

After conferring with Keith, they paid a visit to one of Keith's acquaintances, Old Man Shaw, a tattoo artist in Corpus Christi. Shaw could give Stevie what he wanted, a phoenix-like bird that Keith described as a space eagle, inked across his sunken chest. The bird, Stevie thought, would make him look badder than ever. But he didn't realize that Old Man Shaw didn't believe in anesthesia. Getting any size of tattoo could be a painful experience. A big bird spreading its wings from shoulder to shoulder was close to torture. As Stevie visibly winced in pain, the space eagle shrunk down to a peacock sitting on a swing, its tail drooping down. The bird was slightly off center, since Stevie fidgeted under the needle so much he had to be restrained by his band mates. It was his first tattoo. It was his last tattoo. He developed an obsession with jewelry instead.

If anything, the new, improved Nightcrawlers were even more depraved than their previous incarnation. When Doyle Bramhall's elder brother Ronnie heard about their determination to keep the band together after Marc Benno jacked them around, he decided to move down from Irving to Austin to look after the boys. He rented a house just east of Interstate 35 and let Doyle and Stevie move in. Unfortunately, Ronnie proved just as susceptible to temptations as had his younger brother Doyle, who was sharing a room with his heroin connection and dating a jailed coke dealer's wife. It was a constant party at the house. But despite the around-the-clock abuses, the music was better than ever.

The elder Bramhall had served time as the only white member of a nine-piece band led by singing and dancing blues entertainer Al "TNT" Braggs. Ronnie plugged his white Hammond B-3 organ into the funk of the Nightcrawlers, knowing full well that he was nowhere near the musician that Stevie was. "I would be listening to Stevie playing lead and he would play something so original, so incredible, it was like going into a maze," Ronnie remembered. "And I'd think, 'God! There's no way out!' and he would come right back to where he was supposed to be and be there when it came down. I'd be watching him, and I'd realize that I wouldn't even be playing. I'd just stopped. And I'd look back at Doyle and he'd be just shaking his head going, 'Whew.' "

Despite his considerable talent and growing confidence, around Jimmie, Stevie was still the stupid little shrimp. Whenever he'd ask Jimmie about his playing, Jimmie would lay down the law. "Don't be up here doin' this shit if you don't know what you're doin', and don't start something if you can't finish it."

One evening Stevie went with Ronnie and Doyle Bramhall out to Soap Creek Saloon, which was the old Rolling Hills Country Club, to see the Storm perform. After the gig, Stevie sidled up to Jimmie.

"Hey, how did you play that part, you know where you went . . ."

Jimmie cut him short with a sharp punch in the chest, knocking him to the ground.

"I showed you how to do that once, dammit," he snarled. "I'm not going to show you how to do it again."

Without Marc Benno, the Nightcrawlers still showed enough promise to attract the interest of Bill Ham, who carried considerable clout in rock-and-roll circles as the manager of that "little ol' band from Texas," ZZ Top. Ham was a larger-than-life figure with a striking physical resemblance to country-pop crooner Kenny Rodgers and a professional affinity to Colonel Tom Parker, the Svengali who guided Elvis Presley's career. He had been impressed with Stevie Vaughan the first time he'd heard him and often dreamed aloud how he'd like to put Jimmie and Stevie together in the same band. Jimmie showed little interest in the proposition, although he once offered Ham a pull off his bottle of cheap wine when Ham pulled up to the One Knite in a limousine. Stevie, on the other hand, was open to hearing Ham out, with or without Jimmie's participation. Ham proceeded to woo Nightcrawler, as he dubbed them, by rounding up some of ZZ Top's practice amps and a U-Haul truck and taping a show at The Warehouse in New Orleans. If Ham could score a deal with the demos, he promised them, he'd personally guide their career.

Bill Ham liked to test a band's mettle by putting them out on the road for several weeks. It was the method he'd used to whip ZZ Top into shape before they emerged as the biggest rock-and-roll band in Texas. If Nightcrawler could survive this version of boot camp, they'd prove their worth to Ham. As it turned out, they proved to themselves that they were not yet ready for prime time, judging from their subsequent tour through Hell, with stops in every tank town in the South big enough to support a Greyhound bus terminal and a club with a six-inch riser and an electrical outlet.

Half the gigs had been canceled by the time the band drove into town. The other half had an average attendance of less than twelve. Cynical minds mused whether or not Ham really wanted the band to emerge from the experience in one piece. Stevie was not the only guitarist that Ham had under contract. Two other guitar wizards from Austin, Van Wilks and Eric Johnson, were part of Ham's Lone Wolf Productions stable; so was the band Point Blank, a Dallas group fronted by guitarists Rusty Burns and Kim Davis, who'd played with Stevie in Blackbird. Ham also had Rocky Hill, the brother of ZZ Top's Dusty Hill, who happened to be one of the finest white blues axemen in the state, as well as one of the most uncooperative, unpredictable, messed-up musicians on God's green earth. Many musicians claimed that, keeping all those flashy blues guitarists in his stable was an effective means of ensuring that ZZ Top had no viable competition in the immediate vicinity.

Nightcrawler disintegrated somewhere in Mississippi. Doyle Bramhall and Drew Pennington got off easy. Their women came to fetch them. Keith Ferguson and Stevie were the only ones left to drive the truck back to Texas. Keith was so pissed off at the way things turned out — if only they hadn't hired Drew, if only they hadn't played footsy with Ham — he decided to take it out on Stevie and make the little fart drive all the way home.

Whenever Stevie felt like he was about to nod off, he asked Keith to take over the wheel. Keith would drive just long enough for Stevie to fall asleep, then pull over and shake him awake.

"C'mon, man, it's your turn to drive again."

Settling up with Ham was a pain in the ass. He wanted the backline equipment and the U-Haul truck back, as well as the $11,000 he'd invested, even though he realized he'd probably never see a dime. Paying back Ham was a noble idea, but Stevie was so broke, he was down to stealing steaks from the Safeway. The deal made him so upset that he put his fist through the wall on several occasions, and, according to friends, continued to curse Ham's name for years. But compared to others, Stevie walked away with few negative consequences. Eric Johnson recorded an album in England that Ham was unable to sell to a label. But Ham had invested hundreds of thousands of dollars in Johnson and wanted to see a return before he'd give him a release. The standoff took several years and a considerable sum of money before the artist could break free of the agreement.

All Stevie needed to remember was the day Ham's stretch limo pulled up to La Cucaracha on East Eleventh. Two eyewitnesses recalled that Ham had come to talk about the latest idea he'd hatched, a band he wanted to called Cut and Shoot after the East Texas town of the same name. The left-handed guitarist, Rusty Burns, that Ham brought with him to La Cuke was part of the plan. Ham wanted to match Stevie with Rusty and sell them to Capricorn Records as the next Allman Brothers.

"Can't you see it?" enthused Ham, choreographing the front line of his imaginary band. "You here. Rusty there. Right hand, left hand. Right hand. Left hand. You. Rusty. Can't you see it? Can't you see it?"

Stevie stared at his boots, then lifted his eyes, fixing a gaze on Ham. "No, man," he muttered. "I can't see it."

If this was what the big time was all about, Stevie would be happy working dives like the One Knite and La Cucaracha for the rest of his nights. He knew what he wanted, and it didn't include being told what to play by some yo-yo who thought a band's name or the way they wiggled their butts on stage was more important than the music.

He was approaching his twentieth birthday, but already he felt like a used-up has-been. Benno's deal had completely fucked up. Ham was a control freak. How was he going to play guitar on the moon if all these assholes were always screwing things up? He'd rather hang with the people who sincerely appreciated him just the way he was.

Ray Hennig had only been in Austin a few months, but knew Stevie like a favorite nephew. Hennig ran Heart of Texas Music, an instrument store he'd started in Waco and moved to Austin. Shortly after he opened the South Lamar Boulevard location, Stevie Vaughan became a regular window-shopper, dropping in to check out the rows of new and used guitars Hennig had on display. "He'd look at me and if they looked interesting he'd grab it, bend over and do a little ol' run or two on it, and hang it back up. He was just the kind of guy you're always glad to see come by. Course I knew he wouldn't buy anything 'cause he didn't have any money."

One day Stevie came in and spotted what Hennig described as "an old-rag, trashed-out Stratocaster," a 1959 model that Hennig had put on display in the back. "He grabbed that thing and started feeling around with it, then he'd take it and look at it, turn it over, then he'd set down and do another little old number on it, just picking out chords. I thought, 'Now that would be just about the kind of thing he'd pick out.' So all of a sudden he comes walking up, whispering, 'Hey, Ray? I've been listening to this thing.'

" 'Stevie, what do you want with that old raggedy thing?' I asked.

" 'I don't know. It feels good, man. It feels just exactly like what I'm looking for.'

" 'Well, go over there and hook the old raggedy thing up and see if it works,' I told him. 'Of course, being a Fender, it probably does.' "

Hennig observed that the longer Stevie played, the wider the smile on his face got.

"I love this old thing," Stevie said. "This feels like what I've been looking for all these years. This neck and everything."

"Yeah, but it looks like shit," Hennig replied.

"I don't care what it looks like. It sounds and feels like this is it."

Stevie proposed trading in a newer Strat he owned and returning a Les Paul that Hennig had loaned him if Hennig would let him keep the old Strat. Although another musician was interested in the guitar, he let Stevie take it. He was sure Stevie would bring back the raggedy old thing in a day or two. Stevie never did.

"He lived for that guitar," Hennig said. "It just became part of him. He told me it was the only guitar he ever had that said what he wanted it to say. Isn't that weird? It was like it was alive. That's what he thought. That guitar actually helped him play. That's how much confidence he had in it."

Marc Benno phoned Stevie again in the fall of 1974. He was holed up at Neil Young's house up in Bolinas, north of San Francisco, writing songs with Johnny Perez, the drummer from the Sir Douglas Quintet who had a knack for coming up with catchy, hook-laden lyrics. Would Stevie care to come out and join them? He still felt burned from the LA trip with the Nightcrawlers, and the Bill Ham affair was still fresh in his mind. But he was also between gigs, without a place to stay, and had nothing to lose.

"Send me a ticket," Stevie said.

By day, the three jammed around at Neil Young's country estate, working up new material. By night, they gigged in small clubs around Marin County. The three quickly made friends with area musicians including bassist Chris Ethridge, a founding member of country rock's Flying Burrito Brothers who later landed with Willie Nelson's band; saxman Martin Fierro; and Jerry Garcia, the lead guitarist and figurehead of the Grateful Dead, the icons of the San Francisco psychedelic movement. Garcia enjoyed dropping by the house to pick songs with the trio. He had this little label deal cooking, he told them. Someone was going to give him lots of money to sign musicians and produce records. Benno's combo would be perfect.

Marc Benno was still under contract to A&M. He called Jerry Moss, but Moss wouldn't let him out of the deal, irrespective of his recent lack of productivity. Benno, Perez, and Vaughan eventually headed back to Los Angeles in December to attempt another round of recording sessions at Sunset Sound, supported by the rhythm section of Russ Kunkel and Lee Sklar. They never got further than laying down a few instrumental tracks. Benno floundered for the lines he once delivered so effortlessly. His musicianship had been consumed by bad habits and the nasty divorce he was going through. It would be twelve years before his next album, *Lost in Austin,* would be released. A few days before Christmas, Stevie talked Johnny Perez, a native of San Antonio, into driving to Austin for the holidays.

The two made the long, fourteen-hundred-mile haul in less than twenty hours with Perez behind the wheel and Stevie riding shotgun, fingering the strings of his guitar and urging on Perez. "You can do it, J.P.," he kept saying between strums. "You can do it."

Crusty and bleary-eyed, they drove straight to the doorstep of Speedy Sparks, a former roadie for the Sir Douglas Quintet and a bass player who lived in one of the houses surrounding Red River Motors, an enclave of freelance, rogue mechanics. They walked inside as J.P. made introductions. Stevie shook Speedy's hand and excused himself, plopping down on the sofa so he could put a new set of strings on his guitar. He'd worn out the old set on the drive from LA.

The Christmas holidays were typically one of the slowest times of the year in clubland, what with all the UT students gone and families on vacation. Still, there was enough action for Stevie to realize how much he'd been missing. Marin County was a stone groove, but no one knew blues like his pals in Austin. Enlightenment came at a monster jam one night at the Ritz Theater, a decrepit old movie house on Sixth Street that had recently started booking bands. The improvising had started across the street at a bar called the Lamplite, where Doug Sahm had been sitting in with Jimmie Vaughan's Storm. By the time the action shifted to the Ritz, where Johnny Winter was headlining, Sahm, Winter, the Vaughans, and Denny Freeman were all blazing through a fanatic's repertoire of Texas blues classics.

"J.P., you can go back without me," Stevie informed Perez after the show. Marc Benno could wait. So could David Anderle, who kept bugging Stevie about Charlie Freeman's white Strat that he had loaned him; Stevie not only didn't have it, he couldn't remember where in the hell he'd hocked it. Bill Ham could wait until hell froze over. He wasn't a crook, but Stevie didn't trust him. Why did he always want to change the name of the band or dress everyone up? Stevie Vaughan was tired of sticking his hand in the fire and having it come out black and crispy around the edges every time. This time, he was going to stay in Austin for a while.

LAND OF THE COSMIC COWBOYS

By 1975, the rest of the world was beginning to discover the hip little music scene that was going down in Austin, thanks to the Armadillo World Headquarters, a converted armory at the corner of Barton Springs Road and South First Street. The Armadillo was a loose collective of music freaks spearheaded by Eddie Wilson, a former lobbyist for Texas brewery interests. It began as a cool concept cum crash pad and within two years evolved into concert hall, beer garden, and fine arts center for the counterculture. Jim Franklin, the 'Dillo's first house poster artist, was smitten with the armadillo, a shy, peace-loving creature with a hard-shell exterior whose worst natural predator was the automobile, as evidenced by the numerous carcasses on Texas roads. Franklin's renderings of the passive creature with the nine-banded armor became a symbol for Texas hippies, who had to be tough on the outside even if they were peace-loving individuals in their heart of hearts.

In the tradition of the Vulcan, the Armadillo booked blues acts like Lightnin' Hopkins and Mance Lipscomb. Dallas bluesman Freddie King played the hall so often it became known as "the house that Freddie built." But the real key to the Armadillo's renown was the club's ability to provide common ground for hippies and rednecks in a partying atmosphere where cocaine, country music, and good ol' Lone Star beer mixed together.

The turning point came when Nashville renegade Willie Nelson moved to Austin in 1972 and booked into the Armadillo. Willie was from the old school of country music singer/songwriters who did not try to disguise the accent in their voices. But Willie was a hipster, too, who appreciated righteous weed as much as he enjoyed a shot of tequila. By playing the 'Dillo he confirmed the suspicion that hippies — Texas hippies, at least — could dig real kicker music under the right conditions. Out of this strange cultural cross-pollination sprang the Cosmic Cowboy, a weird half-breed who was part longhair, part goat roper, steeped in rural country traditions but open to new ideas spawned by the LSD generation. The Cosmic Cowboy had his own music, a newfangled musical hybrid known as progressive country, or redneck rock, as defined by the New Riders of the Purple Sage, Gram Parsons, the Byrds, and the Flying Burrito Brothers. But the Cosmic Cowboy didn't need to look to the West Coast for his cues. A slew of singer-songwriters followed Willie Nelson to Austin to create their own new sound. An engaging Dallas folksinger, Michael Murphey, became an overnight sensation with his rousing theme "(I Just Want to Be a) Cosmic Cowboy." Jerry Jeff Walker, a Greenwich Village folkie who wrote the song "Mr. Bojangles," revitalized his flagging career when he moved to Austin, donned a pair of Charlie Dunn cowboy boots, and recorded the album *Viva Terlingua* in a dance hall in the pastoral Hill Country hamlet of Luckenbach. Two songs from that album in particular, "Up Against the Wall, Redneck Mother" and "London Homesick Blues" (with the refrain, "I wanna go home to the Armadillo"), became instant Cosmic Cowboy standards.

Doug Sahm shed his Sir Douglas Quintet trappings and left the friendly confines of San Francisco to get back to his Tex-Mex roots by settling in a house a few steps from Soap Creek Saloon. Commander Cody and His Lost Planet Airmen, a California band of hippies infatuated with western swing music became the unofficial touring band at the Armadillo after recording a live album there. Their compadres, Asleep at the Wheel, took it one step further and moved to Austin for keeps in order to get closer to the music and musicians they emulated. Even Frank Zappa was lured by the Armadillo's magic, recording a live album there in 1975 that ended with the immortal words "Good night Austin, Texas, wherever you are."

Progressive country took on a life of its own, embodied by a bunch of college-aged bohemians known as Freda and the Firedogs, who packed the Split Rail bar every Monday night, launching the careers of a reclusive pianist from Louisiana named Marcia Ball and a west Texas guitar fireball named John X. Reed. The country-rock craze became big enough in

Austin to justify its own radio station, KOKE-FM, Super Roper Radio, which dared to include Creedence Clearwater Revival along with Ernest Tubb and His Texas Troubadours in its music mix. The sound spread to other Texas cities courtesy of touring club acts like Greezy Wheels, a country-rock outfit with a loose and fluid style that might have made them contenders had not their charismatic leader, the Reverend Cleve Hattersley, been sent to prison for dealing marijuana.

Willie Nelson had already set country music on its collective ear with two heavily rocked-up albums, *Shotgun Willie* and *Phases and Stage*. His 1975 follow-up, the all-acoustic *Red Headed Stranger*, would zoom up the pop charts. The dope-smoking, ponytailed prophet wasn't just king of Austin anymore, he was king of America — a superstar whose traveling minstrel show and gypsy caravan had all the magical appeal and organic qualities of the Grateful Dead.

The idea of a bunch of pickers and grinners wearing cowboy hats and playing hillbilly music was a crock of shit as far as Stevie Vaughan was concerned. He'd played the Armadillo on several occasions with the Nightcrawlers and the people running the place treated him well enough. But as much as everyone working at the 'Dillo talked about how much they dug the music, blues bands didn't draw there. Stevie resented all the attention that was being heaped on these Cosmic Cowpie goofballs and the money that these long-haired pretend buckaroos were making. They weren't musicians; they were a bunch of clowns in western outfits.

When Austin writer Chet Flippo penned an article about the local music scene for *Rolling Stone* magazine, he focused on the rise of progressive country and completely ignored the blues players. It didn't mean anything to the musicians. Who gave a shit about *Rolling Stone* anyway? Shirley Dimmick Ratisseau, a diminutive gray-haired book editor and mother of two who'd sung with black bands during the fifties and sixties and championed the young musicians who played the kind of music she liked, fired off a letter to the editor:

"Austin boasts the finest rhythm and blues guitarists anywhere — Jimmie and Stevie Vaughan, Mark Pollack, Denny Freeman, Derek O'Brien, W. C. Clark and Matthew Robinson," she wrote in a letter that appeared in the May 9, 1974, issue. "Most of the bluesmen are so broke that a pickpocket going through their pockets would get nothing but practice. So please don't ignore the other half of Austin's music scene. Makes us feel as unwanted as those for whom Ben Williams sang, 'Come After Breakfast, Bring Along Lunch, and Leave Before Suppertime.' "

Her cause became a crusade. All the blues musicians needed, she decided, was to be heard on record. She conceived the Blue Norther project, hustling financial backing, booking time at Odyssey Sound on Sixth Street, and shuttling in a number of players including Derek

O'Brien, Denny Freeman, Mark Pollock, the guitarist whom she managed at the time, and Paul Ray. She enticed a brilliant blues harp player named Kim Wilson to come down from Minneapolis to play on the sessions.

Wilson was a Detroit native who grew up in California and blew Chicago-style harp in the tradition of Little Walter better than anyone but Little Walter. The first two guys he met in Austin were Stevie Vaughan and Doyle Bramhall. For two weeks, the three club-hopped around the city, begging to sit in with anyone who would let them. Shirley insisted they drive out south of town to Alexander's on Brodie Lane. The Armadillo may have been getting the national attention, but for anyone who dug the blues, there was no place as soulful as Alexander's. It was a musicians' hangout, run by a black family who served up tasty plates of ribs and brisket in exchange for tasty guitar licks from the bandstand. Playing Alexander's wasn't a money deal. It was just cool.

Sunday afternoons were happenings at Alexander's, and on the Sunday afternoon that Stevie, Doyle, and Kim Wilson arrived, Jimmie and the Storm were making it happen. Stevie and Doyle wanted to show off Kim to Jimmie and Lewis Cowdrey, the top harmonica man in town, excepting Mickey Raphael from Willie Nelson's band. Jimmie, however, was in no mood to accommodate sit-ins. He made his little brother, his friend, and their new pal wait until the break. They could play a few songs on their own then. When the trio took over and plugged in, the gathering at the old gas station went bonkers. Even Jimmie's ears visibly pricked up. Doyle and Stevie weren't kidding about this Wilson guy, he realized. He made Lewis sound white bread. Kim had the gift.

"Pretty good, man," Jimmie admitted after their ten-minute show. "Keep in touch."

Shirley's tapes were promising, but every major label she solicited turned them down. Blues didn't sell, they told her, especially low-down blues played by white boys. Dejected, Kim Wilson went back to Minnesota.

But the winds of change were stirring. The Armadillo World Headquarters shifted emphasis from Cosmic Cowboy bands to more ambitious fare. The concert hall introduced Austin audiences to a New Jersey wailer named Bruce Springsteen for the ticket price of a dollar. The eclectic parade of talent that passed through ranged from jazz saxophone legend Dexter Gordon, modern avant-gardist Captain Beefheart, and jazz experimentalist Sun Ra to Irish soul singer Van Morrison, Tennessee fiddler and boogie rocker Charlie Daniels, and New Wave sensation Elvis Costello. Not only was the music good, the price was always right. Typical was the weeknight triple bill of Linda Ronstadt, Little Feat, and Commander Cody presented in the spring of 1974 for a three-dollar cover.

On that same night, about five miles west, the Soap Creek Saloon featured Doug Sahm and Augie Meyer doing their country-rock-Tex-Mex amalgam for the same three-buck premium, joined by an unannounced drop-in guest by the name of Herbie Hancock, who was pounding away on the club's rickety upright piano less than an hour after he'd enthralled a Municipal Auditorium audience with a cutting-edge demonstration of jazz-rock fusion music on his massive synthesizer and keyboard setup. If any club represented the rapidly evolving Austin music scene in the mid-seventies, it was Soap Creek.

"If the Armadillo is Austin's Fillmore, then Soap Creek is its Avalon," crowed KOKE-FM disc jockey Joe Gracey in *Rolling Stone* magazine. The place may have harbored too many Willie Nelson wannabes for Little Stevie Vaughan's comfort, but it would become his headquarters for the next two years, the place where he would develop the sophisticated yet hard-driving style that would become the basis of his legacy.

The Soap was the reincarnation of the Rolling Hills Country Club, where Stevie Vaughan first crashed with his band Blackbird. Patrons had to negotiate a quarter mile of bumpy, unpaved road to reach the club, which was splendidly isolated from the semisophisticated suburban trappings that were beginning to encroach on the edges of Austin. Everything about the place — the slapdash decor, the stuffed sofa by the door, the extremely hip selection of rare 45s on the jukebox, the cigarette burns on the pool tables in back, the wall at the rear of the music room where all the guys leaned back and checked out the women on their way to the restroom — it all spoke of Youth on the Make in the hippest post-hippie, pre-Yuppie outpost in the state.

Music might have been a mere accompaniment to this nightly pursuit of hedonism as far as the regular Soap Creek crowd of movers, shakers, scenemakers, old dogs, and new bohemians was concerned. But they paid close enough attention to applaud an inspired solo when they heard it and kept the dance floor jammed when the groove was in the pocket. When Soap Creek opened in February 1973, the clientele was fed a steady diet of progressive country from bands like Greezy Wheels, Plum Nelly, and Marcia Ball, with regular appearances from the unofficial house bandleader, Doug Sahm. But even Sahm's uncanny ability to touch upon the whole spectrum of native Texas sounds wasn't enough. The regulars started griping to hear something new.

They were primed for something that didn't fit in with the rowdy, long-haired shitkicker stereotype that was becoming a source of embarrassment for anyone who didn't buy their hats from Manny Gammage at Texas Hatters; something that wasn't introspective or so downed out it sounded like everyone in the band was strung out on heroin or reds; something that would make them want to dance and boogie until the break of dawn. Paul Ray's group, the Cobras, was in the right place at the right time.

Carlyn Majewski, who ran Soap Creek with her husband, George, and booked the bands, met Stevie and Jimmie Vaughan not long after Soap Creek opened. After running into Carlyn at the One Knite, Jimmie had asked her to come check out his brother and him. They were holed up at the Austin Motel, a seedy lodge across the street from the Continental Club on South Congress. Carlyn knocked on the door at 3:30 A.M. and walked into a room cluttered with dirty clothes, guitars, and amplifiers. "They were both real gone," she observed. But not so far gone that they couldn't play. With a sly, slightly skewed smile, Jimmie cued Stevie and they worked out on a jump number. Carlyn immediately recognized their immense talent as guitarists.

"That's great," she said. "Now, do either of you sing?"

Stevie responded by singing his ass off.

She was convinced.

"They were good, they knew it, and they wanted me to hear it."

She'd heard dozens of good players around Austin, she told them, but she was looking for bands. And at this particular moment, she noted, Jimmie and Stevie were between gigs.

"Give me a call when you get a band together," she told them.

When they got it together, they got the gigs.

Stevie had picked up a few dates at the Soap with the Doyle, Keith, and Drew version of the Nightcrawlers. But after he came back to Texas following his second go-round with Marc Benno, he didn't have time to think about what he was going to do next before Paul Ray cornered him.

The Cobras, the band that Ray fronted, really didn't need another guitarist and they didn't exactly have to juice their draw, either. Their regular Tuesday night stint at Soap Creek was already an institution, with the crowds growing wilder and more uninhibited by the week, particularly on full-moon nights.

But Paul Ray was no fool. He'd been digging blues music since he was a teenager in East Dallas, naming his first blues band, 1948, in honor of the year that B. B. King began broadcasting on WDIA in Memphis, "The Mother Station of the Negroes." He'd worked with Jimmie Vaughan in both Texas Storm and the Storm, meeting Stevie during his brief stint as Texas Storm's stand-in bassist. Through the years, Paul had given Stevie a place to crash, turned him on to righteous records, and generally looked after his ass. He was like an uncle, like Joe Boy Cook. When Paul caught wind that Stevie Vaughan was back in town and looking for a gig, he extended the invitation to join the Cobras on New Year's Eve, 1974.

The Cobras' lead guitarist, Denny Freeman, was surprisingly game.

Freeman was one of the best stylists anywhere, with a facile touch for jazz chording in the tradition of Kenny Burrell and Wes Montgomery. He, too, was something of a father figure to Stevie going back to his teenage days. Quiet-spoken and unassuming offstage, Denny had a textbook knowledge of guitar, which he played with unusual delicacy, quite a contrast to the little punk who was ready to steamroll through his catalog of licks at the drop of a hat. Denny would have preferred Paul bringing in someone who played another instrument, but he knew Stevie well enough to deal with him. If he got too overbearing, Denny could always retreat to his Fender Rhodes piano and pump up the sound with keyboard fills.

For his part, Stevie went out of his way not to step on Denny's toes. He was the Professor, the experienced blues man who had his act together, unlike almost everybody else. Denny had sheltered him, humored him, and taught him a lot about the guitar beyond mere volume and tone. Stevie was too happy to be part of the Cobras to screw things up. The entire band was impressive. Alex Napier held down bass while drums were first played by John Henry Alexander before a muscle-bound weight lifter named Rodney Craig signed on. Jim Trimmier, who'd played with Stevie in Dallas with the horn band Liberation, did the Cobra's sax fills before being replaced by Joe Sublett.

The Cobras not only sounded sharp, they looked sharp, too, in their thrift-shop pimp suits and pleated pants, a contrast to the faded-denim, tie-dyed casual look that was still in vogue around Austin. Dressing up for Stevie was a big change. Now when he went junking, he wasn't just looking for guitars. Wherever he happened to sleep, he made a point of rifling through closets, looking for baubles and beads that he could add to his stage wardrobe. The Cobras taught him the value of image, that it was an important part of the act, a necessary tool that helped people lock onto what he was playing. Looking good also facilitated the pursuit of young women.

"We dressed a little different, like Superfly pimps," Denny Freeman said. "Our girlfriends were real good-looking and they were wearing makeup and perfume. If you get the girls, you've got it made."

The Cobras got the girls by playing swinging, crotch-grinding rhythm-and-blues and soul music, stuff that would keep the crowd dancing and drinking, hot and horny. Paul Ray, a crooner out of the Bobby Bland/Junior Parker/Joe Scott Duke-Peacock Silk 'n' Soul school, was the band's leader, front man, and song doctor, responsible for coming up with the lion's share of material; his bias leaned heavily to danceable soul and R&B standards — Wilson Pickett's "In the Midnight Hour" and "634-5789," the timeless "Harlem Shuffle," as well as Bland's "Turn On Your Lovelight," and Little Junior Parker's "Next Time You See Me" —

material that contrasted sharply with the darker, plodding I-IV-V straight blues progressions favored by bands like the Storm.

Paul Ray could read a crowd and give them exactly what they wanted. He also had two guitarists who could scorch the heels off anyone's dancing shoes. Instead of the usual etiquette of letting one play while the other held back and filled in on rhythm, Denny and Stevie would often take their leads simultaneously, one player completing a phrase begun by the other, as if they were tuned into the same wavelength. Denny's tasteful elegance usually drew the attention of other guitarists in the audience. But no one could ignore Stevie, even though he kept his head down low and stayed in the background, occasionally stepping forward to the microphone to sing a rendition of "Thunderbird," the Nightcaps song he'd been singing since he was a kid. When it was his turn to take the guitar lead, though, Stevie didn't hold back. He might have been too shy to stare at the faces in the crowd, but he wasn't hesitant about showing off everything he could do with a guitar, at full-force volume. The one show of emotion he allowed was when he pulled up his guitar neck in an over-the-top fusillade of notes, clenching his teeth and closing his eyes in a full-bore grimace that came to be called the Vaughan face.

Through it all, Denny was more than patient. He actually encouraged Stevie to step out more. "I figured I was flashier, more of a hot rod," Stevie said. "But I always looked up to him and followed what he was doing unless he pushed me out front, which he did quite a bit." Just as frequently though, Denny implored him to understand the value of restraint. "It's something I have to learn," Stevie later admitted.

As the Cobras shifted into high gear, the party crowd that hung around them switched to a higher-octane fuel: cocaine. Methedrine connoisseurs scoffed at coke — they called it rich man's speed — and derided it as a weak sister to crank. It was a bogus drug that merely made a person want to do more and more. On the other hand, abusing coke didn't make your teeth fall out. It wasn't even addictive, or so it was thought at the time, which made it all the more appealing to middle-class recreational users. With the Cobras urging their crowd to chug another shot of tequila, shake their booty on the dance floor, and get high all night long, cocaine became the drug of choice almost overnight.

By late 1975, snowstorms regularly blew through Soap Creek's dirt parking lot. Half the people who walked through the door and past Billy Bob Sanders, the affable security man and ticket taker, looked like they had just chomped down on a box of white donuts. But they had little fear of getting busted thanks to Soap Creek's isolation and the laissez-faire attitudes of local law enforcement officials. Even Travis County sheriff Raymond Frank, whose campaign slogan "The Sheriff That Shoots

Straight" was altered to "The Sheriff That Shoots Straights" by his counterculture constituency, was a Soap Creek regular.

Stevie figured he earned every good high someone offered him. It was part of the deal, like getting paid at the end of the night: get someone off with his guitar and they'd get him off later. It was standard operating procedure, the way it was supposed to be. Drugs were an even more effective way of gauging success than money. If it was a good night, there was a party after the show. If the party was happening in the least he knew a solid buzz would come his way. Coke, speed, it really didn't matter, as long as it kept coming. Hell, he'd heard all the rap that you couldn't get hooked on the shit. They didn't call it nose candy for nothing. It made him feel good but not so totally wired that he'd fuck up. He could handle it. It pissed him off when people around him voiced concern that he was doing too much of this or getting behind some bad dope. He didn't need to hear that kind of talk. If he wanted someone to nag him, he'd go see his parents. What he was doing wasn't any worse than what his brother did, and look at where he was at. Fuck up on coke? Forget it. Little Stevie Vaughan, the guitar genius of the Cobras, believed that he'd fuck up on Pepsi first.

The distinction between what was a gift and what a business transaction was often lost on Stevie. All he knew was that the dope dealers had both the bucks and the goods. One night at Soap Creek one of those dealers took him out to his car in the parking lot between sets for a few bumps out of the twenty-gram stash he kept hidden behind the sun visor. The two went back into the club with a pleasant freeze that left their teeth numb enough for root-canal surgery. But when the dealer returned to his car later in the night for a recharge, the coke was gone. He ran back inside and looked no farther than the bandstand before he figured out who had lifted it. "Stevie had it all over his face," the dealer claimed. "I just couldn't believe he'd taken it. I would have given him some if he had asked."

But why ask? The dude didn't have to show him where he kept his stash. What the hell. If he was that upset over a few grams, Stevie would pay him back. Someday.

The Cobras ruled Soap Creek but wanted more. They started carrying their sound out on the road, booking club dates in cities across the state. They started talking about record deals. Unfortunately, the "managers" they talked to about handling their business were typically dealers posing as entrepreneurs, nonstop coke rappers with time and money on their hands but no clue how to put together a record deal. The Cobras' inexperience underscored the city's reputation among industry executives as a backwater burg rife with amateurs. "I keep hearing about the great Austin scene," legendary talent scout Jerry Wexler complained in *Rolling*

Stone magazine. "But whenever I ask who I should sign, nobody seems to know. Is it a mirage down there?"

The do-it-yourself method proved to be a more realistic route for the Cobras. The band recorded a tape of their live material including two originals, "Better Days," which featured Denny's lead work, and "Texas Clover," on which Stevie soloed. Other songs recorded by the Cobras included the jazz-influenced "Boilermaker" and "I Tried Pretty Baby," in which Stevie not only displayed a ferocious Buddy Guy attack on the guitar, but also sang. His vocal performance was tentative and restrained, but it hinted at a distinctive style influenced by both Doyle Bramhall and Hendrix. Gary Heil, a sound mixer and engineer, raised a couple grand to produce, record, and manufacture a 45 RPM single of the songs on the Viper label. Both sides of the record got considerable exposure on KOKE-FM, the progressive-country radio station that occasionally broke format to feature outstanding Austin bands like the Cobras. The irony of hearing your song on the radio while you were penniless was lost on Stevie. He was having too much fun to care. He was a musician, and being a musician opened doors to more important things than money. Sometimes it seemed like he fell in love every night. But one girl completely turned his head around. Her name was Lindi Bethel, a sweet, slender, delicate-looking girl from Corpus Christi.

He met Lindi and Terri Laird, "two health food chicks," he called them, on Wilson Street, where they lived down the block from Denny Freeman. He started chatting Lindi up every chance he got. One night he ran into her and two girlfriends at Soap Creek, where they had been listening to the Storm. When they were ready to leave, they discovered their car had a flat tire. After the show, Lindi asked Jimmie Vaughan to give them a ride home. Jimmie willingly obliged. As he began to pull out of the parking lot, Stevie materialized from out of nowhere, opened the car door, and jumped in, immediately hitting on Lindi. Jimmie turned around and stared darkly at him. "It ain't over yet, little brother," he warned.

But it was over. Lindi did not resist Stevie's advances and the two of them started doing a thing together. She loved his playing. He reminded her of "a white Hendrix," his boundless enthusiasm, his jive talk, and the way he held her. The fact that he was without a car, a pad, and material possessions brought out the mothering instinct in her. She eventually let him move in with her and her roommate, Mary Beth Greenwood, a budding photographer who was dating the jazz-rock guitarist Eric Johnson. In the morning, Stevie would take Mary Beth to her classes at UT, driving her VW. In the afternoon, the three of them hung out in Zilker Park, went swimming at Barton Springs or Lake Travis, cruised the streets, talked about all things spiritual and material. Stevie often brought along the book of Urantia and read Lindi passages from the strange publication that mixed science fiction and pop psychology. While she listened to the words, it all sounded like mumbo jumbo to her. "I didn't really understand much of it," she later admitted. At night they hit the clubs, then the party circuit that began to roar after last call.

Lindi idolized Stevie as much as she loved him and was happy to cook for him, sew stage clothes for him or loan him some of her own threads, and support him when he was short of cash. Since his sense of financial responsibility rarely extended beyond guitars, amps, beer, wine, liquor, and dope, her willingness to chip in on expenses was a godsend. On those rare occasions when he'd be flush with cash, he'd readily blow his paycheck on Lindi and her friends, taking them out to gigs and buying them breakfast at La Reyna Bakery, drinks and dinner at Casita Jorge's, or a late-night slab of barbecued ribs at Sam's on the East Side. At one point, their financial situation became so desperate that Lindi and Stevie went to apply for food stamps. "What's your occupation?" asked the state examiner.

"I'm a musician," said Stevie proudly.

"I'm sorry. That occupation doesn't qualify," came the reply.

Doesn't qualify! Shit! Stevie was so pissed he shot the finger at passing cars as he and Lindi walked home.

Though their lifestyle wasn't high-class, the girls thought it was romantic. "That was the coolest thing in the world. We thought it was so neat to be dating guitar players," said Mary Beth Greenwood. Stevie did not disappoint either of them. One night, he woke up next to Lindi, got out of bed, and headed for the living room. When Lindi went to check on him, he was sitting on the floor, buck naked except for his hat.

"I gotta idea for a song," he said, hunched over a piece of paper, scribbling the words "she's my sweet little thang," the phrase that would provide the lyrical foundation to "Pride and Joy."

As with Glenda Maples, Stevie and Lindi had a stormy relationship. Stevie enjoyed the rush of falling in love, not the pedestrian behavioral patterns necessary to keep a relationship going. He was fanatically protective of Lindi, warning her and her friends to "be good" on those occasions when she would leave the house without him. He demanded that she be faithful to him. But he practiced a double standard. With the celebrity status that the Cobras had brought him came ladies of all shapes, sizes, and colors. "He had to fend off advances from other women," Lindi said. "When I got into the relationship, I already knew his reputation. I took it for granted." But she was still unnerved when he'd stay gone for days at a time, shacking up with someone else, periodic episodes that eventually led to their breakup.

Lindi might have enjoyed looking after her Stevie, but certain members of the Cobras were not so affectionate. To them, Little Stevie was Little Nigger. The name stuck, not because he was the kid who wanted to be black, but because he was such a total fuckup. It was business as usual for the band to drive halfway to San Antonio for a gig only to have Stevie freak out, announcing he had to go back to Austin to get some new strings for his guitar.

Actually, Stevie kind of liked being called Little Nigger. He'd rather be a nigger than a cowboy. And when it got down to it, he really didn't mind having his electricity turned off or not having a place to live or hearing Lindi yell at him for sleeping around. It wasn't his fault if he passed out and woke up in some woman's bed. It was the music's fault. That was what did it. The guitar and the music. And that was all that he cared about anyway. As long as the fingers were touching the strings, nothing else really mattered.

He was maturing in one sense, ready to take on more responsibility. David Murray could tell by the tone of a letter he wrote him while he was in Indianapolis, peddling books for the summer. Stevie began by imparting fatherly advice:

> You must continue with music as you are a rarity. Is that the right word? I mean, there aren't many people your age or older who can play half of what you can. I just hope you can find some other musicians you can play with who are about three or four feet above your head and have the ability to teach you to play the things that you hear. Don't mean to sound like a lecturer, just think highly of your playing. By the way, you did good at the music store when the jerk said something about they don't just let anybody come in and play just to be playing. Why does he think people play?

Stevie then related the progress of his brother's band and the frustrations he was experiencing with the Cobras.

> I'm going to play Wednesday with the Thunderbirds! Jimmie is going to Dallas to get the van fixed so they can go on the road. They have some great gigs coming up. New York State! Canada! They'll be gone for at least six weeks. The agent that booked them wanted a tape from us. I heard this from Paul a couple of days ago. But Paul never got one together, so here we are still in Austin.

The Cobras might have been Little Stevie Vaughan's ticket to the big time if not for Paul Ray's voice. One night in the parking lot at Soap

Creek, a tearful Diana Ray broke the news to Stevie. "Paul has nodes on his throat," she sobbed, choking back the tears. "He's going to have to quit singing." A temporary solution was proposed. He'd take a few months off and let the rest of the band fill in.

Stevie didn't realize it at the time, but it was a cue to consider his career options. He'd already blown a chance to audition for Albert King, his number one blues guitar hero, after sitting in with him. He didn't know if he was ready to leave the Cobras at the time. He sneaked up to Dallas one day to try out for the guitar chair in Pyramid, a popular funk-rock ensemble that promoter Angus Wynne had put together and was managing. Wynne had aggressively courted Stevie after Pyramid's multitalented lead guitarist, Catfish Renfro, was killed in a car wreck in 1976, and sent him an airplane ticket to come to Dallas for a tryout. Stevie made a mighty impression, but the band passed on Wynne's nominee. They didn't want a blues prodigy who could play like Freddie King, Guitar Slim, and Albert King all at once. They wanted someone who could play like Catfish.

David Murray was always on his case about branching out, too. "Man, you oughta have your own band," he'd tell him.

"Little brother, if you take too big a step, you fall flat on your face," Stevie replied.

Paul Ray finally took a leave of absence while the Cobras tried valiantly to fill in the gaps. Stevie seized the opportunity to sing more and more. He had Angela Strehli teach him the words to "Texas Flood," the riveting slow blues by Larry "Totsy" Davis, the bluesman from Oklahoma. That song convinced him he was a decent vocalist, not as deep and soulful as Doyle Bramhall, perhaps, but good enough to cut it with the Cobras. As the nights stretched into weeks, he became so self-assured that he decided it was time to cut and run.

When he gave his notice, the rest of the band was neither surprised nor upset. They had tired of baby-sitting Little Nigger, giving him rides, wiping his nose, and holding his hand. "Being in the Cobras was like going to school for a lot of people," explained Denny Freeman. "If there was something we wanted to do, we would tackle it. And if it had more than three chords in it, we would learn them. Stevie learned that, and started singing. And he was ready to go out and start being Stevie."

His departure may have been ill-timed, since the biweekly *Austin Sun* reader's poll had just voted the Cobras "Band of the Year" and "Best Blues Band." At least this way everybody could figure out who the draw in the Cobras really was — Paul, Denny, the whole band, or the young catdaddy who splattered guitar notes all over the place.

Stevie Ray Vaughan's father, Jimmie Lee Vaughan (*top row, second from left*), poses at age fifteen for a family portrait. Included in the 1936 photograph are Jimmie's brothers (*left to right*) Robert Hodgen, Thomas Everett, and Preston. Laura Bell Vaughan, Stevie Ray's grandmother, sits in the center of the bottom row, flanked by her daughters (*left to right*) Vada, Juanita, Linnie Vee (Jimmie's twin), and Vera Bell.

Fifteen-year-old Jimmie Vaughan (*second from right*) was already a rock star in Dallas when this 1966 publicity shot of the Chessmen was taken. Drummer and lead vocalist Doyle Bramhall sits at far left.

Photo courtesy of Charlie Hatchett

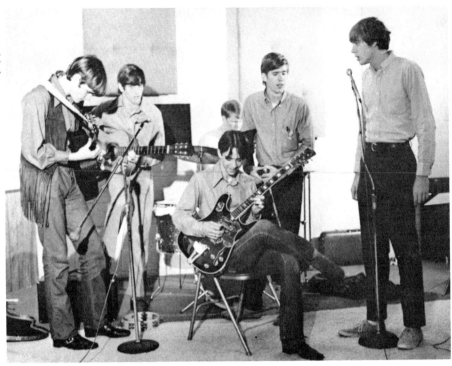

Basking in the glow of his first studio session, Stevie (*center*) sits in with the Cast of Thousands in 1971 as they cut tracks for the locally released album *A New Hi*. Former student body president and future actor/director Steve Tobolowsky stands at far right.

Stevie poses for a publicity shot with the band Blackbird at the Waterloo Social Club in Austin in 1972. *Top, left to right:* keyboardist Noel Deis, drummer John Huff, vocalist Christian Plicque, drummer Roddy Colonna, and bassist David Frame; *bottom*, dueling guitarists Kim Davis and Stevie.

Stevie rockin' in bell-bottoms with the Night-crawlers at the Armadillo Headquarters in Austin, circa 1973

Krackerjack, riding high with their latest guitarist in a 1972 publicity shot. *Left to right:* drummer Uncle John "Red" Turner, singer Bruce Bowland, bassist Tommy "Slut" Shannon, keyboardist Mike Kindred, and Stevie.

Running down the fat strings. Stevie slides a bottleneck, Elmore James–style, with the Cobras at Soap Creek Saloon in Austin, 1976.

Kings of Tequila Night, members of the Cobras take time out for a Coke and a smoke by the Soap Creek Saloon bar, 1976. *Left to right:* vocalist and leader Paul Ray, bassist Alex Napier, Stevie, guitarist Denny Freeman, and drummer Rodney Craig.

Kathy Murray

Early version of the Fabulous Thunderbirds on the stage of the original Antone's, 1975. *Left to right:* Keith Ferguson on bass, Andy Miller on drums, the nattily attired Jimmie "Lee" Vaughan, and harmonica man Kim Wilson, resplendent in turban.

Mary Beth Greenwood

Stevie playing with the Cobras, 1976

Mary Beth Greenwood

Stevie and girlfriend Lindi Bethel look out over Lake Travis, near Austin, circa 1976.

The Vaughan face on display during Stevie's farewell gig with the Cobras at Soap Creek Saloon

Checking out guitarist Ronnie Earl (*left*), Stevie jams at the Rome Inn, circa 1977, with Triple Threat bassman W. C. Clark on vocals.

The brothers Vaughan hanging out in front of Cat-man's Shine Parlor, just down the block from the original Antone's, 1978

A very serious cat still in search of a persona, "Stingray" poses with the original version of Double Trouble. *Left to right:* Miss Lou Ann Barton, Chris "Whipper" Layton, Stevie, Johnny Reno, and Smilin' Jack Newhouse, 1979.

Lou Ann Barton cops a feel onstage at the Armadillo with Double Trouble, 1979.

Mary Beth Greenwood

Stevie and new bride Lenny inspect wedding gifts upstairs at the Rome Inn as Double Trouble band mate Chris Layton looks on, 1979.

Mary Beth Greenwood

6

HOME OF THE BLUES

A year earlier on a hot summer day, David Murray spotted Stevie on the corner of Sixth and Brazos downtown, waving his arms excitedly. He was standing in front of an abandoned furniture store, motioning for David to pull his newly purchased '61 Falcon over to the curb. David whipped the wheel and screeched to a halt. There must be an emergency, the way Stevie was acting.

"Look, look!" he said breathlessly, pointing to the furniture store. David looked but couldn't figure out why Stevie was hyperventilating.

"Man, this is gonna be the happening place. This is gonna be it!"

"What's it?" David asked.

"Antone's, man! Clifford's opening a club. A club for *us*."

Antone's, the home of the blues in Austin, would be the place where Stevie Ray Vaughan would do his postgraduate work and develop the confidence and polish to enable him to become a star. And if it wasn't for Clifford Antone, there would never have been an Antone's. A scion of a family of Lebanese importers from Port Arthur on the Texas Gulf Coast, Clifford ran the Austin location of the family's gourmet grocery business, selling po'boy sandwiches, tins of imported olive oil, and other delicacies from around the world. But Clifford harbored far grander visions than being a successful merchant. He had remodeled the back room of the store into a rehearsal hall, a space filled with all kinds of guitars, amps, and cords where friends like Jimmie and Stevie Vaughan, Doyle Bramhall, Bill Campbell, and Angela Strehli could spin their favorite blues records and create some blues of their own.

The original grocery owned by Clifford's parents was located in the heart of the black section of Port Arthur, and he spent a good part of his teenage years dancing to the white soul-brother sounds of the Boogie Kings at the Big Oaks Club across the state line in Vinton, Louisiana, where eighteen-year-olds could legally drink. But Clifford was a relatively recent convert to real down-home blues. He'd had his head turned around when friends turned him on to the American originals from whom popular British bands were stealing.

That discovery became his life's mission. Clifford liked to fool around on bass in the jam sessions that he presided over in the back of the store after closing time. Jimmie and Kim Wilson joined him often, as did Bill Campbell. Sometimes Stevie showed up, just to goof around. "He'd play songs and hit every note wrong," Clifford laughed. "It was the sourest thing you ever heard."

Antone wanted to do more than just fool around. Damn, he often wondered aloud, wouldn't it be fine if there was somewhere to do this all the time? Wouldn't it be great to bring respect to the ladies and gentlemen who created and championed this incredible musical form? Wouldn't it be something to have a nightclub where they could perform? If he ran a club, Clifford promised, playing blues wouldn't just be tolerated, it would be mandatory. After the city of Austin extended drinking hours to 2:00 A.M. in 1975, he became more determined to turn that dream into something concrete. Bill Campbell told him about seeing a for lease sign go up in front of the old Levine's Department Store on the western edge of the rough-and-tumble Sixth Street strip, a collection of wino bars, transvestite hangouts, conjunto dives, cheap cafés, and porno bookstores. Looking through the glass window, Clifford was overcome by a burst of inspiration (or stupidity or blind faith, depending on whom you asked). Here, he declared, would be a blues club like no other blues club on the face of the planet.

"We didn't enter into it like most people enter into the nightclub business," Antone later explained. "We entered into it wanting to bring the blues, and do anything possible to want to make it happen. The business part never really came into it at all. The idea was the blues guys were getting older and if we were ever gonna see these guys, we had to bring them ourselves. You've got to know that there's such a thing as risk before you've taken a risk. We didn't even know that there was such a thing as risk. Who cares?"

Sixth Street was a throwback to the days of segregation. The majority of businesses on the north side of the strip that stretched from Interstate 35 to Congress Avenue catered primarily to blacks. Businesses on the south side of the street appealed to a Mexican clientele. After dark, both sides of the street were considered dangerous, not the sort of destination frequented by "nice people" or UT students.

The doors of Antone's opened on July 15, 1975. It was the anchor tenant of a block that defined blues in its natural state. Next door was OK Records, a collector's shop brimming with blues 78s and 45s founded by Steve Dean and run by Leon Eagleson and Doty Tullos, who, like Antone, hailed from the Golden Triangle of southeast Texas. Another old pal from back home, Robbie Greig, opened a Cajun seafood café called Moma's Money on the other side of OK Records. Other tenants on the block included an old-fashioned stand-up beer bar, a drug store, an X-rated bookstore, and Ed's Shine Parlor, operated by an engaging figure named Catman, who posted signs in the window that announced "The Professionals Are Here" and now was the time to "Shine 'Em Up." They all complemented Antone's as if they were all part and parcel of a theme park dedicated to the pursuit of the unholy Get Down.

Clifford hired Angela Strehli to run the club. Angela was about as close to a matriarch as there was in Austin's blues scene. She commanded the musicians' respect because she was good-looking, smart, and had sung her share of the blues. She'd been around long enough that most everyone knew the story about how she once lent Muddy Waters three hundred dollars in Chicago. She had spent the Summer of Love in San Francisco and had been through her share of recording trips. Under Strehli's direction, Antone installed a top-of-the-line sound system, staffed the club with bartenders who knew how to mix a drink and cocktail waitresses who knew how to sashay their way to a table. The club proceeded to book an incredible lineup of national and local blues talent. The only thing Clifford worried about was who should inaugurate the whole shebang.

The answer to his dilemma was the undisputed King of Zydeco. Clifton Chenier and His Red Hot Louisiana Band was an all-black, French Creole, working-class band from the swamps of southern Louisiana who played zydeco, an exotic, regionalized brand of jump rhythm and blues. Chenier, who wore a crown to emphasize his royal status, worked the accordion while his brother Cleveland scratched out a rattlesnake rhythm with a handful of can openers across the metal washboard he wore on his chest. Clifton and his band didn't change the course of Western civilization, but they most certainly turned Austin on its ear with a nonstop, four-hour explosion of rhythm and butt-rocking.

Clifton Chenier had already helped Soap Creek Saloon sell a few drinks when he pulled his small trailer decorated with silhouettes of dancing black girls up to the club in October of 1974. Chenier and his band showed all the young bucks that blues wasn't a museum piece to be appreciated only by academics but a modern, danceable sound with vitality and currency. And they validated Jimmie Vaughan's theory about the importance of a band playing as a unit. Every member of the Red Hot Louisiana Band cooked, but no one, not even Clifton, overplayed.

Antone persuaded Leon Eagleson, one of the proprietors of OK Records, who was booking Clifton into Soap Creek, to bring the Red Hot Louisiana Band for his club's grand opening. Spiriting Clifton away from Soap Creek created some bad blood, but Clifford saw it as a birthright. Clifton was "homefolks" to Antone's southeast Texas circle of friends who grew up around French-speaking whites and Creoles. By the time opening night had rolled around, there was a line outside the door that snaked around the corner before Chenier squeezed so much as a note out of his massive accordion.

The paint on the wall was still wet, but no one complained. With Clifton onstage, it really did feel like being back in the swamps. Half the crowd, it seemed, had roots in Lafayette, Lake Charles, Opelousas, Port A, Beaumont, or Bridge City. Patois was fluently spoken. Most of the crowd showed up dressed like cast members from a revival of *Guys and Dolls*. Vintage suits, hats, dresses, heels, and black fishnet stockings were in. Flannel shirts, jeans, granny dresses, and stash bags were out. Clifford and his lieutenants, almost all of them part of the old gang from Port Arthur, favored button-down Oxford shirts, tails out, and slacks.

To the blues loyalists who'd been knocking around the One Knite, Alexander's, La Cucaracha, the Lamplite, Soap Creek, and the Armadillo, Antone's was almost too good to be true. Reality set in the week after Clifton Chenier packed the house when Sunnyland Slim was booked to play. Fewer than fifty customers turned out to see the Chicago legend, leaving Clifford and his crew scratching their heads.

"I thought that if you brought Sunnyland Slim and Big Walter Horton" — as he did the second weekend the club was open — "people would be lined up around the block trying to get in," he said. "There is no way to describe the way people let me down." Fortunately, where Clifford sensed disaster, Sunnyland Slim saw opportunity. He'd never been treated so well by a club owner, even if a whole lotta folks didn't show up to see him. This Antone's Club was something else. He went back to Chicago and started spreading the word among friends. Within weeks, Muddy Waters, Jimmy Rodgers, and every other able-bodied Chicago blues all-star started calling in search of a date.

When they'd show up at the club, they would inevitably ask to see Mr. Antone.

"I'm Mr. Antone," Clifford would say.

"Well, where's your father?"

"He lives in Port Arthur. Why?"

"Then, who owns this place?"

"I do," Clifford would reply, usually drawing a grin from the visiting dignitary.

The opening of Antone's practically saved the new band that Jimmie Vaughan had started up. Jimmie remembered the harmonica player that his brother had brought to Alexander's. He decided to give Kim Wilson a call in Minnesota.

"I'm thinkin' about comin' up there," he told Wilson. For three nights, Jimmie sat in with Kim's band. They played together, partied together, and talked shop together. Jimmie went back home, but he and Kim continued talking. Jimmie finally convinced Kim he had nothing to lose by moving to Texas. They could put a band together, he suggested. The first six months were slim pickings for the group, which they dubbed the Fabulous Thunderbirds. Connie Vaughan (née Crouch), whom Jimmie had finally married, did not take kindly to having Kim as a semipermanent houseguest. After a brief succession of rhythm-section players, the band stabilized around Keith Ferguson, the Houston bassist with the Mexican low-rider look and demeanor, and Mike Buck, a shuffle drummer out of Fort Worth's New Blue Bird Nite Club, who brought along his extensive collection of obscure blues records, introducing the guys to little known legends like Li'l Millet and Count Rockin' Sidney. For a brief period, Lou Ann Barton hired on as featured vocalist, but the chemistry proved too volatile.

The combination of Jimmie and Kim together, though, was pure audio dynamite. Jimmie "Bad Boy" Vaughan, as he liked to call himself, could churn out lead and rhythm lines simultaneously on the Stratocaster that he customized with cheap metallic letters spelling out his JLV initials. But he preferred being a low-profile counterpoint to Wilson, who alternated between singing and blowing distorted wails on his mouth harp. Together, it was as if Little Walter and Muddy Waters had been reincarnated as white boys. Kim and Jimmie had each invested years learning restraint and control, the cornerstones of real black blues, and the result was a dead-on re-creation of the Chess Records sound that exported the electric Chicago blues to the world. The Fabulous Thunderbirds had that sound down cold and they knew it, even if hardly anyone else did.

The Fabulous Thunderbirds, along with Bill Campbell's band, the Houserockers, were Antone's unofficial house bands. Fortunately for both groups, Clifford acted more like a patron of the arts than a bar owner. For the first year the club was open, the T-Birds rarely drew as many paying customers as the Storm used to attract on a Monday night at the One Knite. Those gigs, when they had to carry the evening on their own, were the equivalent of paying their dues. The nights that Antone featured one of the faded legends he'd ferreted out of the woodwork were more like school. Hubert Sumlin, Howlin' Wolf's guitarist, Luther Tucker, who'd done time with Muddy Waters, and Eddie Taylor, Jimmy Reed's right-hand man, were among the visiting professors who did several weeks' residency at a time, hanging around the club and the record store by day and taking over the stage at night.

For Stevie Vaughan, Jimmie Vaughan, and all their compadres eager to soak up blues au naturel, this informal apprentice system was better than a Ph.D. in R&B at the University of Soul. Antone's missionary zeal made it possible for them to learn how Lazy Lester got that sweet sound on the harmonica on "Sugar Coated Love" by asking him point blank. Every week there were informal tutorials and seminars. It was gratifying from the veterans' perspective that these youngsters were so interested in what they were doing. Getting paid a decent wage for their efforts was a pleasant change, too.

Jimmy Reed was reunited with Eddie Taylor at Antone's, using the Thunderbirds' rhythm section as their own band after the T-Birds opened the show, much to Jimmie Vaughan's delight. He had opened for Reed years before in Austin at a dive called the Black Queen, when Reed's severe drug habits caused him to nod out several times during his set. A week after a rejuvenated Reed tore up the stage on Sixth Street, he suddenly died following an epileptic seizure in California.

The Thunderbirds opened for, backed up, or jammed with almost every act that passed through the doors. Clifford Antone orchestrated late-night cram courses after closing that often lasted until sunrise. Antone's was the Thunderbirds' office, rehearsal hall, hangout, and home away from home. It all paid off when Muddy Waters arrived to play a weekend. Since Johnny Winter had opened for him at the Vulcan Gas Company seven years earlier, Waters had been rediscovered by white rock and rollers. The man who had recorded the song from which the Rolling Stones took their name was a respected eminence who was used to adoring younger musicians paying him tribute. Unfortunately, most of those players he heard emulating him were pretty weak. But this band, the Thunderbirds, who opened up for him at Antone's, they were not like the rest. The entire Muddy Waters band became aware of it when they heard the Thunderbirds work out their opening instrumental. Suddenly the curtain of the upstairs dressing room pulled back and black faces peered out in disbelief. The way those boys played, the way they dressed — it had been a long time since they'd seen white boys dressed nice in Italian double-knit slacks — their sense of feel, was something else, especially that harp man with the turban on his head. At the end of the first night, Muddy himself paid Kim Wilson the biggest compliment of his life when he sidled up to him backstage.

"Maybe you can help me out sometime."

Muddy Waters spread the word about the Thunderbirds and Antone's wherever he went. And when Muddy spoke, every musician trying to decipher the roots of Mississippi Delta blues listened. The effect was immediate. Almost overnight, Jimmie was getting calls at the club from all around the country. Would the Thunderbirds consider coming to play their town? Duke Robillard, a T-Bone Walker disciple, was playing lead guitar with Roomful of Blues, in Providence, Rhode Island, when the Thunderbirds passed through Lupo's Heartbreak Hotel, where Roomful was the house band. "Jimmie did it with such flair — putting all these great turnarounds into it," Robillard remembered. "He'd be pumping that bottom, plain and simple, and then he'd put in this turnaround at the end of the verse that would just knock you out. It would create so much tension, it made everybody crazy. Pretty soon, you saw all these guitar players up here with Strats, greasing their hair back, wearing fifties clothes."

Getting out of town boosted the 'Birds draw back home. If they were good enough to play somewhere else, fans reasoned, they must be worth going out to see.

Muddy Waters wasn't the only gentleman able to separate the Thunderbirds from the punk pretenders. Buddy Guy, whom Clifford introduced to Jimmie, came away impressed. "The guy doesn't have any gimmicks or anything; he just plays it like it's supposed to be played," Guy raved to *Guitar Player* magazine. "I was really surprised the first time I played there, because I didn't realize how strong they knew the blues as much as they did. Man, that guy Jimmie pulled that slide out on me, and I just had to stand back in the corner and watch. I've never said no when I've been invited to play Austin, ever since I've been going there, because of guys like Jimmie and his brother and five or six other guys that are raisin' hell, too."

Stevie Vaughan got plenty of chances to raise hell with all the old pros who appeared at Antone's. "Man, I could do that all night," Stevie said after a fierce jam with guitarist Otis Rush. "No way, Stevie," the older musician replied. "I can't keep up with you anymore." Of all the veterans Stevie rubbed shoulders and traded licks with, none was so intimidating as Albert King. Ever since he was a ten-year-old staring at record covers, Stevie had been mesmerized by King's Flying V guitar. The first time King was booked into Antone's, Stevie was waiting at the curb for him as the hulking figure with the pipe clenched between his teeth steered the tour bus with his name on it up to the curb. King was not known as the most gregarious entertainer, and Clifford had already developed a rep in music circles for treating his stars with an uncommon amount of deference and respect, but before King took the stage on his first night, Clifford broke rank and asked a favor. He wanted Albert to let Stevie sit in.

"I wouldn't ask you if I didn't think he was good," he told King. "You're his hero, man. He tunes his strings like you do and everything." If he called him up to the bandstand, Antone hinted, Stevie would hold his own. King grudgingly grumbled his approval. "All right, let him up here."

When King paused in the middle of his set and started talking about bringing up a special guest, Stevie's face turned red, but he did not hesitate. He practically sprinted to the stage and started strapping on his guitar. King was the kind of ruthless performer who could wreck a player's career by shutting him down on the bandstand on a whim. But he was downright jovial when he welcomed the Vaughan boy to plug in, managing even a trace of a smile. He'd taken Antone's word. Now he'd find out who was bullshitting whom.

King had heard countless emulators try to do his style. He was a regular at the Fillmore in San Francisco. He'd seen Clapton and all the rock stars from England attempt his stuff. But no one ever got his tone down stone cold like this young fellow. Stevie worked the strings with such brute power and brash confidence, King was taken aback. It was like the young boy had just twisted the cap off the bottle that contained the secrets of all blues and poured every guitar lick known to man right out onstage. He even sang "Texas Flood," but not before apologizing to the audience for his vocal shortcomings. He wasn't used to singing, he whispered into the microphone. When he finished, King nodded for him to keep going. One song segued into another. Then another. Stevie Vaughan could keep up with Albert King, the crowd could see. He kept up with him for the whole night.

Antone's was wrapped in a mystique more typical of a club that had been operating for fifty years rather than just a few months. The element of danger that permeated Sixth Street made it all the more exciting. When Boz Scaggs, the Dallas native who made it big in San Francisco as a white soul artist, brought an entourage to hear Bobby Bland one night, that mystique was further embellished. Scaggs wanted to see Bland during a break and pushed past a security guard to get backstage. Perhaps he did not hear the guard inform him that Bland was busy changing outfits. Maybe he didn't want to hear him. Whatever the circumstances, rules were rules, even for uppity rock stars. The guard decked Scaggs with a single punch, and removed his person to a sidewalk by the backstage door. A photograph of the coldcocked Scaggs subsequently ran in the pages of *Rolling Stone*. Antone's reputation was spreading fast.

If any single person represented the Antone's attitude, it was Bill Campbell, a strapping, wide-faced figure whose surly reputation preceded him. He was a rogue, a fallen angel, a police character, an excruciatingly funny scam artist, and a mean alcoholic who liked nothing better than to get drunk and dare somebody to fuck with him. He was a rare gem who was actually born and raised in Austin and steeped in the history and perspective of the city's black music scene. Campbell passed. He could play with as much soul, feeling, and tone as any of his black mentors and half the pros who passed through the doors of the Victory Grill, Doris Miller Auditorium, Charlie's Playhouse, and Ernie's Chicken Shack. Campbell wasn't just tolerated in these establishments, he was welcomed there. That he could outdrink, outdrug, and definitely out-insult any foul-mouthed hophead who tried to challenge him, as well as cut him to shreds onstage with his guitar, only added to his mythic stature. When Campbell spoke, his words carried some weight. So when he told Stevie, "If you ever want to get anywhere, you're gonna have to start singin'," Stevie was all ears.

Other young musicians from all across America who were hooked on the blues started showing up on the sidewalk, following in Kim Wilson's footsteps, among them a pianist from Providence named Johnny Nicholas; Keith Dunn, a black harp player from Boston; and Steve Nardell, an Ann Arbor guitarist whose band had cut albums for Blind Pig Records. Denny, Campbell, W. C. Clark, and Jimmie and Stevie became mentors in their own right, their every move watched like hawks by a gang of aspiring youngsters like "Little" David Murray, "Little" Eddie Stout, Anson Funderburg, and the Sexton boys, Will and Charlie, who understudied them while they were barely teenagers.

On many mornings, the staff at Antone's would open the doors to serve sandwiches to the lunch crowd, only to find Stevie Vaughan standing there with a guitar in hand and a goofy grin on his face. He needed to work through some chops, he'd tell them. There really wasn't anywhere else to go. He was twenty-two years old and ready to make some serious moves. Little David Murray was right. It was time to get his shit together. It was time to put together a band of his own.

7

HURRICANE TAKES THE WHEEL

Breaking away had never been easy. It was like a relationship with a woman. Stevie had a hard time saying no, and never wanted to say goodbye, even when a relationship turned sour. It was like that feeling he'd get in the pit of his stomach, that fear of being left all alone. Intimacy had a lot to do with it, too. Women gave him comfort. To him, they were more than just a trophy in an unstated competition between musicians. The long goodbye with the Cobras was true to form, only this time he was the one who cut the cord. Stevie felt grown-up enough to take charge of his own destiny.

He was on a mission now. The spiral notebook he carried with him showed everyone he was serious. He wanted to put together a band that was his ideal, a band with the classy lines of a Mustang, the muscle-bound power of an LTD, the sharp, low-riding cool of a Thunderbird, and the white-trash toughness of a Ranchero. He headed straight for McMorris Ford on Sixth Street.

Stevie bypassed the showroom where all the new models were on display and ducked into the repair shop in back, where he found Wesley Curley Clark fiddling under the hood of a Pinto. Sneaking up from behind, he said, "Look what you're doin' to your fingers. Man, you're a guitar player. You're gonna ruin your hands."

W.C. rose up and turned around in recognition, slapping Stevie on the back and giving him a gap-toothed grin. "Well, at least I've got my own wheels," he jived back. Of all the crazy young musicians who'd crossed his path, Stevie was the one W.C. enjoyed shooting the bull with the most. The kid had a curiosity that wouldn't quit, his enthusiasm was boundless, and he hung on every word coming out of W.C.'s mouth as if it were the Book of Acts. He was a pup thirsty to drink in everything he could about the guitar, chords, rhythms, tones, and timing. W.C. believed that between his curiosity and considerable talent, Stevie had incredible potential, if only he could figure out how to focus. He'd seen him come into his own with the Cobras, giving Denny Freeman a run for his money. Stevie must have been nuts to leave that deal, he figured.

Then again, W.C. knew a few things about moving around to keep his own creative edge sharp. Raised on gospel music on Austin's east side, W.C. was one of the few young blacks who embraced the blues, hanging out as a teenager at the Victory Grill, where he fell under the influence of the little-known guitar virtuoso T. D. Bell. One of W.C.'s greatest gifts was his color blindness. When he was old enough to leave home, he hooked up with Angela Strehli for two years in the band Southern Feeling, doing a lengthy stretch in Seattle making a demo record in search of a label deal that never materialized, and saw about as much of the world as he cared to see touring with Joe Tex, the Navasota soul singer with a string of novelty hits like "Skinny Legs" and "Show Me." Both experiences soured W.C. on the business of music to the point he finally decided to get off the road and settle back home, getting by in a more pragmatic fashion. He sold his equipment and hired on at McMorris Ford as a mechanic, a trade he had taught himself over the years.

Stevie became a regular visitor to the Ford garage, swapping stories with W.C., talking up music, and trying, in Stevie's roundabout manner, to get W.C.'s mind off of crankshafts and back onto more pressing matters. It took him several weeks to finally get to the point.

"I'm trying to put a band together, W.C.," he blurted out one day. "I need you. That's all there is to it."

Now W.C. thought Stevie was going to be a monster of a guitar player if only he kept his head screwed on straight. But McMorris was security like he'd never had before. The problem was that Stevie wouldn't take no for an answer. He kept coming back and pestering him. Finally, W.C.'s resistance began to soften. One reason he quit Joe Tex was that he sensed there was a movement going on in the Austin clubs that he wanted to be a part of. Maybe, just maybe, Stevie was on to something. With little reluctance or fanfare, he gave notice to his boss at McMorris Ford, scrounged up some equipment, and committed to play bass and sing with Stevie.

W.C. was only part of the dream team. Stevie buttonholed every other competent musician that he knew in Austin, jamming with them to see if they generated any sparks together. He looked up a sax player named Jeffrey Barnes he'd known from the One Knite. He auditioned a young female blues belter named Karen Kinslow. He even tried to see how he'd fit in with Stump, a project started by some of the guys from Too Smooth, a popular Mother Earth showband notable for their tight three-part vocal harmonies. After a lengthy culling process Stevie nailed down a group of players that could really kick ass.

Mike Kindred was an old running buddy from Oak Cliff and a Krackerjack veteran who carried around a book of more than three hundred original compositions. Although he was trained as a classical pianist, Kindred got drawn into blues through the Kats Karavan radio show, did the teen rock-and-roll bit with his first band, the Mystics, who had a local hit in Dallas that asked the musical question, "Didn't We Have a Good Time, Baby?" and had been knocking around Austin for six years. Stevie found him between jobs after he'd left a heavily bankrolled pop-rock concoction called Gypsee Eyes.

For drums, Stevie recruited Fredde Pharoah, the rail-thin Dallas Cellar veteran who'd popped the snare for the Storm. But before Stevie made the hiring official, he busted Fredde's chops by reminding him of the time he'd tried out for Fredde's band the Dallas City Blues in the late sixties. The tadpole in bell-bottom pants made an indelible impression on Pharoah. Big Jim Vaughan drove Stevie to the audition and helped him hook up his Gibson Melody Maker guitar to his Showman amp with the Silvertone 10-inch speaker. The kid was good, but Fredde didn't offer him the gig. "He was only fifteen and we were playing late-night club gigs," he said. "No matter how good he was, we couldn't be looking after a kid," he said. In Austin, Stevie decided to turn the tables. After auditioning him, he ribbed Pharoah that he was pretty good, all right, but maybe he was "too old" to play with his new band.

The crowning touch was Miss Lou Ann Barton. Stevie had heard her sitting in with Robert Ealey's band at the New Blue Bird Nite Club in Fort Worth, one of the last real juke joints in Texas, and during her brief stint with the Thunderbirds. She had pouty lips, a gift for teasing men, onstage and off, and a wickedly assertive voice. When she was at the top of her game, she could wrap her pipes around a Brenda Lee, Patsy Cline, or Wanda Jackson country song, then wallow in the emasculating grit of dusky shouters like Koko Taylor, Big Mama Thornton, and Miss Lavelle White without ever sounding out of character. No matter what kind of material she mined, she packed a verbal wallop that could strip the chrome off a trailer hitch.

But Lou Ann didn't even have to open her mouth to hold an audience in the palm of her hand. The microphone was a prop she manipulated with seductive skill and passion, alternately caressing it, hanging on to it for dear life, and berating it like a scorned lover, flicking cigarettes into the crowd for added emphasis. When Stevie took a lead, she'd step back, hands on her hips, eyebrows arched in a challenging expression that said, "Prove it to me, big boy."

Lou Ann was also a foul-mouthed partying lush with a wicked temper and a sexual appetite to match the most deranged male rock and roller. Her sharp tongue and her hard drinking had already proved to be too much for the Fabulous Thunderbirds. She had been bouncing between the band Marc Benno had put together in Dallas, sitting in with Robert Ealey and His Five Careless Lovers in Fort Worth, and doing pickup gigs in Austin. The reputation she brought with her fascinated Stevie. She was a wildcat begging to be tamed, was how he saw it. If the boys in the other bands couldn't handle her, then it was all the more reason for him to try. Lou Ann was a soul sister, a bitch in heat who put as much muscle into her music as he put into his.

Stevie Vaughan's new band actually rehearsed before making their debut on August 8, 1976, at Soap Creek Saloon. They practiced in a vault in the back of Pecan Street Studios on Sixth Street, where Mike Kindred kept a bed. They settled on the name Triple Threat Revue, a handle that suggested a supergroup in the making, one that had too much talent to focus on any one individual. The trouble was trying to figure out who the three Triple Threats were — W.C., Stevie, Lou Ann, Kindred, or Fredde? Actually, everyone in the band had their moment on center stage. Lou Ann did her rave-up of Barbara Lynn's early sixties blues ballad "You'll Lose a Good Thing" (which, true to Lou Ann's roots, came out sounding like "thang"), Irma Thomas's regional smash "You Can Have My Husband (But Please Don't Mess With My Man)," and sneaked in an occasional rockabilly rant; Kindred like to showcase his brooding composition "Cold Shot," which Clark toughened up with an insistent, driving bass line from the book of John Lee Hooker; W.C. sang his soul-tinged originals and an Al Green cover or two while holding down the bottom; Stevie added vocal grit and guitar dynamite; and Fredde shuffled the night away as steady as they came.

Given Triple Threat's considerable depth, it was a golden opportunity for Stevie to broaden his musical horizons. He worked in phrasings picked up from the jazz players that Denny Freeman had turned him on to, absorbed all sorts of weird Asian and African ethnic musics that Kindred dug, and studied the exotic Tex-Mex conjuntos that his buddy Keith Ferguson was into, bands like Cuatitos Cantu, a south Texas group led by a pair of accordion-playing midget twins with six fingers on each hand. Having perfected the licks of Albert King and Otis Rush, Stevie began to reshape their material into his own distinctive sound, a sound incorporated into a swerving jump original called "Love Struck Baby," while road-testing crowd pleasers like "Dirty Pool," left over from the Nightcrawlers days, and "Texas Flood," the Larry Davis dirge that had become his signature.

Stevie and the band hustled up gigs at After Ours, an all-night club downtown, Soap Creek, Antone's, the Continental on South Congress, and the Austex, Steve Dean's wood-framed alkie bar down the street from the Continental — anywhere they could nail down an open date. Sometimes they'd even get a small guarantee instead of crapshooting with the usual 80 percent of the door receipts. Club owners often advertised the band as Stevie Vaughn (sic) and the Triple Threat Revue, much to the annoyance of the rest of the band since Stevie spent most of the time onstage staring at his shoelaces while picking his guitar. Even with zero stage presence, the buzz about Stevie Vaughan's powerful chops was spreading fast.

The band's most dependable gig was a semiregular Sunday-night slot at the Rome Inn. The Rome didn't pay a guarantee and it wasn't exactly a clean, well-lit place. The former pizza parlor had originally opened as a Cosmic Cowboy joint, a favorite hangout for Willie Nelson's band and crew due in no small part to the almost constant coke sniffing that went on in the office upstairs. But after the owners split town owing hundreds of thousands of dollars, the manager, C-Boy Parks, a cook at the Nighthawk restaurant during the day, took over the establishment. True to his own personal bias, Parks started booking blues acts, including Jimmie Vaughan's Fabulous Thunderbirds, who ruled the triangular stage every Monday night.

The T-Birds' Blue Monday gig evolved into the biggest weekly debauch in Austin for professional club crawlers, musicians, music freaks, and party professionals on the make. As sure as Kim Wilson and Jimmie Vaughan would slice through their versions of "The Monkey" and "Scratch My Back," there would be Sherri Phelan, aka Sherri, the Freedom Dancer, on the dance floor, performing a nonstop interpretive dance solo (she was such a Vaughan brothers fanatic that Stevie gave her a laminated permanent pass guaranteeing admission to any show); Miss Ivy, the six-foot-tall shady lady of the evening; Janet Quist, the old Krackerjack groupie who had finally graced the centerfold of *Playboy* magazine; Jimmie's wife, Connie, who always brought along a tableful of female friends who were called the Blues Bitches behind their backs; and another group of girls calling themselves the Whorellas who would egg on the band by throwing pantyhose on the stage and yelling "Fuck me" from the dance floor. Even Billy Gibbons from ZZ Top would frequently drive up from Houston for the night, once bringing along an entire busload of friends to witness the debauchery that he described in the song "Low-down in the Streets" on ZZ Top's album *DeGuello*.

Sunday, Triple Threat Revue's regular night at the Rome Inn, had very little vibe at all. Sometimes, no one showed up to pay their two dollars at the door. The band called those slow nights Pizza Nights be-cause they would walk across the street to Conan's Pizza, where the sympathetic management dished out free food. Triple Threat's reward for staying on the calendar was getting the Blue Monday slot whenever the T-Birds went on the road, which they were doing with increasing regu-larity, and earning C-Boy's respect.

Taking a cue from the Fab T-Birds, Triple Threat also began to hit the highway, booking out-of-town dates at many of the same places Stevie had worked with the Cobras. Even if they lacked a band van, they did have one hell of a mechanic in W. C. Clark. Their circuit included Faces in Dallas, the Cheatham Street Warehouse in San Marcos, where freight trains rumbling past behind the stage often drowned out the music, and the Crossroads in the east Texas college town of Nacogdoches, run by a character named Butthole Bill. Strangely enough, of all the out-of-town gigs, their most rabid following developed in Lubbock, the Hub City of the High Plains of West Texas, 368 miles from Austin.

Lubbock looked like it was created out of a vacuum, a pancake flat, rectangularly arranged community of 100,000 surrounded by cotton fields, feed lots, and pump jacks. There wasn't all that much poetic or picturesque about Lubbock except perhaps for its wicked dust storms in the spring, the lively prairie-dog town in Mackenzie Park, and its small but vibrant music scene, which primarily revolved around folk singer-songwriters Joe Ely, Butch Hancock, Jimmie Dale Gilmore, and Terry Allen before they all left town. Lubbock actually could brag of its rich musical heritage. It was the hometown of Buddy Holly, although it often seemed like the city's leaders were slightly embarrassed by the rock-and-roll world created in part by their not-so-favorite son. They'd rather cite the accomplishments of pop singer Mac Davis or Ralna English from the "Lawrence Welk" show.

Times had changed since the day the music died in 1959, when a private plane carrying Holly, the Big Bopper, and Richie Valens crashed in a snow-covered Iowa cornfield, killing all on board in the first great rock tragedy. The student body at Texas Tech University had grown to 25,000, a good-sized herd of young people ready to cut loose when the weekend rolled around. Tech wasn't UT, but for anyone primed for a party, it was the key reason there was more action in Lubbock than anywhere else between Austin and Albuquerque.

Stevie found some redeeming qualities about the place. He felt like a star in Lubbock. He was always able to draw a supportive crowd and leave with a little cash in his pocket. He was something of a celebrity, too. Hardly anyone in Lubbock had ever heard of the Storm or the Fabulous Thunderbirds, much less of Jimmie Vaughan. No one cornered Stevie after a show to compare him with his brother. Here, they took him at face value and still heaped him with praise. Stevie liked that.

By the time Stevie Vaughan debuted his new band in Lubbock, the hot spot near campus was Fat Dawg's, where Triple Threat set and reset attendance records in a cramped room that could legally accommodate fewer than one hundred people. Stevie considered it the one consistent money gig on the High Plains. But if he'd had his druthers, Stevie would rather have done business with C. B. Stubblefield any day. Stubblefield was a gentle giant of a black man who owned and operated Stubb's Barbecue on East Broadway. On Sunday evenings, he hosted an informal jam session that was attended by every able-bodied musician in town. The music invariably leaned to country and folk, but on rare occasions, like the times Stevie Vaughan dropped in, the smoke-encrusted room would resonate with the sounds Stubb loved most.

The friendship with Stubb began when Stevie had played a date with the Cobras at the Cotton Club on the Slaton Highway. After a Triple Threat gig in Lubbock, Stevie phoned him up. "He said he needed to play at my Sunday jam," Stubb said.

"Play for me? We don't pay anybody to play over here," Stubb told him. "Everybody just comes over here and has a hell of a time."

"I'll tell you the truth," Stevie said in a low voice. "I need to make eighty bucks or I can't get my shit out of my room."

Stubb told him to come over with the band. They showed up Sunday afternoon.

"If ever I saw hungry people, it was them, with a lot of pride," Stubb recalled. "I asked, 'You want a beer? You hungry?' "

"No, we're fine," Stevie said, trying to contain himself.

"These guys can tell you they're fine all they want to, but that barbecue sure smells good," Fredde Pharoah piped up with typical candor. "I want to eat!"

Stevie shot a stare at Fredde, but he wasn't mad, he was thankful. Stubb fixed them all plates of sliced beef, chicken, and ribs drenched in his spicy, mixed-with-love sauce and brought them a pitcher of beer. They could not hide their hunger.

"Boy, you talk about people getting after it!" exclaimed Stubb with no small amount of pride. While they ate, Stubb slipped a quarter in the jukebox and punched up some songs. The second Stevie heard the downhome blues, he jumped up and headed for the jukebox. Food could wait. He wanted to know what in the hell these sides were that Stubb was playing. When "Tin Pan Alley," a dark, dramatic slow blues popularized by Jimmy Wilson and the All-Stars came on, Stevie was floored. This was some very serious music. "Hey, Stubb," he said, "mind if I bring my tape recorder in here sometime?"

That evening, during the jam session, Triple Threat made a cameo appearance that would be a turning point for the band, for Stubb's Barbecue, and for anyone who ever heard a live band in Lubbock, Texas. All the revue came out smoking, but young Stevie floored the house and set it rocking. It was one thing to hear blues on the juke. But no one had ever heard it done live and in person like they did that night. At ten-thirty, Stubb counted out $150 and silently handed it to Stevie as he passed by the counter.

A few minutes later, Stevie came back.

"Hey, man, you all right?" he asked Stubb.

"Yeah, I'm fine," the big man said.

"You gave me too much money here."

"Man, that's eighty dollars. Can't you count?" Stubb grinned.

"This is a hundred fifty!"

"Well, you gotta buy breakfast and a tank of gas to get back to Austin," Stubb said, turning away.

Stevie learned two important things about Lubbock. When they played Stubb's, they were gonna eat well and go home with some money in their pocket.

It was the twenty hours of the day when he wasn't in the spotlight that Stevie Vaughan couldn't deal with. Without a guitar in his hand, he sometimes seemed as hopeless, derelict, and pathetic as a "drag worm," a term used to describe the vagrants and panhandlers who hung out near the UT campus in Austin. He was a fool when it came to money. On one drive back to Austin from Lubbock, he spent half the band's gig money on shiny wristwatches that a black man was peddling outside a convenience store on the highway, giving one to each member of the band. It was hard to get pissed at him. He was terribly shy about the way he looked and embarrassed about his thinning hair, which made him all the more huggable in the eyes of Kelli, Shirley, and the string of girlfriends who followed Lindi. They not only provided companionship and shelter, they gave him fashion advice, loaned him hats and scarves, showered him with jewelry, earrings, and other shiny objects. Everybody wanted to help Stevie, who always seemed to cry out for it even if he didn't think so. Perry Patterson, who owned a small recording studio where Triple Threat noodled around on occasion, even gave him a '65 yellow Chrysler with a black top.

People like Patterson took a shine to Stevie because he played guitar like no one else. His presence made or broke any party, and he would put up with even the most amateur guitar picker as long as the person brought along "party favors." If powdered stimulants were around, it was next to impossible to get Stevie to leave the room until nothing was left. His insatiable appetite for the drugs was the main reason Stevie spent so many nights crashed out on couches and floors, waking up in the morning to ask himself, "Where the fuck am I?"

One of these aspiring guitar pickers with a business head for black-market distribution was Diamond Joe Siddons, a Cadillac-driving hustler with a predilection for Afghan coats. Stevie humored Diamond Joe, showing him riffs in informal picking sessions in exchange for the goodies that Siddons was always packing. He would drop by Diamond Joe's place regularly, bringing along his guitar and the occasional girlfriend for all-nighters. In the morning, Stevie always remembered to leave with his guitar, though at least once he left the girl behind. There was one girl he noticed in the after-hours crowd at Siddons's parties that he would have been happy to take home. Stevie had it bad for Siddons's girlfriend, Lenny Bailey.

A strong-willed, independent party princess with a creamy dark olive complexion, Lenny was fascinated by the spiritual, the supernatural, and those modern mystics — musicians. She grew up a military brat who moved with her family frequently enough and traveled widely enough to speak fluent German. She was enough of a looker to have won the Miss Copperas Cove beauty pageant, representing the central Texas town adjacent to Fort Hood, America's largest army base, where Elvis Presley did his basic training. And she was a challenge. Lenny was just as unpredictable and wild as Stevie could ever hope to be. It wasn't a case of her being able to keep up with him, but the other way around.

Friends knew Stevie's infatuation with Lenny had turned into something more serious the morning he showed up at the house where he was staying in a pair of blue jeans that were two sizes too large. "I'm wearing his pants," he crowed. What he was really saying was that he'd slept with Lenny and walked away in Siddons's Levis. The dreamy, faraway look in his eyes was accompanied by the declaration, "I think this is it." Everyone nodded knowingly. Oh yeah. Sure. They'd heard that line before.

But this time really was serious. After a nasty Fourth of July spat with Siddons, Lenny ran into Stevie at a Mexican restaurant. "He had on a T-shirt and a Hawaiian print pillowcase for a doo-rag on his head," she said. She asked him, "Why don't you come home with me?" He took up her offer. "That was our love-struck day. That was the day he wrote 'Love Struck' and said it was for me."

Siddons, who actually fantasized that he had the guitar chops to keep up with Stevie, was angry and bitter about losing Lenny to the guy he considered a rival. He hung a picture of Stevie on the wall and threw darts at it.

Lenny thought she knew what she was getting into by doing a thing with Stevie; she soon discovered otherwise. "He was so insecure," she explained. "He never wanted to be alone." A major difference between Joe and Stevie was money. Siddons kept a fat roll stuffed in his pockets. Stevie never knew where his next meal was coming from. Lucky for him that Lenny didn't mind becoming part of the musicians' matriarchy. She held down a day job working as a computer programmer at St. Edward's University. It was not unlike having two jobs and two separate lives.

Their typical routine was to go out clubbing, then come home, where, as Lenny described it, they "boinked all night." In the morning, Stevie would sleep in while Lenny would ride her bike to work. He didn't particularly dig the fact she was the one who was bringing home the bacon. That was his role, if only he could ever start making some decent wages. He resented the fact his woman worked for another man who could order her around, just because he was boss.

"Stevie just wanted to play all the time," said Pammy Kay, a friend of the couple's who was dating Doug Sahm. Whenever she went to visit the couple at their rent house on Rabb Road, Pammy Kay would inevitably find Stevie within arm's reach of a guitar or record player. Stevie bought Lenny a bass guitar and taught her a few licks, but it never took. Instead the couple preferred spending many evenings at Pammy Kay's playing Yahtzee, shooting craps, pitching pennies, or drawing pictures with the art supplies she kept on hand while they drank or got high. His artistry impressed Pammy. "His watercolors were misty-looking, but his drawings were very precise. He was a draftsman type of drawer. One time we took pieces of paper and squirted tubes of acrylic paint onto 'em and stuck firecrackers in 'em. Made a great picture."

One house Lenny and Stevie lived in had no stove, so they made do cooking pretzels and pancakes in the fireplace. The couple never did get around to buying a refrigerator. "The first thing we'd do every morning was go get a bag of ice for the ice chest," Lenny recalled. Appliances weren't important priorities, not when the proverbial sex and drugs and rock and roll were in plentiful supply. Strangely enough, the couple were old-fashioned in the sense that they demanded fidelity from each other, at least in principle.

Lenny did not much care for other women, especially women who were attracted to Stevie. "She considered them all bimbos," Pammy Kay said. Just as Stevie would disappear from his old girlfriend, Lindi, for days at a time, Lenny was not averse to following a good-looking man who promised her a good time. It was not unusual for her to borrow a friend's car for an hour and not return it until a week later. But as much as her disappeareances frustrated Stevie, the aura of mystery that swirled around her was a turn-on. It was all part of her otherworldly allure.

"Lenny liked to run the show," explained Pammy Kay. "She got

Stevie into psychic stuff, like throwing stones. She had this friend who used to give Stevie business advice. She'd look at his palm and read his horoscope and tell him when was the right time to sign a contract and stuff."

Stevie had a weakness for the spiritual realm. His own life wasn't shaped by material concerns or rational decisions but by the strange and wonderful gift he possessed, a gift whose origin he could never fully comprehend. He believed in just about anything that wasn't tangible. He swore that he'd do a ninety-degree phase shift of the planet before he died. He tried to talk Jimmie into buying a UFO advertised in one of the tabloids so that when the time came, they would be ready. The ordinary straight world of nine-to-five jobs, family, and responsibility was foreign to him, which was the way he wanted it. His world was determined by whatever direction his guitar took him. Lenny couldn't come along for that ride; no one, not even his band mates could do that. But offstage, she was an extraordinary sidekick. Not for nothing had she been a dealer's girlfriend. Now that her supplier was a thing of the past, she figured out how to keep the party rolling on her own. That way, she figured, she could keep Stevie happy, avoid a day job, and pay the bills at the same time.

At times, too much of a good thing worked to undermine Stevie's performance. There was the time he and Fredde Pharoah scored some exceptionally clean crystal meth. They knew they had to be in Lubbock the next day to begin a three-day gig, but they figured they had plenty of time to get there. Unfortunately, the whacked-out, jabbering duo went for a drive, headed east instead of west, and wound up somewhere north of Houston before they noticed their mistake. As they drove across the length of Texas the next day, Stevie phoned ahead to explain why they had missed the first night of the gig. "Uh, we ran into some car trouble," he uttered lamely.

His obsessions could be touching, even when they were drug-addled. It was two o'clock one morning when Becky Crabtree heard a knock at her door. There stood Stevie with a small guitar in his hand. "You are not gonna believe it. You are not gonna believe it. You are not fuckin' gonna believe it," he babbled.

Becky was terrified. "What? Who died?"

"Me and Lou Ann found a guitar in Lubbock with the skinniest neck. It's a '57 Fender Mustang with this little skinny neck, and I know Tyrone's hands are big enough to play it," he said, referring to the young boy he considered to be his nephew. "Wake him up."

Becky knew there was no way to stop Stevie, and she went down the hall. "Tyrone," she whispered softly. "Wake up. Uncle Stevie's here." Stevie sat down on the bed, strung the guitar, tuned it, and handed it over to his sleepy-eyed little pal. "Check this shit out, man," Stevie said. "Look at this little skinny neck."

Tyrone gently wrapped his left hand around the neck of the guitar. "Yeah," he smiled, as Stevie beamed triumphantly.

His increasingly erratic behavior prompted his fellow band members to confront him. He needed to watch himself or he was going to get hurt, they warned. Stevie responded with a letter that neither admitted culpability nor denied it:

"If band members are so dissatisfied with my leadership of the band, they should go on their own. I will be then able to carry on with my career, recording, working gigs, and on a much higher level. I do understand some of the complaints concerning my health, actions, etc., but also understand all circumstances involved are evolving because of me."

Less than a year after their debut, Mike Kindred and W. C. Clark bailed out of Triple Threat. They were both fed up with Stevie's bad habits and Lou Ann's incessant demands. Both of them were hard to deal with when drunk and downright impossible if they were jacked up on stimulants. Driving to west Texas for three hundred bucks a night was not what they had in mind when Stevie recruited them for the band. W.C. was itching to play guitar again and front his own group. Kindred was looking for a steadier gig and musicians more willing to expand their horizons, though he had talked Triple Threat into adding a samba to the repertoire. W.C. gave his notice first, though Stevie refused to believe him until he didn't show up for a gig. Kindred followed shortly thereafter when Stevie voiced his intent to add a sax to the band.

In the spring of 1978, Triple Threat cut back a notch and became Double Trouble, taking their new name from the Otis Rush song. The sax that Stevie added to the band belonged to Johnny Reno, who had been sitting in with the band in March and April before officially joining the band on Saturday, May 13, 1978. Two days later, Jackie Newhouse, W. C. Clark's replacement on bass, made his bow at the Rome Inn. The old Triple Threat's last gig was opening a show at Soap Creek headlined by a Delaware guitarist named George Thorogood, who was being hailed as the Next Big Thing.

Newhouse and Reno had matriculated with Robert Ealey's house band at the New Blue Bird Nite Club, a soul shack in Fort Worth that had been featuring live dance blues since the forties. In the early seventies, it was home to a new generation of players including Miss Lou Ann, Mike Buck of the Fabulous Thunderbirds, Sumter and Stephen Bruton, Freddie "Little Junior One-Hand" Cisneros, Jim Colegrove, and Gerard Daily, all of whom learned how to play jump blues in its element.

Reno's honking rhythm sax gave the reworked Double Trouble a richer, fuller sound that pushed Stevie's guitar even further out front.

Newhouse had no idea what he'd walked into. He thought he was joining Lou Ann's band. But he saw the potential right away. Stevie played with emotion and control. Most impressive, though, was his intensity. "It came from deep inside," Newhouse said. "You could really feel it. He absorbed a lot of styles, but I don't think he played like anyone else."

For thirty minutes of each set, the spotlight belonged to Lou Ann, who would come onstage to sing a few selections, then split. When Lou Ann was gone, Stevie would step forward to sing his signature "Texas Flood," the old favorite "Thunderbird," as well as Otis Rush's "All Your Lovin' " and Albert King's "Crosscut Saw." In between, the band concentrated on instrumentals in the vein of Albert Collins's "Frosty" and Freddie King's "Hide Away."

A month after Jackie Newhouse signed on, the band members played the toughest gig of all their young careers. Juneteenth, held on or around June 19, was a traditional holiday for Texas blacks, commemorating the day in 1865 that General Gordon Granger, U.S. commander of the District of Texas, read the emancipation proclamation freeing all slaves. One hundred and thirteen years later, the band, worn out and frazzled, still being advertised as Triple Threat, pulled into the backstage area of the Miller Outdoor Amphitheater in Houston's Hermann Park minutes before their scheduled performance. The van they were driving had a flat on the interstate on the outskirts of the city, and now they had to go perform in front of the biggest crowd they had ever faced. And since most of the 30,000 people impatiently waiting for them were black, they were about to learn how valid their credentials really were. Before she'd go on, Lou Ann demanded a bottle of gin to settle her nerves. She took a few belts, steadied herself, then led the group on. The first reaction on both sides of the stage was one of shock and confusion.

"Who are these white punks in the thrift-shop threads, and what are they doing at our celebration?"

The answer came when Miss Lou Ann's sanctified wail cut through the dulling humidity, the pop of the snare jumped out from the back of the band shell, the bass line rumbled up from the bottom, and the guitar man broke out of the box like he was running for his life. It was all the crowd needed to know. Between that cheeky white gal howling and that skinny-assed white boy up there banging on the strings there was some mean inspirational music going down. When it was his turn to step up to the microphone, Stevie squalled something fierce, like someone who'd been born and raised in the bloody Fifth Ward. The applause, the hollers, the waving hands, the shaking hips of the big fat women carrying on at the foot of the stage told the band all they needed to know.

"When they opened the curtains and I saw all those people, I had to drop my head so I couldn't see them," Stevie recalled. "Once I realized that those people enjoyed what we were doing, it was an abnormally satisfying thing." To put it mildly.

The Miller Amphitheater performance in Hermann Park was an encounter with a remnant of Houston that once roared twenty-four hours a day, back when Don Robey ruled the world of bronze entertainment. Everybody in Double Trouble had grown up listening to records with the Duke and Peacock labels that were made here in the fifties and sixties. But it was something else being smack-dab in the middle of it, live and in person. The presence of Koko Taylor, Lightnin' Hopkins, and ol' Big Walter Price standing in the wings watching them run through their stuff told them they were doing all right, no matter what the color of their skin. Somewhere up in heaven, behind the pearly gates where golden Cadillacs delivered the faithful to their appointment with God, Amos Milburn, Houston's Big Daddy of the Big Beat, was smiling.

A few weeks later Double Trouble returned to Houston to repeat their performance in front of a predominantly white audience at Fitzgerald's, an old Polish dance hall where Bill Narum, a graphics artist-turned-promoter had cobilled them with Rocky Hill, the hulking hotshot guitar in town. Rocky was already a star by virtue of being the brother of Dusty Hill, the ZZ Top bass player. Rocky fancied himself just as bad a blues guitarslinger as the Top's Billy Gibbons. Stevie remembered him as something of a buffoon who was a pretty decent player when he and Dusty were in the American Blues in Dallas during the late sixties. But no way was he afraid of Hill, especially not after the Juneteenth concert across town.

The shows were two nights of exceptional posturing and showboating for this level of clubland. Friday night, Rocky stalled for an hour and a half before he went on after following Stevie. On Saturday, Stevie returned the favor and hemmed and hawed for forty-five minutes until the band took the stage. The one-upmanship did not obscure what was obvious to the guitar freaks in the house. When the smoke cleared on Sunday morning, Double Trouble had gained a firm foothold in Houston while Rocky Hill was demoted to the rank of the second-best guitarist in Space City.

The real struggle for Stevie was keeping his personal act together. He fought so frequently with Lenny that it seemed like half the time they were living together and the other half Stevie was either on the couch circuit or crashing with his sleeping bag and record player in a spare room at Lou Ann's house on South Second Street.

Fredde Pharoah got so strung out on speed, he quit the band and headed back to Dallas. He was replaced briefly by Jack Moore, who'd moved down from Boston for the specific purpose of playing blues, not knowing that he'd have to live them, too. But there was another drummer waiting in the wings, one who'd been angling to hook up with Stevie for the past three years. Stevie had regarded Chris Layton as a pretty fair fireplug of a rhythm man ever since he had come to Austin in 1975 from Corpus Christi. He'd met Chris through his roommate Joe Sublett, the Cobras' sax player. Chris had initially joined the resolutely eclectic Dan Del Santo and His Professors of Pleasures before landing a job with Greezy Wheels, the quintessential Austin hippie-cowboy band of the early seventies, that still had a decent club draw and a couple of albums under their big-buckled belts. Stevie saw through Greezy Wheels' stereotype — he *still* hated progressive country music — and heard a drummer who could lock into a groove.

The feeling was mutual. Chris first heard Stevie with the Cobras at Soap Creek shortly after he arrived in Austin and was taken aback with what he called this "human diamond" whose unremitting concentration and power were so thorough and complete once the strap went over his shoulder, "It was like he *was* the music."

On one of the most dogged of the dog days of the summer of 1978, Stevie walked in on Layton with his headphones on, pounding away on his drum kit in the kitchen. A lightbulb flashed above Stevie's head. "I'm looking for a drummer," he announced. It was a done deal. He didn't have to say anything else. Chris didn't need to be persuaded. Greezy Wheels had used up their fifteen minutes of fame long ago. Stevie Vaughan was going places.

The chemistry certainly felt right. In a few minutes, Stevie taught Chris how to play a rub-shuffle to his satisfaction, dragging the stick across the snare on the first and third beats in the style favored by many Dallas-area drummers. Stevie was very particular when it came to the beat. Once Chris got a bead on the beat, Double Trouble had a drummer.

Raised on his parents' Chick Webb 78s, Chris Layton grew up under the influence of Frank Beard of ZZ Top, Santana's Mike Shrieve, and jazz machine Tony Williams, all references that Stevie respected. The minute the subject of Jimi Hendrix came up, they both knew it was a hand-in-glove thang. Layton dug Mitch Mitchell's style as much as Stevie dug Jimi's guitar. And just like Mitchell, Chris could keep up with Stevie and stay with him like white on rice, locking his radar tight on the guitarist's swirling lead. Chris was also a smart guy with good horse sense, rare qualities in a musician, much less a drummer. Without prompting, he began to help book gigs and took charge of rounding up PAs and organizing the books, a job that he took out of frustration with Stevie's managerial incompetence. "Sometimes Stevie'd call us up at eight o'clock for a gig at ten," remembered Chris Layton. "A couple times we ended up playing 'Chitlins Con Carne' at a little place called the Austex Lounge, just Stevie and I — guitar and drums — maybe five people in there. And they were goin', 'Where's the rest of the band?'"

Double Trouble subsisted on regular gigs Sundays at the Rome Inn, Wednesdays at Soap Creek, and every other Thursday at Antone's with occasional trips to the Broadway 50/50 in San Antonio and St. Christopher's, a rough little bucket on Greenville Avenue in Dallas. Once every month or two, they'd play Lubbock, where the Tech sorority girls and bandido bikers had designated Stevie their favorite guitar hero.

A typical Double Trouble night kicked off with a driving shuffle copped from Guitar Slim's old showtime introduction, "They Call Me Guitar Slim," with Stevie altering the lyrics to fit his own self-styled nickname:

They call me Hurricane and I've come to play in your town
They call me Hurricane and I've come to play in your town
If you do not like me I will not hang around

The band dressed like secondhand-store gangsters, Johnny Reno in his sharp pleated slacks, Lou Ann with a low-cut, sleeveless clinging black dress and beret, Stevie with double-knit pants, a button-up shirt, his applejack hat, a soul patch of hair under his lower lip, and the hint of a budding pencil-thin mustache.

After the intro warm-up, the band blindsided the audience with "Tin Pan Alley," the song Stevie first heard on Stubb's jukebox that he thought was one of the meanest, hardest, coldest blues songs ever recorded. Next came a faithful reading of "Thunderbird," the Nightcaps song, Stevie exaggerating his way through the "Get high" chorus like he was Mick Jagger. That was followed by unequal portions of Howlin' Wolf–brand growl and Hubert Sumlin–style steel, quotations from the works of Otis Rush, Buddy Guy, B. B. and Freddie King, with occasional sidetrips into Jimmy Smith and Groove Holmes soul-jazz territory.

Lubbock fans were particularly smitten with the band's dance instrumental "The Rhinogator," a frenzied, compact piece of work to which dancers put their hands on their nose like a rhinoceros, then flopped around the floor in imitation of an alligator out of water — a variation of the Gator, a popular Texas frat-party dance usually performed by extremely inebriated males.

Once they had their instruments in tune and the sound system under control, Double Trouble tended to play over their heads with enough assurance to risk fluffing a line in exchange for the inspiration. "If you blow a note once, blow it again in the same song and it will be all right," Stevie liked to say. As a front man, he was still a little shy, preferring to stay in the shadows and avoid establishing a rapport with the audience. Lou Ann or Johnny could do the between-song patter. From the back of a club, he seemed wrapped up in a cocoon, oblivious to his surroundings. But Stevie was actually keeping a close eye on Layton,

Reno, and Newhouse, but not as close a watch as Chris, Johnny, and Jackie kept on him. With Stevie, they didn't have much of a choice. "He'd never call a tune off, he'd just start playing it," Reno said. "By the first two or three bars we'd know what it was going to be." The only time the band paused much between songs was to replace a string that Stevie managed to bust or call for drinks to the bandstand. In lieu of practicing, the band would just keep playing as long as a club manager would let them. Long after closing time, Stevie would perch at the front of the stage while he and Jack and Chris would jam for hours.

The infusion of fresh talent and Stevie's seemingly unlimited potential did not end the whispers about Stevie's drinking and drugging. It was just that Lou Ann was worse. She had no trouble matching him shot for shot, though offstage she displayed a completely different side, mothering her brood by whipping up fried-chicken-and-mashed-potato dinners for the boys when they were in Austin. Both of them were intimate with the wicked ways of getting down. The key difference between Lou Ann and Stevie was that he was never too high to play.

"Stevie was shooting up speed and drinking a bottle of Chivas Regal before he'd show up at the club," said Nick Ferrari, a Lubbock guitar player and telephone-company employee who recorded Double Trouble dates at Stubb's Barbecue and Fat Dawg's. "He'd be an hour and a half late, out of his fuckin' mind. But I tell you what, when the guy picked up the guitar, he was better than ever. He may not have been able to walk or anything, but he still played fuckin' perfect."

"I didn't know he was that bad in drinking," admitted C. B. Stubblefield. "I knew Lou Ann was bad. She was bad news for him. Muddy Waters said, 'Stevie could perhaps be the greatest guitar player that ever lived, but he won't live to get forty years old if he doesn't leave that white powder alone. You just don't get over that.' Many times I told him, 'Man, I told you what Muddy Waters said.' "

Besides providing too many convenient excuses for getting high, the long hours on the road were the basis for establishing a camaraderie. They weren't really a band. They were trailer trash, a family of missing links from the boonies, traveling down the highway, goofing on a running gag inspired by the free show they played at the Austin State Hospital for the mentally incompetent so they could get their musicians' union card. Lou Ann was Momma, the hillbilly matriarch, and Keith Ferguson, her real-life husband for a short time, was Father. Jackie was Buford. Chris was Harold, or "Haw-wald." Johnny Reno was "Weeno" or "Renozetti." Stevie was Brady (pronounced "Bwaydee"), the illiterate pinhead whose mission in life seemed to be finding "gasoween." Whenever Stevie wanted to poke fun at himself, he lapsed into his "Bwady" character. The play-acting of these "special people" continued at home, where Lenny was

Bitsy, and their friend Pammy Kay was Junior. In addition to looking for "gasoween," their favorite activities were bowling and watching "All My Children."

The romanticism of rock and roll glossed over the not-so-glamorous hard economics of playing music for a living. Fans may have treated them like stars, but everyone still was earning subsistence wages. In Austin, at least one or two members of the band stayed at Lou Ann's because they couldn't afford a place of their own. On the road, they parked at friends' houses, sleeping on sofas and the floor. They scraped together a hundred dollars and two lids of pot to buy a white '64 Econoline van that provided them dependable transportation to Lubbock and back before it blew up and was abandoned in Austin.

Between rent, food, gas, and the payments on his Pinto station wagon, Johnny Reno wasn't making ends meet with Double Trouble. He gave notice and moved back to Fort Worth in the late spring of 1979. "I was frustrated with things not being together, like gig money would get lost or dates would fall through or we'd show up to play and there wouldn't be a PA," Reno said. "Nobody thought about those things and Stevie really resented anybody trying to take on that kind of responsibility because it was his band. He would take care of it. He was really conscious of trying to be a good band leader, because he knew he was taking on something that he hadn't done before. It didn't seem like there was any kind of plan or any kind of idea what direction things were going in. Now that I look back, I can see that Stevie had a plan. He just didn't articulate it very well."

Stevie felt burned. It was like Roddy Colonna, his drummer in Blackbird, going to play gigs at the Holiday Inn, or David Murray, a perfectly good guitar player, wanting to sell books. How could these guys do anything but music? He was mad Reno was abandoning him, but he wasn't going to make a big deal about it. So go ahead and split. He'd learn.

Reno had no regrets.

By playing with someone of his ability and caliber I got better. He went for it every night. If there were five people out there, he was burning. He was always pushing, always trying stuff. Some stuff he didn't make out. He'd do things where he'd spin out. After a certain point, when he started making records, there was a trade-off. He lost a little bit of that excitement of going for really wild shit, trying to play something really fuckin' wild. He traded that for being smoother and executing better instead of standing on the edge and hammering away at something.

With his departure, Double Trouble was stripped down to a three-piece street rod with Miss Lou Ann riding in the rumble seat. The sax-driven soul material was replaced by more twelve-bar blues for Stevie to solo on and more pelvis-grinding ballads for Lou Ann to croon. There was more empty space than ever for the guitar's dirty tones to fill. Even with Lou Ann playing the role of wild card to the screeching hilt, the four were jelling into a tight little unit. Stevie had a band. Now he needed someone to look after it.

Stevie liked the idea of having someone taking care of business, but it seemed like every time he'd get close to finding someone to direct his career or book the band, they'd flake on him — not too surprising considering most of these would-be business types were glorified dealers. In the summer of 1979, he canned the crap and hired his first legitimate business representative in the person of Joe Priesnitz. Priesnitz had come to Austin a year earlier to learn the booking business as an agent for Moonhill, the agency that had a lock on many of Austin's most popular progressive country acts. But Priesnitz saw cowboy rock was headed south and quit to ally with a club owner and booker named Hank Vick. They founded Rock Arts, a regional booking agency with a diverse roster of rock, reggae, and blues club acts. Priesnitz approached Stevie after Vick had taken him to the Armadillo to see Double Trouble open for Robert Gordon.

After a brief meeting with the band, he was designated as Double Trouble's booking agent, responsible for securing engagements for the band in return for 15 percent of their earnings. Priesnitz quickly figured out that regardless of how democratic everyone tried to make it appear, Stevie Vaughan called the shots in this band. "He had this way about him. He was very proud of what he did and how he did it. He didn't want to be told what song to play, how he should be represented. That was pretty apparent from the first meeting."

The first task was coordinating dates around the San Francisco Blues Festival, coming up in August 1979. Organizers of the festival had heard about Stevie, Lou Ann, and company from the Fabulous Thunderbirds, who'd electrified the Bay Area blues scene at the fest the year before. With the help of a fan from Santa Cruz known as Ice Cube Slim, Priesnitz routed the band out west through Lubbock and Santa Fe, setting up a week's worth of dates in northern California in mid-August.

Double Trouble lacked the T-Birds' sense of fashion, and Stevie was no match for Jimmie's animal magnetism, although Miss Lou Ann most certainly rated her own groupies. But when it came to music, they still made quite an impression in the City of Haight, immediately attracting the interest of Robert Cray, the only young black blues guitar player on the West Coast blues scene. Like Jimi Hendrix, Cray was a native of

Seattle who worked both black and white musical idioms. He, too, had seen his musical past and the future pass in front of him when he witnessed the Thunderbirds. Now Double Trouble was working the same effect, so Cray and his band ingratiated themselves to the Texans. "They were real nice guys, but they hadn't been around a lot of guys from the South before," observed Jackie Newhouse. "Cray and Richard Cousins, his bass player, would talk in these outlandish black idioms like, 'Ise gwine a pick some cotton.' They wanted to know what it was like, where we came from."

The San Francisco engagement was further validation that Double Trouble could play with as much feeling as anyone, which made the run out west all the more fun. They played the Keystone clubs in Berkeley, Palo Alto, and San Francisco. They performed live on the Fat Friday broadcast on KFAT-FM in Gilroy, improvising a supergroup out of Chris and Jackie, Stevie on slide, Lou Ann singing, Robert Cray on lead guitar, and Curtis Salgado on mouth harp. Unfortunately, some of the gigs Ice Cube Slim had lined up paid so meagerly the band had to call Priesnitz to wire enough money to get home.

Surviving their first West Coast tour was a milestone. No one had given much thought to the throwaway gig they played at the Armadillo World Headquarters in Austin two weeks before, although in the long run it had a greater impact on Stevie Vaughan's career. The July 27 date was opening for headliner Randy Hansen and his band, Machine Gun. Hansen was a talented guitarist, though not very original. His shtick was doing Jimi Hendrix, down to wearing an Afro wig, headband, and the requisite jewelry and scarves. Stevie had been a Hendrix fanatic since back in '67. As a teenager, he learned Hendrix's songs and emulated Hendrix's flashy style. Even as a dedicated bluesman fixated on the old cats like Muddy and Albert, he still ate up anything to do with Hendrix and the mythology that grew around him after his death. Stevie loved slipping in Hendrix material at parties and late-night picking sessions. He was ecstatic whenever another album of outtakes or live performances sprang from the record company vaults or surfaced out of the bootleg underground. He saw the documentary film *Jimi Hendrix* the day it opened. He often mused about Hendrix dying young and wondered aloud to band mates if he was destined for the same fate. He studied Hendrix's distinctive, biting tone, and learned how to play his guitar behind his back, behind his head and with his teeth, just like Jimi did. Through the years, Stevie had tried to add Hendrix-like inflections to his guitar solos, but more often than not, his band mates told him to knock off the psychedelic shit.

Opening for Randy Hansen was the perfect opportunity for Stevie to show everyone just how experienced Jimi Hendrix had made him. At the end of Double Trouble's set, Stevie launched into a version of "Manic Depression," impressing both the crowd and himself. He knew the material better than he thought he did. Hansen, of course, wallowed in Hendrix to the point that the tribute made Stevie uncomfortable. Hansen was good, but this wasn't the real thing.

After the show, the two Hendrix fanatics hit it off grandly. They compared notes about their hero backstage, traded licks in the dressing room, then went club-hopping around Austin. Hansen even lent Stevie his Hendrix wig, which Stevie proudly wore as a disguise when they hit the joints. Gerard Daily, an obtuse, bop-inspired, self-taught pianist and saxophonist who sat in with Triple Threat and Double Trouble on several occasions, heard an overnight review from two high school–aged coworkers at Conan's Pizza. Hansen was all right, they reported. His Hendrix look was cool, and so was the Hendrix stuff he played. But the opening act's guitarist, Stevie Vaughan, was just as impressive. He didn't exactly play Hendrix note-for-note, but he certainly gave his guitar the kind of workout Hendrix would have.

Among the Rome Inn regulars, that kind of praise was close to heresy. Jimi Hendrix wasn't the blues. That attitude got Stevie wondering about Jimmie. He'd actually shared the same stage as Hendrix and used to do his material better than anyone he'd ever heard. But Jimmie would have nothing to do with Jimi now. He wouldn't have much to do with Stevie, for that matter. The brothers Vaughan had rarely played together, even though they were working the same musical turf more closely than they ever had.

Each Vaughan was headed for the big time. Anyone who heard them knew it. The big bone of contention was who would be first to break on through. Jimmie Vaughan had a decided edge, being older and having rightfully earned his reputation as the toughest no-compromise blues guitar player in Austin, and perhaps the entire cosmos. His reputation attracted the interest of celebrity music people like Bob Dylan and Joni Mitchell, who stopped in to check him out. Ray Sharpe, the Fort Worth legend whose song "Linda Lu" defined the Texas shuffle in a rock-and-roll context in 1959, materialized out of the woodwork to sit in with the T-Birds and came away a believer.

The older members of the Rome Inn crowd who were familiar with the sources of the Thunderbirds' and Triple Threat's material tended to agree that Jimmie was the better guitarist. He had perfected a spare, understated signature that was the perfect counterpoint to Kim Wilson's vocals and harmonica leads, and an antihero's Seen It/Done It/Didn't Need It attitude to go with it. He looked like an antihero, too. The Fab T-Birds didn't show up for gigs wearing T-shirts or tennis shoes; the one time Kim wore jeans to a gig, Jimmie chewed him out. Their vintage suits, shirts with flyaway collars, pleated slacks, and sharp shoes were so sartorially splendid their audience started dressing up, too.

Jimmie's crowd knew that Stevie was good, but they were put off by his flamboyant guitar style. It was over the top, too much to be good. Stevie's loyalists saw it differently. To them, it didn't matter how authentic, deep, or direct the blues he played were. All they knew was that he put his ass on the line every time he unleashed a solo. So what if he overplayed? Hendrix did. So did Clapton and half the players who were working sold-out shows in basketball arenas, even if they weren't one tenth as talented as Stevie. Jimmie's blues may have been high concept as period pieces, but Stevie was on the fast track to guitar-god status. His speed and flash attracted fans too young to have had the Hendrix experience, much less the Freddie King experience. It was Stevie's electric power that drew them like moths to a lightbulb.

The most telling distinction between the Vaughans was how each moved their respective audience. The Fab T-Birds were the penultimate bar band, best appreciated in a pressure-cooker, asshole-to-elbow atmosphere where the music practically forced butts to commence to wiggle. Theirs was a fast and cool crowd of hipsters and scenemakers. Double Trouble drew more of a blue-collar, mainstream rock audience including a sizable contingent of air guitarists who gathered at the foot of the stage, twisting their fingers and hands into spastic contortions in response to the nonverbal vibrations they were picking up from the stage. For them, Stevie was as good as it got.

The advantage was Stevie's when it came to his hands and his single-mindedness. His paws were so big and bony, so strong and sinewy, that he could contort his fingers across the fretboard to bend notes into blues progressions no one, not even Jimmie, could physically duplicate. The index finger on his left hand had become permanently crooked from playing so much on the '59 Strat and the red Rickenbacker with the heavy-gauge strings. On many nights, Stevie played to blood. One evening between sets at Fat Dawg's in Lubbock, he rushed into the office where manager Bruce Jaggers was counting change.

"Man, you got any Superglue?" Stevie asked.

"Yeah. What do you want it for?" replied Jaggers.

"Aw, I pulled this callus loose here on my finger all the way down to the quick."

Jaggers rifled through his desk and tossed him the tube. His jaw dropped as he watched Stevie squeeze the glue onto his bloody finger, reattach the callus, and hold it down.

"Hey, you don't have to do that," Jaggers protested. "Two sets are enough. The crowd will understand."

"Nah," Stevie said, motioning him away. "I've got to do this. I need this." He tossed the tube back to Jaggers and walked back out into the club.

About the only ones in Austin who didn't acknowledge the Vaughan rivalry were the Vaughan boys themselves. They weren't competing, they were just going about their business. "People always wanted to make something out of it," Jimmie told writer Ed Ward. "He was playing lead and I was playing lead and there wasn't room for both of us. It was, we always used to joke about it, like having two organ players."

They were different people. Jimmie was his father's son. He hadn't just inherited his dark features; he could be as hard, cold, and tough as the old man. Stevie was the momma's boy blessed with a sweet disposition who begged to be cuddled and coddled. Stevie showered his brother with expressions of admiration. Jimmie acted like he didn't give a double damn.

On many nights after last call, when the chairs were stacked atop the tables, Stevie would keep Jackie and Chris onstage to run through new material, particularly at the Rome Inn, where C-Boy Parks let the band store their equipment. About three o'clock one morning, a familiar straggler shuffled in to watch the band run through their paces. For the next ten minutes an extremely wasted Jimmie Vaughan heckled his little brother relentlessly.

"You can't play shit," he slurred drunkenly with a cocky half-grin, propping his body against the wall. "Your whole band sucks." Stevie ignored the epithets and focused on his guitar, but the razzing didn't let up.

"You sound like fuckin' Robin Trower!"

That did it. Pushed to the brink, Stevie quietly laid down his instrument, jumped down from the bandstand, and walked over to his brother. Without a word, he balled his right hand into a fist, reared back, punched his brother in the jaw, and sent him sprawling to the ground. He paused a moment to open and close his hand with a wince, then helped Jimmie up.

"You've had too much to drink, man. Go home," he said, his voice quivering. What had he done? He climbed back on the bandstand and hunched over his guitar, tears silently streaking down his cheeks.

8

MEAN AS HOWLIN' WOLF

Jimmie Vaughan beat his brother to a record contract when the Thunderbirds signed in 1979 with Takoma Records, a small, folk-oriented independent label noted for acoustic guitarists John Fahey and Leo Kottke. Their first album, *The Fabulous Thunderbirds*, was hardly a commercial triumph. The recording was flat, the execution dull, and the album itself was impossible to find, given Takoma's poor distribution system. Nevertheless, the music was a convincing reading of modern American blues, Muddy Waters's Chicago colliding with Slim Harpo's Louisiana swamp sound somewhere west of the Sabine River. Though it didn't zoom up the *Billboard* charts, the album was a hit with blues hounds in Providence, Washington, Ann Arbor, San Francisco, and other cities with budding scenes where other young men and women struggled to revive old black music.

The Thunderbirds' forte was playing live, and they became the standard against which all other contemporary bands were judged. For better or worse, Jimmie, Kim, Keith, and Mike indirectly inspired the Blues Brothers, a humorous sendup of the white-boy blues fantasy by "Saturday Night Live" comedians Dan Ackroyd and John Belushi. The sound may have originated in Itta Bena, Mississippi, and at 2120 Michigan Avenue on Chicago's South Side, but the Fab T-Birds served notice that the new power spot where the black-cat bone could be found was in Austin, Texas.

Stevie was an ardent admirer of the Thunderbirds' Just Do It philosophy. "When they first got together, there were a lot of us doing just local club gigs in Austin and every once in a while going into Dallas or Houston or San Antonio and playing a little club with five or ten people in it," he told a writer from *Musician* magazine.

The Thunderbirds went, "Hey, we ain't got no gigs anywhere. We don't have a record deal. We just have a good band. We're gonna get a van and we're gonna put our gear in it and we're gonna find some gigs."

The rest of us around Austin went, "Well, they got balls, man! If they can do that, we can do that too." The Thunderbirds went and they got a record deal that opened doors for people like myself to say, "Maybe there's a chance," even though record companies were telling us that nobody wants to hear that crap.

It was a rough go, knocking around bars, doing three forty-five-minute sets a night, hoping upon hope that someone, somewhere in the crowd would take notice and make a difference. It was great when people would grab Stevie's sleeve as he was packing up after a gig and tell him how good his music made them feel. But for every moment like that there was another "baked potato" gig in some godawful restaurant that doubled as a music room where, as Stevie put it, "You know it's time to go on when the salad bar is moved away from the front of the stage." He performed those gigs without bitching, but he damn sure wasn't going to compromise. The manager would inevitably ask the band to turn down their volume so diners could talk while they were pushing their vegetables around the plate. Stevie wouldn't even listen. Requests like that did not dignify a response. He didn't give a damn whether or not he'd be asked back again. No one was about to rob him of his integrity. Sometimes that was all he had.

Joe Gracey walked in on Double Trouble at the Rome Inn one Sunday night in the spring of 1979. Gracey had worked as the music director and morning-drive disc jockey at KOKE-FM, the progressive country radio station in Austin, until throat cancer robbed him of his voice. But he never lost his passion for music. He began fiddling around with a four-track TEAC recorder in a makeshift studio he'd fashioned out of two windowless office suites in the basement of the KOKE-FM building and was burning miles of tape on any worthy act he could persuade to drop in.

On his way into the Rome Inn, Gracey had walked past a blue panel truck parked outside. Inside the truck were Houston White and Sandy Lockett, the founders of the Vulcan Gas Company, along with guitarist "Fat" Charlie Prichard, and Perry Patterson. Perry ran a little studio called the Hole and the others worked with him. They were recording Double Trouble's live show on an eight-track portable setup. The sight of the equipment and the sound of the band made Gracey see red. "*I* should be the one recording," he thought.

The crew in the truck had been cutting tape on Stevie at Perry's studio in the basement of an old church on Red River Street since the days of Triple Threat. Stevie was such a regular that Patterson gave him a key to the studio. But those sessions were motivated more by the opportunity to hang out and do speed than the desire to make a hit record.

Gracey believed he could do better. He cornered Stevie after the gig and invited him to check out his little operation, which he'd dubbed Electric Graceyland. Stevie was game. He knew Joe from the radio and liked a demo he'd recorded of the Thunderbirds a couple years earlier.

"Let's cut some tracks and see how they turn out," Gracey proposed. If they both liked the results, he'd either try to sell it or put it out on his own little label. Stevie agreed.

Stevie had told friends that he wanted to cut his first record in a cheap hotel in San Antonio, the way Robert Johnson did it in 1936, only with the colors reversed, arranging for a roomful of black technicians to record him in one room while he played solo in the next room over. The Gracey sessions weren't quite like that, but they were close enough. For six months, the band repeated the best parts of their stage show in the windowless ten-by-ten-foot room with bare cinder block walls. Gracey ran wires under the door to the adjacent control room and made the actual recording on a quarter-inch tape at a speed of 7½ inches per second. He found an old fifties-style Shure microphone for vocals, processing them through a little cheap compressor. "We both loved the horrible, nasty sound we got that way," Gracey said.

He operated by a simple code. "I just turned on the tape and let them rip. We overdubbed a few vocals, but the whole thing was mostly live." His inexperience was actually a plus. "They were as green as I was. We were all literally feeling our way through these steps towards being pros."

Lou Ann showed up only when necessary, but Stevie took to hanging out at the basement. "He had a very trusting nature. Once he decided he liked me, it was almost a little scary," Gracey said. "I'd think, 'I've got this kid's total, absolute trust, and I've got to do right by him or I'll go straight to hell.'" Gracey designated him coproducer.

Half the songs the band recorded featured Lou Ann's plaintive vocals: "Hip Hip Baby," a rockabilly rave-up that Gracey envisioned as a country crossover; "Oh Yeah," an uptempo shuffle that was originally recorded by Ray Sharpe; Irma Thomas's paean to true love "You Can Have My Husband"; the Slim Harpo hit "Tina Nina Nu"; "Will My Man Be Home Tonight?," originally by Lillian Offit; and Lazy Lester's "Sugar Coated Love."

The rest were full-blown, unadulterated Stevie: his throw-caution-to-the-wind jump number "Love Struck Baby"; the jangly, amphetamine-charged instrumental "Rude Mood," named in honor of Gracey's envisioned Rude Records label; "Empty Arms," an original that sounded like it had been copped from a Delmark Records classic; and the real-time shuffle "I'm Cryin'." He finally finished "Pride and Joy," the song he'd been working on ever since he sang the first lines to his ex-girlfriend Lindi Bethel. After he recorded it, he took it home and played it for Lenny, but it only pissed her off. She accused him of writing it for someone else. "We got in a big argument," he later recounted. "So I got back in the car and went into the studio and rewrote the words, recorded it, and took it home to her. I'm glad to say I ended up going back to the original."

Gracey regarded both Lou Ann and Stevie as rare birds solidly grounded in blues. But he saw a completely different side to Stevie the night he showed up at Electric Graceland sweating profusely and shaking involuntarily. "He was all freaked out. He told me he'd been taken over by the spirit of Hendrix — literally. He was convinced that Hendrix had spoken to him and entered his playing. It was at that point that he put the Hendrix stuff in the act and started dressing in that cape and Spanish hat. It was a huge, radical shift in his whole persona."

The metamorphosis of Stevie's stage persona from a raghead thrift-shop blues brother to a dashing guitar vaquero would take a few more years to complete, but the music was already there. It did not take long for Gracey's tapes to find an interested investor. Austin impressario John Dyer offered to back Stevie's efforts to the tune of $7,000. It was a nice wad of dough, Stevie thought. He took the money, just like he took whatever happened to come his way, with little thought about what he was getting himself into. Flush with cash, Gracey and Stevie decided to recut the entire LP on a twenty-four-track board in the Nashville home of Cowboy Jack Clement, a producer-engineer whom Gracey regarded as a personal hero.

One fall day in 1979, roadie Jay Hudson packed the band into a van and headed east with a full tank of gas and a perfume bottle containing liquefied crank. They arrived at their fishing-camp motel outside Music City USA wide-awake and chattering like magpies, the driver complaining about the dragons and gorillas that had been running alongside the vehicle for the past three hundred miles.

Clement loaned Gracey his engineer, Curt Allen, the son of singing cowboy Rex Allen. Allen had his own ideas about how a record should sound, and Gracey, lacking the experience, frequently acquiesced. One technique Allen and other Nashville engineers were smitten with was the "LA snare sound," where the snare head was tuned down and muffled to the point it emitted a leather-like sound that conveyed the sensation of the drumstick sinking into the head, rather than rapping on it. By persuading Gracey to use it on the recording, Allen inadvertently doomed the project.

Chris Layton hated the dull LA snare sound and complained loudly. Stevie soon picked up the lament. They wanted an old-fashioned snare that shook and rattled like all the great Chess Records recordings. This Nashville sound was for toothless yahoos. The sessions at Clement's house wrapped in three days and the band went home while Gracey started mixing the tapes.

By the time he arrived in Austin with the mastered lacquers, ready to press the record, the band was in revolt. Stevie didn't want to put the record out and he told Gracey so. "Obviously, they'd talked it over on the way home and were unhappy," related Gracey. "It didn't end right there, but Stevie started telling me how much he disliked the sound. Our relationship became much more a matter of my trying to please him. He was extremely opinionated, as most great artists are, but up until this point, he'd decided to trust Curt and me."

Gracey agreed that the recordings were flawed, especially "Love Struck Baby," which was played way too fast. So he scratched up enough cash to take Stevie, Chris, and Jackie to Cedar Creek Studios in South Austin to recut the track. But even that wasn't enough. No one was happy with the results. Gracey had spent $7,000 of Dyer's money and $6,000 of his own and had nothing to show for it. Broke and broken-spirited, Gracey attempted to salvage the recordings by drawing up a one-page contract that would allow him to release the sides on Rude Records.

Dyer pressured Stevie to sign the paper so he could recoup his investment. Stevie refused. Dyer resorted to street tactics, threatening to break Stevie's fingers if he didn't release the material. When threats didn't work, Dyer began to show up at Stevie's gigs, doing a psych number on his head. "I can't play with that guy out there," Stevie would complain. When the tires of the band's van were slashed outside Al's Bamboo on Oak Lawn in Dallas a year later, everyone in the band blamed it on the botched deal. But Stevie would not back down. He wouldn't release the Nashville tapes. "He was starting to feel his power, and in the year we'd been working together he simply outgrew me," Gracey concluded. "Chris had assumed many of the management functions and he was fencing me off from my artist. I could hardly argue. My little label was more of a dream than a reality."

In a last-ditch effort, Gracey sent the tapes to Rounder Records, the largest folk and roots music independent label in America. When the rejection letter came in the mail, he knew he was whipped.

The recording debacle only aggravated the love-hate relationship between Lou Ann and Stevie. She could be an angel of mercy or the devil in red stretch pants depending on her mood. Stevie dug her when she behaved, even thought he loved her a time or two, but when she was late for a gig or lost her voice from yelling, he got bent out of shape. For her part, Lou Ann wanted to be the Queen Bee. She wanted somebody to back her up, not a guitar star hung up on Hendrix. She didn't need him, or at least that's what her fans told her while the guitar hounds were pestering Stevie to get rid of her. In the middle of a performance at Brother's in Birmingham, Alabama, on their first East Coast tour after they finished recording in Nashville, Lou Ann got so drunk that halfway through a song she fell flat on her back. Staring up at Stevie, she slurred, "You take care of your shit, I'll take care of mine."

Booking agent Joe Priesnitz was getting calls every night from the road, never quite sure if the band had made it through another gig. They dragged their way through Jacksonville, Atlanta, and Charlotte before Tom Carrico, the manager of the Nighthawks, the reigning blues and roots band in Washington, DC, took over the band's bookings for the Northeast. Some nights, like the one when the Hawks shared the bill with Double Trouble on their DC debut only to get blown away, Double Trouble could do no wrong. Other nights were not so fondly remembered. They pulled off two impressive performances at the Lone Star Cafe in New York City, earning their hundred-dollar nightly fee and the praise of songwriter and producer Doc Pomus, who thought Lou Ann was a real diamond in the rough. Following the second night at the Lone Star, the tension boiled over. Lou Ann had drunk herself into a rage, throwing glasses and bottles and screaming at the waitresses.

The band staggered into Lupo's Heartbreak Hotel in Providence, where much to everyone's relief, Lou Ann announced she would henceforth be appearing with the Roomful of Blues, who were still stinging from the loss of their ace guitarist, Duke Robillard, after he split for a solo career. The Lou Ann/Roomful union lasted but a few months before she landed back in Austin, only to be "discovered" by R&B talent scout Jerry Wexler, the guy who complained to *Rolling Stone* back in 1974 that there wasn't any outstanding talent in Austin.

The day after returning to Austin from the East Coast in early December, Stevie, Chris, and Jackie met with Joe Priesnitz.

"What are you gonna do?" Priesnitz asked Stevie.

"Well, I'm fronting the band," he replied.

"Who's gonna sing?"

"Well, I am."

"Can you?" Priesnitz wondered aloud.

Stevie shot him a hard look. Why would he even need to ask? Asshole.

"We can pull this off," Chris Layton reassured Priesnitz. "It'll be great."

Recent experiences on the road and in the studio may have been rough and none too rewarding, but surviving all that and Lou Ann's departure confirmed the band's mettle. More significantly, there was no one left to fight with for the spotlight, the attention, and the glory. Twenty-five-year-old Stevie Vaughan finally had his own band.

The new, improved Double Trouble was now a power trio in the tradition of Buddy Holly's first band, Johnny Winter's group, and the chart-topping ZZ Top. The boys hit the highway after less than a week's rest to open a show for Muddy Waters at the Palace in Houston, followed by three nights in Lubbock. For Stevie, the chance to play with Muddy Waters was better than jamming with the Dalai Lama. When Double Trouble finished their set, Stevie went to his dressing room to change. Lenny was there changing with him. The two were the same size and often swapped clothes. As they stripped down, they snorted up a long line of coke in celebration of doing a show with Muddy. An off-duty police officer working security happened to look through an open window of the dressing room and saw what they were celebrating with. The guard busted them and hauled them off to jail.

Priesnitz bailed the lovers out of jail while wondering if it was all really worth it. Scrounging up gigs for Double Trouble was a hassle, between club owners who complained the band played too loud and the band, who complained about working dumps that passed for nightclubs. When Priesnitz wanted to send talent buyers copies of Stevie's demo tapes, the band leader hesitated. He was so protective of his material that he once erased an entire tape of studio performances at Perry Patterson's Hole after he made a safety copy for himself. With no tapes and little promotional material, Priesnitz often had to resort to the tried-and-true sucker line, "He's Jimmie Vaughan's brother" to get Double Trouble a booking.

For some time, Stevie felt like he was adrift. He may have survived an extremely rough period, but his insecurity could still get the best of him. He needed a rudder, some sort of stability to get him through the long nights of music, drugs, and couch flopping and the days of hanging around, listening to records, getting something to eat. He asked Lindi to come back to him. She refused. On a beer run to the 7-Eleven he asked his friend Mary Beth Greenwood to marry him. She refused. Then Stevie had a dream. He was standing out in a field and he noticed a white church with a fence and a party going on in the backyard. He walked into the backyard and saw a big sign that read "Jimi Hendrix Band Aid." Under the sign was a stage. Howlin' Wolf was playing on the stage and cows were dancing around in the field. Howlin' Wolf called Lenny up to the stage and set her on his knee. "She's as mean as Howlin' Wolf," Stevie thought to himself after he woke up. "I want to marry her."

On December 23, when Double Trouble was booked to play the Rome Inn, Stevie repeated the line to Lenny. Why not take the leap? They called C-Boy Parks, who gave his blessing and offered the Rome Inn as the wedding chapel. They'd tie the knot between sets.

Stevie extended last-minute invitations via telephone. Attendees included W. C. Clark, guitar repairman and luthier Mark Erlewhine, Billy Gibbons's girlfriend Gretchen Barber, Chris and Jackie, Keith Ferguson, Roddy Colonna, and Stevie's old buddy, Cutter Brandenburg, who had settled back in Austin after spending years on the road with Jo Jo Gunne, Andy Gibb, and Ian Hunter. The preacher was summoned from the Yellow Pages.

It was a joyous occasion in a sordid setting. The couple looked like they had not had a lot of sleep over the past week. The bride wore a silk blouse borrowed from the wedding photographer. The groom was attired in work clothes — a wide-brimmed fedora, loud shirt with flyaway collar, vest, and jacket. The office upstairs where the ceremony was conducted had never looked so neat and clean. Beer cans, cigarette butts, roaches, and a hypodermic needle rig had been swept away, leaving the broken-down sofa and well-worn carpet as spotless as they would ever get.

The wedding rings were fashioned from two pieces of wire found on the floor and poetically tied into knots. Once they were pronouned man and wife, Stevie and Lenny kissed and embraced before Stevie led the crowd back to the bar and raced up onto the bandstand in a shower of rice. Shaking his head at the spectacle, Lenny's dad leaned over to W. C. Clark. "They better pick up that rice," he said only half-jokingly. "That's probably going to be the only thing they have to eat."

To most people, the institution of marriage was a cue to settle down and nest. To Stephen Ray Vaughan and Lenora Darlene Bailey, marriage was one more excuse to party, the send-off for an extended sleepless jag during which they could endlessly declare their spiritual and religious affinity for each other. All Stevie owned in the world were his guitars, a small bundle of clothes, and his records. Lenny didn't have much more. "We were a couple of kids, pretending to be married," Lenny explained. "I can't believe we did it."

As Lenny and Stevie rushed headlong into spaced-out connubial bliss, the scene around them was changing rapidly. In fact, Austin was losing many of the attributes that made it so appealing to starving artists and musicians. The city no longer boasted the lowest cost of living in the United States. It was a bona fide boomtown populated by an increasing number of speculators, promoters, builders, land developers, and fast buck artists from all over the country.

The real estate market became so superheated that many of the clubs that Stevie had worked could no longer afford their leases. The Split Rail on South Lamar, the last of the no-cover longhair honky-tonks, disappeared in 1978, replaced by a Wendy's hamburger stand. Antone's was ousted from its Sixth Street location in 1979 so a parking garage could be erected on the site. Soap Creek Saloon was sacrificed for a new, upscale subdivision. Stevie Vaughan, dressed in a baggy white suit and an applejack hat, played "The Sky Is Crying" as part of the closing show at the Rome Inn in 1980 when C-Boy Parks lost his lease and moved on to the Ski Shores restaurant on Lake Austin. (Stevie thought so much of C-Boy that he once bought him a new engine for his car.) On New Year's Eve 1980 the Armadillo World Headquarters shut down for good. Double Trouble was one of the headliners during its last week of shows. The building was leveled and a high-rise office tower was erected in its place. In a rare blow of poetic justice, the project went bankrupt and was foreclosed on several years later.

The second Antone's, located in a strip shopping center on the northwest side of town, was a symbol of the new Austin. It was spacious, modern, comfortable, there was plenty of parking, and the air conditioning actually worked most of the time. But it had all the charm of an airport, and was six miles from downtown, too far away to be much of a hangout for club crawlers used to hitting two or three joints a night.

Location worked against the new Soap Creek Saloon as well. Although it was the funkiest of the new breed of clubs, housed in a building that had already enjoyed a colorful history as an historic country-western roadhouse known as the Skyline Club, the new Soap Creek was so far north on Lamar Boulevard that some folks thought they'd crossed into Oklahoma before reaching it.

Having lost their cachet as hangouts, both Antone's and Soap Creek concentrated on bringing in touring acts like James Brown, Millie Jackson, and Delbert McClinton. One of the few local acts who could attract a comparable draw in these cavernous spaces was the Thunderbirds, who would book a weekend at Soap Creek when they came off the road and walk out with almost $10,000 for their services.

Neither club, though, appealed to the apartment dwellers who worked at Texas Instruments, IBM, or any of the other high-tech computer firms driving Austin's growth north and northwest. Few tears were shed when the state highway department condemned the Soap Creek property in 1981 in order to construct an intersection. That same year, Clifford Antone decided to give up his lease.

Both Antone's and Soap Creek would rise one more time from the ashes when A.J.'s, two extensively renovated clubs closer to town, went bust. George Majewski took the South Congress location around the block from Willie Nelson's Austin Opry House for the new Soap Creek. Clifford Antone assumed control of A.J.'s Midtown in what once was a Shakey's Pizza Parlor on Guadalupe Street near the University of Texas campus for the third and longest-running version of the Home of the Blues.

While the club business was suffering from skyrocketing rents, music remained on a growth curve. Progressive country took a backseat to the sudden explosion of blues, roots rock, reggae, and folk singer-songwriter acts, though the tribal factions had never been more pronounced. Just as the blues revival was a reaction against country rock, the advent of punk and New Wave at venues like Raul's, Club Foot, and Duke's Royal Coach Inn, a club in the building that once housed the Vulcan Gas Company, was a reaction by college-aged kids against the older generation of club mavens. The rancor became so pronounced that Raul's briefly instituted a ban on any bands that played the Continental, which was booking both roots and new music acts.

In the first few months of 1980, Double Trouble toured the South and Northeast as a considerably more stabilized unit. A gig with Willie Dixon at New York's Bottom Line, the city's top showcase room, set off a serious street buzz in Manhattan about the fast-draw blues guitarist who just rode in from Texas. When the word trickled back to Austin about the response Stevie was getting, the serious barflys set their minds to wondering if they had taken Little Stevie for granted. To which the more cynical pundits replied, "If he's so great, how come you can see him practically any night of the week in some dump around town for two bucks at the door?"

The band was starting to attract curiosity-seekers and scenemakers in addition to their loyalists. Their appearance at Third Coast, located in a North Austin strip mall, marked the only time in the club's brief two-year history that the bar ran out of beer, Jack Daniels, and Crown Royal on the same night. In April 1980, Stevie and Lenny appeared in court in Houston and pleaded guilty to possession of cocaine. Lenny took the heavier rap and received five years' probation. Stevie got two years' probation with the stipulations he not leave the state and that he undergo drug-abuse treatment. The cure didn't take. Another requirement was that he "avoid persons or places of known disreputable or harmful character." Unfortunately, that meant most of his friends and the joints where he worked.

9

STEVIE RAY

The money was improving on the bar circuit, but Stevie wanted more. He might have felt more confident than ever when it came to his musicianship, but he realized that in many ways the band was still struggling to get their act together, especially when it came to business. Austin was a music town, not a music-industry town. The prevailing wisdom was that once a band was good enough to merit a deal, they went to New York, Nashville, or Los Angeles in search of a manager, lawyer, and record label.

A four-leaf clover in the form of an outfit called Classic Management made the trip unnecessary for Stevie. Classic, which operated out of Manor Downs, a quarterhorse racetrack located ten miles east of Austin in the town of Manor, had money and connections, which was more than enough to prompt Stevie to shake hands on a deal in May 1980. The scramble to make ends meet had gotten old and debt collectors were resorting to veiled threats.

Stevie's involvement with Classic actually began two years earlier on the night he met Edi Johnson at the Rome Inn. Edi was a very hip single parent who'd raised five children while doing accounting at Manor Downs, a job she took at the suggestion of Eddie Wilson, the former head honcho of the Armadillo World Headquarters. Edi took karate lessons in the afternoon at the Rome Inn. One day, her instructor told her to come back that night to see Stevie play. She decided to check him out. "I'm not an authority on music — it's whatever turned me on — but this did," Johnson said of that first performance.

It was Stevie's birthday and I was wanting to meet him so I bought him a bottle of Crown Royal, which at the time was his opium. I started learning more about him and it seemed the one thing he was lacking was money.

I said to myself, "If the guy is so good, why can't he just do it?" The more I talked to people around, [I learned] nobody would touch Stevie because of his involvement with drugs and his being undependable. Anyway, Stevie was having his tires slashed, so I figured so what? This guy's got talent and whoever went to Stevie with financial backing would have to be the type of person that could live without it for two to five years.

Their friendship grew to the point that one night following a gig at the Steamboat 1874 on Sixth Street, Stevie and Lenny asked Edi to read over a contract tendered by Denny Bruce of Takoma Records, who handled the Thunderbirds. Edi told them not to sign it. "You really need to take this to someone that has more of a background and knowledge than I do," she told them.

"Why don't you be my manager?" Stevie blurted out.

Edi was almost astonished at Stevie's naïveté and impulsiveness as she was by his talent. She wasn't even in the business, and he wanted her to manage him? This business was crazier than she ever imagined. "One night he'd say one thing and the next night he'd say something else, so I had to take that with a grain of salt. But I took the idea and ran with it."

She ran with it straight to her employer, Frances Carr, a scion of a South Texas oil and ranching family, who had opened Manor Downs in anticipation of the state of Texas legalizing pari-mutuel betting. Carr was a horsewoman, first and foremost, but she was also a rock and roller who had worked on the road with the Grateful Dead and promoted concerts. It was through the Dead and their former manager, Sam Cutler, that she met Chesley Millikin, a former show jumper and onetime international corporate sales executive from Ireland who left the fast track in the mid-sixties after consuming his first hit of LSD.

For a time Millikin ran a nightclub in North Hollywood called the Magic Mushroom while sharing an apartment with Steve LaVere, the collector who became legal keeper of the flame of blues guitar master Robert Johnson. It was through LaVere that Millikin met the blues up close, hanging out at the Ash Grove, the landmark LA venue where the white rock and rollers could watch black legends still spry enough to run through their paces. Millikin dug the LA music scene and cultivated friendships with hundreds of musicians. Ever the salesman, he talked his way into the business and worked his way up the industry ladder to become the European label manager of Epic Records, the road manager for the New Riders of the Purple Sage, and a confidant of the Rolling Stones. Carr persuaded Millikin to come to Manor Downs to work with horses and help stage concerts at the track, including appearances by the Dead. But concerts merely scratched Millikin's itch to plunge deeper into the business. Edi knew that Millikin was interested in getting into management and that Carr would provide backing for the right act. Though Carr seemed to be more interested in nuevo wavo rocker Joe "King" Carrasco, Edi was determined to steer her toward Stevie.

Edi brought Frances and Chesley the contract that Stevie had wanted her to check out. Chesley read it over and passed along the word that under no circumstances should he sign it. Always ready for a deal, he figured that if there was interest in Stevie, he was worth checking out. Frances and Chesley's initial impression was that Stevie Vaughan was certainly a talented instrumentalist, although he didn't exactly stand out from the dozens of blues vets Chesley had seen wheezing their way through sets back at the Ash Grove. But the longer he watched the boy sweat his ass off, the more he realized that Stevie took his version of the blues a little further out in space than the old geezers did. Even if the band needed more discipline to be marketed properly in his opinion, it was worth a shot. After a show at the Steamboat, Edi made the introductions and Chesley cut straight to the point.

"Would you like me to manage you?" he asked.

Stevie nodded in the affirmative.

Edi was thrilled. With Chesley's connections, Frances's backing, and her bookkeeping experience, she saw no limits to the band's potential. Even Frances's reluctance to pay her for the work didn't diminish her enthusiasm. "I told her I'd take care of Stevie's books and Classic Management's books at no charge if she'd give me the opportunity," Edi said. "I didn't know what I was doing in the music business. I figured it was graduate school."

Stevie and Lenny figured something different. "Frances needed to lose some money," Lenny later explained. "That's how we thought the deal was going to work." When Classic put Stevie, Chris Layton, and Jackie Newhouse on a weekly salary of $225 plus per diems, Stevie didn't realize that the money was an advance against future earnings, or preferred not to look at it that way. All he knew was that he had a steady paycheck for the first time since he swept up at the Dairy Mart. He called up his old buddy Cutter Brandenburg. He wanted him to be Double Trouble's road manager. This time, though, he wouldn't have to hang around for scraps. He was going to make good money. Cutter was still "pure D 100 percent" loyal to Stevie and said yes, even though he knew that the hardest part of his job was not going to be lugging equipment or fighting off drunks. His toughest task was going to be keeping the peace between Stevie, Lenny, and management.

Frances, a slim, soft-spoken blonde, preferred staying in the background and letting Chesley take the lead. He enlisted his pal, Charlie Comer, a legendary smooth-talking publicist, to help create an image. The two Irishmen were a matched set — one, Comer, a consummate hypemeister with a propensity toward referring to his clients in the self-aggrandizing possessive, as in "my Beatles" and "my Rolling Stones"; the other, Millikin, a brash, arrogant wheeler-dealer who fancied wearing ascots instead of ties, the likes of whom had never been seen in Austin before.

They knew they had a hard sell on their hands. Stevie was a blues guitarist and blues hadn't been regarded as hot commercial property in several decades. Worse, the electric guitar had become passé. It was the waning of the disco era and the dawn of MTV, a period of time when the music industry was looking to synthesizers and hairstyles, not Fenders and Marshall amps, to sell records.

Millikin and Comer brainstormed to come up with a gimmick, trying to find a hook that would put Stevie across. At one point, Classic Management tried to revive the Lou Ann angle by auditioning several female vocalists to see how they'd mesh with their guitar man. They ultimately figured that the way to best sell Stevie was to emphasize his strengths, which for better or worse stemmed from his considerable abilities to manipulate six strings. The one caveat they agreed on was to avoid the blues label at all costs, since they felt it would doom Stevie to the far corners of the retail racks where his role in life would be to satisfy a few thousand blues purists and no one else.

The Emerald Isle think tank concluded the world would be better served by a bona fide "gee-tar hero," one who could rock it up as well as he could get down. And that hero would be Stevie Ray Vaughan, a stage name too good to be true, smacking of double entendre and Texas. Cutter Brandenburg was the one who started addressing his buddy as Stevie Ray, just as he laid claim to nicknaming Chris Layton the Whipper, the guy who could "whip it good," quoting from the band Devo's New Wave dance single "Whip It."

But other than the name change, Millikin and Comer didn't need to manipulate their act to realize their vision. The band did it for themselves. Randy Hansen and Double Trouble reprised their Hendrix tribute double bill at the Austin Opry House on June 18, 1980. Some changes had evidently gone down in Hansen's life since the two guitarists had last seen each other. He shocked the crowd when he stepped onstage and tore off his Afro wig, telling the paying customers he wanted them to know him as an instrumentalist of many talents, not just a Jimi windup doll. The audience, however, was not particularly interested in meeting the real Randy Hansen. They paid their money to hear Hansen do Hendrix, not Hansen do Hansen. He stiffed big time. Double Trouble stole the show by default.

The encounters with Hansen did a number on Stevie's head. He had sworn to Lenny and others that he would never perform Hendrix's music, that he would never do something so blatantly commercial, that his gig was playing his own music. Still, he couldn't help it that whenever he was fooling around, he felt the urge to run the band through a raw rendition of "Manic Depression." Now he decided to start some encores with a solo version of "Little Wing" before Chris and Jackie joined him to rock the house with "Rude Mood." In the six months since Lou Ann had split, he even began singing Hendrix, too, worming "Voodoo Chile (Slight Return)" onto the set list. Sometimes if he really felt possessed, he would even start talking like Hendrix, shifting into a jive, stream-of-consciousness mumble. His command of soul-speak was already quite remarkable; the other band members marveled over the long conversations he could carry on with older, country blacks who had thick, slurred, backwoods accents that no one else could decipher.

Three months after the second Randy Hansen gig, he took the Jimi obsession to the extreme. Stevie Ray Vaughan and Double Trouble were the featured entertainment at the annual Halloween bash at the Ark Co-op, a student dormitory west of the UT campus, where they had played parties before. But the group that showed up for the Halloween show was fronted by a character who bore only a vague resemblance to Stevie. He had an Afro wig, wore blackface, and played and sang just like Jimi Hendrix. "Nobody else could dress like that and get away with it," Cutter said. "Stevie wanted to be black. He said that lots of times."

Being Hendrix for a night was fun, but no way to run a career. Chesley Millikin concluded the first step toward making Classic Management's investment pay off was "to get the band the fuck out of Austin." He began organizing a tour of the East Coast with booking agent Joe Priesnitz, but when he told Stevie about it, the would-be gee-tar hero was less than enthusiastic.

"I can't go, man," he told his manager. "I'm on probation."

Millikin, who knew almost nothing about Stevie's reputation, took a deep breath. "OK," he said. "Let's go see your parole officer."

They met with Stevie's parole officer in Austin. Chesley explained the situation to him, that his client needed to travel out of state in order to continue his gainful employment.

"That's fine," the parole officer drawled flatly. "But he's not going anywhere. He's not leaving Texas."

"Are you telling me that you are going to interfere with this man making a living?" Millikin asked incredulously.

"No, I'm just telling you he's not leaving Texas," the parole officer responded.

"He's a musician! He's getting offers to play around the country, and you're saying no?" challenged Millikin.

The parole officer relented. "Let me think about it."

Soon after the encounter Chesley tried to contact the parole officer. He called him at the office. He called him at home. But he was never able to get through. In disgust he talked with Frances Carr about the situation. She gave him the number of a family friend who happened to be a rather influential attorney. Chesley called the lawyer and told him about the situation.

"I'll call you back in an hour," the lawyer said.

Millikin waited one hour, two hours, three hours. Finally, the phone rang. "I'm sorry, I have to go to the golf course," said the voice on the other end of the line. "But your boy can go out of town. When he comes back he'll have a new parole officer." Sure enough, the parole officer was replaced by a much more understanding individual, one who never objected to Stevie's professional obligations, in or out of Texas.

Chesley had cleared the runway for Stevie's flight to the top. The band bought a step van that Cutter dubbed the African Queen in honor of the popping noise that the engine made. After the gigs, the band would crash in the back of the van while Cutter drove. They played small clubs across the Southeast, working their way up to New York. They were the same old joints they'd seen before, but with some teeth backing them up, Stevie, Chris, and Jackie couldn't help but feel more confident. They'd been vindicated. They were bulletproof. Nothing could stop them now. When managers asked Stevie to turn down the almost painful volume that he insisted on maintaining, Cutter would be on them like a pit bull. "Don't you know you're fucking with a GOD!" he'd shout in their face. On one occasion, in Monroe, Louisiana, a club owner paid Double Trouble just to go away. Stevie's standard response to such situations was "SMA" — suck my ass.

Chesley caught up with the band after a date in Washington, DC. The reality of managing a band duking it out in the trenches of clubland horrified him, prompting Joe Priesnitz to worry that Millikin had been hanging out with the rock aristocracy too long. Following a gig at a Baltimore dump called No Fish Today, he walked in on his star and bass player trading punches in a drunken brawl next to the African Queen. "He was aghast," Priesnitz recalled. "I got railed when he came back. 'How could I put the band in these toilets?' 'Why couldn't I get them into better venues?' "

Equally aggravating to Chesley was the behavior of the young star he was grooming. Stevie did not take direction very well. The manager was supposed to call the shots, not the act. When the two would arrive at an impasse, Millikin would summon Priesnitz for a conference: "Junior is up to his antics again. We've got to talk."

"It was like Khrushchev called Nixon out of bed," Priesnitz said.

> I'd go meet him somewhere and he'd start saying, "Junior doesn't understand. He's just got to change. He's gotta get commercial. We've got to have something to sell to the public."
>
> I tried to tell him the public will come around. He just didn't understand. He didn't see Stevie for what he is. He hadn't a clue what Stevie had been through, never gave him credit for surviving. And Stevie wasn't about to change for him. He did what he did, even though he'd listen to Chesley and try out certain suggestions.

Cutter, Stevie's protector and the buffer between band and management, had his own bones to pick with the new boss. "Chesley loved Stevie, but he was a square peg in a round fucking blues band," said Cutter. "Junior" sometimes chafed at Chesley's heavy-handed style. Being on a salary may have brought security, but the price was not having much say in decisions that affected the band. Nobody had ever pushed Stevie into doing anything against his will, and Chesley wasn't going to be the first.

From the manager's perspective, Stevie was his own worst enemy. As long as Stevie stuck to being the artiste, Chesley could get along just fine with Junior, regaling him with expansive rock-and-roll tales of yesteryear. It was hard not to like him, especially when it was one-on-one, without the band or Lenny around. Chesley liked to pamper Stevie, an indulgence he did not extend to Chris or Jackie. But Stevie wanted the others treated the same way he was, or at least that's what he told them. Either way, the management-artist relationship became more and more adversarial, rather than cooperative. Chesley's position was that he and he alone would call the shots. He wasn't going to have it any other way.

There was one last piece of the puzzle that had to fall into place in order for the picture to be complete. That piece showed up one night at Fitzgerald's in Houston in the person of bass player Tommy Shannon.

When he saw Tommy at the gig, Stevie did not hesitate to invite him up onstage. There was nothing really wrong with Jackie. He was as steady as they came. But with Tommy working the bottom of the sound, something clicked. Cutter saw it that night at Fitz's. "Tommy really laid the foundation and made Chris come to life, and all of a sudden Stevie went double clutch," he said. "He had a life force behind him." Life force or just a dependable beat, the sit-ins continued in both Houston and Austin for several months until finally on the last day of 1980, Stevie, Chris, and Cutter sat Jackie down and gave him notice: Chesley wanted him out, they told him. Tommy Shannon would be the Double Trouble bassist, effective January 2, 1981.

Jackie was relieved more than surprised. "It didn't blindside me," he said. "There was no animosity. It was just getting pretty bizarre." As good as the pay had gotten since Millikin and Carr started backing the band, the drinking and drugging were getting out of hand. The hypocrisy being practiced by management in the name of protecting their investment disgusted Jackie. One minute Chesley would be warning the others to keep Stevie away from dopers; the next, someone would walk in on the star and his manager chasing a long trail of sparkling powder with a straw. But Millikin was just a fall guy. Chris and Cutter were behind the change as much as Stevie and his handler were.

Tommy was like a lost brother. Stevie had idolized Shannon since he played with Uncle John Turner behind Johnny Winter. He'd even played with Slut in the band Krackerjack in the early 1970s. Shannon was self-taught, just like Stevie. He couldn't read a sheet of music but had developed a sixth-sense feel for bending and popping the fat strings of his instrument, adding multiple harmonies to Stevie's leads.

Just as significantly, Tommy knew his way around the rock culture on and off the stage. He was experienced. He could party all night long with the wildest of the wild bunch and still be standing when the sun came up. He had a professorial knowledge of every street drug that had ever been synthesized or cultivated and was familiar with the threshold point of each and every kind of high. He knew what it was like to overdose and how to survive when his toxic level crossed the red line. He knew what it was like to be busted. He knew what it felt like to fail a urine test, to be too broke to hire a lawyer, to hit the big time and see it evaporate. When he showed up to see Double Trouble at Fitzgerald's, music was little more than an avocation. The bassman who had shared stages with Edgar Winter, B. B. King, Freddie King, Little Richard, Elvin Bishop, and Jerry Garcia was working as a bricklayer. Stevie knew that with Tommy around, everything would be all right, even though Shannon's tendency to nod off on a whim earned him the nickname Nappy. Stevie and Tommy immediately became best buddies, often to the detriment of their other relationships. "Stevie really should have married Tommy," Lenny said. "They were that close."

With Tommy, Chris, a manager, a wife, and a steady salary, there was little to distract Stevie from his music. Double Trouble was more of a unit than ever, a chain with no weak links. What had been a remarkably gifted, virtuoso guitarist backed by a bass player and a drummer evolved into a ferocious power trio. The guitar man was still very much the center of attention. Precious few in his line of work could match his raw speed. Fewer still — brother Jimmie excepted — could produce a full-blown ensemble sound by playing rhythm and lead at the same time, working out the melody with his pick held fat-side out, and strumming out chords with his bare fingers. As the lead singer in the band, Stevie developed a vocal style that combined the sweet tones of Doyle Bramhall with the growls of Howlin' Wolf, the grunts of Muddy Waters, the moans of Buddy Guy, and the ethereal soul of Magic Sam. When Stevie sang, "I'm gonna leave you woman, before I commit a crime," people believed him.

Stevie's evolving sense of couture reflected his newfound self-assurance. He trashed the floppy caps, pimp suits, and vintage waif-up-from-poverty look that recalled a secondhand Thunderbird in favor of silk scarves, wide-brim hats, white boots, flamboyant loose-fitting shirts, and kimonos that provided a peek of the phoenix tattoo on his chest. Stevie was beginning to look and act like a star. He was Stevie Ray Vaughan. Stevie Rave On.

He could put a manicured polish on a down-in-the-gutter blues as well as T-Bone Walker, the original Oak Cliff legend. But he also understood Walker's sense of showmanship. Like T-Bone, Stevie didn't mind strutting and shucking onstage, holding his guitar behind his back and sliding the instrument across the floor. It was a gimmick, all right, but if it didn't detract from the obvious talents of T-Bone and Guitar Slim, it would do just fine for him. He borrowed a page from Hendrix's act, too, shaking the headstock of his guitar violently back and forth to conjure a tremelo effect that sounded like the soundtrack to a nervous breakdown. He beat on his guitar so bad that his crew put a bolt through the neck to hold the instrument together. The old and the new, gutbucket blues and supercharged rock and roll, it was all part of the Stevie Ray Vaughan package. "It's my life," he explained in his first official biography. "It's everything. I have been gifted with something, and if I don't take it to its fullest extent, I might as well be farting in the bushes."

10

THE LEGEND OF ZIGGY STARDUST AND THE TEXAS KID

He could almost taste it now. He was so close to getting it, all he had to do was stay on track. His support team would do the rest. It was all a matter of time. At least that's what everyone said. Meanwhile, he was doing just fine, living the high life. He was packing out the Continental and Steamboat, doing decent business at Antone's, and drawing big crowds at Fitzgerald's in Houston and just about everywhere he worked in Dallas. The Texas Music Association bestowed the 1981 Buddy Music Award on Double Trouble. The next deal wouldn't be like the Nightcrawlers, the Cobras, or the Joe Gracey trip. This one would be the one that put him across.

A personal favorite label was Alligator Records, a Chicago-based independent outfit with an impressive roster of contemporary black blues artists including Albert Collins, Fenton Robinson, Son Seals, Koko Taylor, Lonnie Brooks, and Blind John Davis. In February of 1981, Mindy Giles, the national sales representative for Alligator, took time out from a college talent convention in San Antonio to check out the sensation from Austin. Joe Priesnitz had booked Double Trouble for two nights at Skipwilly's on the northeast side of San Antonio, hoping to attract some conventioneers, a deal the band members were not happy with. They never had much of a draw at the club, and the gigs, a 160-mile round-trip drive from home, were on typically slow weeknights. Their doubts were confirmed. On February 18, the second night of their two-night stand, fewer than twenty-five people had paid the cover charge at the door, which wouldn't even cover Double Trouble's hundred-dollar guarantee. Giles and several friends attending the convention arrived at the club just in time to hear a voice over the PA saying, "Thank you and good night."

Stevie noticed the people walking into the door at the last call but paid them little mind. He just wanted to go home. All the band had pulled their shirts off to wring out the sweat when Stevie heard a knock at the dressing room door. He opened it and winced. Oh God. *It was a gurl.*

Mindy Giles apologized for intruding and introduced herself and the people she had brought along with her.

Stevie's eyes lit up.

"Alligator Records!" he exclaimed. "I love your label! What a great label! *Albert Collins!*"

He shot a glance at Layton and Shannon and didn't even give them time to react. "Well, boys," he drawled purposefully. "Put your shirts on. Let's give 'em a show."

Giles and her entourage scooted five chairs onto the dance floor of the empty club. For the next forty minutes, Double Trouble ripped through a repertoire of scorching, rocked-up blues for the tastemakers, concluding the performance with Stevie sitting down on the edge of the stage riser, coaxing sweet after-the-storm notes out of his guitar on an instrumental he called "Lenny," composed at the foot of his wife's bed, a sweet meditation that pulled tears out of Giles's eyes.

"They were beat to hell after playing all night, but they just sparkled," she said.

Stevie was even more excited after he talked to Giles some more. She wanted the band to come to Chicago. Her boss, Bruce Iglauer, would flip when he heard them, she promised. She could hardly contain herself when she called Iglauer the next day to tell him, "I've seen the future of the label."

This time the drive back to Austin went by in a blur. Alligator wasn't some jive-turkey label. It was probably the best blues label going, putting out honest blues by genuine originals. It would be an honor to be on the same roster, Stevie raved on the drive back to Austin. He couldn't wait to tell Lenny, tell Chesley, tell the whole world. Alligator Records wanted to put out a record with his name on it!

That proved to be easier said than done. Giles had a tougher sell than anticipated. None of the clubs in Chicago she'd worked with had ever heard of Stevie Ray Vaughan. They all turned her down at first, but

finally she scraped together three gigs so the band could afford to come to the Windy City. One of those gigs was a showcase specifically for Iglauer at a tiny bar near Loyola University called Jawbone's. It was Bruce's kind of joint. There was no stage per se, only an empty space in the corner cleared out by moving the pool table, and the audience consisted largely of regulars from the neighborhood who had stopped in for a drink or three.

The three unknowns from Texas filled the corner and turned up their instruments to wind-tunnel volume too overpowering to ignore. Giles watched as the regulars took notice. One by one, heads turned and eyes fixed on the band while customers held their hands over their ears. You could almost read the reaction on every customer's lips above the din.

Who is this guy?

The exception was Bruce Iglauer. He was not moved. Midway through the forty-five-minute set, he slipped out of the bar.

"That was a little before I was willing to accept any white artist," Iglauer later explained. "You gotta understand, between '68 and '78 I listened to two albums by white people. Secondly, he didn't sound that original. I thought he did pretty standard material — the Albert King songbook, stuff like 'The Sky Is Crying' and 'As Years Go Passing By.' He and I had difficulties in communicating."

Stevie was bummed out. Of all things, the color of his skin prevented him from joining his heroes on the Alligator roster. Iglauer had no clue how black Stevie really was. Chesley told him to forget about it. Alligator was chump change. He wouldn't have let him do a deal anyhow. "I had no intention of signing with Alligator," Millikin insisted. "I had been in the record business and I knew what the fuck was going on." He had bigger game in his sights. Already, Stevie's version of "Tin Pan Alley" taken from a live broadcast from Steamboat 1874 was the most requested song on Austin's leading rock station, KLBJ-FM. Chesley was fielding calls almost daily from A&R reps at record labels who'd picked up on the buzz about the Vaughan lad. And he still hadn't pulled the ace from his sleeve — his Rolling Stones connection.

Gig money in Austin was improving by the month to the extent touring acts sought Double Trouble to open shows in Texas to help boost ticket sales. When all else failed, there was always the Continental, a compact, friendly club on South Congress that could comfortably hold eighty people. The Continental was run by four music-scene nabobs — Roger One Knite and Roddy One Knite, survivors from the old One Knite, Wayne Nagel, and Summerdog — who loved Stevie so much they gave him a Gibson E-3 and an open invitation for him to play their place whenever he damn well pleased. If there were any holes in Double Trouble's calendar, Cutter Brandenburg, remembering one of Uncle John Turner's old commandments of the music business, would pencil in full-moon nights, and the first and the fifteenth of the month — paydays for state and University of Texas workers — at the Continental.

One opening slot was in front of the Fabulous Thunderbirds, who were celebrating the release of their album *What's the Word?* at the Paramount Theatre. Joe Priesnitz at Rock Arts thought it was a natural pairing, but he learned otherwise when he told his client about the booking. Stevie shook his head. "I'd rather not do that. My band has a different crowd. I want to rock."

Early in 1982, Lou Ann Barton made her major label bow with *Old Enough*. The Asylum record had been produced by Glenn Frey and overseen by Jerry Wexler. Frey was founder and chief songwriter for the Eagles, the definitive LA music-biz band of the seventies, and had accumulated sufficient wealth, fame, and political clout to get his first producer's credit with Lou Ann.

Wexler was in Austin for Lou Ann's album christening date at the Continental, when a crazy, loose jam session broke out climaxing with Jimmie, Stevie, Doug Sahm, and Charlie Sexton crowded onto a stage so small that Stevie had to unplug his guitar cord whenever he wanted to sing a line and walk away from the microphone to plug back in again when he took a guitar lead. Wexler stuck around the next night to see Double Trouble on their own at the Continental. He was impressed enough to call Chesley Millikin.

"I can't do anything for you," he told Millikin. "But a friend of mine, Claude Nobs, can." Nobs was the promoter of the prestigious Montreux Jazz Festival on the shores of Lake Geneva in western Switzerland. This Texas kid was a jewel, Wexler told Nobs, one of those rarities who comes along once in a lifetime. He would be great for the festival's blues night. Nobs agreed after hearing a tape and extended an invitation to Stevie Ray Vaughan and the band to perform at Montreux that summer. Chesley was beside himself. This was the break he'd been waiting for.

Stevie and the band weren't so excited. What the hell was Montreux anyway? None of them had ever heard of the place, much less knew where it was. The idea of spending $10,000 to fly across the Atlantic Ocean to play one gig seemed like a big waste of money, money that Stevie would have to pay back to Classic Management if he ever struck it rich. Chesley ultimately convinced Double Trouble to commit to the gig. What the hell. Stevie'd never seen a foreign country, except for a Mexican border town.

Lou Ann Barton's career immediately slid downhill after the Continental date where Jerry Wexler got so excited about Stevie Ray

Vaughan. The first out-of-town date of the tour to promote her album was at Fitzgerald's in Houston, but she somehow failed to make the second set of the showcase. Leery of being able to keep her under control, Asylum Records executives decided to cut their losses and canceled her West Coast and East Coast dates.

Meanwhile, Chesley Millikin's pal Mick Jagger and Jagger's girl-friend, Jerry Hall, dropped in at Manor Downs to peruse some quarter-horses. When Jagger offhandedly complained about the dearth of competent bluesmen on the contemporary scene, Millikin arched his eyebrows. In a flash, he gave Jagger a video of Double Trouble perform-ing at a festival at Manor Downs the previous summer. A few days later, in New York City, Charlie Watts, the Rolling Stones' drummer, popped the tape into a VCR at Mick's house.

Watts was floored by what he saw. Garbed in a white kimono dec-orated with bamboo leaves, a silver concho belt, and a black hat with a silver band, Stevie Ray Vaughan navigated the realms of the dirty and the low-down like no one Watts had heard in twenty years. The way the Vaughan kid jumped right into Earl King's "Come On" was not imitative or slavish in the least but rather fresh and authentic. He made the song by the New Orleans guitarist sound like he'd written it himself, wielding such flash and might that his guitar sounded like it was on fire, the Vaughan face in full cortorted grimace as he bent the strings on a newly found Strat whose wiring hung out like guts. Watts could tell that the young fellow had a few things to learn about presence, given the way he hung his head low, all shy and retiring, dripping sweat on his instrument as he worked through "Dirty Pool." But even the cynical old rock-and-roll veteran had to admit feeling charged when he saw the Texan duck-walk across the stage on "Love Struck Baby," slinging the guitar behind his head, hopping backwards, and sashaying his hips. The way he tore through Howlin' Wolf's "Tell Me" was like he was Hubert Sumlin's lost brother. He had the audacity to top it off with "Manic Depression." As Watts watched the tape of Stevie unstrapping his guitar and banging it against his Marshall amps, bringing the feedback up to a violent cre-scendo, he made a move for the telephone to call Chesley.

"When can we see the band in person?" he asked.

"How about four weeks?" Chesley said.

A party and showcase was arranged at the Danceteria, a trendy, late-night music club in midtown Manhattan. It would be a semiprivate audition for the Stones and their friends, ostensibly to see if Stevie and his band were right for their record label, Rolling Stones Records. At first the gig had all the trappings of a rough, ill-fated voyage. Amps blew up and guitar straps broke like there was some kind of hex on the band. But when the stage manager tried to cut them off after their allotted thirty-five minutes (a typical New York set, but hardly time to wind up by Texas standards), Ron Wood pulled the curtains open while Mick Jagger yelled, "Let them fucking play."

Stevie and the band gladly accommodated them. If someone was going to stick up for them in a viper pit like the Danceteria, it might as well be the Rolling Stones. "It was the first time I met him," Stevie said of Jagger. "I attacked it. I kept seeing somebody I thought I recognized from Texas, this guy jumping up and down, acting like he was playing with us. Come to find out about an hour later that it was Jagger I'd been staring at. Every time we'd stop, Jagger would say, 'Keep playing.' "

"Fuck it," Jagger slurred, urging the band on. "I'll buy this place."

Celebrities never did much impression-wise for Stevie, especially white ones. There were precious few times he was intimidated hanging around some tight-pants musician who was supposed to be God or someone like him. But the Danceteria show was something else. Every other face seemed like it was out of a magazine. "It was wild. Everyone that you never expected to be there, from Johnny Winter to what's-his-name, the blond-headed guy, Andy Warhol, was there, running around and going nuts," Stevie said. "Ronnie Wood kept saying he wanted to sit in with us, but he never would." Hanging out backstage surrounded by New York's glitterati was a heady trip. Vials of cocaine magically appeared and disappeared. Ron Wood was so hammered he couldn't hit his mouth with a cup. Jagger wandered around, mumbling to everyone around him, "Bloody 'ell, I've peed in me pants."

"I may be vain," Stevie later laughed. "But I'll take a little bit of credit for that." It was true. He had played so good, he made the leader of the World's Greatest Rock-and-Roll Band lose bladder control.

Jagger proceeded to heap praise on Stevie Ray and Double Trouble. He promised Stevie dates on the Stones' forthcoming tour. Charlie Comer, ever on the lookout for a photo opportunity, maneuvered the band to pose with the party hosts. The following week, the image of new kid in town Stevie Ray Vaughan standing next to the wide-mouthed Mick Jagger appeared on the "Random Notes" page of *Rolling Stone* magazine.

In the end, all the band wound up getting out of the showcase was publicity. Despite the wild night at the Danceteria, Jagger later phoned Chesley to tell him the label was passing. His act was a blast to party to, but frankly, Rolling Stones Records wasn't interested in signing a blues band, since blues bands had a rather limited appeal. The label wanted someone with the potential to sell a million records, not 33,000.

"Balderdash!" sputtered Millikin. "He'll sell that in Texas in a week." There would be no deal with the Rolling Stones. Still, the vibe that the Stones created by their mere interest was invaluable. It was more than enough to keep the talent scouts sniffing around.

Back home, in what he thought was a stroke of creative brilliance,

Joe Priesnitz scored two nights opening in front of the Clash in June at the City Coliseum in Austin. When he told the band about it, they blanched. "We don't want to play with them. They're a punk rock band," Stevie protested. "That's ridiculous."

It was a golden opportunity to reach an audience unfamiliar with Stevie or Double Trouble, Priesnitz argued. "Look what they did for Joe Ely in England." Besides, the first show was already sold out and the money was decent.

Priesnitz should have listened to the band. They'd opened for British roots-rocker Dave Edmunds at the Austin Opry House the night before to an appreciative crowd. But when they walked on in front of the Clash's audience, the boos began before Stevie even hit the first note. Jeers, beer cans, and spit flew at the stage. The Clash's trendy crowd had little patience for blues-rock. He'd played some tough gigs before, Stevie thought, but nothing like this. Goddamn punks didn't know shit. Maybe if he would have worn a safety pin through his nose, he would have gotten a little respect. "Fuck it," Stevie told Priesnitz after the show. Let another band open the show the second night.

The same kind of hostile reception almost happened again five weeks later, thousands of miles from Austin. After several changes of planes and flights that seemed to take forever, Double Trouble landed in Geneva, Switzerland, to play the nearby Montreux International Festival XVI. Their July 17, 1982, performance at the Montreux Casino marked the first time an unsigned band had appeared at the prestigious event. Like the audiences' adverse reaction to Muddy Waters's debut in England in 1958 as recorded by blues scholar Paul Oliver, Stevie's full-volume electric blues experience was "meat that proved too strong for many stomachs." The Europeans, accustomed to a quieter, folk blues style, cringed at the sheer volume level emitted by the Texas trio. A few bars into "Texas Flood," some of the crowd began booing, whistling, and heckling. Halfway through the song, others in the audience countered with cheers, drowning out the nonbelievers by the end of the eleven-minute workout. For the remainder of the set, Stevie performed like he was having an out-of-body experience, dazzling the crowd with his fretwork, amusing them by playing guitar behind his back and with his teeth, and pulling out the slide for a rendition of Lightnin' Hopkins's exotically funky "Gimme Back My Wig," leaving the audience as physically and emotionally drained as the band was. They knew that this Stevie Ray Vaughan fellow was really something, they just couldn't quite figure out what. After the show, Stevie freaked out listening to a playback of his performance. When he heard the boos, he wondered if the Montreux trip was going to turn out to be another expensive, star-studded bust.

Chesley Millikin, however, had every intention of squeezing all the juice he could out of the situation. Following the concert on the big stage at the Montreux Casino, he booked the band in the casino's after-hours bar in the basement for two nights running. On the first night, David Bowie introduced himself to Stevie Ray. He told him he had watched the Casino show backstage on a video monitor and was mightily impressed. He had been something of a bluesman himself when he was starting out as a professional musician, honking a saxophone. Would Stevie Ray perhaps be interested in appearing in a music video he was putting out? Stevie told Bowie he was game. What the hell.

On the second night, Chesley Millikin cornered Jackson Browne. He knew Jackson from the old days in LA and had accompanied Browne's guitarist, David Lindley, to the 1967 Newport Folk Festival when Lindley was with the band Kaleidoscope. Chesley implored Jackson to bring the band by the after-hours club and see the new act he was handling. Browne and his group showed up, sitting directly in front of the small stage. The sounds pouring out of the scruffy trio were riveting, like nothing they'd been hearing in La-La land, at least. This was almost like stumbling upon some brilliant primitive hidden away in a Mississippi Delta backwater. When Chesley saw Browne and other members of his band jamming with Double Trouble at seven the next morning, he knew the mysterious tumblers on the lock of the music business were finally lining up. It wasn't exactly a harmonic convergence, but it was close enough. Browne was so moved by the integrity of Double Trouble's music, he told Stevie Ray that they were welcome to use his studio in Los Angeles free of charge if they ever got the inclination to make a record.

Double Trouble returned from Europe as conquering heroes. Half the people they knew back in Texas hadn't heard of Montreux either, but their first Texas gigs confirmed fans fully understood the significance of the festival vis-à-vis Double Trouble's career when the names Jackson Browne and David Bowie came up. Double Trouble sold out a homecoming Club Foot date in Austin that was opened by Little Charlie Sexton, clearing more than $3,000 at the door. The next weekend they earned $5,000 for two nights at Fitzgerald's in Houston.

In the fall of 1982, Stevie decided to take up Jackson Browne's studio offer. When Stevie called Browne, the LA scenemaker seemed to hedge on the deal a little bit. He was really busy. He didn't have time to work with Stevie at his Down Town Studio. The best he could offer him was three twenty-four-hour blocks of time around Thanksgiving. Sure, Stevie said. A three-day deal was better than no time at all, he reasoned. Before Chesley would put his stamp of approval on the project, he demanded that Stevie sign the management contract he'd been dodging for two years. The day before the actual recording was to begin, Stevie formally signed papers with Classic Management, giving Classic a 10 percent interest in the first three albums as well as a cut of Double Trouble's performance earnings.

Down Town Studio was not quite the state-of-the-art recording experience the band had envisioned. Stevie spent the first day trying to get the attention of Greg Ladanyi, Browne's engineer, who was more interested in watching sports on television than cutting tracks. Stevie finally confronted him. "You're watching TV. This is our career." Nodding to Richard Mullen, whom they'd brought along from Texas to help engineer in the studio, Stevie told Ladanyi, "This guy knows what he's doing." Ladanyi willingly yielded his chair. In the remaining two days, the band taped ten songs — six originals and four covers — the final track, "Texas Flood," in a single take before the clock ran out. If the session sounded like a live performance, that's because it practically was. There were two overdubs, both covering mistakes made when Stevie broke strings.

While the band was in the studio, Stevie got a phone call from another Montreux acquaintance. David Bowie was preparing to record another album in New York in January. Forget the offer he'd made to do a cameo appearance in a music video. Would Stevie Ray be interested in playing on his album?

"Yes," he replied.

"Well, then, what are you doing the rest of the next year?" Bowie wanted to know.

"That's a good question," Stevie said. "Let's talk about it later."

Double Trouble lingered around southern California for another week, picking up engagements at the Blue Lagoon in Marina del Rey, which attracted almost every guitar pro in the metropolitan area, and the Cathay de Grande, a seedy dive in the basement of a Vietnamese restaurant in Hollywood where the ultra hipsters of the music scene liked to hang. No one was keen on playing the Cathay. The two-hundred-dollar guarantee was an insult for a band that had just finished making a record at Jackson Browne's, Stevie told his booking agent. But even more than the Blue Lagoon, the Cathay gig served notice to the heavy hitters in the music industry capital that Double Trouble meant serious business.

The band returned to Texas to cash in on their growing word-of-mouth reputation. They packed Antone's on New Year's Eve and again on New Year's, easily breaking their $2,000 guarantee point and walking out with almost $5,000 for the second night. They also paid back some close friends who were doing time for drug busts by playing a free show at the Big Spring Federal Correctional Facility in west Texas.

All the hoopla, the private showcase for the Rolling Stones, the triumph at Montreux, the sold-out club dates, obscured the fact that a record deal still had yet to be sealed. Without one, they were still one giant step away from the big time. David Bowie had taken that giant step a long time ago. Over the years, he had stayed on top by keeping a sharp eye on changing trends. And he wanted Stevie Ray to play on his new album.

It was a weird matchup, the sophisticated pansexual originator of glam rock and the no-frills Texas blues guitarist who worked and slept in the same clothes for so long that his fellow road dogs referred to him as Stinky. Bowie was a master at sensing shifting tastes and felt the need to put some new twists into his act. Now that Eurodisco and synthesizers had become so prevalent, it was time to get one step ahead of the masses again. The signature sound on his new album would be the Texas blues guitar sound.

Stevie wasn't exactly a big fan of the Thin White Duke. He'd heard the *Ziggy Stardust and the Spiders from Mars* album just enough to hate it real bad. "Uncle John Turner used to play it all the time and rave about it," he said. "It didn't just make me not like it, it made me mad. The way it sounded made me mad and when I saw a picture of Bowie on that tour it made me mad." It was sissy stuff, self-indulgent, full of electronic gimmickry, the polar opposite of his kind of music.

But Stevie saw another side of Bowie at Montreux, and the more he learned about him, the more he liked. Hell, the guy even collected Earl Bostic and King Curtis records. Bowie sent him rehearsal tapes to listen to and plane tickets to New York, where he'd booked two weeks in January at the Power Station.

The idea of Stevie Ray as Bowie's lead guitarist pissed off half the studio pros in Manhattan. Who the hell was this bumpkin nobody fresh off a Greyhound bus? That was what Bowie actually wanted. He bragged that his discovery was so retro that he "considers Jimmy Page something of a modernist. The lad seems to have stopped at Albert Collins."

Running through an album's worth of material in three days at Jackson Browne's had been a cakewalk. Working with a perfectionist like popmeister David Bowie was a completely different introduction to the creation of a record. By the time Stevie entered the picture, most of the album's instrumental tracks were complete. Stevie watched carefully from the sidelines as Bowie went into the studio, cut his vocals, and polished the songs' rough edges for another hour or two. Only then did he bring Stevie into the process, commanding Stevie to "plug that blues guitar in." Stevie obeyed, using Albert King as his guide. He required but a couple of takes to complete each track. Though Nile Rodgers from the dance band Chic was officially the producer, it was Bowie who was calling the shots.

Stevie played on a total of six selections, needing only two and a half hours of studio time over a three-day period. The sessions gave him a chance to measure his worth surrounded by the top studio players in the business, mining a genre a world away from the competitive atmosphere of blues guitar cutting contests and three sets a night. He could almost relax and kick back, knowing that all Bowie wanted was a little guitar sting in all the right places. On one cut, "Cat People," Stevie later recalled, "he wanted real slow, Brian Jones kind of parts. I wanted to rip and roar. We tried it and I thought we'd dumped it. The next time I heard the song it was there." For "China Girl" Stevie evoked steamy sexuality with the sensual phrasing that later moved one model in *Hustler* magazine's "Beaver Hunt" to say she fantasized having sex with two men while Stevie Ray Vaughan provided the music. On "Let's Dance," the cut that became the first single off the album, Stevie copped Albert King's licks so directly that King later accused him half jokingly of "doin' all my shit on there."

"Bowie liked what I played," Stevie told the *Dallas Times-Herald.*

When I started listening to the cuts, I had no idea at all what to play, even though he'd already shown me on the rehearsal tape what he wanted. So what I did was go in there and get the best tone I could out of the amp without blowing it up, which I did do to the first one. I killed it. But I finally realized just to go in there and play like I play and it would fit. I'd never played on anything like that before but I just played like I play and it worked.

Still, the guitar man from Texas wasn't exactly awestruck. "I wouldn't necessarily go buy it. But I like what I've heard."

The album *Let's Dance*, Bowie's self-described "commercial debut," was an unprecedented smash, spinning off three hit singles and eventually selling more than 5 million copies, more than three times that of *Ziggy Stardust*, Bowie's previous best-seller. When the single "Let's Dance" shot straight to the top of the pop charts in the United States and England, Bowie realized that a key ingredient of his unprecedented success was Stevie Ray Vaughan's earthy, direct guitar stylings. He asked him to join his Serious Moonlight World Tour, which would last a year, minimum.

The invite was flattering, but it served to tear Stevie up inside. After the Power Station recording sessions, he had stuck around New York to cut some tracks behind Houston guitarist Johnny "Clyde" Copeland. When he returned to Texas, it was business as usual for Double Trouble, setting door-receipt records at the Continental, Steamboat, Antone's, and Fitzgerald's in Houston. The band was doing all right, terrific on the club level, but a record deal remained just out of grasp. Stevie was ferociously loyal to Chris and Tommy, but Bowie's invitation held out the promise of propelling him into the rock-and-roll big top, a world that Stevie claimed he despised while craving it deep in his soul. What would he do: stick with the blues and rule the clubs or see the world courtesy of David Bowie? There was really only one choice. When rehearsals for the Bowie tour began on a soundstage at the Las Colinas studios near Dallas in March of 1983, Stevie Ray Vaughan was there.

He'd agonized over his decision. Moving up to the major leagues gave him pause to reflect back on his own motivations, his talent, and all the people who had nurtured and supported him. "I don't think I'll be going through too much [head expansion] 'cause some of that's been there all along, being the little bitty brother and figuring out how to play a few fast notes. There was always kind of a ridiculous praise." It was a pleasant change that the praise he was beginning to hear had nothing to do with that "little bitty brother" tag he'd been saddled with all his life. It made him all the more resolute about giving credit where credit was due.

"Don't take this wrong and if it doesn't read right, don't put it down," he told writer Joe Rhodes after the Bowie sessions.

> [Jimmie] was born right about the spring equinox, the seed. I'm born right about the autumn equinox, the harvest. He's given me things to grow with, that he doesn't need to flaunt. And I sit here and wave it all around. If he wouldn't have been there I wouldn't have done anything. If he hadn't shown me what to start with I wouldn't have had anything to reap. He is responsible for me having the chance to play. I really believe that. My brother is really the reason I play and I'll always respect him for that. He's the biggest big brother I could ever have.

There was a bon voyage show on Sixth Street before Stevie left for the Bowie tour rehearsals. Double Trouble was going to be put on the shelf while their leader took his shot. Before the last set, a fan made his way backstage to wish Stevie well. Impulsively, the fan asked him if he could get a closer look at his hands.

"OK," Stevie shrugged. "They're just regular fingers," he said, holding them out for inspection.

"No, man," the admirer said, gently caressing them for a moment before letting them go. "You're wrong about that."

While Stevie Ray Vaughan's naive artistry was a plus in making the album *Let's Dance,* it turned David Bowie's tour rehearsals into a nightmare. Before His Ladyship, as Bowie was referred to in his absence, even arrived, Stevie got crossways with Carlos Alomar, the tour's musical director. Alomar was a lead guitarist, too, and keenly aware that he was going to have to compete with Stevie for playing time during the shows. To add to the tension, Stevie couldn't read music like the other band members, making it difficult for him to figure out the parts he was charted to play. Alomar claimed he could deal with the musical shortcomings. What he couldn't deal with was Lenny.

Lenny was starstruck. Being Stevie's wife and everything, she wanted to hang out at the rehearsals. Stevie said he wanted her with him. He liked her company, the coke she usually brought with her, and the relief of not worrying where she might be or who she was consorting with when he wasn't around. Alomar was straight as an arrow and knew that Bowie had long ago lost his tolerance for cocaine and other drug-induced highs. Alomar began to believe that he had to get Stevie off the tour, even if his guitar work was now an essential element of the new Bowie sound. When Bowie arrived after ten days of preliminary rehearsals, Alomar complained about the drugs and the meddling wife. Bowie immediately banished Lenny from the premises, which pissed Stevie off. Amends were made at a birthday party for Bowie, when the star came over to tell Stevie how nice it would be if Double Trouble could open some shows on the tour.

It was the solution to the problem that had been nagging Stevie ever since he agreed to go on tour with Bowie. He wanted to have a taste of the big time, but it bummed him out putting Chris and Tommy on hold, especially when Double Trouble had an album — their very first album — in the can. The possibility of his boys tagging along seemed like the ideal solution.

Chesley Millikin immediately got on the phone to take advantage of Bowie's largesse. With Double Trouble out on the road with Bowie, selling the album to a label would be a given. During two days of downtime for the Bowie tour, he lined up a gig for Double Trouble on "Musicladen," an influential music television program beamed across Europe by Radio Bremen in Germany. When Bowie caught wind of the side action, he balked. He couldn't have one of his support musicians upstaging him, advancing one's career in the midst of Bowie's own tour. Bowie sent word that Millikin would have to relinquish management of Stevie Ray Vaughan for the duration of the tour.

Chesley hit the roof. The nerve of Bowie. Who would be looking out for Stevie's interests? No way. He demanded to renegotiate the contract for Stevie's salary, insisting that Bowie increase the three-hundred-dollar-per-night fee. Chesley sent the contract to Bowie's lawyer, Lee Eastman, Beatle Paul McCartney's father-in-law, in New York. When Stevie and he visited Eastman's office just days before the tour left for Europe, Chesley was confident that something could be worked out.

"Did you change the contract?" he asked Eastman.

"What contract?" Eastman replied. "I don't know anything about any contract."

The writing was on the wall. Chesley looked at Stevie. Stevie looked back at Chesley.

"Let's get outta here," Millikin said.

"I'm with you," Stevie replied. "Shit, man, I'd rather go out with my guys anyway."

For several weeks, it was the talk of the music business. This unknown guitar player was actually blowing off David Bowie. Was he crazy? Didn't these Texans realize who David Bowie was?

"I couldn't gear everything on something I didn't really care a whole lot about," Stevie Ray told a reporter from the *Dallas Morning News*. "It was kind of risky, but I really didn't need all the headaches. We really thought we had something going with our album." Stevie Ray Vaughan, the world would learn, didn't take no shit. Even so, he was upset the way things turned out. When he saw David Bowie miming his own guitar parts on the video of "Let's Dance," Stevie was so furious he couldn't touch a guitar for several days. He called his brother, Jimmie. "Bowie stole my licks," Stevie complained.

"Naw, he didn't steal them," Jimmie consoled him. "He's just playing them 'cause they're the best thing on the album."

As a businessman, Chesley knew that he had taken a risk by pulling Stevie off the Bowie tour. As a believer in his client, he knew in his guts that what he had done was right.

"Telling Bowie to fuck off was the greatest factor for establishing Stevie Ray Vaughan as the working-class guitar hero," he later said.

11

BETTER THAN T-BONE

Perhaps the single most important factor that gave Stevie the courage to jump off the Bowie dream machine was an elderly gentleman with a flattop haircut and a set of teeth big enough for a horse. His name was John Henry Hammond, Jr., and he was a genuine living musical treasure. John Hammond's background was about as far from Stevie Ray Vaughan's as you could get. He was a Yankee, an heir to the Vanderbilt fortune, born and raised in the family's eight-story mansion just off Fifth Avenue in Manhattan. He attended The Hotchkiss School, an elite prep school in Connecticut, and Yale University. But in 1931, Hammond dropped out of Yale to begin an illustrious fifty-year career that helped shape the sound of American music.

Hammond was a promoter, a writer, a talent scout, a protester, and a reformer, a lifelong civil rights advocate who served for many years on the board of the NAACP. He was also a record producer, the consummate tastemaker who recorded a Who's Who of music greats including Fletcher Henderson, Bessie Smith, Chick Webb, Red Norvo, Austin's Teddy Wilson, Mildred Bailey, Count Basie, Harry James, Jimmie Rushing, Pete Seeger, Paul Winter, Herb Ellis, and George Benson. Hammond discovered Billie Holiday, Aretha Franklin, Bob Dylan, and a singer-songwriter from New Jersey named Bruce Springsteen. He also revolutionized the electric guitar's role in popular music when he forced his brother-in-law Benny Goodman to audition a young black Texas-born musician in a purple shirt and yellow shoes named Charlie Christian. Christian's 1939 debut on the song "Rose Room" in front of a packed house at the Victor Hugo restaurant in Beverly Hills turned into a heated forty-five-minute jam session. When the dust settled, the Benny Goodman Quintet was a sextet. If anybody could appreciate Stevie Ray's virtuosity, it was John Hammond. And he most certainly did.

Millikin had been working on the producer for two years, sending him tapes and updates on the band's progress. Hammond's interest turned into aggressive pursuit after his son, John Paul Hammond, brought back a tape from Montreux. "Now I like my son," Hammond said. "But Stevie knocked me out." Stevie's performance brought back memories of the evening in 1936 when Hammond took Benny Goodman to hear T-Bone Walker perform in Dallas. "Everyone was crazy about him," Hammond recalled, thinking back to T-Bone's show-stopping style. "He was a musician's musician. But Stevie is simply better."

When Hammond heard the rough mixes of Double Trouble's recording sessions at Jackson Browne's studio, he heard the potential. From the opening twangs of "Love Struck Baby" to the final plinks of the soulful love song "Lenny," the album had the same honesty and straightforwardness that drew Hammond to the songs of Dylan and Springsteen. Hammond was convinced that he had come across another find. "He brought back a style that had died, and he brought it back at exactly the right time," he said. "The young ears hadn't heard anything with this kind of sound."

Stevie was as impressed by Hammond's credentials as Hammond was impressed by Stevie's musicianship. Hammond's OK meant more than Mick Jagger's boozy compliments or Bowie's officious stamp of acceptance. Mister John Hammond wasn't only the greatest record producer on the planet, he had done more to promote black musicians than any white man in America. The mentor and the artist weren't just mutual admirers. They were soul mates.

John Hammond was bound and determined to release Stevie Ray Vaughan's first album, come hell or high water. He wanted to put the record out on his own HME (Hammond Music Enterprises) custom label that CBS distributed, but HME was experiencing cash-flow problems. The next best thing that Hammond could do was to make sure that Stevie wound up on another CBS label. He passed Stevie's tapes on to Gregg Geller, a vice president of A&R at Epic, which, like HME, was part of the CBS Records group. Geller had been a true believer in Hammond's integrity long before he met him face-to-face at a Bobby Vinton show at the

Copacabana supper club in New York. When Geller, then a young reporter for *Record World*, made a disparaging remark about Vinton to Hammond, the producer vigorously defended Vinton. "I came to understand that John Hammond liked Bobby Vinton because he'd led a regional band in Pittsburgh years before, an honorable calling, as far as Hammond was concerned," Geller explained.

Geller's job was to scout and sign acts, supervise the recording of an album, and finally introduce the finished product to label personnel. Most of the time, his relationship with Hammond extended no further than to playing the role of heavy and formally turning down acts that Hammond had recommended to Epic but didn't have the heart to personally reject. But the Stevie Ray Vaughan tape that Hammond passed along was something else. This was something Geller loved.

"For me, it was instantaneous, because it was so contrary to what was happening, though completely refreshing," Geller said. Stevie played right into Geller's Gap Theory — certain sounds, approaches, attitudes are universal and always good, regardless of their stature in the marketplace at any given time. At that particular moment in history, Linn drums, Fairlight computer keyboards, and Mini-Moog synthesizers had supplanted the guitar as rock's dominant instruments. "I didn't believe that, not for a second," Geller said. "And all of a sudden here comes this guy who could play guitar like ringing a bell. I didn't have to think a whole lot whether this was the right thing to do or not."

Geller caught Hammond's enthusiasm and spread it throughout the Black Rock, CBS's corporate headquarters at 51 West Fifty-second Street in New York City, despite the fact that his superiors at the time were, in his words, "a particularly tone-deaf bunch." The word traveled fast through the hallways and up and down the elevator shaft. The office champion of New Wave, the guy who had signed Elvis Costello to the label and was currently promoting the American debut of Culture Club, an English band led by the cross-dressing Boy George, was going crazy over David Bowie's blues guitarist.

Epic decided to risk releasing the record, and offered Stevie a $65,000 advance — a pittance for a major label, but a good deal for the band, which had invested very little in the recordings since Jackson Browne had donated studio time and tape. It was a good thing they tendered the deal when they did; Chesley had the Elektra label and Irving Azoff, the new president of MCA Records, interested in Stevie Ray. As a kicker, Epic agreed to finance two videos of songs from the album, a novel sales concept that was being championed by a new cable television channel called MTV, short for Music Television. On top of that, Millikin wangled a verbal commitment from the label to work the record on radio for six months rather than the standard six weeks. Once the ink was dry on the contract, Geller began familiarizing the various departments at the label with the new artist and his handlers, who, Geller admitted, "Gave me some pause. But a basic rule of thumb is you don't allow factors like that to inhibit you from being involved with the music that you think you ought to be involved with."

With Hammond patiently riding herd as executive producer, Stevie and the band got down to business, mixing their record at Media Sound studios in New York. Hammond had his eccentricities, timing each song with a stopwatch, but in Stevie's eyes, he could do no wrong. Hammond's message was to keep the fine-tuning process simple, lest the band lose sight of the goal of finishing the album and getting it into the marketplace. His priorities were old school all the way, emphasizing emotion and performance over technical perfection. In that respect, Hammond assured Stevie the product was already in good shape. "Everything he would play was almost letter perfect," he said. "There was no need for him to do anything else."

Stevie absorbed Hammond's philosophy. "When you mix and mix and mix, sometimes you get off about how the record really sounds," he said. "[John] would come in and if things were going really smooth, he'd just listen and come back later. If we had the echo turned all the way up because we'd gotten used to the sound, he'd come in and say, 'Turn that damned thing off,' then laugh and let you know it was OK."

There were still three minor stumbling blocks to releasing the record. One was John Dyer, who financed Stevie's Nashville sessions that Joe Gracey produced. Dyer told Millikin he was going to put the tapes out if he wasn't repaid his $7,000. So Classic Management paid up.

The second hang-up was designing a cover. Chesley wanted to pose Stevie saddled atop a stallion to play up his gunslinger/guitar singer image, but Lenny protested that Stevie couldn't even ride a horse. In the end, the Epic art department hired illustratror Brad Holland to paint a likeness of Stevie from a photograph.

The third hang-up was proving to the record company that Junior could pull off live what he'd done in the studio. Stevie had no doubt he could impress CBS executives. Hell, he had been impressing folks in clubs for fifteen years. He hadn't even been able to really stretch out during the recording sessions because of the time limitations. Chesley lined up a booking at the Bottom Line in New York City in May of 1983 opening two shows for pop-metal rocker Bryan Adams, who was celebrating his birthday with a record-release party in front of a houseful of industry heavies.

Stevie's band and crew worked from a disadvantage from the moment they loaded in their equipment. Chesley had flown in the Grateful Dead's sound man, Harry Poppick, for the gig, but even he couldn't get any respect from Adams's rude and crude crew. John Hammond showed up to hear Stevie's sound check, but Adams was so late, Stevie never got a chance to test his levels. "That's all right," Hammond reassured his flustered protégé. "You'll do fine."

Though Adams's crew wouldn't let Double Trouble check the monitors or the mikes or use any colored gels on the lights, Stevie's feathers were unruffled. This smelled like another break, and no one was going to mess it up, goddammit. He was determined to show Adams and everybody else just what he was made of. He may go on first but it was going to be his show. "We always huddled together before going on," Cutter Brandenburg recalled. "But Stevie was so in control that night, it was different. I can't explain it, except Stevie was talking, saying how relaxed he felt. And he said, 'I'll pull no punches.' "

Stevie led the band out onto the stage and squeezed himself into position, scrunched up in front of Adams's gear. He looked over at Cutter, who was running the lights. "Stevie had on a gold fucking metal shirt," Cutter said. "I hit the switch and when the white lights hit the mother, it blew the crowd's mind. I think Stevie played every lick as loud and as hard and with as much intensity as I've ever heard him. It was ungodly." John Hammond, Billy Gibbons, Johnny Winter, Mick Jagger, the CBS brass, even the paying customers in the audience were summarily knocked out, as reported by *New York Post* critic Martin Porter:

"Fortunately, Bryan Adams, the Canadian rocker who is opening arena dates for Journey, doesn't headline too often," Porter wrote. "As a result, he doesn't have to endure being blown off the stage by his opening act the way it happened at the Bottom Line the other night. By the time that Texas blues guitarist Stevie Ray Vaughan and his rhythm section were finished, the stage had been rendered to cinders by the most explosively original showmanship to grace the New York stage in some time."

"Stevie was relentless," said Chesley Millikin, chuckling over the review. "That's what I loved about him."

As Adams prepared to do an encore at the end of his first show, he cornered Mick Jagger, who was conferring with Stevie in his dressing room.

"Come on, Mick," Adams said. "Do one with us."

"Do your own show, man," ragged Jagger.

The record packaging for *Texas Flood* took two months to complete, shipping nationally in June of 1983. Geller orchestrated the album's promotion along with Al DeMarino, a vice president of artist relations; Bill Bennett, Epic's head of album promotion, who was responsible for getting radio stations to play label product; and Robert Smith, the product manager, who was in charge of physically getting records into stores. DeMarino declared the project a top priority. Product manager Smith made sure all the major chains had plenty of stock and commissioned a simple band-plays-in-bar video for the song "Love Struck Baby" to stimulate interest. Jack Chase, the sales manager of the CBS Group for the Dallas region, assured the big boys that his territory would be Stevie Ray's breakout market. He promised to turn 70,000 pieces of *Texas Flood*, no empty boast considering that Chase had grown up in Dallas, knew both Vaughans, loved them, loved their music, and had his entire staff primed and ready before the masters had been pressed.

Bennett was entrusted with persuading the music directors of radio stations that programmed AOR, or album oriented rock, the heir of free-form and progressive rock radio as defined by the radio and record industries, to play songs from the new albums released by AOR acts contracted to the Epic label. Each week, promo reps across the nation made calls at the important AOR stations in their respective regions to lobby for the addition of their label's product to radio stations' playlists. A significant number of adds typically indicated strong listener response and potential sales, especially if a song remained on the playlist for more than three or four weeks. Popular AOR acts had three or four songs pulled from an album for radio promotion purposes. Those songs that registered the most requests or strongest sales were placed in a category known as Heavy Rotation. The most popular AOR acts crossed over, their sales and airplay justifying the promotion of a song to the harder-to-please music directors of CHR, or contemporary hit, format — what was once called Top 40 — stations.

Bennett's staff had already primed the pump for AOR airplay, the format most suited for Double Trouble's music, by sending out advance tapes to his field representatives. The field reps, in turn, passed along advance tapes to sympathetic radio people. By the release date, AOR radio was ready to jump all over *Texas Flood*. Particularly effective was Heavy Lenny Pietzche, who worked AOR in the crucial and highly influential New York City Tri-State region.

One of the many targets of Bill Bennett's radio promo blitz was a Memphis disc jockey known as Redbeard, the program director and afternoon drive-time announcer at WZXR, Rock 103, one of the top album-rock formats in the South. "Let's Dance" was still fresh on Redbeard's mind when he was handed an advance cassette of Stevie Ray Vaughan and Double Trouble in late May. Bowie's unlikely hit and Stevie Ray's well-publicized break from the Bowie camp had prepared him for something out of the ordinary. "I couldn't believe he was leaving the relative security and limelight of Bowie's band. I was intrigued by that. You'd think an unknown would ride his horse further in that direction. I thought, that's a pretty ballsy move."

What he heard on the advance cassette ran counter to everything

AOR represented at the time. "It was the nadir of the guitar gods, and guitars were very much out of favor." Redbeard liked the first cut, "Love Struck Baby," all right, though the earth didn't exactly move beneath his feet. "Jump tunes are fine live," he observed. "But they don't work on the radio, despite all the swagger and confidence." The second cut, though, "Pride and Joy," he liked. "I thought this would stick out so much in light of what we were playing." Redbeard immediately added the selection to the station's playlist. It was a bold move, perhaps. "But it became a tasty bit of programming."

The station's programming consultant, Lee Michaels, overheard Redbeard setting the song up the first time he aired it. "David Bowie has always had an amazing ability to take totally unknown but very talented individuals and make them into stars," Redbeard said. Michaels, who was consulting more than one hundred of the top AOR stations in the country, was so impressed with the introduction, he typed up a memo about Redbeard's rap to show how an announcer could tie things together with passion. Michaels liked the Stevie Ray tune, too. It had a nice blues feel and some tough guitar like he hadn't heard in quite awhile.

Dozens of other stations followed Redbeard's lead in adding the record. The video for "Pride and Joy" received good exposure on the fledgling MTV. True to Jack Chase's prediction, out-of-the-box sales were strong in the Southwest. More surprising was Canada, where the record went through the roof.

In anticipation of touring behind major-label product, Chesley Millikin pulled the rug from under Rock Arts, informing Joe Priesnitz of the change by letter and thanking him for his services. Priesnitz didn't hear from Stevie until several months later, when he showed up at his office, which was next door to his landlord's. He asked Joe to get the Musician's Union off his back. They were harassing him for money Classic Management still owed Rock Arts. Stevie claimed he didn't know anything about it. He thought Chesley had taken care of the bill. Honest. The impasse was quickly settled through Stevie's lawyer, the future mayor of Austin, Frank Cooksey, who negotiated a partial repayment of the debt. Local 433 and the brothers and sisters of unions in other cities got off Stevie's back, while the band and the booking agency formally severed ties. The last gig Rock Arts booked was a weekend at Steamboat 1874 in Austin for which the band earned $6,400. Double Trouble had come a long way from two-hundred-dollar guarantees.

Stevie Ray Vaughan and Double Trouble's new booking representative was Rick Alter of the Marietta, Georgia, based Empire Agency. Empire was run by Alex Hodges, a soft-spoken gentleman who had quite a résumé for someone in his line of work. Hodges's fraternity brother at Mercer College in Macon was Phil Walden, who taught him a few tricks about buying and selling bands at dances before he started managing a Macon soul shouter named Otis Redding. Hodges became Redding's booking agent and remained with him until Otis died in a tragic plane crash in December of 1967 at the peak of his career. Hodges quit the music business and went to work for the Republican Party in Georgia in Atlanta for two years until Walden sent him a tape of a new band he was managing. They were called the Allman Brothers and they sounded like no one before, mixing a gritty soul sound with a progressive, almost psychedelic, free-form jazz approach to Southern blues. Walden had started up a record label called Capricorn and asked Hodges to help him out. Hodges quit the GOP and started working with the Allmans in Macon.

In a matter of weeks, Hodges was guiding Paragon Agency, a booking concern that represented not only the Allman Brothers but other bands in Walden's Capricorn stable, including the Marshall Tucker Band, Wet Willie, the Charlie Daniels Band, and Hank Williams, Jr. Hodges's acts sold millions of records and a proportionately greater number of concert tickets. Booking dates for Capricorn's acts was just as profitable as cutting label deals.

It was a sweet setup until tragedy struck again. Duane Allman was killed in a motorcycle wreck in October 1971. Bass player Berry Oakley died under similar circumstances thirteen months later. In 1977, Lynyrd Skynyrd, the only legitimate heir to the Allmans' legacy, went down in a private plane crash that claimed the lives of Ronnie Van Zandt and two others.

Paragon survived those accidents and the soap opera surrounding the bust of the Allmans' roadie Scooter Herring for possession of cocaine. Paragon could not survive Capricorn Records' filing for bankruptcy in 1979. The company's phones were disconnected and Walden retreated to the Georgia coast. Ian Copeland, one of the agents Hodges had trained, packed his bags for New York to establish Frontier Booking, or FBI, bringing along John Huie and Buck Williams from Georgia. Copeland's brother was the drummer for an up-and-coming act called the Police, which was enough of a calling card to boost FBI as the top New Wave and punk agency in the business.

Hodges stayed behind in suburban Marietta, outside Atlanta, where he set up his own scaled-down agency, Empire, that specialized in country and rock acts. One of those clients was Asleep at the Wheel, the neo-western swing big band from Austin. The Wheel had a spotty career when it came to records, bouncing around a half dozen labels in a single decade. But they loved the road and happily worked more than 250 one-nighters a year. Hodges respected the band, their leader, Ray Benson, and their readiness to hit the highway at the drop of a ten-gallon hat.

But he was a little dubious when Benson started hyping a tough little three-piece that was kicking up a storm back in his hometown.

There were some persuasive arguments in Double Trouble's favor. The David Bowie connection would certainly sweeten any guarantee, and Hodges respected the business savvy of Chesley Millikin, whom he'd known for more than ten years. He decided to take the bait and began booking Stevie Ray Vaughan and Double Trouble on a relentless tour schedule designed to alert the world to their presence. The band didn't seem to mind. Roadwork was still fun, and this next stretch of miles would perhaps help break them out of the club scene and into the world of arena rock. They ditched the step van for a fancy touring bus but little else changed. "They may be on the road 365 days a year," commented the band's hired driver. "But they're still the band that never sleeps."

Empire was instrumental in securing opening dates in big arenas with Huey Lewis, Men at Work, the Moody Blues, and the Police — acts that were light years removed from Albert Collins or B. B. King — while mapping out headlining gigs for the band that was being billed in Canada as the Legend in the Making Tour, all while Charlie Comer orchestrated the press blitz. It was so effective, it made it hard for Stevie to concentrate on music. Stevie had been the object of worship in several circles of party animals and guitar freaks in Austin, San Antonio, Lubbock, Waco, and Dallas for several years, long enough to expect to receive generous offerings of illicit substances in exchange for playing some inspirational guitar. But by the time *Texas Flood* was released, so many people started showing up with goodies night after night that Cutter and roadie Byron Barr started screening backstage visitors for the band's own protection.

"I was the coach," Cutter fumed. "I beat people up. I literally grabbed 'em out of the fucking restroom and punched 'em in the mouth and threw them down the stairs at Fitzgerald's. I said, 'I don't want these coke rappin' motherfuckers bringing these guys stuff anymore.' Chris and Tommy and Stevie would say, 'Hold us. Don't let us do it.' Then I'd look up at the end of the night and see I lost the fucking battle."

Fans were laying rocks, half grams, and more on everyone even remotely connected to Stevie, turning the debauch into a round-the-clock affair. Stevie entertained his partying pals by passing a handkerchief through his nose. While most coke heads were gradually destroying their nasal cartilage, Stevie was already a step ahead of them. The doctors had removed it years before.

Tennis superstar and guitar freak John McEnroe took a liking to Stevie and brought his girlfriend Tatum O'Neal along to hang out and bask in the attention. At one informal jam McEnroe hosted in a Manhattan rehearsal studio, Eric Clapton showed up. After ten minutes of listening to Stevie wail away on the guitar, he quietly laid his axe down and walked off. Others, like cabaret star Liza Minelli, were so smitten with Stevie they offered their bodies and anything else they could give.

In July, Double Trouble returned to Montreux to reprise their triumphant debut of the year before with an itinerary that continued through several European countries. It was the last tour for Cutter Brandenburg. He had spent fifteen years taking care of rock and rollers, and he had tired of seeing his best friend Stevie getting out of hand. Back in Texas, Cutter's wife had the previous fall given birth to their first child, "Rockin' " Robin. Though Stevie dedicated a tune off the first album to the little boy, Cutter knew the kid needed more than a song. He needed his daddy.

Lenny was challenging Cutter's authority at every turn. She and Stevie would get so high between gigs, they'd pass Tommy and Chris in the hotel hallways and not even recognize them. Lenny toyed with Stevie Ray's insecurities, staying away from gigs, which drove Stevie into a jealous rage. In Paris, she accused Cutter of stealing Stevie's guitar. In London, she scratched off the names of Brian May from Queen and other VIPs that Cutter had put on the band's guest list. On a whim, she took off with Stevie for a couple of days of downtime, during which the rest of the band and crew hit the road for the next destination. Without Lenny and Stevie on board, the band's carnet, the papers that were absolutely essential for carrying backline equipment across borders in Europe, was broken, costing the band thousands of dollars. Cutter had humored Lenny to the point of accommodating her request to put quartz crystals atop the band's amplifiers for healing power. He'd endured her insatiable appetite for cocaine, which only aggravated Stevie's tendency to get loaded. What could he, or anyone else, do? Threaten to fire the star if his old lady didn't get with the program?

The split came in Berlin, where the band played a disco club called the Sector on September 4. Walking around the city, Cutter came across the Brandenburg Gate and other monuments bearing his surname. They gave him the creeps, these cold German symbols. When the management of the hotel refused to let him leave with the bath towels he had ferreted in his suitcase, Cutter went berserk. He destroyed his room, as only a professional roadie could do. He disconnected the pipes under the sink and let the water run. He shoved food way up into the air-conditioning ducts. He poured sodas into the television set. He dumped the refrigerator on its back, opened the door, opened up every can and bottle and poured them back into the refrigerator, shut the door, and stood the refrigerator upright. As he left the hotel, he goose-stepped through the lobby and gave the concierge a *"Sieg heil"* Nazi salute. He had had it. He was done. Fried. Kaput. He knew it. Everyone knew it. The time had come for Cutter to get off the bus.

Cutter may have gone off the deep end, but he thought he was just following his boyhood pal. "Stevie was dying on me, man. He was not punching," Cutter said. "All of a sudden my best friend, the kid that I loved more than anybody, he and I couldn't talk."

After finishing a show in Copenhagen, the band flew back to New York. On the flight, Stevie crossed the aisle to talk to Cutter.

"I love you," he said, putting his hand on his face.

"I love you, too," Cutter replied.

The rest of the traveling circus continued pell-mell, getting crazier by the night. It was symptomatic of the line of work they were in. "Artists get pretty well beyond your control pretty quickly, especially when they get successful," explained Epic's Gregg Geller. By year's end, *Texas Flood* had gone gold, selling more than 500,000 units, though it peaked at number thirty-eight on *Billboard*'s album chart. Stevie tried to maintain his humility, but it was getting harder and harder to keep his feet planted in the ground. He wasn't just a great guitarist anymore. He had ascended to the kingdom where every roadie's shiny Halliburton briefcase had a "No Head, No Backstage Pass" bumper sticker. Whereas his cocaine habit had always previously been kept in check by his bank account, that constraint vanished with sold-out concerts. He was rock royalty, a gentleman of privilege who could have anything he wanted, before, during, and after a show, as long as he gave the customers their money's worth. He would never have to worry again about blowing up someone's borrowed amp. The hospitality rider of his contract specified, among other things, a fifth of Crown Royal backstage before every performance. He enjoyed the luxury of keeping $5,000 in cash stashed in his boot without having to justify to anyone how he spent it. Who said it wasn't a perfect world?

A perfect world for Stevie Ray Vaughan meant a world filled with guitars. His success gave him the opportunity to indulge his single-minded passion as he had never been able to before. So what if he didn't have a car or a refrigerator? Dallas instrument dealer Charley Wirz had been scrounging up guitars for Stevie for years. Now strangers were bringing him their own finds that Stevie passed on to Charley to customize.

He had accumulated quite a harem.

There was "First Wife," the beat-up 1959 SRV Strat that he bought from Ray Hennig in 1974. Wirz installed microphone pickups that were so sensitive you could hear a fingernail click on the plastic pick guard, giving it an exceptionally clear tone. Wirz replaced the stock neck with a copy of the Fender maple neck given to Stevie by Billy Gibbons.

There was "Lenny," the '64 Strat that his guitar tech, Byron Barr, had found in an Oak Cliff pawnshop. Lenny Vaughan gave the guitar to Stevie for his birthday, with the understanding she would repay Barr after taking up a collection from friends. But part of the debt lingered until Barr confronted Stevie: "I said, 'It's yours, man, now I want my dough.' He offered me a bicycle. I think I ended up with a little bit of cash and a real cool jacket."

There was the yellow Strat that had been hollowed out by the previous owner, the guitarist from the sixties psychedelic band Vanilla Fudge. Charley rigged it with a stock treble Fender pickup to give it the distinctive sharp, ringing tone heard on the lead of "Tell Me" on *Texas Flood*. There was "Charley," a white '61 Strat that Wirz wired with Danelectro pickups and rewired in a configuration that only he had the blueprint for, and a very slick-looking orange 1960 Strat.

There was also the '59 Gibson hollow-body 335 with a wide dot-neck tailor-made for his big hands, the '48 Airline with three pickups, a prototype Rickenbacker, and an alleged '28 National Steel that Byron Barr gave him. Billy Gibbons also gave Stevie a custom Lurktamer built by James Hamilton with his name spelled out in inlaid pearl script along the neck, designed by Austin artist Bill Narum. The Lurktamer was shaped like a Strat, only with a thicker body, and an ebony fretboard wide enough to accommodate his wide paws.

Wirz and his assistant, Rene Martinez, souped up almost all of Stevie's guitars with bass frets, the biggest ones available, to punch up his sound with more guts and sustain and reduce the wear and tear his callused fingers and telephone-wire-sized strings wreaked on the metal bars. All the Strats were rigged with five-way switches on the pickups to vary the tones. Byron Barr and his father stamped some heavy-duty wang bars on a metal press specifically for Stevie and installed them on the bass side of the bridge in emulation of Otis Rush. By switching on the middle pickup and turning the tone knob down, grabbing the wang bar and shaking the guitar on the floor, he could coax a threatening rumble out of the instrument. Otherwise, he limited his use of effects to the wah-wah pedal for the Jimi Hendrix rave-ups and an Ibanez Tube Screamer to warm up the sound.

Live and in person, Stevie Ray Vaughan put his toys to good use. The secret to his sound was simple. "I use heavy-gauge strings, tune low, play hard, and floor it," he liked to say. His balls-to-the-wall style set a new standard for rock-and-roll guitar, a standard against which all other performances were measured. He may have adopted the extravagant tastes of a man who could afford all the clothes he wanted, but he retained the cocksure toughness of a bad boy fresh off the streets, evidenced by the muffdiver imperial beard he cultivated under his lower lip and the burning Kool cigarette he jammed into the guitar neck just below the low E string tuning peg. Stevie Ray Vaughan in concert was a no-holds-barred affair. He hardly acknowledged his audiences, much less Shannon and

Layton, who kept their eyes riveted on their leader lest he swerve off into uncharted territory. He didn't need smoke pots, light shows, exploding stage effects, or friendly chatter to connect with the audience.

All he had to do was grasp the plastic pick, fat end out, between his fingers and thumb, and let fly, boiling it all down to a man and his guitar. He treated the battered Strat in his hands like a love-hate object, delicately handling it like it was some wondrous, lighter-than-air confection, then mangling it like it was a tool possessed that needed to be exorcised of its evil demons. He seduced it, fondled it, fought it, tangled with it, and beat full chords out of it by banging the strings with his fist until he coaxed out an electronic cry of mercy. He was a contortionist, working the strings while he held the instrument behind his back, balanced on his shoulder like a violin, then stood on it, one hand on the neck, the other jerking up on the vibrato bar like he was trying to rip it out of the guitar.

His voice wailing right along with the guitar, balling his right hand into the air for added emphasis, he sang downtrodden laments like the tragic "Texas Flood" with the sad wisdom of a three-time loser. He fell into a loping shuffle automatically like he'd been working in the same house band on Harry Hines Boulevard back in Dallas for decades. Crowds had little knowledge of those references, other than their being elements of Texas blues. But they did know who Jimi Hendrix was. Even the most vociferous skeptics who doubted the ability of any other Hendrix clone to cop the master's riffs were floored when they heard Stevie Ray take off to roam the range of space and time with the same abandon as the black dude with the hippie headband.

A sweaty scowl slapped on his face, Stevie flashed his brown-stained teeth in fearless loathing at the wood and metal. If the artist had to suffer to create, then he was holding up his end of the bargain. Other than an occasional "Thank you very much," there was nothing to say. He let his guitar do the talking. For once in his life, that was more than enough.

When the house lights went up, he was a publicist's wet dream, ready to accommodate the well-wishers, celebrities, and hangers-on with encouraging words, an autograph, or by posing for a souvenir snapshot, willing to stick around until the last fan went home.

It was a hard life he had chosen, though you couldn't tell from the sleek tour bus, the spacious first-class hotel rooms, the eager crowds, the backstage adulation, and the party that went on forever. Those comforts never fully compensated for the long hours of traveling, the lack of privacy, and the constant demands on everyone's time, especially Stevie's. The first time around was a fresh new experience. By the second time and third time they'd played the same city, the bloom had fallen. Instead, there was the lament: "When do we get a break?"

Chesley Millikin ignored the pleas. "As they got bigger and richer, they complained they had to work so much," he acknowledged. "Bottom line was that if they were in town for more than a week, they got into trouble." Besides, hanging around Austin was no way to sell records. In this business, you had to seize the moment, and that moment, Millikin believed, was right now.

Behind the scenes, the gulf between Stevie Ray Vaughan and Double Trouble and Classic Management continued to widen. Stevie wanted to have more input in decisions that affected him. Chesley thought Junior should stick to his art. They were business partners, not bosom buddies. "Chesley was over here saying this is what Stevie should be doing," observed Edi Johnson. "And Stevie was over here saying, 'Why aren't you asking me what I wanna do?' "

Millikin chalked up his client's attitude to the Locked-in-the-Bus syndrome. "These fuckers got him in the fucking bus, snorting cocaine up the ass, telling him, 'You're the greatest, Stevie, old boy, we love you, man. Can we get more money?' Everybody decided they could manage Stevie better than I did.

"Stevie liked the idea of carrying the weight," claimed Millikin. But it aggravated the manager to no end that his client insisted on splitting the earnings equally with the rest of the band. "To me, that was an absolute outrage," he said, especially in light of Classic Management receiving a relatively paltry 10 percent of the band's gross for their services when other management firms were taking 25 percent off the top. Chris and Tommy could get lost in the desert as far as Chesley was concerned. "I could go out and get $12,500 for Stevie Ray Vaughan, his guitar, and his amp. I couldn't get 1,250 *cents* for Double Trouble."

Edi Johnson realized the grumbling was more than idle talk when she walked in on the band in a hotel room in Austin toasting a pending partnership with their road manager of the moment, Geoff Torrance, who had ambitions of running the whole show. He was immediately relieved of his duties.

The band had no idea what kind of money was coming in or going out. In many respects, they still acted like they were living hand-to-mouth. Hygiene was still a low priority. Despite Stevie's tendency to sweat profusely while performing, he rarely did laundry. After the coke bust in Houston, he was so scared of being popped again that he made it policy to refuse maid service in hotels, no matter how long he was camped in one room. "Stevie did not wash clothes," recalled road manager Jim Markham. "When he'd take his socks off, we'd throw them in the trash. He would wear the same clothes for five days in a row, on- and offstage, sleep in them too." The funk felt good to Stevie. "He wanted to be a nigger," Markham said. "Deep in his psyche, he was pissed that he wasn't black."

Accolades poured in, for which the Texas guitarslinger had a simple, economical explanation: "We just worked our butts off." It took Albert King to burst his bubble. Cobilling a concert in Toronto in the fall of 1983, King pulled Stevie aside after the gig for a little heart-to-heart. He was proud of all Stevie'd accomplished, but he was bothered with the way he was coping with his status. He felt like Stevie's daddy sometimes, and like a daddy, there were some things he needed to say.

"I been watching you wrestle with that bottle three, four times already. But the gig ain't no time to get high," he admonished him. Stevie heard Albert's words, but didn't give them much weight. He had his act together. There wasn't anything wrong with doing a little shit. He could handle the alcohol and cocaine. He was at the top of his game — everyone around him told him so, every day, no matter where he was.

Both the mastery of his instrument and his wasted physical state were becoming more evident with each performance. It was almost as if playing music were a purification ritual, a spiritual and physical process that enabled Stevie to consume superhuman quantities of drugs. Onstage the meat of Stevie's fingers sliced through any hint of pretense. Midway through every set he was awash in sweat, a guitar ascetic consumed by an inner fire, a warrior locked in the sweat lodge of his music. Every performance was physically grueling, to the point of being almost pornographic in its total emotional abandon. Watching him writhe, fidget, and immerse himself in his music was almost too painful to watch. When he stepped offstage, he was ready for a drink, a toot, and a chance to do it all over again.

12

CARNEGIE HALL

The struggle paid off. But Stevie still was less than fulfilled. Something was missing. It wasn't Lenny, whose erratic behavior kept him more off balance than ever. It wasn't Chesley, although Stevie didn't exactly trust him like he used to. It wasn't Tommy or Chris. They were partners for the long haul. It was this strange feeling of emptiness nagging at the pit of his stomach. He was a big-time star, and he still wasn't right.

In the midst of an increasingly tight schedule, Double Trouble managed to squeeze in nineteen days of studio time in the middle of January 1984 for a follow-up album. Compared to *Texas Flood*'s miracle seventy-two-hour turnaround, the second effort was done at a positively deliberate pace. There was certainly no problem in digging up enough material. Some of the best songs in the band's live sets didn't make it onto the first album. It was just a matter of getting it down on tape.

Sticking to the formula that worked the first time around, the emphasis in the studio was on replicating the excitement and spontaneity of a live performance. The album was made at New York's Power Station, where Stevie had cut *Let's Dance* with David Bowie. Unlike with the sessions for the first album, though, the band had to strike their equipment after each session and set up all over again every day, causing problems with getting a consistent sound and moving Stevie to swear, "I'll never record again without block time."

John Hammond, who only supervised the mixdown and mastering of *Texas Flood*, was on hand for the entire recording. Initially, this led to some tension in the studio. "The first thing I had to get past was this stumbling block," Stevie later explained to radio producer David Tarnow. "I was looking at John Hammond with so much awe, sometimes it was like looking at my father." Stevie's skittishness was no doubt due in part to his own habits, and the fact that the seventy-three-year-old Hammond was a lifelong teetotaler. Unlike in his dealings with his father, however, Stevie was able to be up front with Hammond. "We brought it right out in the open and laughed about it," Stevie recalled. "God bless his ears, and God bless his heart too."

There were moments during the recording when Hammond would space out. At one point, he wondered aloud when Stevie was going to show up, when the guitarist was actually sitting right next to him. But no one minded the brief memory lapses. Hammond wasn't there to run the show. He was a steadying influence, a wise eminence on call to remind everyone it's better to hear a mistake in an inspired performance than sacrifice soul for a flawless rendition. He invoked his Keep-It-Simple philosophy whenever necessary. Stevie listened to Hammond and by doing so avoided the pitfalls of too much money, too much time, and too much of too much spent on making an album. How could he not listen? Ignore John Hammond?

Stevie sought help on the album from other people as well. He invited his brother, Jimmie, into the recording sessions, marking the first time the Vaughan boys had worked together in the studio. Jimmie added some tasty guitar licks to the songs "Couldn't Stand the Weather" and "The Things (That) I Used to Do." The chance to work together was a positive experience for the boys. For once, Jimmie was helping out his kid brother, who, despite his increasing high profile, was still in awe of his elder sibling's musical abilities if not his reputation. It was great fun, and the end result sounded like it.

As Stevie's reputation grew, his friends sought to protect him. But while some were well-meaning, they only served to make things worse. Sid Morning, a guitar-playing cohort from Austin who loved to party with Stevie Ray and frequently put him up when he needed a place to stay, thought he was coming to his buddy's defense when he confronted Frances Carr. During band rehearsals before the recording session, Sid had an earful of the complaints he was hearing from Stevie about the management. When Carr showed up at the rehearsal hall, Morning confronted her. "Isn't it true Stevie's broke because of you?" he asked the woman who had invested hundreds of thousands of dollars in Stevie Ray's career.

"We want to audit your books," he said, speaking for the band. Morning's reaction was typical. Everyone thought they knew what was best for Stevie Ray, and Stevie Ray seemed only too willing to take anyone and everyone's advice. Carr, on the other hand, felt more estranged than ever.
Couldn't Stand the Weather was a major turning point in Stevie Ray Vaughan's development. His singing improved. "I'm getting to be more relaxed," he said. "I haven't taken any voice therapy or anything, but I've learned how to open and close my throat in different ways to make it easier to sing."

He strived hard to shake his gunslinger image. Being the fastest draw in town was no longer enough. He wanted to be the tastiest, nastiest, funkiest, and most nitty-gritty guitar player of them all, a reflection of his determination to mine as many musical veins as possible and prove to the world he was no one-trick "blooze" pony. He even delved into jazz with "Stang's Swang," a song inspired by the organ sound of Jimmy Smith and Grant Green that he'd been doing since the Rome Inn days. Fran Christina of the Thunderbirds and saxophonist Stan Harrison sat in for the session. Christina was so on-the-money, he got his drum track done on the first take.

Hammond's favorite cut on the record was "Tin Pan Alley," the guaranteed showstopper for Double Trouble. From the first ominous notes of the first run-through, everyone in the studio knew that Stevie was laying down one of the greatest collisions of controlled technique and raw emotion in a blues recording, complemented by a husky, reflective vocal more typically associated with teddy bears like Bobby "Blue" Bland.

"I heard a pistol shoot/It was a forty-four/Somebody killed a crapshooter 'cause he couldn't/Shake rattle and roll"

A conversation between Stevie and his engineer, Richard Mullen, over an SRV original, "Empty Arms," that ended up on the cutting-room floor, demonstrated that he was still consumed with getting the black thang down cold. Mullen wanted Stevie to try a faster version of the song.

Stevie responded in his best Old Tired Negro's voice: "I wuz wantin' to play it both ways, but I wants a drink 'fore I do damn near anythin'."

When Mullen insisted, Stevie, still in character, replied, "Hey muthafucka, do I tell you how to toin da knobs?"

"Yes, you do, as a matter of fact," the engineer said.

Resuming his normal manner of speech, Stevie chuckled, "I figured I had my foot in my ass on that one."

Couldn't Stand the Weather also unveiled to his record-buying public his Jimi Hendrix fixation. The band recorded several Hendrix compositions, eventually selecting a wholly consumed rendition of "Voodoo Chile (Slight Return)." Hammond liked the cut so much he wanted to title the album *Voodoo Chile.* Some industry insiders saw the song's inclusion as a shrewd marketing move, but Stevie had a considerably humbler explanation. "More people are asking me why we did it, trying to read some kind of big meaning to us doing that song," he told writer Joe Rhodes. "People don't understand that it's something that we've done for a long time and really wanted to do. It is still just as good as it was having people see him for the first time."

Since Hendrix's death in 1970, Hendrix analogies had been thrust upon practically every guitar hero in the business, most notably Randy Hansen, Ernie Isley of the Isley Brothers, Frank Marino of Mahogany Rush, Yngwie Malmsteen, and Robin Trower. The mere inclusion of "Voodoo Chile" on his album prompted the inevitable comparisons again, which irritated Stevie just a little. "Why do people want to make it out to be more than it is?" he asked. Stevie believed younger fans needed to hear this tremendous music, and it was part of his mission to turn them on to it, just as he was turning on fans to Albert and Albert, B.B., Freddie, Buddy, and Muddy. "Some of the distance that people put between playing music and playing Hendrix music is kind of strange to me," he explained. "Granted, it's hard to play . . . but that doesn't mean you shouldn't try."

Mindy Giles of Alligator Records once asked him about his fixation, wondering what was going on when he was playing Hendrix with his eyes closed.

"What do you mean?"

"Well, uh, are you a vessel, are things moving through you? It's not your mind working, it's some other things functioning."

"Oh, you mean, is it Jimi? Like getting in me?" he asked matter-of-factly.

"Yeah," Giles nodded her head.

Stevie smiled beatifically.

"Yeah."

The parallels were certainly there. Like Jimi, Stevie Ray Vaughan worked with only the support of a bass and drums. Like Jimi, he exhibited an amazing command of feedback, volume, and distortion. Like Jimi, he could play lead and rhythm simultaneously with the rare ability to rattle out massive chord clusters and piercing barrages of single notes with incredible precision, drenching them in exotic tones produced by pickup switches, wah-wah pedals, and overamplification. Stevie paid almost as much attention to his amps as he did to his guitars, preferring two Fender Super Reverbs when he played live, sometimes augmenting them with a custom 150-watt Steel String Singer, designed and built by Howard Dumble of Los Angeles, that Stevie described as "the King Tone Console — that's S-O-U-L." The significant differences were Hendrix's considerable talents as a writer and musical innovator and Stevie's ability to sing Jimi under the table, with twice the control and range.

In the five months between the album's completion and release, the band guested at Charlie Daniels's annual Volunteer Jam in Nashville, did a short swing through the Southeast and Midwest, opened for the Police in Honolulu, and made a Scandinavian tour. Frances Carr, the head of Classic Management who preferred to stay in the background when it came to guiding Stevie's career, came out front for this tour to road-manage the band. "I've got to give her a lot of credit," said roadie Byron Barr, who was surprised to have Frances help him load and unload the band's equipment onto countless trains in the frigid March weather. "She was good. She had a lot of guts." Drugs were hard for the band to score in Norway, Finland, and Sweden, a situation that enhanced the quality of the music and made life on the road less sordid. "It was like traveling with a bunch of kids," Frances recalled. "It reminded me of the early days with the Grateful Dead." The one thing that annoyed the band was that ice was never provided at the venues in Europe, a dilemma that Frances resolved by going outside and collecting snow for the boy's drinks. Despite their conflicts over money, Frances and Stevie got along well one-on-one. "He was like a replacement for my big brother after he died," she said.

Upon returning to the States, Double Trouble taped television appearances on the Public Broadcasting System's "Austin City Limits" and the syndicated "Rock of the 80s" series, and did a string of New York–area dates. *Texas Flood* was voted Best Guitar Album in the *Guitar Player* magazine Reader's Poll, which also named Stevie winner of the Best Electric Blues Player category (beating out no less than Eric Clapton) and Best New Talent, making him the first Triple Crown champ since Jeff Beck collected three prizes in 1976.

Stevie Ray Vaughan and Double Trouble were nominated for four Grammy awards, winning the Best Traditional Blues Category for their Montreux debut version of "Texas Flood," which appeared on the *Blues Explosion Montreux '82* compilation album released by Atlantic Records. At the Grammy presentation, Stevie teamed up with George Thorogood, the Delaware guitar ace he'd opened for at Soap Creek Saloon five years earlier, to pay tribute to the rock-and-roll guitar godfather, Chuck Berry. It was a performance that Stevie was not proud of. "[George] told me he was going to turn all the way up and if I didn't, I wouldn't be heard. And I figured, 'Just let him go.' There was a lot of respect there that Chuck Berry should have gotten that I'm not sure he got. The whole point was to have him perform and give him an award for being Chuck Berry. That's what I thought was the disappointing thing. I'm not trying to run Thorogood down, but I thought he was real disrespectful to Chuck Berry in doing what he did. We were there to say thanks to him."

A few days later, the band flew into Austin to perform a sneak preview of the album material at the Austin Music Awards. During the short break at home Stevie filmed two surprisingly impressive videos. "Couldn't Stand the Weather" was a mood piece in which he played his way through a horrendous storm that was generated by an industrial fan and gallons of water. The song, Stevie said, carried a world message about "stopping all this damn fighting before someone comes and takes it all away." The second video, "Cold Shot," was a humorous, vaguely auto-biographical story about a guy who only wants to play his guitar, and a nagging, overweight wife who is willing to throw her husband out of the window to get him to stop. Both videos helped deflect industry criticism that he was an exceptional talent with not a shred of visual presence.

All the groundwork paid off by the time *Couldn't Stand the Weather* hit the streets in late May of 1984. Two weeks after its release, it debuted at 144 on the *Billboard* pop album chart. Stevie Ray's second album sold a lot faster than his first, turning 242,000 pieces in the first 21 days. Momentum kept it on the list of the top 200 selling albums in the United States for 38 weeks. Both videos were in steady rotation on MTV, which the industry no longer considered a novelty but an essential promotional tool. The album material, the videos, the touring, and Stevie's obvious talent all contributed to *Couldn't Stand the Weather* reaching platinum status, signifying sales of 1 million units, despite the fact the record never moved higher than number thirty-one on the charts.

It was about that time that the gold album for *Texas Flood* arrived at the Manor Downs offices. Stevie, on a brief break, rushed over to see it for himself. He hugged the framed award like a long-lost family member and happily posed for photographs. The contentment on his face told the whole story. He'd worked all his life for this. He'd earned it. No one could take it away. Tommy hung his gold record on the wall of his room at the Imperial 400 Motel on South Congress, his permanent address in Austin.

Stevie Ray Vaughan's life had been simplified to that of a bona fide rock-and-roll star: tour till you couldn't anymore, take a break and rest, tour some more, then cut an album and start all over again.

In July, he asked Angela Strehli to open dates in Dallas, Houston, and Austin. Strehli's guitarist was David Murray, the kid Stevie had taken under his wing when he was still with the Cobras. Stevie'd just bought a red '75 Caprice and wanted to take David for a ride. He drove around the block and pulled into the 7-Eleven across the street from the auditorium and adjacent to a hobo camp. One of the street persons hanging near the entrance hit Stevie up for spare change. Stevie gave him a five, suggesting, "Why don't you get something to eat?"

But the panhandler followed him inside. "Hey, man, on 'Couldn't Stand the Weather' that rhythm part kinda sucked," he said to Stevie, who was buying a pack of Kools. "You can do a lot better than that." He was referring to one of Jimmie Vaughan's contributions to the album. Stevie paused and held in his breath, slowly stating, "Man, my brother's the greatest rhythm player I ever heard."

The street person was taken aback. He reached into his pocket and offered Stevie his fiver back.

Stevie was steamed. He waved the man away. "Naw, keep it."

The band made a short jaunt to Europe in August and appeared on "Rockpalast," a live concert series from Germany televised throughout the European continent, sharing the bill with the English haircut band the Alarm and Little Steven Van Zandt from Bruce Springsteen's E Street Band. The following month, Stevie Ray and Double Trouble headlined the Delta Blues Festival in Mississippi, sharing the bill with Albert King, Bo Diddley, and Son Thomas. The night was uncharacteristically cold, but as Stevie leaned into his guitar on the wooden stage surrounded by cotton fields, he was warmed by the fact that he was good enough and credible enough to be on a bill with the same people who invented the music he dedicated himself to. After the concert, the blues masters offered Stevie the greatest gift they could, their respect for him as a musician and for what he was doing to reinvigorate the power of the blues.

Those bookings were mere warm-ups leading to the big one in New York, a night at Carnegie Hall on October 4, the day after Stevie turned thirty. Carnegie Hall was the sight of John Hammond's legendary Spirituals to Swing concert in 1939 that introduced New York's high society to Sonny Terry, Big Joe Turner, Big Bill Broonzy, and Sidney Bechet, among others. But subsequent appearances by blues artists in New York's premier concert hall were few and far between. Stevie's booking was not only a personal feather in the hat, it recognized his role in bringing the blues back to prominence. He understood the significance of the date by assembling his own all-star revue.

Joining Chris and Tommy were Jimmie Vaughan on guitar; George Rains, a swinging drummer from Fort Worth who'd done time with Boz Scaggs, Doug Sahm, and the Antone's house band; New Orleans's Mac Rebennack, aka Dr. John, on additional keyboards, a last-minute replacement for Booker T. Jones; and the Roomful of Blues horn section from Rhode Island for a high-tone tip of the bolero hat to T-Bone, who used to front brassy big bands himself. For the featured female vocalist, he selected Angela Strehli. In Stevie's ideal world, if he'd really been born black and reincarnated as Robert Johnson, Angela would have been his Bessie Smith.

Stevie dressed the male musicians in silver-studded, skin-tight, royal-blue velvet Mexican mariachi outfits custom-sewn by a tailor in Nuevo Laredo, just across the Rio Grande from Texas. They prepared by rehearsing six and a half days in Austin, one and a half days with the full ensemble, then went to the Caravan of Dreams in Fort Worth for a full-dress-rehearsal performance on September 29.

In New York, the revue rehearsed for two days on a soundstage, then did a quick run-through at Carnegie Hall the afternoon before the performance. Stevie Ray–mania was in full force in the Big Apple. Although his hotel was only a half block away from the venue, he found it necessary to take a limousine to avoid being mobbed on the street. But when the lights finally went down, all the preparation and hype seemed worth the effort.

"It was a strange sight, the Texas boys in those funny clothes, playing a place that has chandeliers in the lobby and carpet on the floor," wrote a reviewer for the *Dallas Times-Herald*. Many of the 2,200 people sitting in the high-class seats were expecting the country blues of Leadbelly or Big Bill Broonzy. Instead, Stevie hit them with a blast of heavy-metal blues, spraying notes around the acoustically perfect auditorium with the fattest-gauge strings anyone could sling on an electric guitar.

"Stand up," shouted one fan to the dignified types in the crowd, who were somewhat put off by the volume and by the rowdier fans in their "Stevie Fucking Ray" T-shirts. "This isn't *La Traviata*."

Stevie was more than a little nervous. He rushed through his first couple of numbers and didn't settle down until the middle of "Voodoo Chile," when he looked over and saw Tommy watching him like a hawk. He relaxed and swung his guitar behind the back and over the shoulder, which drove the T-shirts in the audience nuts. But for all the promised fireworks, the big-band concept never fully jelled. Instead of the tight, compact dynamics of Double Trouble, the playing was loose, bordering on sloppy. It would have been fine if this was a late-night improvisation in a chicken shack instead of a show at the most distinguished concert facility in America. Still, it was a breath of fresh air that Stevie needed. "We won't be limited to just the trio, although that doesn't mean we'll stop doing the trio," he said after the show. "I'm planning on doing that, too. I ain't gonna stay in one place. If I do, I'm stupid."

The technical flaws did not detract from the pervasive feeling of triumph. The Hurricane of Texas guitar, old Stingray, Skeeter, Stevie Rave On, had pulled it off in the temple of the perfect note. After the show MTV threw a party for him at a downtown club. When his limo pulled up to the door, he recognized a familiar face standing outside the velvet rope at the entrance. It was Diamond Joe Siddons, the boyfriend Lenny dumped for him. He told the doorman Siddons was OK and walked him through. Inside, Stevie glad-handed an hour's worth of well-wishers and worked his way to the table where his parents were sitting. When he finally reached them, he bent over and hugged Big Jim Vaughan until they both had tears streaming down their cheeks.

13

SERIOUS TROUBLE

Though he was successful enough to start making good on his monetary debts, Stevie was downright passionate about repaying the emotional and artistic debts he had accrued on his climb to the top. The Carnegie Hall show gave Stevie the chance to repay his parents by showing them that he had indeed made good. In his whacked-out rock-and-roll reality, being with his folks at his party was a way of finally inviting them into his home, a chance to prove to them that he loved them, an opportunity for him to make up for his failures as a son and their shortcomings as parents. For Big Jim and Martha, being honored guests of their son's was flattering, yet strange. The boy was a star, but he seemed to be missing something. He was rich and famous, yet he looked lost to them, with that glazed expression. Maybe he was having a hard time holding his liquor. Something was wrong about the whole deal. They just couldn't put their finger on it.

Stevie had reached out to Jimmie by inviting him to perform with him onstage at the most triumphant gig of his life. As his reputation grew, Stevie was able to take his big brother off the pedestal that he had put him on, and actually play guitar with him as an equal for the first time in his life. There was still tension between them as professionals, but as brothers, Stevie swore that he could tell Jimmie was finally enjoying his company.

A month later, there was a chance to pay homage to some of his other musical gurus in a setting even more intimidating than Carnegie Hall. Double Trouble was on a tour of Australia, and had just finished three consecutive sold-out nights at the Sydney Opera House, when Stevie got word that he was invited to pick up an award in Memphis. Nothing, no tour, no amount of acclaim, no fat guarantee was going to stop him from getting it.

The fifth annual W. C. Handy National Blues Awards had two prizes to hand out to Stevie Ray Vaughan — Entertainer of the Year and Blues Instrumentalist of the Year. It was the first time in the history of the event that a white person had won either category. For Stevie, this was better than the Nobel Prize. The band interrupted the Australian swing and flew to Memphis. They checked into the Peabody Hotel, where Tommy developed an obsession for the marching ducks that are paraded into the lobby of the ornate hotel every day. "I'd like to shoot one and take it home for Thanksgiving," he repeated over and over.

The Handy Awards ceremony at the Orpheum Theater climaxed with an all-star picking session on B. B. King's classic "Every Day I Have the Blues," during which Stevie was uncharacteristically subdued. How could he help it? He was surrounded by stars, the *real* stars — Albert King, cats who actually played with Howlin' Wolf and rode in cars with Muddy Waters. He was humbled. He felt shy and alone on the stage of the Memphis theater. He kept his head down, focusing on the right hand feeling up the strings, just like he was little Stevie all over again back at Antone's, trying to cop a new lick or two from one of these gentlemen. He was a blues guitar player. These guys *were* the blues.

(He didn't grovel at the feet of all black musicians, by any means. Once, at a party in Austin, he had gone up to meet the pop sensation Prince, who was sitting in a chair surrounded by security guards, valets, and assistants. Stevie was so put off by the scene that he sneaked up behind the entourage, leaned over a table, and blurted, "Yeah, you might be the Prince, but I'm the King Bee!")

If the Handy Awards signified a genuine sense of worth to Stevie Ray Vaughan, they underscored the struggle he had in dealing with his success as a white man playing black music. Stevie was making more money and selling more records than Muddy or Howlin' Wolf sold. As Stevie moved up to the rock arena high life, he fretted about his ability to play and feel the music he was raised on in clubs. Rich folks, so the old saw went, could neither play nor understand the true blues experience. Homesick James Williamson, an obscure Chicago veteran, summed up the resentment, when he was asked about this young turk Stevie Ray

Vaughan. "He's a disgrace to the human race," Williamson complained. Vaughan's guitar style, he insisted, was "too loud and disrespectful."

Most black musicians didn't share Williamson's opinion. Unlike Led Zeppelin and ZZ Top and other rock bands who copped black material without acknowledging the source, Stevie went out of his way to credit his teachers and his teachers' teachers.

B. B. King was especially pleased that the young fellow had won the Handy Awards. Stevie reminded him of many of his own idols — Blind Lemon Jefferson, Lonnie Johnson, Django Reinhart, T-Bone Walker, Charlie Christian — people that he had looked up to but could never duplicate. King was grateful for what Stevie was doing for blues, too, making it more popular than ever among young people. "He was sorta like the rocket booster that you put on the spaceship to make it go a little further," he explained.

But when Stevie buttonholed King backstage, he didn't want to talk guitars. He wanted to talk about maintaining his sanity. How the hell did B.B. manage to stay on the road for most of his adult life without getting messed up, strung out, or dead?

"A man doesn't have to get high off of other things to play well," a ponderous King later reflected. "A man can get as high as he wants to just off the music. We talked about that. When we was talking about it, there was a little something happening at that time that made us discuss it," he said, without alluding to the specifics of the low-down tendencies Stevie was showing around his professional peers.

King had a right to wax philosophical. With the exception of an expansive paunch, he appeared none the worse for wear despite a relentless regimen of playing 350 dates a year. He knew the life well enough that he recognized the musical ambiguities that go along with live performance. Stevie's Hendrix predilection was a plus in his book. "A lot of blues purists don't accept me," he said.

I'm not accepted in the world of rock and roll or jazz. I'm just B. B. King. The reason for that is I don't do a lot of the things that a blues player is supposed to do. . . . It's not because I can't have it or I'm not allowed to have it. It's because I haven't had the desire to take a drink. If you've seen a Scotch bottle around here, I didn't open it. Even the style — my butt is not out. I've got it covered. I don't mind wearing a shirt and tie. I guess I got too much gut up here to wear a vest. In so many words I'm trying to say a lot of the things we do is not the way everybody thinks a blues guitarist should be.

Stevie did not quite get the message.

During the Australia/New Zealand blitz an encounter with Eric Clapton once again opened his eyes to the thin blue line he was walking. "He was leaving the hotel [in Sydney] and I went out to talk with him, hangover and the whole bit, you know? He was sober, of course, and was really calm the whole time while I sat there downing two, three shots of Crown. And he just sort of wisely looked at me and said, 'Well, sometimes you gotta go through that, don'cha?' He didn't tell me what to do. He told me how it had been for him."

Albert King continued to weigh in, too, trying to get Stevie to get a handle on himself. "You get high when you're working 'cause you're having too much fun and you don't see the people fuckin' you around." This warning gave Stevie pause. "You wake up one day back in the clubs without a whole lot to show for what you've been through," King concluded wearily.

It was a routine now, this strange world so out of perspective. Hotel rooms, guitars, tour buses, limos, dressing rooms, soundchecks, interviews, jets, shows, radio stations, handshakes, deli platters, charters, parties, Crown. Coke. Lots of it. Mounds of it. Sparkling piles of pretty powder. Go for days, if he wanted. Play. Keep going. Stevie Ray's savior, time and again, was Tommy. He was his main man. He was his sidekick. He was willing to go with him to score if they needed some. And they always needed some. He was his surrogate big brother. "Tommy lived with Stevie Ray Vaughan," recalled road manager Jim Markham. "He called him every day of his life. He did everything Stevie did. . . . If Stevie went to an interview, Tommy did too. If Stevie got fucked up, so did Tommy."

"Stevie would have been dead a long time ago if it hadn't been for Tommy," said Keith Ferguson. "He'd listen to Tommy. Tommy had been there and back. He knew to say 'Don't do that, you'll fuck up, you'll get hurt.' Everybody that doesn't play thinks Tommy was such a fuckup, but Stevie could learn from Tommy getting burned. He remembered all that shit — that acid's weirder on you than coke."

As his personal habits were egging him on into the abyss, Stevie Ray's professional relationship with Classic Management grew more strained. Edi Johnson flew back to Austin with Stevie before the band returned to Australia and New Zealand. Ever ready to acknowledge his musical debts, he found it impossible to deal with the business end. He didn't understand everything about the books, but no one would explain it to him either. OK, if he needed $5,000, he'd get it, and they took care of him and the band on the road, treated them first-class all the way, but he didn't like the talk about Frances wanting her investment back and how they were actually in the red. How could he be losing money when thousands of people were paying ten to twenty bucks to see him perform every night? He didn't dig this kind of treatment. Once again, Edi tried to mediate between client and manager. The strain was getting to everybody. "You need to sit down and talk with Chesley, air out what you're thinking," she advised him. Back at the office, Edi was chewed out for trying to intervene. Chesley made it plain that he did not want to be Stevie's minder. If Edi wanted to baby-sit, then fine. He had a job to do and nothing, not even the rising tide of dissension would get in the way.

Stevie resented Chesley's decision-making style. It was *his* career. He had a right to know what was going on. He wanted a sympathetic ear when he complained about the demands being placed on him and the band. He wanted someone who understood him as a person, who understood his music. The hair on the back of Stevie's neck bristled whenever he heard Chesley shout, "Play da blooze" in that caustic Irish accent. It had never been a sweetheart deal, he reminded himself. Before he'd even signed his deal with Epic, Stevie had asked several well-to-do friends for a loan so he could buy his way out of Classic Management.

The band had accrued a sizable tab in the forms of salaries, per diems, and travel expenses over the first three years of their agreement. At the same time, the overhead had become so massive that it was eating up earnings and then some. There were dozens of mouths to feed. Several current and past employees filed lawsuits against Stevie, the band, and Classic Management. Among them were Richard Mullen for back payment of engineering fees and Cutter Brandenburg for the share of points on *Texas Flood* that Stevie had promised him.

He forgot about all the business entanglements and endless career demands whenever he managed to squeeze in what little downtime he had at Antone's. Other clubs had come and gone, but Clifford's place was still home. More often than not, someone like Denny, Angela, or Derek would be working the stage, a perfect excuse for reconnecting with the people and the music that made it all worth it in the first place. Lenny and he were treated like honored guests there, double shots of Crown Royal materializing at their table without their even having to ask. And when it got late and someone inspiring was playing, he'd jump up and head for the stage, especially if one of his idols or Tommy or Chris was spotted in the building. That was a sign that the guy in the shorty kimono was about to make an appearance.

For all of his musical sophistication, Stevie was in many ways still a little kid when it came to trusting people, giving away money to the down-and-out who could hit him with a moving story, accepting the advice of anyone with an opinion about him and his career, and going on shopping sprees in airport gift shops. While he was touring Australia, a stranger sold him a handful of stones that he said were opals. Stevie later realized that the stones were bogus. He telephoned Edi Johnson and complained about being burned. "Well, Stevie, what do you want me to do?" Edi replied. "Fly to Australia and have an argument with the guy who sold them to you?"

A man in his position, it slowly began to dawn on him, needed to realize everything came with strings. One fan gave Stevie a Doberman puppy. Stevie took the dog back to his house and was immediately cornered by the snarling critter. A few days later, the person who had given him the dog called up to ask when Stevie was going to rent a two-bedroom house so they could live together.

Then there was the time when Isaac Tigrett, one of the owners of the Hard Rock Cafe, lured Stevie up to a party at his penthouse apartment in the Stoneleigh Hotel in Dallas with the promise of presenting him with a Gibson Flying V guitar. Not just any Flying V, but one that had belonged to Jimi Hendrix. Stevie showed up at the party loaded. He said hello to Dan Ackroyd and the other guests who'd assembled there, and sure enough, out came the Flying V. He held it like a fragile piece of china, sat down, and blowing on the strings, slurred, "Watch, man. It'll bring life back to 'em." He began to play, bending over in concentration, completely oblivious to the rest of the room. When it came time to leave, Stevie thanked Tigrett for the gift, and headed for the door. Tigrett stopped him. He had only wanted to show Stevie the guitar. He wasn't giving it to him. After a big row, Stevie gave him back the guitar while spewing "fuck you"s as he angrily stamped out the door.

His willingness to trust people's good intentions may have been a weakness. But one of his greatest strengths as an entertainer was the way he related to the public, his fans. He was gracious and accommodating to anyone who approached him, always willing to sign an autograph, listen to a story, or stand for a snapshot. He relished personal contact with those who liked his music; he liked to hear that his music made others feel so good. Part of the process of getting used to the Life, though, was learning to separate the adulation from the bullshit. "All the people mean well — 99 percent of them, anyway," he said. "Then there's the people that just want to impress their girlfriends. If they really were my friends to begin with, it's good to see them. But if it's somebody who really took a dump on me every time they got the chance, I'll be happy to be their friend now. Just don't come up to me with your girlfriend, because I'll make the truth real clear."

He was good to his fans because he was the ultimate fan, had been ever since he'd been captivated by those first crazy sounds blaring out of his transistor radio and record player. One of Stevie's first heroes was Lonnie Mack, whose 1963 hit "Wham" fired Stevie's passion for the electric guitar. He finally met the Memphis man one night at the Rome Inn in 1980. Lonnie had come to Austin looking for musicians for his new band, which he wanted to call South. It blew Stevie's mind standing up onstage, looking over at the door. He'd just started the rumbling intro of "Wham" when he saw the big guy himself walk in. It was a gas.

Since he felt Double Trouble was beginning to percolate, Stevie passed when Lonnie offered him a slot in his band. Five years later, though, he jumped at the chance to produce Lonnie's album for Alligator Records. It could have been an uncomfortable arrangement, considering the fact that the president of Alligator, Bruce Iglauer, had declined an opportunity to sign Stevie because he was white. Since then, Iglauer had broken his own color barrier by signing Johnny Winter before Mack and had begun to appreciate Stevie's work. "In retrospect, he had very big ears. He had grown into the potential." Besides all that, Iglauer knew that Stevie's participation would help sell records.

Stevie wasn't at all uncomfortable with the arrangement. For him it was realizing a dream. "The way I look at it, we're just giving back to him what he did for all of us," Stevie said, talking about the guitarist who hadn't had a hit record in twenty years. "It wasn't a case of me doing something for him — it was me getting a chance to work with him. You know, the way people come into your life when you need them, it's wonderful and it happens in so many ways. It's like having an angel. Somebody comes along and helps you get right."

Despite the obvious love and respect the two guitarists had for each other, the recording setup made Iglauer nervous. "The whole session came together in a weird, casual kind of way," he recalled. Actually, the "weird, casual" vibe of the four-week sessions at Cedar Creek studios in South Austin was normal in light of the personnel. The burly, bearded Mack was an avowed iconoclast, a blue-collar rock-and-roll antihero who didn't care for drugs and had rejected celebrity status in favor of working the roadhouses around his native Indiana and Cincinnati. Stevie was a young superstar, with an entourage of coked-up buddies. "They were always taking a lot of breaks," observed Iglauer with a touch of cynicism.

Stevie's title of coproducer was largely ceremonial. He made it clear from the start that Lonnie was the boss. "They were his tunes, and I just tried to help him by doing the best I could to do what he wanted to do with the record," he later told *Guitar World*. "A lot of producing is just being there, and with Lonnie, just reminding him of his influence on myself and other guitar players. Most of us got a lot from him. Nobody else can play with a whammy bar like him — he holds it while he plays and the sound sends chills up your spine. You can't do that with a Stratocaster. I just don't want to sound like I was trying to direct the record."

Mack preferred recording songs in one take, sometimes improvising lyrics while the instrumental tracks were being polished. The only time the producer would nitpick was when he was recording his own guitar fills. Fueled by his desire to provide a perfect complement to Mack's twanging, and a plentiful supply of Budweiser, Crown Royal, and the stimulating powder that seemed to materialize whenever he did, Stevie spent hours upon hours trying to dub in his parts, using a scaled-down version of his usual amp setup. Even so, his work on the album had a fresh, one-take feeling to it and great clarity. He even got down-home country, playing his National Steel guitar on one cut, "Oreo Cookie Blues." During the entire process, he kept contact with Iglauer to a minimum, hardly acknowledging him. He may have been jacked up and blitzed, but he didn't forget.

Although expenses were well below the recording budgets Stevie was now accustomed to, Iglauer fretted about cost overruns. "It went way over budget and I thought it would never recoup." The fretting was unnecessary. *Strike Like Lightning* outsold all of Alligator's previous releases when it hit the streets in April of 1985, turning more than 70,000 units. Neither of Mack's two subsequent albums for Alligator sold half as many. "It makes me wonder what the record could have done if Stevie's picture would have been on the cover," mused Iglauer.

It was much easier for Stevie to deal with his musical responsibilities than his personal ones. No matter how many times he was unfaithful to her, Stevie was still very much attached to the tough broad who got her kicks keeping her mate guessing. After finishing the Lonnie Mack project, Stevie and Lenny Vaughan finally took a vacation alone together, going to the Caribbean resort of St. Croix, in the Virgin Islands. It was the honeymoon they never had and an attempt to patch things up between them. He hadn't had a real break in three years. She hadn't either, as far as she was concerned. But kicking back in the idyllic setting took some getting used to. He had a musician's moontan, not a suntan. What was he going to do? Try to put some color on the peacock on his chest?

"He handled it," Lenny said afterward. "I couldn't believe it. No 7-Elevens, no cassettes." But his obsession shadowed his every step. "Of course, he talked music," she said. "The, uh, work mode was always there. He gets that look, you know?"

Certainly, Stevie wasn't the easiest guy to live with. For one thing, he wasn't around much. Even when he was around, he was still possessed by the guitar more than he was with Lenny. His fingers twitched involuntarily when he didn't have one in hand. He was constantly sketching pictures of his ideal designs. "He even played in his sleep, saying things like, 'That B note should not be flat,' " Lenny Vaughan recalled. "He figured out how to play a Hendrix lick in a dream."

When they married in 1979, Stevie didn't have much else but his guitar and Lenny. Stevie hadn't married Lenny because she was a nice quiet girl. He had married her because she was tough and independent enough, he felt, both to keep his life in order and live her own. He needed Lenny to look after him, and she tried to do just that. She had once paid the bills with her day job. She still sat in on Stevie's business meetings. She was wary of Frances and Chesley from the beginning, partially out of jealousy perhaps, but also because she was honestly concerned that Classic Management was bleeding Stevie, spending money that didn't need to be spent and hitting him with bills that were really the responsibility of the organization.

"She always felt that Stevie should have been taken care of better, that management was supposed to provide the artist with a comfortable living so that he can do his art," said Edi Johnson.

When Stevie began to make money, things changed. Suddenly, he was the one who was taking care of Lenny, not the other way around. Lenny was jealous of the people around Stevie, and angry at him for ignoring her. She thought he still acted as if he were crashing in Austin, using his cash for splurges while others paid his bills. What about that red '75 Chevy Caprice Classic with white leather seats and his name stenciled on the driver's door that he paid for with $5,000 cash? Or him offering twice what they were asking for a belt buckle with five playing cards depicting a full house? He could be a saint of generosity, but he couldn't get it together to buy a refrigerator or a house. It was always rent, borrow, or lease, like he thought it all would end tomorrow. Living on the edge like he'd always done was much more to his liking. If he wanted to prove his love to Lenny, he'd rather give her a gram than a Frigidaire. "He wouldn't give me money, but he would give me drugs," Lenny remembered. "I would say, 'Here's what we'll do. Every time you get yourself a gram, instead of getting me one we could put that money in a savings account. . . .' He got really angry with me when I suggested that."

Before *Texas Flood*, Stevie tried to involve Lenny more directly in the band business by putting her in charge of T-shirt sales at gigs. Chesley Millikin nixed the plan in favor of hiring an experienced merchandiser. "She was absolutely and totally unreliable," he said, citing the time Stevie deposited his first $5,000 check into a bank account only to have it cleaned out by Lenny. "I sat Stevie down one time and said, 'Your wife is not acting in your best interests and I am,' " Chesley Millikin said. "In a way, she was good for him. He believed in love and marriage and all of that, it was just very hard for him to deal with. She pushed him. His moments in the sun were always clouded by her actions." Once she called Stevie's hotel room in Norway and Frances answered the phone. Lenny went ballistic. "I just want you to know I just flushed a baby down the toilet," she screamed hysterically when Stevie grabbed the telephone receiver.

"Chesley didn't want her to have her hand in it in any way," said Lenny's friend Pammy Kay. "He wanted her to be a stupid little bimbo. He considered her a troublemaker." Lenny's own unpredictable tendencies made it worse. She once missed four consecutive flights to a Fourth of July concert in Minnesota, which Stevie blamed on management instead of her. Why wasn't Classic taking care of her travel plans? he hollered over the phone.

Stevie's fame and all the support it required — the managers, roadies, guitar techs, security, and everyone else whose jobs depended on him — left Lenny feeling like a leftover groupie. "I remember one day I wanted to slap her," said Sue Sawyer, who was the West Coast publicist for Epic Records. "Stevie was doing press all day at the Greek Theater. It was almost sad because I could see she married this guy and his career had taken off and she was left on the outside. He had things to do. She wanted something to do. So she kept coming in the room, asking, 'Where's my husband? What's he doing?' I had to keep telling her, 'Go sit down, go away, he'll be done in a while, be patient.' "

Sawyer had seen the behavior before. Lenny was just more dramatic. "She didn't really care what any of us thought, so she didn't have a problem marching into a room in her loud voice and asking for her husband."

The long absences from each other bred suspicion and doubt. Stevie was always on the road, and Lenny wasn't cut out to be a sailor's wife. Stevie was as jealous as she was and demanded fidelity on Lenny's part, even though, true to his profession's moral code, he fooled around constantly. Lenny still felt betrayed about the Playboy pinup in Dallas who allegedly gave him an infectious disease that he passed on to her several years before. They had problems communicating. Lenny told Stevie to hold his guitar while he talked with her. It helped him focus. She took to writing down what she wanted to tell Stevie. He wrote down his responses. "He wrote much better than he talked," she surmised. "It wasn't a rap, it was what he was feeling."

They actually communicated best over the phone, ringing up four-digit monthly bills as they chatted with each other on an almost daily basis. The phone calls exasperated some members of Stevie's crew. One minute he would be determined to lay down the law to Lenny, then he would talk to her and change his mind completely. Sometimes, he called up and asked Lenny to put their dog T-Bone on the phone. Stevie enjoyed barking long distance with the runt of the litter that Frances Carr gave him.

When he was in Austin, Lenny tried to make the most of her limited time with Stevie. To separate her husband from his fellow road dogs, she moved their belongings to Lakeway, a planned resort development on

Lake Travis, thirty miles west of Austin, then to Volente, a settlement across the lake, where they took up residence in a building that once housed a restaurant. By staying out of town, she reasoned, she could keep him at arm's length from bad influences. It had the reverse effect. A visitor who happened to be packing some uncut blow would simply stay over until it was gone. Sometimes, Edi Johnson would have to spend an entire day with Stevie and Lenny, just to get Stevie to sign a check, a formality he studiously avoided as long as he could.

Stevie told Lenny that she was always welcome to come on the road, but that meant long hours of hanging around, hearing about everybody bitching behind her back, while Stevie was treated like nobility. She hated the shitty looks she was always getting from the roadies. Who did they think they were anyhow?

The road did have its small advantages, especially when it took them to LA, New York, and the occasional foreign destination. They never had to clean up their room on the road. The meals were paid for. It was cool getting the star treatment all the time, which included the snow flurries that seemed to follow the entourage wherever they went. That was always fun. Expensive, maybe, but it was never much trouble getting more money.

For all the good times that rocking and rolling all night and partying every day implied, too many jags with an ounce of 90 percent pure Peruvian flake could prove fatal. That realization was driven home when Stevie's guitar procurer and good friend Charley Wirz died suddenly of a burst aorta. The Vaughan brothers played "Amazing Grace" at his funeral. Stevie and Lenny both knew they'd jacked themselves up to excessively dangerous speeds and came near hitting the wall on several occasions. They just didn't want to do anything about it.

"Right now, for us, it's like there's no perspective," Lenny said at the time. "Perspective is hard when you don't even have a place to sit down and think about what has happened to you. You're not going to believe this, but the other day I found a quotation I had written on the bottom of my corn-bread recipe. It was something about success not being a destination but a journey. That may sound stupid, but it's almost true for us." It wasn't an adventure anymore. It was a job. "You get kind of possessed. It's all-consuming and the demands continue to grow," she said with a sigh. "So he just keeps going."

As much as she tried to fight it, Stevie didn't belong to just her anymore. He belonged to everyone. "She took care of him in her way. She wanted him to have a home," said Nick Ferrari, who lived with the couple for a few months before Stevie's career took off. "Stevie loved her. I don't know how, but he did. Lenny had this whole deal about visions that this was going to be good luck or bad luck. And they believed in karma. Karma was big back then. There was the theory that they both had been black once. I think he finally saw the light, that he was just a regular person who had hangups like all the rest of us had." The problem was, the life he was leading was anything but normal.

After the vacation, Double Trouble flew to Japan for six nights of concerts, followed by more domestic touring. "I don't remember anything about Japan," Tommy later confessed. "I was too messed up." Just as in his relationship with Lenny, Stevie began to feel that the music was getting kind of stale. He could fill up any empty space by himself by reeling off a flurry of licks, but he longed to add another dimension to the music that he'd been missing since the old Triple Threat Revue days. The four years he'd been with Chris and Tommy was the longest period of time he'd ever stuck with one lineup, a lineup that was so in-synch, "He'd set the tone and we'd just follow," remembered Chris Layton. But the trio format that had once liberated him was beginning to lose its spark. The Carnegie Hall concert convinced him to make some adjustments.

Stevie thought what the band needed was another guitarist, someone like Denny Freeman, whom he played with in the Cobras. Ever since he'd recorded *Couldn't Stand the Weather*, he felt the need for a supporting guitar. His own guitar and vocal tracks were usually recorded separately in the studio, but when he reprised the material in concert, he sometimes found it difficult to sing and play those parts at the same time. With a rhythm player or a second lead to fall back on, he could concentrate on singing his lines without having to worry about fluffing the musical fills. At his urging, Derek O'Brien, the Dallas guitarist who was leading the Antone's house band, was hired to play four Texas dates as the fourth member of Double Trouble in anticipation of preproduction for album number three.

The move was made over Chesley Millikin's loud protestations. Granted, Stevie needed something to expand his musical horizons. But not another guitar player, not when Junior could not be improved upon. "I met Derek O'Brien in the parking lot of [Austin's] Palmer Auditorium and said, 'No.' I refused to handle him in the band," Millikin said. "To me it was a totally unnecessary expense and made absolutely no sense." Stevie was a "media darling," and Millikin's job was to protect that franchise.

Stevie thought Derek made a lot of sense and was angry with his handler. But he acquiesced in the end, compromising with Chesley by adding another instrument. He wanted to hire Reese Wynans as keyboard player. Reese was road-tested and album-ready, with a string of credits that included stints with Captain Beyond, Jerry Jeff Walker, Joe Ely, and most recently Delbert McClinton. Stevie was a fan of Jimmy McGriff, Jimmy Smith, Groove Holmes, and the fat sound of the Hammond B-3 organ, an electric instrument that he said "sounded like wood." Wynans was hired after the tall, quiet-spoken figure jammed with the band in Austin. "Now that we've got Reese, we're gonna be Serious Trouble," Stevie crowed.

With two albums under their belts, Stevie, Chris, and Tommy had developed strong, specific ideas about how Double Trouble should sound on record. The Epic brass, mindful of the strong sales of the band's previous releases, accommodated them with the financial wherewithal and artistic license to do it their way. This time, the album would be made at the forty-eight-track Dallas Sound Labs, with additional over-dubbing at the sixteen-track Riverside Sound in Austin. Double Trouble would produce themselves with Richard Mullen as coproducer. Three and a half weeks of solid studio time were blocked out so the equipment could stay put without being disturbed. A new monitor system was installed in the studio and the two Vibroverbs, the twin Super Reverbs, the Leslie, and every other amp that he owned were brought in specifically to afford Stevie and the band the luxury of recording together in the same room without needing headphones. They weren't going to rush this one.

Stevie was excited about the approach. "It's helping us a lot because we've gotten to work on individual technique and things, so that we've come down to playing more like we wanted to play in the first place," he said.

We've always been forced to work a lot faster than this before, and we play so many gigs on the road that we don't have the time to listen to ourselves as closely as we should all the time. You go and play for an hour and a half and then [it is] off to the next place, and you don't get a chance to catch what's changing in your music, what's working and what's not working. We love to play shows — don't misunderstand me on that — but it's hard to ask, how did we improve, or did we? We have fun when we play, but the studio is a blessing that a lot of people forget about.

The leisurely pace of the recording time turned out to be a curse, not a blessing. "The routine was to go to the studio, do dope, and play Ping-Pong," said Byron Barr, the roadie who worked as assistant to the band in the studio.

It was pathetic. They'd be there from eleven A.M. to five A.M. and four hours of that, they'd be doing dope. It was out of control. And the band got on my ass.

I mean, my role became Drink Boy. Which is OK when

you're in a lackey role, but I don't think it should be primary. The Crown Royal had to be *here* on Stevie's amp, and Tommy's screwdrivers had to be in the exact right spot when they got ready to cut a song. Or if they had to stop because a drink wasn't there, *I* was fucking up. Man, I got in their shit. I said, "Man, you guys, you're blowing it, man. That's all you care about is It [their code word for cocaine], and you ain't pulling it off."

The band was doing everything possible to avoid the fact that in spite of everything that had been done to make the recording go smoothly, they couldn't manufacture inspiration. The ideas didn't flow for Stevie at all. He would take a lead break and someone would say, "Man, that sounds just like such-and-such." The more frustrated he got, the more cocaine he whiffed. He experimented with different kinds of alcohol to give his voice a different quality. When he wasn't in the studio, Stevie holed up in his room smoking, drinking, and doing more dope.

"Ah, I've seen it before," Chesley Millikin observed to Byron Barr when informed of the decadent scene in the studio. "Next, it'll be heroin to kill the pain."

Though he didn't start shooting junk, Stevie knew he was consumed with "It" and drinking way too much. He even alluded to it publicly, albeit cryptically, in a *Guitar World* interview. "Some big changes have taken place. I haven't resolved all my problems, but I'm working on it. I can see the problems at least, and that takes a lot of pressure off. I've been running from myself too long and now I feel like I'm walking with myself."

He just refused to confront himself.

Stevie realized that his best work was essentially playing live even in the studio, but as the amount of drugs escalated, so did the complexity of the approach needed to re-create that simple and direct feeling. Typical was the roundabout way they came to cut "Empty Arms," a Stevie original that the band had recorded during the *Couldn't Stand the Weather* sessions but didn't make it onto the album.

"We had been doing it faster and in a different feel," Stevie later explained in *Musician* magazine. "I played drums, Tommy played bass, and I went back and played a rhythm part. Then I played an organ part on my guitar through a Leslie, sang it, played the solo, and then had the keyboard player play a piano part on it. We actually recorded the song in C and it was real slow . . . so we sped it up to D with a Unispeed. The whole song is all in different keys to record things. But my solo and my guitar parts are all in D and I sang in D. But just to find things we would go back and forth between the two."

Songwriting never came easily to Stevie, especially as his mind became increasingly obliterated by Crown and coke. Searching for new material, he called on his old friend and former band mate Doyle Bramhall. After the Nightcrawlers and his marriage had both disintegrated in Austin, Doyle had moved back to the Dallas–Fort Worth area, playing drums and singing with Freddie King, Lou Ann Barton, Johnny Reno, and other blues bands before starting a band of his own. Doyle had toned down his own act of shooting heroin, boozing, and carrying on like a wild hyena when he met Barbara Logan, the woman who convinced him to go straight. Stevie still looked up to Doyle and respected the fact that he'd sworn off drinking. Doyle was only too happy to oblige Stevie with the right kind of lyrics for the melodies he was working on.

Doyle's lyrics were straightforward and simple and the music was highly derivative of the shuffles, breakdowns, and ballads both of them had been playing and listening to all their lives. His material fit Stevie like a glove, and the comfort Stevie felt working with someone who was almost part of his family was obvious. Doyle volunteered two songs for the new album, "Change It" and "Lookin' out the Window," which he wrote while looking out his window watching his partner Barbara work in her garden. Doyle's songs hit the note, especially after saxman Joe Sublett, Stevie's mate from the Cobras, added rhythm honks to the latter song.

"Say What!," whose only lyrics were the chant "Soul to soul," the inspiration for the album title, played on the expanded band's strengths. The tune was built around a funky groove that sounded more than a little like Jimi Hendrix's "Rainy Day, Dream Away," due in no small part to the underwater sound of the guitar, an effect created by the very same wah-wah pedal Hendrix used on his recording of "Up from the Sky" (and which Jimmie Vaughan had passed along to Stevie).

There was still plenty of gritty material to satisfy traditionalists, particularly "Ain't Gone 'n' Give Up on Love," which once again borrowed heavily from Albert King, with enough flash and fire to satisfy the guitar-god worshipers. The Earl King composition "Come On," reinterpreted by Hendrix as "Come On (Part II)" was updated by Stevie and released as "Come On (Part III)." Stevie's most emotional composition for the album was "Life Without You," a somber anthem of remembrance, dedicated to the memory of Charley Wirz, the guitar dealer from Dallas who had supported Stevie with instruments and a compassionate ear for many years. His musical epitaph became a part of every Double Trouble performance, inspiring Stevie to put aside his guitar playing and speak directly to the audience in free-form raps that touched on love, respect, and racism.

After the lengthy, difficult go in the studio, Stevie was ready to hit the road again. He'd hardly resumed touring when he made a brief appearance in front of 30,000 baseball fans who showed up at the Houston Astrodome on April 10 for the opening day of the 1985 National League season. He had been asked to perform the "Star Spangled Banner" at the event, which also celebrated the twentieth birthday of the world's first domed stadium. He didn't know the song real well, and he wasn't much of a baseball fan, but he was willing to oblige. Jimi had played the national anthem before; it would be a goof to try it himself.

Baseball great Mickey Mantle was on hand to commemorate the first home run in the stadium, which he'd hit in an exhibition game. Former ballplayers driving Corvettes circled the warning track while elephants marched onto the field. Track star Carl Lewis threw out the ceremonial first pitch. And Stevie Ray Vaughan played an electric, spaced-out version of the national anthem on his guitar.

Unlike with Jimi Hendrix's performance of the "Star Spangled Banner" at Woodstock, the Astrodome crowd was not moved, showering Stevie Ray Rock Star with a round of boos.

Astrodome publicist Molly Glentzer, writing in the *Houston Press*, described the entertainer as barely coherent:

"As Vaughan shuffled back behind home plate, he was only lucid enough to know that he wanted Mickey Mantle's autograph. Mantle obliged. 'I never signed a guitar before.' Nobody asked Vaughan for his autograph. I was sure he'd be dead before he hit 30. (I didn't realize he was 31.)"

Stevie left the building before the second inning of the game, which the Astros lost.

Another promotional appearance turned into an even bigger disaster. When Stevie refused to do an interview at a Philadelphia radio station, the management threatened to pull his records from their playlist and the playlists of the other stations they owned. Chesley finally convinced Stevie to do the interview, but when the DJ asked, "Who do you think you are to blow off an interview with our radio station?" Stevie exploded. "You go straight to fucking Hell," he shouted over the air and stormed out.

Stevie's performances became increasingly erratic. It wasn't that he was fucking up, it was just that he was going through the motions, playing fast and hard but without the soul. The diagnosis was too much of a bad thing. "There were many times when I'd find Stevie absolutely comatose on the couch before a show," Chesley Millikin recalled. "Sometimes I didn't think he could possibly play. But as soon as he hit the stage, he was able to plug himself in and come alive."

Reese Wynans added a great deal to the band's stability onstage and provided a musical safety net for Stevie as the band resumed a relentless touring schedule through the spring. In fact, Reese soon became comfortable enough in the SRV family to start asking questions about how the band business was run and where all the money was going, questions that did not endear him to management. How was Double Trouble making between $5,000 and $25,000 a night and still losing $30,000 a month? "I couldn't believe how naive they all were," he said later. Didn't the band realize who was paying for the limo rides, the chartered planes, the bottles of Moët & Chandon that were being popped over business lunches? Didn't they care? Perhaps, he suggested, an examination of the company books was in order.

Chesley Millikin reacted defensively. The band had run up quite a tab on Frances Carr's account over the years, a sum in excess of $100,000, which they were now balking at repaying, either in installments or in one lump sum. Lenny convinced Stevie the debt didn't need to be settled ever. Frances was born rich. She wasn't hurting. Classic Management was still only pulling down 10 percent off the top and wanted at least 15 percent. Stevie insisted on keeping the band on full salaries even when they were off the road, "scratching their fuckin' arses when other drummers and bass players were driving cabs when they were off the road," according to Millikin.

"They were the ones bleeding him, while they were telling the world how much they loved him and how much they meant to him. What I wanted Stevie to do was get rid of the band. He was griping about the amount of work he was doing. It was fine to gripe about it, but it was necessary to keep this schedule going to keep these fuckers fed."

All Stevie knew was what everyone was telling him. He was the star and the managers worked for him, not the other way around. It was like Lenny said: Frances didn't need the money she said she was owed. She needed to lose money, at least that's what he'd heard when they met. The friction led to the hiring of the New York accounting firm Joseph Rascoff & Co. The New Yorker's performance proved to be less satisfactory than Classic's. After a few months they were replaced by an accountant in Los Angeles the band contracted to keep their financial records. Neither bookkeeper publicly objected to Classic's handling of the band.

If Chesley felt any vindication, it came from Stevie's wheelchairbound father, Jim Vaughan, who took him aside at a concert to speak with him about his boy. "Without you," Big Jim told him, "Stevie would never have gone anywhere."

Life on the road had deteriorated to the point that Jim Markham couldn't even get Stevie out of bed. After futilely calling and knocking one morning, Markham got a maid to unlock the door. Inside he found Stevie and Lenny lying naked on the bed. "Everything else was scattered all around like a tornado had hit. I didn't know if they were dead or not," Markham said. "It took me five minutes, shaking him with my hands, to wake him up. He finally came around and focused his eyes and realized it was me."

"What the fuck are you doing in my room?" Stevie shouted. "Don't bother me. Don't ever do that again. Get the fuck out."

Later that day, Markham gave his notice. "I don't want to be the one to find you dead." Stevie begged him to stay, to the point of giving him a guitar and crying. But Markham was unmoved.

"I've been in this business too long and seen bands come and go, and if you don't take advantage of this opportunity you're going to fall. I'm not gonna be around you for that. I'm not gonna see that happen to you."

On the first of June, Double Trouble returned to Austin for a concert on the banks of Town Lake. The 15,000 fans in the audience cheered Stevie and Double Trouble's performance loud enough to convince the band they were still kicking ass and taking names. Older acquaintances weren't so sure. Mike Steele, who had put Stevie up in his house ten years before, spotted his ex-roommate taking the stage for the closing jam with Lonnie Mack. Steele took up a position on the side of the stage where he could get Stevie's attention. He was proud of all his friend had done, and he wanted to tell him to his face. He waved several times until he thought he caught Stevie's attention, but on second glance, he realized Stevie's eyes were so glassy, so empty and vacant, he was staring right through him. He couldn't have seen him if he'd wanted to. Mike Steele walked off the side of the stage and into the night, softly saying a prayer for his old friend.

14

SEVEN GRAMS A DAY

Get high, everybody, get high. It was a way of life, seven days a week. It was hard, fatiguing, and never-ending, but it sure beat work and wasn't a sellout nine-to-five gig. *Soul to Soul* debuted on the Billboard Top 200 in October. It did not get the same critical response as the first two albums had. *Rolling Stone* critic Jimmy Guterman gave the record a mixed review, saying that although "there's some life left in their blues rock pastiche, it's also possible that they've run out of gas." The album peaked at 34 and hovered on the charts through the summer of 1986, eventually turning gold. But sales did not match *Couldn't Stand the Weather*, suggesting Stevie Ray and Double Trouble were plateauing.

Jimmie's band, the Fabulous Thunderbirds, had heard the same knocks against their albums, which straddled the line between blues and rock and didn't sell that well. The Vaughan brothers were able to commiserate over the difficulties of making records during most of the fall of 1985 when their bands toured together, playing fifty one-nighters from October to the end of the year.

Stevie's sweetest-money date during the tour was a performance at the Fair Park Coliseum in Dallas. Before the concert, Stevie agreed to host a guitar clinic at Arnold and Morgan music store in the Dallas suburb of Garland. The December 15 Sunday-afternoon invitation-only promotion cosponsored by KTXQ-FM was supposed to be a homecoming of sorts. Stevie used to hustle rides to the store billed as the "Musical Supermarket of the Southwest" and spend all day testing out their guitars. Back then he was a bothersome, guitar-possessed kid. Now, he was a famous wreck.

He showed up late and irritated, accompanied by Rene Martinez, a longtime employee at Charley Wirz's guitar shop whom he'd hired as his full-time guitar technician. "The place was packed, ninety percent males, and they were like going to church," recalled Q-102 program director Redbeard.

> They put Stevie in a little anteroom. He was nervous, walking around this tiny room like a caged cat. He seemed to have a hard time concentrating. It was obvious that he was preoccupied with something. He finally came out and sat on this folding chair in the middle of this little riser.
>
> I don't know if the people that put this together didn't tell Stevie that it was a guitar clinic or whether he didn't want to do that, but it turned out to be him just showing some rudimentary guitar things and he went off into a stream-of-consciousness rap and his consciousness was pretty much I think altered by some chemical substances. It was extremely rambling and disjointed. He started saying that he wasn't happy with the *Soul to Soul* album at all, that he was going to remix it, and then he paused and looked very pointedly at the audience and he said, "And it *will* be remixed."
>
> He didn't really tell anybody anything about the guitar and he certainly didn't show anybody anything. He didn't really play. It kind of broke down. It seemed to be over in about twenty minutes. But nobody in the audience razzed him. They were very attentive.

Later that night, from the stage, Stevie continued to ramble, mumbling vaguely political remarks like, "We ain't got no business hurting people" and standard shtick like, "I hope you all have enjoyed yourself tonight. I'm doing the best I can." For their efforts that night, Double Trouble collected $49,000.

Double Trouble and the Fabulous Thunderbirds continued touring through the first two months of 1986, moving on to Australia and New Zealand in March. If there was an unspoken competition between the brothers — Double Trouble was a much stronger draw than the Thunderbirds — they didn't show it. In fact, Jimmie and Stevie had worked up a slick routine for Double Trouble's encore of "Love Struck Baby" during which they'd play a twin-neck guitar together, Stevie working the lower neck while Jimmie wrapped his arms around him from behind, working the upper neck. The symbol of big brother hugging little brother spoke volumes about their relationship.

"I'm so proud of him you can't imagine it," Jimmie told John Parker from the *Adelaide News* during the tour. "He don't owe me nothing. He's already paid me back a thousand times by just being himself. As a guitarist you could say he's in fourth gear and I'm in first. It's really hard to compare us so I don't even try."

Stevie was just as complimentary. "What kills me is when people compare Jimmie and me in our playing," he said. "I play probably 80 percent of what I can play; Jimmie plays one percent of what he knows — he can play just about anything. Once I walked into his house, and he was trying to play bass pedals, guitar, and harmonica, all at the same time."

One of the two most significant stops on the tour was Auckland, New Zealand. The band bus was pulling up to the hotel before the gig when Stevie noticed a drop-dead beautiful young girl walking down the street. He demanded the driver stop the bus and jumped out and ran after her. He returned to the hotel empty-handed and sullen-faced. He didn't find her. But he was definitely obsessed. Before and after the show, all he could talk about was the girl that he'd seen. "I gotta find her. I gotta find her," he said repeatedly. After the show, he was sitting in a lounge in the hotel, knocking back glasses of champagne, when she materialized in the doorway. Stevie's eyes grew large and round as silver dollars. He bared his teeth in a wide smile and walked over and introduced himself, vainly trying to conceal his excitement.

Stevie knew that this meeting was not just some drunken infatuation. It was karma. It was destiny. They were meant to be, this striking female and him. He excused himself from the party and escorted his dream girl up to his hotel room. The next morning, when it was time for the bus to depart, Stevie called downstairs and begged Chesley Millikin to wait another thirty minutes. The band and crew sniggered. Stevie must have been waylaid by another admirer. But they weren't doing the Bad Thang in his hotel room. They had been talking all night, and there was still so much to say.

The girl's name was Janna Lapidus and she was a seventeen-year-old fashion model. Stevie was transfixed by her round eyes, full lips, and translucent olive skin. With her calm, confident, reassuring manner and her exotic Kiwi accent, she represented a whole new world to Stevie, a world of innocence and new ideas. They continued their acquaintance by telephone, first through the remainder of the Australian tour and later by long distance from the States. He'd fallen out of love with Lenny. Now he'd found someone new to fall in love with all over again.

Getting lovestruck was a diversionary tactic. In spite of rave reviews and sold-out houses, band and management were splitting apart before everyone's eyes. The other significant date on the Australian tour was in the west coast town of Perth. It was there that Chesley Millikin decided to jump off the bus before it crashed. Classic Management would cease representing Stevie Ray Vaughan and Double Trouble effective June 1, 1986. A lawyer was hired to make the split official. Millikin recommended Al DeMarino as the right guy to take over the management duties for Stevie. DeMarino had been the band's A&R rep at Epic when *Texas Flood* was released by CBS and was the former manager of Sly and the Family Stone. On their return from Australia, Stevie met with De-Marino in New York at the Fifth Avenue apartment belonging to Frances Carr's mother. At the meeting, Stevie was visibly stoned and DeMarino demanded too big a cut. The deal collapsed on the spot. But there was another out.

Booking agent Alex Hodges had shut down Empire the year before and moved to Los Angeles to become an agent with International Creative Management, ICM, one of the biggest booking agencies in the nation. At ICM, Hodges represented Stevie and a number of other artists. When Stevie finally secured the legal clearance to break from Classic Management and eliminated DeMarino from consideration, he asked Hodges to help draw up a list of prospective managers. Hodges produced eleven names.

"No, that's twelve," Stevie corrected Alex. "You're on that list, too." Almost by default, Hodges won the job as personal manager of Stevie Ray Vaughan and Double Trouble, resigning his position at ICM, and handing over booking chores to his colleague Alex Kochan.

One of the main reasons Stevie was inclined to hire Hodges was his willingness to listen. He liked Alex's calm demeanor and got along famously with his son, Alex II. Unlike Chesley, Hodges was a Southerner who had been intimate with blues people since the early sixties. Alex agreed the band needed more breaks to keep their sanity and promised they would have a greater voice in important decisions affecting them. His new clients weren't exactly intimidating, but Hodges knew his new job wasn't going to be easy.

Stevie Ray and Double Trouble were a hard-driving road band cut from the same cloth as the Southern rockers on Capricorn Records he'd worked with in the early seventies. Handling a bunch of gonzo musicians, some of them almost permanently blitzed out of their gourds, was nothing new. It was the other baggage they'd brought with them that posed a challenge to Hodges. The numbers didn't lie. Double Trouble was in deep financial trouble. The albums were generating some income. So was the placement of songs on movie soundtracks like the brat-pack film *Sixteen Candles*, Ron Howard's *Gung Ho*, and *Back to the Beach*, in which Stevie appeared as himself playing the instrumental "Pipeline" with Dick Dale, the King of the Surf Guitar. The song not only made it onto the movie's soundtrack but was released as a single. But the band still owed Classic Management in excess of $100,000 in unpaid personal loans from the early years. Lawsuits were pending not only with Cutter Brandenburg and Richard Mullen but with songwriter Bill Carter, all of them seeking moneys they were owed. Stevie's biggest complaint about Chesley's management style had been that Chesley forced the band to work too much. Ironically, one of the first things Hodges did was to recommend that the band book a series of concerts. The boys were deep in the hole, they needed money, and the quickest way they could generate cash was by playing music in front of as many fans as possible.

By the spring of 1986, Stevie was little more than a coke-sniffing, whiskey-chugging, guitar-playing automaton. The easiest way to handle him was to make him as comfortable as possible, give him whatever he wanted, and make sure he got to the show on time. Unfortunately, Stevie found it all too easy to allow others to support his bad habits, even though he knew he had a problem. He'd started drinking when he was six, sneaking sips from his father's drinks and nips out of the family liquor cabinet. In the ensuing twenty-five years, he had worked his way through the *Physicians' Desk Reference*, dabbling briefly in psychedelics and pot before finding his poisons of preference — alcohol, methamphetamine, and, ultimately, cocaine.

His habits had become almost as legendary as his fret work. He'd always pushed himself, physically and creatively. He was strong as a bull and could put more licit and illicit substances in his body than ten wussies. Being a celebrity only made it worse. No one working for him or around him questioned the baggie of coke he stashed in his boot. So what if he became a *Naked Lunch* variety Coke-noid whose brain worked like a "berserk pinball machine flashing blue and pink lights in an electric orgasm"? Getting high was part of the rock-and-roll life, right?

The abuse got so excessive that doing shit before and after a performance wasn't enough. Roadies improvised ways for Stevie to have easy access to a snort during a show, without the inconvenience of leaving the stage. One method, piling some powder atop the lip of a beer can in order to have a whiff while having a swig, was scrapped because it left a tell-tale white mustache on his upper lip. The most effective plan was dissolving a half gram into a drink, the same method of administration preferred by onetime cocaine enthusiast Sigmund Freud, except that Freud mixed his stimulant with water. Stevie used Crown Royal.

He was out of control. He knew it. Everybody — the band, the crew, management, the record company, his wife, his friends — knew it. No one knew how to stop it. Dozens of people were depending on him for their livelihood. There was no other way to keep everybody in the organization paid and fed than to keep going and stay out on the road. But in order to advance his career and satisfy both the record company and his audience, he had to squeeze in time to make records and find or compose the material for them. He'd somehow managed to juggle his way through three albums and at least five years of constant roadwork, staying one step ahead of himself with his Crown and coke cocktails augmenting the natural high of performing, and by avoiding sleep at all costs. Now, in the summer of 1986, even the superhuman Stevie Ray was cracking under the strain.

Though he had been seeing a lot of Jimmie, his older brother was in no position to help. Jimmie was cutting his own path of destruction with alcohol and pharmaceuticals. On one occasion, he was kicked off an airline flight for making obscene overtures to a flight attendant, and rumors about his other escapades earned the Thunderbirds the nickname the Turdburglars among some band road crews in Great Britain. As with Stevie, there was no way to make Jimmie stop as long as he was able to play his music. Besides, the image of deranged rock-and-roll pirates drinking, drugging, raping, and pillaging their way across the stages and hotel rooms of the world was considered by many to be a romantic notion. Inebriation was a badge of macho courage, not a liability to a real, dedicated rock-and-roll motherhumper.

The situation on the home front was just as grim. During one three-month stretch of touring, Stevie had sent his earnings to Lenny to live on and pay for upkeep on their residence in Travis Heights. When Stevie came back to Austin, the house was padlocked, the electricity had been shut off, the dog was missing, and Lenny was nowhere to be found. She'd squandered his road earnings on dope while running around with other men that one acquaintance glibly described as "police characters."

There was nowhere to seek refuge. Stevie called up his old girlfriend Lindi Bethel, hoping that she would understand. Lindi was sympathetic, but soon grew so tired of Stevie's deranged 3 A.M. ramblings that she changed her telephone number. At one point, Stevie went to visit Keith Ferguson to cry on his shoulder. Keith, who'd left the Thunderbirds under a cloud of controversy, could see that his friend Skeeter was in bad shape. His solution was to take him for a ride over to Austin's East Side, to the house of some Mexican compadres, where a backyard barbecue was in progress. For a few hours at least, the skinny-assed dude who everyone else knew only as Keith's friend played dominos, shot the bull with a bunch of strangers, ate slow-smoked brisket, and reveled in the *simpatico* atmosphere. It was a wonderful respite, being in a place where for once he was Stevie again, not Stevie Ray.

Peace in Austin was well-nigh impossible anymore. His marriage was finished. Going home only made things worse. He didn't even want to talk to Lenny. He needed rest and relaxation away from her, the band, his friends, everyone, with the exception of a sweet costume designer from Canada named Jacqueline he'd been seeing, maybe, and that knockout girl he'd met in New Zealand. He decided to lay low in LA, near Alex Hodges.

He sought shelter at Tim Duckworth's. Duckworth was an old Texas acquaintance who picked guitar, wrote songs, and liked to roar until dawn. He'd run into Stevie at a concert a few months earlier in Austin and told Stevie to give him a call if he was in southern California. When Stevie asked to stay at his place for a few days after the Australian tour, Duckworth gladly put him up. One of the first things he did to take the heat off Stevie was to screen him from Lenny's phone calls, which infuriated Lenny.

Stevie hung around long enough for Duckworth to recognize that his troubles weren't just of the female variety. Anyone could see that Stevie had been pushing himself too hard and was headed over the brink. Duckworth went to Alex Hodges with a proposal. Stevie didn't know it, but he needed Tim as his personal assistant, someone who would stay around him and make sure he'd get to the gig in time with his head screwed on half straight.

Hodges was dubious at first. With Double Trouble's overhead and back bills, the last thing he needed was another mouth to feed on the road. But he listened. "I couldn't dislike the guy," he said. "He convinced me he wanted to take care of Stevie. It didn't look like he was a prodigious abuser. He simply said, 'I'm *really* concerned about Stevie. I'm concerned he's gonna kill himself.' "

Hodges knew that he couldn't give Stevie the sort of personal attention he needed, so he sprang for the bucks and hired Duckworth to take care of his star. Lenny was even more livid. "Stevie hated Tim," she later insisted. "The only reason they hired him was to keep Stevie from me. And I was his wife."

No matter what Stevie thought about his personal assistant, he liked hanging out in LA, which was convenient in light of all the guest sit-ins he was doing. He played the abbreviated guitar lead on "Living in America," the comeback hit single for Soul Brother Number One, James Brown. He later took part in a recording project for Don "Miami Vice" Johnson, probably the goofiest gig he had ever done. At least he wasn't alone: Ron Wood of the Rolling Stones and Dickie Betts, formerly of the Allman Brothers, also lent their names, talents, and credibility to Johnson's vanity record.

The cameos were sandwiched between tours for Stevie and the band. The shows were opened by Bonnie Raitt, with whom he'd developed an intimate friendship, and Robert Cray, who was dying to have Stevie play on his album.

For all his status, Stevie was still in awe of the Hollywood glitterati. After the 1986 Grammys, where the cut "Say What!" from *Soul to Soul* was nominated for "Best Rock Instrumental," he went with Jimmie and Connie Vaughan to the lounge at the Continental Hyatt House to see Kenny Burrell demonstrate why the brothers and Denny Freeman held his records in such high regard. Both Vaughans were impressed enough to introduce themselves and humbly request Burrell's autograph.

Etta James didn't recognize Stevie at all when he came to see her at the Vine Street Bar and Grill a few weeks later. She knew anyone with a purple cape draped around his shoulders was somebody, or at least thought he was, but she didn't put two and two together until her regular audience-participation number, during which she roamed the room, selecting patrons to sing a line or two into the microphone. When she pointed the mike at Stevie, he cut loose in a rich, full-bodied warble that had such warmth and feeling, James jumped back while the house roared their approval. She realized then who Stevie was, called out his name, and handed the mike back to him to sing some more.

On the road, someone gave Stevie the telephone number of Mitch Mitchell, the drummer for the Jimi Hendrix Experience who was living in LA. Stevie called him up and struck up a friendship, stoking his Hendrix obsession. The gear he carried on the road included an artist's portfolio containing blown-up stage shots of himself along with one blowup of Jimi.

In the midst of all the shoulder rubbing and the endless roadwork, pestering calls started coming from the Epic A&R department. A fourth recording was stipulated in Double Trouble's contract with Epic and the time had come for delivery. The answer was a live album. Stevie, Tommy, Chris, and Reese figured that anything would be better than going through the creative torture that they had suffered during the *Soul to Soul* sessions, and Stevie was in a lot worse shape in 1986 than he had been in 1985. Doing it live had been their meat and potatoes from the get-go. They proved it in west Texas biker bars, in Butthole Bill's joint in the piney woods, in Manhattan's classiest midtown venue, and at outdoor mass gatherings in front of fifty thousand roaring fans. What could be simpler?

Live Alive turned out to be the messiest Stevie Ray Vaughan and Double Trouble record of them all. The tip-off should have been the need to do a live album in the first place. Live albums by established major-label acts were considered an easy way out in all but the most exceptional situations. They were fillers, a cheap and efficient means to satisfy contractual obligations without the pressure of providing new material.

The recordings that ultimately comprised *Live Alive* were rife with technical and stylistic defects. Performances recorded at Double Trouble's third Montreux appearance in 1985 were so flawed that the band decided to try again on more familiar turf, in Austin and Dallas. The Austin shows sold out in minutes, as fans showed their support for their hometown hero. Over the course of two nights, almost 4,000 fans watched Stevie struggle to perform, his music so jagged, so jacked up, so meandering and uninventive that it resembled white noise more than guitar pyrotechnics. Perhaps the most telling sign of what was going down behind the scenes was Stevie's rap in the middle of "Life Without You," in which he talked about the need for people getting together and loving one another, while invoking "Africa" as the source of all healing. "We got to figure out the right way to go around and make people not understand their bullshit," he spoke into the microphone. "I might be white, but I ain't stupid. Neither are you." As an indication of how desperate the situation was, the song and the rap were included in the final cut of the album.

The Dallas gig went no better. The band had to face the reality that patching together a live album from substandard gigs was going to be more work than going into the studio in the first place.

On one particular song, Chris Layton was asked to do the impossible and recut his entire drum part, vainly attempting to match his lines to a concert track riddled with fluffs, slips, and bungles. Once studio time to fix the tracks had run out, the band used off-days while on tour to fly to studios for late-night audio-duct-taping sessions. Exhausted, drunk, and stoned, Stevie and Tommy often passed out in the studio while the technician dozed at the board. "It was supposed to be a live album," Tommy recalled, "but we ended up overdubbing just about everything from studio to studio all across America." Engineers were constantly fussing with Stevie and the band over the mixes, vainly trying to capture something that just wasn't there. The project was way over budget, and Epic accountants, lawyers, and A&R staff started leaning heavily on Alex Hodges. Get the album done. Now.

In the midst of all the demands, there were gigs to play and bills to pay and people to see. Stevie insisted on personally answering all his fan mail. He loved for people around him to play their guitars, too, urging on even the rankest amateur with a patience Jimmie would never tolerate. When a kid who'd never played guitar before won a private lesson in a contest sponsored by a local radio station, Stevie invited him into his hotel room and spent an hour coaching and encouraging him, telling him, "C'mon. You can do it. It's fine."

The professional demands were aggravated by his tendency to push himself to the limit. His daily intake was up to two eight balls, or seven grams of coke, in addition to a fifth of Crown Royal. He insisted to friends that there was a medical reason for his massive drug habit. He'd been taking a prescription inhalant that he claimed contained cocaine for his blocked sinuses since he was a child. For once in his life, his broken nose, that physically deformed crutch, was a convenient excuse.

He certainly could see no reason to slow down. Staying on the road meant staying high and doing what he knew how to do best. The actual act of making music was still pretty much a charge. He always answered the bell when he heard the roar of the crowd. It was the rest of the rock-and-roll circus that was pulling him down. He fell into a routine of staying up for one or two or three nights — as long as the stimulant effect would allow — before coming down hard for twelve to eighteen hours, unplugging phones, shutting drapes, and hanging the Do Not Disturb sign outside the door. Upon awakening, he immediately medicated himself with a shot of Crown Royal, sometimes enhanced by dissolving a gram of coke into the glass. The simultaneous alcohol and drug abuse fed on each other. The more coke he inhaled, the more Crown he could knock down. The more he drank, the more he needed It to keep drinking. His stature, his job, his life, his pocketbook all depended on it.

It wasn't much of a Blues Thang anymore, except for the feeling that he was crying inside. Chris tried his best to be supportive. Tommy was of little help because he tended to get just as bent as Stevie. Reese stayed at arm's length. He was a hired hand and tried to do his job like a professional. What anyone did when they weren't onstage was their own business. That same attitude was pervasive among the crew. They worried behind his back, but no one wanted to say anything at the risk of pissing off the main man.

One of the few bright spots making *Live Alive* was working on Stevie Wonder's "Superstition," which brought the two Stevies together. Stevie Ray had been goofing around with the song ever since he first heard the record. At the suggestion of a few friends, the band recorded the song in Texas for *Live Alive*. When Stevie Wonder caught wind of Double Trouble's intent to do further overdubs of the song for the album in Los Angeles, he offered use of his Wonderland studio. The two Stevies became instant telephone buddies, calling each other up to exchange ideas and musical tidbits. Wonder even made an appearance in a music video of the song. It was too good to believe. The man who inspired junior-high classmates to tease him and call him Little Stevie was now his friend.

The band also had hopes for "Willie the Wimp," an original midtempo blues composed by Bill Carter and Ruth Ellsworth based on the death of a Southside Chicago street hustler who was buried in a coffin sculpted like a Cadillac Deville. "Willie the Wimp in his Cadillac coffin" was an instant classic in the Stevie Ray songbook, appropriately outlaw, slyly humorous, grundgingly studomatic (Willie was a pimp, as well as a wimp), and veneratingly negrodelic.

Most of July was spent holed up at the Record Plant and Wonderland studios in LA, the whole organization held hostage by a looming deadline, overblown budget, and the mercurial whims of a leader who could barely tie his own shoes. The two-night stand at the Greek Theater in Los Angeles at the end of the month that kicked off the resumption of touring was a welcome relief. For ninety minutes at least, the band that needed no gimmicks to sell seven thousand tickets could forget the second-guessing of the record company bozos. The Greek was for the fans.

The shows were by no means perfect. Before the first show, Stevie had spent the entire day graciously doing press with Epic's West Coast press liaison, Sue Sawyer. In order to accommodate him and make him as comfortable as possible over the course of a dozen interviews, Sawyer dutifully filled and refilled his glass with Crown Royal. Stevie was drunk to the point of slurring words by the time he took the stage. But he pulled the show off, wrapping up by calling up Hank Ballard to help him sing "Look at Little Sister," a Ballard original, and Mitch Mitchell, who made the encore of "Voodoo Chile" as real as it ever could be. Mitchell later accompanied Stevie back to his mixing sessions at the Record Plant.

Though there was still some unfinished business on the album, the band was all too happy to get out of LA and back on the road. For all the built-in drawbacks, it was the one environment where every night was a fresh start and practically every performance concluded with Stevie being declared King by thousands of loyal subjects.

The tour, with Bonnie Raitt opening, continued to San Diego, where Hank Ballard showed again, and on to Santa Cruz, where Stevie visited with Little Doyle, the sixteen-year-old son of Doyle Bramhall. Doyle had been raised by his mom in nearby Santa Rosa, but had inherited his dad's love of blues music. On the first night of a two-night stand at the Santa Cruz Civic Auditorium, Stevie unexpectedly called young Doyle up to accompany him on guitar. He was more than a little impressed with the way Doyle played and carried himself in front of an audience. The following evening, Doyle showed up again, dressed in full-blown rock-star regalia, anticipating Stevie's call.

Rene Martinez, Stevie's guitar tech, opened both Santa Cruz shows, entertaining the throng with an impressive demonstration of flamenco technique and closing out with a crowd-pleasing version of Mason Williams's guitar instrumental hit, "Classical Gas." Fans and critics who were aware that Stevie was at less than top form continued to heap praise on his skills. Dave Gingold, writing a review in the *Santa Cruz Sentinel* went so far as to suggest, "Maybe it isn't too late for Fabulous Thunderbird Jimmie to take up clarinet."

The caravan steamed on to Salem, Oregon, to perform a free concert on August 6, a triumphant return to the Oregon state penitentiary, where their Labor Day appearance the year before inspired the inmates' local Jaycee chapter to start up a roadie's school. That expertise came in handy when the band's equipment truck got lost on the way to the prison and a new backline had to be scrounged at the eleventh hour.

Following their performance in front of five hundred inmates, a convicted armed robber named Jimmy Bernhard, aka Skinny Jimmy, who served as the prison entertainment committee chairman, made a presentation declaring the members of Double Trouble Honorary Convicts.

"Convicts have learned to be content with less; therefore, we guard what we have against those who would take from us," the proclamations read. "That which we so zealously protect, we offer freely to Stevie Ray Vaughan. He has twice given us one of his most beloved possessions: his music. . . . His gift to us prompts us to offer him our most treasured possession: brotherhood."

Stevie, Tommy, Chris, and Reese were given a tin cup hand-made by inmates. "After all," said Skinny Jimmy proudly, "we have some of the best printers, forgers, and engravers right here."

The tour jumped from the Pacific Northwest to Memphis. Stevie had promised to help out Lonnie Mack, who was having his live performance at the Orpheum Theater videotaped for the pilot of a Public Broadcasting System series called "American Caravan." But those plans were suddenly put on hold when Stevie got word that his father, Big Jim Vaughan, had taken a turn for the worse.

15

VOODOO CHILE

Stevie had known for several years that his father, Jimmie Lee
Vaughan, had Parkinson's disease, or at least something like it. He had
heard about his dad suffering through the early stages of the illness,
suddenly losing control and falling to the floor after a seizure or spasm. As
the frequency of the attacks increased, Big Jim's musculature had deteriorated, until he was confined to a wheelchair. Martha quit her job at the
Portland Cement Company to look after him. The larger-than-life man
who had loved and terrorized the two Vaughan boys for decades was a
thin, weak, sputtering figure, and his condition broke Stevie's heart.

"They mean a lot to me," Stevie had said of his parents shortly
before his debut album, *Texas Flood,* was released.

Dad has asbestosis. He's suing the people that make fiberglass.
He got laid off, and never has worked again. He sits around
and feels worthless 'cause he can't do anything. That's one
thing I want to do, buy them a farm or something, somewhere
close to a hospital. He's had a bunch of heart attacks. I'd like
to figure out some way to set him up with something he can do
that won't really strain him. He worked hard, too hard. Now

he can't do anything. They need time to fall in love again. They need time to be old people in love, kiss on each other and stuff. I'm a hopeless romantic. I'm fixin' to cry if I don't stop this.

Stevie wanted badly to do something for his parents, but he himself was so strapped for cash and so tore down that there was little he could do except invite them to shows. During the holidays, Stevie did his best to show up and reach out to his father, even though Big Jim's attitudes and the attitudes of the rest of his kinfolk drove him nuts. At Christmastime one year, Stevie went to a family gathering where he noticed a cartoon on the buffet table beneath the covered dishes. It depicted a white man fishing in a lake. The white man had a watermelon on the end of the line, bait for several blacks swimming around in the water. The cartoon so offended Stevie that he stormed out of the house.

Patching up a relationship between a father and son is difficult. It is impossible when the son is drunk and coked up all the time and the father is out of his mind on medication, aggravated by years of anger, bitterness, and frustration. "I was sitting over there in the living room and Jim was giving me this cold stare," remembered Stevie's uncle Joe Cook. "All of a sudden, he said, 'Joe, you're a son of a bitch.' Martha was horrified. She scolded him, saying, 'Jim, shame on you.' I just smiled and said, 'Jim, it takes one to know one.' A few nights later, he said to me, 'I'm sorry, I'm sorry.' "

Just as often as Big Jim would snarl something mean-spirited, he'd break down and cry for what appeared to be no reason. Once Martha came in and asked what was wrong. Her husband, tears welling in his eyes, blurted, "I just love those boys and their music."

When Stevie got the call that his father had suffered a severe heart attack, he flew to Dallas immediately and joined Jimmie and Martha at the hospital. Everyone knew Daddy was going fast. Stevie was devastated, but he had obligations to fulfill, the television taping in Memphis with Lonnie Mack. Lonnie was one of his musical fathers, someone who could provide him with comfort in his time of need.

"When he sees something that needs to be talked about, he'll talk," Stevie said of Mack. "He understands. He's deep, real deep, and a warm kind of deep."

Few people outside of the band and crew knew what Stevie was going through. Still, during his regular rap in the middle of "Life Without You," the song he wrote about losing his friend Charley Wirz, he did a little testifying from deep in the heart.

"Please remember to tell the people you care about that you love them," he told the audience. "Tell them out loud. Because you may not get a chance later on."

On August 27, 1986, three days after the heart attack, the time had come for Jimmie Lee Vaughan to end his painful struggle with death. The staff at Dallas's Medical City Hospital decided to remove the elder Vaughan from the life support systems that were keeping him breathing. Big Jim passed away shortly thereafter. Stevie returned to Dallas from Memphis on the day of his father's death and joined Jimmie in trying to console their mother. Neither was quite prepared for the responsibility, and they sought to ease their own pain the best way they knew how before the funeral. But even Stevie's grief had to be rushed. Minutes after Big Jim's coffin was lowered into the ground at Laurel Land Cemetery on August 29, Stevie, his band, and his manager were whisked by limousine to the Red Bird Airport, where a Learjet was waiting to fly them to Montreal. Upon landing, they were escorted directly to the stage of the Miller Beer festival at Jarry Park. Montreal was one of the biggest paydays of the year. The show had to go on. Crying would have to wait.

Big Jim's death only underscored the obvious. After the funeral in Dallas, an eternally optimistic Epic field rep confided to Redbeard, the radio programmer, that at the pace Stevie was going, he wouldn't live another six months. He was coming apart at the seams. A sickness was gnawing away at his insides, a sickness he tried to deny. During one bout of illness, he asked Tim Duckworth to lay purple cloth across his body. Purple had healing powers, he believed, and he once gave Tim a book on the subject. But no spiritual edge could compensate for Stevie's conviction that he had to keep playing no matter how bad he felt.

Following Montreal, Stevie flew back to Los Angeles to continue mixing *Live Alive*. With a five-week, twenty-eight-date swing across Europe hovering on the horizon, he was under the gun. He remained in LA while the rest of the band and the crew shipped out for Scandinavia in preparation for the Continental tour, which began on September 12. Finally, even Stevie had to go, leaving Tim Duckworth behind to courier the mixed-down reference tapes to Copenhagen for everyone's approval.

The first leg of the tour through Denmark, Germany, Holland, France, and Belgium was a critical and financial success. The houses were full and the fans were rabid despite the artist's deteriorating condition. Standing there in the lights, banging and thrashing and sweating seemed so natural, so automatic, so in-the-groove. But Stevie's tank had emptied. He was running on fumes.

The tour stopped in Paris for a two-night stand, September 23 and 24, at the Olympia Theatre. Mitch Mitchell had hipped Stevie to a bar in an alley by the backstage entrance off Rue Caumartin. He and Jimi Hendrix used to duck in there when they played the same venue fifteen years earlier. During some downtime after the soundcheck, Stevie made his way down to the bar and drank a toast to Hendrix.

Two days later, on September 26, there was a note waiting for Stevie when the band checked into their Munich hotel before their performance that evening at the Circus Krone.

Keep playing the blues.

The Rev. Willie G

Billy Gibbons was in town with Frank and Dusty to play the Circus Krone the next night, which happened to be a rare day off for Double Trouble. That afternoon Stevie showed up at ZZ Top's soundcheck. The band wasn't around, so Stevie did the soundcheck for them.

After the show, ZZ's manager, Bill Ham, had a word with Stevie. "I took Stevie backstage and sat him down and told him it looked to me like he was about to kill himself . . . what he was doing was not fair to his loved ones, his fans, and most of all to himself. I remember being appalled that whoever was responsible for Stevie's life and career had not intervened to rescue this talented young man from what appeared to be a downward spiral."

The tour continued to Pfalzbau in Ludwigshafen, Germany, on September 28. After the show, Stevie, Chris, and Tim were walking to a restaurant when a wave of nausea suddenly seized Stevie. He doubled over, throwing up blood-flecked vomit. He regained his composure, walked several paces, and went into convulsions again. The pattern repeated itself for several blocks.

"I need a drink," Stevie finally huffed.

"That's the last thing you need," Chris told him.

"I know. I need one, though."

Chris and Tim walked him back to the hotel, where Stevie settled down. They thought everything was fine. Then suddenly Stevie started gasping for air. A panicked look crossed his face. He began shaking uncontrollably and started turning pale.

His eyes glazed over.

"I need help. I need help," he cried weakly. An ambulance was summoned and five paramedics rushed in to administer a glucose and saline solution intravenously. The color returned to Stevie's face. He was taken to a local hospital, where a doctor gruffly checked his vital signs, said he'd had too much to drink, then sent him back to the hotel.

Chris phoned Alex Hodges.

"Stevie needs help. We've got to stop this thing," he said. It wasn't the first time Hodges had heard those words, but this time, Chris sounded adamant.

"*He* said he needs help. Who's that doctor in London who helped Clapton and everybody get off heroin?" When he got off the phone with

Chris, Hodges searched for a reference. He knew that Stevie had finally reached the end of his rope. He didn't even have enough left to hang himself.

On the following night, September 29, Stevie struggled through a show at the Volkshaus in Zurich, leaning on Chris and Tommy to help him make it. The next morning, they all flew to London, where a scheduled string of interviews and a television appearance on "The Wogan Show" were immediately canceled. Tommy, Chris, and Reese checked into the Kenilworth Hotel. Stevie was taken to the London Clinic on Devonshire Place and put under the care of Dr. Victor Bloom, the man who had nursed Eric Clapton back to health after his own collapse four years earlier.

Bloom diagnosed the problem as severe internal bleeding. Alcohol was eating holes in Stevie's stomach. The condition was aggravated by his habit of dissolving cocaine in his Crown Royal. The coke recrystalized in the stomach, ripping Stevie's guts apart. Had the situation gone unchecked, Bloom predicted, his patient would have been dead in a month. He prescribed an immediate four-week rest at the clinic, followed by further rehabilitation in the United States.

Stevie was facing the biggest challenge of his life, and he knew he needed help to make it through. "Momma," he said in a breaking drawl on his mother's answering machine, "I got some trouble over here, some things I got to do. I sure would like you to come over." Martha Vaughan immediately booked a flight to London. Stevie then asked Tim to track down Janna Lapidus, the girl from New Zealand he'd fallen in love with the previous spring. Though she was only seventeen, Janna agreed to come to London, too, making her own travel arrangements.

There was still some unfinished business — an engagement the next evening at the Hammersmith Palais that Stevie desperately wanted to play. The Thursday, October 2, engagement would be his last for quite some time.

"I'm grateful to be here," he told his fans at the start of the performance. "You don't know *how* grateful."

Even he didn't realize how grateful. His skin was as pale as a corpse's. He was weak. He started his rap during "Life Without You," informing the audience that his mother was with him that evening, telling them, "That's a love thing." He had reached the point where he was ready to give it all up, yet, one more time, he satisfied the fans enough to earn an encore, returning to the stage wearing a large Indian headdress.

The headdress was the brightest of all his stage plumage, but it was so heavy he had to hold his chin up to keep it from falling over his face. After finishing the encore, Stevie kept the headdress on while he was being escorted off the stage and down a gangplank. He couldn't see where he was going and slipped, falling off the narrow walkway, suffering scrapes and bruises. The fall told him all he needed to know.

Icing down his leg afterward, he made it plain to James Fox, a reporter for the *London Observer*, that after almost twenty years of hard and fast living as a musician, he could read the writing on the wall. He had no other choice but to reassess his career and his personal life. "I've got stomach trouble and I'm exhausted. I've been on the road without stopping. I've got to look after myself now. I hope maybe I can go home and stay with my mother."

Subsequent dates in Holland, Finland, Sweden, and Norway and a seventeen-date run through the eastern and midwestern US were canceled. Even so, Double Trouble had racked up 242 concert dates that year. The band and crew flew home. Tommy immediately checked himself into a rehab facility in Austin. The big lunk was more of a brother than ever. Martha Vaughan, Janna Lapidus, and Tim Duckworth stayed behind to look after Stevie.

If he was truly committed to getting his life turned around, the London Clinic would be a good place to start. It wasn't exactly boot camp. The clinic stressed abstention without requiring it. If patients needed a drink, a shot, a smoke, or a snort, they would be accommodated, but only under controlled circumstances. But Stevie wanted to stick with his vow to get right. On one occasion he felt so shaky, he told Duckworth he needed a drink, but Tim kept talking to him and the urge passed. It wasn't like being in prison or anything. During the day, he'd take shopping excursions to Harrods' department store and flea markets and sight-seeing expeditions to the zoo, the Tower of London, and Windsor Castle, enjoying the company of his mother, the girl he was infatuated with, and his assistant.

One afternoon Eric Clapton dropped by while Tim had taken Martha on an outing. Stevie immediately phoned up Jimmie to tell him about his visitor. He appreciated the way Clapton could be so reassuring without passing judgment. Any fool could tell him he'd fucked up. Clapton understood. He'd experienced the same pressures, faced the same temptations, and overcome the same obstacles. Clapton had inspired Stevie as a guitar player. Now he came to inspire his young friend to get his act together. He'd done a stretch at the clinic and pointed out his favorite places to take walks in all the nearby parks and other sights worth checking out in the neighborhood. The following day, carts full of flowers were wheeled into the room, filling it with color and fragrant smells. The cards read "Compliments of Eric Clapton."

While in London, Stevie looked into the Charter rehabilitation program, which had a good reputation in the United States. Unlike the London Clinic, the Charter program stressed total withdrawal from drugs and alcohol. A month's stay was booked at the Charter Peachford Hospital facility in Atlanta. Martha Vaughan had a sister nearby that she could stay with, and Alex Hodges kept an office just a few miles away.

The flight from London to the United States was a challenge. Before he boarded, Stevie admitted to Tim that he was so afraid of flying, he'd never taken off without having a drink to calm him down. There was just too much time and not enough to do. Midway across the Atlantic, Stevie borrowed some money from his mother. He was going to buy some duty-free cigarettes, he told her. Stevie made his way tentatively down the aisle and conferred with a stewardess, who poured him a double shot of Crown Royal. Stevie knocked it straight back. When he returned to his seat next to Martha Vaughan, he began to sob uncontrollably.

They arrived in Atlanta on a Monday afternoon. Stevie wrote one last request to Duckworth. He needed just a little more time before checking into Charter.

> I will be wanting to go into the Charter clinic tomorrow *evening*.
> So I can sleep late and take care of some "pre-entry" business etc. . . . and start off with a full program day the next morning.
> Also Janna will be calling me mid afternoon. Please help me so this way.
>
> > Love and Dag,
> > SRV

On Wednesday, he was ready. He said goodbye to Tim Duckworth and thanked him for holding up his part of the bargain, for keeping him alive. He talked to Janna and his mother. Physically, he was drained. There really had been nothing left in him when he was taken to the London Clinic. Mentally, he felt rejuvenated, like there was a chance for a new start if only he could keep focused. This time, though, it wasn't the guitar he would have to concentrate on. It was his mind and his body. He was going to pull up, by God. He had to pull up. And no one else could do it for him.

16

STEVIE V.

The neatly manicured hospital grounds in the upscale suburb of Marietta looked nice enough. It reminded Stevie of a resort or a Club Med, where there are planned activities to keep you busy all day. He thought handling the program would be no problem. It was October 16, and he'd already made it through seventy-two hours straight, long enough to figure out how close to the edge he'd come this time. Way too close. There were no options left. He had to stop. Really. The choices were getting clean and sober or dying. He craved a drink and a line, but he knew, this time, he had to get straight.

Charter wouldn't be some sort of jail, boot camp, or high school, he figured. Pay attention to the lectures and stay out of trouble and there would be coffee to drink and cigarettes to smoke and hang time with other people trying to clean up, too.

He quickly learned that would not be the case the moment he began to go through the admission proceedings. He was handed a list of symptoms that identify the characteristics of addiction. As he read it over carefully, his expression changed from mildly upbeat to horrific. The traits that were described told him more than he wanted to know. He had scraped the bottom. He wasn't a privileged celebrity anymore, he was just another lush whose bottle had finally run dry. He couldn't sink any lower. He broke down crying.

The press release announcing the hospitalization of Stevie Ray Vaughan downplayed the severity of his condition. It stated the musician "would spend 30 days in a Georgia convalescent clinic after being diagnosed as suffering from extreme exhaustion, complicated by an overindulgence in alcohol." The abuse wasn't "chronic, but the pressure of touring has caused him to drink more than he should just lately."

By the time the words filtered down to Redbeard, the program director at Q-102 in Dallas, it sounded practically like a cover-up. "There must have been a wonderful spin put on that story, because the way we got it was that he had decided to take some time off the road," he said. "We didn't get the fact that he literally collapsed and was taken to the hospital in London. And we naively, I guess, accepted it."

The odds are heavily weighted against an addict actually beating his or her habit, even one who spends from $12,000 to $20,000 to undergo the highly regarded Charter program at one of the eighty-four rehabilitation units operated by the Atlanta-based corporation. Fewer than half of the more than 70,000 patients who enter a Charter facility each year overcome their chemical dependency for more than six months. The limited goal of the program is to provide the first step toward achieving sobriety. It is up to the individual to do the rest. Stevie knew the rehab routine. He had tried to clean up once before and had actually gone without drinking or doing coke or anything else for three months before climbing back to the bottle and the blow. "I decided that I was such a jerk sober that I might as well drink and have fun," he reasoned.

The roller-coaster ride was over now. Going into Charter was an acknowledgment that he had to come to grips with his sickness. Like rehabilitation programs offered by National Medical Enterprises, the Hospital Corporation of America, Community Psychiatric Centers, and others, the twenty-eight-day Charter treatment was an intensive group and individual counseling experience based on the twelve-step program developed by Alcoholics Anonymous.

Ever since humans first discovered the pleasures of intoxicating drink and the horrors caused by overindulgence, the medical establishment has struggled to find a cure for alcoholism, experimenting with remedies including cabbage, strychnine, arsenic, opium, morphine, horse antibodies, gonorrhea innoculations, hot-air boxes, electrical nerve tonics, and molten lead. But it wasn't until the early twentieth century that a failed Wall Street investor and rummy named William Griffith Wilson devised a truly effective treatment for human dependency on alcohol and other addictive chemicals.

On a dark November afternoon in 1934, Bill Wilson welcomed an old drinking buddy into his drafty Brooklyn brownstone, set up two glasses on the white oilcloth-covered kitchen table, and offered his friend a drink of gin. His friend refused. Instead, he launched into conversation that would lead Wilson to quit alcohol and found Alcoholics Anonymous. "In the kinship of common suffering," Wilson later wrote of that afternoon, "one alcoholic had been talking with another."

Recovering alcoholics have been talking to each other ever since, providing mutual support along the path to recovery. A loose-knit fellowship of meeting groups that refuses outside funding, charges no fees, and requires only that members have a desire to stop drinking, Alcoholics Anonymous today is comprised of more than 88,000 groups in 134 countries helping more than a million and a half alcoholics in the US alone. With the 1939 publication of *Alcoholics Anonymous*, known as the Big Book because of the thickness of its original pages, Bill W., as he called himself in adherence to the code of privacy that he created, established a series of steps that he and his fellow travelers followed on the road to recovery. Despite the fact that the American Medical Association initially described the Big Book as having "no scientific merit or interest," Bill W.'s twelve steps are today the basic tenets for more than 90 percent of the alcohol and chemical dependency recovery programs in the United States, as well as a dizzying array of self-help groups dealing with everything from eating disorders to emotional problems.

The twelve steps became Stevie V.'s ten commandments. His daily routine was simple. He got up early, exercised, ate breakfast, and then participated in a variety of intensive group and one-on-one therapy sessions. Some sessions dealt exclusively with the biological aspects of chemical addiction. Others concentrated on tearing down his denial mechanisms, getting him to open up emotionally and face the truth about himself and his addictions, a gentle, confrontational approach that was an essential part of Charter's no-tolerance, restrictive framework. For someone who had never allowed himself to admit his weaknesses and had grown accustomed to being indulged by well-meaning coworkers, fans, and sycophants, just being there was liberating.

The private journal he began keeping, recording his past and present experiences in a notebook, helped him sort out the conflicting feelings he once had and still was having. As it had in his relations with Lenny, writing things down on paper gave him time to organize his thoughts and to express himself when the words wouldn't come out of his mouth the right way. The meetings, too, helped him work through the maze that had landed him in Atlanta. He started attending AA sessions outside as well as inside the hospital. Though the Alcoholics Anonymous credo forbade any formal affiliation with a recovery facility, local groups provided H and I, or hospital and institution, committees to come in and talk

Classic Management
Chesley Millikin
Managing Director
P.O. Drawer T • Manor, Texas 78653 • 512-272-5581

Rock Arts, Ltd   512/327-5320
97 West Bee Caves Rd. No 101 • Austin Texas 78746

His first Guitar Star promotional shot, 1980

Back at Lee Park in Dallas,
Double Trouble plays a
free concert honoring Freddie King for a handful of
fans, 1980. The Fender
Stratocaster was purchased
four days earlier.

Power Trio: Stevie Ray Vaughan and Double Trouble, with Jackie Newhouse on bass, at Steamboat 1876 in Austin, 1980

Star Time. Stevie Ray shares a laugh with new pal Mick Jagger after Double Trouble's 1982 New York showcase at the Danceteria. Lenny Vaughan looks on admiringly as Ron Wood pulls on a beer and Tommy Shannon checks out the scene.

Let's Dance. Producer Nile Rodgers strains to glean the secret of Stevie Ray Vaughan's magic guitar as David Bowie hones in on the camera, 1983.

Dennie Turner

Above: Chris "Whipper" Layton, whippin' it good, Austin, 1982

Right: Tommy "Slut" Shannon, steady like a rock, Austin, 1982

Above left: The Legend and his Discovery. Stevie Ray relaxes in the studio with John Hammond, 1983.

Above: Demonstrating a little showmanship in the tradition of T-Bone Walker at Pine Knob Theatre, Clarkston, Michigan, 1987

Left: Live from Carnegie Hall, 1984

Getting the gold for
Couldn't Stand the Weather,
Double Trouble with Reese
Wynans (*second from left*),
Lenny Vaughan (*fourth
from left*), Chesley Millikin
(*fourth from right*), and Epic
brass, 1984

Family reunion in Dallas
with (*left to right*) Stevie's
cousin Sammy Klutts and
Jim and Martha Vaughan,
1985

In the summer of 1986,
Jimmie lends support for
an encore at the end of a
sold-out performance at the
Austin Opry House. The
concert was recorded for
the album *Live Alive*.

W. A. Williams

W. A. Williams

Low-down jam with the Wham! Man, Lonnie Mack, in Cincinnati, summer 1988

Making it slow and sweet at Deer Creek, Noblesville, Indiana, 1989

Harold I. Dozier

Mother and son, Dallas, 1989

W. A. Williams

A new and improved Stevie Ray plants a smooch on Janna Lapidus, summer 1987.

John Saller

August 27, 1990. Federal investigators rummage through the wreckage at Alpine Valley.

Last Call

with patients in rehab facilities. Some AA groups even paid rent to clinics and hospitals in order to hold meetings on a regular basis at recovery institutions.

As he acclimated himself to the regimen, Stevie began to understand that the Charter people weren't like his teachers, the principals, the coaches, his father, his brother, his managers, or other authority figures who'd always tried to run his life. The folks at Charter were on his side. They weren't going to spank him, threaten him, bully him, beat him up, or fence him in. They were like Albert King, B. B. King, and Eric Clapton. They were there to help him grow and get better.

Stevie V. discovered the participants in the program were no better or worse than he was. Everyone was a fallen angel here, regardless of how big or how bad their particular habit had been. Their common bond was that they all had the desire to piece their lives back together.

He threw himself into recovery with the same passion, determination, and sense of purpose that he had once used to teach himself how to play the guitar, practicing a phrase that moved him so many times he couldn't help but absorb it. School never motivated him like this place did. Here, ducking classes to sneak out to the playground for a smoke was out of the question. If he didn't want to get with the program, the exit door was always open. He had to be committed or else he wouldn't make it. "This place is just intense," he marveled. "You don't have a lot of time to slough off. There's a lot of work to be done."

Without the resolve, no program could have helped Stevie. But he was more than ready. Before entering the hospital, he had come to accept the first step of the twelve-step healing process. He knew he was a head case, that he had no willpower when it came to amber liquid and white powder, that they had seized control of him. Getting high had been a priority for more than twenty years. He had built up so much resistance, accumulated such a remarkable level of toxic tolerance, and was able to use his music so successfully to work through his highs that he no longer had any idea what it would take to cop a buzz. Some days he could knock back a quart of Crown Royal without feeling a thing. Other days he could take just one sip and get thoroughly wasted. Mood swings became so exaggerated that there were times he would try to say hi to people he knew and would fall apart instead, weeping.

Perhaps the scariest realization of all was what the chronic abuse had started to do to his gift. The music had been gradually dissipating along with his physical strength and emotional stability. All he had to do was think back to all the tapes he'd been sifting through to find material for the *Live Alive* album. Nothing sounded right. Every performance he had considered from two years' worth of live recordings was so flawed it either needed overdubbing, editing, or polishing. It had been a while since he'd felt possessed by the muse, regardless of what his fans, his friends, his band mates, the crew, and the record company told him. His once effortless stylings had turned tentative and choppy. In place of new, innovative ideas, he recycled a few tried and true riffs, reprising them by rote. He masked the shortcomings with volume and attack, keeping one step ahead of the inevitable by staying on the road, where he began every night with a clean slate.

Owning up to all that was merely the beginning. If he was going to make it all the way through the twelve-step program, he would have to undergo a transformation, one in which he would have to confront a power greater than himself, a power that would give him back his life.

Bill W., the primary catalyst for Alcoholics Anonymous, described his own spiritual transformation as a moment when "the room lit up with a great white light" and he was "caught up into an ecstasy which there are no words to describe." Stevie Ray Vaughan was certainly no stranger to that sort of realm. He just had to get in touch with it.

In the book *The Varieties of Religious Experience*, the theoretical inspiration for Bill W.'s Big Book, Harvard philosopher William James wrote, "A musician may suddenly reach a point at which pleasure in the technique of the art entirely falls away, and in some moment of inspiration he becomes the instrument through which music flows. So it is with the religious experience."

Stevie could recount many occasions when he felt like he had no control over the sounds produced by his fingers and guitar. "There've been nights when I started playing chord solos, and I didn't know any of the chords," he recalled. But it hadn't been the cocaine or meth coursing through his veins that was doing it. It was him. He had just been too far gone to take notice.

"Pain is not the price, but the very touchstone of spiritual rebirth," Bill W. once wrote. Stevie Ray's pain was his salvation. The cry of the blues could leave him and the audience feeling spent, but the same spirit could be used to lift them all up, too, shifting, in William James's words, "the habitual center of his personal energy" from dissipation to sobriety. It all depended on how you made use of your tools.

The next phase of recovery required Stevie to share his experience with others. "The spiritual approach was as useless as any other if you soaked it up like a sponge and kept it to yourself," wrote Dr. Robert Smith, whose first day of sobriety, June 10, 1935, is regarded as the actual founding day of Alcoholics Anonymous.

For most of his life, Stevie had managed to avoid confronting his insecurities, his low self-esteem, and his shyness by hiding, first behind his mother's skirt, later behind his guitar. He had spent most of his youth and his entire adult life keeping his head down, his eyes watching his hands move the strings, seeking peace out of sound, repeating the quest night after night, validated by screams of approval. The twelve-step program forced him to reveal the warmth and compassion that had been hiding beneath the gunfighter's hat, the scarves, the jewelry, and all the accoutrements of luxury and stardom.

Gritting his teeth and white-knuckling his way through a session didn't cut it at Charter. He had to maintain eye-to-eye contact and speak directly with others, listening to what they had to say, even if the words were not what he wanted to hear. He had to string words and sentences together to express himself clearly. Slurred one-liners delivered with a cocksure swagger didn't floor this audience.

"In group therapy, after you get to talking about it, and you open up and start telling what's bothering you, and you get to the root of the matter, you start to trust people," he later explained. "I had not dealt with a lot of problems and resentments that I had built up for years. That's the main thing."

In many respects, the transition from coke rap to therapy rap was seamless, the difference being that the therapy rap grew from a positive, healing experience, rather than a destructive, convoluted exercise in pretzel logic. The democratic group confessionals that formed the core of the twelve-step program and AA fellowship were little different from the early-morning hotel-room bull sessions that followed performances, only this time he didn't need any "It" to keep the conversation going. A shot of love would do just fine.

"There were a lot of things I was running from," he told writer Bill Milkowski.

> And one of them was me. I was a thirty-two-year-old with a six-year-old kid inside of me, scared and wondering where love is. . . . I came to realize that the alcohol problem, the drug problem, and the fear were all symptoms of an underlying problem that's called lack of love. Once you really become an addict or an alcoholic, the drink and drugs just take the place of people you care about and those people who care about you. You forget about love, you reject love. You become consumed by fear. . . . I was scared that somebody would find out I was scared. And now I'm finally realizing that fear is the opposite of love.

The biggest hurdle of all was making sure he held on to everything he was learning at Charter. Fortunately, he had plenty of support. A cousin entered the Charter Peachford program with him, and they compared notes on their progress. Tommy Shannon, who had taken his own

pledge of sobriety on the same day as Stevie and entered a similar program in Austin, cheered Stevie on through telephone calls and letters.
Although Tommy had tried to clean up several times before, he knew that
like Stevie, he couldn't afford to backslide again: "It was getting real
destructive, real sick, just a dead-end street," he said. "If we hadn't quit,
we'd have either ended up in a hospital or dead." Martha Vaughan stayed
by Stevie's side, visiting regularly. Janna kept in touch. Even Jackson
Browne dropped by to let Stevie know others were behind him.

Stevie composed letters to friends to update them on his progress.
This is the one Keith Ferguson received:

> Hey, cat, how are things with you? Finally got back my
> strength and energy and trying to pick up the brain cells and
> put some marbles back in the bag. All's goin' good. These guts
> of mine are in sad shape. Doc Bloom in London said my
> stomach x-ray showed the stomach of a sixty year old man.
> Sure feels a lot better these days. How's the Tailgators, An-
> gela, Den den, Derek and all dat har har? Have you talked to
> Tommy? How's he doing. Hope he's doing good. People un-
> derstand that we can't speak to anyone on the phone or in
> person at first when we come in here and are seen that we are
> working on this little program for ourselves. We don't have a
> choice but to be a little selfish about it, shit. I'm fighting for
> my life and I finally see that there's nothing wrong with being
> selfish about helping myself. I can't just let myself run out of
> gas, but shit I miss you folks! How's Clifford? Hope the club
> is doing well. Who's been there lately? Everybody probably.
> I've got to go to a lecture so I guess I gots to go. Say hi to
> everybody.
>
> > Love you all,
> > Stevie

The word began trickling out. Stevie had cleaned up.

It was with more than a touch of cruel irony that Epic released *Live
Alive* while Stevie was at Charter. The album, intended for an audience
largely comprised of blue-collar beer drinkers, bikers, and stoned-out
electric-guitar freaks, was a testament to Stevie's excesses, not his talent.
He didn't have to look further than the "V" section of any record shop to
remind himself of how low he could go.

While at Charter, Bonnie Raitt played a solo date in Atlanta and
Stevie left the hospital to see her. When she called him up onstage, he
hesitated momentarily. He hadn't stood on a stage in what seemed like a
month of Sundays. But he couldn't turn down the woman who was one

of the closest friends he'd made since he started riding the touring circuit. The mere act of picking up the guitar with a clear head was intimidating at first, until exhilaration took over. Stoned or sober, there was nothing like playing guitar.

Stevie checked out of Charter recharged and revitalized. It was one day at a time now. To stick with that philosophy, he rearranged his life. He moved his worldly possessions from Austin to Dallas. For fifteen years, Austin's music community had nurtured his talent and provided him with an accepting environment in which to learn and grow musically. Now the rest of him had to catch up. The excesses that were part and parcel of the musician's lifestyle in Austin convinced him he needed "a new playground," as he described it. All of his old friends and acquaintances, it seemed, were users, abusers, or suppliers. Some new faces were in order.

Stevie hadn't spoken with Lenny since the previous spring. The hospital staff arranged to set aside time for Lenny to visit Stevie in Atlanta, but she never showed. In February of 1987, Stevie filed for divorce. Cleaning up helped him see exactly how destructive their relationship really had been. Lenny fought the proceedings even though she knew the marriage was over. If Stevie was going to cut the ties, she was going to make sure she got what was coming to her. The divorce, not recovery, would hold up recording plans for more than a year.

The Charter program hipped Stevie to the importance of family values. More than ever, he felt the need to be near his mother. Daddy died before he saw his boy sober. He wasn't going to screw it up with his surviving parent. "I figured I could be close by her and learn to know her again," he explained. "It was a real neat thing to tell her that I needed her and for that to work out."

Martha lived in the same modest house in Oak Cliff where the boys were raised. Rather than move back home, Stevie opted for a modern condominium at 4344 Travis in North Dallas just off the Knox-Henderson exit of the North Central Expressway. As happy as Martha Vaughan might have been about her son coming back to Dallas and straightening out his life, she was less enamored of his decision to have Janna Lapidus move in with him. Living with an eighteen-year-old girl to whom he was not married conflicted with her Christian values.

The gradual recovery process that began in London and continued in Georgia carried over to Dallas. The new anchor in his life would be the Aquarius chapter of Alcoholics Anonymous. Attending meetings became as much an obsession as scoring coke had once been. The Aquarius group was a homecoming of sorts, reuniting him with the extended musical family he'd grown up with. His sponsor, Bruce M., was an old band mate from the Nightcrawlers. Half the people who showed up for meetings, it seemed, had either played in a band or hung out with him at one time or another — his high school girlfriend, Glenda M.; Billy E. from Krackerjack; Phil C. from the Chessmen and Texas Storm; Robin S., another Chessmen veteran; and Joe K., who could burn the strings off a Strat almost as well as Stevie could.

The Aquarius group provided Stevie a congregation of equals to share with and a pulpit to preach from. For years, he'd spoken somewhat inarticulately about the need for peace, love, brotherhood, and understanding. The twelve steps provided all the eloquent references he needed. Just as he was a focal point onstage, Stevie V. became a focal point at meetings, freely admitting his foibles and shortcomings, providing a role model for getting right.

"If I can do it," he frequently stated, "anyone can."

When a longtime friend attending the Aquarius meetings suffered a relapse, he rode her relentlessly, calling her every morning and leaving a message from the twelve-step book on her answering machine. He was as obsessive about her recovery as he had once been about his girlfriends or his guitars. There were even occasions when he yelled and screamed, trying to knock some sense into her. "He was real protective," she recalled. "He'd interfere with your life. He'd tell you how he did it, how you should do it, and he did it out of love. He was very persistent to the point of arrogance. He was bull-headed. He tried to run my life. I got so tired of it, I didn't talk to him for six months." Eventually, though, she returned to the fold.

After meetings, he'd often take Martha or Janna to lunch at the 8.0 Restaurant, or the veggie sandwich café across Greenville Avenue from the old Nick's Uptown, or at La Suprema organic Mexican food bakery, where his favorite dish, spinach enchiladas, was renamed in his honor. The man who once guzzled Crown Royal for breakfast was now obsessed with maintaining a healthy, well-balanced diet. He gave up red meat and abstained from using even Tabasco sauce because it contained alcohol. He became a regular shopper at the Whole Foods Market natural grocery.

When he attended family functions, he asked to be treated like Stevie, Martha Vaughan's boy, not Stevie Ray, the rock star. Still, it was hard to shake the stage persona. He expressed frustration at being unable to be a real person to his mother while they were shopping for records. Martha shot him a stern look, then laughed. "Maybe if you'd take off that hat, they'd stop coming up to you."

Taking inventory of his life allowed him to rediscover the things about being a kid that he never took the time to do, or was too messed up to consider doing. He read children's books, and voiced regrets that he never completed high school. He got in touch with the music that had turned his head around in the first place by regularly tuning in Soul 73

KKDA, an AM station that programmed vintage blues, classic soul, and gospel music for an older, black audience. He rediscovered records that hadn't been on the turntable for years. Just looking at the cover of a Bobby Bland or a Johnny Guitar Watson album brought back a flood of memories. "It's like I've just found them, a newborn kid, remembering all the feelings I used to have," he said.

Mike Rhyner had known Stevie since they were both kids playing in bands in Oak Cliff. After he'd moved back to Dallas, Rhyner became reacquainted through his wife, Renee, who was Janna Lapidus's modeling agent in Dallas. "He'd be normal people when he had downtime, going to restaurants, movies, hanging out," Rhyner said. "He made it very comfortable. He was just totally without any ego. To have his talent, his gift, he didn't have the ego you'd expect to go with it. Once, he got a call from Eric Clapton, wanting him to do a show in England. He turned to me and asked, 'What do you think?'

"*What did I think?* I didn't know what to say. What did I know about it?"

Stevie V. gradually developed the will and the strength to lead a sober life. But another challenge lingered: could he be clean and still perform the role of the consummate guitar ace, one of the few white boys who really grasped the meaning of black blues? According to the myth, you had to live the blues to play the blues. After all, the word itself was derived from the expression "blue devils," a phrase commonly used in seventeenth-century England to describe the hallucinations caused by delirium tremens. Without the alcohol and drug elixirs, would the desire still be there? He'd seen other people's creative fires snuffed out by cleaning up. Bill Campbell, Austin's original white-boy blues guitarist and one of Stevie's mentors, went through several years of hell and two changes of scenery before regaining his form after he quit drinking in the late seventies. The image of Campbell playing second guitar in a hack lounge band — and a poor second guitar at that — was still etched in his mind.

If, as legend had it, Stevie Ray Vaughan had to make a pact with the devil to play the blues, he was determined to cut himself a good deal. The mojo hand he'd carried with him since he first picked up a guitar was still in his pocket. The muscles that propelled his mighty forearms, his long, bony fingers, had not atrophied. The grits 'n' gravel voice remained. Just because he was rejecting the sloppy-drunk life that the blues evoked didn't mean he had to reject the music.

Old friends provided an outlet to test himself. On New Year's Eve 1986, he jammed with old pal Lonnie Mack. "We won't be bringing in the new, if we take with us the old," he told the crowd during his rap on the song "Life Without You." "Let's everybody set off this new year and the rest of our lives with a true feeling of love. . . . It's all you have to give, so give it freely."

Three weeks later, he showed up at the Redux Club on Lower Greenville Avenue in Dallas. Robert Cray was performing two shows that were being taped for later broadcast on Q-102. During the break between the shows, radio station program director Redbeard noticed a stranger pop into Cray's dressing room. "He just lit up the whole room with this huge, beaming smile, with all this warmth radiating around him." Redbeard thought it was someone imitating Stevie Ray Vaughan, since the Stevie he remembered was always solemn, aloof, and preoccupied.

But it was Stevie Ray, all right, the new, improved version. He gave Cray a big embrace, then recognized Redbeard. The radio man extended his hand in greeting, but instead, Stevie wrapped his arms around him. Then he placed a hand on each of Redbeard's shoulders and looked him straight in the eyes with a wide smile.

"Hugs. Not drugs."

17

REDEMPTION

The sights and sounds seemed so familiar yet oddly foreign. A dank dressing room, stale with the sweat of a thousand athletes. The row of guitars in their stands placed just so in front of the phalanx of speakers, amplifiers, and other electronic gizmos. The faint sounds of recorded music being played on the sound system gradually being drowned out by the rising hum of expectation. Soft words of encouragement offered by his compadres while running through the last-minute preparations. Escorts leading the way through the dark with flashlights in hand. The roar of recognition when the voice on the PA called his name. The blinding glare of the lights that blurred the crowd into one big mass. The breathless rush that enveloped his entire being the split second the pick made contact with the taut coiled wires. Going through the routine without being stoned made all these sensations so strange, so deliciously new, so positively liberating. All these people — most of them didn't give a flip what had gone down since they saw him last. They just wanted him to lift them up again with his instrument the way he used to. And here he was, doing it all over again.

It was January 30, 1987, a full two months since Stevie completed the Charter program, and Double Trouble was back on familiar turf, working the barnlike Fair Park Coliseum in East Dallas. The show was both a homecoming and a coming-out party, celebrating the first concert of Stevie's second life.

If anyone doubted that he could pull it off, Stevie answered them in a New York minute. Gazing out over the crowd, clear-eyed and brimming with confidence, he drawled, "It's sure good to be back home, live and alive," and got to work, releasing a tremendous flood of teeth-rattling licks from his dammed-up soul. His toes curled up, he got goose bumps, he screwed his face up in the patented Vaughan contortion and let rip. The rock-and-roll army huddled around the lip of the stage thrust their fists into the air in time with Chris Layton's jarring snare pops and Tommy Shannon's self-assured rhythm lines, embellished by the hallelujahs Reese Wynans coaxed out of his sanctified B-3.

It was almost too easy. You didn't have to be a genius to see it or hear it. *Dallas Morning News* reviewer Russell Smith described the reading of "Texas Flood" as "almost epic" and called "Voodoo Chile" "scorching." But this was no mere ninety-minute show plus encore. When it came time to do his rap on "Life Without You," Stevie confounded those who expected the standard drivel they were used to hearing. ("Hey, he plays a bitchin' guitar. If he wants to prattle on with the hippie shit, let him.") The message now was quite specific, based on real-life experience: "We've got to quit tearing our bodies up and give ourselves a chance."

The fire in his belly blazed. He still had the chops. He felt like a guitar hot rod again, regardless of the battle he was fighting around the clock. From Dallas, the band resumed touring like they'd never stopped, heading to the East Coast to make up postponed dates including a stop at Radio City Music Hall in New York. In March, Stevie Ray and DT worked the college spring break circuit, drawing bigger crowds on the beach than even the Miss Tan Line contests at South Padre Island in Texas, Honolulu, Hawaii, and Daytona Beach, Florida. He stopped in Hollywood to attend the premiere of the campy *Back to the Beach*, the movie that included his "Pipeline" duet with Dick Dale, one of two songs that would earn Stevie Grammy nominations for Best Rock Instrumental. He also squeezed in an appearance in Jennifer Warnes's music video for "First We Take Manhattan," a Leonard Cohen composition that both Stevie and Cohen played on.

In mid-April, he taped a B. B. King video special for Cinemax, joining Eric Clapton, Albert King, Phil Collins, Gladys Knight, Billy Ocean, Chaka Khan, and pioneering white blues harmonica player Paul Butterfield (who died a few days later) in an all-star tribute to one of Stevie's great influences. He beamed broadly trading licks with Albert on "The Sky Is Crying." Then it was back to the highway with a vengeance.

For Stevie, work was therapy. The road regimen had been fine-tuned to suit his sober outlook. It helped a great deal that his best friend, Tommy, had taken the cure too. So had others in the Double Trouble camp, including guitar technician Rene Martinez, and Wild Bill Moundsey, Chris Layton's drum tech. It was getting infectious, as if Stevie started a movement. Bonnie Raitt, whose career was on the rocks due to her destructive habits, had gotten her act together, too, and, after a period of readjustment, was rewarded with unprecedented popularity. The pseudonym Stevie used when registering at hotels spoke volumes: instead of his old aliases, Lee Melone or Mr. Tone, he signed in as Iza Newman. The whacked-out lost weekends that went on forever were history, replaced by a level of professionalism and pride in his work that brought along with it a strange sense of inner peace.

Alex Hodges, whose personal touch had moved Stevie to hire him as manager the previous year, made a special effort to make sure promoters were aware of Stevie Ray's transformation and were prepared to accommodate his act's peculiarities and needs. A new, no-nonsense tour manager, Skip Rickert, was hired. The hospitality rider attached to the band's contracts was radically altered. Crown Royal was crossed off the list, replaced by raw vegetables, fruit juices, and sparkling water. Tour itineraries issued to the band and crew listed the closest AA meetings to the gig and hotel. When they couldn't make a meeting, they held their own. At the same time, those not on the program were acknowledged by designating "wet" and "dry" buses and dressing rooms.

"Reese and Chris aren't alcoholics," Stevie explained, "though us alcoholics sometimes resent the fact that other people can drink." When he wasn't working on the guitar or the twelve steps, Stevie found new diversions. On the road, he went bowling or tooled around arena parking lots on a motorized skateboard. On visits to Austin, he and Tommy channeled their energies into pumping iron at Big Steve's Gym or shooting hoops instead of speed.

Temptations were still all around him, as everyone realized after an outdoor September gig at the Pier in New York City. Gregg Allman and his band had opened the show and Allman got so coked up afterward that an EMS unit had to be summoned to his hotel to administer CPR. But Stevie vowed that he wasn't going to fall off the wagon. A motivating factor in staying straight was the level of popularity he had attained. The large venues he was working were a long way from the gin mills of his youth. Ticket sales and merchandise revenues, not bar receipts, were the economic bottom line at this level of performing. And Stevie sold tickets and T-shirts. His no-bullshit attitude toward playing music had made him a paragon of integrity, in sharp contrast to the overproduced stage spectacles other touring acts hawked to the public. People came to a

Stevie Ray Vaughan concert to hear the man play guitar, not for the staging. And Stevie Ray was playing better than ever.

In early November, during a brief break from the road, he showed up at Antone's the night the Irish rock band U2 and producer T-Bone Burnett dropped by after playing the Frank Erwin Center. It was a public birthday party for Lou Ann Barton. Angela Strehli, Jimmie Vaughan, and Dr. John were among the music people on hand to help her celebrate. Jimmie brought along his lap steel and Stevie brought a Strat and Janna. Before the music started cranking full force, he ran into Shirley Ratisseau and one of her daughters, who shared a table with Stevie and Janna. When Stevie found out Shirley's other daughter had been ordained a Methodist minister, his eyes brightened.

"Where is she? How do I get in touch with her?"

"What's the deal?" Shirley asked Stevie. "Why do you want to know? Are you thinking of getting married?"

He glanced toward Janna and smiled slyly. The mere suggestion of a wedding had already caused some friction at home when Stevie told his mother they were thinking of tying the knot in Australia.

"Don't say nothin'," he whispered.

Later that night, the Antone's stage was a bluesbusters' gangbang, as guitars clanged and twanged and U2's charismatic lead singer, Bono, made up lyrics about the curves of Lou Ann's legs because he didn't know the words to any blues standards.

Before Ratisseau rose to leave, she and Stevie played the game they used to play in the bars fifteen years before.

"You really played great tonight, Stevie," she told him.

"Yeah, but who's better?" he asked.

"Jimmie is, dear."

Stevie nodded in agreement. It was the answer he wanted to hear. They smiled across the table, then he walked around to give her a long hug.

"Wait! Wait!" he said excitedly. He reached into his back pocket and fetched out his wallet. He fumbled with it until he produced a card. It was his personal business card. He handed it to Shirley, then opened his arms wide, beaming.

"See how proud I am."

The year following his vow of sobriety was the most private and the most public phase of his life and career. He tried to focus on himself, for once, instead of just his guitar, while professionally expanding his horizons. He cut himself off from many of his old friends who were also his "enablers," the folks who once provided the substances he thought he needed for inspiration.

Breaking away from one of those enablers, his soon-to-be ex-wife,

Lenny, had been the stickiest parting of them all. He filed for divorce on the grounds of "conflict of personality" that made their marriage insupportable. She accused him of adultery. Their battle by proxy was strung out over fifteen months, the exchanges becoming so heated that at one point Lenny's lawyer called Stevie's actions "oppressive and tantamountive [sic] to blackmail." While the lawyers got heavy with accusations and counteraccusations, Stevie maintained an appearance of innocence throughout the painful proceedings. "At one meeting, Stevie and I were sitting with all the lawyers around a table," Lenny remembered, "and Stevie was going on and on about how great I was and everything. I looked at him and said, 'Stevie, this really isn't the time to be talking like that.' "

The battle wound up in court, and the final decree was not granted until June 1, 1988. The price for Stevie's part of the settlement was not cheap. He had to pay lawyer's fees that approached $130,000. Lenny was to receive $50,000 as a lump-sum settlement as well as one fourth of all the royalties from Stevie's first four albums, which translated into a substantial annuity.

Stevie's split with Classic Management was not so expensive. His lawyers settled with Chesley and Frances Carr in the spring of 1987, agreeing to reimburse Classic Management a portion of the money they claimed they had fronted Double Trouble to get the band rolling. Still, Classic figured they wound up on the losing end of the deal to the tune of almost $90,000.

It wasn't cheap, but at least his marriage and Classic were behind him. He preferred talking about other aspects of the past he had shed. If someone asked about drug or alcohol abuse, he jumped at the opportunity. His message was incorporated into his music, sweetening the line "I'm not gonna give up on love/Love's not gonna give up on me" with the words "or you" tagged on the end. "I thank God I'm alive and well enough to be here today," he told his concert audiences time and again. "I've had a second chance."

Stevie's evangelical zeal was part of a long-standing tradition of God-fearing Christians tossing aside the secular heathenism of rock and roll in favor of the Good Book, a tradition almost as old as the music itself. Jerry Lee Lewis and Aretha Franklin first developed their musical might in the sanctified shelter of the House of God. So did R&B shouter and piano pounder Little Richard and screaming rockabilly pioneer Wanda Jackson. Even the Beatles, the band that John Lennon once accurately stated was "more popular than Jesus," went through their own phase of religious enlightenment on a pilgrimage to India where they learned transcendental meditation from the Maharishi Mahesh Yogi.

Religion has always been rock's most consistent wild card. Bob

Dylan, the articulate voice of protest in the sixties, couldn't decide whether he was Orthodox Jew or Jesus freak during most of the seventies. Carlos Santana rejected Latin blues-rock for a more abstract realm of music influenced by his interest in Buddhism and Christianity. Likewise, jazz guitar great John McLaughlin rejected worldly musics for something more ethereal after he embraced the teachings of Sri Chimoy. Then there were those like Eric Clapton, whose embrace of traditional, fundamentalist Christianity helped him kick several addictions before backsliding.

If Stevie had tried to preach sobriety twenty years, even ten years earlier, his career might have fizzled, the way Little Richard's, Wanda Jackson's, Dylan's, and Santana's careers stalled when they were caught in the spirit of the Holy Ghost. But times had changed. Stevie's fans didn't mind it when he preached at them from the stage, telling them to "leave the damn drugs alone, they will kill you," even as they took a hit of Wild Turkey or snorted a little nose candy. It was cool. He was just trying to take care of himself the way he took care of them with his music.

Not everyone bought into the rap. Talk is cheap, the conventional wisdom went, and relapse is even cheaper. When the alternatives were redemption or jail, enlightenment could be so much lip service put out for public consumption while the hypocrisy of the message was played out on mirrors behind closed doors. Hey, he was still willing to let beer companies sponsor his gigs, wasn't he? Some insisted that Stevie still got high on the sly. Others remembered debts that Stevie never paid. Stevie was an asshole when it came to dope, hogging all the blow, promising to pay someone later for a little charge today. How come he was suddenly OK?

Several of his former running buddies, including those who thought of themselves as fellow guitarists first and cokeheads second, swore they could detect the passion had gone out of his guitar playing. Was his mind hijacked by the Moonies or some other fanatical religious cult, they wondered aloud, a cruel trade-off of his old habits for a crutch that was no less demeaning? Stevie and Jimmie used to joke about how their father, Big Jim, would get drunk on Saturday night, only to appear sanctimoniously remorseful in church on Sunday morning. In some respects, Stevie was no different, though his church was a concert hall and the stage his pulpit.

He recognized his tendency to want to testify. "Sometimes I wonder whether people want to hear it, or if they'll think it's stupid or silly," he mused. But while he was adamant about refraining from talking about it unless someone asked, he was willing to risk alienating some of his hardcore fans if it meant helping one person who needed it. "Now I realize that I'm responsible to stay sober and to reach out to anybody who's got a problem. Hell, if it hadn't been for people reaching out to me, I may not have made it," he said.

He made a point of seeking out old friends he might have done wrong in the past. He cornered C. B. Stubblefield, the Barbecue Czar of Lubbock, backstage after a concert in Austin.

"I've changed my lifestyle," he told Stubb. "I haven't had a beer and I don't do all that other shit no more, and I feel good. I look out at the audience and it's not just a bunch of people glaring at me or waving at me. Hell, I can see everybody. And I can hear my music and I feel real good. I thought about you from one end of this world to the other, more than you think."

Brother Stevie Ray's witnessing rubbed some AA participants the wrong way. Ever since 1940 when Rollie Hemsley, a well-known catcher for the Cleveland Indians, became the first public figure to acknowledge that he got with the program, internal debate within AA circles raged about what is and isn't proper when talking about the twelve steps. The stated guidelines include the suggestion that AA participants "always maintain personal anonymity at the level of press, radio and films."

In a letter to one McGhee B., AA cofounder Bill W. warned that "excessive personal publicity or prominence in the work was found to be bad. Alcoholics who talked too much on public platforms were likely to become inflated and get drunk again." Stevie adhered to the code by never referring publicly to Alcoholics Anonymous, although he talked freely about the twelve-step program, which was considered OK. His willingness to open up was welcomed by a significant number of recovering alcoholics, despite AA's tradition of anonymity, in no small part due to Stevie's high public profile and his particular line of work.

One of those who approved was W. A. "Bill" Williams, a reformed lush who had seen the light and, as a nondenominational lay preacher, devoted his life to working the streets of his hometown, Cincinnati. Carrying the word of the Gospel did not lessen Williams's appreciation of rock music, which led to a sideline trade taking photographs of touring music performers.

One of the acts he shot during the summer of 1987 at the Riverbend outdoor amphitheater was the reconstituted Allman Brothers, which featured the Tolar brothers, his old running buddies from Cincinnati. Seeing the Tolars performing with one of the great American rock bands made Williams proud, but rather than schmooze with them after their set, something made him hang around the stage for the headline act. He vaguely remembered hearing Stevie Ray Vaughan and Double Trouble shortly after the release of their second album, but he wrote off the guitarist as a "Hendrix clone." Try as he might, no one came close to touching Jimi in Williams's book. What he heard that night had more to it than mere Hendrix reproductions, he thought to himself. But it still didn't move him. Not until Stevie started talking to the audience about addictions during the rap portion of "Life Without You."

Williams believed in using every possible opportunity to give witness to his salvation through Christ. He was accustomed to having his message fall on deaf ears. That was the price for working all the low-rent joints he frequented. But the words coming out of Stevie's mouth, not the sound of his guitar, hit Williams like manna from heaven. "He started sharing from his heart about almost killing himself. I saw somebody with a platform who was using it not to promote sex, drugs, and rock and roll, but promoting his music and the importance of being good to people."

Convinced of Stevie's sincerity and the significance of his message, he cornered him after the show to let him know he'd reached at least one person that night. They plunged into a deep discussion about the spirit, redemption, and the importance of evangelism. One crew member who heard Williams talking with Vaughan backstage innocently kidded him, saying, "Hey, Stevie, you going to church or something?"

"We looked at each other, then at the sky," Williams remembered. "That was when it clicked."

He went out of his way to make as many shows around the Midwest as time and his limited budget would allow, not just to take pictures of Double Trouble, but to read the Scriptures together with Stevie, Tommy, and other crew members in recovery, sharing personal experiences from before and after their long, twisted journeys to reality.

Ten days after celebrating his birthday, marking his thirty-third year on earth, Stevie V. marked a far more important milestone. October 13 marked a full year of sobriety. The one-year chip he received from the Aquarius group back in Dallas meant more to him than all the gold and platinum discs he'd collected from the record industry: selling a million albums was a lot easier than surviving the 8,760 hours since his last drink.

18

IN STEP

There wasn't a lot of time to contemplate what had gone down, what was happening now, and what was around the next bend. The calendar was crammed too full to do that. There were debts to retire and charts to climb. Work didn't feel like the burden it once had become, but more like a pleasure, the way it was back in the clubs, when money was the least of his motives or concerns. During the month of February 1988, Stevie and Janna flew to New Zealand and filmed a commercial for the Europa Oil Company. In it, Stevie played guitar, rode a motorcycle, and sat on the front end of a plane in pursuit of a hot babe, played by the noted native New Zealander Janna Lapidus.

Two months later, Double Trouble did a three-week run through the Northeast, opening up shows on the first leg of Robert Plant's North American tour. In July, it was the summer festival circuit in Italy, Germany, Holland, and nine other European countries where Stevie was hailed as the guitar great of his generation.

Deals and offers tumbled in. Tough-guy actor Mickey Rourke huddled with him to discuss a screenplay he was developing for a film called *The Ride*. He envisioned casting Stevie Ray in the role of a half-Indian biker whose character had a younger brother that Rourke wanted Charlie

Sexton to play. Actor and playwright Sam Shepard included Stevie's version of "Voodoo Chile" in the soundtrack of his film *Far North*. Robert De Niro called, too. The molar-grinding "Rude Mood" provided the perfect background music for the trailer advertising the De Niro–Charles Grodin movie *Midnight Run*.

He also squeezed in time to appear in the "Stevie Wonder's Characters" special for MTV, in which he reprised his studio role playing guitar behind Wonder on "Come Let Me Make Your Love Come Down." For "Superstition," he shared lead vocals with the original Little Stevie and Jody Watley. Stevie Ray Vaughan wasn't just the main guitar man for the 'ludes and Jack Black generation anymore.

The problem he faced now was convincing his record company. In the middle of his comeback, the Sony Corporation of Japan paid $2 billion for CBS Records Inc., which included Stevie Ray Vaughan's label, Epic. Manager Alex Hodges figured that the corporate realignment provided a good opportunity to reposition Stevie Ray Vaughan and Double Trouble and boost their profile at the company. On May 17, 1988, he presented the new regime with a Report of Career Achievement that he hoped would convince company executives to gear up the promotional push necessary to boost Stevie into the superstar stratosphere.

Hodges's dog-and-pony show detailed all the various Grammys, Handys, and other awards Stevie had won, recounted his exceptionally strong box-office receipts, tabulated worldwide album sales of more than 3 million units over the previous eighteen months despite Stevie's longest career break since junior high school. The buildup led to the point that Hodges wanted to prove. His client was alive and well. His potential was greater than ever. Stevie Ray Vaughan, the bad boy of the blues, could be as big as or bigger than Hendrix or Clapton.

The bigwigs were unmoved. The Sony brass stroked the manager and his act with compliments and encouragement, but there was no significant commitment of additional funds. Stevie Ray Vaughan's records were solid gold sellers, all right, but they couldn't compare to products like Michael Jackson's *Thriller*, which sold almost 40 million units worldwide. And yet, the momentum did not stop, could not stop. Product and ticket sales continued a steady upward curve. Never again would they flatten out or drop.

Onstage, Stevie continued to improve. The coked up, frazzled edge that marked earlier shows was replaced by an approach defined by subtlety and understatement, moving Bruce Nixon, the *Dallas Times-Herald* music critic and longtime Stevie-watcher to call Vaughan's Starplex concert in mid-July his "most polished, and certainly his most thoroughly professional performance."

By the fall of 1988, he'd toured long enough to demonstrate to one and all he could still dazzle an audience and pack a house. Now he wanted to make a document that would reflect his rebirth and erase the memory of *Live Alive*, that lingering, embarrassing reminder of how out of control he had been. Road-tested and revitalized, legally divorced and in love, Stevie jumped at the chance to get back into the studio and see what was in him.

October, November, and December of 1988 were blocked off to work on the first studio album since 1985's *Soul to Soul*. This time, his approach was textbook in its methodology. In order to come up with material, he huddled once again with Doyle Bramhall, who next to his brother was the major influence on his music.

Ever since he recruited Jimmie into the Chessmen, Doyle had been both a willing and often unwitting mentor to Stevie. Doyle was the bedrock foundation of the Nightcrawlers, even though A&M Records thought it was Marc Benno's band and Bill Ham believed it was Stevie's. He had contributed songs on every one of Double Trouble's studio albums. He'd set another sort of example, too, first as an unreconstructed gonzo wildman, and later as the first of Stevie's friends to get with the twelve-step program.

Doyle knew what Stevie was talking about when he expressed his desire to do songs with themes that meant more than just getting a new girl or driving a fast car or roaring until the break of dawn. Previous Double Trouble albums were primarily showcases for the guitar. Stevie wanted this one to be personal and up front, a monument to the struggles he and his friend had endured. Slip in a message or two with the music, and maybe someone else might find inspiration.

The collaborators began by airing out their thoughts. "Before we'd write anything down, we would talk for hours and days about what was going on with us," Doyle told writer Brad Buchholz. "Then we would end up making little notes to ourselves."

They were both surprised when they discovered how similar their notes were. A lot of what they discussed focused on recovery from addictions and the difficulties they endured working their way out of the morass their habits had created. They agreed there was no easy way to do it.

The terrifying blank spots that marred the making of *Soul to Soul* and *Live Alive* did not manifest themselves this time around. Writing songs with Doyle was a kick, a process as nourishing as AA meetings. "In a lot of ways during the whole time I was using, part of me didn't grow — emotionally, mainly, spiritually, and some parts mentally," Stevie said. "Being around Doyle was an adventure."

Doyle had been locked into the twelve steps for a decade, but for many of those years, he had been a "dry drunk," someone who had put the cork in the bottle but who continued to think like an alcoholic and had not achieved true sobriety. As they worked together, Doyle's thoughts drifted to this nagging dilemma. One day as he was driving home from Stevie's house, a phrase stuck in his craw. He stopped the car, pulled out a piece of paper, and jotted it down.

Stevie had been experimenting with a 6/3 blues shuffle riff. At one point he began to play the shuffle for Chris, who picked up his drumsticks and began to beat out a rhythm on a telephone book while Tommy played bass. The melody was still fresh on his mind when he was talking on the phone with Alex Hodges. He was giving his manager a progress report when Doyle burst into the room and breathlessly sang, "A wall of deni-alll . . ."

Stevie quickly bid Alex adieu, hung up the phone, and turned around to face Doyle.

"Say whaaat?"

The song that evolved summed up what Stevie, Doyle, Tommy, and millions of others had learned from recovery.

"We're never safe from the truth/but in the truth we can survive."

It was a basic element of the twelve steps, Stevie explained to writer Timothy White. "We always try to hide from the truth, thinking we can, when in fact if you try to cover up those things that really are too hard to look at, they end up coming out like razor blades or explosions in our lives and tear things up." Stevie knew this for a fact. In his own attempt to hide from the truth, cocaine crystals had torn his insides up like so many razor blades.

"Wall of Denial" wasn't the only paean to the twelve-step program the Bramhall/Vaughan team came up with. "Tightrope," which Stevie began to articulate before his rehabilitation, needed Doyle's perspective before it could be declared finished. There was an important statement that needed to be made: "My heart goes out to others/who are there to make amends."

Even fuckheads could redeem themselves.

"Crossfire" echoed the theme of overcoming addictions through mutual support, both in the lyrics written by the songwriting team of Bill Carter and Ruth Ellsworth, and in the music that the band created, the only song Stevie ever recorded that listed Tommy and Chris on writing credits.

Stevie was wise enough to know that people would dismiss his message if he laid it on too thick. In keeping with AA's Rule Number 62 — "Don't take yourself too seriously" — the album kicked off with Doyle's celebratory "The House Is Rockin'," a full-tilt boogie that promised loyalists that the party hadn't stopped.

There were other selections of a more conventional nature. "Let Me

Love You Baby" lifted a few ideas from zydeco king Clifton Chenier's stomper "All Night Long"; the instrumental "Travis Walk" was inflected with a distinctive south Louisiana backbeat. The title for "Scratch-N-Sniff" was lifted from an old Fab T-Birds poster. Though considerably less weighty than some of their message-laden tunes on the album, they, too, were part of Stevie's life.

"I didn't want them just to be something with some preaching lyrics and kinda go by the wayside," he explained. "What's going on in those songs, what they mean to me, is why I'm alive now."

That was as good a reason as any to name the record *In Step*.

Once the songs began to take shape, the band started rehearsals in Austin. Chris Layton had introduced Stevie to Stephen Bruton, a guitar touring pro who agreed to sublease his South Austin home to Stevie while he was on the road. The two Steves had more in common than they ever suspected. Bruton grew up in Fort Worth, thirty miles west of Oak Cliff, in a household where music was a given. His parents, a drummer and singer by training, owned a record store. Like Stevie, Steve had a big brother who was also a guitarist. Stephen Bruton had done a fifteen-year stretch as Kris Kristofferson's lead player and was about to join Stevie's friend Bonnie Raitt as her guitarist. Most significantly, Steve Bruton had recently quit drinking and drugging after more than twenty years of serious over-the-top abuse.

When he came over to check out the house, Stevie was distracted by Bruton's collection of guitars and amps. In a matter of minutes, he cajoled Bruton into letting him take some equipment with him to Los Angeles, where he would begin recording. Bruton consented, with the caveat, "You break, you pay."

They both proceeded to engage in a little picking session. Bruton played a few lines or chords, and Stevie followed. Stevie threw in a tricky lick only to have Steve fill in the blanks without hesitation. The exercise began in the midafternoon. Somewhere around 3 A.M. they both stopped long enough to exchange knowing grins.

"You know, a few years ago, we'd have finished half an ounce between us by now," Bruton joked.

"This is even better," Stevie replied.

The recording sessions at the Sound Castle and Summa Studios in LA and Kiva Studios in Memphis were a sharp contrast to the chaos that distinguished the making of *Soul to Soul*. Jim Gaines was hired as producer, largely on the strength of his work with Carlos Santana. It didn't hurt that he had a roundabout connection to Austin blues, having engineered a never-released project by Southern Feeling, Angela Strehli's and W. C. Clark's band, in Seattle fifteen years before.

Stevie and the band's extensive preparations made the actual recording process relatively cut-and-dried. For once, they weren't dead set on trying to capture the excitement of a live show, but concentrated on crafting a studio album that they could be proud of. "We went ahead and kicked out the idea that if you play it more than three times you're wanking," Stevie explained. There was no more blaming the drink mixer or snorting another line when something went wrong. If there was a problem, the band confronted it, talked about it, and fixed it.

That approach left room for unexpected moments of serendipity. Not surprisingly, the most eloquent song turned out to be one without words. Stevie had started the composition many years before, playing snatches of it during the 1984 *Couldn't Stand the Weather* sessions. Over time, lyrics appeared and disappeared, and the melody was tweaked around. But when he sat down to do the tune for this album, the first take of what Stevie titled "Riviera Paradise" was the keeper.

There was nothing particularly remarkable about the way he went about it. He picked up the maple-neck Strat, the same one he had used to record "Lenny" on his first album, dimmed the lights in his recording booth, and turned his back to the people sitting behind the console on the other side of the glass. Gaines let the tape roll, mixing in Chris's delicate rhythms and Tommy's bass line while Stevie played away in a world of his own. When he noticed that the tape was running out, Gaines gestured frantically to Chris to wrap up the song. The producer caught Chris's eye and, with a few flourishes, he brought the song to a close. Eight seconds later the tape ran out.

"To me the song was a much needed chance to turn the lights off in the studio and basically — I don't know how to put it any other way — pray through my guitar," Stevie said. The band tried to do more takes of the song, but they came out sounding like Muzak. The first version would do just fine. It was a fitting close to *In Step*, Stevie Ray Vaughan's last recording with Double Trouble.

He dedicated the album to John Hammond. The man with the golden ears had passed away the previous year, but not before Stevie personally told him about his own sobriety. Hammond appreciated the gesture. Back in the fledgling years of the record business, at a time when very little was known about addictions and how to beat them, Hammond strongly supported any artists who tried to kick their drug or alcohol habits.

In Step hit the retail racks in July 1989, just in time for an extensive string of domestic dates paired with another of Stevie's old heroes, the British guitarist Jeff Beck. Billed as "The Fire and Fury Tour," the performances gave Stevie a chance to work with an artist whose hits he had once interpreted in front of his high school speech class, and whose music formed part of the bedrock of his musical education.

"It's been a lifelong thing to me, listening to you, man, and for me it's an honor to be out here with you now," Stevie said to him during a dual interview. "I'm not just being a parrot talking shit. This is the real deal."

Beck returned the compliment. He talked about playing with Hendrix, an experience that made him feel "like a peanut." "I felt very amateurish alongside him, because he lived and breathed it," he said, directing his comment to Stevie. "You're very similar to Jimi in that way. I'm not in love with the guitar as much as you are or Jimi is — was. I just pick it up and play it sometimes."

Though there was a keen sense of anticipation since Beck had been off the road for eight years, the tour had mixed results. The forty-five-year-old Beck was a technician conversant in many languages of the instrument who was working for the first time with one of the best stage drummers in rock, Terry Bozzio. Stevie's dynamics came from the heart and soul, not the head. Unlike the gentleman guitarist he was sharing the bill with, he acted possessed onstage, as if he were letting the spirit take hold and tell his fingers where to go. While Beck and his band ordered drinks from hotel bars, comparing their lot to that of the mythical Spinal Tap, Stevie was still hugging people backstage, telling them, "I'm alive today, and I'm happy."

The two acts alternated opening and closing the bill, although they informally agreed to close the shows together, typically on a standard like "Goin' Down," the Don Nix composition that became a Freddie King standard. When the two did go *mano a mano*, the contest wasn't as close as an impartial observer might have expected. Stephen Bruton caught the show in Los Angeles. Beck was brilliant, as usual. Vaughan, however, was exceptional. "He was hitting hyperspace. He took it away." They even sold out Madison Square Garden in New York, after which Stevie split uptown to the Beacon Theater to sit in with his favorite guitar player, Jimmie Vaughan.

But no concert meant quite so much as the one at the Frank Erwin Center in Austin. It was a poetic return for Stevie. He not only shredded Beck at the end of the night while effusively heaping praise on his counterpart, he had the greater satisfaction of collecting more cans of food donated by ticket buyers for his favorite charity, the Capital Area Food Bank, than Bruce Springsteen had a few months earlier. The incentive for fans to bring a can was the promise to meet Stevie backstage. The helpless waif who once sold aluminum cans for guitar strings was able to help others eat.

In Step went gold, then platinum, and earned Stevie Ray Vaughan and Double Trouble another Grammy for Best Contemporary Blues Recording of 1989. When Stevie stepped up to the podium at the awards ceremony in early 1990, he was as humble as he was clean. Holding up his award in front of the glitterati of the biz, he thanked them, then declared, "Now let's get Buddy Guy one."

Guy was another mentor of sorts. Stevie'd first jammed with George "Buddy" Guy at Antone's in the mid-seventies. Over the years, they continued to share the stage at every opportunity. Stevie helped Buddy open up Legends, his nightclub in Chicago, and he never tired of praising Guy's relentless guitar attack because, he, too, approached it from the heart. "Buddy's style is not necessarily such a technical style, it's more like raw meat in a lot of ways," he explained. "He plays from a place that I've never heard anyone play. A place inside."

The black blues legends remained his favorites. He once gave $5,000 to Larry Davis, who had been credited for writing "Texas Flood." When Stevie later learned that Fenton Robinson, the lead guitarist in Davis's band, was the actual composer, he laid some cash on him, too. Sometimes the payback came in the form of recognition, turning his audience on to his heroes. At Fort Lauderdale's Sunrise Music Theater, Stevie introduced Otis Rush, who stepped out onstage in his standard cowboy hat and cowboy boots, carrying his righty-played-lefty Gibson Stereo 345 guitar like a Colt .45 for renditions of Muddy Waters's "Got My Mojo Working" and T-Bone Walker's "Stormy Monday."

Taping a live performance for MTV on the Riverboat President during the New Orleans Jazz and Heritage Festival, Stevie shared the limelight with B. B. King, Katie Webster, the queen of Louisiana swamp boogie, and Albert Collins, the Houston-born "Master of the Telecaster" who'd watched the kid grow up on Texas stages. Collins didn't need Stevie's goodwill. He was a solid road draw on his own. But he appreciated the younger guitarist's acknowledgments. "He did a lot for us blues players, keeping the blues happening," Collins said. "He made the blues a young and old thing to listen to."

Even his frustratingly brief solo on James Brown's comeback single, "Living in America," was satisfying for the blackness his guitar lines lent to a tune that was otherwise white-bread.

His efforts to give credit where credit was due actually solidified his standing as the musical equivalent of basketball star Larry Bird: he was the best white man in a black man's game. It was all in keeping with his lifelong desire for a different skin color. "Stevie's only regret was that he was not born black," remarked former manager Chesley Millikin. Lenny and he had often speculated that they'd been born black in previous lives. The worst thing he could say about his own playing when he had a rare off night was "I sounded really white tonight."

For all the praise being heaped on him, he never hesitated to return the favor. In October of 1989, he was the linchpin of a tribute to W. C.

Clark for "Austin City Limits," a Public Broadcasting System series taped in Austin. Stevie joined Jimmie, Denny Freeman, Angela Strehli, Lou Ann Barton, Derek O'Brien, and George Rains in a tribute to one of the father figures of the Austin blues scene. During the performance, Clark couldn't help being struck by the vaguely familiar feeling of someone looking over his shoulder. He glanced back after he hit a particularly nasty lick and saw not-so-Little Stevie peering at his fretboard, asking the same question he used to ask almost every night.

"How'd you do that, man?"

19

HILLBILLIES FROM OUTER SPACE

Of all the people Stevie Ray Vaughan was indebted to, no one was tougher to pay back than brother Jimmie. The Fabulous Thunderbirds finally broke into the big time in 1986, about the same time Stevie Ray was flaming out. Their ticket was the Top 10 hit "Tuff Enuff." But by the summer of 1989, the band was coming unraveled at the seams too. Jimmie and Kim Wilson, the vocalist and harp player, found themselves increasingly at odds. The old plodding I-IV-V progressions had finally gotten to Jimmie. He wanted to delve into new territory like the Hawaiian steel guitar music he was discovering and straight jazz. Kim felt like the band had a responsibility as official keepers of the American blues flame. Their record company didn't care what style it was, they just wanted another hit record. The rancor between the two musicians moved one maven at Ardent Studios in Memphis who witnessed the band's last recording session to describe the standoff as "the most tension I've ever seen in a studio, and I've seen Alex Chilton [the Memphis pop and punk singer who led the Boxtops and Big Star] beat up his girlfriend between cutting tracks."

Hot Number, the Fabulous Thunderbirds' follow-up album to *Tuff Enuff* was again produced by British roots rocker Dave Edmunds. But this time around, Edmunds's magic touch did not do the trick. The album was a creative and financial failure, despite Jimmie's vow to infiltrate the charts again with "the dirtiest fuckin' record that's gonna be out." Kim Wilson's alleged disdain for commercial success — "As far as I'm concerned, mainstream is kind of like a piss puddle comin' out of a wino on Sixth Street," he said — was belied by the song he wrote that was floated out as a single. "Powerful Stuff" was a blatant attempt to reprise "Tuff Enuff" but minus the spark or the hook.

Stevie knew that Jimmie had sunk to the creative pits. He also knew that if anyone could benefit from cleaning up, it was his brother. Drugs had derailed the Chessmen, played a significant role in Jimmie blowing his first chance at a recording contract, and were influencing his visible disinterest in playing T-Bird rhythms. The guy once known as Chief for his propensity to "go Indian" with too much drink and too much toot displayed all the symptoms of being consumed by his own image, an image that he tried to dress up, at one time or another, with cheap Italian suits, women's clothing from Neiman-Marcus, and soul perms.

Jimmie and Stevie had played music with each other in their bedroom, in Jimmie's band Texas Storm, and shared stages at the Armadillo, the South Door, the T-Bird Riverfests, and all across North America, Australia, and New Zealand. Through it all, the quiet brotherly rivalry always lingered, even though Stevie and even Jimmie publicly offered nothing but praise for each other. Now that he'd gotten his life and his career back on track again, Stevie decided it was time to put up or shut up. He approached Jimmie with a proposal: a Vaughan brothers album.

C'mon, man. I'll make the time, if you'll make the time. If I can do it, you can, too.

The project made more sense than ever. Both Vaughans were conveniently obligated to the same record company. Their respective fans would certainly dig the collaboration if for no other reason than to figure out once and for all which Vaughan wielded the hotter hands. Besides, both Jimmie and Stevie were ripe for a change of scenery. Jimmie had been punching the clock as a Thunderbird for fifteen years. Stevie, Chris, and Tommy had been a combo for almost a decade. Working together would give them each a break and put some real meaning into the brothers' relationship.

The prospect of cutting a whole record with Jimmie intrigued Stevie, made him giddy. Getting Jimmie to do it straight was the real challenge. He laid down the gauntlet.

If I can do it, anyone can.

Of all the people he had testified in front of, there was no one he wanted to reach as badly as Jimmie. The fearful, insecure little brother who was only good enough to play bass, the impish kid who used to show up at the studio with a Baggie full of white powder for inspiration, he was the one who had to take the lead now. Jimmie may have taught Stevie how to play the guitar, but it was Stevie who wanted to show Jimmie a few pointers on how to live the rest of his life.

Let's see what we can do straight.

Jimmie swallowed his pride long enough to listen. He'd used up eight lives already, maybe more. The kicks had gotten stale. He knew he was ripe for a change. He took Stevie's advice and entered rehab. When he emerged, he joined Stevie to do the album they'd waited all their lives to make.

"It's like a long-delayed homecoming," Jimmie said afterward. "I feel like I've found a brother I'd lost for years." The feeling was mutual.

The Vaughan boys began their collaboration by going back to *their* roots and retreating to the garage of Jimmie's South Austin home, just fartin' around like a couple of flat-topped teens with an itch to hold a guitar. They worked on songs that were touchstones of their youth, some of them predictable, some of them odd relics that could have only come from growing up in Oak Cliff in the sixties: Booker T. and the MGs, Creedence Clearwater Revival, Bob Wills and The Texas Playboys, and exotic Hawaiian fare inspired by the steel guitar Jimmie liked to fool around with, as well as the usual suspects — the Alberts (King and Collins), the Kings (Freddie and B. B.), Eddie, Hubert, Lonnie Mack, Guitar Gable, pedal-steel ace Herb Remington, and the jazz organ sounds of Jimmy Smith and Groove Holmes. As they discussed material over the phone and ran through numbers in Jimmie's garage, they realized they had become so adept at their chosen line of work they didn't even need a backup band for the album. Jimmie always thought he could drum as well as his drummers (and more often than not, he could) and Stevie knew enough bass to rate playing with Jimmie back when he was still in high school. The prospect of playing all the instruments themselves was tantalizing, because with this record there were no limits and no expectations. "We just wanted to do all the stuff that we've been wanting to do for years and couldn't for one reason or another," Jimmie said.

They hired Nile Rodgers to produce the record. Stevie had liked Rodgers ever since he'd watched him oversee David Bowie's *Let's Dance* album, and Jimmie felt good about him after they met. Rodgers would certainly free up both brothers from any preconceived notions about what the album was supposed to be. If nothing else, they could count on Nile to push them toward the unexpected.

Very Vaughan, as the album was tentatively titled, got under way at the Dallas Sound Labs the day after Stevie wrapped up his Jeff Beck tour. From a distance, the closed session suggested a tense atmosphere, Mr. Understatement against the Right Reverend Louie Kablooie Over-the-

Top. As it turned out, the one-upmanship was limited to the praise they continually heaped on each other. Jimmie freely complimented Stevie. Stevie was so reverential he went out of his way to defer to his brother and give him more than his equal share of the spotlight. Instead of acting like rough, tough guitarslingers squaring off for a shoot-out, they behaved like two long-lost goofballs.

What else could have precipitated the vocal debut of Jimmie Vaughan on the boastful brag "Good Texan" and on "White Boots," a thoroughly stupid song about teenage lust written by Billy Swan and Jim Leslie? "It was amazing they got him to sing," declared Mike Buck, the Thunderbirds' former drummer. "The only time I'd heard him sing before was trying to do Lazy Lester drunk in some dressing room."

After finishing demos in Dallas and Austin, the brothers headed to Ardent Studios in Memphis and really went to work. Nile Rodgers persuaded Jimmie and Stevie to focus on their guitar work and leave the rhythm tracks to studio pros. The brothers agreed. After all, twenty-five years had already slipped by. If they farted around too long, it might take another twenty-five before the final mixdown was finished. Rodgers brought in two players he liked to use, bassist Al Berry and drummer Larry Aberman, neither of whom had worked with either Vaughan or knew much about them. "Roll and I'll just feel something," said Stevie, kicking off the album with a quote that captured the extremely loose mood of the project.

Doyle Bramhall cowrote three compositions with Stevie about longing and redemption — "Hard to Be," "Telephone Song," and "Long Way from Home." Jimmie did a watery sendup of a Hammond B-3 organ with his lap steel for the instrumental titled "Hillbillies from Outerspace," a not-so-veiled reference to themselves.

"Tick Tock," a Memphis-styled soul groove, was written with the assistance of song doctor Jerry Lynn Williams, a Fort Worth native who'd "fixed" projects by Eric Clapton and ZZ Top, among others. The song carried the message of making amends before it's too late, since "time's tickin' away," a sweet reverie that recalled Otis Redding at his most circumspect. Jimmie came up with the melody line twenty years earlier while sitting on his front porch shortly after he had arrived in Austin.

The album was actually pretty light on the six-strings. The one time they let their guitars go balls to the wall was on "D/FW," a frenzied homage to Lonnie Mack and every great two-minute-and-thirty-second instrumental that was ever pressed as a 45 single. The closest they came to a cutting contest was a meditative instrumental titled "Brothers." To record the song, they faced each other in a sound booth and swapped Jimmie's white Strat back and forth, picking out lines over the rhythm tracks. Rodgers objected to this less-than-professional recording technique — the guitar strap got caught in one handoff, and the two players couldn't help but give each other some grief, as brothers are wont to do — but finally relented. The version that ultimately appeared on the album was a remarkable piece of mobile musicianship. This time around when they copped riffs from guitarists they idolized, they copped from each other.

During a break in the recording in mid-March, Stevie flew to his former hometown to attend the Eighth Annual Austin Music Awards to pick up a passel of honors that included Record of the Year for *In Step*, Single of the Year for "Crossfire," Musician of the Year, Record of the Decade for *Texas Flood*, and Musician of the Decade.

"I just want to thank God I'm alive," he told the crowd during one of several acceptance speeches. "And I want to thank all the people that loved me back to life so that I could be here with you today." More than anything, the awards validated his struggle up the ranks in Austin. Working the clubs might have been the hard way out. But it was honest, at least. Besides, if he could do it, anyone could do it.

Stevie and Jimmie learned a lot about each other, as musicians and as people, while making the record. "He's a little gentler than I knew," Stevie said, tapping his chest, "here. Maybe part of the reason that we tried so hard was because we had each other to impress." Jimmie nodded in agreement, sounding more than a little like a younger brother. "This record was just personal," he said. "Playing from your heart." Taping a promotional video for the album, Stevie talked about how much the project meant to the both of them. "We've probably got closer makin' this record than we have been since we were little kids. And I needed it. I can honestly say I needed it."

When the basic tracks were finished, Double Trouble and the Fabulous Thunderbirds headlined together at the New Orleans Jazz and Heritage Festival. Following that event and the T-Bird Riverfest on Town Lake in Austin, Jimmie announced his retirement from the Fabulous Thunderbirds. Kim Wilson could have the band. He had his own agenda now.

20

THE OTIS EXPRESS

"See this," Stevie Ray Vaughan said to Bill Milkowski of *Guitar World* magazine, pointing to the white pin on his lapel emblazoned with an image of Jimi Hendrix. "You know, there's a big lie in this business. The lie is that it's okay to go down in flames. Some of us can be examples about going ahead and growing. And some of us, unfortunately, don't make it there and end up being examples because they had to die. I hit rock bottom, but thank God my bottom wasn't death."

Music was a gift. So were the twelve steps. "Where I got the idea, I'm not sure, whether it be in Sunday school when I was a little kid or what," he said. "But I do know that it is a gift, and I know that my life is a gift right now."

The intensity of Stevie Ray's performances was due in part to his understanding that his gift could be taken away at any moment. "The way I like to look at it is if that's the last time I ever got to play, I better give it everything I've got. Because it sure would be a drag to look back and go, 'Well, I blew that one.' " Just as he did when he was a sixteen-year-old crooning "Crossroads" at the Cellar, just as he did keeping up with Denny Freeman lick for lick in the Cobras at Soap Creek, and just as he did when he snapped his head back and let himself go, gnawing at his guitar strings with his teeth for the edification of a paying crowd of three at the Rome Inn, Stevie Ray Vaughan, sobered-up superstar, made every performance count. "He played like every note was his last," said Stephen Bruton. "That's how you're supposed to play. He did it."

Stevie had the remarkable ability to connect with his audience, even if they numbered in the thousands. He had matured enough to figure out the value of a more facile touch, as if he were giving a private concert in the living room of every ticket holder in the arena. He had dreamed of playing guitar for a living ever since he was a kid. Now, he was more driven than ever: he played guitar because he had to.

"For me it's a need to play that stuff," he remarked. "I've seen that kind of sound heal me and other people. I'm not saying that I am a healer; I'm saying that wherever those kinds of feelings and emotions come from or through, music is a healer. If I hadn't had the music to play, I probably would have been dead a long time ago."

Scholars have compared rock performers to shamans, or healers in traditional societies. In Stevie Ray's case, healing was no theoretical bullshit. Healing was part of the power of music, he often told friends. He'd seen it for himself almost ten years earlier.

Back in the days when Double Trouble regularly gigged at Fitzgerald's in Houston, one of the band's loyal fans was seriously injured in a horrible car wreck. A friend contacted Cutter Brandenburg, the band's road manager, and told him the kid wasn't going to make it. Cutter passed the word on to the band, and they all decided to pay the fan a visit in the hospital. They weren't prepared for what they saw. "This guy was a mess," Cutter recalled. "It was frightening. We were way above our field here. We wanted to make somebody feel good — this guy was about to die."

Unlike his band mates, Stevie wasn't repulsed by the sight of the mangled fan in traction. He hugged him. He kissed him. He played guitar for him. The others had a hard time getting Stevie to leave. "I think through Stevie's love and dedication he gave the guy something that hadn't been there before," observed Cutter. "Stevie took the time that nobody else did, to say 'I love you and I'll play for you.' "

The young man did eventually recuperate and got well enough to attend a Double Trouble show at Fitzgerald's. That night, Cutter noticed a change come over Stevie, a strange sense of calm that seemed connected to knowing the boy he'd visited in the hospital was in the crowd. "I don't know if Stevie healed him," Cutter said. "But I do know that both of those two motherfuckers think he did something."

Stevie found an articulate advocate for the healing power of his music in Michele Sugg, a clinical social worker at Yale Psychiatric Institute at the Yale University School of Medicine, where some of her patients were Double Trouble fans. One male teenager in particular who had been a heavy-duty abuser played Stevie Ray music constantly. Sugg knew enough about the band to point out that Stevie was straight. Her patient didn't believe her at first but finally came around to accepting the sobriety of his kick-ass guitar hero. The example helped him to clean up. His justification, he told Sugg, was "Stevie Ray Vaughan did it."

Sugg became a friend to both Stevie and Janna Lapidus. She attended dozens of performances and had lengthy discussions with both of them about music and Stevie's struggle to get sober and stay that way. A presentation Sugg made to her colleagues at Yale about the healing power of music cited studies describing the correlations between bodily rhythms and music and included Stevie Ray Vaughan's point of view. He believed that music was a part of each person's soul. He felt that the body, like music, was nothing more than a bunch of vibrating molecules, and that each individual's being responded to a particular musical chord. "The chord goes through a progression during someone's lifetime," he told Sugg once over the phone. "How to find that chord, I'm not real sure. I don't think you can look at somebody and say, 'I bet you're an A, and this girl's a B-flat.' "

At Sugg's behest, he wrote numerous postcards and letters to her patients, discussing the intricacies of the recovery process. He even composed an inspirational message for the institute's newsletter that concluded: "Today seems a difficult time. Hang onto your faith because the difficulty will pass. This is the miracle of healing. May God bless you all. Stevie Ray Vaughan."

Stevie and Janna became so interested in the work of the institute that Michelle made arrangements for them to visit Yale in late August of 1990 to explore other ways in which he could put his gift of music to work as a healing mechanism.

There was so much to do, so much to say, he began to be obsessed about making the most of every moment. "Every day I live now, it's kind of like borrowed time," he told a Kansas City concert audience in the spring of 1990, testifying during "Life Without You." It wasn't just a stage rap anymore. It was God's truth. The clock was doing more than marking time, it was ticking down, on him, on everyone. In an interview with fellow guitarist Larry Coryell, Stevie spoke about death, Jimi Hendrix, and himself, confiding, "I don't know why he died and I'm still alive, going through a lot of the same problems."

He tried to laugh off the eerie feelings he'd get. Whenever the band chartered private airplanes, he kidded that they were flying the Otis Express, a reference to the fate of Alex Hodges's former client soul singer Otis Redding's tragic death in a plane crash in 1967.

With the imminent release of the Vaughan brothers' album and

Chris Layton's wife, Betty, expecting their first baby in November, Double Trouble geared up for one last sweep across the country, this time in tandem with the British soul shouter Joe Cocker. Though Cocker hailed from an earlier generation of rockers, the pairing, dubbed the Power and Passion Tour, actually made a lot of sense. Joe's unique sandpaper voice was as much an instrument connected to the soul as Stevie's patented guitar tone. Their respective audiences were similar in their appreciation of rhythm-and-blues music, a key factor in explaining why it was one of the few package shows to fill the seats in outdoor amphitheaters during June and July in a summer marked by otherwise sluggish ticket sales. Neither possessed so large an ego to demand top billing; as on the Beck tour, the acts alternated as headliners.

"I hear you're a friend of Bill's," Stevie Vaughan said to Phil Grandy, Cocker's lead guitarist, before their first date at the Shoreline Amphitheatre in Mountain View, California, on June 8. Grandy vaguely remembered Vaughan from his association with David Bowie. Like many other session players in New York at the time, he was insanely jealous that Bowie would pluck out this Texas cowboy to play the guitar parts that he should have been playing. But a lot of water had passed under the bridge since then.

"Yeah," Grandy informed him, he was a friend of Bill's, he was in recovery, too. "Just a few months."

"That makes you the most important person here, doesn't it?" Stevie said reassuringly. "You're the newest member among us."

The meetings that Grandy attended with Stevie in the cities they were playing and on the tour bus helped him stay the course. So did Stevie's constant support. "If I was having a hard day he'd say, 'Philly, come up now. NOW!' If I had to cry I'd cry right there and he'd hold my hand and let me get through it."

Phil was just as impressed with Stevie's musicianship as he was with his heart. "His 'Voodoo Chile' at the end of the night scared me," said Grandy, who would approach his new friend after his set and comment, "Stevie you're touching some sacred ground."

"I don't want to be like Hendrix," he'd reply. "I want to *be* Hendrix."

"That's as close as you're gonna get," Grandy would tell him.

"It was spooky because if you know what that song's all about it was Jimi's premonition about death," said Grandy.

When Cocker was performing, Stevie would rifle through the dressing room, lifting scarves and other clothes from Cocker's bassist, T. M. Stevens, then wear them onstage when he joined Stevens for jams at the end of the night.

For all the camaraderie and the relatively relaxed pace of his sober life, the cumulative effect of touring was beginning to catch up with Stevie again. He had been performing more than two hundred dates a year for a full decade. Singing was beginning physically to hurt him, causing a condition he called "hamburger throat." He tried to alleviate the pain with massage therapy and acupuncture. But it was so intense, he had to resort to cortisone shots, which puffed up his face and gave him a mild buzzed-out feeling, a source of obvious discomfort. On top of that, he was trying hard to kick his last bad habit, cigarettes, by chewing wads of Nicoret gum.

Even his hands hurt. His fingers were getting ripped up so badly that he committed what in the past would have amounted to heresy by asking Rene Martinez to dress the sharp edges of his frets by filing them down and to use lighter-gauge strings.

The Cocker-Vaughan tour wound its way to Dallas on June 17 as part of the Benson and Hedges Bluesfest, where Stevie headlined over B. B. King, Dr. John, and Irma Thomas in front of more than 13,000 homefolks at the Starplex outdoor theater. Three weeks later, on July 7, the Cocker-Vaughan show played the Garden State Arts Center in Holmdel, New Jersey. Equipment-truck driver Henry Gonzales recalled the crew had a great deal of trouble loading in for the performance, so much trouble in fact that Rene Martinez loudly complained about the uselessness of the union stagehands who wouldn't allow Stevie's crew to touch their own equipment.

After his set, Stevie led the rest of the band off the stage as a stagehand closed the curtain. No one noticed as the curtain caught the corner of a thirty-foot-tall, six-foot-wide wooden baffle used for symphony performances. Without a sound, the baffle hurtled down toward center stage. It missed Rene Martinez and Stevie and crashed directly into his guitars, which were still on their stands. "First Wife," Number 1, the beat-up '59 Strat he'd played for a decade and a half, was broken in three pieces along the neck.

Stevie's eyes reddened and tears started to well up when he saw the damage, but he quickly regained his composure. "See," he said, sauntering up to Phil Grandy, holding the mangled pieces of wood and wire that had once been his pride and joy.

"It's still in tune."

Rene Martinez furiously went to work, grafting together a new old instrument in time for the concert at Jones Beach Theater in Wantagh, New York, the following evening.

Another ominous incident occurred in Seattle a few weeks later, as the tour was winding down. A fan handed a roadie a bulging white envelope to pass on to Stevie. The envelope contained a rubbing of Jimi Hendrix's gravestone. When Stevie opened it up, he read the words

"James Marshall Hendrix — Forever In Our Hearts" and his face went pale. "Get that outta here," he growled. "It's too weird."

A play date in Anchorage followed, with Stevie and some of the crew hiring a bush pilot to take them salmon fishing on the following day. On July 30, Stevie, Double Trouble, and Jimmie went to Minneapolis to make up a rained-out date that would be the last of the Power and Passion Tour. The next day, Alex Hodges stopped by for lunch before Stevie took off for a short vacation in Hawaii and New Zealand with Janna. On the fourteenth of August, Hodges spoke with Stevie by phone about possible directors he was lining up to shoot videos for the brothers' album, which finally had a title, *Family Style*. But Stevie was more interested in hearing about Hodges's son, Alex II, who had been seriously injured in a car wreck. Stevie was worried the kid had fallen off the wagon. He wanted to help him through his crisis.

The short vacation was a chance to recharge the batteries. Stevie returned to the United States invigorated and ready to finish the mop-up dates that would wrap up the summer season with Double Trouble, going first to New York City, where he'd leased an apartment with Janna, who was getting a lot of modeling work. He joined the band and crew in Kalamazoo, Michigan, for an outdoor gig, then headed around Lake Michigan for two gigs near Chicago, which sounded more like a holiday than work since he would be sharing the bill with Robert Cray and Eric Clapton.

The normally volatile business of concert promotion turned even more cutthroat in Chicago during the summer of 1990. Three sheds — industry slang for large, outdoor venues — were locked in a ruthless battle to secure major acts with the potential to sell tens of thousands of tickets. The promoters in charge of booking Alpine Valley, Ravinia, and Poplar Creek knew that by the time the season ended on Labor Day, at least one of them would be knocked out of business. When International Creative Management agent Bobby Brooks started calling promoters to let them know that his client, Eric Clapton, would be passing through Chicagoland in late August, the sheds scrambled to come up with the most attractive offer.

After intense negotiations, Joseph Entertainment secured the date. Their shed was Alpine Valley, a small winter ski resort in southern Wisconsin, about eighty miles from Chicago's Loop, where summer concerts were staged. Clapton's fee for two nights was a reputed $1 million, less production expenses.

To bolster Clapton's drawing power, Robert Cray, the Seattle-born blues and soul stylist who was touring with the Memphis Horns, and Stevie Ray Vaughan and Double Trouble were added to the lineup, which was billed as An Evening with Eric Clapton and His Band. The advance sales of more than 60,000 tickets for the Saturday, August 25, and Sunday, August 26, dates more than justified Clapton's guarantee.

The first night went smoothly enough. Surprise guests Bonnie Raitt and Jeff Healey, the former a longtime friend of Stevie's, the latter a disciple of his guitar stylings, appeared at the end of the show to join Clapton, Cray, Stevie, and Jimmie Vaughan, for a not-so-informal picking session, much to the delight of the assembled crowd.

The second evening, August 26, promised even more fireworks. On the helicopter flight from Chicago to the concert on Sunday afternoon Eric Clapton, the man who had jammed with Jimi Hendrix, Albert King, B. B. King, Freddie King, and every other guitar player on earth, leaned over to Buddy Guy, the Chicago wildman who would appear that night as an unannounced special guest, to ask a question.

"How am I going to follow this guy?" he said, referring to Stevie Ray Vaughan, who had played like a man possessed the night before in marked contrast to Clapton's restrained performance.

Guy shrugged.

"Well, just do the best you can," he advised.

It was a hot, humid midwestern summer night, the kind of still evening that seems to put a slow-motion brake on reality. The muggy weather was a sharp contrast to the air of expectation that filled the Double Trouble part of the backstage area. With the exception of a mop-up date in Lubbock and a concert in London, this was their last show before what would be the longest break the band had taken since Tommy Shannon hired on as bassist in 1981.

Mark Proct, Jimmie's manager, showed up for the gig wearing one of the black polo shirts embroidered with two guitars crossed at the neck and the initials SRV and JLV that Jack Chase, the CBS branch manager in Dallas, had made. The shirt spoke volumes. This was the brothers' deal. No one from either Double Trouble or the Fabulous Thunderbirds was being recruited for the Family Style touring band.

Before the gig, Clapton, Stevie, Jimmie, and Robert Cray posed for photographer Robert Knight, who was shooting an advertising layout for Fender guitars. They all were Strat men, as good an endorsement of Leo Fender's craftsmanship as anyone could desire.

Stevie Ray Vaughan followed Robert Cray's opening set by strolling onstage wearing a floral-print vest over a billowy white shirt, his face shielded by the trademark broad-brimmed hat, looking for all the world like the fastest gun in Dodge City. With little fanfare, he immediately got down to business, warming up with an introductory jump boogie whose groove was pinned down by Reese Wynans's pumping organ grind. Not saying a word, the band seamlessly segued into "The House Is Rockin'," Stevie and Doyle Bramhall's party anthem from *In Step*, which immediately commenced the 30,000 fans in the house with no roof to swanging their butts.

The set built up its own momentum with a perfunctory reading of "Tightrope" followed by a tip of the gaucho hat to Guitar Slim on "The Things (That) I Used to Do," during which Stevie dredged the aural equivalent of cries, moans, and field hollers out of the primordial mud from which all subsequent great electric guitar licks have emanated. He led into "Let Me Love You Baby" and "Leave My Girl Alone" with some stage patter about the need to please your woman and keep her happy. He then paused long enough to make a dedication "to everybody in the world who's suffering for any reason, that they might find some happiness soon, if not now." He'd distilled his message to the abstract. Suffering was a part of the human experience, regardless of the cause. Everyone could use a little healing sometime.

The balm he offered came in the form of "Riviera Paradise," the wordless contemplation from *In Step* that once and for all placed him on equal emotional footing with Jimi Hendrix. Every delicate run that skittered up and down the frets elicited roars of approval from a crowd paying such close attention, they seemed more like a bunch of friends sitting in the living room than a swollen mass of faces. Jimmie came out to join the band for the final triad of "Goin' Down," "Crossfire," and "Voodoo Chile," the climax that brought the audience roaring to their feet.

It was Eric Clapton's turn next, playing music from a quarter-century's worth of blues and rock classics. Clapton, like Stevie, had never stopped improving his craft, never stopped exploring the possibilities of his instrument. It was an odd juxtaposition, hearing the elder statesman run through his repertoire with skilled restraint, following the young Texan who had grown up emulating Clapton's version of "Crossroads" at sock hops and battles of the bands.

As Clapton ended his set, the late evening faded into early morning, and a thick fog descended on the huge crowd, enveloping them like the smoky haze in a low-rent blues joint. It was an eerie sight, 30,000 people trying to peer through the mist so they could see the tiny figure onstage approach the microphone to introduce the final portion of the concert. With its engagingly polite English accent, the amplified voice of Eric Clapton echoed from the public address system to the surrounding hillside.

"I'd like to bring out, to join me here, a big treat — the best guitar players in the entire world: Buddy Guy, Stevie Ray Vaughan, Robert Cray, Jimmie Vaughan."

Standing in a semicircle, the five briefly tuned up while sizing up one another. For Buddy Guy, Jimmie and Stevie Ray, it was a throwback to a 3 A.M. jam at Antone's. For Cray, it was a chance to match licks with elders and contemporaries who inspired him to dig deep into the blues. For Clapton, the master of blues-inspired, rock-and-roll electric guitar, it was an opportunity to bring together three generations of players, paying respects to Buddy Guy while acknowledging the contributions of the three younger players who picked up where he left off.

"It's in A — I mean it's in E, it's in E," Clapton told them. The men all knew what key it was in. They went right to work.

The nightcap Clapton had selected was "Sweet Home Chicago," an appropriate choice since that's where the musicians and the vast majority of the fans were headed when the music was over. Most of them had a slow bumper-to-bumper crawl out of the Alpine Valley Amphitheater, down a congested two-lane farm road and another fifty miles of interstate highway to look forward to. But only a fool would try to beat the traffic and miss what was going down where the spotlights were burning. Fog or no fog, juke joint or amphitheater, this jam was going to be serious.

Behind Guy's gritty vocals, the five electric-guitar players interplayed with an ease and intimacy more typical of a motel room picking session. After Guy's opening lines, each player took a turn working notes and chords out of his instrument, revealing to one another and the audience beyond bits and pieces of what they knew about making a guitar sing. Clapton ripped off a run of crisp, staccato notes, clean enough for a studio take. Cray rattled out florid clusters of sound, then one-upped Clapton by punching out some impossibly high squeaks at the bottom of his fretboard. Jimmie Vaughan and Guy preferred an earthier, more direct approach that emphasized economy over excess, aiming their breaks below the belt, as if they were running their fingers up the thighs of a big-legged woman instead of a guitar neck.

And then there was Stevie Ray. The first time around, he demonstrated a textbook knowledge of subtlety, precision, and circumspection from the instant his index finger pressed the fat, nickel-wound top E string, grinding it against a thick metal fret. He played his passage, acknowledged the applause, and waited for his turn to come again. The second time around, he cut loose, using passion and pure force to push the notes out, bending strings so forcefully that each note shimmered and shook with the pressure of his fingertips. Following the second lead, Clapton shook his head with a disapproving smile, rather than nodding to the next player.

"You're on a roll, Stevie Ray," he seemed to say. "Do it again."

The Texas kid shook the sweat from his face, sucked in his gut, and lowered his head out of view, clenching his teeth. With his large, bony right hand he stroked his instrument, making it howl. Moving both sweaty hands in a contorted blur along all six strings, he summoned up a sonic roar pierced by a flurry of sharp single notes and chunks of growling chords wrapped so tightly around the song's loping rhythm that they threatened to consume it altogether.

Come on. Baby, don't you want to go?

Jangling, furious and refined, intricate and brute, the solo answered the call that Robert Johnson, the Mississippi Delta blues guitarist who sold his soul to the devil at the crossroads, had issued into a wire recorder in a San Antonio hotel room fifty-four years earlier.

Standing on the stage of the amphitheater, rivulets of sweat coursing over his busted-up nose, down his chin, and over the body of his instrument, Stevie Ray Vaughan confirmed to one and all that he belonged there. On this night, at least, he was the best guitar player in the whole wide world.

"He just sort of kicked everybody's ass and nobody seemed to fight back," Jimmie remembered. "Stevie was on a cloud or something." Buddy Guy didn't know where it was coming from, just that whatever Stevie was doing worked a strange number on even him.

"I had goose bumps," he said.

The song ended. The lights went up. The roadies immediately began tearing down equipment while the musicians hugged and traded compliments backstage. Stevie autographed posters, compared calluses with the other performers, talked with Clapton about some future dates they were planning for London's Royal Albert Hall, and discussed the possibility of going to Paris in September for a Hendrix tribute. But while Stevie usually lingered until he shook hands with the last fan, he seemed preoccupied with getting back to Chicago. Tommy had already hopped a helicopter after Double Trouble's set. Now Stevie scurried between Joseph Entertainment representatives, tour manager Skip Rickert, and members of Clapton's crew trying to hustle a ride on the next helicopter out.

Rickert had reserved a helicopter with Omni Flights, the charter company that was providing Clapton's entourage an airborne detour above the inevitable traffic snarl leading out of Alpine Valley toward Chicago.

Peter Jackson of Clapton's crew told Stevie there were three seats left on one of the Bell 206B JetRangers. Jimmie and his wife, Connie, could take the other seats.

"Let's go," Stevie said. He wanted to get back to his hotel to call Janna and get the first commercial airline flight back to see her. Shortly before lift-off, Stevie learned there was a mix-up. Only one seat was available, though another helicopter would be leaving shortly thereafter. Stevie ran back to Jimmie.

"Hey, man. Do you mind if I take the seat?" he asked. "I really need to get back."

"Sure," Jimmie replied.

The fog was thickening and settling in when Stevie strapped himself in next to Bobby Brooks, Clapton's agent; Colin Smythe, Clapton's assistant tour manager; and Nigel Browne, Clapton's bodyguard. It was 12:40 A.M. when pilot Jeffrey William Browne guided the helicopter skyward from the Alpine Valley golf course, its landing lights flashing through the soup. Seconds later, Browne sharply banked the machine into the backside of a three-hundred-foot-high hill. There was no explosion. No fire. No cries for help. No one heard a thing. As the other copters flew past, the blood flowed out of the crash victims' bodies onto a meadow of Queen Anne's lace and bittersweet, twisted metal strewn over an area of some two hundred square feet. It was August 27, 1990, the fourth anniversary of Jimmie Lee Vaughan's death.

Eric Clapton, Buddy Guy, and Clapton's manager, Roger Forrester, were on a helicopter that took off behind Stevie's. Guy, who was nervous about flying in the fog, joked with Clapton how he could cook better than he could play guitar and what kind of meal he was going to serve him the next day. Roger Forrester told the United Kingdom's Sky News that he noticed the helicopter in front "suddenly disappeared from view" but had given it no further thought.

Chris Layton, Jimmie and Connie Vaughan, and Mark Proct were waiting for their helicopter to land so they could leave, but the fog had become so thick, the pilot changed his plans and landed at a strip at the old Playboy resort in nearby Lake Geneva, where his passengers drove to board the flight.

At 1:30 A.M., the Federal Aviation Administration was notified that a helicopter had failed to arrive in Chicago. The downed helicopter had set off an emergency radio beacon and officials used the SARSAT, or search and rescue satellite system, to pinpoint the site. Meanwhile, Skip Rickert landed at the airport with the last load of passengers. Since one helicopter had been in use when he left the airport before the concert, he didn't think anything was amiss when he only counted three parked on the tarmac.

FAA officials dispatched ground crews to Alpine Valley. At 6:50 A.M., two sheriff's deputies discovered the wreckage scattered on the hillside. William Bruce, an investigator from the National Transportation Safety Board, arrived on the scene shortly thereafter. He'd seen scores of crash sites before and knew well enough from his experience to judge this one as "a high-energy, high-velocity impact at a low angle."

Skip Rickert had hardly rested his head on a pillow when the telephone rang. Alex Hodges was on the line.

"There's been an accident," he said in measured tones. One of the helicopters was missing, the one that Stevie was on.

"This has got to be a cruel joke," protested Rickert.

"I wish it was," Hodges said with an audible sigh.

Rickert called Jimmie and gathered everyone else in his room. The Walworth County coroner's office asked Jimmie and Eric Clapton to return to the scene of their triumph only a few hours earlier. They were shepherded into a limousine for a long, silent ride back to Wisconsin. In the pale morning sunlight, they were guided to the hillside, where they were asked to sift through the mangled wreckage to identify the bodies. Jimmie saw the hat. Walking back to the car, Jimmie wished that he had some token of remembrance, something of Stevie's that he could cling to. Someone came up to the car and knocked on the window. "We found one other item," he said. Jimmie recognized Stevie's Coptic cross. He took it and placed it around his neck.

21

SLIGHT RETURN

The news of Stevie's death was already beginning to leak out. Radio stations picked up an Associated Press wire story about a missing helicopter, speculating that Eric Clapton, Stevie Ray Vaughan, and/or members of their bands and crews were aboard. Calls to their respective management groups and publicists yielded little more information. By 9 A.M., the actual details were made public. Eric Clapton's American press agent, Ronnie Lippin, initially denied that there had been a last-minute seating switch, saying, "It's just the Hollywood version, trying to rewrite *The Buddy Holly Story*." Stevie Ray Vaughan's publicist, Charles Comer, later confirmed that there had indeed been such a switch.

Henry Gonzales didn't make it out of Alpine Valley with Double Trouble's equipment truck until shortly after dawn. Rather than fight the traffic, he decided to take a nap. When he woke up, he drove to a café for breakfast and returned to the truck to start the long drive back to Austin. He'd locked his cassette tapes in the back, so he turned on the radio, which he rarely listened to. A few minutes later, he heard the news. He pulled off to the shoulder of the road and broke down crying, a pattern that would repeat itself numerous times that day.

Janna Lapidus woke up wondering why Stevie hadn't called her after the show like he'd promised he would. Martha Vaughan and her brother Joe Cook spoke over the phone while listening to their radios. They feared the worst.

A young woman who was helped through her own recovery by Stevie sought comfort remembering what he had told her about death after she'd lost a close relative.

"This is when people change," he had said. "It's not that they die. I can't physically see them or talk to them, but they are there. You can't hear them, but it doesn't mean they're not there."

Skip Rickert went into automatic, quickly rearranging travel plans to get everyone back to Dallas as soon as possible. His hotel room became a bivouac headquarters.

Eric Clapton was booked to play an outdoor concert in Bonner Springs, Kansas, that same night. He decided the only way to overcome his grief was to carry on with the gig. He didn't mention the accident out of respect for the people he later called "my companions, my associates and my friends." In Dallas, 2,000 fans spontaneously gathered in Kiest Park in Oak Cliff, just a few blocks from Stevie's boyhood home, to mourn his passing.

In Austin, the switchboard of rock radio station KLBJ was swamped by sobbing callers who didn't want to believe the news. Something must be done, they said, like when John Lennon died and those seeking solace gathered in Zilker Park where the radio station organized a wake in a large meadow. More than 5,000 fans and friends brought candles, radios, photographs, flowers, and messages, all of them paying tribute to the man they considered their neighbor, their bud, the local boy who'd made good. "I always felt he was playing for all of us, sort of like he was representing everyone in Austin," said one construction contractor. "That made his success feel very personal for all his fans and his death seem like even a greater loss."

Jody Denberg, the disc jockey who monitored the live radio feed from the park, chucked the station's regular music programming to play Stevie's music all evening, drawing a huge roar from the crowd every time he said, "Rave on, Stevie Ray Vaughan."

Cutter Brandenburg, Stevie's sidekick and most trusted roadie, the one person whose business transactions with Stevie were above reproach, showed up, but the spectacle just made him feel uncomfortable. He got in his car and drove to Robert Mueller Airport, just in time to find Tommy Shannon and Chris Layton walking off a flight from Chicago. For one last time, he helped them with their bags and gave them a ride home. In the end, just as in the beginning, Cutter was the reliable one who held it all together.

In a more private display of affection, scores of new faces showed up at AA meetings around town. They came not as friends of Bill W., but as friends of Stevie V.

W. C. Clark, Lou Ann Barton, David Murray, and other musician friends gathered at Antone's to pay tribute to the fallen member of their clan. Susan Antone tried to keep the doors of the club locked out of respect for Stevie, but a line had formed outside the door. People wanted to come in to buy Stevie Ray T-shirts.

In Lubbock, a mental health counselor named Ivah Villalobos shed a tear. She'd been eagerly anticipating Stevie's long-awaited return to Lubbock, only two weeks away. In a previous life, Ivah was Miss Ivy, one of the Rome Inn regulars who subscribed to the theory that "if you remember the seventies, then you didn't have a good time." Miss Ivy had fed and housed Stevie on many occasions back in the old days in Austin because, as he liked to tell her, she was "honest from the get." She hadn't seen Stevie for years, but she wanted him to talk with her sixteen-year-old stepson about the dangers of drugs. "He was still cool, as far as the kids were concerned." She knew she could entice him over to the house by cooking him a plate of enchiladas. More than helping her stepson, seeing him again would have righted a wrong that had nagged her ever since she served time in jail for her involvement with a speed lab.

"In all the time we knew each other, he and I had never been straight."

In Chicago, Buddy Guy went ahead and performed at his Legends nightclub. A much anticipated jam with Carlos Santana was carried out with a sense of duty, not joy. "My head ain't right yet," he apologized.

In the midst of their grief, Jimmie and Martha Vaughan made funeral arrangements. On a blistering-hot Friday morning several thousand family members, friends, associates, and fans gathered at the Laurel Land Memorial Park in far south Oak Cliff to say goodbye. It was a diverse group, including many people who would have been prone to fight, argue, or file a suit against one another had they met under any other circumstances. Charles Comer, who rarely appeared in public to orchestrate his public relations coups, stood in the parking lot, directing family members and celebrities to the private ceremony conducted inside the Laurel Land chapel at ten-thirty that morning. Martha Vaughan wore a suit of purple, the color Stevie believed had healing power. Sitting next to her was a stunned Janna Lapidus, dressed in white. Pallbearers included manager Alex Hodges, guitar tech Rene Martinez, tour manager Skip Rickert, production manager Mark Rutledge, stage manager Bill Moundsey, Chris Layton, Reese Wynans, and Tommy Shannon.

Dr. John played piano as Stevie Wonder sang the Lord's Prayer. Buddy Guy became so choked up, he left while everyone else filed outside for the public funeral service.

The public service at high noon was an intimate sharing experience and a rock-and-roll circus. The family and invited celebrities sat under a canopy near the casket, grouped around a blown-up photograph of Stevie Ray. A rope separated them from two thousand fans and admirers broiling under the blazing sun. As the temperature gauge pushed past the century mark Lenny Vaughan, whose loud wails punctuated the private service, was shepherded by Uncle Joe Boy Cook to a spot out of eyeshot of the immediate family. Chesley Millikin and Frances Carr came to pay their respects along with friends from Kimball High who hadn't seen Stevie in twenty years.

The service was mercifully brief. Bruce "BC" Miller, Stevie's AA sponsor, invited Dr. Barry Bailey, a local preacher he had seen on television, to conduct the service. Bailey, the charismatic minister of the First Methodist Church in Fort Worth who had worked with Alcoholics Anonymous for decades, led the crowd in reciting the AA Prayer:

"God, grant me the serenity to accept the things I cannot change, the courage to change the things I can, and the wisdom to know the difference."

Bailey read the twenty-third psalm — "The Lord is my shepherd" — and reflected for a few moments on Stevie's life. Miller recited the twelve steps and read selections from two chapters of the Big Book, "How It Works" and "A Vision for You." Record producer Nile Rodgers talked for a few moments about the album *Family Style*. "In the song 'Tick Tock,' Stevie sings the refrain 'Remember,' " Rodgers said, his voice choked with emotion. "He was trying to tell me and all of us, 'Remember my music. . . . And just remember that it is a gift that we get.' Some of us are touched by God, and Stevie was one of those who was definitely touched by the hand of God. Thank you for making me your brother. I'll always remember."

The mourners applauded Rodgers and listened to a recording of "Tick Tock." Bonnie Raitt, Jackson Browne, and Stevie Wonder followed with an a cappella version of "Amazing Grace." The healing words floated out over the perspiring congregation like a cool breeze.

"How sweet the sound/that saved a wretch like me."

Bailey read the Prayer of St. Francis, the words to which had been found in Stevie's pocket at the crash site, and asked the gathering to join hands while reciting the Lord's Prayer, ending the ceremony as if it were a twelve-step meeting. The family was escorted away from the site while the stars filed into their limos.

Finally, the multitudes of regular folks behind the rope were allowed to file past the closed casket to say their last goodbyes. Among them was Tyrone Fullerton, Stevie's nephew who had never known the rest of the Vaughan family. He paused to place a rose on the casket before a security guard told him to keep moving. Others walked past to pay their own silent tributes until there was no one left in line. True to form, Stevie always stayed to visit with the people who made the extra effort to see him, touch him, have him write his name on a piece of paper, and speak with them. This time, though, the bus wasn't leaving.

Later that afternoon, out of the public eye, Stevie's body was laid to rest in Veteran's Section 15 of Laurel Land Cemetery in a gently sloping field of grass burned brown by the white-hot summer sun. The casket was lowered into a hole that had been dug next to the marker identifying Jimmie Lee Vaughan, Mason and World War Two navy veteran. To one side, fifty yards away, was a Pearl Harbor memorial, with the inscription, "They Live If You Remember." Nearby, amid the scattering of live oaks, were replicas of a cannon and the Liberty Bell.

Though he never served in the military, Stevie Ray Vaughan belonged here. He was a veteran, too, a decorated, battle-scarred survivor.

In the days that passed, some fans fretted that drugs might have been a factor in the crash, that somehow Stevie Ray Vaughan had fallen from grace. The coroner's report quelled those worries by explicitly detailing the cause of death: exsanguination caused by severing of the aorta. There was no evidence of drug use. Stevie had died just as he had lived for the final 3 years, 317 days, and 40 minutes of his life, clean and sober.

It did not take long for Stevie Ray Vaughan the man to be replaced in the public eye by Stevie Ray Vaughan, the legend. Dying tragically at the age of thirty-five made him an immediate object of worship in the great rock-and-roll tradition. Dying under such tragic circumstances after overcoming his own personal battles with the demons of booze and drugs elevated him to something just short of sainthood.

The first hint of a death cult came with the release of *Family Style* on September 15, two and a half weeks after the fatal crash. On the heels of posthumous tributes that appeared in *Rolling Stone, Newsweek, Time, People, U.S. News & World Report*, and hundreds of other publications around the world, the album shot straight to *Billboard*'s Top 10, a feat neither Jimmie nor Stevie had accomplished by themselves. The content of the record made it all the more remarkable. Despite the fact the record eventually won two Grammys — one for best rock instrumental performance ("D/FW") and the entire album for best contemporary blues recording — many loyalists and purists hated it. If there were guitar blues on *Family Style*, they were happy, loopy blues, the zany kind preferred by Louis Jordan and Louis Prima, not the mean, rusty straight-razor Howlin' Wolf kind of blues.

Family Style was one of the few uplifting achievements that marked an otherwise dark period for Jimmie Vaughan. His brother was gone, and now, more than ever, he had to look after him, speak for him, be responsible for his actions. For the first time in more than twenty years, he was a guitar player without a band, a man with no immediate goals, an artist without the desire to do what had driven him since he was old enough to think for himself. He was still grappling with the daily challenges that come with drying out. Suddenly, through little of his own doing, he was a millionaire saddled with a world of responsibilities.

Jimmie and his wife, Connie, searched Stevie's personal belongings looking for a will. They came up empty. A probate court would decide how his estate would be settled. Jimmie and Martha Vaughan formally petitioned the court to be named coexecutors of Stephen Ray Vaughan's estate. As part of the legal proceedings, they inventoried Stevie's possessions at the time of his death: $173,000 in various bank accounts; 100 percent of the stock in his music publishing company, Ray Vaughan Music, Inc.; 34 guitars in various stages of repair; 12 speakers; 31 amplifiers; and a few personal effects, including a CD player, a strobe tuner, a motorized skateboard, jewelry, a video camera, and the 1975 Chevrolet Caprice.

The real wealth was in the future royalties from the 27 songs he had published, the 6 albums he had recorded, and 132 video and audio recordings of his performances, described in the probate papers as varying in quality from sentimental to commercially viable. The family's lawyers estimated the value of the unreleased recorded material as $20,000, an extremely conservative figure designed to protect the estate from excessive taxation. When the estate was finally probated, Jimmie and Martha were designated coexecutors of Stevie's estate.

Jimmie stated that he didn't want Stevie's legacy to wind up like Jimi Hendrix's, which eventually was controlled by a Caribbean-chartered investment group. He and Martha strived to protect Stevie's name by carefully screening each and every request for commercial and noncommercial projects related to the late guitarist. Try as he might, some of Jimmie's decisions rubbed Stevie's intimates, friends, and associates the wrong way.

He told Stevie's former manager Alex Hodges that his brother was gone and no longer needed a manager. Jimmie then placed his own manager, Mark Proct, in charge of managing Stevie's music business affairs. Proct, who originally came to Austin to mix sound for the western swing band Asleep at the Wheel, had some familiarity with Stevie's career, once working as Double Trouble's road manager for several weeks before being relieved by a permament replacement.

Janna Lapidus had lived with Stevie and been introduced to his friends as his fiancée, but Jimmie saw it otherwise. Stevie, he felt, had made it plain to him that the relationship was not as binding as many others were led to believe. Though Martha had once advised her son to draw up a will that would include Janna, she and Jimmie rebuffed several attempts by Janna to make a claim on Stevie's estate. Were they destined to be married or was she an immature, spoiled whiner trying to dig for gold? After a year's grace period, the family strongly suggested Janna give up the leased car and the Travis Street condominium that she and Stevie had once shared. She waited until what would have been Stevie's thirty-seventh birthday, then packed her bags for Tokyo, where the Wilhemina Agency had lined up some lucrative modeling assignments.

In the midst of sorting out the tangled estate, Jimmie paused to step back and assess his own career. After a long and wild ride, one so excessive and demanding that it almost killed his brother and himself several times over, what else was there left to prove? The recent chain of events convinced him to take a break from the public eye.

For the first year and a half, his public performances were limited to Eric Clapton's Royal Albert Hall concerts in London the last week of February 1991, where Robert Cray, Buddy Guy, Clapton, and Jimmie reprised the final Alpine Valley jam session; and sit-ins with Bob Dylan's band at the Austin City Coliseum, Lazy Lester at Antone's, and with Clapton at concerts in Dallas and New Orleans. At the request of Junior Brown, an Austin guitarist who shared a common love of Hawaiian guitar, Jimmie went in the studio to play rhythm ukelele on Brown's "Lovely Hula Hands" and a country-western guitar lead on "My Wife Thinks You're Dead" for an album that Brown was making.

He redirected his artistic energies to preparing his custom '51 purple Chevy coupe and his green, metal-flaked, lowered '63 Riviera for the Grand National Car Show in Oakland, where he had been made a member of the prestigious West Coast Roadsters car club, and renewed a long-smoldering interest in painting.

He struggled to get a grip on his personal life. His daughter, Tina, moved to Austin to live with Jimmie and Connie after graduating from high school in Dallas. He reached out to make amends with his nineteen-year-old son, Tyrone Fullerton, inviting the young man to go with him to a recovery meeting. He didn't doubt his paternity anymore and pledged to be there for Tyrone whenever he needed him. He even let his boy drive his beloved Violet Vision Chevy.

Jimmie also had to face the music that his brother had made. He spent almost a full year after the crash culling through Double Trouble studio tapes to create new composites from several different guitar tracks, drum tracks, and bass tracks with the aid of a Diaxis machine for the posthumous album *The Sky Is Crying*. Standouts included an instrumental version of the Hendrix classic "Little Wing" that was edited down from an extended Hendrix jam recorded during the *Couldn't Stand the Weather* sessions and the incomplete but achingly prophetic "Life by the

Drop," written by Doyle Bramhall and his partner Barbara Logan for *In Step*, on which Stevie played solo on the acoustic guitar.

Released shortly after Stevie's birthday in October 1991, *The Sky Is Crying* debuted at number ten on the *Billboard* album chart. The record went platinum less than three months after it hit the streets, racking up sales in excess of 1.5 million units. A video of a 1983 Double Trouble performance at El Mocambo in Toronto, released during the summer of 1991, rocketed up *Billboard*'s music videocassette sales chart, knocking opera singer Luciano Pavarotti out of the top spot. Even the disastrous *Live Alive*, which never made it onto *Billboard*'s Top 200 album chart, was finally certified gold. A promotional video of "Little Wing" released by Epic was a seven-minute history of the blues that included visuals of Leadbelly, Hendrix, Buddy Guy, Stevie Ray, and the Fender guitar factory.

In the spring of 1992, under pressure from Epic, Jimmie began sifting through tapes of performances for a representative album of a Stevie Ray Vaughan live set. After listening to hundreds of hours, Jimmie chose a 1980 performance of Stevie Vaughan and Double Trouble, featuring Stevie, Chris Layton on drums, and Jackie Newhouse on bass. The recording was made at Steamboat 1874 on Sixth Street in Austin and broadcast live on KLBJ-FM, an Austin radio station owned by Lady Bird Johnson. It was released in the fall of 1992 under the title *In the Beginning*.

As Jimmie came around to get on with his own career, he went into the studio to record tracks with boogie king John Lee Hooker, something that Stevie had been scheduled to do before his death. He also opened up a production office to prepare for a record of his own.

Regardless of how his future work would be received, Jimmie Vaughan's place in rock history was secure. He was more than the guy who almost single-handedly deconstructed rock guitar, showing other players that true virtuosity lay in playing less, not more. He was Stevie Ray Vaughan's greatest influence.

Stevie's death had left Chris and Tommy in a state of shock and without a job. "We don't know what we're going to do," Chris said two days after the crash. "We went from riding in vans to flying in jets together and all of a sudden . . ." Tommy was stunned. "Stevie was the best musician I ever played with, the best friend I ever had, and the best person I've ever known," he said.

The answer came at the Austin Rehearsal Complex, where Chris rented a space to practice his drumming. One afternoon he began fooling around with Tommy; Doyle Bramhall's son, Doyle II.; and Charlie Sexton, a Stevie disciple who first began performing roots-rock and blues in Austin at the age of nine before embarking on a failed attempt to become an LA teen idol. In a matter of weeks, the informal jam band had a record deal. In April 1992 the Arc Angels, named after their practice hall, the Austin Rehearsal Complex, debuted on Geffen Records. In August, Doyle II entered the Betty Ford Clinic to detox.

After Stevie's death, Reese Wynans returned to play the B-3 at Antone's and rejoin Joe Ely's road band. Doyle Bramhall, Sr., continued working clubs around Dallas and Austin, still crooning the line "Mona Lisa was a man" from "Grits Ain't Groceries" in the familiar style that meant so much to his younger protégé. He and his girlfriend, Barbara Logan, moved from Fort Worth to Wimberley, a resort town in the Hill country. "I'm so happy here," he told writer Brad Buchholz. "There are so many times, walking around out here that I find myself saying, 'Thank you, Stevie.' Because if it weren't for Stevie, I might not be living here right now.' " Or certainly not as comfortably. Marc Benno, the original leader of the Nightcrawlers, who was beginning to perform and record again while surviving comfortably on his extensive catalog of songs, moved in down the road from Bramhall.

Up in Austin, the specter of Stevie Ray Vaughan was everywhere. It was like one hard-core fan explained to a reporter for the *New York Times:* "He never died around here." Vans filled with young idealistic musicians still pulled into town in search of fame, fortune, and creative freedom. Denny Freeman, Derek O'Brien, Kim Wilson, George Rains, and Paul Ray were the elders now, imparting wisdom and knowledge to a whole new generation of younger talent including guitarists Sue Foley, Ian Moore, and Chris Duarte. Austin's black bluesmen from the east side, including Victory Grill guitarist T. D. Bell, piano player Erbie Bowser, and Blues Boy Hubbard found themselves indirect beneficiaries of Stevie's success, to the point of having records of their music released for the first time in their lives. "If it wasn't for young whites and older whites, the blues scene would be zero," Bell told Mike Clark of the *Austin Chronicle.* "But what's really happened is that the whole scene is getting mixed, to the point where people think whites started it, that Stevie Ray Vaughan was the first blues guitarist in Austin. And it's because we lost it, turned it loose. So who are you going to blame?"

Recovery became contagious. With Jimmie's help, Lou Ann Barton finally got straight and revived her career. Even the chamber of commerce, the convention and visitor's bureau, and the city council got the message about what music meant to the city and what the city represented to struggling musicians. The Austin music scene, long ignored by the establishment as a bohemian quirk, became part of the city's corporate relocation sales pitch as well as a civic point of pride. "Welcome to Austin, the Live Music Capital of the World," blinked the electronic sign above the baggage claim area at Robert Mueller Airport. Despite the lip service being paid, serious misunderstandings remained between music people and the larger "straight" world. Petitions to re-name Auditorium Shores for Stevie stalled, as did fund-raising efforts to erect a statue in his honor. Some business leaders misguidedly believed that memorializing Stevie Ray Vaughan was the equivalent of condon-ing drug abuse.

There were other, more personal tributes to Stevie. His portrait hung over the bar of Antone's, between images of Muddy Waters and Clifton Chenier, above a string of blinking Christmas lights. Buddy Guy finally fulfilled Stevie's wish and got his own Grammy in 1992 for the Best Contemporary Blues Recording, an album that included the instrumen-tal, "Rememberin' Stevie." John Lee Hooker and Bonnie Raitt dedicated albums in memory of Stevie Ray Vaughan. Young bands like Nirvana and Pearl Jam picked up on the sensory-overload guitar sound pioneered by Hendrix and reinterpreted by Stevie. Even Eric Clapton turned to deeper blues, listening to a lot of Stevie Ray Vaughan music. On the one-year anniversary of Stevie's death, clusters of fans improvised altars of candles, photographs, guitar picks, and other mementos in grottos at the Rock Island limestone outcropping in Zilker Park.

Stevie's uncle, Joe Boy Cook, composed a poem in memory of his nephew, entitled "A Texas Ray of Sunshine," which he recited in front of several hundred fans gathered at the Texas Theater in Oak Cliff to mark what would have been Stevie's thirty-seventh birthday.

> *I hear a blues riff in the still of the night.*
> *Is that you little boy blues?*
> *Your cross was found on some faraway hill,*
> *They say where wild flowers grow.*
> *Are you up there somewhere playing your blues?*
> *Oh Lord I think I know . . .*

Joe Cook kept thinking back to the time he got a telephone call from his famous nephew.

"Where are you at?" Joe asked him.

"I'm in a plane thirty-five-thousand feet over Dallas, just callin' to say 'Hi,' " Stevie said.

Shortly after Stevie's death, Joe Boy was lying in bed in his North Dallas home when he heard a wind chime that sounded like a guitar. Joe didn't know of any wind chimes near his house. "Maybe, that's Stevie passin' by," he thought to himself. "Just callin' to say 'Hi.' "

Despite the good intentions of friends and family, the most moving memorial to Stevie is the one he created himself, his music. Time keeps tickin' away. Cruising along the edge of a ridge in Oak Cliff, Double Trouble's version of the Jimi Hendrix composition "Little Wing" blasts out of the car radio as the last red and yellow streaks of a setting sun illuminate the Emerald City skyline of downtown Dallas. Beyond the Trinity River flood plain and the gleaming, mirrored glass towers with their neon frosting and flickering lights, a fat burnt-orange harvest moon slowly rises up the hazy twilight backdrop. The wistful melody, charged with Stevie's sweat-stained funk, is a wordless hymn to some higher power, a power that gave Stevie Ray Vaughan the ability to pull heart and soul out of wood and metal. As darkness falls over Oak Cliff, the message rings louder and clearer than ever. Great guitar player. An even greater man.

ACKNOWLEDGMENTS

While there are only two people credited as authors of this book, the project could not have been realized without the help of many, many others, chief among them our editor, Michael Pietsch, our original editor, Colleen Mohyde, whose belief in the project made it a reality, and our agent, Madeleine Morel.

Our researchers and transcribers, including Veronica O'Donovan, Betty Milstead, David Meyerson, David Kulko, Rebecca Borden, and Lori Roos, brought thoughts and words onto the printed page. Craig Keyzer's encyclopedic knowledge of Stevie Ray Vaughan's recorded material gave us a tremendous ears-on advantage, and Kent Benjamin, Frank de Santis, David Tarnow, and Tim Hamblin also provided audiovisual support. Thanks also to Mare-Mare Garrard and Debbie Phillips for logistical support.

In Dallas, we wish to thank Joe Cook, Bill Minutaglio, Diane Jennings, Robert Wilonsky, Kirby Warnock, Scott Phares, Kim Davis, Mario Daboub, Dave Swartz and all the Nightcaps, Jim Lowe, Craig Hopkins, Homer Henderson, Phil Bennison, Billy Knight, Connie Trent, Mark Pollock, Tony Dukes, Chris Lingwall, Patrick Keel, Douglas Green, Chuck Nevitt and the Dallas Blues Society, Angus Wynne, Terri

Denton, Redbeard, Christina Patoski, Stephanie Stanley, Chris Brooks, Johnny Reno, Ann McGee-Cooper, Sumter Bruton, Pat Savage, A. J. Davis, Goofy, Fredde Pharoah, Mike and Renee Rhyner, Alan Govenar, Sammy L. Klutts, J. W. "Red" Klutts, Lenny Vaughan Cobb, David Cobb, Craig Hopkins, Bruce Yamini, John Kenyon, Scott Weiss, Mike Griffin, Joe Dishner, Ronnie Bramhall, and W. P. Durrett. Although circumstances did not allow us to work closely with her on this project, we wish to thank Martha Vaughan for the generosity she displayed during the course of our research. We are also grateful to the staff of the Dallas City Collection at the Dallas Public Library.

In Austin, we thank Clifford Antone, Gretchen Barber, Joe Priest-nitz, Margaret Moser, Steve Dean, Casey Monahan, Deb Freeman and the Texas Music Office–Office of the Governor, Jody Denberg, Ed Ward, Jay Trachtenberg, John Wheat and the Center for American History at the University of Texas at Austin, David Bennett, French Smith III, Nelson Allen, Gerard Daily, Lois Loeffler, Derek O'Brien, Susan Piver, Sarah Brown, Dennie Tarner, Micael Priest, Charles Ray, Jo Rae Di-Menno, Woody Roberts, Henry Gonzales, Sherri Phelan, Mary Beth Greenwood, Edi Johnson, Chesley Millikin, Frances Carr, Cutter and Peggy Brandenburg, Tim Hamblin, Byron Barr, Roddy Colonna, David Murray, Kathy Murray, Martha Grenon, Alex Napier, Mike Steele, C. B. Stubblefield, Ed Mayberry, W. C. Clark, Mike Kindred, Jackie New-house, Greg Martin, Steve France Goteski, Jay Hudson, Tary Owens, Mike Buck, Keith Ferguson, Kim Wilson, Eddie Stout, the Continental, the One Knite, Gary Oliver, Dana Whitchair, Cliff Hargrove, David Alvarez, Walter Morgan and the gang at KUT-FM, Jim Trimmier, Dale Bramhall, Becky Bramhall, Tyrone Fullerton, Marc Benno, Pammy Kay, Ernie Durawa, Speedy Sparks, Doug Sahm, John Kunz, Charlie Pri-chard, Ray Benson, Houston White, Sandy Lockett, Joe Gracey, D. K. Little, Jim Finney, Jim Franklin, Ray Hennig, Lindi Bethel, Martin Coulter, Charlie Hatchett, Martin Bernard, Nels Jacobsen, Michael Point, Darcie Jane Fromholz, Michael Corcoran, Joe Frank Frolik, Stephen Bruton, John T. Davis, John Burnett, John Morthland, Greg Curtis, Doug Hanners, Bill Narum, Billy Bob Sanders, Nicolas Russell, Carlyn Majer, George Majewski, J. W. Williams, David Arnsberger, Jay Hudson, Kathleen Hudson, Benny Rowe, Sugar Bear, Blues Boy Hub-bard, Jim Ramsey, Mark Erlewine, Eddie Wilson, T. D. Bell, Erbie Bowser, Tanya Rae, and Junior Brown. Others we wish to thank for keeping our lives interesting include Frank Cooksey, Susan Antone, Chris Layton, Dan Forte, Richard Mullen, Tommy Shannon, Reese Wynans, Jimmie Vaughan, Lou Ann Barton, Gary Heil, Paul Ray, and Mark Proct. We are also grateful to the staff at the Austin History Center of the Austin Public Library, and to Richard Lariviere, John Broders, Sarah

Wimer, Martha Harrison, and Karla Renaud for their support and encouragement during the writing process.

Around the globe, we'd like to acknowledge the contributions of David Anderle, Denny Freeman, Bill Bentley, Alex Hodges, Tom Marshall, Charles Comer, Tim Duckworth, Sid Morning, Sue Sawyer, Bob Merlis, Nick Ferrari, Dede Ferrari, Dr. Barry Bailey, Joe Rhodes, Ronnie Lippin, Fred Goldring, Johnny Perez, Angela Strehli, Bill Campbell, David Gans, Dennis McNally, Ice Cube Slim, Mike Goodwin, D. J. Adams, Mindy Giles, Tom Marker, Bruce Iglauer, Michele Sugg, Frank DeSantis, Phil Grandy, Walter Dawson, Richard Luckett, Nick Tosches, Gregg Geller, Skip Rickert, W. A. Williams, Shirley Dimmick Ratisseau, James Luther Dickinson, J. Gillespie, Huey P. Meaux, Aaron Schecter, Frank Motley, Mr. Jesse Hernandez, Pepi Plowman, Johnny Hughes, Ivah Villalobos, B. B. King, Leon Eagleson, Marion Wisse, David Tarnow, Jim and Linda Markham, and Christian-Charles de Plicque.

Finally, close to home, our love and thanks to Diana, Joe, and Amelia, and to Kris, Jake, and Andy.

NOTES

CHAPTER 1: DON'T TOUCH MY GUITAR

Interviews

J. W. "Red" Klutts, Sammy L. Klutts, Joe Cook, A. J. Davis, Jim Lowe, Connie Trent, Mario Daboub, Roddy Colonna, Cutter Brandenburg, Ronnie Bramhall, Dale Bramhall, Alex Napier, Melanie Grey, Lou Thompson, Chris Lingwall, Greg Martin

Articles

Davis, John T. "Guitarists Lose Loved One." *Austin American-Statesman*, August 29, 1986.

Ward, Ed. "Blues Brothers." *Musician*, May 1987.

Forte, Dan. "Brothers: Jimmie Remembers Stevie." *Guitar Player*, March 1991.

White, Timothy. "Stevie Ray Vaughan: Talking with the Master." *Musician*, June 1991.

Forte, Dan. "Stevie Ray Vaughan." *Guitar Player*, October 1984.

Aledort, Andy, and Robert Knight. "Now and Forever: Stevie Ray Vaughan." *Guitar for the Practicing Musician*, May 1991.

Minutaglio, Bill. "Stevie Ray Vaughan." *Dallas Morning News*, March 17, 1985.

Swenson, John. "Stevie Ray Vaughan: 1954–1990." *Rolling Stone*, September 4, 1990.

Buchholz, Brad. "Going Solo." *Dallas Morning News*, December 29, 1991.
Jennings, Diane. "Stevie Ray Vaughan: No More Wild and Crazy Days for This Guitar Guru." *Dallas Morning News*, June 10, 1990.

Books

Rockwall County History. Rockwall, Tex.: Rockwall County Historical Society, 1984.
Liles, Allen. *Oh Thank Heaven! The Story of the Southland Corporation*. Dallas: The Southland Corporation, 1977.
Govenar, Alan. *Meeting the Blues*. Dallas: Taylor Publishing Company, 1988.
Schutze, Jim. *The Accommodation: The Politics of Race in an American City*. Secaucus, N.J.: Citadel Press, 1986.
Oliver, Paul. *The Story of the Blues*. Radnor, Pa.: Chilton Book Company, 1982.
Dance, Helen Oakley. *Stormy Monday: The T-Bone Walker Story*. New York: De Capo Press, 1989.
Harris, Sheldon. *Blues Who's Who: A Biographical Dictionary of Blues Singers*. New York: De Capo Press, 1979.

CHAPTER 2: FUCKHEAD

Interviews

Christian-Charles De Plicque, Richard Goodwin, Mike Rhyner, Chris Lingwall, Stephanie Stanley, Christian Brooks, Billy Knight, Dale Bramhall, Ronnie Bramhall, Benny Rowe, Greg Martin, Allen Stovall, David Faulkner, Keith Ferguson, Alex Napier, Cutter Brandenburg, Peggy Brandenburg, Roddy Colonna, Scott Phares, Fredde Pharoah, Tary Owens, W. P. Durrett, Elizabeth Knodle, Joe Dishner, Clyde Williams, Bruce Yamini, Ann McGee-Cooper, Jim Trimmier, Connie Trent, Mike Kindred, Angus Wynne III, Stephen Bruton

Articles

Forte, Dan. "Brothers," op. cit.
Forte, Dan. "The Fabulous Thunderbirds." *Guitar Player*, July 1986.
Milkowski, Bill. "Stevie Ray Vaughan: Hendrix White Knight." *Guitar World*, May 1984.
Davis, John T. "The True-Blue Soul of Stevie Ray." *Austin American-Statesman*, July 16, 1985.
Forte, Dan. "Stevie Ray Vaughan." op. cit.
White, Timothy. op. cit.
Minutaglio, Bill. op. cit.
Jennings, Diane. op. cit.
Resnicoff, Matt, and Joe Gore. "Stevie Ray Vaughan and Jeff Beck: Of Meat and Fingers." *Guitar Player*, February 1990.
Evans, Christopher. "Remembering the Cellar." *Fort Worth Star Telegram*, May 25, 1984.
Neer, Dan. "Up Close: Stevie Ray Vaughan." Interview on CO-NOT. MediaAmerica Radio, 1991.

Books

Govenar, Alan. op. cit.
Wright, Lawrence. *In the New World: Growing Up with America, 1960–1984.* New
    York: Knopf, 1988.
Minutaglio, Bill, and Holly Williams. *The Hidden City: Oak Cliff, Texas.* Dallas:
    Elmwood Press and the Old Oak Cliff Conservation League, 1990.
Henderson, David. *Jimi Hendrix: Voodoo Child of the Aquarian Age.* New York:
    Doubleday & Co., 1978.
Murray, Charles Shaar. *Crosstown Traffic: Jim Hendrix and the Post-War Rock 'n' Roll
    Revolution.* New York: St. Martin's Press, 1989.

CHAPTER 3: LOST IN AUSTIN

Interviews

Denny Freeman, Ray Benson, Charlie Hatchett, Roddy Colonna, Cutter Branden-
    burg, Alex Napier, Christian-Charles de Plicque, Becky Bramhall, Sandy Lock-
    ett, Houston White, Keith Ferguson, Bennie Rowe, Greg Martin, Tary Owens,
    Stephanie Stanley, Mike Tolleson, Angela Strehli, Shirley Dimmick Ratisseau,
    Mike Kindred, Charlie Prichard, Pepi Plowman

Articles

Forte, Dan. "The Fabulous Thunderbirds." op. cit.
Eschenbrenner, Bob. "Stevie Ray Vaughan: Weathering the Storm." *The Music Pa-
    per,* December 1989.
Flippo, Chet. "Austin: The Hucksters Are Coming." *Rolling Stone,* April 11, 1974.
Minutaglio, Bill. op. cit.
Blodgett, Elaine. "The Vulcan Gas Co." *Austin Chronicle,* August 9, 1985.
Swenson, John. op. cit.

Books

Wilson, Burton. *Burton's Book of the Blues: A Decade of American Music, 1967–1977.*
    Austin, Tex.: Edentata Press, 1977.
Fowler, Gene, and Bill Crawford. *Border Radio.* Austin, Tex.: Texas Monthly Press,
    1987.
Ivins, Molly. *Molly Ivins Can't Say That Can She?* New York: Random House, 1991.
Handbook of Texas. Austin, Tex.: Texas State Historical Association, 1952.
Brammer, Billy Lee. *The Gay Place: Being Three Related Novels.* New York: Vintage
    Books, 1983.
Lomax, John. *Cowboy Songs and Other Frontier Ballads.* New York: Sturgis & Wal-
    ton, 1910.
Joplin, Laura. *Love, Janis.* New York: Villard Books, 1992.
Dalton, David. *Piece of My Heart: The Life and Times of Janis Joplin.* New York: St.
    Martin's Press, 1985.
Friedman, Myra. *Buried Alive: The Biography of Janis Joplin.* New York: William
    Morrow & Company, 1977.

Malone, Bill C. *Country Music, U.S.A.: A Fifty Year History.* Austin, Tex.: University of Texas Press, 1968.

CHAPTER 4: CRAWLIN' TO LA

Interviews

Cutter Brandenburg, Christian-Charles de Plicque, Roddy Colonna, Billy Knight, Marc Benno, Ronnie Bramhall, David Anderle, Leon Eagleson, Doty Tullos, Becky Crabtree, Keith Ferguson, Margaret Moser, Gary Oliver, David Murray, Eddie Stout, Denny Freeman, Mark Pollock, Ray Hennig, Johnny Perez, Speedy Sparks, J. W. Williams

Articles

White, Timothy. op. cit.

Books

Booth, Stanley. *Rhythm Oil: A Journey through the Music of the American South.* Pantheon: New York, 1991.
Harris, Sheldon. op. cit.

CHAPTER 5: LAND OF THE COSMIC COWBOYS

Interviews

Mike Tolleson, John Burnett, Ray Benson, Shirley Dimmick Ratisseau, Kim Wilson, Clifford Antone, Mark Pollock, Greg Martin, Mickey Raphael, Carlyn Majer Majewski, Margaret Moser, Mary Beth Greenwood, Lindi Bethel, Denny Freeman, Gary Heil, David Murray, Angus Wynne III, Mike Buck, Tony Dukes, Bill Campbell, Woody Roberts, Leon Eagleson

Articles

Flippo, Chet. op. cit.
Dimmick, Shirley R. "In Defense of Austin Blues." *Rolling Stone,* May 9, 1974.
Soap Creek Collection, Barker Texas History Center, University of Texas at Austin.

Books

Menconi, David Lawrence. "Music, Media and the Metropolis: The Case of Austin's Armadillo World Headquarters." Master's thesis. The University of Texas at Austin, 1985.
Reid, Jan. *The Improbable Rise of Redneck Rock.* Austin, Tex.: Heidelberg Publishers, 1974.
Wilson, Burton. op. cit.
Govenar, Alan. op. cit.

CHAPTER 6: HOME OF THE BLUES

Interviews

David Murray, Angela Strehli, Bill Campbell, Steve Dean, Clifford Antone, Kim Wilson, Kathy Murray, Mike Buck, Patrick Keel, David Dennard, Leon Eagleson, Keith Ferguson, Mark Erlewine, Bill Bentley

Articles

Forte, Dan. "The Fabulous Thunderbirds." op. cit.
Point, Michael. "The Austin Blues: Stevie Ray Vaughan, 1954–1990." *Spin*, September 1990.
Patoski, Joe Nick. "Play That Funky Music White Boys." *Texas Monthly*, April 1978.

Books

Govenar, Alan. op. cit.

CHAPTER 7: HURRICANE TAKES THE WHEEL

Interviews

W. C. Clark, David Murray, Fredde Pharoah, Mary Beth Greenwood, Mark Pollock, Tony Dukes, Jackie Newhouse, C. B. Stubblefield, Nick Ferrari, Dede Ferrari, Johnny Reno, Houston White, Lenny Vaughan Cobb, Pammy Kay, Dr. Barry Bailey, Becky Bramhall, Stephen Bruton, Bill Narum, Joe Priestnitz, Martin Bernard, Gerard Daily, Lois Loeffler, Bill Bentley, Stephanie Stanley, Christian Brooks, Mike Steele, Margaret Moser, Steve Dean, Keith Ferguson

Articles

Rhodes, Joe. "Stevie Ray and the Bowie Tour." *Dallas Morning News*, April 17, 1983.
Forte, Dan. "Stevie Ray Vaughan." op. cit.
Neer, Dan. "Up Close: Stevie Ray Vaughan." op. cit.
Bentley, Bill. "The Vaughans — Mainline Blues." *Austin Sun*, April 28, 1978.
Davis, John T. "The True-Blue Soul of Stevie Ray." op. cit.
Ward, Ed. op. cit.
Moser, Margaret. "Stevie Vaughan & Double Trouble." *Austin Sun*, July 27, 1978.

CHAPTER 8: MEAN AS HOWLIN' WOLF

Interviews

Joe Gracey, Houston White, Sandy Lockett, Cutter Brandenburg, Chesley Millikin, Joe Priestnitz, Lenny Vaughan Cobb, Mary Beth Greenwood, Gretchen Barber, Roddy Colonna, Martin Bernard, Mike Kindred, Jody Denberg, Wayne Bell

Articles

Coryell, Larry. "Stevie Ray Vaughan interview." *Musician*, December 1989.
White, Timothy. op. cit.
Milkowski, Bill. "A Good Texan." *Guitar World*, December 1990.

CHAPTER 9: STEVIE RAY

Interviews

Edi Johnson, Chesley Millikin, Frances Carr, Lenny Vaughan Cobb, Cutter Brandenburg, Joe Priestnitz, Jackie Newhouse, Byron Barr

Articles

Roberts, Jim. "Tommy Shannon: New Life with the Arc Angels." *Bass Player*, September 1992.
Price, Mike H. "Little Stevie: Coming of Age." *Texas Jazz*, August 1982.

CHAPTER 10: THE LEGEND OF ZIGGY STARDUST
AND THE TEXAS KID

Interviews

Bruce Iglauer, Mindy Giles, Chesley Millikin, Wayne Nagel, Jim Hudson, Cutter Brandenburg, Byron Barr, Joe Rhodes, Lenny Vaughan Cobb, Edi Johnson, Craig Keyzer, Bill Bentley, Sid Morning, Joe Rhodes, Frances Carr

Articles

"Stevie Vaughan." *Buddy Magazine*, July 1981.
Rhodes, Joe. "Stevie Ray Vaughan: Guitar Hero." *Rolling Stone*, August 1983.
"Random Notes." *Rolling Stone*, June 10, 1982.
Nixon, Bruce. "Stevie Vaughan: Blues to Bowie." *Guitar Player*, August 1983.
Erika, "Fantasy." *Best of Hustler Beaver Hunt*, Fall 1991.
Forte, Dan. "Stevie Ray Vaughan." op. cit.
Rhodes, Joe. "Stevie Ray Vaughan Makes Debut." *Dallas Times-Herald*, April 17, 1983.
Minutaglio, Bill. op. cit.

Books

Palmer, Robert. *Deep Blues*. New York: Penguin, 1982.
Edwards, Harry, and Tony Zanetta. *Stardust: The David Bowie Story*. New York: McGraw-Hill, 1986.
Hopkins, Jerry. *Bowie*. New York: Macmillan, 1985.

CHAPTER 11: BETTER THAN T-BONE

Interviews

Chesley Millikin, Gregg Geller, Cutter Brandenburg, Frances Carr, Byron Barr, Redbeard, Joe Priestnitz, David Kulko, Alex Hodges, Ray Benson, Edi Johnson, Bill Narum, Mark Erlewine, Jim Markham

Articles

Minutaglio, Bill. op. cit.
Swenson, John. op. cit.

Nixon, Bruce. op. cit.
Porter, Martin. Review of Bryan Adams show. *New York Post*, May 1983.
Forte, Dan. "Blues Brothers: Stevie Ray." *Guitar World*, July 1989.

Books

Hammond, John, and Irving Townsend. *John Hammond on Record: An Autobiography with Irving Townsend*. New York: Summit Books, 1977.
Dannen, Fredric. *Hit Men: Power Brokers and Fast Money Inside the Music Business*. New York: Random House, 1990.
Patoski, Joe Nick. "Southern Rock." In *Rolling Stone Illustrated History of Rock and Roll, 1950–1980*, edited by Jim Miller. Revised and updated edition. New York: Rolling Stone Press/Random House, 1980.

CHAPTER 12: CARNEGIE HALL

Interviews

David Tarnow, Frances Carr, Sid Morning, Craig Keyzer, Joe Rhodes, Byron Barr, David Murray, Bill Minutaglio, Chesley Millikin

Articles

Forte, Dan. "Stevie Ray Vaughan." op. cit.
Rhodes, Joe. "Stevie Ray Vaughan at Carnegie Hall." *Dallas Times-Herald*, November 28, 1984.
"Reader's Poll." *Guitar Player*, January 1984.
McBride, James. "You Can Take the Boy out of Texas, But You Can't Take Texas out of Blues' Golden Boy Stevie Ray Vaughan." *People*, March 25, 1985.
Davis, John T. "Stevie Ray to Answer Carnegie Call." *Austin American-Statesman*, October 2, 1984.

CHAPTER 13: SERIOUS TROUBLE

Interviews

Bill Minutaglio, David Murray, Bill Jones, B. B. King, Keith Ferguson, Edi Johnson, Lenny Vaughan Cobb, Cutter Brandenburg, Michael Corcoran, Connie Trent, Bruce Iglauer, Frances Carr, Pammy Kay, Sue Sawyer, Nick Ferrari, Byron Barr, Mike Steele, Jackie Newhouse, Mindy Giles

Articles

Minutaglio, Bill. op. cit.
Menconi, David. "With Respect, 'Blood and Memories,' the Late Mr. Vaughan Rave On." *Blues Access*, vol. 1, no. 4, Christmas 1990.
Milkowski, Bill. "Stevie Ray Vaughan: Stevie Comes Clean." *Guitar World*, September 1988.
Nixon, Bruce. "It's Star Time: Stevie Ray Vaughan." *Guitar World*, November 1985.
Roberts, Jim. op. cit.

Davis, John T. "The True-Blue Soul of Stevie Ray." op. cit.
White, Timothy. op. cit.
Buchholz, Brad. "Going Solo." op. cit.
Aledort, Andy. "Remembering Stevie Ray." *Guitar for the Practicing Musician*, March 1992.
Glentzer, Molly. "Brotherly Blues." *Houston Press*, September 13, 1990.
Point, Michael. "Stevie Ray Comes Back to Play." *Austin American-Statesman*, June 1, 1985.
Davis, John T. "Stevie Ray Vaughan Flashes Serious Style." *Austin American-Statesman*, June 3, 1985.

CHAPTER 14: SEVEN GRAMS A DAY

Interviews

Mark Pollock, Redbeard, Chesley Millikin, Alex Hodges, Michael Corcoran, Fredde Pharoah, Keith Ferguson, Mary Beth Greenwood, Tim Duckworth, Lenny Vaughan Cobb, Sue Sawyer, Richard Luckett, Bill Bentley, Sid Morning

Articles

Guterman, Jimmy. *Soul to Soul* review. *Rolling Stone*, April 19, 1986.
Nixon, Bruce. "Stevie Ray Vaughan Shows Fans 'How To.' " *Dallas Times-Herald*, December 17, 1985.
"Blues Legend on Special Mission." *The News* (Adelaide, Australia), March 24, 1986.
Point, Michael. "Hometown Hero." *Austin American-Statesman*, July 17, 1986.
Gingold, David. "Stevie Ray Vaughan." *Santa Cruz Sentinel*, August 8, 1986.
Milkowski, Bill. "Stevie Ray: Stevie Comes Clean." op. cit.
Donahue, Michael. "Drugs and Alcohol Took Him Down but Not Out." *Memphis Commercial Appeal*, May 8, 1987.
Forte, Dan. "Soul to Soul." *Guitar Player*, March 1991.
"Stevie Ray Vaughan." *Statesman Journal* (Salem, Oreg.), August 7, 1986.

Books

Ashley, Richard. *Cocaine: Its History, Uses and Effects*. New York: St. Martin's Press, 1975.
Burroughs, William. *Naked Lunch*. New York: Grove Press, 1966.

CHAPTER 15: VOODOO CHILE

Interviews

Joe Rhodes, Joe Cook, Mindy Giles, Tim Duckworth, Lenny Vaughan Cobb

Articles

Davis, John T. "Guitarists Lose Loved One." *Austin American-Statesman*, August 29, 1986.

Kronke, David. "He Found Life Upbeat after Ending Addictions." *Dallas Times-Herald*, August 28, 1990.
Fox, James. "Stevie Ray Vaughan." *Observer*, October 5, 1986.
Milkowski, Bill. "Stevie Ray Vaughan: Stevie Comes Clean." op. cit.
Forte, Dan. "Soul to Soul." op. cit.

CHAPTER 16: STEVIE V.

Interviews

Tim Duckworth, Redbeard, Tary Owens, Keith Ferguson, Joe Cook, Marc Benno, Mike Rhyner, Michele Sugg, Stephen Bruton

Articles

Jennings, Diane. op. cit.
Smith, Russell. "Dallas Born Rocker Kicks His Addictions." *Dallas Morning News*, January 25, 1987.
Milkowski, Bill. "Stevie Ray Vaughan: Stevie Comes Clean." op. cit.
Resnicoff, Matt, and Joe Gore. op. cit.
Racine, Marty. "Guitar Whiz Battles a Flood of Troubles." *Houston Chronicle*, January 31, 1987.
Eschenbrenner, Bob. op. cit.
Davis, John T. "Exhaustion Sidelines Stevie Ray." *Austin American-Statesman*, October 7, 1986.
MacCambridge, Michael. "Blazing New Trails." *Austin American-Statesman*, November 25, 1989.

Books

Kurtz, Ernest. *A.A. The Story: A Revised Edition of Not-God — A History of Alcoholics Anonymous*. San Francisco: Harper & Row, 1988.
Wilson, William Griffith et al. *Alcoholics Anonymous Comes of Age*. New York: A.A. Publishing Inc., 1957.
Pittman, Bill. *A.A.: The Way It Began*. Seattle: Glen Abbey Books, 1988.
Twelve Steps and Twelve Traditions. New York: Alcoholics Anonymous World Services, 1953.
James, William. *The Varieties of Religious Experience*. New York: New American Library, 1958.
Govenar, Alan. op. cit.
Oxford English Dictionary. Second edition. Oxford: Clarendon Press, 1989.

CHAPTER 17: REDEMPTION

Interviews

Skip Rickert, Alex Hodges, Shirley Dimmick Ratisseau, Lenny Vaughan Cobb, Chesley Millikin, Frances Carr, Edi Johnson, W. A. Williams, David Bennett

Articles

Smith, Russell. "Vaughan's Return Is Red Hot." *Dallas Morning News,* January 31, 1987.
Eschenbrenner, Bob. op. cit.
Milkowski, Bill. "Stevie Ray Vaughan: Stevie Comes Clean." op. cit.

Books

Govenar, Alan. op. cit.
Kurtz, Ernest. op. cit.

CHAPTER 18: IN STEP

Interviews

Skip Rickert, Alex Hodges, Stephen Bruton, Chesley Millikin, W. C. Clark, Lenny Vaughan Cobb

Articles

Milkowski, Bill. "Stevie Ray Vaughan: Stevie Comes Clean." op. cit.
Nixon, Bruce. "Stevie Ray Vaughan." *Dallas Times-Herald,* July 1988.
Buchholz, Brad. op. cit.
Resnicoff, Matt, and Joe Gore. op. cit.
White, Timothy. op. cit.
Eschenbrenner, Bob. op. cit.
Coryell, Larry. op. cit.
Pond, Steve. "Alone Together." *Rolling Stone,* January 25, 1990.
"A Wisconsin Helicopter Crash Claims a Blues Legend-in-Making." *People,* September 7, 1990.

Books

Dannen, Fredric. op. cit.

CHAPTER 19: HILLBILLIES FROM OUTER SPACE

Interviews

Mike Buck, Henry Gonzales, Richard Luckett, Stephen Bruton, Skip Rickert, Alex Hodges

Articles

Forte, Dan. "Blues Brothers: Stevie Ray." op cit.
Birnbaum, Larry. "Red Hot Rhythm & Blues: The Fabulous Thunderbirds." *Downbeat,* February 1986.
Point, Michael. op. cit.
Milkowski, Bill. "A Good Texan." op. cit.
Forte, Dan. "Brothers." op. cit.

CHAPTER 20: THE OTIS EXPRESS

Interviews

Stephen Bruton, Cutter Brandenburg, Michele Sugg, Phil Grandy, Joe Cook, Dale
Bramhall, Henry Gonzales, Richard Luckett, Alex Hodges, Skip Rickert, Don
McCleese, Mindy Giles, Tom Marker, David Arnsberger, Doug Sahm

Articles

Milkowski, Bill. "Stevie Ray Vaughan: Stevie Comes Clean." op. cit.
Eschenbrenner, Bob. op cit.
Forte, Dan. "Blues Brothers: Stevie Ray." op. cit.
Coryell, Larry. op. cit.
Bonny, Helen Lindquist. "Music and Healing." *Music Therapy*, vol. 6a, no. 1, 1986.
Aledort, Andy, and Robert Knight. op. cit.
"A Wisconsin Helicopter Crash Claims a Blues Legend-in-Making." op. cit.
Rzab, Greg. "The Last Show." *Guitar Player*, March 1991.
Ressner, Jeffrey. "Dense Fog May Have Caused Crash." *Rolling Stone*, October 4,
1990.
Johnson, Dirk. "Stevie Ray Vaughan Killed with 4 Others in Air Crash." *New York
Times*, August 28, 1990.
Gamino, Denise. "So Long, Stevie Ray." *Austin American-Statesman*, August 28,
1990.

Books

Eliade, Mircea. *Shamanism: Archaic Techniques of Ecstasy*. Princeton, N.J.: Princeton
University Press, 1964.
Taylor, Rogan P. *The Death and Resurrection Show: From Shaman to Superstar*. Lon-
don: Anthony Blond, 1985.

CHAPTER 21: SLIGHT RETURN

Interviews

Alex Hodges, Henry Gonzales, Richard Luckett, Joe Cook, Skip Rickert, Jody
Denberg, Cutter Brandenburg, Ivah Villalobos, Becky Fullerton, Dale
Bramhall, Michele Sugg, Chesley Millikin, Dr. Barry Bailey, Tyrone Fullerton,
John Logan

Articles

Ressner, Jeffrey. op. cit.
Point, Michael. "Vaughan Anniversary to Pass Quietly." *Austin American-Statesman*,
August 22, 1991.
Schoemer, Karen. "The Laid-Back No-Frills Road to a Music Conference in Texas."
New York Times, March 18, 1992.

DISCOGRAPHY

compiled by Craig Keyzer

ALBUMS AND ALBUM APPEARANCES WITH DOUBLE TROUBLE

Blues Masters Vol. 3 (Texas Blues), 1992, Rhino, 71123

In the Beginning, 1992, Epic, ET 53168

Up Close — Stevie Ray Vaughan, 1991, MediaAmerica Radio (radio program distributed on CD)

The Sky Is Crying, 1991, Epic, ET 47390

Interchords — Stevie Ray Vaughan and Double Trouble, 1991, Epic, ESK 4418 (promotional)

In Step, 1989, Epic, OET/EK 45024

Back to the Beach (movie soundtrack), Dick Dale, 1987, Columbia, SC 40892 (with Dick Dale)

Atlantic Blues — Guitar, 1986, Atlantic, ATC 81695-1

Live Alive!, 1986, Epic, EGT/EGT 40511 (with Jimmie Vaughan)

Soul to Soul, 1985, Epic, FET/EK 40036

Couldn't Stand the Weather, 1984, Epic, FET/EK 39304 (with Jimmie Vaughan)

Blues Explosion, 1984, Atlantic, 780149-1

Texas Flood, 1983, Epic, FET/EK 38734

APPEARANCES ON OTHER ALBUMS

The Blues Guitar Box 2, Lonnie Mack, 1991, Sequel, NXT 185
Alligator Records 20th Anniversary Collection, A. C. Reed, 1991, Alligator, ALC-105/6
The Blues Guitar Box, Lonnie Mack, 1990, Sequel, TBB 47555
Stevie Ray Vaughan: October 3, 1954–August 27, 1990, Epic, ESK 2221 (limited tribute edition)
Family Style, The Vaughan Brothers, 1990, Epic, ZT/ZK 46225 (with Jimmie Vaughan)
Under the Red Sky, Bob Dylan, 1990, Columbia, C 46749 (with Jimmie Vaughan)
Bull Durham (movie soundtrack), Bennie Wallace, 1988, Capitol, 90586
Distant Drums, Brian Slawson, 1988, CBS, 42666
Loaded Dice, Bill Carter, 1988, CBS, BFZ 44039 (with Jimmie Vaughan)
Characters (CD only), Stevie Wonder, 1987, Motown, MCD 06248 MD
I'm in the Wrong Business, A. C. Reed, 1987, Alligator, AL 4757
Emerald City, Teena Marie, 1986, Epic, FE 40318
Famous Blue Raincoat, Jennifer Warnes, 1986, Cypress, 661111
Gravity, James Brown, 1986, Scotti Bros., 5212-2-SB
Rocky IV (movie soundtrack), James Brown, 1985, Scotti Bros., 40203
Living for a Song, Roy Head, 1985, Texas Crude
Heartbeat, Don Johnson, 1985, Epic, 40366
Twilight Time, Bennie Wallace, 1985, Blue Note, BT 85107
Strike Like Lightning, Lonnie Mack, 1985, Alligator, AL 4739
Soulful Dress, Marcia Ball, 1983, Rounder, 3078
Texas Twister, Johnny Copeland, 1983, Rounder, 2040
Let's Dance, David Bowie, 1983, EMI-America, SO-17093
A New Hi, Cast of Thousands, 1971

APPEARANCES ON VIDEO

Little Wing, 1992, Epic, promotional video
Live at the El Mocambo, 1991, Sony, 19V-49111
Pride and Joy, 1990, CBS, 17V-49069
Tick Tock, 9/90, Epic, promotional video
Bull Durham, 1988, Orion, 8722 (music only)
Back to the Beach, 1987, Paramount, 31980
B. B. King & Friends: A Night of Red Hot Blues, 1987 HBO 90074, IEI ID 6871HB, or ATL 50203
Gung Ho, 1986, Paramount, 1751 (music only)
Rocky IV, 1985, CBS, 4735 (music only)

SINGLES

Wham! b/w Empty Arms, 1991, Epic, 34-74198
The Sky Is Crying b/w Chitlins Con Carne, 1991, Epic, 34-74142
Tick Tock b/w Brothers, The Vaughan Brothers, 1990, Epic, 73576
    (with Jimmie Vaughan)

Madre Dollisima b/w Jesus, 1989, Polygram (with Adelno Fonciari)
Pipeline b/w Love Struck Baby, 1987, Columbia, 07340 (with Dick Dale)
Superstition b/w Willie the Wimp, 1986, Epic, 06996
Superstition b/w Pride and Joy, 1986, Epic, 06601
Heartache Away b/w Love Roulette, Don Johnson, 1986, Epic, 06426
First We Take Manhattan b/w Famous Blue Raincoat, Jennifer Warnes, 1986, Cypress,
    661115-7
Look at Little Sister b/w Change It, 1985, Epic, 05731
Living in America b/w How Do You Stop?, James Brown, 1985, Scotti Bros., ZS8
    69117
Living for a Song, Roy Head, 1985, Texas Crude
Love Struck Baby b/w Rude Mood, 1983, Epic, A 3689
Without You b/w Criminal World, David Bowie, 1983, EMI, B-8190
Modern Love b/w Modern Love, David Bowie, 1983, EMI, EA 158
China Girl b/w Shake It, David Bowie, 1983, EMI, EA 157
Let's Dance b/w Cat People, David Bowie, 1983, EMI, EA 152
My Song b/w Rough Edges, W. C. Clark & The Cobras & Stevie Vaughan, 1979, Hole
    Records, HR-1520
Other Days b/w Texas Clover, The Cobras, Viper, 30372

TWELVE-INCH SINGLES

Living in America, James Brown, 1985, Scotti Bros., 4Z905310
Modern Love b/w Modern Love, David Bowie, 1983, EMI, 12 EA 158
Let's Dance b/w Cat People, David Bowie, 1983, EMI, 12 EA 152

COLLECTOR'S TAPE-OGRAPHY

compiled by Craig Keyzer

Included in the following list are TV appearances, radio broadcasts, studio sessions, live concerts, videos, and interviews known to exist in private collections. We have included as much information as we have been able to gather on these unreleased tapes of Stevie Ray Vaughan's performances. If you have corrections, additions, or more information on particular performances, please send your information to: SRV, P.O. Box 31516, Aurora, Colo. 80041.

Demo recordings, Austin, Tex., 1972, with Blackbird
Studio recordings for A&M Records, Los Angeles, Calif., 1973, with Marc Benno and the Nightcrawlers
Demo recordings for Lone Wolf Productions, The Warehouse, New Orleans, La., 1974, with Nightcrawler
Studio outtakes, Austin, Tex., 1975, with the Cobras
Unreleased album, Austin, Tex., 1975, with the Cobras
Hole Sound Recording, Austin, Tex., 1977, with Triple Threat Revue
50-50 Club, San Antonio, Tex., summer 1978, with Lou Ann Barton and Double Trouble

Stubb's Barbecue, Lubbock, Tex., summer 1978, with Lou Ann Barton and Double Trouble

Fat Dawg's, Lubbock, Tex., 12/78, with Lou Ann Barton and Double Trouble

The Rome Inn, Austin, Tex., 1978, with Lou Ann Barton and Double Trouble (video)

Juneteenth Blues Festival, Houston, Tex., 6/19/79, with Lou Ann Barton and Double Trouble

Fat Friday, Gilroy, La., 8/20/79, with Lou Ann Barton and Double Trouble, Robert Cray, and Curtis Salgado (radio broadcast)

Jack Clement's home studio, Nashville, Tenn., 11/79, with Lou Ann Barton and Double Trouble

Electric Graceyland, Austin, Tex., summer and fall 1979, with Lou Ann Barton and Double Trouble

Steamboat 1874, Austin, Tex., 1979, with Lou Ann Barton and Double Trouble

Steamboat 1874, Austin, Tex., 4/1/80, with Double Trouble (radio broadcast — includes seven songs not released on *In the Beginning*)

King's Bay Inn, Norfolk, Va., 7/22/80, with Double Trouble

Fort Worth, Tex., 8/30/80, with Double Trouble

Cheatham St. Warehouse, San Marcos, Tex., 1980, with Double Trouble and Charlie Sexton

Private Mother's Day Party, Dallas, Tex., 5/81, with Double Trouble

Harling's Upstairs, Kansas City, Mo., 7/4/81, with Double Trouble

Tornado Jam, Manor Downs, Manor, Tex., 7/11/81, with Double Trouble (Tommy Shannon on bass for this and all following Double Trouble tapes) (video)

Fitzgerald's, Houston, Tex., 8/14/81, with Double Trouble

Chef's, Baton Rouge, La., 9/9/81, with Double Trouble

Steamboat 1874, Austin, Tex., 10/3/81, with Double Trouble, Stevie's birthday

Fitzgerald's, Houston, Tex., 10/14/81, 10/15/81, 10/19/81, with Double Trouble

Barton Creek benefit, Antone's, Austin, Tex., 3/7/82, with Double Trouble, Kim Wilson, Omar and the Howlers

Montreux Festival, Montreux, Switzerland, 7/17/82, with Double Trouble and Johnny Copeland (video/audio)

Antone's, Austin, Tex., 1982, with Albert King

Demos for CBS Records, Down Town Studios, Los Angeles, Calif., 8/82, with Double Trouble

Fitzgerald's, Houston, Tex., 12/18/82, with Double Trouble and Johnny Copeland

Austin, Tex., 2/2/83, with Double Trouble

Houston, Tex., 2/23/83, with Double Trouble

Antone's, Austin, Tex., 2/2/83, with Double Trouble

The Continental Club, Austin, Tex., 2/28/83, with Double Trouble

The Ritz, Dallas, Tex., 3/19/83, with Double Trouble

Fitzgerald's, Houston, Tex., 3/26/83, with Double Trouble and Alan Haynes

Rehearsals with David Bowie for "Serious Moonlight" tour, Las Colinas Soundstage, Dallas, Tex., 4/27/83

Unreleased Alan Haynes Single, "I Need Love," 1983; Stevie plays six-string bass

The Bottom Line, New York City, 5/9/83, with Double Trouble

Tennis Rock Expo, Pier 84, New York City, 5/23/83, with Aerosmith, Buddy Guy, Clarence Clemmons, and John McEnroe

The Agora, Dallas, Tex., 6/3/83, with Double Trouble and Eric Johnson

Fitzgerald's, Houston, Tex., 6/20/83, with Double Trouble

The El Mocambo, Toronto, Ontario, 7/11/83, with Double Trouble (television broadcast)

Rosa's, Colorado Springs, Colo., 8/15/83, with Double Trouble

Rainbow Music Hall, Denver, Colo., 8/16/83, with Double Trouble

Reading Festival, England, 8/27/83, with Double Trouble (radio broadcast)

West Berlin, Germany, 9/6/83, with Double Trouble (television broadcast)

Paradiso Theater, Amsterdam, Netherlands, 9/9/83, with Double Trouble (radio broadcast)

The Music Hall, Houston, Tex., 10/6/83, with Double Trouble (with interview)

City Coliseum, Austin, Tex., 10/7/83, with Double Trouble

The Spectrum, Philadelphia, Pa., 10/19/83, with Double Trouble (radio broadcast)

Ripley's Theater, Philadelphia, Pa., 10/20/83, with Double Trouble (radio broadcast)

Gilly's, Dayton, Ohio, 10/83, with Double Trouble

McNichols Arena, Denver, Colo., 11/28/83, with Double Trouble

Toronto, Ontario, 11/30/83, with Albert King (television broadcast)

"Austin City Limits," Austin, Tex., 12/13/83, with Double Trouble, Lonnie Mack, Fabulous Thunderbirds, Angela Strehli (television broadcast)

The Beacon Theater, New York City, 12/28/83, with Double Trouble

The Palace, Hollywood, Calif., 1983, with Double Trouble (radio broadcast)

Couldn't Stand the Weather sessions, Power Station Studios, New York City, 1–2/84, with Double Trouble

CBS Record Convention, Honolulu, Hawaii, 3/9/84, with Double Trouble, Jeff Beck, Jimmie Vaughan, and Angela Strehli (video)

The Astrodome, Houston, Tex., 5/84 (performs "The Star Spangled Banner" on slide guitar before baseball game) (video)

The Palladium, Los Angeles, Calif., 6/16/84, with Double Trouble

The Music Hall, Houston, Tex., 7/19/84, with Double Trouble

Pier 84, New York City, 8/1/84, with Double Trouble

The Omni, Atlanta, Ga., 8/8/84, with Double Trouble

Lorelei Festival, Munich, West Germany, 8/25/84, with Double Trouble

Carnegie Hall, New York City, 10/4/84, with Double Trouble, Tower of Power Horns, Dr. John, Jimmie Vaughan, and Angela Strehli

The Spectrum, Montreal, Quebec, 1984, with Double Trouble (radio broadcast)

"Solid Gold," Los Angeles, Calif., 1984, with Double Trouble (television broadcast)

"The Grammy Awards," Los Angeles, Calif., 1984, with George Thorogood and Chuck Berry (television broadcast)

Budokan Theater, Tokyo, Japan, 1/21/85, with Double Trouble (video)

Yubinchukin Hall, Tokyo, Japan, 1/24/85, with Double Trouble

Soul to Soul sessions, Dallas Sound Labs, Dallas, Tex., 3–5/85, with Double Trouble (Reese Wynans now on keyboard)

Auditorium Shores, Austin, Tex., 6/1/85, with Double Trouble

Chicago Blues Festival, Grant Park, Chicago, Ill., 6/7/85, with Double Trouble (audio/video)

Red Rocks Blues Festival, Morrison, Colo., 6/19/85, with Double Trouble

Jazz & Blues Festival, Stockholm, Sweden, 7/7/85, with Double Trouble (radio broadcast)

Montreux Festival, Montreux, Switzerland, 7/15/85, with Double Trouble and Johnny Copeland

Albert Hall, Toronto, Ontario, 7/27/85, with Double Trouble, Albert Collins, and Jeff Healey

Dallas, Tex., 8/1/85, with Double Trouble and Eric Johnson

Seattle, Wash., 9/1/85, with Double Trouble and Bonnie Raitt

McDonald Arena, Springfield, Mo., 10/5/85, with Double Trouble

C. U. Events Center, University of Colorado, Boulder, Colo., 10/8/85, with Double Trouble

"In Session," 10/85, with Albert King (television broadcast)

Cowboys for Indians Benefit, Berkeley Community Theater, Berkeley, Calif., 10/14/85 (solo acoustic set)

Veteran's Memorial Coliseum, Phoenix, Ariz., 10/29/85, with Double Trouble

Memorial Auditorium, Burlington, Vt., 10/31/85, with Double Trouble

Milwaukee, Wis., 12/7/85, with Double Trouble

Newport Jazz Festival, Newport, R.I., 1985, with Double Trouble (television broadcast)

"Rock Influences," Capitol Theater, Passaic, N.J., 1985, with Double Trouble (television broadcast)

Boston, Mass., 1985, with Double Trouble (radio broadcast)

SEVA Benefit, Los Angeles, Calif., 1985 (solo acoustic set)

Rockefeller's, Houston, Tex., 1/31/86, with Double Trouble, John Lee Hooker, and Robert Cray

Memorial Hall, Kansas City, Mo., 2/8/86, with Double Trouble and Jimmie Vaughan

"Saturday Night Live," New York City, 2/15/86, with Double Trouble and Jimmie Vaughan (television broadcast)

Royal Oak, Mich., 2/22/86, with Double Trouble

Fair Park Coliseum, Dallas, Tex., 4/8/86, with Double Trouble

Dallas, Tex., 6/9/86, with Double Trouble and Eric Johnson

Pier 84, New York City, 6/26/86, with Double Trouble and Jimmie Vaughan

Farm Aid II, Manor Downs, Manor, Tex., 7/4/86, with Double Trouble (television broadcast)

Starfest, Dallas, Tex., 7/19/86, with Double Trouble

Red Rocks, Morrison, Colo., 7/24/86, with Double Trouble and Taj Mahal

"Rockline" interview, 12/8/86 (radio broadcast)

Fox Theater, Atlanta, Ga., 12/31/86, with Double Trouble and Lonnie Mack (radio broadcast)

Redux Club, Dallas, Tex., 1/21/87, with Robert Cray (radio broadcast)

Majestic Theater, San Antonio, Tex., 2/1/87, with Double Trouble

Park Center, Charlotte, N.C., 2/10/87, with Double Trouble

"MTV Mardi Gras," on board the SS *President*, New Orleans, La., 2/28/87, with Double Trouble, Dr. John, Katie Webster, Jimmie Vaughan, Kim Wilson, B. B. King, and Albert Collins (television broadcast)

Ocean Center, Daytona Beach, Fla., 3/25/87, with Double Trouble (television broad-
    cast)
Civic Auditorium, La Porte, Ind., 5/10/87, with Double Trouble
Red Rocks, Morrison, Colo., 6/17/87, with Double Trouble
Poplar Creek, Hoffman Estates, Ill., 6/20/87, with Double Trouble
Mann Music Center, Philadelphia, Pa., 6/30/87, with Double Trouble (radio broad-
    cast)
Kingswood, Toronto, Ontario, 7/23/87, with Double Trouble (video)
Des Moines, Iowa, 8/30/87, with Double Trouble (video)
Zoo Amphitheater, Oklahoma City, Okla., 9/12/87, with Double Trouble
Maple Leaf Gardens, Toronto, Ontario, 5/10/88, with Double Trouble (video)
Apollo Theater, Manchester, England, 6/88, with Double Trouble
Pistola Blues Festival, Piazza del Duomo, Milan, Italy, 7/3/88, with Double Trouble
    (video)
Red Rocks, Morrison, Colo., 8/5/88, with Double Trouble and Jimmie Vaughan
The Stone Pony, Asbury Park, N.J., 12/29/88, with Double Trouble
"Characters," 1988, with Stevie Wonder and Jody Watley (television broadcast)
"Don't Mess with Texas," 1988 (television commercial)
Mid-Hudson Civic Center, Poughkeepsie, N.Y., 6/27/89, with Double Trouble
Riverfest, St. Paul, Minn., 7/30/89, with Double Trouble
Legends Club, Chicago, Ill., 7/30/89, with Buddy Guy on Buddy Guy's
    birthday
"Music Link," Red Rocks, Morrison, Colo., 8/21/89, interview and performance
    with Double Trouble (television broadcast)
"The Arsenio Hall Show," Los Angeles, Calif., 8/89, with Double Trouble (television
    broadcast)
"Beach Boys Summer Show," 8/89, with Double Trouble (television broadcast)
"MTV Promo," 9/89, interview with Jeff Beck (television broadcast)
"Night Music," Los Angeles, Calif., 10/12/89, with David Sanborn and Maria
    McKee (television broadcast)
"Late Night with David Letterman," New York City, 10/89, with Double Trouble
    (television broadcast)
"Austin City Limits," Austin, Tex., 10/10/89, with Double Trouble, Jimmie
    Vaughan, W. C. Clark, Kim Wilson, Angela Strehli, Lou Ann Barton, Denny
    Freeman, Derek O'Brien, and George Rains (television broadcast)
Met Center, Minneapolis, Minn., 10/25/89, with Double Trouble
    and Jeff Beck
The Pavilion, Chicago, Ill., 10/28/89, with Double Trouble and Jeff Beck
Skydome, Toronto, Ontario, 11/2/89, with Double Trouble and Jeff Beck (video)
Philadelphia, Pa., 11/7/89, with Double Trouble and Jeff Beck
Madison Square Garden, New York City, 11/11/89, with Double Trouble and Jeff
    Beck (video)
RPI Fieldhouse, Troy, N.Y., 11/12/89, with Double Trouble and Jeff Beck
The Omni, Atlanta, Ga., 11/19/89, with Double Trouble and Jeff Beck
The Sundome, Tampa, Fla., 11/22/89, with Double Trouble and Jeff Beck
McNichols Arena, Denver, Colo., 11/29/89, with Double Trouble and Jeff Beck
    (radio broadcast)

Tingley Coliseum, Albuquerque, N.M., 11/30/89, with Double Trouble (radio broadcast)

Sports Arena, Los Angeles, Calif., 12/1/89, with Double Trouble and Jeff Beck

Oakland Coliseum, Oakland, Calif., 12/3/89, with Double Trouble, Jeff Beck, and Carlos Santana

The Ritz, New York City, 12/31/89, with Double Trouble

"MTV Unplugged," 1989, solo acoustic (television broadcast)

"After Hours," 1989, with Double Trouble (television broadcast)

"Tennessee Volunteer Jam VIII," 1989, with Double Trouble (television broadcast)

"The Tonight Show," Burbank, Calif., 1989, with Double Trouble (television broadcast)

"Thrill of a Lifetime," 1989, with Double Trouble (television broadcast)

Newport Jazz Festival, Newport, R.I., 1989, with Double Trouble

"David Letterman 8th Anniversary Special," Universal Amphitheater, Universal City, Calif., 2/1/90 (television broadcast)

Music Hall, Omaha, Neb., 4/22/90, with Double Trouble

Auditorium Shores, Austin, Tex., 5/4/90, with Double Trouble

Sound on Sound Studios, New York City, 5/12/90, interview, with acoustic guitar

"The Tonight Show," Burbank, Calif., 6/15/90, with Double Trouble (television broadcast)

"Late Night with David Letterman," New York City, 6/90, with Double Trouble (television broadcast)

Star Lake Amphitheater, Pittsburgh, Pa., 6/28/90, with Double Trouble

Columbus, Ohio, 7/14/90, with Double Trouble

St. Louis, Mo., 7/15/90, with Double Trouble (video)

Starflight Theater, Kansas City, Mo., 7/16/90, with Double Trouble

Fiddler's Green, Denver, Colo., 7/17/90, with Double Trouble

"Live 1990," 1990, with Double Trouble (radio broadcast)

MTV Vaughan Brothers' Profile (*Family Style* sessions), MTV, 1990, with Jimmie Vaughan (television broadcast)

Milwaukee, Wis., 8/25/90, with Double Trouble

Alpine Valley, East Troy, Wis., 8/26/90, with Double Trouble and Jimmie Vaughan (Stevie Ray Vaughan's last concert with Double Trouble)

Alpine Valley, East Troy, Wis., 8/26/90, with Eric Clapton, Jimmie Vaughan, Buddy Guy, Robert Cray, playing "Sweet Home Chicago." Stevie Ray Vaughan's final performance

ABC, CBS, CNN news reports, 8/27/90 (television broadcasts)

"Night Flight — Tribute to Stevie Ray Vaughan," 9/90 (television broadcast)

INDEX

Past Masters

General Editor   Keith Th[...]

Schopenhauer

Christopher Janaway is Senior Lecturer in Philosophy at Birkbeck College, London, and author of *Self and World in Schopenhauer's Philosophy* (1989).

Past Masters

Forthcoming

Christopher Janaway

SCHOPENHAUER

Oxford New York

OXFORD UNIVERSITY PRESS

Oxford University Press, Walton Street, Oxford OX2 6DP

Oxford New York
Athens Auckland Bangkok Bombay
Calcutta Cape Town Dar es Salaam Delhi
Florence Hong Kong Istanbul Karachi
Kuala Lumpur Madras Madrid Melbourne
Mexico City Nairobi Paris Singapore
Taipei Tokyo Toronto

and associated companies in
Berlin Ibadan

Oxford is a trade mark of Oxford University Press

First published 1994 as an Oxford University Press paperback
Reissued 1996

British Library Cataloguing in Publication Data
Data available

Library of Congress Cataloging in Publication Data
Janaway, Christopher.
Schopenhauer / Christopher Janaway.
p. cm.—(Past masters)
Includes bibliographical references and index.
1. Schopenhauer, Arthur, 1788–1860. I. Title. II. Series.
B3148.J35 1994 193—dc20 93–40149
ISBN 0–19–287685–6

10 9 8 7 6 5 4 3

Printed in Great Britain by
Biddles Ltd
Guildford and King's Lynn

Preface

The status of Schopenhauer's work is somewhat enigmatic. He is recognized as a profound and erudite thinker, but he is not what one would call a philosopher's philosopher. Philosophical specialists may enjoy his marvellous style and find his ideas provocative, but they do not usually model themselves on him: to someone schooled on Kant or Aristotle, he is apt to come over as too wayward and too 'literary'. Yet philosophy is what he is doing, with few concessions, and many readers he has inspired have regarded him as the paradigm of the deep, difficult metaphysician. It is a pity if the general or literary reader rejects him because he is too philosophical; and if the philosopher rejects him because he does not appeal only to philosophers, that is simply foolish. Although the chief drawback with Schopenhauer is that his 'system' seems to collapse under even the gentlest analytical probing, our loss is great if we let that blind us to his strengths. At his best, Schopenhauer displays a gift for cogent and lucid debate, and for exposing the flaws of his predecessors. But what should also earn our respect is Schopenhauer's lack of complacency. He does not play safe, but risks confrontation with problems that ought to make us feel insecure. He asks what the self is, and can give no easy reply. He presses on into the greatest insecurity, asking what value one's existence may have—and his conclusion here is even less comfortable. Within the classical restraint of his prose, he faces up to these concerns both as a philosopher and with all the resources of his personality. If we can bring back into a single focus the genuine, probing philosopher and the imagination that excited Wagner, Hardy, and Proust, along with many others, then we shall be seeing Schopenhauer in his true light.

I would like to thank John Atwell, David Berman, Anthony Grayling, and Fiona Janaway for their helpful comments on an earlier draft of this book, many of which I have heeded. Thanks also to Catherine Clarke and a reader for Oxford University Press for their assistance with the final version.

C. J.

August 1993

Contents

Abbreviations and works cited

Schopenhauer's works are referred to as follows, in translations by E. F. J. Payne, unless otherwise stated. Some very minor changes are made to some quoted passages.

B   *On the Basis of Morality* (1841; Indianapolis/New York, 1965).
F   *On the Freedom of the Will* (1841), trans. K. Kolenda (Oxford, 1985).
M1–M4   *Manuscript Remains*, vols. 1–4, ed. A. Hübscher (Oxford/New York/Hamburg, 1988–90).
N   *On the Will in Nature* (1836; New York/Oxford, 1992).
P1, P2 *Parerga and Paralipomena*, vols. 1 & 2 (1851; Oxford, 1974).
R   *The Fourfold Root of the Principle of Sufficient Reason* (1813, 1847; La Salle, Illinois, 1974).
W1, W2 *The World as Will and Representation*, vols. 1 & 2 (1819, 1844; New York, 1969).

1 Schopenhauer's life and works

Arthur Schopenhauer was born in 1788 in Danzig, and died in Frankfurt am Main in 1860. There are a number of photographs taken during the last decade of his life, from which we derive our most immediate sense of the man. He looks unconventional and grimly determined, but the sparkle in his eye is that of someone vigilant, incisive, and capable of mischief—not altogether different from the persona which emerges from his writings. At the end of his life Schopenhauer was just beginning to enjoy a measure of fame. His philosophy, however, is not a product of old or middle age. Although most of the words which he published were written after he settled in Frankfurt at the age of 45, it was in the years between 1810 and 1818 that he had produced the entire philosophical system for which he became celebrated. As Nietzsche later wrote, we should remember that it was the creative, rebellious energy of a man in his twenties which produced *The World as Will and Representation*. The mature Schopenhauer occupied himself in consolidating and supplementing the position he had presented in this masterpiece, which was, until very near the end of his life, neglected by the intellectual world.

Independence of spirit is the trait most characteristic of Schopenhauer. He writes fearlessly with little respect for authority, and detests the hollow conformism which he finds in the German academic establishment. But behind this is the significant fact that he was also financially independent. When he came of age in 1809, he inherited wealth which, with astute management, was sufficient to see him through the rest of his life. His father, Heinrich Floris Schopenhauer, had been one of the wealthiest businessmen in Danzig at the time of Arthur's birth. A cosmopolitan man, committed to the liberal values of the Enlightenment and to republicanism, he left Danzig when it was annexed by Prussia, and moved to the free city of Hamburg. Arthur had in common with his father a love of French and English culture and a horror of Prussian nationalism. The name 'Arthur' was chosen because it was shared by several European

1

languages—though the intention here was chiefly to fit the infant for his envisaged career in pan-European commerce. Later Arthur felt he had also inherited his father's intense, obsessive personality. His father's death in 1805, probably by suicide, was a great blow to him.

Schopenhauer received a broad and enriching education in school, enhanced by the travel and social contacts that his wealthy family made possible. Sent to France at the age of 9 when his sister was born, he acquired fluent French. After some years of schooling, at the age of 15 he embarked with his parents on a two-year trip to Holland, England, France, Switzerland, and Austria. He saw many of the famous sights of the day, and at times was deeply affected by the poverty and suffering he witnessed. While his parents toured Britain, however, he was consigned to a boarding-school in Wimbledon, whose narrow, disciplinarian, religious outlook (a marked contrast to the education he had hitherto received) made a negative impression that was to last. This episode says much about Schopenhauer's character and upbringing. He was a seething, belligerent pupil who would not submit to the stultifying practices that surrounded him, and he seems quite isolated in his defiance. His parents wrote to him, his father niggling about his handwriting, his mother gushing about the wonderful time they were having and pleading with him to take a more reasonable attitude, but neither showed much inclination to see things from his point of view. It is tempting to view the situation as a microcosm of his later life. As his life progressed, it became clearer that it would not be constructed around close relationships with others. He began to see company as like a fire 'at which the prudent man warms himself at a distance' (*M1*, 123), and resolved to be lonely even when with others, for fear of losing his own integrity. He later wrote that five-sixths of human beings were worth only contempt, but equally saw that there were inner obstacles to human contact: 'Nature has done more than is necessary to isolate my heart, in that she endowed it with suspicion, sensitiveness, vehemence and pride' (*M4*, 506). He was prone to depression, and confessed 'I always have an anxious concern that causes me to see and look for dangers where none exist' (*M4*, 507).

Some writers on Schopenhauer's personality have looked to his relationships with his parents, and what they have found is not surprising. His father was an anxious, exacting, and formidable man, very ambitious for his son. Johanna Schopenhauer, née Trosiener, also from a successful business family in Danzig, was quite different. A lively, sociable person, she had literary aspirations which culminated in a career as a romantic novelist, making her during her lifetime more famous than her son. She was a significant force in his life, but relations between them were never warm. In her marriage too, as she herself wrote, she saw no need to 'feign ardent love' for her husband, adding that he did not expect it. After Heinrich Schopenhauer died, the independently minded Johanna was free to embark on her own career, and moved to Weimar, where she established an artistic and intellectual salon frequented by many of the luminaries of the day. Arthur benefited from some of the relationships he established in this circle, notably with Goethe, and with the oriental scholar Friedrich Majer, who stimulated in him a life-long interest in Indian thought. However, his relationship with his mother became stormy, and in 1814 she threw him out for good, never to see him again.

By the time this happened Schopenhauer had abandoned the career in business which his father had projected for him, and had found his way into the life of learning. In 1809 he went to the University at Göttingen, from where he was to move on to Berlin two years later. He attended lectures on a variety of scientific subjects, having originally intended to study medicine; but he soon gravitated towards philosophy. The Göttingen philosopher G. E. Schulze played a decisive role in Schopenhauer's career when he advised him to begin by reading the works of Plato and Kant. Though Schopenhauer was, by any standards, a widely read and scholarly thinker, it is fair to say that his reading of these two philosophers provoked in him the fundamental ideas that shaped his philosophy from then on. The Hindu Upanishads, which he learned of through Friedrich Majer, were the third ingredient which he later blended with Platonic and Kantian elements to make something quite original in *The World as Will and Representation*.

When he moved to Berlin, Schopenhauer heard lectures by Schleiermacher and Fichte, two of the philosophical heavyweights of the day, though, true to form, he was fairly contemptuous of them, and certainly did not seem to think he was there to absorb what they had to say. His lecture notes and marginal annotations to the books he was reading (preserved in the *Manuscript Remains*) show him keen to object and debate, and, for a young student, he reacts with an almost uncanny sureness of his own position. This too is a pattern that was not to vary greatly. Schopenhauer did not learn in association with others, by exchanging ideas and submitting himself to scrutiny. He learned, and wrote, by relying on his own judgement and treating other people's ideas as raw material to be hammered into the shape he wanted. What he could not use he sometimes decried as rubbish, with a witty style of mockery that usually succeeds in keeping the reader on his side. Schopenhauer would have made far less of himself without such single-minded determination, but the same feature has its compensating weakness: it can be a virtue for a philosopher to exhibit more give and take, more sense of dialogue and self-criticism, than Schopenhauer sometimes does.

When Schopenhauer was ready to write his doctoral thesis, in 1813, war broke out. Schopenhauer had an aversion to fighting, and even more of an aversion to fighting on the Prussian side against the French. He fled south to Rudolstadt near Weimar and there completed his first work, *On the Fourfold Root of the Principle of Sufficient Reason*, which gained him his doctorate at Jena, and was published in an edition of 500 copies in the same year. The book takes a stock academic topic, the principle of sufficient reason (which says that, for everything that is, there must be a ground or reason why it is), lays out concisely the ways in which it has been dealt with in the history of philosophy, then proceeds to a four-part explanation of the different kinds of reason. The systematic framework is derived from Kant, whose thought Schopenhauer has clearly assimilated, though not uncritically. There are enough twists to make this the beginning of something new, and more than a hint of what is to come in his major work. Schopenhauer always considered *The Fourfold Root* essential to understanding his thought, and undertook a revision of it for re-publication in 1847.

Another early publication is the essay *On Vision and Colours*, of 1816. This short book is a product of his involvement with Goethe, whose anti-Newtonian theory of colours had been published at the beginning of the decade. In discussing this theory, Schopenhauer and Goethe came to know each other quite well. Schopenhauer did not regard it as a central project of his own, but understandably did not turn down the invitation to work with one of the greatest men he was ever likely to meet. Goethe, forty years his senior, recognized the rigour of Schopenhauer's mind, and regarded him as someone with great potential, but was less concerned to foster his talent than to receive help in his own intellectual endeavours. The brief period in which they worked together is the one exceptional collaboration in Schopenhauer's career—but still he did not have it in him to become anyone's disciple. His own work *On Vision and Colours* diverged somewhat from Goethe's thinking, and he did not disguise the fact that he thought it superior. The partnership tailed off, Schopenhauer disappointed, though not crushed, by Goethe's lukewarm response. He later sent Goethe a copy of *The World as Will and Representation*, and had an apparently cordial meeting with him in 1819. But by now the two had parted company. As Goethe was to say, they were like two people who eventually shook hands, one turning to go south, the other north.

Schopenhauer's true destination is revealed in Volume I of *The World as Will and Representation*, which he completed in Dresden and published in 1818, although 1819 is the date that stands on the title-page. The dispassionate, Kantian exercise which Schopenhauer carried out in *The Fourfold Root* of 1813 did not reveal the driving force of his philosophy. It did not address questions concerning suffering and salvation, ethics and art, sexuality, death, and the meaning of life, but it was in these areas that his preoccupations already lay. The collected *Manuscript Remains* show Schopenhauer's greatest book in a process of composition over a period of almost ten years. Adapting the thought of both Plato and Kant, he had become convinced that there was a split between ordinary consciousness and a higher or 'better' state in which the human mind could pierce beyond mere appearances to a knowledge of something more real. The thought had aesthetic and religious overtones: Schopenhauer wrote of both the artist and the 'saint' as possessing this 'better consciousness'—though it should be said straightaway that his philosophical system is atheist through and through. He also struck one of

5

the keynotes of pessimism, saying that the life of ordinary experience, in which we strive and desire and suffer, is something from which to be liberated. Such thoughts were well established in Schopenhauer's mind by 1813.

The idea which allowed his monumental book to take shape was his conception of the will. In the finished work, as its title indicates, Schopenhauer presents the world as having two sides, that of *Vorstellung* (representation), or the way things present themselves to us in experience, and that of *Wille* (will), which is, he argues, what the world is *in itself*, beyond the mere appearances to which human knowledge is limited. The will is not easy to define. It is, to begin with, easier to say what it is not. It is not any kind of mind or consciousness, nor does it direct things to any rational purpose (otherwise 'will' would be another name for God). Schopenhauer's world is purposeless. His notion of will is probably best captured by the notion of *striving towards* something, provided one remembers that the will is fundamentally 'blind', and found in forces of nature which are without consciousness at all. Most importantly, the human psyche can be seen as split: comprising not only capacities for understanding and rational thought, but at a deeper level an essentially 'blind' process of striving, which governs, but can also conflict with, the conscious portions of our nature. Humanity is poised between the life of an organism driven to survival and reproduction, and that of a pure intellect that can rebel against its nature and aspire to a timeless contemplation of a 'higher' reality. Though he does still envisage a kind of resigned 'salvation', Schopenhauer thinks ordinary existence must involve the dual miseries of pain and boredom, insisting that it is in the very essence of humanity, indeed of the world as a whole, that it should be so.

Many have found Schopenhauer's philosophy impossible to accept as a single, consistent metaphysical scheme. But it does have great strength and coherence as a narrative and in the dynamic interplay between its different conceptions of the world and the self. What is set down at the beginning should be treated not so much as a foundation for everything that is to come, but as a first idea which will be revealed as inadequate by a second that seems to undermine it, only to re-assert itself in transformed guise later on. There is a superficial resemblance here to the method of his contemporary Hegel, though everything to do with Hegel was anathema to Schopenhauer, and in other respects they could hardly differ more as writers. Thomas Mann likened Schopenhauer's book to a great symphony in four movements, and it is helpful to approach it in something of this spirit, seeking contrasts of mood and unities of theme amid a wealth of variations. Certainly there have been few philosophers who have equalled Schopenhauer's grasp of literary architecture and pacing, and few whose prose style is so eloquent.

For all this, the great work went virtually unnoticed for many years after its publication. Schopenhauer was embittered, but he was not one to think that the world was right and he was wrong; he continued throughout his life to believe in the supreme value of his work. In 1820 he was awarded the right to lecture at the University in Berlin, after speaking before a gathering of the faculty chaired by Hegel, the professor of philosophy. Schopenhauer duly presented himself to lecture, under the stunning title 'The whole of philosophy, i.e. the theory of the essence of the world and of the human mind.' But he had chosen to speak at the same time as Hegel. Two hundred attended the lecture of the professor, who was at the peak of his career, and the unknown Schopenhauer was left with a pitiful few. His name was on the lecture-schedule in later years, but he never returned to repeat the experience, and this was the end of his lecturing career. Hegel was the epitome of everything that Schopenhauer disliked in philosophy. He was a career academic, who made use of the institutional authority which Schopenhauer held in contempt. He upheld the Church and the State, for which Schopenhauer, an atheist and an individualist, had no time. Although thoroughly conservative himself, Schopenhauer regarded the political state merely as a convenient means for protecting property and curbing the excesses of egoism; he could not stomach Hegel's representation of the state as 'the whole aim of human existence' (*P1*, 147). Hegel was also an appalling stylist, who seemed to build abstraction upon abstraction without the breath of fresh air provided by common-sense experience, and Schopenhauer—not alone in this—found his writing pompous and obscurantist, even dishonest. The emblem at the head of Hegelian university philosophy, he says, should be 'a cuttle-fish creating a cloud of obscurity around itself so that no one sees what it is, with the legend, *mea caligine tutus* (fortified by my own obscurity)' (*N*, 24). It is not true to say that Schopenhauer's philosophy was based on opposition to Hegel—Hegel was far from his mind as he created his major work—but Hegel's triumphant success, coupled with his own continuing lack of recognition, nevertheless produced in him a rancour which dominated much of his subsequent career.

During the 1820s Schopenhauer was at his least productive. He travelled to Italy, suffered during and after his return journey from serious illness and depression, and continued an affair with Caroline Richter, a chorus girl at the National Theatre in Berlin. He planned a number of writing projects, such as translations of Hume's works on religion and of Sterne's *Tristram Shandy*, but nothing came of them. His notebooks were full, sometimes with invective against Hegelianism which he reworked for inclusion in later works, but he completed no more publications while in Berlin. It is especially sad that the English publisher he approached about translating Kant's *Critique of Pure Reason* and other works should have turned him down. Schopenhauer's English was good, his feel for literary form superb, and his knowledge of Kant's work intimate. One can only speculate how the history of ideas would have been affected had he succeeded in making Kant more accessible to the English-speaking world at this comparatively early date. (By contrast, a result of his scholarship to which we are indebted is the rediscovery of the first edition of the *Critique*, which was re-published in 1838 partly thanks to his efforts.)

In 1831 cholera reached Berlin, apparently claiming Hegel among its victims, and Schopenhauer left the city. After some indecision he settled in Frankfurt, where he was to continue living an outwardly uneventful life, balanced between writing and recreation—theatre, opera, walking, playing the flute, dining out, and reading *The Times* in the town's library. Now he was able to produce more books. In 1836 he published *On the Will in Nature*, which was designed to support his doctrine of the will by putting forward corroborative scientific evidence from independent sources. It is still a work of interest, although arguably it does not stand very well on its own apart from *The World as Will and Representation*. However, in 1838 and 1839 Schopenhauer entered for two essay competitions set by the Norwegian Royal Scientific Society and its Danish counterpart, and the two occasions produced a pair of fine self-standing essays, *On the Freedom of the Will* and *On the Basis of Morality*, which were published together in 1841 under the title *The Two Fundamental Problems of Ethics*. In terms of doctrine these pieces are not radical departures from his earlier work, but both are well-constructed and persuasive pieces in which local parts of the grand design are presented with clarity. They can readily be recommended to a student of ethics today. In the essay on freedom Schopenhauer presents a convincing case for determinism, only to say, as some more recent philosophers have, that the deeper issues of freedom and responsibility are scarcely resolved thereby. This essay was rewarded with a gold medal by the Norwegians.

The second essay, part of which is a thorough criticism of Kant's ethics, suffered a different fate in Denmark: despite its being the only entry, the Royal Society refused to award it a prize. It had not, they judged, successfully answered the question set—and they took exception to the 'unseemly' manner in which a number of recent philosophers of distinction had been referred to. Who did they mean, asked Schopenhauer in his Preface to the essays: Fichte and Hegel! Are these men the *summi philosophi* one is not allowed to insult? It is true that Schopenhauer had not been playing the conventional game of academic politeness, but now he seizes the chance to let rip with all the means at his command. He produces an escalating series of allegations about the emptiness and confusion of Hegel's philosophy, throwing in a picturesque quote from Homer about the chimaera which is a compound of many beasts, and ending

> Further, if I were to say that this *summus philosophus* of the Danish Academy scribbled nonsense quite unlike any mortal before him, so that whoever could read his most eulogized work, the so-called *Phenomenology of Mind*, without feeling as if he were in a madhouse, would qualify as an inmate for Bedlam, I should be no less right. (*B*, 16)

In 1844 a second volume of *The World as Will and Representation* was published along with a new edition of the first volume. Schopenhauer was wise in not trying to re-write his youthful work. What he provides instead is a substantial elaboration of the original, clarifying and extending it with the benefit of mature reflection. The second volume is actually longer than the first, and the two combine well to produce a single work. They were published together again in a third edition in 1859, the year before he died. Schopenhauer's final new publication was another two-volume book, entitled *Parerga and Paralipomena*, which appeared in 1851. The imposing title means 'complementary works and matters omitted', and the contents range from extended philosophical essays to the more popular 'Aphorisms on the Wisdom of Life' which have often been published separately. Somewhat strangely, it was this late work, which was reviewed favourably first in England, that led to Schopenhauer's becoming well known. There was demand for new editions of his writings, and he even became a topic for German university courses. He received many visitors, and much correspondence, including the complete libretto of the *Ring of the Nibelung* from an ardent fan, Richard Wagner, of whose music, incidentally, he did not think very highly. In the first fifty years after his death Schopenhauer was to become one of the most influential writers of Europe. Though he made no claim to be a poet, the verses which came to stand at the very end of *Parerga and Paralipomena* (P2, 658) are no doubt an honest reflection of what he felt in his last years:

1856

Finale

I now stand weary at the end of the road;
The jaded brow can hardly bear the laurel.
And yet I gladly see what I have done,
Ever undaunted by what others say.

2 Within and beyond appearance

Appearance and thing in itself

Schopenhauer's philosophical thinking is easiest to grasp if one first sees the backbone that runs right through it. This is the distinction, which he found in Kant, between appearance and thing in itself. The world of appearance consists of things as we know them by the ordinary means of sense experience and scientific investigation, in other words, the empirical world. Appearance is not to be understood as straightforward illusion: the things that meet us in our empirical knowledge are not hallucinations, but, to use the Greek word for appearances, they are the phenomena that make up the world. However, there is still the question whether the whole world consists only of these phenomena. Should we regard 'what there is' as being exhausted by our empirical knowledge? We can at least conceive of a reality independent of what we could experience, and this is what Kant meant by talking of things 'in themselves'.

Kant's achievement was to show that knowledge was limited: we could never know how the world was in itself, only how it could appear to us, as scientists or ordinary perceivers. The pretensions of traditional metaphysicians to know about God, the immortality of the soul, or a supernatural order pervading the whole universe, were therefore doomed. According to Schopenhauer's assessment (in his 'Critique of the Kantian Philosophy' (Appendix to *W1*, 417–25)), Kant had added to this destructive achievement two others that were more positive. The first was the idea that the world of appearance had fundamental and necessary organizing principles which could be discovered. The second was the view that ethics could be separated off from the sphere of appearance, and was not knowledge in the way that science was: when considering ourselves as beings who must act and judge things to be right or wrong, we were not dealing with how matters lay in the empirical world.

First, let us take the idea that appearance, the world as we know it, has a necessary structure. Kant thought that the world of appearance must occupy space and time. It is obviously hard to imagine there not being space or time, but Kant went further and argued that without them there could not be a knowable world at all. A similar point applies to cause and effect, and to the principle that things can endure unchanged through time. The rules of the empirical world are that it must contain enduring things, arranged in space and time, and having systematic effects upon one another. Nothing else, Kant argued, could ever count as an empirical world that we could know. However, his most startling claim is that all these rules are not present in the world as it is in itself. They are all rules simply about how the world must be *if* we are to be able to experience it. So space and time, cause and effect, relate only to the way in which things have to appear to us. Take away the experiencing subject, and none of the world's structure would remain.

The second positive point from Kant concerns our view of ourselves. As well as trying to understand the world, we are called upon to act and make decisions, and these will ultimately be governed by questions of morality. Kant argues that morality can work only if each of us conceives himself or herself purely as a rational being, who is constrained by duty, and has freedom to choose the principles on which he or she will act. No kind of empirical investigation could reveal us to be such purely rational, free beings: if you like, there are no such things in the physical world. Nevertheless, it is a conception of ourselves which we must have. So, even though my knowledge is limited to the empirical world, I cannot ever believe that what I am is limited in the same way. Kant's idea, simply put, is that I must think that *in myself*, beyond appearances, I am a free and purely rational agent.

Now when Schopenhauer came across the Kantian philosophy as a student at Göttingen, he found it convincing, but incomplete. He embraced the distinction between appearance and thing in itself. On the appearance side, he wanted to modify Kant's views, but was happy to agree that the empirical world did not exist in itself, and was given its structure by rules of space, time, and causality imposed by us. It was, however, on the side of the thing in itself that he felt Kant had fudged his account. What *is* the world really, in itself? And what am I? This was the double riddle which Kant had left by distinguishing appearance from thing in itself, and claiming that it was only of appearances that one could have knowledge. The conception of the thing in itself gave rise to other philosophical problems which had been much discussed in the German academic world. Both Schopenhauer's first teacher, Schulze, and Fichte, whose lectures he heard in Berlin, were prominent in the debate. In presenting his solution to the riddle, claiming that the thing in itself, both in the world and in the microcosm of the human being, was *will*, Schopenhauer was addressing a burning problem of the day, and to some extent trading on a familiar post-Kantian idea.

The better consciousness

At the beginning, the young Schopenhauer was reading not only Kant, but also Plato, and here he encountered another way of understanding the difference between what appears and what 'really is'. What 'really is' for Plato is a set of unchanging entities called Ideas or Forms. Individual things are imperfect, they come and go, but this does not affect the fundamental order in the universe which is constituted by absolute and eternal Forms. Plato thought that the greatest achievement for humanity would be to gain an understanding of these eternal Forms, such as Justice itself, Goodness itself, and Beauty itself. The human soul would be elevated to a plane where it transcended the limitations of mere opinion and mortal appetite, gained an apprehension of absolute standards of value, and achieved a release from conflict and suffering. At a crucial phase in his development Schopenhauer succumbed to this vision. Even though the Kantian thing in itself was supposed to be beyond the limits of human knowledge, while Plato's Ideas were the objects of knowledge *par excellence*, Schopenhauer conflated what the two were saying, and formed a Platonic view about what an insight into the thing in itself beyond appearance would be like. For many years he thought he had made an important discovery: '*Plato's Ideas* and *Kant's thing-in-itself* . . . that these two are one and the same is as unheard of as it is sure and certain' (*M1*, 377). Although he did come to see that the positions of the two great philosophers were in fact distinct, the fusion created in his mind had acquired an energy of its own. He believed that empirical consciousness, limited as it was to the

13

phenomena of space, time, and causality, was something inferior which we should aspire to escape from, if possible. Only if there was a 'better' consciousness could human beings find anything that was of true value.

The term 'better consciousness' appears only in Schopenhauer's earliest unpublished manuscripts. It was not a very well-focused concept, and he abandoned it. But his later ideas about the value of art and about resigned detachment from life are continuous with his early view. In 1813, for example, he wrote the following in his notebooks:

> As soon as we *objectively consider, i.e. contemplate* the things of the world, then for the moment *subjectivity* and thus the source of all misery has vanished. We are free and the consciousness of the material world of the senses stands before us as something strange and foreign which no longer wears us down. Also we are no longer involved in considering the nexus of space, time and causality (useful for our individuality), but see the Platonic Idea of the object. . . . This liberation from temporal consciousness leaves the better eternal consciousness behind. (*M1*, 50)

Ordinary consciousness is seen as something to which 'misery' attaches; if only we can break the Kantian rules that limit knowledge to appearance, we shall enter into a realm in which both we ourselves and the objects of our direct 'contemplation' are timeless. This 'liberation' Schopenhauer thinks may be found in art, and in the attitude to the world which he calls that of the 'saint'. Both the artistic genius and the saint supposedly contemplate reality from a standpoint which transcends ordinary empirical understanding. Many recent commentators have played down the influence of Plato, and treated Schopenhauer as a rather unorthodox Kantian. But the 'better consciousness' is dramatically un-Kantian; Schopenhauer's own assessment that Kant and Plato were united in his philosophy is nearer the mark, even if the two make themselves felt in quite different ways.

In fact, Schopenhauer was prone to cite three influences: 'I do not believe my doctrine could have come about before the Upanishads, Plato and Kant could cast their rays simultaneously into the mind of one man' (*M1*, 467). What of the third influence?

Schopenhauer's knowledge of Plato and Kant, and his notion of the 'better consciousness', were already formed when he encountered the Upanishads, the sacred Hindu writings which he acquired in 1814 (in a Latin version taken from the Persian and entitled *Oupnek'hat*) and which he described in his late years as 'the consolation of my life' (*P2*, 397). We may note two principal ideas which impressed Schopenhauer in the Hindu writings he studied: one is *Mâyâ* or illusion, the other the identity of the individual with the world as a whole, embodied in the powerful Sanskrit saying *'Tat tvam asi'* ('This art thou'). Schopenhauer often refers to our ordinary experience as not penetrating the 'veil of *Mâyâ*'. This is not the common sceptical thought that we cannot trust our senses to tell us about the material world, but rather the idea that the material world of our experience is not something eternal, and not something we should ultimately put our trust in. Schopenhauer thinks that the world of material things which we experience and can investigate in science must be cast aside as of no genuine worth by comparison with the timeless vision open to artists and saints. The suspension, or denial, of one's complete differentiation from the rest of the world ('This art Thou') will be a feature of that timeless vision. Schopenhauer had to work out how one's understanding of both the world and the self would be transformed on abandoning ordinary empirical consciousness, and what came to play a central role here was the notion of losing the sense of oneself as a separate individual. Some of his ideas have a kinship with Buddhism which he later emphasized, though the relationship here was one of convergence rather than influence (*W2*, 169).

The Fourfold Root

While all these thoughts began to form, Schopenhauer set himself to write his doctoral dissertation, *On the Fourfold Root of the Principle of Sufficient Reason*. In it he makes no mention of the 'better consciousness', and deals simply with the principles governing ordinary experience and reasoning. He was obviously satisfied with the answers he reached, since he later retained them substantially unchanged, and frequently refers back to the dissertation. The fact that he produced an expanded version of the dissertation in 1847 confirms his statement that it is to be considered part of his complete system of thought. The text of *The Fourfold Root* we usually read today is this later version.

Schopenhauer begins *The Fourfold Root* with the single principle of sufficient reason which was the stock-in-trade of the eighteenth-century academic tradition associated with Leibniz and Christian Wolff. The principle states simply: 'Nothing is without a ground or reason why it is' (*R*, 6). Nothing is self-standing; everything is in relation to something else which is the reason for its being, or the explanation of it. However, there are, according to Schopenhauer, four distinct ways in which something may relate to a ground or reason, associated with four different kinds of explanation, which, he claims, none of his predecessors has clearly distinguished. The most familiar kind are causal or physical explanations, where we explain one event or state in terms of its relation to another which caused it. Then there are cases where we explain why some judgement is true by relating it to the grounds for its truth, such as an empirical observation or another truth from which it can be inferred. Thirdly, there are mathematical explanations—in which we explain, for example, why a triangle has the properties it does. Finally, there is explanation of what people do. We explain actions by relation to motives, which are their reasons, or causes, or both. In all these cases we are dealing with relations imposed by the mind, Schopenhauer thinks, and in each case the relation is one of necessity. Hence, in his terms, there are physical necessity, logical necessity, mathematical necessity, and moral necessity. Once we understand what the mind is doing when it operates with these relationships, we will have understood the forms that all explanation takes, and hence the true significance of the principle of sufficient reason. Let us deal with the four kinds of relation in turn.

By far the most substantial section of *The Fourfold Root* is devoted to the principle of causal explanation. An obvious class of objects the mind can grasp is that of the particular perceptible things that occupy space and time, and make up empirical reality. Space and time, as we saw, provide the basic structure of empirical reality. But space and time are not perceivable; what we can perceive is what fills space and time, and that, for Schopenhauer, is simply matter (*R*, 46). Were there not both time and space, there could be neither distinct material things, nor change, and so nothing for causality to apply to. Now the principle of causality states that every change in the world of material things must have a cause, or, as Schopenhauer puts it, 'every state that appears must have ensued or resulted from a change that preceded it' (*R*, 53). The principle allows of no exceptions: what we usually call the cause of some event is merely a particular change that preceded it, but that change must itself have ensued from some previous changes, and so on. By ensuing, Schopenhauer means following regularly, or 'as often as the first state exists'. Cause and effect are related in such a way that, if the first occurs, the second cannot but occur. This relation is seen as one of necessity.

Schopenhauer has a simple, uncluttered view about the nature of empirical reality. Individual material things exist in space and time. A material thing is something capable of interacting causally with other material things. And every change that occurs to a material thing is the necessary result of some preceding change that occurs to a material thing. One complication, however, is that Schopenhauer is not a realist about material things, but an idealist: that is, material things would not exist, for him, without the mind. He holds, with Kant, that the whole structure we have just described exists only as something presented to us as subjects, not in itself. When Schopenhauer says that empirical things in space and time are objects, he means that they are *objects for a subject*. 'Object' in his parlance means something met with in experience, or in the subject's consciousness. Space and time are the fundamental forms brought to experience by us. So the material occupants of space and time would not exist if it were not for the subject, and the causal connections which obtain between the states of material things are connections which we, as subjects, impose.

In Schopenhauer's account of perception, the human intellect 'creates' the world of ordinary material things (*R*, 75), and does so by applying the principle of cause and effect to sensations received by our bodily senses. We apprehend some change in our bodily state. The intellect then applies the principle of causality, and projects as cause of the sensation a material object 'outside' in space—and this projection is the object which we say we perceive. Thus the principle of causality is doubly important to Schopenhauer: it not only governs all interaction between material things, but is responsible for our construction of those very material things in the first place. The account has a certain ingenuity, but is troubling. For one thing, where do bodily sensations come from? They must surely be originally caused in the body by something prior to the operation of the intellect, but Schopenhauer does not discuss what that prior cause might be. Secondly, how do we apprehend the initial sensation? It cannot be that the mind perceives the sensation as a change in a material thing (the body), and yet if it does not do so, why is the principle of causality, which governs changes of material things, called into operation at all?

Schopenhauer's second class of objects for the mind is made up of *concepts*. Concepts are, for Schopenhauer, mental representations which are by nature secondary: he calls them 'representations of representations'. The basic representations are experiences of things in the material world, such as a particular tree; the concept *tree* is, by contrast, a general representation formed to stand for many such objects, by leaving out the detailed elements of what is experienced in each case. Schopenhauer is fond of emphasizing that concepts are always at least one step removed from direct experience, for which he uses the Kantian term *Anschauung* (intuition or perception). He thinks that a concept, to be of much use to us, must always be capable of being cashed out in terms of experience. Concepts such as *being, essence*, or *thing*, have the least cash value in these terms (R, 147, 155). As we shall see, Schopenhauer also takes the view that in some areas, such as art and ethics, abstract conceptual thinking can actually stand in the way of genuine insight.

Nevertheless, possession of concepts is a distinctively human characteristic for Schopenhauer, raising us above the consciousness of which other animals are capable. Other creatures, in his view, can have a perception of material things existing in space and time, much as we do—in a remarkable passage he laments the fact that 'in the West where [man's] skin has turned white' we have ceased to acknowledge our kinship with animals whom we demean as 'beasts or brutes' (R, 146). But the other animals do lack conceptual representations, and so lack the ability to make

18

judgements, to reason, to have a language, or an understanding of past and future. Thinking, or making judgements, is the fundamental function of concepts. Schopenhauer calls a judgement a combination or relationship of concepts, though he is not very clear about what this relationship involves. He is more interested in the idea that a judgement can express knowledge, and it is here that the principle of sufficient reason comes in again. 'If a judgement is to express a piece of *knowledge*, it must have a sufficient ground or reason; by virtue of this quality, it then receives the predicate *true*. *Truth* is therefore the reference of a judgement to something different therefrom' (*R*, 156). It is a familiar thought that a judgement amounts to knowledge if it is true and sufficiently grounded in something outside itself. Schopenhauer's brief remarks appear to make no distinction between a judgement's having a sufficient ground and its being true. Whether he would accept a notion of truth as correspondence with the way things are, independently of grounds for judging them to be so, remains obscure.

What Schopenhauer succeeds in establishing is that true judgements may be grounded in quite different ways. They may be grounded in another judgement, as when we argue, conclude, or infer (*R* 157–8) from one truth to another. They may, on the other hand, be 'empirical truths', grounded not in another judgement, but in experience. For example, our judgement 'There is snow on the trees' may have its justification in the evidence of our senses. On the other hand in the syllogism: 'There is snow on the trees, Snow is a white substance, Therefore, there is a white substance on the trees,' the truth of the final judgement is grounded simply in the truths of the two premises. Schopenhauer calls this a 'logical' or 'formal' truth, meaning simply one whose ground is based on deduction, rather than observation. There are two other kinds of truth in his account, which he calls transcendental truth and metalogical truth. These occur respectively when a judgement is founded on the conditions of experience or on the conditions of thought in general. A notable transcendental truth is 'Nothing happens without a cause', which is neither grounded in observation nor on deduction from any other truths, but is an underlying principle on which all experience is based. (Schopenhauer is here following Kant closely.) Metalogical truths are supposedly a kind of judgements where, if we try to go against them, we cease to be able to think properly at all. One example Schopenhauer gives is 'No predicate can be simultaneously attributed and denied to a subject': we cannot think, for example, 'Snow is and is not white'. The principle of sufficient reason itself is a truth of this kind, Schopenhauer claims, though in some of its guises, especially the principle of causality, it appears as a transcendental truth (*R*, 162).

Schopenhauer's third class of objects in *The Fourfold Root* is made up simply of space and time. Once again, we are close to Kant, who thought that we can have knowledge not only of the particular things that fill space and time, but of the basic properties of space and time as such. Geometry and arithmetic, on this view, are bodies of knowledge concerning position in space and succession in time, but they are neither scientific empirical knowledge, nor a matter of mere logical deduction. With this view of geometry and arithmetic, which would now be disputed, Kant arrived at the idea that we must be able to grasp space and time in a pure, non-empirical way in our minds. Schopenhauer follows suit, and produces his third form of the principle of sufficient reason. The relation between a triangle's having three sides and its having three angles, for example, is that the one is grounded in, is a sufficient reason for, the other. But, Schopenhauer argues, this relation is not that between cause and effect, and is not that between a piece of knowledge and its justification either. We must distinguish not only the ground of becoming (change grounded in causes) and the ground of knowing (knowledge-claims grounded in justifications), but also the ground of being. If we say that a triangle has three angles because it has three sides, the ground we are referring to is simply the way that space, or one facet of it, is.

The final form of the principle of sufficient reason has application to only a single object for each subject. Each of us can be aware of himself or herself as a subject of will. We experience our own states of wanting and making decisions, and can always ask Why? (*R*, 212). Our willing, we assume, is preceded by something which is its ground, and which explains our action or decision. This prior something is what Schopenhauer calls a *motive*, and the principle in operation is what he terms the 'law of motivation', or the principle of the sufficient reason of acting. It states simply that every act of will can be explained as ensuing from some motive. The connection between motive and act of will is one of cause and effect, the same as holds universally for changes in the material world. Motivation is thus, as Schopenhauer puts it, 'causality seen from within' (*R*, 214).

The limits of sufficient reason

The Fourfold Root is a remarkable sustained attempt to separate different forms of explanation which the tradition before Schopenhauer had not always distinguished. We may certainly sympathize with his request that henceforth 'every philosopher, who in his speculations bases a conclusion on the principle of sufficient reason or ground, or indeed speaks of a ground at all, should be required to state what kind of ground he means' (*R*, 233). However, clarifying the framework which governs our experience and reasoning was only one part of Schopenhauer's task. He remarks in the enlarged edition of 1847 that none of the relationships he has dealt with applies beyond the phenomena out of which our experience is composed: the principle of sufficient reason would not apply in any of its forms to the world considered as thing in itself (*R*, 232–3). He also reminds us that 'the sublime Plato' degrades phenomenal reality to what is 'always only arising and passing away, but never really and truly existing' (*R*, 232).

In his 1813 notebooks Schopenhauer returned to his task of revealing what lay beyond all these subject-imposed modes of connection. Now something of great iportance occurred: as he proceeded in his investigations, it became clear that revealing the nature of the thing in itself and clarifying the 'better' Platonic consciousness were two distinct enterprises. The thing in itself was a hidden essence working away underneath the order we imposed on the objects of our experience. It was also his own inner nature, something in him that drove him on—it was the world, as it were, surging up within him. To this hidden nature he gave the name *will*, and with it he now associated the 'misery' which ordinary life had to offer. By contrast, if only he could cease *being* this will, and cease imposing all subjective forms of

21

connection, the same world would take on a wholly different aspect, revealing itself spread out before him in timeless objective glory as a panoply of Platonic Ideas. Schopenhauer's philosophy really took shape once he attained this distinction between thing in itself (will) and Platonic Ideas: the first the murky reality underlying the empirical world in which the individual toils and tries to understand the connections of things, the other an exceptional vision to aspire to, of all connections undone and a brighter reality contemplated without striving and pain.

3 The world as will and representation

Schopenhauer's greatest work, *The World as Will and Representation*, is divided into four books, with a long appendix on Kant's philosophy in Volume I. Each of the four books sets out a distinct movement of thought. The first presents the world as representation, or as it is for our experience. The second book adds that this same world (and we ourselves within it) must be viewed under another aspect, as will. We called the appearance/thing in itself distinction the backbone of Schopenhauer's philosophy: now 'the world as representation' is what falls on the 'appearance' side of this line, while 'the world as will' is the thing in itself. But then in Book 3 aesthetic contemplation emerges as a cessation of willing in the individual, which transforms the world of objects into a timeless reality of Ideas, and finally Book 4 intensifies Schopenhauer's pessimistic view of the ordinary life of desire and action, and advocates an abolition of the will within oneself as the path to what is ethically good, and ultimately to a kind of resigned mystical salvation.

Representation

In its first aspect, then, the world is representation. The world, in other words, is what presents itself in a subject's experience. (A more old-fashioned translation of the German *Vorstellung* gives us 'the world as idea'—but to retain this could be misleading because of Schopenhauer's use of *Idee* for a Platonic Idea elsewhere in the system.) Schopenhauer begins by expounding an idealist position. This is the view that the material objects which we experience depend for their order and their existence on the knowing subject. He calls his position transcendental idealism, which is Kant's term, but he also emphasizes his continuity with Berkeley, as he sees in the latter's doctrine that 'to be is to be perceived' the initial glimmer of the truth in idealism—Kant's contribution being to explain how what is perceived constitutes a world of objects when it is governed by the necessary rules of space, time, and causality. Schopenhauer's account of the world of empirical things is what it was in *The Fourfold Root*: empirical things consist of matter, which fills distinct portions of space and time, and which is in causal interaction with other such portions. But his idealism says that without the subject of experience, all such objects would not exist.

To be more specific, it is *individual* things that would not exist without the experiencing subject. What we experience in the ordinary course of our lives are distinct things. One table is an individual distinct from another, one animal or person likewise. But what is the principle on which this division of the world into individual things works? Schopenhauer has a very clear and plausible answer: location in space and time. Two tables are distinct individuals because they occupy distinct portions of space, or of time, or of both. Now if you take this view, and also think, with Kant, that the organizing of things under the structure of space and time stems from the subject, and applies only to the world of phenomena, not to the world as it is in itself, then you will conclude that individuals do not exist in the world as it is in itself. The world would not be broken up into individual things, if it were not for the space and time which we, as subjects, impose. Here then are two important tenets of Schopenhauer's philosophy. Space and time are the principle of individuation, or in his favoured Latin version, the *principium individuationis*; and there can be no individuals on the 'in itself' side of the line.

Schopenhauer has four main arguments for idealism. One alleges that we cannot imagine anything which exists outside our own minds, because 'what we are imagining at that moment is . . . nothing but just the process in the intellect of a knowing being' (*W2*, 5). This is reminiscent of a controversial argument attempted by Berkeley, who thought that an unperceived tree could not be imagined. Schopenhauer's use of the argument is not very convincing, however, because even though *my imagining* a world independent of my mind does presuppose my own mind, the existence of a world independent of my mind does not. A second argument is the claim that idealism is the only viable alternative to scepticism. Scepticism maintains that we can have no certain knowledge about the existence or nature of material things, because all that we can be certain of is what falls within our own consciousness. If you deny idealism (the argument runs) and think that the world of material things has to exist wholly outside a subject's consciousness, then you will have to admit that scepticism wins the day, and that we can never have certain knowledge about a world of material things. If we wish to preserve our entitlement to *knowledge* concerning the world of things that occupy space and time and follow causal laws, the solution is to accept that they do not lie outside our consciousness.

Schopenhauer's third argument adds to this by suggesting that realism—the alternative to idealism—saddles itself with two 'worlds', one of which is redundant:

> According to realism, the world is supposed to exist, as we know it, independently of this knowledge. Now let us once remove from it all knowing beings, and thus leave behind only inorganic and vegetable nature. Rock, tree, and brook are there, and the blue sky . . . But then let us subsequently put into the world a knowing being. That world then presents itself *once more* in his brain . . . Thus to the *first* world a *second* has been added, which, although completely separated from the first, resembles it to a nicety. . . . All this proves absurd enough, and thus leads to the conviction that that absolutely *objective* world outside the head, independent of it and *prior* to all knowledge, which we at first imagined we had conceived, was already no other than the second world already known *subjectively*, the world of the representation, and that it is this alone which we are actually capable of conceiving. (*W2*, 9–10)

Schopenhauer is here in a territory littered both before and after him with debates of some complexity. The three arguments so far discussed can be found already in Berkeley. They are, however, not decisive for quite simple reasons. The realist may reply to the 'scepticism' argument by saying that if the choice is between scepticism and idealism, then scepticism is the better option. The idea that material things depend on the subject for their existence may seem too high a price to pay for a guarantee of knowledge. Also the argument only says that *if* we can have any certain knowledge, idealism must be preferred. One might settle for not having certain knowledge, and insist that the empirical world must nevertheless be conceived as existing independently of the

25

subject's consciousness. To the third argument, that the world of things existing outside consciousness is redundant, the realist can reply simply that this world outside consciousness would be *the* world. It is only the idealist who wants to say that the *picture* of material things which we have in consciousness is already a world of material things. The realist does not accept this, and makes a clear distinction between the one world existing independently of us, and our picture of it. However, Schopenhauer's points correspond to familiar parts of the debate, and are valuable against some opponents. A realism which said both that we can be certain only about what lies within consciousness, and that the world outside consciousness exactly resembles the picture we have built of it, would be threatened by his criticisms.

The fourth argument for idealism is the one which Schopenhauer most relies on. It rests on the concepts *subject* and *object*. The subject is that which knows or experiences, the object that which is known or experienced. The world of representation, for Schopenhauer, requires both. He makes two large claims: first, that nothing can be both object and subject, secondly that there can never be a subject without an object, or an object without a subject. It is the last point which he takes to establish idealism, and indeed to make it something obvious. Nothing can be an object for experience without there being a subject to experience it or think about it. But why must we think of material objects in space and time in this way? Schopenhauer would argue that the point of calling them objects is to indicate that they can and do fall within our experience. But then he also requires us to believe that whatever we can experience must exist only in relation to our experiencing it. This simple principle is central to Schopenhauer's position. Because of it, he does not think that idealism can be seriously doubted, once one properly understands it. But it is surely a questionable principle.

A fair proportion of Book I of *The World as Will and Representation* is devoted to the distinction between perception and conceptual reasoning. As we saw in the previous chapter, Schopenhauer thinks that we share our perceptual abilities with other animals, but that concepts and reasoning are what mark us out from them. Perceiving the world is the business of what he calls intellect or understanding, and he suggests that conceptual thinking and judgement play no part in this. On the other hand, manipulating concepts to form judgements, relating judgements to one another as premiss and conclusion, and so on, is the business of what he calls reason. By playing down the significance of reason and treating concepts as more or less faint abstractions out of direct experience or intuition, Schopenhauer paves the way for a close assimilation between the human mind and that of other living creatures.

Will

As we cross from the First Book into the Second, a sudden reversal takes place. In the world as representation, what am I? The world spreads out before me, containing individual material things in space and time which change according to causal laws—but I myself am just the subject which is distinct from every object that it experiences, including that object which I call my body. Something is missing. I seem to be 'a winged cherub without a body' (*W1*, 99), the world confronting me as something alien to which I do not belong.

> For the purely knowing subject as such, this body is a representation like any other, an object among objects. Its movements and actions are so far known to him in just the same way as the changes of all other objects of perception; and they would be equally strange and incomprehensible to him, if their meaning were not unravelled for him in an entirely different way. Otherwise, he would see his conduct follow on presented motives with the constancy of a law of nature, just as the changes of other objects follow upon causes, stimuli, and motives. But he would be no nearer to understanding the influence of the motives than he is to understanding the connexion with its cause of any other effect that appears before him. (*W1*, 99–100)

Schopenhauer is generating a puzzlement in order to make us receptive to the central idea of the whole book, which is now unveiled:

> All this, however, is not the case; on the contrary, the answer to the riddle is given to the subject of knowledge appearing as an individual, and this answer is given in the word *will*. This

and this alone gives him the key to his own phenomenon, reveals to him the significance and shows him the inner mechanism of his being, his actions, his movements. To the subject of knowing, who appears as an individual only through his identity with the body, this body is given in two entirely different ways. It is given in perception of the intellect as representation, as an object among objects, liable to the laws of these objects. But it is also given in a quite different way, namely as what is known immediately to everyone, and is denoted by the word *will*. (*W1*, 100)

What Schopenhauer means is that when I act (when I do something) my body moves; and my awareness of its movement is unlike my awareness of other events that I perceive. I am 'outside' other objects, or they are 'outside' me—but my own body is mine in a uniquely intimate way. This can be expressed by saying that other events are merely observed to happen, whereas movements of my body are expressions of *my will*. Schopenhauer's account of acts of will is anti-dualist. A dualist would maintain that the mental realm and the bodily realm are distinct, and that *willing* (or volition) was an event in the mental realm, while the movement of the body was something distinct that occurred in the physical realm. Schopenhauer denies this:

> The act of will and the action of the body are not two different states objectively known, connected by the bond of causality; they do not stand in the relation of cause and effect, but are one and the same thing, though given in two entirely different ways, first quite directly, and then in perception for the understanding. (ibid.)

Wanting, striving, and trying are to be seen as things that we do with our bodies, not as events that occur in detachment from our bodies. They manifest themselves in physical reality, but also retain an 'inner' aspect, because each of us knows what he or she strives for, in a direct, non-observational way. Thus what Schopenhauer calls the 'action of the body' is neither in a wholly mental or a wholly physical realm, but is one single occurrence which presents two aspects: we each have 'inner' awareness of something that is also part of the ordinary empirical world, and can be observed as such.

28

This account of acts of will is a decisive step for Schopenhauer, since it places the human subject firmly within the material world. If striving towards ends is setting the body in motion, then, while we will, we are rooted in the world of objects. Schopenhauer thus cannot conceive of a subject of will as being anything other than bodily. He also makes the converse claim that our bodily existence is nothing other than willing. Whenever we undergo feelings of fear or desire, attraction or repulsion, whenever the body itself behaves according to the various unconscious functions of nourishment, reproduction, or survival, Schopenhauer discerns *will* manifesting itself—but in a new and extended sense. What he wants to show is that ordinary conscious willing is no different in its basic nature from the many other processes which set the body, or parts of it, in motion. Admittedly, willing to act involves conscious thinking—it involves the body's being caused to move by motives in the intellect—but it is, for Schopenhauer, not different in principle from the beating of the heart, the activation of the saliva glands, or the arousal of the sexual organs. All can be seen as an individual organism manifesting will, in Schopenhauer's sense. The body itself is will; more specifically, it is a manifestation of will to life (*Wille zum Leben*), a kind of blind striving, at a level beneath that of conscious thought and action, which is directed towards the preservation of life, and towards engendering life anew.

This interesting idea is wrapped up in the much wider claim that the whole world in itself is will. Just as my body's movements have an inner aspect not revealed in objective experience, so does the rest of the world. Schopenhauer seeks an account which makes all fundamental forces in nature homogeneous, and thinks that science is inherently unsatisfying because it always tails off without explaining the essence or hidden inner character of the phenomena whose behaviour it accounts for. His unifying account of nature is that all natural processes are a manifestation of will. This is likely at first sight to be dismissed as fanciful—but we should heed Schopenhauer's warning that he is vastly extending the concept 'will':

> hitherto the identity of the inner essence of any striving and operating force in nature with the will has not been recognized, and therefore the many kinds of phenomena that are only

different species of the same genus were not regarded as such . . . Consequently, no word could exist to denote the concept of this genus. I therefore name the genus after its most important species, the direct knowledge of which lies nearest to us, and leads to the indirect knowledge of all the others. But anyone who is incapable of carrying out the required extension of the concept will remain involved in a permanent misunderstanding. (*W1*, 111)

So we must not transfer 'will' simple-mindedly from human actions to the whole of nature. It serves only as the most convenient term where none yet exists. Nevertheless, this aspect of Schopenhauer's philosophy is puzzling. What is the 'required extension' of the concept? Perhaps it is an extension of sense: if 'will' is now to have a new meaning, this might save Schopenhauer from claiming something ridiculous. But this line should not be taken too far. Schopenhauer insists that 'will' is not interchangeable with 'force', for example (*W1*, 111–12), and that the issue is not a mere 'dispute about words'. In saying that all processes are will, 'we have in fact referred something more unknown to something infinitely better known, indeed to the one thing really known to us immediately and completely' (*W1*, 112). To subsume willing under force (or energy, which has also been suggested) is not Schopenhauer's intention. The global doctrine of will can tell us something informative only because we have some grasp of what willing is from our own actions. An alternative interpretation is that Schopenhauer is keeping the sense of 'will' fixed, and simply widening the range of phenomena that it refers to. He does say that in mechanics '*seeking* shows itself as gravitation, . . . *fleeing* as reception of motion' and similar things (*W2*, 298); he is prepared to speak in remarkable terms of 'the powerful, irresistible impulse with which masses of water rush downwards, the persistence and determination with which the magnet always turns back to the North Pole, the keen desire with which iron flies to the magnet' (*W1*, 117–18). How are we to take this? If meant literally, it is merely embarrassing. But perhaps he is doing something more subtle here, and attempting to teach us our own kinship with nature by rhetorical means: the behaviour of the inorganic world is to an extent '*like* the vehemence of human desires' and so 'it will not cost us a great effort of the imagination to recognize once more our own inner nature, even at so great a distance'. This is not to say that iron really desires anything, or that water rushes because it wants to.

What we usually call willing is supposed to be a clear guide to the way the world is. So 'will' must still be understood in terms of its application to human actions; however, we must enlarge its sense at least far enough to avoid the barbarity of thinking that every process in the world has a mind, a consciousness, or a purpose behind it. For the most part, Schopenhauer assures us, the world operates blindly and 'in a dull, one-sided, and unalterable manner'—and the same is even true of many manifestations of the will within each human individual. The following passage states Schopenhauer's view as clearly as any:

> only the *will* is *thing in itself* . . . It is that of which all representation, all object, is the phenomenon, the visibility, the *objectivity*. It is the innermost essence, the kernel, of every particular thing and also of the whole. It appears in every blindly acting force of nature, and also in the deliberate conduct of man, and the great difference between the two concerns only the degree of the manifestation, not the inner nature of what is manifested. (*W1*, 110)

This surely means that every force in nature, those that involve conscious purpose and those that do not, must be understood as some form of striving or end-seeking, even if in highly attenuated form.

Two more peculiarities of this doctrine should be noted. First, if the will is the thing in itself, it is not something occupying space and time. Space and time are merely the subject-imposed structure of the world as representation, and the thing in itself is what remains when the world as representation is thought away. Given Schopenhauer's idea that space and time are the principle of individuation, the thing in itself cannot be split up into separate individuals. Beyond representation, space, and time, it is simply the world as a whole that is to be conceived as will. Secondly, there can be no causal interaction between the will, as thing in itself, and events in the ordinary empirical world. Causality too is something which operates only at the level of empirical changes occurring to individual material things, not at the level of the thing in itself. Kant seemed to require that the thing in itself could impinge upon us causally, rather like some empirical object, and Schopenhauer was well aware that this claim was the stumbling-block of Kantianism for many of his contemporaries. Schopenhauer himself avoids the problem, and never claims that the will as thing in itself is a cause. But then what is the relationship between the world in itself and the things and events that lie within our empirical knowledge? Schopenhauer talks sometimes of the will's 'manifestation' in empirical reality, but his preferred term is 'objectification'. This means just that the world shows to us the side of it which we can experience. We have to think of the single will and its objectification in a multitude of phenomena as two sides of a coin, two aspects of the same world.

A big problem here concerns the knowability of the thing in itself. Schopenhauer's doctrine of the will is metaphysical. Metaphysics, for him, gives an account of the fundamental nature of reality, but uses the data of experience as the only possible guide: 'the solution to the riddle of the world must come from an understanding of the world itself . . . the task of metaphysics is not to pass over experience in which the world exists, but to understand it thoroughly, since inner and outer experience are certainly the principal source of all knowledge' (*W1*, 428). Strictly speaking, our knowledge reaches only as far as the phenomena of inner and outer experience. So we do not—cannot—know the bare thing in itself. When I am conscious of my own willing in action, what I know is a phenomenal manifestation of the will, not the thing in itself. Nevertheless, it is this knowledge of my own willing which is to provide the key to knowing the nature of the whole world in itself. How?

As we saw, Schopenhauer sets up a contrast between experience of the world of material objects, and 'immediate' awareness of one's own willing. Sometimes he writes as if the latter amounted to knowledge of the thing in itself directly: 'my body is the only object of which I know not merely the one side, that of the representation, but also the other, that is called *will*' (*W1*, 125); 'Everyone finds himself to be this will, in which the inner nature of the world consists' (*W1*, 162); 'a way *from within* stands open to us to that real inner nature of things to which we cannot penetrate *from without*' (*W2*, 195). This may suggest direct cognitive contact with the thing in itself inside us, and a further inference that everything in the world has a similar inner nature. But we must wonder how this can be achieved, if the thing in itself is strictly unknowable. When he is being more careful, Schopenhauer says that even the act of will which we know 'immediately' is an event in time, and is therefore part of our representation, rather than the thing in itself. Still, he says, the thing in itself, though it 'does not appear quite naked', has 'to a great extent cast off its veils' in our 'inner' awareness of action (*W2*, 197). In consciousness of our own willing we are still on this side of the divide between representation and thing in itself, but we can say that we come closer to knowledge of the thing in itself. This is still troubling, however. If knowledge of our acts of will is the nearest we get to the thing in itself, and if even here we do not know it directly, what grounds do we really have for claiming to know what it is?

As an exercise in metaphysics, Schopenhauer's doctrine of the will as thing in itself is so obviously flawed that some people have doubted whether he really means it—perhaps *will* is just a concept which explains a wide range of phenomena, and is not supposed to extend to the unknowable thing in itself? On the other hand, if that were the whole of his position, he could offer no 'solution to the riddle' in the way that he clearly intends. Given such problems, it is perhaps not surprising that his metaphysics has had few followers. Nevertheless, to stop there would be shortsighted. Schopenhauer's more restricted notion of the *will to life*, which characterizes observable aspects of human and animal behaviour, is an interesting and powerful idea. His conception of will expressing itself within humanity, and the polarity he discovers between our being governed by the will and our escaping it, enables him, as we shall see, to present large tracts of our lives in a new light. It enables him to explain thought-processes as having an organic, survival-directed function, to show the influence of unconscious drives and feelings on the intellect, to suggest that our picture of ourselves as rational individual thinkers is in some sense an illusion, to place sexuality at the core of human psychology, to account for the power of music and the value of aesthetic experience, to argue that ordinary life is inevitably unfulfilled, and to advocate the renunciation of individual

The world as will and representation

desires as the route to reconciliation with our existence. It has been these applications, rather than the bald metaphysical statement that the thing in itself is will, that have had the most influence on philosophers, psychologists, and artists of later generations.

4 Will, body, and the self

Unity of body and will

Schopenhauer's claim 'My body and my will are one' (*W1*, 102) has a number of different aspects to it. The first, as we saw, is the idea that *acts* of will are movements of the body. Schopenhauer takes a robust line on this, saying that 'every true, genuine, immediate act of the will is also at once and directly a manifest act of the body' (*W1*, 101). This would suggest, somewhat perversely, that there can be no such thing as a willing which goes unfulfilled because one's muscles or nerves do not function in the right way. (Would Schopenhauer say that stroke victims have not 'genuinely' willed, if their bodies fail to move as they want them to?) But Schopenhauer is trying to oust the traditional division between mental and physical, and to supplant it with a division between will on the one hand, and intellect and reason on the other. Perception, judgement, and reasoning are all functions of what he has called representation. We observe the way a state of affairs is in the world of objects, judge that it should be altered or preserved, and form the intention to act. Schopenhauer's chief point is that none of this is yet *willing*. The operations of perception, thought, and intention are quite separate preparatory events which may trigger the will—the body, that is—into action. He plays down the gap between willing and the movements one carries out with one's body, concentrating instead on the gulf between representing the world of objects, and being in goal-seeking motion within it.

Schopenhauer's other evidence for the unity of will and the body is that almost everything that impinges on the body sets off some reaction of the will, and that conversely, when the will is aroused, there are always bodily manifestations. The list of mental states included under the heading of the will is extensive:

all desiring, striving, wishing, demanding, longing, hoping, loving, rejoicing, jubilation, and the like, no less than not willing or resisting, all abhorring, fleeing, fearing, being angry, hating, mourning, suffering pains—in short, all emotions and passions. For these emotions and passions are weaker or stronger, violent and stormy or else quiet impulses of one's own will, which is either restrained or unleashed, satisfied or unsatisfied. In their many variations they relate to the successful or frustrated attainment of that which is willed, to the endurance or the overcoming of that which is abhorred. Consequently, they are explicit affections of the same will which is active in decisions and actions. (*F*, 11)

Sometimes, Schopenhauer admits, when the bodily senses are affected our reaction is neutral, and does not rouse the will in any of these ways—but only rarely. For the most part, such an occurrence is to some degree painful or pleasant, welcome or irritating. Similarly, when we are in one of the mental states on Schopenhauer's list, there is usually a characteristic bodily accompaniment: the heart beats faster, the blood drains from our face or suffuses it. Thus 'every vehement and excessive movement of the will, in other words, every emotion, agitates the body and its inner workings directly and immediately' (*W1*, 101). For Schopenhauer these considerations tend to show the identity of the body with the will. They do at least suggest a close affinity between bodily existence and the empirical manifestations of willing in Schopenhauer's broader sense.

A representation in the conscious mind which causes the body to move in action is what Schopenhauer calls a *motive*. We share some kinds of motive with other animals that perceive the world. For example, behaviour in a cat which is caused by perceiving a predator or some food, would be classed by Schopenhauer as willing brought about by a motive. Humans, on the other hand, are distinctive in being able to act not just on perceptual motives, but also on rational ones: representing matters conceptually, we reason ourselves to a conclusion about what to do, and this process plays a causal role in setting us into action. A cat may eat because it senses food and is hungry, a human being because doing so is judged the best course of action. But willing manifests itself in the body's movements in the same way in both cases. Different kinds of willing really differ, for Schopenhauer, only in the causes that precede them. He makes a basic distinction between three kinds of cause. They are motive, stimulus, and cause pure and simple (as found in mechanical and chemical changes).

So far 'willing' has stood for a range of mental states which have bodily manifestations, including active striving, the emotions, and feelings of pleasure and pain. But some manifestations of the will in the body are not what we should call mental states at all, and are of a kind which we share even with lowlier parts of nature. Plants behave in certain ways in reaction to light, moisture, gravity, and so on. They do not perform actions, and their movements and modifications are not caused by motives, for the simple reason that they have no minds with which to perceive. The plant's turning towards the sun is caused by a *stimulus*, rather than by a motive. Nevertheless, Schopenhauer is prepared to call such plant-behaviour a manifestation of will, because he thinks it can only be understood as goal-directed, even if there is no mind present to entertain the goal. Having located will in bodily movement, and distinguished it from representation, he sees an affinity between the plant's movement in response to stimuli and those of the cat and the human brought about by motives. It is clear that human beings and animals also respond to stimuli—the involuntary contraction of the pupil of the eye provides but one example. This occurrence, for Schopenhauer, is equally a manifestation of the will—though not an *act* of will, because it is not caused by a conscious representation of the world.

Will to life

Schopenhauer's conception of the will is not restricted to the body's episodic reactions to motives and stimuli, for he claims that 'the whole body is nothing but the objectified will' (*W1*, 100), meaning that the way in which the body grows and develops, and the way in which its parts are organized, reveal a principle of striving towards ends which is 'blindly' at work:

> Teeth, gullet, and intestinal canal are objectified hunger; the genitals are objectified sexual impulse; grasping hands and nimble feet correspond to the more indirect strivings of the will which they represent. (*W1*, 108)

37

What underlies and explains the body's functioning, indeed its very existence, is its being directed towards life—or what Schopenhauer calls *will to life*. (The usual translation of *Wille zum Leben* as 'will to live' is linguistically correct, but what Schopenhauer has in mind is more inclusive; it is a striving not just to live, but also to engender life and to protect offspring. (See *W2*, 484–5.) In other words, *life*, rather than *living*, is the common end of all *Wille zum Leben*.) Schopenhauer is boldly seeking a single hypothesis to explain the ways in which all life-forms grow, function, and behave.

It is easy to think that the idea of the 'will to life' is wrongly fixated on the idea that there are purposes in nature. However, although Schopenhauer speaks of 'purposes' or 'ends' being fulfilled by behaviour patterns and the workings of particular organs, he clearly does not think that organisms entertain any conscious purposes—for the will works 'blindly':

> we see at once from the instinct and mechanical skill of animals that the will is also active where it is not guided by any knowledge. . . . The one-year-old bird has no notion of the eggs for which it builds a nest; the young spider has no idea of the prey for which it spins a web; the ant-lion has no notion of the ant for which it digs a cavity for the first time. . . . Even in us the same will in many ways acts blindly; as in all those functions of our body which are not guided by knowledge, in all its vital and vegetative processes, digestion, circulation, secretion, growth, and reproduction. (*W1*, 114–15)

So, despite superficial appearances, Schopenhauer does not simply wish to understand nature in anthropomorphic terms. Although he asks us to interpret the world using concepts applied first to ourselves, the notion of the will to life has the effect of demoting humanity from any special status separate from the rest of nature. First, in our bodies, the same 'blind' force operates as throughout nature: we are organized to live and to propagate life not by any conscious act of will. Secondly, there is a close continuity between even the conscious, purposive willing of human action and the life-preserving functions and instincts at work elsewhere. In our seeking of mates and providing for offspring, we are driven by the same instincts as other animals. And Schopenhauer sees the human capacities for perception, rationality, and action as an offshoot of the same wider principle which leads insects to build nests, feathers to grow, and cells to divide. In this respect, the will to life can seem quite a forward-looking notion. Another crucial feature is Schopenhauer's steadfast opposition to anything approaching an external or divine purpose for nature. Even though it is 'a single will' which expresses itself throughout the multiplicity of phenomena, this means only that all behaviour is of the same striving or goal-directed kind. All life-forms strive towards life; but there is no co-ordinated purpose to nature, rather the kind of purposelessness and conflict which are usually associated with Darwinism. Schopenhauer derides those 'pantheists' and 'Spinozists' who think the world divine, but have not 'the remotest idea why the whole tragi-comedy exists' (*W2*, 357).

On the other hand, Schopenhauer does believe that the various species of animate and inanimate things in the world are eternal and static. There are not only individuals which we happen to classify as ants, or oak trees, or magnetic fields. Rather, each individual is of a *kind*, and the kinds that can exist are fixed. Thus, while individual things come and go over time, *the ant* or *the oak tree*, as a kind, is a permanent feature of empirical reality. Schopenhauer has two ways of expressing this point, which he frequently repeats. One is to say that the will (the thing in itself) manifests or objectifies itself in a series of *grades*. The other is to say that *the ant* and *the oak tree* as such are Ideas, or as he often puts it '(Platonic) Ideas'. The most adequately objective knowledge we could have would be of the nature of these abiding forms 'fixed in the nature of things'. Such objective knowledge would not consist in knowing the thing in itself in its naked form, which is impossible, but in knowing the timeless patterns of the things that are experienceable by us.

The following passage shows quite well how Schopenhauer uses his doctrine of the will to life and his notion of the order of Ideas in nature:

> everywhere in nature we see contest, struggle, and the fluctuation of victory ... Every grade of the will's objectification fights for the matter, the space, and the time of another. ... This universal conflict is to be seen most clearly in the animal

kingdom. Animals have the vegetable kingdom for their nourishment, and within the animal kingdom again every animal is
the prey and food of some other. This means that the matter in
which an animal's Idea manifests itself must stand aside for
the manifestation of another Idea, since every animal can
maintain its own existence only by the incessant elimination
of another's. Thus the will to life generally feasts on itself, and
is in different forms its own nourishment, till finally the
human race, because it subdues all the others, regards nature
as manufactured for its own use. (*W1*, 146–7)

Intellect as an outgrowth of will

Now we come to a step in Schopenhauer's argument whose importance cannot be overestimated. He claims that all our knowledge of the empirical world is the product of the kind of organism
we are. The structure of knowledge and of its objects depends on
the kind of manifestation of will to life which its subject happens
to be. Everything the reader was told at the outset about the world
of representation, the forms of space, time, and causality which
govern the objects of our experience, and the concepts and judgements which we can obtain from them by abstraction—all of this
is merely a surface beneath which lurks the driving force of our
nature, the will. We grow into creatures who can perceive, judge,
and reason, in order to fulfil the ends of life: survival, nourishment, and reproduction. In Schopenhauer's narrative this is a
marked change of fortune for the human subject. The capacity for
knowledge on which we pride ourselves suddenly appears as
merely a way in which a particular species manipulates the environment that impinges on it, so as to foster its well-being:

> [the intellect] is designed for comprehending those ends on the
> attainment of which depend individual life and its propagation.
> But such an intellect is by no means destined to interpret the
> inner essence-in-itself of things and of the world, which exists
> independently of the knower. (*W2*, 284)

To establish this picture, Schopenhauer has to claim not only
that all biological functions are manifestations of will to life, but
also that knowledge, perception, and reasoning are biological

functions. This he does by espousing a particularly blunt form of materialism: states of mind are states of the brain. If, instead of regarding our processes of thought and perception from the point of view of self-consciousness, we take an 'objective' view of them, we must conclude them to be 'nothing more than the physiological function of an internal organ, the brain' (*W2*, 273). The whole world of individual objects in space and time consists only of our representations, and representations are brain-functions. So the brain, the 'pulpy mass in the skull', supports the whole world of objects—Schopenhauer's materialist account of mental states combines with his idealism to produce the claim that the empirical world of individual things is a product of the brain's functioning. For fear of saying such things, people in the past invented the notion of an immaterial soul, but Schopenhauer will have none of that:

> We say fearlessly that this pulpy mass, like every vegetable or animal part, is also an organic structure, like all its humbler relations in the inferior dwelling-place of our irrational brothers' heads, down to the humblest that scarcely apprehends. (*W2*, 273).

Finally, the brain is a biological organ, and so it cannot be exempt from Schopenhauer's doctrine of the will to life:

> the *will-to-know*, objectively perceived, is the brain, just as the *will-to-walk*, objectively perceived, is the foot; the *will-to-grasp*, the hand; the *will-to-digest*, the stomach; the *will-to-procreate*, the genitals, and so on. (*W2*, 259)

So the position is this: our capacity for knowledge of empirical objects resides in the functioning of the brain, the brain is an organ of the body, and all organs of the body have developed in order to propagate life. Our much-vaunted knowledge is thus a derivative feature of what we are; the primary element in us is the will that manifests itself in the body as a whole. Conscious actions, caused by perception of the world and reasoning about it, are merely one way in which this will in our bodies is set into motion. The individual human subject is different from other kinds of striving thing in the world only by virtue of the fact that the particular organization of his or her brain gives rise to self-consciousness and reasoning. But these capacities are only the tip of an iceberg, whose bulk is the will. Our predicament is to be driven by this will, whether we like it or not, into conflict, pain, and frustration. Schopenhauer still holds out the hope of rising above this predicament, but, as we shall see, the will within us must be suspended or turn against itself before we can exploit the capacities of our intellects to their full potential. Knowledge must eventually 'throw off its yoke, and, free from all the aims of the will, exist purely for itself, simply as a clear mirror of the world' (*W1*, 152). But for that to happen is very much an exception.

The self

What am I? Schopenhauer can say that I am an individual item in the world, a living, bodily thing of a certain species, which is capable of self-conscious thought and action. But he makes it something of a puzzle how I can think of myself in this way. In his philosophy the self is seen successively as a subject of experience and knowledge, a subject of will and action, a bodily manifestation of will to life, and a pure mirror of timeless reality. Sometimes it is as if a struggle for dominance is being waged between these different conceptions. The dichotomy between *subject* and *object*, which is the starting-point for the whole of *The World as Will and Representation*, is especially important here. As we saw, he explains that the subject is that which knows, the object that which is known by it. But this must leave us in some doubt about what a subject is.

A subject of representation is, for Schopenhauer, a single consciousness in which many diverse experiences of objects are united. Material things and conceptual thoughts are representations for the subject. But the subject itself is the 'I' that thinks and perceives, as opposed to the things thought and the things perceived. It is vital to understand that Schopenhauer's subject of representations is not any part of the world of objects. It is not a thing at all. It is not in space or time, does not interact causally with objects, is not visible, not identified with the body, or even with the individual human being. His favourite metaphorical images for it are the eye that looks out on the world but cannot see itself, and the extensionless point at which light-rays focus in a concave mirror. The subject is where experiences all converge, but it is never itself an object of experience: 'We never know it, but it is precisely that which knows wherever there is knowledge' (*W1*, 5). Schopenhauer is not alone in having such a view of the subject. It is recognizable as a version of Kant's conception of the pure 'I' of self-consciousness (apperception); moreover, says Schopenhauer, 'the fine passage from the sacred *Upanishad* applies: "It is not to be seen: it sees everything; it is not to be heard: it hears everything; it is not to be recognized; it recognizes everything" ' (*R*, 208). Wittgenstein later borrowed Schopenhauer's image of the eye that cannot see itself and the idea that the subject was not part of the world.

Schopenhauer's attitude to this pure subject of representation is ambivalent. On the one hand, he says that 'Everyone finds himself as this subject' (*W1*, 5). We are conscious not only of what we think and perceive, but of *being* that which thinks and perceives; moreover, he suggests, we cannot avoid the idea that that which thinks and perceives is distinct from every object of which it is conscious—even the body, which is 'an object among objects'. At the same time, however, each of us is an individual distinct from others. Each of us is closely associated with one particular part of the material world, and, as a subject of action or will, each of us must be a bodily thing. We seem to be two kinds of subject at once: subject of willing, which is essentially embodied, and subject of knowledge, which knows everything objectively, including its own body and acts of will, and hovers outside the world of individual things altogether. Our conception of ourselves ought, perhaps, to be split. Yet we think of the 'I' that thinks and perceives and the 'I' that acts as one and the same. Schopenhauer calls this a 'miracle *par excellence*', saying that 'the identity of the subject of willing with that of knowing by virtue whereof . . . the word "I" includes and indicates both, is the knot of the world, and hence inexplicable' (*R*, 211–12).

One may think that Schopenhauer inadvertently refutes his own conception of the pure subject which is not an object. For he admits that it provides at best an incomplete and perplexing way of thinking of oneself, says that it is inexplicable how 'I' could refer both to this pure subject and to the acting, material body, and even has to invoke the notion of a 'miracle' to get round the problem. We may also not be convinced that we do 'find our-selves' as the pure knowing subject, or that this is a conception which a philosophical account of self-consciousness needs to use at all. However, Schopenhauer's difficulties are not simply a matter of ineptness on his part—they go deep into an area of enduring perplexity. Each of us is not *merely* an object in the world; some account needs to be given of one's awareness of being oneself, of being 'inside' one's experience and seeming to be distinct from the rest of the world. Schopenhauer is not a dualist: he eschews any notion that souls, spirits, or immaterial substances constitute part of reality. Reality is material, and what each of us refers to using 'I' is, partly, an active, material thing in the world. But he is surely right in saying that that cannot be the end of the story. It seems true that I somehow 'find myself as a subject', however precisely we account for that. Some philosophers more recently have suggested that there is a fundamental, perhaps insuperable problem in trying to square 'subjective' and 'objective' views of ourselves. The underlying difficulty which Schopenhauer reveals is a substantial philosophical issue.

The struggle between competing views of the self is made even more intense by Schopenhauer's materialist account of the workings of the intellect as brain-functions, and his doctrine that the individual's body is an expression of will-to-life.

> That which in self-consciousness, and hence subjectively, is the intellect, presents itself in the consciousness of other things, and hence objectively, as the brain; and that which in self-consciousness, and hence subjectively, is the will, presents itself in the consciousness of other things, and hence objective-ly, as the entire organism (*W2*, 245).

> That focus of brain-activity (or the subject of knowledge) is indeed, as an indivisible point, simple, yet it is not on that account a substance (soul), but a mere condition or state. . . . This *knowing* and conscious *ego* is related to the will, which is the basis of its phenomenal appearance, as the image in the focus of the concave mirror is to that mirror itself; and, like that image, it has only a conditioned, in fact, properly speaking, a merely apparent reality. Far from being the absolutely first thing (as Fichte taught, for example), it is at bottom tertiary,

since it presupposes the organism, and the organism presupposes the will. (*W2*, 278)

We need to tease out two distinct elements here. One is Schopenhauer's materialism, the other his view that the will is our essence.

We can consider ourselves both subjectively and objectively. If we are considering ourselves objectively, as things occurring in the empirical world, then materialism is the most plausible and consistent position to take, according to Schopenhauer. To be a materialist pure and simple would be 'one-sided' (*W2*, 13), because materialism can never give a proper account of what it is to be a subject who experiences and understands the world: 'materialism is the philosophy of the subject that forgets to take account of itself'. But one side of the truth is an objective account of ourselves as things inhabiting the empirical world, and the only choice here is to conceive of ourselves as material occupants of space and time, falling under causal laws. So what from one viewpoint we call thought and perception are, from the other viewpoint, processes of the material brain and nervous system. From this objective point of view, the subject which we take ourselves to be is—in Schopenhauer's most extreme claim about it—'merely apparent'.

But even this unsettled combination of subjective and objective views about oneself is not the complete predicament which Schopenhauer places us in. For brain and organism are not merely part of an inert, material reality. They are expressions of the blind will in nature, enabling life to exist and propagate itself. The will is primary, and lies beneath the division between subject and object altogether. The larger contrast between will and representation re-asserts itself here. The subject that represents and the object that is represented are both, in a sense, illusory, because in the world in itself the division between subject and object does not exist. Even if I the subject disappeared, and along with me all the individual objects that make up my experience, the will would still be there in itself, continuing to strive and throw up new life-forms. And the most fundamental point about the self, for Schopenhauer, is that this same will is exactly what now strives away within the bodily organism that has produced me the subject.

5 Character, sex, and the unconscious

Will and intellect

For Schopenhauer, the primary element in human beings is the will. The intellect is only secondary; Schopenhauer explains it as a particular manifestation of the will to life in the brain and nervous system, and 'a mere tool in the service of the will' (*W2*, 205). Schopenhauer invents many images for the relationship between intellect and will, but his favourite is that of the sighted, lame man who is carried on the shoulders of the strong, blind man. The intellect is conscious, and is our window on the world, but the driving force which takes us where we are going is deeper down inside the psyche, inside the body or organism which we also are. The doctrine of the primacy of the will has many applications which are broadly psychological or ethical. Schopenhauer is in some respects a forerunner of twentieth-century views about the unconscious mind and the influence of sexuality on our behaviour, both of which emerge from his considerations of the opposition between intellect and will. His ethics also depends on the idea that the core of each individual, which makes them the person they are, is not the intellect, but the enduring, underlying will.

Once again we find that the individual's sense of his or her identity is something of a precarious affair. The self is a kind of compound between the will and the intellect. Although objectively the intellect is an expression of will as well, in our own self-consciousness we can distinguish the intellect as that part of us which is occupied with conscious perception and thought. The subjective symptoms of this split are various kinds of conflict and domination of which we may be aware: a 'strange interplay within us' between the intellect and the will (*W2*, 207). For example, the will is a comparatively primitive part of us, and not sophisticated enough to react to imaginary ideas in a different way from genuine beliefs:

> If . . . we are alone, and think over our personal affairs, and then vividly picture to ourselves, say, the menace of an actually

present danger, and the possibility of an unfortunate outcome, anxiety at once compresses the heart, and the blood ceases to flow. But if the intellect then passes to the possibility of the opposite outcome, and allows the imagination to picture the happiness long hoped-for as thereby attained, all the pulses at once quicken with joy, and the heart feels as light as a feather, until the intellect wakes up from its dream . . . We see that the intellect strikes up the tune, and the will must dance to it; in fact, the intellect causes it to play the part of a child whom its nurse at her pleasure puts into the most different moods by chatter and tales alternating between pleasant and melancholy things. (*W2*, 207–8)

On the other hand, our ordinary experience of the world is suffused with the positive or negative significance that comes from the will:

In the immediate perception of the world and of life, we consider things as a rule merely in their relations . . . we regard houses, ships, machines, and the like with the idea of their purpose and their suitability therefor. . . . Let us picture to ourselves how much every emotion or passion obscures and falsifies knowledge, in fact how every inclination or disinclination twists, colours, and distorts not merely the judgement, but even the original perception of things. Let us recall how, when we are delighted by a successful outcome, the whole world at once assumes a bright colour and a smiling aspect, and on the other hand looks dark and gloomy when care and sorrow weigh on us. Let us then see how even an inanimate thing, which is yet to become the instrument for some event we abhor, appears to have a hideous physiognomy; for example the scaffold, the fortress to which we are taken, the surgeon's case of instruments, the travelling coach of loved ones, and so on. (*W2*, 372–3)

We tend not to use the intellect in a 'pure' fashion. The way we confront the world of objects in experience and thought is driven by the will—further evidence for Schopenhauer that the will is primary in us. He has many more examples of the bias the will exerts:

> Our *advantage*, of whatever kind it may be, exercises a similar secret power over our judgement; what is in agreement with it at once seems to us fair, just, and reasonable. . . . A hypothesis, conceived and formed, makes us lynx-eyed for everything that confirms it, and blind to everything that contradicts it. What is opposed to our party, our plan, our wish, or our hope often cannot possibly be grasped and comprehended by us, whereas it is clear to the eyes of everyone else. (*W2*, 217–18)

Anybody wishing to describe the mind as a centre of pure perception and reasoning would have to overcome the considerable evidence Schopenhauer amasses (from anecdote, general observation, and introspection) for the contrary view, that our experience is largely governed by what fits our own aims, instincts, and emotional needs.

Where Schopenhauer shows uncommon insight is in his theory of the unconscious, one of the more important and influential aspects of his theory of the will. Since the will is something that operates independently of our conscious representation of reality, it can be credited with desires, aims, and feelings which are not consciously entertained by the thinking subject, but which nevertheless control his or her behaviour. One example (which he says is 'trifling and ridiculous', but nevertheless 'striking') is that when adding up our finances 'we make mistakes more frequently to our advantage than to our disadvantage, and this indeed without the least intention of dishonesty, but merely through the unconscious tendency to diminish our *debit* and increase our *credit*' (*W2*, 218). But this is merely a small instance of a widespread principle. Schopenhauer says that the intellect is often excluded from 'secret decisions of its own will'. I do not consciously decide what I wish to happen in a particular situation, but at a certain outcome I feel 'a jubilant, irresistible gladness, diffused over my whole being . . . to my own astonishment . . . (O)nly now does my intellect learn how firmly my will had already laid hold of the plan' (*W2*, 209).

The will is here a part of the individual's mind which adopts attitudes and guides overt behaviour despite remaining out of sight of the conscious intellect. Schopenhauer even recognizes a process similar to Freud's much later idea of repression:

this will . . . makes its supremacy felt in the last resort. This it does by prohibiting the intellect from having certain representations, by absolutely preventing certain trains of thought from arising, because it knows, or in other words experiences from the self-same intellect, that they would arouse in it any one of the emotions previously described. It then curbs and restrains the intellect, and forces it to turn to other things . . . We often do not know what we desire or fear. For years we can have a desire without admitting it to ourselves or even letting it come to clear consciousness, because the intellect is not to know anything about it, since the good opinion we have of ourselves would inevitably suffer thereby. But if the wish is fulfilled, we get to know from our joy, not without a feeling of shame, that this is what we desired (*W2*, 208–10).

In another interesting passage, Schopenhauer sees this mechanism as responsible for some forms of madness:

Every new adverse event must be assimilated by the intellect . . . but this operation itself is often very painful, and in most cases takes place only slowly and with reluctance. But soundness of mind can continue only in so far as this operation has been correctly carried out each time. On the other hand, if, in a particular case, the resistance and opposition of the will to the assimilation of some knowledge reaches such a degree that . . . certain events or circumstances are wholly suppressed for the intellect, because the will cannot bear the sight of them; and then, if the resultant gaps are arbitrarily filled up for the sake of the necessary connection; we then have madness. (*W2*, 400)

Sexuality and gender

Schopenhauer exaggerates in saying that all previous philosophers have 'ignored' sexual love ('I have no predecessors' (*W2*, 533)), and his dismissal of Plato's contribution in particular is unwarranted (*W2*, 532). Nevertheless, in talking so bluntly about sexuality, and in making it such a cornerstone of his philosophy, he is again unusually forward-looking for his day. Sex is ever-present in our minds, according to Schopenhauer, 'the public secret which must never be distinctly mentioned anywhere, but is always and everywhere understood to be the main thing' (*W2*, 571). 'It is the ultimate goal of almost all human effort; it has an unfavourable influence on the most important affairs, interrupts every hour the most serious occupations' (*W2*, 533). None of this is surprising on Schopenhauer's theory. The impulse to sexual intercourse is at the very core of our being, as an instinct which is the most direct and powerful manifestation of will to life in our bodies: 'the genitals', he is fond of telling us, 'are the focus of the will'.

Schopenhauer explains instinct as 'an action as if in accordance with the conception of an end or purpose, and yet entirely without such a conception' (*W2*, 540). Sexual behaviour and anatomy are directed at reproduction in a purpose-like manner. Reproduction may at times also be a conscious purpose, of course, but to the extent that his or her behaviour manifests instinct, the individual's conscious purposes are irrelevant. According to Schopenhauer, the procreative 'purpose' which sexual activity and its elaborate, all-pervading surroundings are directed towards, is actually a 'purpose' of the human species, a built-in drive to generate itself over again, for which the individual acts as a mere vehicle. The seriousness with which individuals pursue sexual goals reflects the magnitude of this underlying species-purpose.

Thus Schopenhauer sees the individual's sexual behaviour as at the beck and call of an impersonal force. His most striking way of putting this is to say that it is the will to life of the as yet unconceived offspring which draws a male and female partner together. Their view that they are acting wholly in their own interests out of individual desires towards another individual is a 'delusion' (*W2*, 538), and this delusion itself is a means by which 'nature can attain her end'. The 'longing of love' celebrated in poetry of all ages is on this account truly something external to the lover, and hence so powerful that the individual can scarcely contain it:

this longing that closely associates the notion of an endless bliss with the possession of a definite woman, and an unutterable pain with the thought that this possession is not attainable; this longing and this pain of love cannot draw their material from the needs of an ephemeral individual. On the contrary, they are the sighs of the spirit of the species . . . The species alone has infinite life, and is therefore capable of infinite desire, infinite satisfaction, and infinite sufferings. But these are here imprisoned in the narrow breast of a mortal; no wonder, therefore, when such a breast seems ready to burst, and can find no expression for the infinite rapture or infinite pain with which it is filled. (*W2*, 551)

Schopenhauer also believes that once the ends of the species are fulfilled between lovers, their rapture and their delusion must eventually ebb away:

Forsaken by [the spirit of the species], the individual falls back into his original narrowness and neediness, and sees with surprise that, after so high, heroic, and infinite an effort, nothing has resulted for his pleasure but what is afforded by any sexual satisfaction. Contrary to expectation, he finds himself no happier than before; he notices that he has been the dupe of the will of the species. (*W2*, 557)

Of course, individuals will continue to feel sexual desire as a desire of their own directed towards a particular person, and will be conscious of the person's physical and mental attributes. Schopenhauer gives us a detailed list of the qualities that men supposedly look for in women (right age, health, proportion of skeleton, fullness of flesh, beauty of the face—in that order) and that women supposedly look for in men (right age, strength, courage). Looking away from such details, however, all the features of attraction are to be explained in the same way: they result from unconscious principles of selection through which the will of the species works to ensure the character of its next generation. Where the intention of intercourse is expressly not to generate offspring, Schopenhauer is nevertheless determined to explain subjective attraction in terms of life-generating instincts. Even the case of homosexuality does not deter him: such a widespread practice must 'arise in some way from human nature itself', he thinks, though his explanation for it is somewhat desperate. Very young and very old males, he supposes, have deficient semen, and are following an instinct to discharge it in non-procreative fashion, thus still subserving the 'will of the species' for the best possible offspring.

Character, sex, and the unconscious

Some may find surprising another of Schopenhauer's convictions: that it is the intellect which we inherit from our mothers, and the will from our fathers. Not many philosophers have thought of the intellect as a female characteristic, and the capacity for emotions as male. Schopenhauer is convinced that there is empirical evidence for his claim, but he also gives another argument in which he shows his true colours. The will is 'the true inner being, the kernel, the radical element', while the intellect is 'the secondary, the adventitious, the accident of that substance' (W2, 517). So, the argument continues, we should expect the more powerful, procreative sex to impart the will to its offspring, while the mother, the 'merely conceiving principle', is responsible for the merely secondary intellect. The agenda here is to make sure that the female comes out as superficial and secondary, the male as substantial, radical, and primary. What is inherited from the father is the 'moral nature', the 'character', the 'heart'. The view that the intellect is female in origin thus results from a cross-fertilization between Schopenhauer's doctrine of the metaphysical primacy of the will and his fairly conventional prejudice that the female must be secondary to the male.

Schopenhauer's disparaging view of women, concentrated to most corrosive effect in the short essay 'On Women' (P2, 614–26), has earned him some notoriety. To what extent it should single him out from any of his contemporaries and predecessors is debatable. On the one hand, he is perhaps especially worthy of note because of his attempt to imbue gender differences with such metaphysical significance, and because he gives such prominence to sexuality in human life. On the other hand, it may be thought that his actual views are fairly commonplace for his time. What is not in question is the vehemence of his rhetoric on the topic:

> Only the male intellect, clouded by the sexual impulse, could call the undersized, narrow-shouldered, broad-hipped, and short-legged sex the fair sex; for in this impulse is to be found its whole beauty. (P2, 619)

> Throughout their lives women remain children, always see only what is nearest to them, cling to the present, take the appearance of things for reality, and prefer trivialities to the most important affairs. Thus it is the faculty of reason by virtue

whereof man does not, like the animals, live merely in the present . . . In consequence of her weaker faculty of reason, woman shares less in the advantages and disadvantages that this entails. (*P2*, 615–16)

There are a few compensating virtues. Schopenhauer allots to women the greater share of humane loving-kindness, which for him is of supreme moral worth; he also thinks they are more down-to-earth and practical than men (the intellect at work again); but he is convinced that they cannot reason very well, and have shallow characters. Their interests are 'love, conquests, . . . dress, cosmetics, dancing'; they regard everything as a means to winning a man; dissimulation is inborn to them 'just as nature has armed the lion with claws and teeth, the elephant and boar with tusks, the bull with horns, and the cuttle-fish with ink that blackens water' (*P2*, 617). Women may be talented, but artistic geniuses can, apparently, only be male: 'generally speaking, women are and remain the most downright and incurable Philistines' (*P2*, 620–1). Occasionally, one glimpses a portrait of the novelist, socialite, and mother, Johanna Schopenhauer:

the original maternal love is purely *instinctive* and therefore ceases with the physical helplessness of the children. In its place, there should then appear one based on habit and reasoning; but often it fails to appear, especially when the mother has not loved the father. . . . Property acquired by the long and constant hard work of men subsequently passes into the hands of women who in their folly get through it or otherwise squander it in a short time. . . . The vanity of women . . . is bad because it is centred entirely on material things . . . and hence society is so very much their element. (*P2*, 625–6)

Conventional male sentiment mixed with personal bitterness— the result is scarcely edifying. But no account of Schopenhauer's philosophy ought to suppress these ideas, which were clearly important to him.

Character

We have seen that in Schopenhauer's view the will is the primary element within us, the intellect only secondary and 'adventitious'.

Character, sex, and the unconscious

In this, the will often has the role of an impersonal force which is greater than the individual, attaching to the species or to the world as a whole, and expressing itself in each individual equally. However, Schopenhauer also believes that each person has a distinct character. And here too the intellect is secondary. It is not intellectual abilities and traits, or continuity of consciousness, that marks out the true core of one's separate identity as an individual.

> The older we become, the more does everything pass us by without leaving a trace. Great age, illness, injury to the brain, madness, can deprive a man entirely of memory, but the identity of his person has not in this way been lost. That rests on the identical *will* and on its unalterable character; it is also just this that makes the expression of the glance unalterable. . . . Our true self . . . really knows nothing but willing and not-willing, being contented and not contented, with all the modifications of the thing called feelings, emotions, and passions. (W2, 239)

Each human being's character is unique for Schopenhauer, though since we all belong to the same species, the differences may sometimes be very slight. Individual character comes into its own in explaining and predicting actions. An action follows on from motives, but only in combination with the character of the agent. The same set of objective circumstances, perceived and comprehended in the same way by different people, may lead them to act in quite different ways. Offer a large bribe and some will take it, some will politely decline, and others will turn you over to the authorities. The motive, in Schopenhauer's sense (that is, the external state of affairs as apprehended by the intellect) can be the same in all three cases, and the intellect itself can, if you like, be working in exactly the same way. But the character is what differs. If we knew each person's character thoroughly, and all the motives they were exposed to, we could predict all their actions without any remainder. In another of Schopenhauer's beloved Latin tags, *operari sequitur esse*, 'acting follows from being': what we *are* partly determines how we act. The principle is no different from that by which we predict the varied behaviour of different natural substances under the same influence: 'the effect of the same motive on different people is quite different; as the sunlight gives to wax white colour and to chloric silver black, so the heat makes wax soft, but clay hard' (*F*, 50). This doctrine of character has consequences for freedom, responsibility, and morality, as we shall discover later.

Schopenhauer sees the character as a person's 'being', something distinct from the collection of all the person's actions put together. The actions follow from the being, each of them bearing the stamp of the person to whom they belong. This may make the character sound mysterious, but Schopenhauer assures us that we only ever learn about it, in other people or even in ourselves, from its empirical manifestations—just the way we learn about the character of wax or chloric silver, in fact. We observe many actions, and come to know someone's degree of honesty, courage, or compassion over the course of time. Similarly with ourselves: until we see how we fare in action, we may be quite wrong about the qualities of character which we possess. So Schopenhauer says that character is *empirical*. It is not identical with the series of actions I carry out, yet is discovered only from observation of those actions.

Schopenhauer maintains that each person's character is both constant and inborn. We can neither choose nor change what we are. We can be educated to understand the world and ourselves better, giving us better, more refined motives on which to act, but the self that these motives prompt into action really has not altered: 'Under the changeable shell of his years, his relationships, and even his store of knowledge and opinions, there hides, like a crab under its shell, the identical and real man, quite unchangeable and always the same' (*F*, 51). Schopenhauer thinks that many of our ordinary attitudes bear out this claim: we assume not just identity of the person, but constancy in the moral character as well. When we have gone on trusting someone to behave in a certain way, and have eventually been disappointed, 'we never say: "His character has changed," but "I was mistaken about him" ' (*F*, 52). For example, we say, on this view, not that someone used to be honest and courageous, but is now deceitful and cowardly; rather that the extent of their deceitfulness and cowardice was not fully apparent until now. As further evidence for constancy of character Schopenhauer cites the fact that we recognize others as the same after many years from the manner in which they act, and that we feel responsibility and shame for things we ourselves did forty years before.

With the claim that character is inborn we again find that human beings are to be treated very much on a par with other parts of nature. You would not try to produce apricots from an oak tree, says Schopenhauer. Human beings clearly have inborn species-characteristics. Why are people so loathe to accept that there is inborn courage, honesty, or wickedness at the level of the individual? Schopenhauer's evidence, such as it is, leads him to think that the human individual at birth cannot be a mere blank slate which awaits experience before it forms any character at all. Before we can have knowledge or perceive the world very well, we are creatures of will, reacting with positive or negative feelings to what impinges on us. Even at this stage, there is a basic core to the person which is not moulded by what he or she has intellectually apprehended of the world.

Schopenhauer also has the notion of *acquired character*. Especially when we are young, we may not correctly understand what our character is. We do not know what we really like, or want, or can succeed at. Acquired character is a better self-understanding, which one comes to have by gaining an insight into one's true constant character—an idea in some ways reminiscent of Nietzsche's later notion of 'becoming who you are'. This enlightened idea is, however, at odds with the rest of Schopenhauer's account. For it seems that before I have attained the acquired character, I may embark on ventures that go against my real nature—which ought to be impossible if my inborn, unchanging character determines all my actions.

Sometimes, however, Schopenhauer says things about the character which are even more puzzling.

> however old we become, we yet feel within ourselves that we are absolutely the same as we were when we were young . . . This thing which is unaltered and always remains absolutely the same, which does not grow old with us, is just the kernel of our inner nature, and that does not lie in time. . . . (W)e are accustomed to regard the subject of knowing, the knowing I, as our real self . . . This, however, is the mere function of the

brain, and is not our real self. Our true self . . . it is which produces that other thing, which does not sleep with it when it sleeps, which also remains unimpaired when that other thing becomes extinct in death. . . . The *character itself* . . . is still exactly the same now as then. The will itself, alone and by itself, endures; for it alone is unchangeable, indestructible, does not grow old, is not physical but metaphysical, does not belong to the phenomenal appearance, but to the thing in itself that appears. (*W2*, 238–9)

Here it is unclear what kind of thing the character is. On the one hand it is unique and attaches to oneself as an individual. On the other hand it is 'not in time', it is 'not physical but metaphysical', and even 'remains unimpaired' when the individual dies and his or her subjective consciousness disappears. The problem, bluntly, is this: is my 'real self', or 'the kernel of my inner nature', something that attaches to the finite individual that I am, or is it the thing in itself, beyond space, time, and individuation altogether? If the former, it is neither outside of time nor unaffected by my own death. If the latter, it does not serve to explain my personal identity at all. Schopenhauer seems to stumble into a quite elementary difficulty. But in a way his confusion has a more profound point behind it. For he wants to claim in the end that our individuality, seemingly so fundamental to us, is not only a source of torment, but some kind of illusion: 'at bottom every individuality is really only a special error, a false step, something that it would be better should not be' (*W2*, 491–2). The Third and Fourth Books of *The World as Will and Representation*—its great second half to which we now turn—explore the possibilities of escaping from individuality, and from the will which lies at our core.

6 Art and Ideas

Aesthetic experience

Aesthetic experience deliberately reverses the trend of Schopenhauer's book, for in it the will of the subject is suspended. As long as we exercise the will, or are governed by it, we shall be forced to consider a thing in a great mesh of relations to other things and to ourselves: Do we want it? Can we use it? Is it better than something else? What made it the way it is? What will it make happen? Just as our intellects are organs developed to subserve the will, so all the usual connections which we employ in order to understand objects are will-governed: we perceive in order to manipulate, in order to live. Only if we cease to will at all can the object stand out in our consciousness stripped of the relations of time, place, cause, and effect.

Schopenhauer belongs to a tradition which equates aesthetic experience with a 'disinterested' attitude towards its object, and is often cited as one of the chief proponents of such a view. The idea is that to experience something aesthetically, one must suspend or disengage all one's desires towards it, attending not to any consideration of what ends, needs, or interests it may fulfil, but only to the way it presents itself in perception. In Schopenhauer's case, aesthetic experience must always be an extraordinary episode in any human being's life, since he has argued that the will is our essence, and that our 'ordinary way of considering things' is permeated by will:

> so long as our consciousness is filled by our will, so long as we are given up to the throng of desires with its constant hopes and fears, so long as we are the subject of willing, we never attain lasting happiness or peace. . . . Thus the subject of willing is constantly lying on the revolving wheel of Ixion, is always drawing water in the sieve of the Danaids, and is the eternally thirsting Tantalus.

When, however, an external cause or inward disposition suddenly raises us out of the endless stream of willing, and snatches knowledge from the thraldom of the will, the attention is now no longer directed to the motives of willing, but comprehends things free from their relation to the will. Thus it considers things without interest, without subjectivity, purely objectively . . . Then all at once the peace, always sought but always escaping us on that first path of willing, comes to us of its own accord, and all is well with us . . . (F)or that moment we are delivered from the miserable pressure of the will. We celebrate the Sabbath of the penal servitude of willing; the wheel of Ixion stands still. (*W1*, 196)

After the brisk formality of the opening book on the world as representation, and the incipient gloom as we descend into the world as will, the Third Book of *The World as Will and Representation* has a character of brightness and joy which testifies to the importance of the aesthetic for its author.

Schopenhauer states the central problem of aesthetics in an acute way—it is: 'how satisfaction with and pleasure in an object are possible without any reference thereof to our willing' (*P2*, 415). (His view of aesthetic enjoyment is similar in some respects to that put forward by Kant in his *Critique of Judgement*, though Schopenhauer makes little of this connection, and does not rate Kant's work on aesthetics as among his best.) In the usual run of events, pleasure or satisfaction arises from the fulfilment of some desire or end. What we call happiness is usually felt on attaining one of our ends, or it may be the temporary absence of anything further to strive for. But these kinds of pleasure and happiness, since they depend on willing, also carry with them the permanent possibility of suffering. In the first place, all willing 'springs from lack, from deficiency, and thus from suffering' (*W1*, 196). Secondly, when any particular desire is stilled, the subject of willing soon experiences another deficiency. Thus to be driven by the will is to oscillate between suffering and satisfaction, and Schopenhauer is convinced that the suffering lasts longer, the satisfaction being only a temporary return to neutral before another lack is felt.

The problem for aesthetics is how there can be any kind of pleasure other than that which is contained in this oscillation. If pleasure is defined as the fulfilment of a lack or the satisfaction of a desire, then a totally will-less state of contemplation ought to be one in which one cannot experience pleasure at all. Clearly, the positive gain of being in such a state would be the loss of the possibility of suffering, and Schopenhauer makes a great deal of this point. But how could a will-less state leave room for real pleasure? Sometimes Schopenhauer writes as if it could not, as if aesthetic contemplation were a state purely of knowledge, a dispassionate registering of objective reality—'we have stepped into another world, so to speak, where everything that moves our will, and thus violently agitates us, no longer exists. . . . Happiness and unhappiness have vanished' (*W1*, 197). Yet he is also prepared to describe aesthetic experience in terms such as 'peace' and 'blessedness', and as a special kind of pleasure or enjoyment. He even states that when 'all possibility of suffering is abolished . . . the state of pure objectivity of perception becomes one that makes us feel positively happy' (*W2*, 368). These different claims can be reconciled by saying that the usual kind of happiness (and unhappiness) depends on willing, while the aesthetic kind depends on the cessation of willing.

This might be thought sufficient to give aesthetic experience the value which Schopenhauer wishes to assign it. However, his version of the 'aesthetic attitude' theory is unusual in linking the state of will-less contemplation with the achievement of the most objective kind of knowledge. For him, an experience undergone in the absence of subjective desires and aims will be one which distorts the world as little as possible, so he can maintain that aesthetic experience is valuable not only for the calming effect of escaping from one's own will, but because it uniquely displays things as they eternally are. Aesthetic experience, in other words, has high cognitive value, not merely the enriching or therapeutic value of entering into a certain psychological state.

Objectivity and genius

The subject ordinarily experiences material objects that occupy space and time, their causal connections to one another, and bodily acts of will following upon motives. But Schopenhauer believes that we can in exceptional moments gain access to a timeless reality that is not carved up into individuals. Beyond the realm of individual things and events lies the Idea, to which 'neither plurality nor change' belongs: 'While the individuals in which it expresses itself are innumerable and are incessantly coming into existence and passing away, it remains unchanged as one and the same, and the principle of sufficient reason has no meaning for it' (*W1*, 169).

Schopenhauer begins his Third Book with a disquisition on Platonic Ideas and their relation to the thing in itself. His claim will be that artists, and all engaged in aesthetic experience, discern, however fleetingly, the timeless reality of Ideas. Hence he owes us an attempt to set the metaphysical record straight first: what are these Ideas? He calls them 'the most adequate objectivity' of the thing in itself. This sounds obscure but is in fact quite a simple notion. The thing in itself cannot be known; but a knowable object which presented reality to the subject with the least possible degree of subjective distortion would be the 'adequate objectivity' of the thing in itself. Thus Schopenhauer explains:

> the Platonic Idea is necessarily object, something known, a representation, and precisely, but only, in this respect is it different from the thing in itself. It has laid aside merely the subordinate forms of the phenomenon, all of which we include under the principle of sufficient reason; or rather it has not yet entered into them. But it has retained the first and most universal form, namely that of the representation in general, that of being object for a subject. . . . Therefore, it alone is the most *adequate objectivity* possible of the will or of the thing in itself; indeed it is even the whole thing in itself, only under the form of the representation. Here lies the ground of the great agreement between Plato and Kant, although in strict accuracy that of which they both speak is not the same. (*W1*, 175)

Some strain is evident in the way that the Idea seems forced to serve as both thing in itself and representation, when these two categories were supposedly mutually exclusive at the outset. Also, although he recognizes that the equation of Kant and Plato would be wrong 'in strict accuracy', he is still prepared to make the extremely dubious statement that 'the inner meaning of both doctrines is wholly the same' (*W1*, 172). Some commentators have regarded the Ideas as an awkward, hasty afterthought. This is not wholly a fair assessment, however, as the Ideas were one of the earliest parts of the system to fall into place, and figured in the account of the will's objectification in nature in the Second Book. What we should hold on to is the notion that nature contains not only a multiplicity of individual things and events, but unchanging single kinds to which they belong. There are not only horses, but the species *horse*, not only pools and fountains but the repeatable molecular structure H_2O, not only many bodies falling to the ground at different times and places, but a ubiquitous gravitational force. Schopenhauer thinks of such kinds as timeless Ideas, and our apprehension of them as the most objective knowledge of the world we can ever attain. Schopenhauer follows Plato in claiming that Ideas exist in reality, independently of the subject. They are not concepts. Concepts are the mental constructs we make in order to grasp reality in general terms; but Ideas are parts of nature awaiting discovery. For Schopenhauer, they are not even discovered by conceptual thinking, but by perception and imagination.

What would consciousness of Ideas themselves be like? Schopenhauer has a dramatic answer. Once we abandon the guidance of the principle of sufficient reason,

> we no longer consider the where, the when, the why, and the whither of things, but simply and solely the *what*. . . . [We] let our whole consciousness be filled by the calm contemplation of the natural object actually present, whether it be a landscape, a tree, a rock, a crag, a building, or anything else . . . and continue to exist only as pure subject, as clear mirror of the object, so that it is as though the object alone existed without anyone to perceive it, and thus we are no longer able to separate the perceiver from the perception. . . . What is thus known is no longer the individual thing as such, but the *Idea* . . . at the same time, the person who is involved in this perception is no longer an individual, for in such perception the individual has lost himself; he is *pure* will-less, painless, timeless *subject of knowledge* (W1, 178–9).

'At one stroke', Schopenhauer continues, the particular thing 'becomes the Idea of its species', and the perceiving individual 'becomes the *pure subject of knowing*' (W1, 179). What Schopenhauer must mean is that I see the particular as embodying a universal Idea, and momentarily lose consciousness of myself as an individual. His claim is that one cannot know Ideas if one retains an awareness of oneself as an individual separate from the object contemplated ('we apprehend the world purely objectively, only when we no longer know that we belong to it' (*W2*, 368)) — and conversely that one cannot fail to be knowing an Idea, once one's contemplation turns one into this 'pure mirror' of reality.

Although Schopenhauer clearly thinks that natural beauty often gives rise to aesthetic experience (witness the examples of tree, rock, and crag), it is to art that he gives most attention. He is fairly orthodox for his day in believing that the production of art requires something called genius, which must be distinguished from mere talent. But he does give his own account of what genius is. It consists, he writes, 'in the knowing faculty having received a considerably more powerful development than is required by the *service of the will*' (*W2*, 377). The person of genius has two-thirds intellect and one-third will, the 'normal person' is the other way round. It is not that the genius is lacking in will—such people usually have strong emotions, for example— but rather that their intellect is capable of detaching itself from the will to a much greater extent, and has the power to function autonomously:

> the *gift of genius* is nothing but the most complete *objectivity* . . . the capacity to remain in a state of pure perception, to lose oneself in perception, to remove from the service of the will the knowledge which originally existed only for this service. In other words, genius is the ability to leave entirely out of sight our own interest, our willing, and our aims, and consequently to discard entirely our own personality for a time, in order to remain *pure knowing subject*, the clear eye of the world; and this not merely for moments, but with the necessary continuity and conscious thought to enable us to repeat by deliberate art what has been apprehended. (*W1*, 185–6)

The genius stands for something impersonal, which Schopenhauer hints at with the metaphor of 'the clear eye of the world'. The genius is not only an individual, but 'at the same time a pure intellect that as such belongs to the whole of mankind' (*W2*, 390). Abandoning the will that manifests itself in this particular individual, and letting the intellect soar free of it, the genius has an uncommon ability 'to see the universal in the particular' (*W2*, 379). It is important that this is a capacity for heightened *perception*. A great painter or sculptor *sees* with more intensity and more detail, and has greater ability to retain and reproduce what is seen. But perceiving merely what is present to hand is not enough: '*imagination* is needed, in order to complete, arrange, amplify, fix, retain, and repeat at pleasure all the significant pictures of life' (*W2*, 379). Thus genius, in whichever art form, may go one better than actual experience: a great work of art may reflect reality all the better when the picture it conveys is a heightened one, having more clarity and definition than is ever contained in ordinary experience itself.

The true province of genius is imaginative perception, and not conceptual thinking. Art which is structured around some proposition, or worked out on a wholly rational plan, is dead and uninteresting by comparison. One example is where pictorial art turns to a symbolic form of allegory, and can be grasped only by deciphering images according to a code, something alien to art as such, in Schopenhauer's view (*W1*, 239). Another is when 'imitators' or 'mannerists' set themselves to produce according to a formula which they note to have been successful in some other work. The result is offensive: prior deliberation can always be discerned, and the constituent elements they have minced together can always be 'picked out and separated from the mixture'. The concept, 'useful as it is in life, serviceable, necessary, and productive as it is in science, is eternally barren and unproductive in art' (*W1*, 235).

Geniuses are rare because they are in a sense unnatural. In the great majority of people, the workings of the intellect are subordinate to the attainment of individual ends, as Schopenhauer's theory would predict. The intellect is an instrument of the will, and is not 'designed' for purposeless imaginative work which grasps and relays eternal Ideas. By the same token, people possessed of genius are commonly viewed as oddities. With its heightened imagination and tendency to distract from the immediate connections of things, genius has some resemblance to madness. Geniuses do not accommodate to the expectations of their own time and place, unlike people of mere talent, who are admired for the ability to produce what is wanted when it is wanted (*W2*, 390). The genius is also prone to impracticality, because of the degree to which his intellect works independently of the end-seeking will. (I say 'his', because Schopenhauer does not recognize female genius, even though the intellect is supposedly a female inheritance. The difference is presumably supposed to be that women's perception always remains superficial and never rises to 'the universal'.)

The arts and their value

Schopenhauer commands respect among historians of aesthetics for his deep and varied knowledge of the arts. While he has a single theory of aesthetic appreciation as the will-less contemplation of Ideas, he appreciates many different art forms, from architecture through painting of different genres, to poetry and drama, and eventually to music, which he sets apart from the rest. His aesthetics is not an inflexible metaphysical monolith: its core is fleshed out with elegance and sensitivity.

Before discussing the various arts, Schopenhauer makes a substantial qualification to his theory. He has claimed that whenever we have an aesthetic experience there occurs both a subjective cessation of willing and an objective insight into the realm of Ideas. However, he now admits that the value of a particular object of aesthetic experience can reside in one or other of these factors almost to the exclusion of the other:

> with aesthetic contemplation (in real life or through the medium of art) of natural beauty in the inorganic and vegetable kingdoms and of the works of architecture, the enjoyment of pure, will-less knowing will predominate, because the Ideas here apprehended are only low grades of the will's objectivity, and therefore are not phenomena of deep significance and suggestive content. On the other hand, if animals and human beings are the object of aesthetic contemplation or presentation, the enjoyment will consist rather in the objective apprehension of these Ideas. (*W1*, 212)

In other words, the cognitive import of aesthetic experience may often be quite low. This may invite the thought that the single unifying element in his aesthetics is really the notion of pleasure-able will-free contemplation, or even that his aesthetics is not unified. However, he deserves credit for realizing that the arts are regarded both as a release from the pressures of living, and as an intense form of knowledge.

The Ideas form a hierarchy of higher and lower grades of the will's objectification. The lowest are the all-pervading natural forces, the highest the Idea of humanity. Architecture is the art form that deals with the lowest Ideas concerning the beha-viour of solid matter: gravity, cohesion, rigidity, and hardness (*W1*, 214). Buildings must also be of practical use, so that their potential to be pure art is, or should be, restricted. But the real core of architecture as an art is the conflict between gravity and rigidity. All the parts of a fine building should be relevant to making this conflict manifest to the observer, and should appear necessary rather than arbitrary: merely decorative elements be-long to sculpture, and not to architecture as such. Also, it matters what materials a building is made from. An edifice which turned out to be of wood or pumice-stone would be a kind of sham, because materials less substantial than stone are not suited to bring out the Ideas of gravity and rigidity. We must be able to grasp in our perception the striving of the blocks towards the earth, and the counter-striving of the rigid elements which pre-vent them from falling. All else is irrelevant—mere beauty of shape is not a peculiarly architectural feature. The only other aspect to architecture that Schopenhauer acknowledges is light. The illumination of a building serves to reveal its fundamental structure more clearly, while that structure, by intercepting and reflecting light, 'unfolds [light's] nature and qualities in the purest and clearest way, to the great delight of the beholder' (*W1*, 216). Similar to architecture is 'the artistic arrangement of water' (*W1*, 217), which is less developed as an art simply because it is less useful than the making of buildings. The construction of foun-tains, waterfalls, and lakes does for the Ideas of fluidity, mobility, and transparency what architecture does for those of rigidity and cohesion.

Horticulture and landscaping provide a parallel in the realm of plants, although here Schopenhauer reckons that it is predomin-antly nature rather than art that does the work. Only in depictions of vegetation in painting does art come into its own. Our aesthetic enjoyment of a landscape painting whose subject is entirely vegetative or inanimate is one where 'the subjective side of aesthetic pleasure is predominant', residing in pure, will-less knowing, rather than in apprehending Ideas (*W1*, 218). But painting and sculpture become more concerned with the objective depiction of Ideas when they take animals and finally human beings as their subjects. Schopenhauer sees no important difference between confronting a person or animal face to face, and looking at an artistic representation—except that the abilities of a genius allow art to provide us with exemplars of greater beauty than nature actually provides: the genius 'impresses on the hard marble the beauty of form which nature failed to achieve in a thousand attempts, and he places it before her, exclaiming as it were, "This is what you desired to say!" ' (*W1*, 222).

With depicted animals, as with animals themselves, the most beautiful individual is the one most characteristic of the species (*W1*, 220)—the lion, for example, in which we are best able to see the universal Idea of *the lion* embodied. Here, what we enjoy is less the calm of will-less contemplation, more our getting to know the animal which we see in the painting or sculpture: 'we are occupied with the restlessness and impetuosity of the depicted will' (*W1*, 219). With humn beings, it is also true that the beautiful individual is the one most characteristic of the species. But there are also considerations of individual character and expression: a portrait ought to bring out the universal Idea of humanity, but of course must render the particular character of the sitter. Is this not an objection to Schopenhauer's theory that the point of art is always to express Ideas? May the strength of a work of art not lie in its conveying something particular and even arbitrary? Schopenhauer attempts to preserve the unity of his theory by maintaining that 'each person exhibits to a certain extent an Idea that is wholly characteristic of him' (*W1*, 224). But if apprehending an Idea is not always apprehending something timeless, universal, and potentially common to many individuals, it surely becomes less clear what sense we may attach to the notion.

Many paintings depict scenes from history, or from some particular legend or biblical story. But again, Schopenhauer urges that what makes them artistically significant is the extent to which they express something universal about mankind. Particular historical circumstances are irrelevant: 'it is all the same as regards inward significance whether ministers dispute about countries and nations over a map, or boors in a beer-house choose to wrangle over cards and dice' (*W1*, 231). Schopenhauer is fond of contrasting the arts with history. He takes a high-handed line, and often uses the opportunity to disagree with the Hegelian conception of history. In his view, the essential kernel of human beings is always the same, not liable to local variation or change over time. Thus he makes the startling pronouncement that 'The chapters of the history of nations are at bottom different only through the names and dates; the really essential content is everywhere the same' (*W2*, 442). History, he maintains, co-ordinates merely facts about the changing surface of humanity, and can never get beyond this. The contrasting form of discourse is poetry: 'paradoxical as it may sound, far more real, genuine, inner truth is to be attributed to poetry than to history' (*W1*, 245). 'Genuine, inner truth' is supposedly truth about what does not change, that is, the Idea of humanity.

Poetry emerges as the art form which is able to express the Idea of absolutely anything in the world, but which reigns supreme in portraying the diverse characters and actions of mankind. Again Schopenhauer distinguishes carefully between concepts, which are abstract representations formed by the subject, and Ideas, which can be accessed in direct experience and are part of the fabric of nature itself. The task for the poet is to use the conceptual means which poetry has in common with other linguistic practices, towards the distinctive end of revealing an Idea to the mind of the reader. It is this that marks poetry out as an artistic use of language, and as the province of genius—for the writer cannot make an Idea perspicuous to the reader unless he or she first has sufficient objectivity to perceive it. Poetry can be called 'the art of bringing into play the power of imagination through words' (*W2*, 424). It differs from the visual arts not only in using language, but in the degree of work that must be done by the imagination of the recipient. Schopenhauer says much that is of interest about the different genres and styles of poetry: lyric, epic, and tragic, romantic and classical (which he prefers). Sometimes the poet finds the material, the Idea of humanity in him- or herself, the result of which is lyric poetry. At the other end of the spectrum lies drama, in which the writer depicts humanity from an objective point of view.

Schopenhauer gives particular attention to tragedy, as the 'summit of poetic art' (*W1*, 252). While he is not alone in considering tragedy a supreme art form, it has especial importance for him because it is uniquely able to portray human life in what he regards as its true colours, containing the right degree of unfulfilled desire, conflict, and unmitigated suffering: 'It is the antagonism of the will with itself which is here most completely unfolded at the highest grade of its objectivity' (*W1*, 253). But seeing the Idea of humanity revealed in all its terrible truth is not the end of the matter. Schopenhauer requires that we understand also the ultimate human achievement (as he will later argue it to be) of resigning oneself, and turning against the will to life: 'we see in tragedy the noblest men, after a long conflict and suffering, finally renounce for ever all the pleasures of life and the aims till then pursued so keenly, or cheerfully and willingly give up life itself' (*W1*, 253).

Witnessing the depiction of suffering and resignation in tragedy, we learn by suffering in some measure ourselves. The best kind of tragedy, in Schopenhauer's view (which admittedly leaves out many famous instances of the genre) is where a catastrophe occurs in the course of a more or less ordinary life through no particularly grave fault of the protagonist. This kind of tragedy 'shows us those powers that destroy happiness and life, and in such a way that the path to them is at any moment open even to us. . . . Then, shuddering, we feel ourselves already in the midst of hell' (*W1*, 255). Is there room for pure aesthetic pleasure amid such terror—amid such perturbations of the will? Schopenhauer's answer invokes the Kantian conception of the sublime, in which the contemplation of something potentially destructive, viewed from the vantage point of present safety, brings a pleasurable sense of elevation. Schopenhauer gives this his own twist, however. What we rise to, above our shudderings at the depicted pain and misery of the tragedy, is, he claims, a sense of the serene abandonment of all willing which beckons from the very highest plateau that human life can reach. 'What gives to everything tragic . . . the characteristic tendency to the sublime, is the dawning of the knowledge that the world and life can afford us no true satisfaction, and are therefore not worth our attachment to them' (*W2*, 433–4).

Music

Schopenhauer's philosophical theory of music is set apart from his account of the other arts, and has enjoyed something of a life of its own in musical circles and in aesthetics. It remains one of the most striking theories of the power of music to express emotion, even if, like other attempts to explain this phenomenon, it is not ultimately convincing. Schopenhauer's view is that music is a 'copy of the will itself' (*W1*, 257). Whereas all the other art forms present us with Ideas which are the experienceable manifestation of the will, music bypasses these Ideas, and is 'as *immediate* an objectification and copy of the whole *will* as the world itself is'. The will expresses itself once as the whole world of particular phenomena and universal kinds into which they fall; it expresses itself over again as music. There are two parts to Schopenhauer's view. One attempts to explain the significance of music in terms of states of feeling and striving that we are familiar with in ourselves. The other draws a large-scale analogy between the range of phenomena in nature and the different elements of which music consists.

Here is Schopenhauer's idea about music and conscious strivings:

> The nature of man consists in the fact that his will strives, is satisfied, strives anew, and so on and on; in fact his happiness and well-being consist only in the transition from desire to satisfaction, and from this to a fresh desire . . . Thus, corresponding to this, the nature of melody is a constant digression and deviation from the keynote in a thousand ways . . . (M)elody expresses the many different forms of the will's efforts, but also its satisfaction by ultimately finding again a harmonious interval, and still more the keynote. (*W1*, 260)

Schopenhauer contends that the progression of musical notes through time is immediately understood by the human mind as an analogy of the progress of our own inner strivings. Here are some of the many examples he gives:

> as rapid transition from wish to satisfaction and from this to a new wish are happiness and well-being, so rapid melodies without great deviations are cheerful. Slow melodies that strike painful discords and wind back to the keynote only through many bars, are sad, on the analogy of delayed and hard-won satisfaction. . . . The *adagio* speaks of the suffering of a great and noble endeavour that disdains all trifling happiness. (*W1*, 260–1)

> The effect of the *suspension* also deserves to be considered here. It is a dissonance delaying the final consonance that is with certainty awaited; in this way the longing for it is strengthened, and its appearance affords the greater satisfaction. This is clearly an analogue of the satisfaction of the will which is enhanced through delay. (*W2*, 455–6)

Many have found these ideas reflected especially in the composition of Wagner's *Tristan and Isolde*.

A popular prejudice is that music expresses the emotion of the composer or performer. But this is decidedly not Schopenhauer's view. Music, for him, has the peculiarity of expressing what might be called impersonal emotions:

> music does not express this or that particular and definite pleasure, this or that affliction, pain, sorrow, horror, gaiety, merriment, or peace of mind, but joy, pain, sorrow, horror, gaiety, merriment, peace of mind *themselves*, to a certain extent in the abstract, their essential nature, without any accessories, and so also without the motives for them. (*W1*, 261)

If a person experiences some particular joy or sorrow in life, usually some 'motive' or representation of the way things are gives rise to the emotion. Emotions tend to be about something. But Schopenhauer is proposing that in music we grasp directly and non-conceptually the essential shape, as it were, of feeling joy or sorrow, without any content—without any representation of what the emotion is about. Listeners thus recognize the pure ebb and flow of the will, of striving and satisfaction, in which their own life consists, but without their own desires being engaged, without feeling emotions themselves, and so without any risk of pain. The account remains intriguing, though we may question whether it really captures the essential nature of the emotions, or explains just how the listener is supposed to apprehend them.

Schopenhauer's other central thought about music is that it parallels the world in the range of expressions of will which it achieves. The bass is like the lowest grade of the will's objectification, 'inorganic nature, the mass of the planet' (*W1*, 258). The melody on top is analogous to 'the highest grade of the will's objectification, the intellectual life and endeavour of man' (*W1*, 259). All the parts in between, with their intervals from one another, are the various manifestations of will throughout the inorganic world and the plant and animal kingdoms. Hence, music is not merely an expression of conscious human strivings, but a copy of the will in its great diversity, and hence a re-run of the whole phenomenal world. This idea, though fanciful, is a rather fine one. Whether or not Schopenhauer's views about music can be subscribed to literally, one can understand why musicians have often been drawn to him. No other philosopher has given music such a weighty role, and few have come nearer to the impossible achievement of evoking its pleasures in a purely verbal medium.

7 Ethics: seeing the world aright

Against Kant's ethics

In Schopenhauer's view, the ethical sphere parallels the aesthetic in that prescriptive rules, and conceptual thought in general, are not the essential thing:

> Virtue is as little taught as is genius; indeed, the concept is just as unfruitful for it as it is for art, and in the case of both can be used only as an instrument. We should therefore be just as foolish to expect that our moral systems and ethics would create virtuous, noble, and holy men, as that our aesthetics would produce poets, painters, and musicians. (*W1*, 271)

This suggests that people will either have intuitive ethical insight or they will not; and we know that Schopenhauer thinks an individual's basic character cannot be altered. Moral rules, in that case, are useful only in channelling and curbing people's behaviour: you can train an egoistic person so that his or her behaviour has less disastrous consequences, but not make him or her into a good person. Since he takes this view, Schopenhauer's philosophical ethics will not itself be prescriptive. Nor will it attempt to debate whether moral laws are universally binding, or consider what reason one has to obey them, or indeed give any theory of 'moral law' at all.

Schopenhauer's ethical theory does not stand entirely under Kant's shadow, any more than his theory of knowledge or his aesthetics—yet the shadow is always present. Kant's ethics is an ethics of duty, and tries to formulate an imperative to which the actions of the ideally rational being must conform. Schopenhauer's, by contrast, is an ethics of compassion. It tries to explain the difference between good and bad in terms of a divergence of attitudes which individuals may take towards one another, and towards the world as a whole. Morality for Schopenhauer is not a matter of duty or of 'ought'; nor can it be founded in rationality. It is a matter of 'seeing the world aright', to use Wittgenstein's later phrase. But to reach his position Schopenhauer first has to argue with Kant in some detail.

The essay *On the Basis of Morality* contains a succinct and powerful discussion of Kantian ethics, in which Schopenhauer brings forward many objections, chief among them the objection that Kant's idea of an imperative, 'You ought', is a theological notion in disguise. The language in which Kant speaks here has biblical overtones, and, to the atheist Schopenhauer, the very idea of an absolute command either trades surreptitiously on the assumption of an absolute being who may issue it, or it is unfounded. When Kant later tries to show how ethics requires an idea of God, Schopenhauer is reminded of a conjuror who, to our great surprise, pulls out of the hat something which he had planted there all along (*B*, 57). On the other hand, if there is no God, we should not simply swallow the idea of an absolute, universal imperative in the first place.

To whom, in any case, would the Kantian imperative be addressed? Not to human beings as such, but to 'all rational beings'. Schopenhauer is again scathing:

> we know *reason* as the exclusive attribute of the human race, and are by no means entitled to think of it as existing outside that race, and to set up a *genus* called 'rational beings' differing from its sole species, 'man'. Still less are we justified in laying down laws for such imaginary *rational beings in the abstract* . . . We cannot help suspecting that Kant here gave a thought to the dear little angels, or at any rate counted on their presence in the conviction of the reader. (*B*, 63–4)

Kant's moral imperative has to be issued to rational beings in the abstract, because his ethics sets out to be non-empirical, and to rest wholly on principles knowable a priori—that is to say, knowable in advance of experience. But this itself is something that should be queried, according to Schopenhauer. Practical morality—decision-making and judgement—is concerned with the actual conduct of individual human beings who occupy the empirical realm. This should also be the focus of the theoretical discussion which Schopenhauer calls 'morals'. He charges that Kant's moral imperative is by contrast purely formal, and so without any 'real substance' (*B*, 76).

What about the Kantian appeal to rationality? Schopenhauer points out that rational behaviour is not always morally good behaviour: 'Reasonable and vicious are quite consistent with each other, in fact, only through their union are great and far-reaching crimes possible' (*B*, 83). In other words, if one is evil, rationality will not make one any *less* evil; it may simply make one a more efficient and deadly exponent than an evil person who cannot think straight. Reason is instrumental, concerning the means towards some end which one has. An imperative will therefore motivate a rational being to action, only if he or she has an interest or end already in view. Since *human* beings are material, striving individuals who manifest the will to life, their ends tend to be egoistic. Egoism is the 'paymaster' required to cash out any formal imperative (*B*, 89): what will rationally motivate me to act in any particular case will be considerations about whether I can achieve *my* own ends.

One final criticism is perhaps worthy of mention. Schopenhauer is affronted by Kant's idea of the 'dignity of man'—our supposed 'unconditioned incomparable value'—and by the idea that human beings must be treated as 'ends in themselves'. One ground for his criticism is that something can be a 'value' or 'end' only if it is the fulfilment of something specific that is willed. 'Unconditioned value' and 'end in itself' would in that case be disguised contradictions. More significantly, Schopenhauer finds this elevation of the human species at the expense of other animals 'revolting and abominable'. Other species are supposed to lack such dignity, and not to be ends in themselves, solely through lacking reason; but the consequence is that, in philosophical morals, animals

> are mere 'things', mere *means* to any ends whatsoever. They can therefore be used for vivisection, hunting, coursing, bull-fights, and horse racing, and can be whipped to death as they struggle along with heavy carts of stone. Shame on such a morality . . . that fails to recognize the eternal essence that exists in every living thing, and shines forth with inscrutable significance from all eyes that see the sun! (*B*, 96)

Schopenhauer sounds almost our contemporary here. At the same time, his lack of confidence in any special value attaching to humanity or to rationality is an important element in his pessimism. As we shall see, being an individual of the human species is neither a dignified nor a good thing as such.

Freedom and determinism

Schopenhauer believes that actions are caused by a combination of one's unchanging character and a motive occurring in one's consciousness. This is the basis of his claim that all actions are determined, and that, in one important sense, there is no freedom of the will. But his discussion of the issue, especially in its concentrated form in *On the Freedom of the Will*, is of considerable subtlety. As well as arguing for determinism, he makes an important distinction between different senses of 'freedom', and finishes with the reflection that the truth of determinism does not make us any less inclined to feel responsible for our actions— a fact which he rightly says still requires an explanation.

Schopenhauer brings to light a distinction, which is often overlooked, between freedom to will and freedom to act. Freedom to act is the ability to do something, if one wills to do it. This freedom can be removed by external obstacles to action, by constraining motives, laws or threats of various consequences if one acts, or by impairment of the subject's cognitive faculties. Being in prison, being at gunpoint, or having sustained brain-damage are, for example, all ways in which there can be some obstacle to one's doing what one wills. Schopenhauer accordingly lists physical freedom, moral freedom, and intellectual freedom as the three species of freedom to act. The deeper question, however, is whether I have any freedom to *will* this or that course of action. Schopenhauer arrives at his admirably straight answer to this question by examining the only two available sources of evidence: consciousness of ourselves and consciousness of things other than ourselves.

Consciousness of ourselves is powerless to tell us whether we could ever have willed otherwise than we did. In self-consciousness we are aware of doing what we want to do, by being aware of our action itself and of the motives that bring it about. But once I have chosen one course of action, say, going to Frankfurt, can I tell whether I *could* equally have chosen to go to Mannheim? The problem is this:

Everyone's self-consciousness asserts very clearly that he can do what he wills. But since we can conceive of him as willing quite opposite actions, it follows that if he so wills he can also *do* the opposite. Now the untutored understanding confuses this with the proposition that he, in a given case, can also *will* the opposite, and calls this the freedom of the will. . . . But whether in a given case he can *will* the one as well as the other . . . calls for a deeper investigation than the one which mere self-consciousness could decide (*F*, 23).

The question is not whether one can want or wish to do each of two opposite actions, but whether one could will them—remembering that (barring obstacles) willing is acting, for Schopenhauer. I went to Frankfurt, and I am aware that if it had been my will to go to Mannheim, I could have done that. The question is: could that have been my will? Schopenhauer's sensible answer is that, from examining my own knowledge of my actions and motives, I cannot decide this question.

On the other hand, if one looks at the causal relation between the external world and the subject who wills, one is bound to treat the case as one treats any other cause–effect relationship. I cannot regard myself alone as the one part of the world that is exempt from the principle of sufficient reason; so, if the state of affairs which caused me to go to Frankfurt were exactly repeated, it could only cause me to go to Frankfurt. It makes no difference that part of the cause is a process of rational deliberation. Schopenhauer contends that if my character, and the motive—my representation of reality—were to remain the same, then I could not have willed otherwise. In this sense, there is no free will. We think we have it, but all that we have is the freedom to do what we will, with which it is so easily confused.

The argument is already cogent, but the way in which Schopenhauer caps it shows his peculiar skill as a philosophical writer. Imagine a man standing on the street at six o'clock in the evening, he says, musing on the following thoughts: 'the working day is over. Now I can go for a walk, or I can go to the club; I can also climb up the tower to see the sun set'—and so on—'I also can run out of the gate, into the wide world, and never return. All of this is strictly up to me, in this I have complete freedom. But still I shall do none of these things now, but with just as free a will I shall go home to my wife.' Schopenhauer's comment?

> This is exactly as if water spoke to itself: 'I can make waves (yes! in the sea during a storm), I can rush down hill (yes! in the river bed), I can plunge down foaming and gushing (yes! in the waterfall), I can rise freely as a stream of water into the air (yes! in the fountain), I can, finally, boil away and disappear (yes! at a certain temperature); but I am doing none of these things now, and am voluntarily remaining quiet and clear water in the reflecting pond. (F, 43)

After stating his case for determinism, however, Schopenhauer reserves the right to a 'higher view'. 'For there is another fact of consciousness which until now I have left completely aside', he says: 'This is the wholly clear and certain feeling of the *responsibility* for what we do, of the accountability for our actions, which rests on the unshakable certainty that we ourselves are the doers of our deeds' (F, 93–4). As some philosophers have said recently, the truth of determinism does not take away this 'certain feeling' that we are accountable for our actions, that they are in some sense 'up to us'.

Schopenhauer now turns to a distinction in Kant's ethics, namely that between a person's empirical character and their intelligible character, 'one of the most beautiful and profound ideas brought forth by that great mind, or indeed by men at any time' (F, 96). This is another aspect of the backbone distinction between appearance and thing in itself with which we have dealt all along:

> the empirical character, like the whole man, is a mere appearance as an object of experience, and hence bound to the forms of all appearance—time, space, and causality—and subject to their laws. On the other hand, the condition and the basis of this whole appearance . . . is his intelligible character, i.e. his will as thing in itself. It is to the will in this capacity that freedom, and to be sure even absolute freedom, that is, independence of the law of causality (as a mere form of appearances), properly belongs. (F, 97)

The basic idea is quite simple: if I cannot escape from causal necessity as part of empirical reality, then an aspect of me that is beyond empirical reality may do so. Schopenhauer points out that when we hold someone accountable we blame the person for his or her character, or for what he or she *is*, using actions merely as evidence for this. He suggests that I must be responsible for what I am—my intelligible character behind appearances, from which issue all my actions. Freedom is not eliminated, but moved out of the empirical realm.

Here Schopenhauer faces some serious problems. One is that, on his own view, my character is inborn and unchanging. In what sense can I then be responsible for being what I am? Another problem is that *I* seem to disappear from the world in itself. The thing in itself is not split up into individuals—a crucial claim throughout Schopenhauer's philosophy. '*My* will as thing in itself', my intelligible character, ought not to be separate from the world as whole; and so it is hard to see how I could be held responsible for 'what I am in myself'. Schopenhauer is right in saying that we do regard a person as responsible for actions, thinking of the person as their true source, regardless of their place in a causal chain of events. But, although his may be an acute diagnosis of the problem of free will, Schopenhauer's solution is not really credible.

Egoism and compassion

What then is the true basis of morals, according to Schopenhauer? The answer may be given in three stages. One concerns the single principle which, he claims, all moral actions conform to, namely: 'Injure no one; on the contrary, help everyone as much as you can' (which he gives in Latin: *Neminem laede, imo omnes quantum potes, juva.*) The second stage of the answer is an attempt to explain the basic psychological attitude which alone can spur people on to moral actions, namely compassion or sympathy. Ultimately, however, the basis of morals is not reached until the third stage, in which we are given a metaphysical account of how the compassionate attitude is both possible and justified.

The '*Neminem laede*' principle can be broken into two parts: 'Injure no one' and 'Help everyone as much as you can'. Actions which conform to the first part Schopenhauer calls instances of voluntary justice, while those which conform to the second are instances of disinterested philanthropy, or 'loving-kindness' towards other human beings (and presumably towards animals too: in line with his earlier censure of Kant, Schopenhauer adduces the fact that we *do* feel compassion towards animals (B, 175–8)). No action except those of pure justice or philanthropy can count as having true moral worth (B, 138–9). Schopenhauer takes it as a premiss that such acts, however rare and surprising, are acknowledged to occur, and are universally regarded as being good. Examples range from self-sacrifice in battle to someone's returning a lost object which they could have kept without any consequences, or giving alms to a beggar when they stand to gain nothing from doing so. Justice and philanthropy both stem from compassion, which manifests itself either as pure concern to promote the well-being of another, or as pure distress at the suffering of another.

Every human being, according to Schopenhauer, has some element of compassion in their character (B, 192). But there are vast differences in the proportion of compassion with which we are endowed. Some are overflowing with it, some have virtually none in them. Schopenhauer thinks that only actions from compassion have moral worth, and that we judge primarily what a person *is*, using their actions merely as evidence. If we follow him in all this, we shall have to admit that some human beings are greatly more good than others, and that some, though they might occasionally act from compassion, are not good. Whether or not that is a problem, it pales into insignificance compared with the difficulty of explaining how, on his view, compassion is possible at all, and how it can be an incentive to action.

If some part of everyone's make-up is compassion, what is the rest? Schopenhauer's claim in full is this:

> Man's three fundamental ethical incentives, egoism, malice, and compassion, are present in everyone in different and incredibly unequal proportions. In accordance with them, motives will operate on man and actions will ensue. (B, 192)

Schopenhauer helps us with a succinct explanation of the three incentives. Compassion is the incentive to seek the well-being of another (or to alleviate their woe). Malice is the incentive to seek the woe of another; egoism that to seek one's own well-being. We may wonder whether the logic of this triad is quite right: is not malice really a kind of self-seeking, a kind of egoism? In Schopenhauer's defence, the reply must be that some malice at least is not egoistic. Much that we can set down as cruelty is done at the behest of one's own gain in some form or other: it is then a means to an egoistic end. But what Schopenhauer means by pure malice is something as exceptional as pure philanthropy: the kind of depraved or 'devilish' action where the agent sets aside his or her own well-being as an aim, simply in order to harm someone else (*B*, 136)—what one might call disinterested malice. The triad of egoism, malice, and compassion, is thus a genuine threesome, although many cruel and wicked actions do not arise from malice proper.

Nevertheless it is the egoistic incentive that compassion most has to contend with, because it is egoism that makes up the bulk of each individual: 'The chief and fundamental incentive in man as in the animal is *egoism*, that is, the craving for existence and well-being' (*B*, 131). Each individual is a material organism in which will to life expresses itself: hence striving for one's own ends is fundamental to each individual. Indeed, so fundamental is it on Schopenhauer's theory that one must wonder how compassionate action is possible at all. If action is always a bodily striving of the individual towards some end of its own, compassion, which is supposedly the only genuine moral incentive, ought never to move any individual to action. Egoism is 'colossal' and 'natural':

> every individual, completely vanishing and reduced to nothing in a boundless world, nevertheless makes himself the centre of the world, and considers his own existence and well-being before everything else. In fact, from the natural standpoint, he is ready for this to sacrifice everything else; he is ready to annihilate the world, in order to maintain his own self, that drop in the ocean, a little longer. This disposition is *egoism*, which is essential to everything in nature. (*W1*, 332)

Egoism 'towers over the world' (*B*, 132) to such an extent that, without the constraint of laws embodied in the State, individuals would be engaged in *bellum omnium contra omnes*, a war of all against all (*B*, 133). All this suggests that action motivated by pure concern for the well-being of others should be not only rare, but so contrary to our nature as to be impossible. Schopenhauer has to admit that compassion is one of the mysteries of ethics. His only choice is to say that compassion is a primitive anti-egoistic trait which, as a matter of sheer fact, is present in us. But how compassion can 'reside in human nature' (*B*, 149) is deeply mysterious given that the human being is a naturally egoistic expression of will to life.

The metaphysics of morals

The final stage of Schopenhauer's ethics, however, seeks to rest the compassionate attitude on a metaphysical foundation. Compassion turns out to reflect a view of oneself and the nature of reality which differs from that implicit in egoism, and is superior to it. Schopenhauer can thus say that compassion is a good thing not only because it tends to decrease the sum of suffering in the world, but because it embodies a truer metaphysical picture.

The initial thought is that it is possible for me to feel compassion only if 'to a certain extent I have identified myself with the other person, and in consequence the barrier between the I and the non-I is for the moment abolished' (*B*, 166). Schopenhauer takes rather literally the idea contained in 'compassion' or 'sympathy' (German *Mitleid*) that one person 'suffers with' another. Thought for my well-being has to yield its place in my motivation to thought for another's well-being; and it would be inexplicable how that could happen unless I could make the other's suffering and well-being intimately my own concern. Only if I share your suffering, in some sense feeling it as my own, can your well-being, or the alleviation of your woe, come to motivate me. To be compassionate, someone must, says Schopenhauer, 'make less of a distinction than do the rest between himself and others' (*B*, 204).

But now he can argue that the compassionate person is committed to a different metaphysical view:

> The *bad* man everywhere feels a thick partition between himself and everything outside him. The world to him is an *absolute non-I* and his relation to it is primarily hostile.... The

good character, on the other hand, lives in an external world
that is homogeneous with his own true being. The others are
not non-I for him, but an 'I once more'. His fundamental relation to everyone is, therefore, friendly; he feels himself intimately akin to all beings, takes an immediate interest in their
weal and woe, and confidently assumes the same sympathy in
them. (*B*, 211)

Which is the correct view of the world? The appearance/thing in
itself dichotomy will tell us. From the point of view of the world
of representation, governed by space and time which are the
principle of individuation, reality consists of separate individuals,
of which any moral agent is one. So the person who thinks 'Each
individual is a being radically different from all others . . . everything else is non-I and foreign to me' (*B*, 210), is right about the
world of appearance. But beneath this lies the world as thing in
itself, which is not split up into individuals, but just is *the
world*—whatever there ultimately is. So the supposedly more
profound view is the one which considers individuation to be
'mere phenomenon' rather than ultimately part of reality. From
this point of view, no one is distinct from anything else in the
world, and so can recognize 'in *another* his own self, his own true
inner nature' (*B*, 209). Schopenhauer's Indian thoughts come to
the fore suddenly: the conception of the world as composed of
separate individuals is *Mâyâ*—'i.e. illusion, deception, phantasm,
mirage' (*B*, 209), while knowledge of the deeper, more correct,
non-individuating view, is expressed in the Sanskrit *tat tvam asi*:
this art thou (*B*, 210).

At first sight this idea seems so extreme as to expunge the
possibility of compassion altogether. If I really believed that you
were not distinct from me, the attitude with which I regarded you
could only be a strange kind of egoism. Genuine compassion, on
the other hand, surely presupposes belief in distinctness as a
minimum condition. An even more graphic objection is that, if
the world in itself is without individuation, it does not even
contain *me*: it certainly does not contain me as this bodily, willing
human being, nor does it contain the thinking 'I' that I regard
myself as being from a subjective point of view. It is hard to see
how the belief in the illusoriness of all individuals, including the

individual which I am, could support a compassionate attitude between the individual that I am and the individual beggar to whom I give money.

But perhaps this is too simplistic a response. What Schopenhauer has recognized is the possibility of an attitude to the world which does not take one's existence as a particular individual to be of paramount significance: a 'universal standpoint' as opposed to a particular one (*W2*, 599–600). In order to adopt this standpoint, one need not abandon the belief in separate individuals altogether. Compassion is supposed to motivate actions which one must carry out as an individual, towards other individuals. What might ground such actions is the idea that, though individuals are separate, there is nothing of any fundamental importance about the individual which I am. If the beggar and I are both equal portions of the same underlying reality, equal manifestations of the same will to life, then from the point of view of the world as a whole, it is a matter of indifference whether my ends are promoted and the beggar's thwarted, or vice versa. This thought seems genuinely capable of grounding a compassionate outlook. The belief that I simply am not an individual separate from the rest of reality is not what does the work here; rather it is that, though being an individual (and naturally egoistic) thing in the world, my perspective does not always have to be one of identification with the individual that I am. As in Schopenhauer's account of aesthetic experience, I need not accept the natural standpoint of individuality as the one from which I must always regard things. In the next chapter we shall see that the individual's renunciation of his or her individuality not only makes aesthetic value and moral worth possible for Schopenhauer, but is the only attitude which can compensate for his or her existing at all.

8 Existence and pessimism

Ineliminable suffering

Awakened to life out of the night of unconsciousness, the will finds itself as an individual in an endless and boundless world, among innumerable individuals, all striving, suffering, and erring; and, as if through a troubled dream, it hurries back to the old unconsciousness. Yet till then its desires are unlimited, its claims inexhaustible, and every satisfied desire gives birth to a new one. No possible satisfaction in the world could suffice to still its craving, set a final goal to its demands, and fill the bottomless pit of its heart. In this connexion, let us now consider what as a rule comes to man in satisfactions of any kind; it is often nothing more than the bare maintenance of this very existence, extorted daily with unremitting effort and constant care in conflict with misery and want, and with death in prospect. Everything in life proclaims that earthly happiness is destined to be frustrated, or recognized as an illusion. The grounds for this lie deep in the very nature of things. (*W2*, 573)

The Fourth Book of the *World as Will and Representation* is its austere final movement. Schopenhauer's style matches the greater seriousness of the discussion (*W1*, 271), which, together with the topics in ethics we have already looked at, addresses—to use a hackneyed phrase—the human condition itself. Few writers have the insight and eloquence to make a philosophically interesting contribution in this area, but Schopenhauer is undoubtedly one of them.

Schopenhauer looks around the world and finds it full of suffering—frustration, tedium, pain, and misery. It might be thought that this is just a matter of personal propensity. Someone else might point out the occurrence of good fortune, innocent joy, contentment, and reward for honest toil—so is not Schopenhauer merely carrying out a highly selective inventory? If so, his pessimism would be superficial and gratuitous. But this is not the case. Whether we agree with him or not, he has arguments for

85

far-reaching conclusions about the value that can attach to human existence. It must contain suffering, and cannot be preferable to non-existence. It would even have been better for reality not to have existed. These claims make Schopenhauer a pessimist in a philosophically interesting sense.

The first point is that suffering is ineliminably present in the existence of any human individual. As material, living creatures, our ordinary existence is such that we must strive towards ends. But, Schopenhauer argues, a being who strives, and who is conscious of his or her ends and of whether they are fulfilled, is a being who suffers. Part of this can be understood in terms of egoism. Among a multitude of individuals, each of whom must strive in order to exist, conflicts of ends will occur, and, barring the mysterious intervention of compassion, suffering will result. Since compassion is not ubiquitous, nor even widespread, one's life as a human individual among others will be very likely to contain episodes in which one suffers, and episodes in which one brings about suffering.

However, willing itself is closely intertwined with suffering in another way. First, willing could not spring from a state of total sufficiency and contentment. A being strives only if it experiences a lack or deficiency, and experiencing a lack is already a form of suffering. Secondly, in the course of events one does not attain some of the ends for which one strives. If one does not achieve an end, one's original lack is prolonged, which, together with the consciousness of not achieving one's end, is further suffering. Perhaps we can imagine a being that was always successful in its strivings—but that is of little help to Schopenhauer. For what happens when we achieve an end towards which our striving has been directed? The resulting state is called satisfaction or happiness; but, he claims, this state is of value only relative to the deficiency which it removes. Satisfaction can occur only in a being that has suffered, and it has any value only relative to some particular episode of suffering. Schopenhauer puts the point by saying that satisfaction is negative, and pain positive. Pain is something which we feel, but satisfaction is an absence; to be satisfied is simply to return to neutral by wiping out a felt deficiency. And the mere state of feeling no deficiencies, and so having nothing to strive for, has no positive value in its own terms. If it continues for any length of time it is simply boredom, which Schopenhauer often mentions as one of the pervasive features of life. Finally, the attainment of ends never makes striving cease altogether. 'Every satisfied desire gives birth to a new one': whatever striving of ours is successful, we shall soon continue to strive for further ends, and hence to suffer further. Therefore, striving cannot eliminate suffering as such. While we exist, nothing we can undertake to *do* will stop us from willing, or, therefore, from having to suffer.

It is important for Schopenhauer that life's containing suffering is not redeemed by suffering's having any positive point. Many lives, as a matter of fact, strike a balance between suffering and contentment which suffices to make them bearable:

> This is the life of almost all men; they will, they know what they will, and they strive after this with enough success to protect them from despair, and enough failure to preserve them from boredom and its consequences. (*W1*, 327)

But if we consider simply that there is suffering, and ask whether existence containing suffering is something good, we cannot say that suffering is redeemed by some good over and above existence itself. If suffering in general is to be redeemed, it must be by its being simply good to exist as a human individual, come what may. And, as we shall see, that is something which Schopenhauer denies outright. But so far, if we accept Schopenhauer's argument, we can at least conclude that the happiness attainable by any human being must be bound up with suffering. To imagine an existence free of suffering is to imagine an existence that is not that of a human individual.

Death

What attitude should any of us take towards the most obvious fact about our existence: that it will cease? We do tend to fear death, not on any good rational ground, according to Schopenhauer, but because we are manifestations of will to life: a 'boundless attachment to life' is inborn in us as much as it is in all animals (*W2*, 465). We might be right to fear dying, if that process involved pain, but then the object of fear would be pain, rather than being dead. Schopenhauer presents a couple of familiar arguments for the view that fear of being dead is irrational. One is the argument from symmetry: we did not exist for an infinite time before birth, and that is a matter of indifference to us, so we ought to regard similarly our not existing again. The other is Epicurus' argument that precisely *because* it involves our non-existence, death should not be feared: to something that does not exist, it cannot matter that it does not exist.

Schopenhauer does, however, offer a more positive consolation. He accepts that death is the cessation of the individual human being, but maintains that this is not the only way in which it should be regarded. The opinion of many in contemporary Europe vacillates between the view of death as absolute annihilation and the notion of immortality. But both opinions are 'equally false' (*W2*, 464). This becomes apparent from a 'higher standpoint' which once again exploits the distinction between thing in itself and phenomenon. The individual that I am is merely part of the world of phenomena. It occupies certain portions of space for a certain time, after which it ceases to exist. From the point of view of the individual, death is annihilation, and it would be absolute annihilation of me, if this particular phenomenal individual were all that I am. However, if I am also something in myself, outside all time and change, then death cannot be my end:

> the greatest equivocation really lies in the word 'I' . . . According as I understand this word, I can say: 'Death is my entire end'; or else: 'This my personal phenomenal appearance is just as infinitely small a part of my true inner nature as I am of the world.' (*W2*, 491)

'My true inner nature' here must refer to the same thing as 'the world', because reality *in itself* is not subject to any individuation. The 'higher standpoint' thus yields the thought that I am the world; and, thinking this, one can take the supposedly consoling view that the ephemeral individual to which 'I' usually refers is really not worth worrying about.

Once again Schopenhauer is trying to loosen the hold of the usual identification which we make of ourselves with an individual. The world manifests itself as me here and now, but after I cease to exist, the same world will manifest itself in the same way as other individuals of the same species, each of which will find itself as the subject of consciousness, refer to itself as 'I', pursue its ends, experience suffering and satisfaction, and cease to exist in turn. Reality in itself, I am supposed to think, is indifferent between one such manifestation of will and another. Nature itself does not grieve over the destruction of any particular part of itself, and will carry on existing without me. If I share with all other phenomena the same 'inner nature', then the very core of what I am carries on, regardless of the passing of phenomena. Indeed, 'carries on' is a misleading way to put Schopenhauer's point. Reality in itself is eternal in the sense of timelessness. I have my 'now', and every other phenomenon that was or will be has its time, which for it is equally a 'now'. But from the point of view of reality in itself, time is an illusion. Hence the phenomenal fact that some particular thing will not exist later than now is not a fact about reality in itself.

Two concerns arise here: that this may not be convincing as an exercise in metaphysics, and that it might fail to be consoling even if it were thus convincing. The notion that the thing in itself is undifferentiated and timeless stems from Schopenhauer's ideal-ist doctrine of space and time, and may well be questioned if we have doubts about that doctrine. The really troublesome point, however, is the idea that *I* am somehow present in the timeless, undifferentiated world. Schopenhauer has previously told us that 'I' refers to the material, striving, human being, and to the pure subject of consciousness which we find ourselves as, and which would not exist were it not for the human being with his or her bodily organs. But how could anything to which 'I' refers remain if the human being ceased to exist, taking with it the subject's consciousness? What we said when discussing the compassionate person's non-egoistic world-view applies again to the higher per-spective on death: it is impossible to find *myself* in the picture of ultimate reality that it requires.

The question whether Schopenhauer's higher view of death could be consoling is a difficult one. He tries to inculcate the thought that one's own death has no great significance in the order of things. But if one accepted his reasons for taking this attitude, ought one not to think that one's life has just as little significance? And is that a consoling thought? Schopenhauer appears to think so:

> death is the great opportunity no longer to be I . . . Dying is the moment of that liberation from the one-sidedness of an individuality which does not constitute the innermost kernel of our true being, but is rather to be thought of as a kind of aberration thereof. (*W2*, 507–8)

In fact, Schopenhauer recognizes two distinct outlooks for which his view of death might be a consolation. The first, the *affirmation of the will to life*, is the outlook of someone who would, as it were, stand on the earth with 'firm, strong bones':

> A man . . . who found satisfaction in life and took perfect delight in it; who desired, in spite of calm deliberation, that the course of his life as he had hitherto experienced it should be of endless duration or of constant recurrence; and whose courage to face life was so great that, in return for life's pleasures, he would willingly and gladly put up with all the hardships and miseries to which it is subject. (*W1*, 283–4)

This person could be consoled by Schopenhauer's doctrine of our indestructibility by death: 'Armed with the knowledge we confer on him, he would look with indifference at death hastening towards him on the wings of time. He would consider it as a false illusion' (*W1*, 284). Such a person would think that living as an individual is fine, but that the cessation of this life is powerless to detract from that.

Schopenhauer suggests that suicide stems from this same attitude of affirmation towards life. The explanation of this (which seems at first bizarre) is as follows: if I regard the pleasures of life as of positive value, despite its pains, I always run the risk that life's pains will come to outweigh its pleasures. If I continue to want life for its potential positive side, but come to believe that only suffering is available, the solution is to stop living. However,

> Far from being denial of the will, suicide is a phenomenon of the will's strong affirmation. For denial has its essential nature in the fact that the pleasures of life, not its sorrows, are shunned. The suicide wills life, and is dissatisfied merely with the conditions on which it has come to him. Therefore he gives

up by no means the will to life, but merely life, since he destroys the individual phenomenon. (*W1*, 398)

Thus the character who wills the endless recurrence of his or her life (from whom, again, Nietzsche seems to have learned something), and the character who ends his or her life when suffering becomes too great, really take one and the same stance of affirmation. Both, though, would be missing something else: they would not have come to know the truth as Schopenhauer sees it, that 'constant suffering is essential to all life' (*W1*, 283). The alternative outlook, which encompasses this truth, consists in the *denial of the will to life*. Recognizing that suffering pervades any existence as an individual manifestation of will to life, and that achieving ends can never be divorced from suffering, this attitude ceases to look for any positive value in the life of the individual human being, even from its passing moments of satisfaction. This provides a unique attitude to death:

> to die willingly, to die gladly, to die cheerfully, is the prerogative of the resigned, of him who gives up and denies the will to life. . . . He willingly gives up the existence that we know; what comes to him instead of it is in our eyes *nothing*, because our existence in reference to that one is *nothing*. The Buddhist faith calls that existence *Nirvana*, that is to say, extinction. (*W2*, 508)

Denial of the will

The will to life must be denied—'if salvation is to be attained from an existence like ours' (*W1*, 405). Salvation is a religious doctrine, and Schopenhauer is keen to link his philosophical discussion with Christianity, Brahmanism, and Buddhism, claiming that the core of all these religions, leaving aside mythical trappings and recent doctrinal accretions, is really the same. Even God is not to the point: the philosophical import is available to an atheist quite as much as to a theist (*W1*, 385), and is that we must renounce, or say No to, our nature as human beings, if we are to find true value in existing. The real self is the will to life (*W2*, 606), and since this is also what must be denied, salvation lies in self-denial or self-renunciation. 'In fact', he says, 'nothing else can be stated as the aim of our existence except the knowledge that it would be better for us not to exist'. (*W2*, 605)

In 'denial of the will to life', one turns against the particular manifestation of will to life found in oneself, which means turning against the body, and against one's own individuality. Thus one ceases, as much as possible, to strive for one's own egoistic ends, ceases to avoid suffering or to seek pleasure, ceases to desire propagation of the species, or any sexual gratification—in short, one looks down on that willing part of nature which one is, and withdraws from one's identification with it. Such an apparently unpalatable state is made to seem worthy of attainment by Schopenhauer's elevated prose:

> we can infer how blessed must be the life of a man whose will is silenced not for a few moments, as in the enjoyment of the beautiful, but for ever, indeed completely extinguished, except for the last glimmering spark that maintains the body and is extinguished with it. Such a man who, after many bitter struggles with his own nature, has at last completely conquered, is then left only as pure knowing being, as the undimmed mirror or the world. Nothing can distress or alarm him any more; nothing can any longer move him; for he has cut all the thousand threads of willing which hold us bound to the world, and which as craving, fear, envy, and anger drag us here and there in constant pain. (*W1*, 390)

> Then, instead of the restless pressure and effort; instead of the constant transition from desire to apprehension and from joy to sorrow; instead of the never-satisfied and never-dying hope that constitutes the life-dream of the man who wills, we see that peace that is higher than all reason, that ocean-like calmness of the spirit, that deep tranquillity, that unshakable confidence and serenity, whose mere reflection in the countenance, as depicted by Raphael and Correggio, is a complete and certain gospel. Only knowledge remains; the will has vanished. (*W1*, 411)

Despite its kinship with the tranquil contemplation of the beautiful, the denial of the will is not to be reached by an aesthetic route. It is reached first by a saintly life, one whose justice and philanthropy arise from the insight that egoism, individuation, and the whole phenomenal world are a kind of delusion. The supposed knowledge that all things are identical at the level of the 'in itself' leads to the total surrender of egoism, and to the embracing of all suffering as one's own. This 'knowledge of the whole' then becomes the '*quieter* of all and every willing' (*W1*, 379), and turns the will against its natural state of self-affirmation. Another, secondary route to the same state is through suffering itself. This is more common, according to Schopenhauer, since the saintly life is not only rare, but extremely hard to sustain in the face of the allurements of the will (*W1*, 392). There are those, however, in real life or in tragic art, whose own individual pain is of such duration or intensity that their will to life is broken. Then, as a 'gleam of silver that suddenly appears from the purifying flame of suffering', the state of salvation may arrive in which they renounce all their desires, rise above themselves and above suffering in a state of 'inviolable peace, bliss and sublimity'. (*W1*, 392–3)

Schopenhauer points to numerous practices and experiences which he thinks bear out his descriptions of self-renunciation:

> Quietism, i.e. the giving up of all willing, asceticism, i.e. intentional mortification of one's own will, and mysticism, i.e. consciousness of the identity of one's own inner being with that of all things, or with the kernel of the world, stand in the closest connexion, so that whoever professes one of them is gradually led to the acceptance of the others, even against his intention. Nothing can be more surprising than the agreement among the writers who express those teachings, in spite of the greatest difference of their age, country, and religion. (*W2*, 613)

The ascetic, not content with willing the well-being of others, actively seeks to counter the ends of the will as it expresses itself in the body. ('One's own woe' is thus a fourth *incentive* to action, to be set alongside those of egoism, malice, and compassion (*W2*, 607).) Schopenhauer describes the ascetic thus: 'His body, healthy and strong, expresses the sexual impulse through the genitals, but he denies the will, and gives the lie to the body' (*W1*, 380). Voluntary abstention from sexual activity—that most powerful manifestation of will to life—is accompanied by intentional poverty, non-avoidance of injury or ignominy from others, fasting,

Existence and pessimism

self-castigation, and self-torture. Since all these occurrences are pursued as deliberate ends, asceticism cannot be identical with total will-lessness. The latter must occur unpredictably as the 'sudden gleam of silver' arising out of suffering; one can deliberately engineer suffering, but true salvation does not come about by intention or design.

Mysticism, meanwhile, is simply 'consciousness of the identity of one's own inner being with that of all things'. Schopenhauer claims to have arrived at a philosophical delineation of the state which mystics achieve in subjective experience. But since this experience cannot be communicated, he arrives at the limits of philosophy:

> when my teaching reaches its highest point, it assumes a *negative* character, and so ends with a negation. Thus it can speak here only of what is denied or given up. . . . Now it is precisely here that the mystic proceeds positively, and therefore, from this point, nothing is left but mysticism. (*W2*, 612)

Schopenhauer's book, having begun with the words 'The world . . .', does indeed end with '—Nothing'. The phenomenal world is negated by those whose will has turned against it, and they embrace sheer nothingness in return; but then, from their altered point of view, the whole of this world can be set at nought. Having given up placing any positive value in the human round of happiness and suffering, the will-less subject finds a new value in the very rejection of what has ordinary human value.

However sympathetic or unsympathetic we may be to Schopenhauer's final doctrine, we must surely worry whether it is really coherent at all. We have often enough questioned whether I can think of *myself* as existing in a world deprived of all differentiation between individuals. But, even setting that aside, someone might ask: how can I acquiesence in a tranquil vision of my identity with the kernel of the world, if that kernel is the detested will to life, the very thing which it is so desirable for me to escape? There is, however, a reply to this worry. We must not forget Schopenhauer's distinction between knowing and willing. To *know* the whole world as an all-pervading, purposeless will to life is not the same as colluding with that will as it expresses itself in one's own body—it is not the same as willing on behalf of this particular individual. Salvation is achieved by knowledge for Schopenhauer, but not by knowledge that any good state of affairs obtains. To see the world as a whole from which I am not distinct is of value because it liberates me from the treadmill of striving, happiness, and suffering—but not because I come to understand the world as a good thing. The world is not a good thing, and nor am I, for Schopenhauer. But some value can be salvaged if I stand back and know the terrible place from a universal standpoint, rather than carrying on willing in unquestioning identification with one small part of it.

A final concern about the denial of the will is whether it is always bound to be an act of will. If I have a choice whether to affirm or deny my will to life, then, at some higher level, I must be willing to deny the will. This would not be a contradiction if the 'higher' willing, which discriminates between affirmation and denial, was of a kind not subordinate to the will to life: I could then decide at will to deny my will to life. But if Schopenhauer were to think that all willing is a form of will to life, and that the denial of will to life is something I undertake at will, then his position would be quite incoherent. The best resolution of this problem is to say that denial of the will simply occurs in a subject, and is not a consciously undertaken act. One's natural compassion for every being, or the degree of one's suffering, overcome one's egoism to such an extent that it becomes impossible to strive any longer for the ends that arise out of one's own parochial existence. His other description of this is 'the will to life turning against itself'. At the end of the *World as Will and Representation* he writes not of 'those who have denied the will', but of 'those in whom the will has turned and denied itself' (*W1*, 412). It is important that the agency here is not straightforwardly *mine*. Just as it is not I who originlly throw myself into life, so it is not I who turn against the will to life. The 'agent' here is the will to life, which turns against itself. So denial of the will really is *not* an act of will of the person in whom it happens. However, Schopenhauer sometimes writes as if it were. Those in whom the will has turned must constantly 'struggle' against affirmation of the will, which is the body's natural state; they must 'strive with all their might to keep to this path by self-imposed renunciations of every kind' (*W1*, 391). The will to life within in me is recalcitrant, and reverts to affirming itself, even if it has previously been broken by saintliness or intense suffering, so here is a case where *I* must continue to will its denial after all.

Pessimism

Schopenhauer's philosophical pessimism resides in two connected theses: that for each individual it would have been better not to have been born, and that the world as a whole is the worst of all possible worlds. The argument for the first starts from the point that, for the ordinary, striving human being, life must contain suffering, and from the claim that all satisfaction is purely of negative value, being the cessation of suffering. Schopenhauer moves from here to the idea that no satisfaction achievable within human existence can compensate for the suffering that it must also contain. It is as if, in the balance, no satisfaction can weigh anything at all by comparison with any suffering, however small. The mere existence of evil in the world makes it something whose non-existence is preferable to its existence—we should wish, not only not to have come into existence ourselves, but that this world in which we must suffer had not come about (*W2*, 576). All in all, our condition is 'something that it were better should not be' (*W2*, 577).

Now this argument is not one that we have to accept. It is quite plausible that our life has no purpose, that it must contain suffering, and that no satisfactions can ever expunge the evil of any single pain: in this sense the line Schopenhauer quotes from Petrarch, '*mille piacer' non vagliono un tormento*', 'a thousand pleasures do not compensate for one pain' (*W2*, 576), is correct. Also, it may be true that existence is *not guaranteed* to be better than non-existence. And if, as Schopenhauer claims—again with some plausibility—'nine-tenths of mankind live in constant conflict with want, always balancing themselves with difficulty and effort on the brink of destruction' (*W2*, 584), then the total of individual lives that are better than non-existence may be much smaller than we like to think. Still it does not follow that everyone should consider their actual existence worse than non-existence. The crucial premiss needed for this is that *any* suffering contained in a life makes non-existence preferable to it. But this step commits us to thinking that seventy years of content-ment are rendered worthless by a single episode of pain—and that is surely incredible. We should question more strenuously the idea that all satisfaction is negative—the idea that while pain is *felt*, satisfaction is a mere restitution of neutrality. It is true that however many parts of one's life are happy, they do not take away the pain of the parts in which one suffers. But it should be equally true that the mere fact of suffering does not take away the value of the parts in which one does not suffer, which may happen to be quite numerous.

Schopenhauer is scathing about optimism, the view that this is the best of all possible worlds—'The absurdity is glaring!' he says (*W2*, 581). His strongest attack is the argument that this is rather the worst of all possible worlds, which goes as follows: 'Take "possible" to mean "what can actually exist and last". Then, since "this world is arranged as it had to be if it were to be capable of continuing with great difficulty to exist" (*W2*, 583), we can see that a worse world than this could not continue to exist. There-fore, this is the worst world that is possible.' This is a curious argument. Schopenhauer cites a number of pieces of evidence for the claim that the world is continuing to exist only with great difficulty. Nine-tenths of the human race live on the margins of extinction, many species have entirely disappeared, a very small change in temperature or the composition of the atmosphere would extinguish life altogether, the planet could easily be de-stroyed by collisions within the solar system, or by the forces beneath its own crust. So perhaps there are many possible worlds that are more remote from catastrophe than the present one—and if so, it may be salutary to be informed of that. But we can clearly imagine many changes distinctly for the worse in this world which would fall short of destroying it or its inhabitants. Many people nowadays believe the environment is becoming gradually less and less favourable for life. But if Schopenhauer were right, this view would be untenable: the end of the world would have to be as nigh now as it ever could be—and there appears no reason to accept this extreme view.

Schopenhauer's arguments for these extreme pessimist doctrines therefore fail to convince. However, his pessimism succeeds in advancing something less extreme and wholly believable, which is this: to think that we are *meant* not to suffer, that we somehow deserve happiness, or that the world owes us the fulfilment of our purposes, is a mistake—as is also the belief that being alive is simply a good a thing, whatever it brings. His protracted, moving discussions of the vanity or worthlessness (*Nichtigkeit*) of life enable us to escape from these optimistic delusions into a view which is harder, but arguably more humane: that life itself has no purpose, that suffering is always part of it, and that its end may sometimes be welcomed.

Despite this, it is sometimes suggested that Schopenhauer is not in the end a genuine pessimist at all. For it is not as if he really thinks that no value is ever attainable in life. Aesthetic contemplation, artistic genius, a life of philanthropy and justice, asceticism, and renunciation of the will, all are supreme values awaiting some human individuals, at least. The individual who escapes from the will achieves nothing less than 'salvation', which seems to be a state whose value is unassailable. All of this is true; but it conflicts with 'pessimism' only if you think pessimism is the view that nothing is of any value at all. It does not conflict with Schopenhauer's views that non-existence would have been preferable and that the world is the worst possible world. The values of will-lessness are genuine, but only by being, according to Schopenhauer, some amelioration of the worst situation possible. Someone might object that a worse world still would be one in which even the salvation of will-less resignation was not open to us. But Schopenhauer's reply would be that in that case existence would be so intolerable that no one who really understood its nature would be able to endure it. It would, in that sense, not be a possible existence.

Finally, even Schopenhauer's notion of salvation must itself be called pessimistic in a definite sense, if we consider that the only value worthy of the name in his scheme of things depends upon self-renunciation. Resignation and aesthetic tranquillity are achieved by an attitude of detachment from the human individual that strives for life, and from the whole tapestry of ends that are woven into life. If this living individual remains *what I am* in the world of representation, and will to life *what I am* in myself—no immaterial soul, no rational essence, no part of any divine plan— then *what I am* is not only worthless, but is the very obstacle that must be broken down before true value is glimpsed. To feel the full weight of Schopenhauer's *solution* to the problem of existence is thus to encounter a kind of self-loathing in which dwells the deepest pessimism of all.

9 Schopenhauer's influence

Schopenhauer regarded himself as building a philosophical system which unfolded a 'single thought' (*W1*, xii). But the system, which is vulnerable to many criticisms, has not usually been the basis of his appeal. His lasting importance as a philosopher rests more on his manner of unfettered probing and blunt questioning, on his demolition of traditional certainties and on the new insecurities he confronts. The old ideas of the immortal soul, the divine purpose, and the dignity of man have died, for Schopenhauer, and should not be revived. The human species is a part of nature, and rationality gives it no especially elevated status. The human individual is embodied and restlessly active, an animal who strives and suffers, whose core is sexuality and egoism. The identity of the individual becomes problematic through and through. Our mind is that of an organism adapted to the ends of living, and is split between the conscious, knowing, and seemingly unworldly self with which we try to identify, and the unconscious, natural will which seems alien but is truly what drives us on. Life has no purpose. Being ourselves is not something which has any positive value. Schopenhauer argues himself into a predicament in which existence itself is a problem, and then presents the exceptions of genius and saintliness, aesthetic experience and the submergence of individuality, as the only ways of salvaging value. Such uncomfortable, challenging thoughts represent his distinctive contribution to modern culture.

Although there has never really been a Schopenhauerian school of philosophy, his influence on the history of thought has been both great and varied. In the late nineteenth and early twentieth centuries he was at the forefront of European culture: his books were widely read, provided the material for many academic dissertations and published treatises, and were seized upon with enthusiasm by intellectuals and artists. He had some philosophical followers, but was perhaps more notable for attracting people who fell in love with his writing, turned over or wrestled with his thoughts, and then put them to their own creative use. In the

1850s Wagner fell under the Schopenhauerian spell, which became a major stimulant in the writing of *Tristan and Isolde* in particular. In the 1860s something similar happened to Nietzsche, and to Tolstoy; in the 1880s and 1890s he was read by Thomas Hardy, Thomas Mann, and Marcel Proust, and in the 1900s by the young Wittgenstein. We find characters in *Buddenbrooks* and *À la Recherche du temps perdu* who read Schopenhauer, or discuss reading him; and he is mentioned in *Tess of the d'Urbervilles*. In all, there are many more notable artworks than can be catalogued here which bear the stamp of Schopenhauer's thinking, some directly, some more obliquely. The list of artists who became involved with his philosophy could continue for example, with Mahler, Richard Strauss, Turgenev, Lawrence, Beckett, and Borges.

Schopenhauer's appeal cannot be divorced from his own stature as a literary writer. His beautiful prose and his grasp of structure and drama—every step in the narrative marked by a powerful image and timed for maximum effect—make the transition from philosophical system to novel or opera stage almost as smooth as it could be. No single doctrine occupied all these writers and musicians equally, but the strongest impressions were undoubtedly made by his aesthetic theory, his philosophy of music, his recognition of the unconscious, his treatment of the overpowering sexual drive, his pessimism, and his questioning of the value of human existence. In some ways, it is strange that the period of Schopenhauer's most intense influence does not stretch much beyond the 1920s, into the decades when many of those we have mentioned had themselves become well-established cultural figures. This time of frustrated strivings in the economic sphere, when the futility of the First World War was compounded by yet more agonies, and widespread interest in psycho-analysis was changing people's views about the human personality—was this not Schopenhauer's true era? Yet by the middle of this century he was not such a well-known writer, one main reason being that none of the main streams of contemporary philosophy paid him any real attention.

Of those who succumbed to Schopenhauer, the earliest, Wagner and Nietzsche, seem to have been the most deeply affected, and it is in the understanding of these two that an exploration of the link with Schopenhauer is of most help. Wagner was no philosopher, and he sometimes confessed that, despite his constant re-readings, he was struggling to make out what was going on in Schopenhauer's work. Clearly the idea of music as the direct expression of the strivings of the will was one that spoke to him, but so did the idea of the denial of the will. He wrote in a letter to Liszt 'I have ... found a sedative which has finally helped me to sleep at night; it is the sincere and heartfelt yearning for death: total unconsciousness, complete annihilation, the end of all dreams—the only ultimate redemption.' Wagner clearly felt that Schopenhauer's doctrine crystallized some of his own insights, and gave him a fresh outlook on his own existing work: 'Now at last I could understand my *Wotan*.' He comes closest to Schopenhauer's actual philosophy in his operas when the characters Tristan and Isolde express their deep longing to cease existing as individuals. The capacity of erotic love to overpower the individual is also one of Schopenhauer's themes, of course. Wagner, however, contrives to make the longing for nonexistence turn into the climax of erotic love, instead of the complete negation of it which Schopenhauer calls for—in other words, even at his moment of supreme debt to the philosopher, he does not exactly follow him.

One of the things that brought Wagner together with the young Nietzsche was their devotion to Schopenhauer, whom they had discovered independently. Even though Nietzsche had also experienced a kind of emotional 'conversion' to Schopenhauer's philosophy, his relationship with it was to be quite different. In his first publication, *The Birth of Tragedy*, Nietzsche uses the pair of symbolic deities, Apollo and Dionysus, to account for the awesome artistic achievement of Greek tragedy. Apollo stands for the beautiful dream-like image of the individual hero, Dionysus for the terrifying but intoxicating glimpse into the cruel world underlying individuation, which will destroy the hero. In attempting to explain this pair of symbols, he calls on Schopenhauer's distinction between representation and will. Although the book is a unique outpouring, much of which has little directly to do with Schopenhauer (as Nietzsche himself later commented), his reading of Schopenhauer was decisive in providing the shape and the impulse of it.

However, it is what happened later that gives Schopenhauer a greater significance for Nietzsche. He turned away from his former 'master', to the extent of saying that he 'went wrong everywhere'. As Nietzsche's own philosophy developed, Schopenhauer continued to be a guiding star of a special kind—the one to steer away from. In the *Genealogy of Morals* he diagnoses Schopenhauer's doctrines as outlets for his own personality, saying in particular that the elevation of aesthetic tranquillity shows Schopenhauer's relief at escaping from his own abhorred sexual impulses; moreover 'he would have become ill, become a *pessimist* (for he was not one, however much he desired it), if deprived of his enemies, of Hegel, of woman, of sensuality and the whole will to existence, to persistence.' Perhaps—but what would Nietzsche have become without his Schopenhauer, his convenient summation of errors? He has already told us in the Preface: 'What was at stake was the *value* of morality—and over this I had to come to terms almost exclusively with my great teacher Schopenhauer.'

Nietzsche is very much concerned with the loss of value. He agrees with Schopenhauer that existence must contain suffering, and is basically without a point. But he revolts against the idea of renunciation and asceticism as a way to salvation. Plumbing the depths of the Schopenhauerian vision is a necessary step, but there must be an alternative to the 'life-denying' attitude of seeking to escape from the will and despising the individual material being that one is. Nietzsche's proposed solution is that of a creative self-affirmation ('Become who you are!), embracing one's pain and even one's cruelty as true parts of oneself. His notion of the will to power, based more than verbally on Schopenhauer's 'will to life', attempts to supplant the latter as a description of the fundamental drive that organizes human behaviour, and, in some way, the whole universe. Will to power is not primarily a political doctrine, but an attempt to find an explanation of human behaviour, cognition, and cultural beliefs by positing an underlying tendency towards increase and mastery, both over the world and over oneself. Though he repudiates Schopenhauer's metaphysical doctrine of the thing in itself, and seeks to discredit philosophical metaphysics altogether, Nietzsche's notion of will to power shows striking parallels with Schopenhauer's conception of the will. In particular, the idea that will to power can be both conscious and unconscious, that it has an organic basis in the individual, and that it is omnipresent, make it appropriate to call it a successor to Schopenhauer's doctrine.

While Schopenhauer is in the forefront of Nietzsche's critique of philosophers, many of the methods for that critique have also been suggested by Schopenhauer. For example, Nietzsche's view that metaphysical doctrines and beliefs about ethical values do not derive from 'pure' reasoning, but are always informed, covertly, by the need to come to terms with suffering and the will to master oneself or one's surroundings, clearly has its origins in Schopenhauer's doctrine that the will shapes our intellectual processes. Schopenhauer's idea that the world is structured by the mind of a particular species of living organism is reflected in Nietzsche's conviction that there are no absolute truths or values, only perspectives and fabrications that help us to cope with life. Schopenhauer also, of course, provides the most naked instance of the ascetic ideal which Nietzsche sees as underlying so much of Western culture—'Man would rather will *nothingness* than *not* will.' Aside from such doctrinal influences, Nietzsche's writing displays its involvement with Schopenhauer often in fine-grained detail. He will appropriate Schopenhauer's nuances of voice and terminology even at the moment of greatest divergence from his doctrines. To read Nietzsche without a knowledge of Schopenhauer is to lose a recurring sub-text, and one of the key points of orientation in his often bewildering progress.

Among Nietzsche's contemporaries, philosophical interest in Schopenhauer was widespread. He was commonly studied as an important successor to Kant, and philosophers who were significant in their day, such as Hans Vaihinger, and Nietzsche's friend, the orientalist and metaphysician, Paul Deussen, produced new systems which took off from Schopenhauer's. In the twentieth century he was highly thought of by members of the Frankfurt School who were dissatisfied with the optimism of orthodox Marxism, in particular Max Horkheimer. However, it is fair to say that to date the only major philosopher apart from Nietzsche to be influenced by Schopenhauer has been Wittgenstein. Wittgenstein, like Nietzsche, did not come across Schopenhauer's works in an academic setting. He read them as part of the stock of ideas with which Viennese high society was furnished (an illustrative little detail is that Gustav Mahler, another 'disciple', while staying at the Wittgenstein family house a few years earlier, had given Bruno Walter Schopenhauer's complete works as a present). In fact, not to have read Schopenhauer would have been the odd thing for a young person from a cultured family such as Wittgenstein's.

Wittgenstein's earliest philosophical work, leading up to the *Tractatus*, seems at first sight to have little in common with Schopenhauer. He had worked with Frege and Russell in the new methods of formal logic, which became the basis of a movement that attempted to repudiate idealism and the supposed excesses of German metaphysics. It used to be common to apologize for Wittgenstein's interest in Schopenhauer as a youthful aberration. But it was certainly more than that. In the *Tractatus* Wittgenstein uses Schopenhauer's images when talking about the 'I': it is an extensionless point, like an eye that cannot see itself, a limit—not a part—of the world. The 'I' is not among the facts that make up the world. Nor is there any value in the world. Value, whether ethical or aesthetic, seems to come from an attitude to the world as whole, not to any particular facts within it. 'To view the world sub specie aeterni (under the aspect of eternity)'—another of Schopenhauer's ideas—'is to view it as a whole', and this is a mystical feeling, says Wittgenstein. The well-known image of philosophy as the ladder which one discards after climbing it is also reminiscent of Schopenhauer's view of the relationship between philosophy and mysticism.

There hangs over the *Tractatus* the sense that it is about something that appears only obliquely in the text. Its author said that the meaning of the book was an 'ethical' one, and in the book it transpires that ethics cannot be put into propositions, but must show itself. Wittgenstein was clearly troubled by the thought that once the world had been described in language, the really big questions, such as what the 'I' was, how it related to the world, what the point of the world was, and where good and evil came from, were left entirely untouched. As he struggled with these issues, the map on which he attempted to plot them was provided to a large extent by Schopenhauer's philosophy. This is particularly clear from his early notebooks, where the repeated vocabulary of 'subject' and 'object', 'will' and 'representation', 'world' and 'I' acquires any semblance of intelligibility only when viewed as an attempt to think things through with Schopenhauer's help.

Another area where Wittgenstein was clearly influenced by Schopenhauer is the theory of action. From his earliest writings through to his mature works, Wittgenstein worried about whether there is a mental act of will that is separate from bodily movement. The problem became central to his examination of whether the mental was in any sense 'hidden', and had a big influence on action-theory in analytical philosophy. The basic idea that Wittgenstein often seems drawn to is that willing is identical with acting, rather than being some purely 'inner' mental process. It is easy to see that this idea is essentially Schopenhauer's, and, although he does not mention his predecessor's name very often in this connection, the terms in which he discusses it reflect its ancestry.

Apart from the arts and philosophy, Schopenhauer's influence also extends into psychology, through his conception of the unconscious and his idea that sexuality is at the basis of personality. A very popular work in its day, now more or less forgotten, was Eduard von Hartmann's *Philosophy of the Unconscious* of 1869. This was a strange hybrid in which the author tried to combine some of Schopenhauer's ideas with some of Hegel's, and attempted a kind of *rapprochement* between optimism and pessimism. His chief modification of Schopenhauer's notion of the unconscious was to suggest that it must comprise not only will but also Idea, and somehow be in pursuit of rational ends. This work made the unconscious a theme for widespread study in the latter part of the nineteenth century, and served at the same time as a kind of channel for interest in Schopenhauer. Although Schopenhauer was not the first or only philosopher to discuss the unconscious, he probably made the greatest contribution before Freud.

Freud himself certainly consulted Hartmann's work, and does make reference to it. It is has often been pointed out, too, that he must have been familiar with Schopenhauer's ideas from the academic environment in which he moved. Nevertheless, Freud tried to distance himself from Schopenhauer, saying, in a well-known passage,

I have carefully avoided any contact with philosophy proper.
. . . The large extent to which psycho-analysis coincides with
the philosophy of Schopenhauer—not only did he assert the
dominance of the emotions and the supreme importance of
sexuality but he was even aware of the mechanism of repression—is not to be traced to my acquaintance with his teaching.
I read Schopenhauer very late in my life.

One almost hesitates to point out that Freud must have known at
some level what to avoid reading, in order to preserve this title to
originality. In any case, it is pretty certain that the great attention
paid to Schopenhauer in academic and cultural life during this
period was an important factor in making Freud's work possible,
whether he was aware of it or not.

C. G. Jung is another influential psychologist who was impressed by Schopenhauer. He reports that he read Schopenhauer
from his seventeenth year on (putting us, again, in the 1890s), and
agreed with his picture of the world as full of confusion, passion,
and evil: 'Here at last was someone who had courage for the
insight that somehow the foundation of the world was not in the
best of ways.' Should we in the 1990s pass a different judgement?
Though Schopenhauer's metaphysics is not credible as a system,
his doctrines concerning subjectivity, action, striving, suffering,
individuality, renunciation, and aesthetic elevation—the troubling or consoling thoughts that have excited so many influential
thinkers—are surely still as alive and challenging as ever.

Further reading

A recent full biography of Schopenhauer is:

SAFRANSKI, RÜDIGER, *Schopenhauer and the Wild Years of Philosophy* (London, 1989).

The following are treatments of Schopenhauer's work as a whole from a philosophical point of view:

GARDINER, PATRICK, *Schopenhauer* (Harmondsworth, 1967).
HAMLYN, D. W., *Schopenhauer* (London, 1980).
YOUNG, JULIAN, *Willing and Unwilling: A Study in the Philosophy of Arthur Schopenhauer* (Dordrecht, 1987).

Recent books which focus on certain philosophical themes more than others:

ATWELL, JOHN E., *Schopenhauer: The Human Character* (Philadelphia, 1990).
ATWELL, JOHN E., *Schopenhauer on the Character of the World: The Metaphysics of Will* (Berkeley and Los Angeles, 1995).
JACQUETTE, DALE (ed.), *Schopenhauer, Philosophy and the Arts* (Cambridge, 1996).
JANAWAY, CHRISTOPHER, *Self and World in Schopenhauer's Philosophy* (Oxford, 1989).
WHITE, F. C., *On Schopenhauer's Fourfold Root of the Principle of Sufficient Reason* (Leiden, 1992).

For a lively and sometimes idiosyncratic account of the place of Schopenhauer's philosophy in the history of ideas, see:

MAGEE, BRYAN, *The Philosophy of Schopenhauer* (Oxford, 1983).

Two collections of articles reflect a variety of perspectives on Schopenhauer:

FOX, MICHAEL (ed.), *Schopenhauer: His Philosophical Achievement* (Brighton, 1980).

Further reading

VON DER LUFT, ERIC (ed.), *Schopenhauer: New Essays in Honor of his 200th Birthday* (Lewiston, N. Y., 1988).

The latter volume contains an extensive bibliography.

Index

Index

OXFORD

MORE OXFORD PAPERBACKS

This book is just one of nearly 1000 Oxford Paperbacks currently in print. If you would like details of other Oxford Paperbacks, including titles in the World's Classics, Oxford Reference, Oxford Books, OPUS, Past Masters, Oxford Authors, and Oxford Shakespeare series, please write to:

UK and Europe: Oxford Paperbacks Publicity Manager, Arts and Reference Publicity Department, Oxford University Press, Walton Street, Oxford OX2 6DP.

Customers in UK and Europe will find Oxford Paperbacks available in all good bookshops. But in case of difficulty please send orders to the Cash-with-Order Department, Oxford University Press Distribution Services, Saxon Way West, Corby, Northants NN18 9ES. Tel: 01536 741519; Fax: 01536 746337. Please send a cheque for the total cost of the books, plus £1.75 postage and packing for orders under £20; £2.75 for orders over £20. Customers outside the UK should add 10% of the cost of the books for postage and packing.

USA: Oxford Paperbacks Marketing Manager, Oxford University Press, Inc., 200 Madison Avenue, New York, N.Y. 10016.

Canada: Trade Department, Oxford University Press, 70 Wynford Drive, Don Mills, Ontario M3C 1J9.

Australia: Trade Marketing Manager, Oxford University Press, G.P.O. Box 2784Y, Melbourne 3001, Victoria.

South Africa: Oxford University Press, P.O. Box 1141, Cape Town 8000.

ACCEL·WORLD 01

KUROYUKIHIME'S RETURN

REKI KAWAHARA
ILLUSTRATION BY **HIMA**
DESIGN BY **bee-pee**

"That's..."

PINK PIG

Avatar of Haruyuki,
a boy in the lowest
school caste

"Don't
you want
to go further,
boy...to
accelerate?"

KUROYUKIHIME

Avatar of Umesato Junior High
School student council vice president

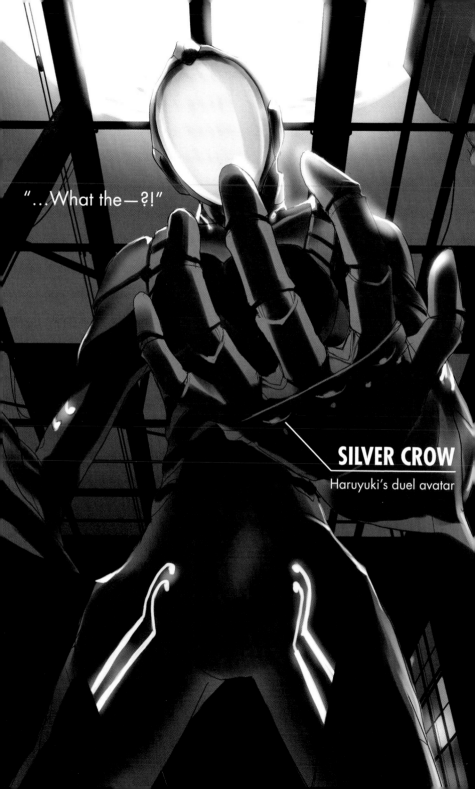

"...What the—?!"

SILVER CROW
Haruyuki's duel avatar

HARUYUKI
is the···

"Silver Crow"
in the
Accelerated
World.

"Haruyuki Arita"
in the
Real World.

"Pink Pig"
in the
Umesato Junior
High School's
Local Area
Network.

▶▶▶ *ACCEL • WORLD* Ø1

KUROYUKIHIME'S RETURN

Reki Kawahara
Illustrations: HIMA
Design: bee-pee

YEN ON

NEW YORK

■ Kuroyukihime = Umesato Junior High School student council vice president. Trim and clever girl who has it all. Her in-school avatar is a spangled butterfly that she programmed herself.

■ Haruyuki = Haruyuki Arita. Grade Seven at Umesato Junior High School. Bullied, on the pudgy side. He's good at games but shy. His in-school avatar is a pink pig.

■ Chiyuri = Chiyuri Kurashima. Haruyuki's childhood friend. Meddling, energetic girl. Her in-school avatar is a silver cat.

■ Takumu = Takumu Mayuzumi. A boy Haruyuki and Chiyuri have known since childhood. He currently attends a different school from Haruyuki and Chiyuri. Beautiful boy who belongs to the kendo team.

■ Araya = Umesato Junior High delinquent. Main bully to Haruyuki.

■ Neurolinker = Portable terminal that connects with the brain via a wireless quantum connection and supports all five senses with images, sounds, and other stimuli.

■ Brain Burst = Neurolinker application sent to Haruyuki by Kuroyukihime.

■ In-school local net = Local area network established within Umesato Junior High School. Used during classes and to check attendance. Umesato students are required to always be connected to it.

■ Global connection = Connection with the worldwide net. Global connections are forbidden on Umesato Junior High School grounds, where the in-school local net is provided instead.

▶▶▶ACCEL•WORLD

1

The yellow message light blinked in the top right corner of the virtual blackboard.

Haruyuki, who had drifted off during class, shifted the focus of both his eyes, pulling his neck back automatically. As he did, the deep green of the blackboard filling his field of vision faded suddenly to translucency, and the figure of the teacher standing beyond the orderly rows of student backs became clear.

The classroom, his classmates, and the teacher were all real, but the transparent blackboard and the closely packed equations on it were not. The Neurolinker around the back of Haruyuki's neck projected the numbers and symbols the teacher wrote in the air directly into his brain.

The math teacher, a man in his early forties, continued with his whispered explanation of one formula while running an empty hand along a blackboard only he could see in areas that seemed particularly difficult somehow. His voice was nowhere near loud enough to reach Haruyuki's ears as actual sound, but the Neurolinker twined around the teacher's neck amplified and clarified it, conveying it to Haruyuki.

When Haruyuki brought his gaze back in, the blackboard materialized once again, covered in even more equations than before. It seemed unlikely that the message he had received was a compressed file sent by the teacher packing up today's homework. And given that he was separated from the global net right now, that meant the sender had to be another student in his school.

In the six months since he'd started junior high, Haruyuki had long abandoned the hope that one of the girls might have broken school rules to send him a friendly message. He desperately wanted to drop the message unopened in the trash in the lower left corner of his eyeline, but if he did that, he'd have no idea what was going to happen to him later.

Reluctantly, taking advantage of the teacher's turned back, he raised his right hand in the air (this action was real rather than virtual) and clicked on the mail icon with the tip of his finger.

In an instant, *bubibaborububiru*, a sound without any actual character, and graphics like a flood of primary colors assaulted Hiroyuki's senses. Then the real message played—not text, but voice.

Piggy, today's command order! (Several voices laughing gleefully in the background.) *Bring two yakisoba buns, one cream melon bun, and three strawberry yogurts to the roof five minutes after lunch starts! If you're late, it's pork bun punishment for you! And if you squeal, it's the pork roast punishment! Got it?!* (Another explosion of laughter.)

Haruyuki mustered every ounce of willpower to fix his neck in place and not look in the direction of the eyes he could feel burning a hole through his left cheek. He knew he'd only be even more humiliated by the sneers of Araya and his underlings A and B if he allowed himself a glance.

Since you obviously couldn't record messages like this during class or add in these kinds of visual and auditory effects, the message had to have been prepared in advance. Those guys had too much free time on their hands. And then that "command order" stuff! Totally redundant! Idiots! Complete morons!

Although he could curse them out in his head, Haruyuki couldn't even answer this message, much less utter his curses out loud. Because if Araya was an idiot the likes of a cockroach, indestructible no matter how the world moved forward, Haruyuki was an even bigger idiot for being bullied by him. If he possessed even the tiniest bit of courage or the ability to act, it'd be an easy thing to submit the several dozen messages he'd saved, including this one, to the school as evidence and get those guys in trouble.

But Haruyuki inevitably ended up thinking about what would come after that.

People could talk all they wanted about how half of our lives were lived in the virtual network now that Neurolinkers were so ubiquitous that basically everyone in the country had one, but in the end, human beings only existed according to the lowest common denominators chaining them to their flesh-and-blood bodies. Three times a day, you get hungry; you go to the toilet; if you get hit, it hurts, and you cry as a consequence. It's all so miserable you could die.

Linker skills determining which school you went to and how far you made it in the world, these were nothing more than the enormous network industry's branding strategies. What determined the value of a human being at the end of the day were simply the primitive parameters of appearance and physical strength. This was the conclusion Haruyuki reached at the age of thirteen, having reached sixty kilos when he was in fifth grade and never having run a fifty-meter dash in less than ten seconds.

He was forced to spend the five hundred yen his mother charged to his Neurolinker in the morning for lunch money to buy buns and yogurt for Araya and the rest, and still he ran over budget. He had a little of the seven thousand yen saved up from his allowance, all the money he had in the world, but if he spent that now, he wouldn't be able to buy the Linker game coming out later that month.

Haruyuki's ample build got terrible mileage. If he skipped just one meal, he ended up dizzy with hunger. Even so, he had no choice but to suffer through it today. At least he still had one trick to get through the day, a full dive, only allowed during lunch.

Sucking in his round body as far as it would go, Haruyuki headed for the second school building, which held nothing but special classrooms. And because everything from science experiments to home ec cooking classes were conducted virtually now, the building no longer served any purpose, and few people went near it. Particularly during lunch, the place was devoid of students.

Haruyuki's special hiding place was the boys' washroom in one corner of the dusty hallway. Trudging into this refuge, he stopped with a sigh and looked at the mirror above the sink.

Staring back at him from the cloudy glass was the fat bullied kid, so hopelessly clichéd that if this were a TV show, people would roll their eyes at the stereotype. His hair had a strong will of its own, springing up here and there, and the curves of his cheeks held not even a hint of definition. His uniform tie and silver Neurolinker were eaten up by his flabby neck as if they were a tightening noose.

There was a time when he'd tried to do something about his appearance, when he pushed himself hard, practically giving up eating and forcing himself to go running. But the result of that effort was that he collapsed during lunch from anemia and ended up with the lunches of several female students, a now-legendary story that haunted him. Ever since, Haruyuki had been determined to ignore his real self—at least while he was a student.

He yanked his eyes away from the mirror and moved farther into the washroom, entering the private stall at the end. He made sure the door was locked and sat on the toilet with the lid down. The creaking and squeaking of the plastic under his body were old friends. He leaned back against the tank, relaxed, and closed his eyes. He chanted the magical incantation to release his soul from this cumbrous form:

"Direct link."

Receiving his voice command, the Neurolinker moved up from audiovisual mode to full sensory mode on the quantum connection level, and the weight and the sense of hunger strangling his stomach disappeared from Haruyuki's body.

The hardness of the toilet seat and the tightness of his school uniform were also gone. The laughing voices of students echoing in the distant schoolyard, the scent of cleansers filling the washroom, and even the featureless door in front of him melted into inky darkness and disappeared. Full dive. Even his sense of gravity was severed, and Haruyuki plunged into the darkness.

Soon, however, his entire body was enveloped by a gentle floating feeling and rainbow-colored lights. The avatar he used during full dives began forming from the tips of his hands and feet. Black, hoof-shaped hands and feet. Plump limbs and a ball-like torso a vibrant peach-pink. He couldn't see them, but he should also have had a flat noise protruding from the center of his face and large ears hanging down. In short, he was a pink pig.

Wearing this ridiculous avatar, he dropped down with a *thud* in the middle of a fairy-tale forest in the Ministry of Education's recommended design.

Giant mushrooms grew everywhere, and in the center of a patch of grass framed in a circle of light from the particularly bright sun, a crystalline spring bubbled up from the ground. On its outer edge, enormous, hollow trees formed a circle and towered over the area. The inside of each tree was divided up into several levels you could use to chat or play, connected by stairs. This virtual space was the in-school local net for Umesato Junior High School, a private institution in Suginami City, Tokyo.

The majority of other figures passing through the forest or laughing in groups of twos and threes were, like Haruyuki, also not human. Roughly half were silly animals walking on two legs, while the rest were fairies with wings sprouting from their backs (although they couldn't actually fly), tin robots, or robed mages. All were avatars of Umesato Junior High students and teachers diving in the local net.

Students could choose from a wide selection of base avatar forms and customize them. If you had the patience, you could also construct a completely original avatar from scratch, taking advantage of the editor provided. The result was ultimately a combination of the technology available and taste of a junior high school student, but even so, the black knight avatar Haruyuki created and unveiled in April had garnered a lot of attention.

...The sad majesty of that avatar. Sighing, Haruyuki glanced down at his current form. In the blink of an eye, Araya had ripped off his black knight avatar and forced him to use this default pig.

Obviously, in terms of originality, this pink pig could not be beat. No one else would make such a deliberately masochistic choice. Desperately sucking in his round body just like he did in the real world, Haruyuki set his sights on a single tree and headed out at a trot.

As he did, he noticed an unusually large throng of people gathered beside the spring at the heart of the forest. Casting his eyes in that direction as he ran, Haruyuki slowed his pace unconsciously. In the middle of the ring of students, he spotted a marvelously rare avatar, the kind you hardly ever see.

It wasn't pulled from the default settings. She wore a jet-black dress studded with transparent jewels. In her hand, a folded black parasol. On her back, the wings of a spangled butterfly shot through with rainbow-colored lines. With a face white like snow framed by long, straight hair, the avatar was so perfectly gorgeous, it was hard to believe it was handmade. The design skill involved was beyond anything Haruyuki could ever have hoped to achieve. It could easily have passed for a pro's work.

Haruyuki knew the girl. Her slender body leaning casually against a giant mushroom, a weary expression on her face as she attended to the compliments of the avatars surrounding her, she was in eighth grade and the vice president of the student council. This shockingly beautiful form was for all intents and purposes a flawless re-creation of her real-world body, thus her nickname: Kuroyukihime.

That a creature like this and someone like Haruyuki could share even the single commonality of both being students at Umesato seemed impossible to him. Just turning his virtual gaze on her, Haruyuki felt the awareness of his diminutive stature that tortured his consciousness swell unpleasantly, and he forced himself to focus the path in front of him again.

The destination he was barreling toward at full speed was a large tree with recreation rooms inside. It was basically an arcade, but naturally, there were absolutely no commercial games like RPGs or war games or such.

It was all educational stuff, like quizzes or puzzles or wholesome sports games, but even so, a number of students gathered in groups in every corner, laughing and chatting. All of them were on full dives from their own desks or the cafeteria. During the dive, their flesh-and-blood bodies were left defenseless, but messing with people in the middle of a dive was a clear violation of etiquette, so no one besides Haruyuki worried about it. He had returned to his classroom after a dive in the local net to find the pants on his uniform pulled down maybe a month or so after school started.

Hiding his flesh body in the toilet and wanting to avoid other eyes even in the virtual world, he started climbing the stairs carved into the tree that was his destination. The higher he climbed, the less popular the games. After passing baseball, basketball, golf, and tennis, and even ignoring the Ping-Pong floor, he finally arrived at the virtual squash corner.

There wasn't a single student in the room. The reason for the floor's lack of popularity was clear. Squash is sort of like tennis, but you hit the ball with a racquet in a space enclosed from top to bottom and on all sides by hard walls. The ball bounces back, and the player silently returns it over and over. It was a thoroughly lonely sport.

In reality, Haruyuki liked first-person shooter games the best, the kind where players run around a battlefield carrying a machine gun, and in those games, he was good enough to hold his own against guys in the states (the home of the FPS). It was also a popular genre in Japan, of course, but there was no way something like that would be available on the school network. When he was in elementary school, Haruyuki had killed pretty much all of the guys in his class with a single handgun, and from the next day on, he had been bullied mercilessly. Ever since, Haruyuki had promised himself he would never again play the same games as the kids at school, no matter the genre.

He walked over to the right edge of the deserted court and held up the control panel with one hand. The panel accessed Haruyuki's student ID number and retrieved his saved level and high scores. Since the middle of the first term, he had been killing time here during his lunch hour, focusing exclusively on this game. As a result, he'd achieved a staggeringly high score. He was actually getting tired of squash, but it wasn't like he had anywhere else to go.

Haruyuki grabbed the racquet that popped up from the panel and held it firmly in his pink right hand with its black hoof. After the words GAME START appeared, a ball dropped down out of nowhere. He hit it with everything he had, pouring every ounce of today's misery into the racquet.

Thk! Leaving a momentary flash, the ball flew up like a laser and struck the floor and the forward wall before returning. Aided by reflex more than sight, Haruyuki returned the ball with a backhand, taking a step to the left in line with the optimal solution to which his brain automatically guided him.

The real Haruyuki obviously could not move like this. But this was an electronic world, free of the chains of meatspace. Watching the ball and moving his body were just quantum signals traveling back and forth between his brain and the Neurolinker.

The ball abruptly lost its substance, leaving nothing but a faint trace of light on the court. The *thwack* it made sounded several times a second, echoing like a machine gun. Still, Haruyuki made his pig's body leap and dance and his racket sing in every direction.

Dammit, who needs reality anyway?

The scream of resentment pierced the back of his brain, unable to shut out his problems even while tackling the game at top speed.

Why do we need dumb stuff like a real classroom or a real school? People can live entirely virtually already. I mean, the world stinks with grown-ups actually doing just that. So much so that they even did those experiments way back when, where they turned a per-

son's entire consciousness into quantum data and tried to build a real parallel universe.

And yet despite all that, they toss groups of us kids into real-life cages to learn group life and develop some kind of morals, or for whatever other idiotic reasons they have. All well and good for Araya and them, probably helps them relax a bit and save their allowances. But for me...I don't know what else I can do.

A bell sounded, and his game increased a level in the corner of his vision.

The ball accelerated abruptly. The angle of return was also irregular, and the ball came powering along, drawing an arc from an unexpected direction. Haruyuki's reaction time gradually started to lag.

Dammit! I have to accelerate, have to go faster. So fast I can break through every wall in the virtual world and even the real world and go somewhere without people! Fast!

The racquet cut through the air with a *whoosh.* The ball, now nothing more than a beam of light, grazed Haruyuki's cheek, passed behind him, and vanished. The words GAME OVER dropped down accompanied by a silly, sad trombone sound effect and bounced around on the court. Without glancing at his blinking high score, Haruyuki turned back to the panel to restart the game, head hanging.

At that moment, a voice suddenly rocked Haruyuki's sacred hiding place.

"Oh!! So this is where you locked yourself up!!" The screech was so high-pitched it was like lightning bolts in his ears, or rather his brain. Stiffening his back with a start, Haruyuki turned around to find a student avatar in the same animal class as his.

Even so, it didn't have the slightest bit of the silliness of Haruyuki's pig. The slim, supple cat was covered in silver fur tinged with purple, with blue ribbons tied on one ear and the tip of her tail. It hadn't been put together from scratch right from polygons, but each of the parameters had clearly been tinkered with.

A touch of anger rose up in her golden eyes, and the cat opened wide her mouth with its small fangs and cried out again, "Lately, you've just disappeared the whole lunch hour, Haru, so I came looking for you! Games are great and all, but you don't have to play this kind of lame game, you know. You should come and play with the rest of us!"

"...I can do what I want. Leave me alone."

Haruyuki tried to leave it at that and return to the court, but the silver cat stretched her neck out and peered at the GAME OVER display. "Huh, what's that...level one fifty-two, score two million six hundred thirty thousand?! You're...," she shouted in an even higher voice—

Amazing!

Or at least that's what Haruyuki was briefly, faintly hoping for when the cat betrayed him abruptly.

"An idiot! What are you even doing, skipping lunch for this?! Come down right now!!"

"...I don't want to. There's still half an hour left for lunch. You go."

"Well, if you're going to be like that, I'll just have to use force."

"Go ahead if you can," Haruyuki answered under his breath and clenched his racquet tighter.

There was no "collision detection" in avatars in the school network. Under the pretext of preventing improper behavior, students were not permitted to touch the avatars of other students. So naturally, forcing another person to log out was completely out of the question.

Sticking her slim tongue out as far as it would go, the cat avatar shouted, "Link out!"

She disappeared immediately, leaving a swirl of light and a ringing noise in her wake.

Once the pest had finally gone, Haruyuki blew a vague sadness out his nose in a short breath. That was when it happened.

An impact, a *thud*—no gentle love tap—struck his head, and the surrounding scene faded away. From the other side of the darkness, the real world returned, a point of light zooming up around him. Feeling his own weight pressing on him heavily, Haruyuki blinked frantically and tried to focus his eyes.

He was in the boys' washroom stall where he'd started. But instead of the blue-gray door that should have been before him, Haruyuki saw something unexpected.

"You...Wha...?"

Standing, arms crossed and imposing, in front of him was a lone female student. The ribbon on her blazer was green, showing that she was in seventh grade just like him. Her physique was small, weighing in at less than a third of Haruyuki's mass. Her short bangs were pulled up to the right and held there with a blue pin. Her large, asymmetrical eyes—outlined by small, catlike lids—burned with anger, glaring at Haruyuki.

Her left hand held a small basket while her right was stretched out directly above Haruyuki's head and clenched tightly in a fist. Seeing this, he finally understood why he had been suddenly yanked out of his full dive. She had punched him with that tiny fist, and the impact had activated the safety on his Neurolinker, which had then automatically disconnected.

Normally, the safety was activated when your shoulders were shaken or someone called out to you in a loud voice, and nervous girls would set it so that they linked out the second anyone got within a meter of them. The fact that Haruyuki hadn't noticed the intruder until she hit him on the crown of his head was because he had hidden himself in the toilet stall and dropped the safety to the lowest level.

"Y-you!!" Haruyuki shouted, stunned, at the only girl in the school he could talk to without panicking. "What are you doing?! This is the boys' toilet! And I locked the door...Are you stupid or something?!"

"You're the stupid one," Chiyuri Kurashima, Haruyuki's childhood friend, strong enough to climb over the partition wall in the boys' toilet still in her skirt, shot back contemptuously as she slipped a hand behind her to unlock the door.

Bouncing out of the stall with a light movement, she finally smiled faintly at Haruyuki, who was squinting involuntarily at the sunlight slipping off her chestnut-colored hair. "Come on, come out already," she urged.

"…Fiiiiine." Swallowing a sigh, Haruyuki yanked himself up, causing the toilet lid to creak. He followed Chiyuri toward the door, asking the question nagging at him. "…How'd you know I was here?"

She didn't answer right away. "I was on the roof, too. So I followed you," she informed him briefly after sticking her head out of the boys' toilet and checking the situation outside before stealing into the hallway.

Which meant…

"…You saw?" Haruyuki mumbled, arresting the foot that was about to step out of the washroom.

Chiyuri looked down like she was trying to find the right words, leaned back against the interior wall, and then finally nodded sharply. "I won't butt in with them anymore. If that's what you want…I don't have much choice. But you should at least eat. It's bad for you not to." A somehow forced smile graced her face, and Chiyuri held out the basket in her left hand. "I made you a lunch. I can't guarantee it'll be good, though."

I'm pathetic, Haruyuki thought.

His own mind, always trying to find something other than pity in the things Chiyuri said and did, was deeply and unrepairably pathetic.

Because Chiyuri had a proper boyfriend. Another childhood friend, the opposite of Haruyuki in every way.

His mouth moved on its own, and Haruyuki heard himself say in a strangely flat voice, "Leftovers from the one you made for Taku?"

Chiyuri's face clouded over abruptly. Unable to see her eyes under those tightly furrowed brows, Haruyuki dropped his gaze to the floor of the hallway.

"No. Taku eats the school lunch. This…it's just sandwiches—ham and cheese—and potato salad. It's your favorite, right?"

Haruyuki tried to gently push back the white basket entering his field of view. But his sluggish, real-world meat body knocked the basket out of Chiyuri's hand in a sudden jerk far removed from his intention. The moment it hit the ground, the lid popped open, and from inside the light blue parchment paper, neatly triangular sandwiches flew out—one, two—and fell apart.

"Ah!"

Instinctively, he went to apologize, but inside his brain, it was suddenly hot, and the words he should have uttered refused to take shape. Unable to even lift his head, he stepped backward, still staring at the floor, and cried out as he turned aside, "N-no thanks!!"

He felt the acute desire to log out of this place right away, but that was clearly impossible. If only he could at least have fled desperately…but his real body was thick and good for nothing; he couldn't even escape the small, sobbing voice behind him.

Lower than low, Haruyuki ignored his afternoon classes and the homeroom that followed, dashing out of the classroom as if fleeing the scene. Banishing from his mind the voice telling him that he should go wait for Chiyuri outside her classroom two doors down or at the school gates or somewhere along the road home, he made a break instead for his other hiding spot, the library.

Spaces like libraries had functionally ceased fulfilling their original roles long ago. However, there were some grown-ups who thought that, just like the school itself, paper media was essential to a child's education, and the walls were lined with the spines of brand-new books set atop bookcases that could only be considered a waste of space and resources.

But then, thanks to this attitude, he was guaranteed precious personal space within the school, so he couldn't complain. Carrying two or three books for camouflage, he locked himself up in one of the reading booths along the wall and stuffed his body into the narrow chair before executing the order for a full dive at a volume just barely loud enough for the Linker to catch.

Precisely because it had only been a few minutes since classes ended, the school net was deserted. He needed to hole himself up in his usual refuge while the net was still empty, and he cut through the grass at top speed to climb the tree building.

Naturally, the virtual squash corner was bare. To be honest, he would have preferred a bloodstained battle game to this simple racquet sport to banish the gloominess in his heart, even temporarily, but given that he couldn't connect to the global net, he was stuck with the school net and its limited selection of gaming apps.

Although his hunger was already more than he could bear, he didn't feel like going home straightaway. He had no idea what he should do, what he should say if he ran into Chiyuri on the way home. Well, first off, he should apologize, but he wasn't so sure he could make his mouth do what he wanted it to.

That day, it was just like this.

On the verge of remembering another time a long time ago when he had made Chiyuri cry like that, Haruyuki shut his eyes tightly. Keeping them closed, he brought his right hand up to the control panel and logged in.

Fumbling, he gripped his racquet, changed the orientation of his body, and faced the court before opening his eyes and trying to beat back the heaviness in his heart using the ball that dropped down when—

Haruyuki froze.

The primary colors of the 3-D font in the center of the court displayed a different number from the one he remembered.

"Level…one sixty-six?!"

More than ten levels higher than the one Haruyuki had achieved just a few hours earlier.

For a second, he wondered how this could have happened given that scores are managed by student ID, but he soon figured it out. Because Haruyuki had been forcibly logged out when Chiyuri hit him on the head, the game had been disengaged with him still logged in. So someone could have picked up where he left off and destroyed his score.

However…

Someone other than him getting a score like this?!

The one thing that had kept Haruyuki's pride from crumbling completely was his VR game technique in the full dive environment. Obviously, this didn't include quiz and board games, where winning depended on how smart you were, but when it came to shooters or action or racing games where what mattered was how fast your reflexes were, it was a point of pride for Haruyuki that there wasn't a soul in school who could best him.

But he never made a show of this. Since elementary school, he'd had it drummed into his head—often painfully—that nothing good came of making himself conspicuous. Up to now, he'd been of a mind that he didn't actually need to confirm his superiority, but...this awe-inspiring squash score...

Just then.

A voice behind him. Not Chiyuri's. It was a girl, but her voice was lower and sounded smooth like silk. "So you're the one who got that ridiculous score?"

Turning around trepidatiously, Haruyuki saw: a dress inlaid with silver in the darkness. An umbrella piercing the floor like a cane, a sword. Snow-white skin and inky black eyes. Kuroyukihime.

Even though she was an avatar, there was not even the faintest hint of digital about her appearance, almost a type of extreme beauty. The most popular person in school moved forward noiselessly. A faint smile playing across her red lips—the only part of her entire body with any color—Kuroyukihime continued, "Don't you want to go further, boy...to accelerate?"

If you do, come to the lounge at lunch tomorrow.

Leaving just these words to linger, Kuroyukihime abruptly logged out.

The time her avatar had existed in Haruyuki's field of vision was likely not even a full ten seconds. The event was just too impossible; he could even have believed it had been a bug on the local net server or an illusion, but the incredible score still floating above the court was real enough.

Unable to muster up the desire to try for a new high score,

Haruyuki ended his dive and sat in the library reading booth, staring off into space. Three lines looped endless in his ears. Kuroyukihime's tone was not like that of a regular girl their age, but he didn't feel it was out of place in the slightest given her incredibly powerful presence. It actually made him see at least part of the reason she was so tremendously popular, not just with the boys but with the girls as well.

Haruyuki finally left the school on wobbly legs, his body essentially on autopilot as he made his way home. Had it not been for the traffic prediction display in the audiovisual mode of his Neurolinker, he likely would've been run over at least two or three times.

When he arrived at his deserted luxury condo in Koenji, Haruyuki immediately warmed up a frozen pizza, scarfing it down with a soda. His parents had gotten divorced ages ago, and though he lived with his mother now, she never got home before midnight. He only ever saw her when she gave him his lunch money just as he was about to leave for school.

His once-empty stomach now full of junk food, Haruyuki retreated to his room. Normally, he'd do his routine check on the global net, run around a battlefield in Europe for a few hours, and go to bed after giving his all to his homework, but today at least, he didn't feel like doing anything. Maybe because too many things had happened his brain felt heavy, as if it were swollen, and Haruyuki flopped down onto his bed after taking off his Neurolinker.

His sleep, though, was nothing particularly restful. The sneers of Araya and his gang, Chiyuri's tears, and Kuroyukihime's mysterious words played over and over in his head, turning up in his dreams, toying with him.

Don't you want to go further . . . to accelerate?

The Kuroyukihime in his dream was not her avatar but the actual vice president of the student council. Even though he had only ever seen her onstage at school assemblies with an aloof, expressionless look on her face, for some reason in his dream, a mischievous, almost inviting smile curled up at the corners of her lips, and she whispered in Haruyuki's ear. *Come here.*

2

Right, it was all a dream. Including the meeting on the local net yesterday, Haruyuki thought as he entered the classroom the next day (a Wednesday), having come to school with a glum face as always.

Araya and his thugs kept sending Haruyuki prank mails during a class that was more déjà-vu than anything else. Being shaken down for lunch two days in a row was a first; the order was the same yakisoba and cream melon buns as the previous day. *Do they really like them that much?* Haruyuki wondered, closing his mail and rising out of his seat as the lunch bell rang.

Sluggishly, he headed not for the rooftop where Araya had summoned him but the lounge next to the student cafeteria on the first floor of the school.

Unlike the closely packed, long, cheap tables that littered the cafeteria, refined, round white tables were arranged spaciously around the semicircular lounge. With its unbroken view of the trees in the courtyard dyed in autumn colors on the other side of its large window, the lounge was without a doubt the most elegant space at Umesato Junior High School.

Thus, it was an unwritten rule that grade-seven students were not allowed to use it. The ribbons and neckties of the students gathered around the tables were all blue (grade eight) or dark red (grade nine), with not a spot of green to be found.

Half of the students were laughing and chatting with cups of coffee or tea in one hand while the other half, eyes closed, had entrusted their bodies to the tall-backed chairs. They weren't sleeping; they were on full dives in the school net.

Haruyuki first hid his large body awkwardly behind the decorative plant at the entrance to the lounge and peered around the room. He half believed she would totally not be there because the thing yesterday was a dream...but...

"...She's here..."

He gulped down air unconsciously. At a table by the window in the very back of the lounge was gathered a particularly conspicuous group. Six students, grades eight and nine, comprised the assemblage, and when he really rubbed his eyes and looked, Haruyuki found that he knew all their faces. Likely all student council members. Each of them, boy and girl, was comely in a different way.

Among them, the one with the strongest presence was a girl with a blue ribbon wearily flipping the pages of a hardcover book. Her straight hair, nearly down to her waist, was a jet black rarely seen these days, while the legs peeking out from her dark gray pleated skirt were wrapped in similarly black tights. For some reason, even the open-collared shirt under her blazer was a brilliant black. No mistake, this was the most popular girl at Umesato Junior High: Kuroyukihime.

If you moved in a straight line, the table in the back was probably no more than twenty meters from the lounge entrance. But to Haruyuki, the distance might as well have been infinite. There was absolutely no way he could undertake the hazardous journey of cutting through the seniors to get there.

Do a right about-face and get out of here. Buy the bread and the yogurt at the cafeteria counter, and take it to Araya and them on the roof. Then hide out in the toilet in the second school building and kill some empty hours in a single-player game on the local net.

Shit. Dammit. I'll go.

Clenching his teeth, Haruyuki came out from behind the plant and stepped into the lounge.

It was no persecution complex; the eyes of the seniors gathered around the tables definitely held hints of reproach and displeasure. He might have gotten a pass if he had just started school or something, but halfway through the second term, he should have been fully aware of the rule that grade-sevens were not allowed. Fortunately, no one raised their voice in reproach against him.

He intently carried his heavy body forward on trembling legs, slipping through the tables, breathing becoming faint, until he finally arrived at the very back table the student council members were occupying.

The first to raise her face was an eighth-grade girl sitting in the very front. Tilting her head and causing ripples in her light hair, she turned a smiling, slightly puzzled face toward Haruyuki and said gently, "Oh…did you need something?"

Unable to get a *yes* out, Haruyuki mumbled, "Er…um… uh…"

At that moment, four of the other council members looked over at Haruyuki. Their faces contained no malice, but the displeased looks from around the table were hard to handle. Just when he was about to pass out from sheer nervousness, the final person at the table at last raised her face from her book.

Kuroyukihime's face, which he was seeing for the first time up close and with his flesh-and-blood eyes, was orders of magnitude more beautiful than the avatar he had seen (supposedly) yesterday. Below sharply defined eyebrows under neatly trimmed bangs were eyes that looked black even as they shone brightly. If her avatar was a black rose, then she was a black narcissus. Although he didn't know if anything like that even existed.

Haruyuki steeled himself for a look of *What is this ugly grade-seven?* to appear on this beautiful face. But, surprising him to the core of his being, Kuroyukihime brought that slight smile he remembered to her pale lips and said briefly, "Well, boy. You came."

She closed the hardcover book with a *snap* and invited Haruyuki, still standing stiffly, to join her, as she glanced around at the other council members at the table.

"I'm the something. Sorry, can you vacate?"

The last part was directed at the ninth-grade boy sitting next to her. When the tall senior with short hair stood up with a bemused look on his face, she directed Haruyuki to the chair with the palm of her hand.

Mumbling his thanks, Haruyuki pulled his round body in as much as possible and lowered himself onto the seat. The slender chair creaked magnificently, but Kuroyukihime appeared not to notice at all and, after digging around in the left pocket of her blazer, pulled out something long and thin.

It was a cable. A thin, silver line, with small plugs at both ends of the shielded cord. After bringing her long hair around to the back with her left hand and inserting one plug into the terminal of the Neurolinker (naturally painted piano black) attached to her surprisingly thin neck, Kuroyukihime casually offered the other plug to Haruyuki. Now a large stir arose among the students in the lounge, all of whom had been carefully studying these events. Mixed in with the din were cries of something akin to distress: "No way!" and "She can't be serious."

Haruyuki was equally taken aback. Beads of sweat appeared suddenly on his face.

Direct wired transmission.

Kuroyukihime was inviting Haruyuki to "direct." Normally, communication happened only through Neurolinkers wirelessly connected to that area's network server, with several layers of security as intermediaries. Connecting directly with a wire, however, rendered 90 percent of these protective barriers useless. If you had the Linker skills, you could peek into the other user's private memory and even set up a malevolent program.

Which is why, normally, directing was limited to people the user trusted implicitly: family, maybe lovers. Put another way, 99 percent of male/female couples directing in public were dating.

Even the length of the cable reflected this level of intimacy, in a custom that had no scientific foundation.

The XSB cable Kuroyukihime was currently holding out was about two meters long, so the problem in this case wasn't the length. Staring fixedly at the glittering silver terminal, Haruyuki managed somehow to squeeze his voice through his throat and ask, "Uh…um, what am I supposed to…"

"You can't do anything besides stick it in your neck, can you?" she asserted without missing a beat.

Very close to passing out now, Haruyuki took the plug with a shaky hand and fumbled to put it in his own Neurolinker. The moment he did, a warning flashed in front of his eyes: WIRED CONNECTION. As this message faded, only the figure of Kuroyukihime before him was alive against the backdrop of the lounge.

Although her lips, still toying with a faint smile, did not move a millimeter, her smooth voice sounded in Haruyuki's brain. *"Sorry to ask you to come all the way over here, Haruyuki Arita. Can you neurospeak?"*

The skill of having a conversation without moving your lips, going only through the Linker. Haruyuki nodded and replied, *"I can. Um…what exactly is this about? Some kind of elaborate… prank or something?"*

He thought she might get mad, but Kuroyukihime tilted her head slightly to the side and murmured softly, *"I suppose…in a certain sense, that's probably exactly it. Because right now, I am sending an application program to your Neurolinker. If you accept it, the world you have known until now will be completely and utterly destroyed and then rebuilt into something you can't even conceive."*

"M-my world…destroyed…?" Haruyuki repeated, dumbstruck.

Already, the student council members at the table were staring with deep interest in where this would go and the students making a fuss around them had essentially disappeared from his view. Only Kuroyukihime's words reverberated in his brain over and over.

The student clad in black smiled again at Haruyuki's confusion, raised her right hand, and quickly flicked the tip of her supple, pale finger.

Followed by a beeping sound.

And holo dialogue: OPEN BRAIN BURST2039.EXE? YES/NO Despite the fact that this was supposedly his own familiar system display, Haruyuki almost felt like the window had its own secret, independent will and was pressing him for a decision.

In terms of common sense, opening an unknown app sent by a direct connection from a person you didn't know very well was the very definition of indiscretion. The obvious thing to do would be to yank out the cable right now. But Haruyuki couldn't do that for some reason. Instead, he looked down at his own body, wedged in tightly on the chair.

My world. My reality.

This dull body. Dull face. Endless bullying, escaping to the net. And more than anything else, me doing absolutely nothing to change any of it. My own self, giving up. I just tell myself it's fine this way and nothing's going to change anyway.

Haruyuki shifted his gaze and stared into Kuroyukihime's pitch-black eyes. And then after a five-second pause, he raised his right hand and poked the YES button with the tip of his finger. He saw her white face suddenly colored with a slight surprise, and a slight satisfaction dripped into his heart.

"Just what I was hoping for. As long as this world . . . breaks," he mumbled, while at nearly the same time, an enormous blaze leapt up to fill his field of vision. The wild flames that had engulfed him, causing him to stiffen up instinctively, finally focused in front of him to form a title logo. The design style was definitely nothing new, with a roughness that brought to mind a certain type of fighting game in fashion at the end of the last century.

The text that appeared: BRAIN BURST.

This was how Haruyuki and the program that would revolutionize the world he knew met.

The installation continued for nearly thirty seconds. For a Neurolinker app, it was pretty huge.

Haruyuki swallowed hard and stared as the indicator bar displayed below the burning title logo finally reached 100 percent. Kuroyukihime had said it would destroy his world. What did that actually mean?

The indicator disappeared, and the logo vanished as if it had burnt itself up. The remaining orange flames produced text reading WELCOME TO THE ACCELERATED WORLD in a small English font, which quickly turned into sparks and scattered. What did that mean: *accelerated world*?

For ten seconds or so, Haruyuki sat and held his breath, waiting for something to happen. However, no sign or omen of the change to come appeared either in his body or in the scene around him. As usual, sweat was trickling down under his uniform, and the critical gazes inflicted on him from the surrounding tables seemed to grow even more intense.

Letting out a long, thin breath, he looked at Kuroyukihime suspiciously. *"Um…this Brain Burst program, what exactly…"* he asked in neurospeak, and the black-clad senior murmured something far removed from Haruyuki's doubts, the smile on her lips never disappearing.

"So you've managed to install it. Although I was certain you had the aptitude for it."

"A-aptitude? For this program?"

"Mm. Brain Burst can't even be installed in people without high-level cerebral nerve reaction speed. For instance, high enough to get an absurd score in a virtual game. When you saw those phantom flames, the program was checking your brain's reactions. If you didn't have the aptitude, you wouldn't have even been able to see the title logo. But…still, you surprised me somewhat. After all, the old me hesitated for nearly two minutes about whether or

not I should accept such a dubious program. I worked out a whole speech to persuade you, and it seems that I wasted my time."

"O-oh...I'm sorry. But, um, it...it doesn't seem like anything's happening. Is it an app you launch instead of a resident app?"

"Don't be impatient. You need to mentally prepare yourself a little first. We can get to the detailed explanations once you do. We have plenty of time."

Haruyuki glanced at the clock continuously displayed in the bottom right of his field of vision. Lunch break was already nearly half over. It didn't exactly seem like they had so much time as all that.

Almost painfully aware of the way the room around him was a mix of curiosity and disgust, Haruyuki leaned forward. The chair beneath him groaned. It was a sound he was used to hearing, but it almost felt as if even the chair were laughing at how ugly and ridiculous he was, and he bit his lip. No one could possibly love him the way he was now. If he could change everything, he'd do it, no matter what the change ended up being.

"I'm already prepared. Please tell me what this program is—" He had gotten this far when the voice he least wanted to hear rang out from the lounge entrance behind him.

"Hey! Pi—Arita! You got a job to do!!"

Reflexively, he flinched and jumped out of his seat. He turned around to see Araya standing red-faced in front of him, even though he normally never came down from the roof before the end of lunch.

At the same time as the expression on Haruyuki's face shifted from shock to terror, Araya's shifted from rage to doubt. By standing up, Haruyuki had revealed the slender figure of Kuroyuki-hime, who had been completely hidden in his enormous shadow, along with the cable extending from her Linker and connecting to Haruyuki's.

Even frozen in place, Haruyuki was keenly sensitive to the nearly imperceptible shift in the mood of everyone around him except the members of the student council. They must have all instantly grasped the nature of the relationship between the large Araya wearing the same green necktie as Haruyuki, small vertically but big horizontally. But the mood of the students was of course not a reproach of Araya, but rather a sense of consensus, as if to say, *Oh, of course.*

Stop. Just stop now, Haruyuki fervently chanted to himself. He seriously hated the idea that Kuroyukihime would know he was being bullied. He offered a stiff smile to Araya with the intention of communicating that once his business here was finished, he would go right away to buy the buns and come up to the roof, so please just be quiet and wait a minute or two.

Upon seeing this, Araya's florid face grew even redder in fury. Haruyuki shuddered as he watched Araya's lips move to form the word *pig* soundlessly. He had completely misunderstood the meaning of the smile on Haruyuki's lips as he directed with the most popular student in school.

Eyes glittering as he raised them, Araya slipped without a word through the hedges separating the cafeteria from the lounge. He approached in a straight line, stepping on the heels of his indoor shoes and making a scuffing sound. Subordinates A and B trailed after him, slightly nervous looks on their faces.

It's all over, Haruyuki thought, taking a step backward.

Araya was so tall and sculpted of solid muscle from karate that it was hard to believe he was also thirteen. On this body, he wore a too-short blazer and a light purple shirt that was conversely way too long, and his pants too were sloppily wide. His hair, dyed a nearly white gold, stood up in points like the flower holders in flower arrangements, and with his very thin eyebrows, piercings decorating both ears, and his almond eyes, he was the very definition of danger.

Umesato Junior High School was a high-level private school focused on getting kids into university, but in this era of extremely low birth rates, almost no junior high schools still had entrance examinations. Thus, martial artists like Araya sometimes signed up with the idea of an easy ride.

Having been easily taken down by this type since his first day of school, Haruyuki flinched and stared up at Araya standing in front of him, practically leaning against the smaller boy as he glowered down at him.

"You making fun of me?" As these words issued between lips twisted into a sneer, Kuroyukihime's clear real-world voice resonated crisply and clearly before Haruyuki could try to force some menial apology from his mouth.

"You're Araya, yes?"

After a moment's surprise flitted across his face, Araya smiled flirtatiously. Even a guy like this could apparently be pleased that *the* Kuroyukihime had remembered his name. But the words that followed astonished not only Araya but Haruyuki as well.

"I heard about you from Arita. That you might have been sent to junior high school from the zoo."

Araya's jaw dropped suddenly, and Haruyuki stared in dazed amazement at how it trembled. "Wh-wh-wha—" The sound Araya was making was exactly what Haruyuki wanted to scream.

Wh-what are you talking about?!

However, he had no chance to give voice to that thought. Araya emitted a fierce, angry bellow. "What the hell?! That's it! You are so dead, piiiiig!!"

Haruyuki froze with a start while Araya tightened his right hand into a fist and raised it up high. At the same moment, a sharp voice within his brain gave Haruyuki an order. "*Now! Shout it! 'Burst link'!*"

Haruyuki couldn't tell if he shouted the short command with his real voice or in neurospeak. But the sound became a vibration that seeped into every corner of his body.

"*Burst link!!*"

The sound of a screeching impact shook his world.

All color instantly disappeared, leaving only a transparent blue spreading out before him. The lounge, the students watching events play out with suspicious eyes, and even Araya in front of him—all were dyed a monochromatic blue.

And everything was frozen.

Haruyuki stared dumbfounded at Araya's fist, which should have been striking him in another second, suspended a few dozen centimeters in front of him.

"Wh-whoa!!" he cried out involuntarily, leaping a step back. As a result, Haruyuki saw something even more incredible.

His own back. His own rounded back, now the same pure blue as Araya, was unnaturally frozen in a ridiculous flinching posture. It was almost like his soul alone had escaped his flesh.

In which case, what was he now?! When, shocked, he looked down, and he saw there his familiar pink pig. There was no mistake, it was the avatar Haruyuki used on the local net. No longer understanding anything about anything, he turned around unsteadily.

Where he saw yet another strange sight.

On the lounge chair, Kuroyukihime was sitting gracefully, knees neatly pressed together, back straight. However, her body and the cable stretching out from her neck, all of it was colored a transparent blue, like a crystal.

And standing next to her was her avatar, clad in the black dress with the swallowtail butterfly wings and parasol folded into it, a mysterious smile on her lips.

"Wh-what's going on here?!" Haruyuki yelled at her, unable to hold back. "Full dive?! Or…an out-of-body experience?!"

"Ha, neither," Kuroyukihime's avatar informed him cheerfully. "Right now, we are operating in the Brain Burst program. We're accelerated."

"A…accelerated…?"

"Exactly. Everything around us looks like it has stopped, but in fact, it hasn't. Our consciousnesses are moving at extremely high speeds."

Kuroyukihime took a few steps, causing the silver gems decorating the hem of her dress to glint, and stopped beside the real

Haruyuki and Araya, frozen and blue. With the tip of her parasol, she indicated Araya's fist in a right straight punch trajectory. "This fist, although we can't see it, is moving very slowly, crawling forward. Like the hour hand of a clock. If we waited like this for quite some time, it would eventually traverse these eighty centimeters, and we would be able to watch it sink slowly into your cheek here."

"Y-you're kidding... No, wait, I mean... J-just hold on a minute." Haruyuki cradled his head in his pig hands and desperately tried to make sense of this information. "S-so, uh... then this means our souls haven't actually left our bodies, right? Then all of this is just thinking happening in our heads basically?"

"You learn fast. That's exactly it."

"But that's crazy! If you're saying that just our thinking and our impressions are accelerated, then this... There's no way I should be able to move around like some out-of-body experience and see my own back or even stand here and have a conversation with you!"

"Mm, that's a very natural concern, Haruyuki." Nodding professorially, Kuroyukihime swung her black hair, twisted into a long roll over her shoulder, and moved to the side of the table. "This blue world we see is the real-time world, but we are not viewing it optically. Go ahead and take a look under the table."

"O-okay..." Haruyuki crouched down with the body of his pig, smaller than his real-world body, and peered under the blue table. "Th-that's..."

Strange. The table was wood, and the top was shot through with a fine wood grain. But the underside was smooth like plastic, without the slightest hint of texture.

"What is this... It's like it's a polygon...?"

Kuroyukihime nodded casually at Haruyuki as he brought his face back up. "Exactly. This blue world is a 3-D image reconstructed from images captured by several social cameras in the lounge, and our brains are seeing it through our Neurolinkers. Areas that are blind spots for the cameras are supplemented by estimates. Which is why there is no point in trying to look up the skirt of that girl there."

"Social cameras" were officially "social security surveillance cameras," and the whole of Japan was covered with them, the goal the maintenance of public order. Guarded by the secure protective wall of the government's image monitoring network, there was no way at all for the general population to sneak a look through them—or that was how it was supposed to be.

As this tidbit popped into his head, Haruyuki's eyes reflexively followed the legs of the female student council member as they stretched out under the table, confirming that the graceful lines disappeared at the edge of her skirt.

Kuroyukihime glanced over at Haruyuki hurrying to stand up. "Don't look at my legs. They're in the view of the cameras."

"I—I won't." Working hard to fix his gaze in one place, Haruyuki shook his head. "A-anyway, I basically get the logic of what we're seeing. It's a 3-D movie of the real world in real time... Using our avatars as proxies, we're looking at stuff around us and talking via the direct connection, right?"

"Right. Your school local net avatar is being used here as a stopgap."

"I'd rather have something else," he mumbled, sighing heavily. He shook the pig head, got his thoughts sorted, and looked at Kuroyukihime's avatar once again. "But...that's only the start of it. What I really want to know...What exactly is *accelerated*? I've never heard of Neurolinkers equipped with a function that stops time like this!"

"Of course you haven't. Only people with the Brain Burst program can call up the acceleration function hidden in the Neurolinkers," Kuroyukihime said, almost under her breath, raising her left hand and gently nudging the extra-large Neurolinker wrapped around the neck of the frozen real Haruyuki. "Do you know the principle behind the operation of the Neurolinker, Haruyuki?"

Haruyuki nodded as he watched her touch "her" neck with a

slim finger, giving him a start for some reason. "Y-yes...I don't know all the details, but I know it connects wirelessly with your brain cells at the quantum level to send in images, sound, and sensations while simultaneously canceling out the reality of your own senses."

"Right. In other words, the principle behind it is fundamentally different from the headgear-style virtual reality machines of the twenty-twenties or the implants of the thirties. A quantum connection is not a physiological mechanism. Thus, you don't have the burden on the brain cells, and you get this unexpected excess...or so a certain person out there realized."

"What do you mean...excess?"

Kuroyukihime responded with another question, as if Haruyuki's query was slightly off the mark. "Have you ever touched a computer from the twenties?"

"Y-yeah, sure. We have one at my house."

"Then you probably know what they called the basic operating frequency of the computers."

"The...base clock?"

Kuroyukihime nodded with satisfaction. "Yes. Depending on the set scale, you overclocked the signal, which carved up time like a pendulum on the motherboard, to run the CPU. And human brains, our consciousness works the same way."

"What?!" Haruyuki's eyes widened, breath shooting out of his large pig's nose. "N-no way! Where is this pendulum inside us, then?"

"Here," Kuroyukihime replied immediately. Embracing the real, blue Haruyuki from the front, she poked the center of his back with her right hand, eyes upturned as if playing a joke.

"Wh-what are you doing?"

"Right now, your clock is a little faster. You probably get it already. It's your heart! Your heart's not merely a pump to send out blood. The beating of your heart makes it a basic clock generator determining the driving speed of your thoughts."

Swallowing hard, Haruyuki pressed on the chest of his pig

body. Kuroyukihime continued, still touching the area above his heart, almost as if she was teasing him.

"For instance, when you try to stop your body, your heartbeat will speed up depending on the situation. Like a race-car driver's. Why? It's because you need to *accelerate* your thoughts—your awareness of the situation, your judgment. Or like a pair of lovers touching each other. You accelerate to more deeply experience each minute, each second."

Kuroyukihime slowly dragged the tip of the finger on Haruyuki's chest upward, stopping at his neck. "With each beat of your heart, the quantum pulse signal generated is sent back to your central nervous system, driving your brain—that is, your thoughts. So what do you think happens when the Neurolinker around your neck captures that signal and overclocks you?"

Haruyuki felt a shudder run up his back. "Your thoughts... are accelerated?"

"Exactly. And the Neurolinker lets you do that. Without any kind of negative impact on your body or your brain cells. Right now, in this exact moment, our Neurolinkers are overclocking the signal generated by a single heartbeat, riding the wireless quantum signal and sending information to our brains. In fact, it's doing so at a rate of more than a thousand times the norm!"

"A thousand... times..." Haruyuki could no longer do anything other than repeat the words fed to him, dumbfounded. In his almost drugged awareness, Kuroyukihime's smooth voice made even more of an impact.

"Your thoughts are accelerated a thousandfold. Which means one second of reality is a thousand seconds. Do the math and you're experiencing sixteen minutes and forty seconds."

This was more than F1 racers. This was basically more magic to stop time than it was technology.

However, before Haruyuki could start to wonder what specifically would be possible if he were to make full use of this marvelous phenomenon, Kuroyukihime muttered, "Oh!" as if just realizing something.

"…?"

"No, sorry. I got caught up in explaining things, and I ended up using a bit too much time. I completely forgot that the real you is about to be sent flying."

"Hah…" Haruyuki hurried to his feet and went around to the other side of his frozen blue self.

Araya's punch had definitely moved quite a bit during the five minutes or so (or the point-three seconds) they had spent talking. It was now only less than fifty centimeters from the real Haruyuki's round cheeks.

Araya's face was reproduced so perfectly, lips twisting to expose his brutal excitement, that it was hard to believe it was created using images from the social cameras hidden in the ceiling. *What exactly about this is fun? No, it's probably fun. I mean, me standing there aimlessly in front of his fist with that blank look on my face. I'm basically a bit player in his story.*

Haruyuki turned back to Kuroyukihime, depressing thoughts rolling around in his brain. "So…how long does this acceleration last?"

"In theory, forever. But due to the limits of the Brain Burst program, the longest you can stay accelerated is thirty felt minutes, or one-point-eight real seconds."

At Kuroyukihime's cool response, Haruyuki widened his round, pink pig eyes. If his real-world self had been frozen like this for nearly two seconds, then Araya's punch would travel the remaining distance and smash in the bridge of his nose in no time.

"H-he's going to hit me, isn't he?" Haruyuki cried, imagining himself being sent flying frame by frame.

But Kuroyukihime laughed lightly and added by way of explanation, "Ha-ha! Don't worry. Of course, you can stop the accelerated state when you want to."

"O-oh…you can? Then I better go back to reality and avoid this punch…"

"Simple. Ha-ha, this way of using acceleration is the easiest to understand. You carefully watch the situation with a reaction speed not possible in flesh and blood, and after careful deliberation, you release the acceleration and leisurely take action."

Just as she noted, accelerated, he now understood what needed to be done given the trajectory and aim of Araya's punch, which due to his terror he hadn't even been able to analyze—much less avoid—the many times he had been hit before now.

Once he released the acceleration, it would be enough to move about fifteen centimeters to the left. Swallowing hard, he carved the thought into his head and looked at Kuroyukihime for the command to release the acceleration.

But before he could speak, the beautiful girl in black dropped a bomb in a light tone. "But don't avoid it. He's actually daring to hit you here, Haruyuki."

"Wh—" Haruyuki's pig nose twitched before he shouted, "I—I don't want to! It's going to hurt!"

"Hurt what?"

"Huh...? What do you mean 'what'?"

"I'm asking you whether it's going to hurt your body or your mind."

The smile disappeared from Kuroyukihime's avatar. Without waiting for Haruyuki's response, she put a black high heel forward sharply.

Her slim form, nearly half a meter taller than Haruyuki's pig body, crouched down, and Kuroyukihime stared into his eyes well within his personal space. He swallowed and stood bolt upright.

"This isn't the first time you have been punched by this student, Araya."

"N-no." For some reason, Haruyuki nodded even though he had so desperately wanted her not to find out about the bullying.

"So then there are two reasons why he has not been dealt with before now. One is, of course, that you have just meekly accepted his behavior. And the other is that Araya has cleverly set the scene of his violence and extortion beyond the view of the social cameras."

It was true that any direct bullying that happened to Haruyuki was always in places where students didn't go, like the shadow of the ventilation units on the roof or behind the school. So that was to avoid not the eyes of other people but the cameras?

The expression on Kuroyukihime's face was complicated, and she stretched herself upright smoothly. "Unfortunately, while they are few, there are students like him even among the eighth and ninth graders. They have their own sort of network, and apparently, an illegal app that warns them when they are in view of the social cameras is quite popular with their crowd. That lot would never give themselves away in front of the cameras. Even as a new student, he would surely have had that drilled into him."

Glancing at Araya's dyed blue face with eyes like ice, Kuroyukihime continued in a quiet, strong voice. "But he is still a child, after all. At my earlier provocation, he forgot himself and is lashing out violently here in front of all these cameras. Understand? This is your chance, Haruyuki. It would be easy to dodge this punch, but if you do, Araya will come to his senses and run off. Your opportunity to punish him as he deserves will again recede ever further from view."

And then Araya would inflict further pain on Haruyuki. He could only too easily imagine that Araya's revenge would make everything up to now look like a game. A shudder ran down his spine as Haruyuki looked at his real self and Araya's fist approaching that face.

The thug's bony right hand tapered to rough points, and if it hit him, it would hurt enough to make him cry. It was a pain he had become disgustingly familiar with over these last six months. But—

What had really been bleeding was not his body but his heart. His pride, which had been steadily shredded.

"Um." Haltingly, Haruyuki asked Kuroyukihime, "If I managed to master Brain Burst, would I be able to beat him in a fight?"

All expression disappeared from her beautiful face, and she stared directly at Haruyuki. "You probably could. You're already a Burst Linker, which means you have a power greatly exceeding that of the unaccelerated. If you were so inclined, you wouldn't have to settle for just one punch; you could beat him for as long as you wanted."

I am so inclined. Is there some reason I wouldn't be?

I'll neatly dodge Araya's karate and make him into something even uglier than a pig. I'll smash his nose, knock out all his front teeth, pull out every single one of those precious golden hairs from his head when he's bowed down before me, weeping.

Clenching his teeth with a crunch, he sighed heavily and told Kuroyukihime in a shaking voice. "...No, I won't do it. I'll get hit like a good boy. I won't get the chance again, after all."

"Mm." Smiling with satisfaction somehow, Kuroyukihime nodded slowly. "A wise choice. Now, let's try to minimize the damage while maximizing the effect, hmm? Once the acceleration runs out, you leap back to the right with everything you've got. Don't forget to turn your head to the right as his fist hits you."

"O-okay." Moving directly behind his real self, Haruyuki checked the trajectory of Araya's punch. She was right, if he leapt while turning his face, he could mitigate most of the bite from Araya's karate technique.

Nodding, he looked to see exactly what he'd be leaping into. There was a table to the left, but a large space opened up behind him to the right, with no obstacles before the big window looking out onto the courtyard. Except for one person.

"Oh no...I can't. If I jump from here to there, I'll end up slamming into you."

There was only about a meter between Haruyuki standing and the real Kuroyukihime sitting on the chair. If he hit her slim form with his enormous bulk, he couldn't be sure what would happen to her.

However, the avatar in the black dress merely shrugged lightly.

"It's not a problem; this way is more effective. Don't worry, I'll make sure to dodge. I won't get hurt."

"...O-okay." It was certainly possible to do if you knew in advance what was going to happen. He was forced to nod. "We're very nearly out of time here. Hurry and line up with your real self."

She poked his back and Haruyuki took a step forward to align his pig avatar with his blue self. Kuroyukihime seemed to have sat on the chair behind him; the position of her voice was lower.

"All right. Now I'm going to teach you the command to release the acceleration. Be strong. 'Burst out'!"

"Burst out!"

Haruyuki took a deep breath and put everything he had behind the shout.

A jetlike roar approached from a distance, shattering the surrounding silence. The blue world gradually took on its former color. In the left of his field of vision, Araya's static fist began to move, bit by tiny bit. From a sluggish snail's pace, it gradually sped up and drew nearer to Haruyuki's cheek.

As he prepared to leap back to the right as instructed, pushing off with both legs, he twisted his head earnestly to the right. The punch chugging toward him touched his skin, sinking in slightly.

And then the world returned.

As the noise around him rushed in, Haruyuki felt the fist digging into his left cheek. He felt his teeth driven into the inside of his cheek, his lip splitting. It was probably bleeding a little, but the pain was definitely about half that of the other karate punches he had suffered through however many times before this.

At the same time, his large body flew spectacularly through the air action-movie style. Fervently hoping she would manage to jump clear of him, Haruyuki collided with the chair behind him. For a brief moment, he smelled something good, felt her soft hair.

The chair clattering to the floor was followed immediately by an ominous *thud*.

His back slamming into the floor, Haruyuki stopped breathing momentarily. Even as he gasped for air, he was yanking his head around to check on Kuroyukihime. She was supposed to have dodged, but what his widening eyes saw was her slender figure, limbs splayed out like a broken doll, eyes closed, head up against the lounge window.

Below the disheveled bangs, a single trail of blood ran down a cheek so white it was nearly translucent.

"Ah...ah!" Swallowing a scream, Haruyuki tried to stand up. But at that moment—

"Don't move!!"

Kuroyukihime's think voice hit his brain through his still directly connected Linker. Freezing instinctively faceup on the floor, Haruyuki responded. *"B-but you're bleeding!!"*

"Don't worry. It's just a little cut. I told you, aim to maximize the effect. After this, you'll never have to deal with Araya again."

Staying still as instructed, Haruyuki moved just his eyes from left to right.

Araya, right fist still stuck out in front of him, looked down at Haruyuki and Kuroyukihime, mouth agape. The blood slowly drained from his face, and his thin lips trembled a few times, as if spasming.

The total silence that descended on the lounge was shattered by the terrible screams of the girls at the surrounding tables.

"Aaaaaaah!!"

Araya and subordinates AB put up almost no resistance when they were thrown out by the male council members. The three of them, white as ghosts, knees knocking, were half dragged away by the teachers who had come running, faces red with anger, and Kuroyukihime was taken straight to the hospital, held by another female council member.

Haruyuki himself just got a little bandaging in the health

room, and as the school doctor's hand disinfected and patched him up, the words Kuroyukihime had uttered immediately before the direct cable was pulled reverberated in his ears. *"Oops, I forgot to tell you. Do not take off your Neurolinker before you come to school tomorrow. And you can't make a global connection, not even for a second. Got it? Under no circumstances. Promise."* He couldn't even begin to guess at the intent behind these instructions. The entire two hours he spent in the health room, his whole body was enveloped in a strange feeling of detachment.

He had no idea how he was supposed to process and digest all of the things that had happened to him in just these past two days.

But at the very least, it seemed like he wouldn't need to worry anymore about things like his shoes disappearing from his shoe locker or weird stuff being put in the shoes if they stayed there. Mechanically, he changed out of his school shoes into his street shoes, and when he was about to leave school grounds, he did as instructed and disconnected his Neurolinker from the net. Wondering once again what the point was, he turned toward the school gates and started walking.

"Haru!"

A small voice reached his ears, and his legs stopped short.

When he looked around, he noticed a small figure casting a shadow on the school wall, colored in the evening light. Aware of his face stiffening up involuntarily, Haruyuki said her name.

"...Chiyu."

It wasn't that he'd forgotten. He'd forcefully chased the events of the previous day out of his head, and now they instantly replayed in the back of his brain. *Ah! What should I do? Okay, I have to apologize, first things first.*

As he panicked, Chiyuri Kurashima approached with a difficult look on her face, sinking slightly on the soft synthetic surface of the schoolyard.

"Uh...um...yesterday, I—"

"Haru, I heard about what happened at lunch," Chiyuri said, cutting through Haruyuki's flustered incoherence.

40   Accel World: Volume 1

"Huh? Lunch…oh, oh!"

"I heard he hit you and you seriously went flying! Are you hurt? Are you okay?" Pulling her thick eyebrows together tightly, Chiyuri brought her face in closer, and Haruyuki unconsciously brought his left hand up to cover the bandage on his mouth. There was no way he could tell her that he was actually the one who had sent himself flying so spectacularly.

"Y-yeah, I'm okay. I just cut my lip a bit. I'm not hurt anywhere else."

"You're not? Oh good."

A faint smile crossing her still terribly stiff face, Chiyuri glanced around. Apparently due to this one incident at lunch, Haruyuki had immediately become a topic of conversation at school, and the students heading home around them were all staring openly.

"Anyway, it's good to walk home together sometimes," Chiyuri said in a hard voice, and she started walking without waiting for an answer.

Sometimes? We haven't done that once since we started junior high, Haruyuki thought, but if he shouted out in protest and ran off, it would just be a repeat of his stupidity yesterday. Whatever else happened, he had to apologize for that stuff.

Jogging after Chiyuri, who stalked forward in long strides unsuited to her stature, Haruyuki put a slight distance between them to walk alongside her. In this manner, they passed through the school gate and walked along the large road with only the sound of the in-wheel motors of passenger vehicles breaking the silence.

Normally as soon as Haruyuki left school, the people, bicycles, and cars moving around him were automatically marked as colored symbols in his vision, allowing him to walk even with his eyes closed, but he couldn't use the navigation while disconnected from the global net. Just as he started to wonder again why exactly Kuroyukihime had given him an instruction like that, Chiyuri to his right casually mentioned that very name and nearly made him jump.

"I heard you were directing with Kuroyukihime in grade eight. For real?"

"What?! Th-that's..." He was about to ask how she knew that, but, thinking better of it, realized that was about right. More than Araya and his fist, the directing probably made the bigger splash at school. "Yeah, well..."

Without even looking at him nodding, Chiyuri stuck out her small lips and started walking even faster. Haruyuki knew only too well from long experience that this was an expression of her very worst mood and wondered again why she was in such a state. To which he was again quick to tell himself that that was about right. If some idiot who had knocked over and dumped out her homemade lunch was doing weird things with some other girl without so much as an apology, it wasn't just Chiyuri. Anyone would obviously be mad.

"B-but it wasn't anything special. It was... I just copied an app from her." Haruyuki tried to explain it away, an unpleasant sweat running down his back even though it was October. However, the look on Chiyuri's face did not soften, and he began to intently put together a dialogue in his head, even more certain of the need to apologize for the sandwich incident.

"A-anyway, about... about yesterday..." He had finally gotten this much out of his mouth when they heard a voice ringing out ahead of them, and Haruyuki swallowed the rest.

"Heey! Haru! Chiii! What a coincidence. You headed home now?"

Chiyuri's legs stopped on a dime, and Haruyuki lifted his face. He saw a boy the same age as them smiling broadly with a hand raised on the escalator leading to Kannana Ring Road.

His blue-gray uniform had a raised collar, unlike that of Umesato Junior. In his right hand, he held a refined, old-fashioned black schoolbag, and a kendo bamboo sword case was slung over his shoulder. His longish hair was parted cleanly in the middle, and the face below it was beautiful, clear—best and most aptly described as "fresh."

"Oh... Taku." Blinking rapidly several times, Chiyuri smiled.

Even though she was in such a bad mood. After thinking this, Haruyuki muttered his third *That's about right* in his head. *I mean, she did just run into her boyfriend while walking along with an annoying jerk who dropped her sandwiches.*

As Haruyuki and Chiyuri's childhood friend Takumu Mayuzumi jogged toward them, bamboo sword case bouncing, he turned a cheerful, open smile toward Haruyuki.

"Hey, Haru! It's been ages!"

"Hey, Taku. Has it been that long?" Haruyuki asked, glancing up at Takumu's face, ten centimeters higher than his own.

"It has. I haven't seen you in two weeks already in meatspace. You never come to the condo events."

"Like I'd show up at a sports meet," he returned, screwing up his face, and Takumu laughed as if to say, *You never change.*

The three of them had all been born the same year in a skyscraper condo complex in Kita-Koenji. However, Haruyuki probably wouldn't have become such good friends with this boy who had everything he didn't based solely on that coincidence.

Ironically, it was because Takumu was so good at his studies and managed to get into a famous K–12 school in Shinjuku that Haruyuki was able to hang out with him without fear. Takumu had never had to see Haruyuki's pathetic self targeted for bullying the second he had started at the local public elementary school.

Haruyuki had forced (or rather begged) Chiyuri, who had gone to that same elementary school, never to tell Takumu about the bullying. If he found out, Takumu might have tried to help him, calling out the gang of brats and taking them down with his bamboo sword.

But Haruyuki had the feeling that even if he stopped getting bullied, he wouldn't be able to keep being friends with Takumu.

"That reminds me." Haruyuki was first to open his mouth while the three of them walked side by side, something he almost never did at school. "I saw the videos of the city tournament on the net the other day. You're amazing, Tak; only in seventh grade and already winning."

"I was just lucky. I was super lucky," Takumu said as he laughed, scratching his head. "The guys who would've given me trouble got knocked out in the prelims. And then there was Chi here coming to cheer me on."

"What? Me?!" Chiyuri cried from the other side of Takumu, eyes wide. "I—I mean, I was just watching from the corner, that's it."

"Ha-ha-ha! What are you talking about? You were really hollering! Stuff like *Kick his teeth in!*" Takumu raised his laughing voice cheerfully. "And on top of that, you even told me you wouldn't give me lunch if I lost. And you looked serious, too, Chi."

"Oh, come on! I'm not listening to you anymore!"

Watching Chiyuri increase her pace while covering both ears, Haruyuki nudged Takumu with his left elbow. "So that's what all that screaming about the final match was."

"Well, you know. Ha-ha-ha!"

He laughed with Takumu.

It's definitely better this way, Haruyuki thought.

His choice two years ago hadn't been a mistake. After all, the three of them were able to talk like this now, just like they used to. He didn't want to ruin this relationship.

At that moment, Takumu said lightly, almost like a counterattack: "So Haru, you got to have the Chi special for lunch yesterday, huh?"

"Huh? Oh, that's, well…" Seeing Chiyuri's back suddenly stiffen, Haruyuki was slightly panicked. *Crap, I still haven't apologized. What should I do? Should I apologize now? Or maybe e-mail her once I get home—*

No, wait.

How did Takumu know that?

Haruyuki's legs became tangled, and Takumu caught him with a "Whoa!" as he was about to fall. He was unaware even of this as his thoughts raced feverishly.

Chiyuri had made those sandwiches because she knew that Araya and his gang were stealing his lunch money. She definitely wasn't one for cooking, so he had wondered why…but could it be that she had actually done it on Takumu's advice? In which case, that meant that Chiyuri had talked to Takumu. About the fact that Haruyuki was being bullied. If she hadn't, he wouldn't have said that just now.

The inside of his head suddenly went incandescent, and unconsciously, Haruyuki pushed away Takumu's hand on his right elbow.

"H-hey! Haru?" Takumu inquired doubtfully, but Haruyuki couldn't bring himself to look up at that face.

Letting his gaze roam around, Haruyuki's eyes met Chiyuri's, an almost-frozen expression on her face. Her lips moved, and she looked as if she was about to say something. Before she got the chance, though, Haruyuki shouted, "Ah! Sorry, there's just this show I want to watch! I'm gonna run ahead! See you, Taku!"

He took off running. His legs insisted on getting tangled up, and he nearly fell more than once, but Haruyuki didn't stop.

The two of them were probably going to talk about him again. About how they could help Haruyuki. Just imagining the conversation, he was overcome with a sensation like the top of his heart was being twisted off. It was too ironic that just when Araya was finally disappearing through a seriously miraculous turn of events, he found out Takumu had already known all about it.

He kept running, legs constantly in motion, until he passed through the entrance to his condo building and dove into an elevator.

The dream Haruyuki had that night was probably at the top of the list of his all-time worst bad dreams.

The bad kids from his elementary school, Araya and subordinates AB, and some outlaw students he didn't know kept tagging one another out to square off against Haruyuki and knock him around. A slight distance away, Chiyuri and Takumu held hands and watched. More than the pain all over his body, it was their pitying expressions that he had the most trouble enduring.

As the dream progressed, the number of spectators increased. His mother appeared next to the couple (Chiyuri and Takumu), and then even his father—who had left them a long time ago—showed up. The residents of his condo and his classmates joined as well, forming a circle and looking down at Haruyuki as he crawled along the ground.

Now it wasn't just pity on their faces but scorn. Too many people to count pointed their fingers at ugly, miserable Haruyuki and laughed.

I hate this. I hate it here.

With this thought in mind, he looked up at the remote, dark sky and saw a shadow there. A single bird, wings blacker than the night, spread its wings, soaring lightly.

I want to be up there, too. Higher. Farther.

I want to fly.

To the other side.

"*Is that your wish?*"

3

Haruyuki opened his eyes with a start.

When he looked at his clock by the white light coming in through the window, the display said six thirty in the morning. Which meant he had been asleep nearly twelve hours.

His entire body was drenched in sleep sweat, a slimy coating on his skin composed of the vestiges of his nightmare. Despite this, he couldn't remember the details of the dream.

Kuroyukihime's final words to him the day before came dimly to mind. Could the instruction not to remove his Neurolinker all night have had some connection with his dream?

Wondering about this vaguely as he showered and changed into his uniform, Haruyuki ate a breakfast of cereal and orange juice alone in the kitchen, put his dishes in the dishwasher, and, to complete his set of predeparture rituals, knocked on his mother's bedroom door.

"I'm leaving for school," he called into the dim light inside her room, whereupon he heard an unintelligible croaking from the bed. Apparently, she'd had quite a bit to drink the night before.

His mother took her terminal in hand, and he waited for her to charge five hundred yen to his Neurolinker. "Haruyuki, your Linker's disconnected." Her voice was unexpectedly tinged with annoyance.

Oh crap. He hurriedly put a hand to his neck. After he connected to the global net, all the while feeling like he had forgotten something, his electronic balance quickly increased with a ring denoting the transaction.

"I'm leaving, then," he said again but with no response this time. Quietly closing the bedroom door, he put on his sneakers in the foyer and left the apartment, taking the elevator to the first floor and making his way through the lobby, muttering "Good morning" to other residents of the building whose faces he barely remembered.

Just three seconds after he slipped out through the automatic doors to step into the condo courtyard, an intense shrieking noise echoed in his brain, and the world blacked out around him. In an instant, the town, sparkling in the morning sun, sank into the darkness of night.

What the—?! Acceleration?! But . . . why? All by itself?!

He held his breath as letters in the familiar flaming font arranged themselves before his eyes: HERE COMES A NEW CHALLENGER!!

He felt like he had seen this sentence somewhere before. But before he could follow the memory trail, the flaming text blinked out, and something even more mysterious appeared atop of his field of vision.

First, in the center, the number 1800. Then, to the left and right, blue bars stretched out abruptly, with a somewhat thin green bar growing below them.

Finally, the flaming text in the center of his view: FIGHT!!

The number changed to 1799.

Not knowing what to do, Haruyuki simply stared at the four-digit number as it counted down. Eighteen hundred seconds. Thirty minutes. It was a number he had heard somewhere. Right, wasn't this the time limit for acceleration that Kuroyukihime had mentioned?

But this time, Haruyuki hadn't even said the *B* of the "burst link" command to start the acceleration. Also, the color of the world—it wasn't blue, it was full-dive. And he basically had no idea what all the *challenger* and *fight* stuff was about. He looked around, desperately trying to get even the most tenuous grasp on the situation before quickly realizing something.

The crisp October morning had vanished without a trace, but the space around him was still the same area in front of his building that had been burned into his memory. On one side, the familiar two-lane road, and on the other, convenience stores and office buildings. When he turned around, the high-rise condo from which he had just emerged pierced the darkness, towering above him.

However, the jam of cars that should have been bumper-to-bumper on the road toward Shinjuku and the school-bound students filling the sidewalks were gone. Instead, the road was cracked and caving in everywhere, guardrails and signs were twisted, and the buildings' windows were very obviously broken.

Bricks were piled up at the intersection a little way away, almost like a barricade, and flames of something burning licked up at the sky from a metal drum. Traces of destruction also marred Haruyuki's condo, which was in a terrible state, with crumbling concrete pillars and large holes in the exterior walls.

Struck by the urge to run back inside and check the state of his own apartment, Haruyuki staggered around a few steps and peered into the entrance through the bricks. He then opened his eyes wide in silent amazement. The interior of the building was just a flat gray surface spreading out boxlike, almost like the time he'd poked his head into a polygon building in a game.

No. Not almost *like.* Exactly *like.*

This was reality and also not reality. Haruyuki was currently in a full dive on the virtual net using the accelerated function, and the scene around him was a 3-D movie reconstructed from social camera images. Just like the frozen, blue world he'd seen in the lounge the day before. But he had never experienced this level of detail in a virtual space. It was impossible for him to pick out the pixel pitch. Even the lone pebble rolling by his feet was inscribed with a level of crispness that was overwhelming.

So then what body did he have? Haruyuki looked down, expecting to find his familiar pink pig avatar. "...Wh-what is this..." Dumbfounded, his voice slipped out involuntarily.

Legs, torso, arms—his whole body was polished silver and thin like wire. Almost like a robot, but far removed from a game or anime fighting robot.

Panicking and bringing his hands to his head, the tips of his fingers merely slipped over the smooth helmetlike curves and found nothing like a nose or a mouth. He looked around for a moment and, seeing the cracked windows in the wall of the mixed residential building across the road from his building, he ran over, feet clanking against the pavement.

The figure the large window reflected back at him was clearly a metal robot, from tip to toe. His body was very thin and small, only the streamlined head was awkwardly large. In a word, a total small fry.

If I at least had some horns on my forehead... or both my eyes shone gold like beacons. As Haruyuki silently grumbled at the unknown avatar designer, he saw several human shapes squirming behind his reflection in the glass on the other side of the road.

Metal body cowering, Haruyuki turned around with a gasp. He didn't know when they had shown up, but looking his way were exactly three figures standing in the shadow of the ruined local convenience store. Under cover of darkness as they were, he could only make out their silhouettes, which were all much larger than his own.

The shadows huddled together as if discussing something. Unconsciously, Haruyuki strained his ears.

"... too, but he looks like the jumpy type."

"And I don't have his name in memory. Maybe a newbie?"

"But he's metallic. That's gotta mean something."

They're—They're not NPCs. Haruyuki felt it instinctively. Their demeanor, their tone—he was sure they weren't the creation of some program; they were real, live people. But this was the accelerated virtual net. Which meant they had also installed Brain Burst, just like Haruyuki and Kuroyukihime.

In which case, they probably knew what this was all about. *I'll just go and ask them*, Haruyuki thought, and he stepped nervously into the road, advancing to the white center line. Abruptly, he felt a new pair of eyes on him. He stopped moving and ran his gaze quickly over the scene.

There they were. Never mind the group of three down there. He didn't know where they had appeared from, but on the roofs of the abandoned buildings, on top of piles of bricks, strange silhouettes were staring down at Haruyuki from all directions. However, they didn't come any closer, and…they seemed to be waiting for something.

At a loss, Haruyuki, in the middle of the road, shifted just his gaze. In seemingly no time, the count in the top of his field of view had gotten down to 1620. There was no change in the two bars stretching out to the right and left of the numbers. And he hadn't noticed until now, but underneath the bars were small English letters.

The text on the left side read SILVER CROW, and on the right was ASH ROLLER.

I know this screen configuration. I totally know this screen, Haruyuki thought, hit by a powerful sense of déjà vu.

It wasn't anything new. This kind of game program had swept through the arcades of Japan more than thirty years before Haruyuki was born, at the end of the 1900s. And just recently, too, he felt like he had seen something like this. It was—

Standing stock-still, searching his memory, he jumped at the sound of a sudden explosion behind him. He tried to turn around, lost his balance, and fell on his backside with a *thump*. A remarkably large silhouette towered above him.

A motorcycle. And not the motor-drive type he was used to seeing. It was saddled with something like the guts of the internal combustion engines that had been outlawed ages ago, and those guts were roaring and rumbling. The front fork was ridiculously long, and the tire wedged between it was also so thick as to be a joke. A faint burning scent wafted up from the rough gray treads.

Haruyuki turned his eyes upward and timidly took in the rider straddling the leather seat on the other side of the exaggeratedly bent handle bars. Body encased in studded black leather, boots on each firmly planted foot, arms crossed over the chest. His head was tucked inside a helmet, also black, but the visor was a flashy thing with a skeleton design.

Haruyuki listened, dumbstruck at the creaking voice coming from within. "The Century End stage! It's been forever. Allllllll riiiiiiiight!" From one of the folded arms, an index finger popped up into the air and waggled left to right. "And as a special bonus, my opponent is a shiny newb. Super all riiiiiiiight!"

Bringing up his right boot, the skeleton rider laid it on the handle bar and rubbed it dexterously. As he did, a thunderous, booming roar sent Haruyuki flying once more.

No matter which way he looked at it, this guy didn't seem brimming with warm friendlies. More importantly, if Haruyki's memory served, this was a battle stage. So then this rider was…

"Wh-whoa…" Haruyuki retreated slowly and turned around. "Whoaaaaa!" He started running in earnest, thin robot legs clanking.

Behind him, the engine roared once again, and the sound of the tires squealing against the pavement threatened to pierce his eardrums. A mere second later, he felt an incredible impact and a sharp pain in the middle of his back before he was flying high up into the night sky. At the same time, the blue SILVER CROW bar in the top right of his view shrank abruptly.

Spinning around in space, Haruyuki thought, *I knew it. So then this is a fighting game, I'm a newbie who doesn't know his left from his right, and my opponent is a veteran player who figured that out five minutes ago.*

There's no way I'm going to win.

*   *   *

"Ha-ha-ha! So you're already being hunted? That's because you broke your promise to me, boy."

Lunch break.

Kuroyukihime, directly connected to Haruyuki in the lounge again just like the day before, laughed smoothly at the mere thought, shaking her head, bandaged under her bangs to encourage healing. Although awful to look at because of the bleeding, her injury was apparently nothing more than a cut. She had stopped every word of gratitude and apology he had in his vocabulary with a wave of her right hand.

"I-it's not funny. I thought I was going to die. I mean, I know it's my fault for accidentally connecting to the global net, but..."

Watching with amusement as Haruyuki stuttered, Kuroyukihime lifted her teacup from the table and brought it to her lips. Next to the saucer was a shrimp gratin with steam rising from it, untouched just like the large plate of pork curry in front of Haruyuki.

The student council members sitting at the table with them had already begun moving their chopsticks and spoons, and Haruyuki's stomach made a slight, pathetic sound. However, Kuroyukihime's lecture or explanation or whatever it was didn't seem like it was likely to end anytime soon.

"But, well, I suppose it's saved me the trouble of having to explain it all to you. The cost of the lesson was somewhat high, but you do understand now, yes?"

"Understand... what?"

"The truth about the Brain Burst program. It's no sweeping conspiracy or mystery, it's just—"

Haruyuki nodded sharply and mentally articulated the end of Kuroyukihime's cutoff sentence. *"It's just a fighting game. Encounters using the real world as a stage. It's crazy."*

"Ha-ha, it certainly is quite crazy, something to really make people talk."

"I mean, think about what you could do with this amazing of acceleration technology! And you go with a fighter?! The genre was already obsolete thirty years ago!"

At this, Kuroyukihime tilted her head slightly as if thinking, a sarcastic-looking smile slipping out from somewhere. *"Hmm, I think you need to phrase it slightly differently. Better to say that we Burst Linkers are accelerated to play fighting games. Conversely, we fight so that we can continue to be accelerated. We must. This is the one unpleasant part of this program."*

"Wh-what do you mean?"

"Mm... I should probably explain the rest to you in the field. Go ahead and accelerate."

"O-okay..."

Haruyuki let go of his unfinished business with the large plate of curry in front of him and shouted the "acceleration" command as instructed after straightening up on his chair.

"Burst link!"

A clang slapped his body and his consciousness, and the students around him stopped moving instantly. At the same time, all color vanished, only to be replaced with that transparent blue.

Kuroyukihime in front of him was also static, but her avatar in its bewitching black dress soon stepped out of her neat, uniformed figure, a soul escaping the body. Haruyuki slipped off his chair in his pink pig body and stepped forward so that he wouldn't have to see the rotund real-life self he was leaving behind.

"So... what are we doing?"

"You have a new icon in the left of your field of vision, yes?"

Shifting his gaze as instructed, he realized that there was, in fact, now a burning *B* mark among the app start-up icons lined up there. He raised his left hand and clicked on it.

"That's the menu for the fighting game software Brain Burst. You can see your own status and battle results and look for Burst Linkers around you to challenge them. Try pressing the DUELING button."

Nodding, Haruyuki clicked the bottom-most button on the menu. Immediately, a new window opened, and after a momentary search display, a list of names appeared.

That said, there were only two names on it. Silver Crow, the name he had seen that morning, which probably referred to Haruyuki himself, and one more. Black Lotus.

He had absolutely no doubt that this was Kuroyukihime's Burst Linker name, but he lifted his head briefly to confirm. As expected, the black swallowtail avatar nodded lightly.

"Right now, because we're cut off from the global net and only connected to the school's local net, there's just you and me on the list. Or at least there *should* just be us."

"Yes... Black Lotus." He wanted to say something like *What a pretty name* or *It suits you perfectly*, but, of course, there was no way lines like that would flow out of his mouth all smooth and cool. Haruyuki's pig nose simply twitched.

"All right, then. Now click on my name and ask to fight me."

"Wh-what?!"

"I'm not saying we're going to fight for real. We'll just let the time run out and end in a draw." With a faintly wry smile, Kuroyukihime made a small, encouraging noise.

Haruyuki lightly clicked her name on the list, all the while wondering at the fact that here he was playing one-on-one in a day and age when massive battle games with tens of thousands of people connecting on the same field were not uncommon. He selected DUEL from the pop-up menu that appeared and subsequently YES from the YES/NO dialogue that followed.

In an instant, the world changed again.

All the students disappeared instantly from the frozen blue lounge. Color returned to the pillars and tables, which decayed as if weathered, and a thick layer of dust clung to the windows. The sky was dyed a deep orange, and a dry wind blew up from somewhere, stirring grasses he didn't know the names of sprouting up from the floor.

The familiar 1800 was carved out in the top of his line of sight.

Blue bars stretched out on both sides, followed finally by the flaming text FIGHT!!

"Hmm...a Twilight stage? You pulled a rare one." Kuroyuki-hime's voice echoed beside Haruyuki, whose eyeballs rolled in his head as he took in the scene. "The properties of this stage are burns well, collapses soon, and unexpectedly dark."

"U-uh-huh..." Nodding, Haruyuki took a look at his body and saw that at some point, his pink pig frame had transformed into the thin silver robot. He shifted his gaze, wondering what form Kuroyukihime had taken, but standing before him was the same black dress avatar, not even slightly altered.

"That's your duel avatar, hm? Silver Crow, good name. Good color. I like the form, too." Kuroyukihime's hand stretched out to stroke the smooth silver head.

The definite sensation of being touched made Haruyuki realize all over again that this was a real virtual reality, a place where the childish no-touching code—ostensibly for protection—did not exist.

"Th-thanks. It's kind of wimpy, but I can't redo it. Right? So who came up with the design and the name? But wait—duel avatar?"

"Just like the name, an avatar for fighting. The design is by the Brain Burst program and you yourself. Last night, you had a very long, scary dream, didn't you?"

"...I did." He couldn't remember the details, just intuitively felt that it was an incredible nightmare. Unconsciously, he rubbed his thin robot arms with his hard palms.

"That was because the program was accessing your deep images. Brain Burst carves up and filters the player's desires, fears, and obsessions to compose your duel avatar."

"My...images. Fears and...desires," Haruyuki mumbled, looking down at his body again. "This...this tiny, weak, smooth body is what I wished for? I mean sure, it's true I'm always thinking it'd be better if I lost some weight...even so, a little more hero-like—"

"Ha-ha-ha! It's not as simple as that. What the program reads is not your ideal image but your feelings of inferiority. In your case, you should probably just count yourself lucky you didn't end up with that pink pig as is as your duel avatar. Although I like that one, too."

"P-please don't say that. I hate it." He quickly considered putting together a new black knight avatar for the school's local net as he asked, "But then does that mean that Brain Burst also made your school avatar? That's the image of your inferiority complex? But it's so beautiful…"

"No." Eyes darkening slightly, Kuroyukihime lowered her face. "This is one I put together myself with an editor. I… For my own reasons, I've sealed off my actual duel avatar. I'll tell you the reason one of these days, when the time comes."

"Sealed…?"

"Unfortunately, my duel avatar is ugly. The epitome of hideous. Although that's not the reason I've sealed it away… Anyway, enough about me."

Kuroyukihime shrugged, and her face quickly found its usual mysterious expression. She petted Haruyuki's helmet head once again with a pale hand. "This morning you were thrust into a fight with another Burst Linker through the global net. You fought with this brand-new avatar. And you were thoroughly defeated. Correct?"

"Uh, well, pretty much. He crushed me." Haruyuki reluctantly remembered the fight stage he had been abruptly pulled into before school. He had been smashed, rammed, and sent flying by the rude rider in the skeleton helmet straddling the bike in the dark ruins, and his health gauge had dropped to nothing in the blink of an eye.

Together with a pathetic sound effect, the text YOU LOSE had appeared in front of him, and then… "I'm pretty sure… It showed my name and level one, and then some weird number. Burst… points, I think? That went from ninety-nine to eighty-nine."

"Good, it's good you remembered. Burst points! Those are the very things that send us into this merciless battlefield." Nearly shouting, Kuroyukihime took a few steps toward the window and whirled around. She thrust the parasol she held in both hands down onto the floor with a sharp *snap*, and a small shard of the cracked pavement flew off. "Burst points are, simply put, the number of times we can accelerate. Accelerate one time, lose one point. The initial value immediately after installation is one hundred, but because you accelerated once in the lounge yesterday, you used up a point. And then you ended up using another point earlier."

"Gah…s-so how do we pay for them? Are we actually charged real money?"

"No," Kuroyukihime countered crisply. "There's only one way to increase your burst points: win Duels. If you win, your points go up ten for a same-level battle. However, your points drop ten if you lose. Like you did this morning."

Turning her face sharply to the twilight sky on the other side of the window, Kuroyukihime continued, almost murmuring. "Acceleration is extremely powerful. It goes without saying that winning fights means earning a perfect score on a test or winning big at certain types of gambling or sports becomes child's play. The freshman player who broke the record for home runs at the big Koshien tournament this summer was a high-level Burst Linker."

"Wh—"

"Therefore." She cast the baffled Haruyuki a somehow sad glance. "Once we've tasted this forbidden nectar, we have no choice but to keep accelerating forever. And to earn the burst points that permit us to do so, we have no choice but to keep fighting forever."

"J-just wait a minute." *That talented heavy hitter was a Burst Linker? No, that's not the issue. Isn't there something off about Kuroyukihime's story?* Haruyuki thought hard and then opened his mouth. "Uh…um, before, you said if you win in a Duel, you get ten points, and if you lose, you drop ten points, right? Then that means...since you use points accelerating, the points all Burst Linkers share only go down. So people who aren't good at fighting naturally lose all their points...What happens then?" "You really do catch on quickly. It's simple. You lose Brain Burst." Her dark eyes almost burning, Kuroyukihime stared directly at Haruyuki. "The program is automatically uninstalled and can never be reinstalled. There's no point in changing Neurolinker models, either. It recognizes you by your unique brain waves. People who have lost all their points can never accelerate again." After relaying this in a bleak tone, she added, "Although it's not the case that the total pool only diminishes because new people join in the fight, like you. That said, right now, the trend is a slight decline."

But Haruyuki barely heard this last part. "You lose...Brain Burst."

Even though he had only tasted the power of acceleration two or three times, his back seized up at the mere thought. And it wasn't just that he wouldn't be able to accelerate. For Haruyuki, there was also the fact that he would lose his one point of contact with Kuroyukihime, who lived in a totally separate world. Once again, he felt the weight of those ten points taken from him by that skull rider.

"Now then. What are you going to do, Haruyuki?"

Faced with this nearly whispered question, Haruyuki lifted his head. "What do you mean?"

"At this point, you can still go back. To the regular world, without acceleration or fighting. You won't see those idiots who were bullying again, I guarantee it as a student council member."

"I—I..." *I don't care about acceleration or Brain Burst or whatever. I just don't want to be away from you.* Of course, he couldn't say anything like that. Instead, he clenched his silver fist and replied, "I still have to repay you."

"Oh?"

"You gave me Brain Burst and pulled me out of that hell. I can at least see that you didn't do it to steal my initial hundred points. If you had, you could've told me anything; you had millions of options. So there must be something you want me to do. Some objective that was worth taking the time to check my squash game score and lecture me from square one about acceleration. Am I right?"

"Hmm. An astute inference."

Through his silver mask, Haruyuki stared squarely at the beautiful avatar with her faint smile. "I...I'm actually not the type of person who gets to talk to you like this. I'm not cool. I'm a blob, a crybaby, I hold grudges, I get jealous of the only two friends I have, I run away at the drop of a hat. I really am a waste of skin. I'm basically the worst."

What am I saying? he thought, but the words poured out of him and he couldn't stop talking. His expressionless, mirror-like avatar was some consolation, at least. "Even so, you reached out to me, you directed with me, and I know it's just because I was kinda good at that game, I know you didn't have any other reason, but I—I wouldn't even, I mean."

Seriously, what am I saying here? Get it together before you talk. Aah, this is exactly the kind of time you need to accelerate. Except you're already accelerated.

Spiraling deeper into panic, Haruyuki felt compelled to bare everything in his heart. "So...so I want to live up to your expectations. I want to properly repay the...m-mercy you showed me. I don't know what I can do, but if you're having some trouble, I want to do anything and everything to help. So I...I won't uninstall Brain Burst. I'll fight...as a Burst Linker."

What the—? I should've just said that last part! How could I have said all that other stuff?

Having finished vomiting words, Haruyuki made his thin avatar even smaller and stared down, acutely embarrassed. He braced himself for the fact that there was no doubt she was thinking that Mr. Self-Conscious here had gotten the wrong idea about things somehow when the staccato pace of her response shook his sense of hearing.

"*Mercy?* Don't use words like that."

Lifting his eyes slightly in shock, he saw her face twisted with more obvious emotion than he had witnessed in her these few days. "I'm nothing but a foolish, helpless junior high student. I'm a human being, the same as you, standing in the same place, breathing the same air. To say nothing of the fact that at this stage, we are both Burst Linkers, exactly equal. You're the one creating a distance. Do these two virtual meters feel that far to you?" Silently, she extended her pale right hand.

They do, Haruyuki murmured to himself. *You have no idea how terrifying it is for someone like me to even be seen by someone like you, who has everything. I'm happy to be your servant. Just being a pawn to be moved on your orders is an unexpected happiness. If I take your hand now, you'll end up with expectations of me you shouldn't have. Poisonous expectations you'll definitely end up regretting several times over.*

It's the same with Chiyuri and Takumu. I'm satisfied being their happy, fat friend. If they would just quit pitying me and sympathizing with me, I couldn't ask for anything better.

The voice that came out of Haruyuki's mouth was dry, like the trees in the virtual twilight. "You rescued me from hell. That's... For me, that's a life's worth of happiness. I don't need anything else. Nothing at all."

"Is that so?" Kuroyukihime murmured, lowering her hand. A hard, heavy silence ruled the stage for a brief while. It was her voice that broke the tension, smooth as if nothing had changed at all. "I gratefully accept your aid. It is true that I currently have the tiniest, troublesome problem. I'd like your assistance in resolving the matter."

Haruyuki nodded, holding his breath momentarily. "I'll do whatever I can. What do you need?"

"First of all, I need you to learn how Duels work. Go ahead and click on your name displayed below your health gauge. Open

'Help' and check what all the normal and special attack commands are for your duel avatar."

"S-special attack?" he parroted, staying the hand about to reach up.

"Mm. When the program creates your duel avatar, it allocates your already fixed potential according to your attributes. Some excel at attacking, others have solid defenses, and peaky types aim to settle battles in a single move with a special attack. But the overarching principle is that the general potential of duel avatars at the same level is exactly equal. You were crushed in your first fight, but it's not because your opponent was stronger. You simply didn't know how to fight."

That bike guy (Ash Roller) was level one just like Haruyuki. Did he really have the same battle ability as Silver Crow, even though he had seemed so overwhelming? If he did, then this small, slender robot avatar definitely had to have an incredible special attack. Heart pounding, Haruyuki stretched out a silver finger and clicked on his name.

A semitransparent window popped open.

The movement of his body was depicted by a simple, human-shaped animation with the name of the technique displayed to its right.

First up, a motion readying the right fist against the upper thigh before being thrust forward. Normal attack: Punch.

Next. A motion pulling in the right leg and jamming it forward. Normal attack: Kick.

And finally, the special attack. Cross both arms, open them to the left and right, and thrust the head out. This one was called Head Butt.

That was it. There was nothing else.

"Um," Haruyuki muttered, dazed. "Normal attacks, Punch and Kick...and all I have for a special attack is a Head Butt."

"Oh?" Hearing this, Kuroyukihime put the fingers of her right hand to her lower jaw and tilted her head. Her expression didn't seem to change, but, unable to face her any longer, Haruyuki quickly hung his head. Just imagining a tinge of disappointment floating up in those black eyes made his whole body suddenly hot. Before he knew it, his mouth was opening on its own. "No, it's fine. I mean, I expected this. Take one look at this avatar, and you can clearly see it's no good. I'm sorry I can't live up to your expectations. It's fine if you kinda leave me be. Just think of me as a lottery you didn't win."

"You...idiot!!"

Haruyuki lifted his face, his whole body shaking with a start. Before he knew it, Kuroyukihime was standing in front of him, beautiful eyebrows raised, looking down at him with eyes like raging fires.

"I won't tell you how to live your life; as junior high students, we're on the same level. However, when it comes to Brain Burst, I have more than six years more experience than you. Were you not listening? When I told you that all the duel avatars have equal potential? Or have you already forgotten?"

"B-but it's just that my only attacks are Punch, Kick, and Head Butt..."

"In which case, you most certainly have some strength somewhere to compensate." Her gaze softening slightly, Kuroyukihime continued as if admonishing him. "It was your heart that gave birth to this duel avatar. If you don't believe in it, then what does that say?"

"That the person who is least able to believe in me is me," Haruyuki murmured to himself as he nodded. "I'm sorry. I believe... maybe not in myself, but at least in what you say."

As she listened, Kuroyukihime's face opened up slightly— although just into a bitter smile—and Haruyuki's shoulders relaxed a little.

"It seems you need to learn something else before how to fight. Strength—" For a brief moment, the bitter smile became faintly melancholy. "*Strength* is by no means simply a word indicating victory. I spent a fair bit of time learning this. And by the time I learned the lesson, it was already too late."

Haruyuki couldn't understand the meaning behind the words she quietly spun out. He tilted his head and started to ask, but she didn't give him the chance, suddenly changing tracks.

"Time's almost up."

Looking, he saw that the counter with its original 1800 had just barely twenty seconds left.

"So shall we make the next lecture a hands-on lesson?"

"Y…es? What do you…?"

Haruyuki stared, puzzled, and Kuroyukihime flashed him a bold smile.

"Of course, you'll go and get them back. Your ten points."

At the time that the Duel ended with a draw screen, the acceleration released.

The moment they returned to the real-world lounge, Kuroyukihime yanked out the direct cable without giving Haruyuki a chance to say anything. "Now then! Let's eat, Arita. It'll get cold on us." She grinned and picked up her small spoon off the table.

Having no other choice, Haruyuki reached out to the plate of curry rice in front of him. In his perceived timeline, he'd brought it over from the counter more than thirty minutes ago, but as it was still steaming hot, his stomach clenched.

The same critical looks from the surrounding tables that he'd gotten the day before shone a spotlight on Haruyuki, and he wanted to abscond with his curry to some corner of the cafeteria. But he couldn't combat his empty stomach. He'd shoveled three quick bites into his mouth when he heard one of the seniors at the same table start talking to Kuroyukihime, and his throat clamped shut.

"Kuro, isn't it about time you told us? We're seriously dying of curiosity here. We really want to understand exactly what your relationship is with the young man here."

Haruyuki lifted his head with a start to recognize the fluffy-haired student council member he'd seen there yesterday. He was pretty sure she was the eighth-grade clerk.

"Mm." Kuroyukihime placed her spoon beside the gratin dish

and gracefully lifted her teacup, looking rather thoughtful. The students around her fell instantly silent. "To be blunt, I told him I liked him, and he blew me off."

The world was full of shrieks and cries of surprise. Spoon in mouth, curry in hand, Haruyuki fled.

"Uh…um, the thing is!!" After spending the two remaining hours of the afternoon under laser-like scrutiny, Haruyuki diagonally behind Kuroyukihime objected somewhat awkwardly as they headed toward the school gates. "What were you thinking?! Everyone's going to pick on me now!! They will totally be picking on me!!"

"It was a proud declaration." After a quiet laugh, Kuroyukihime continued, her expression composed. "I didn't go so far as to tell the truth, did I? And I don't think you were as displeased as you'd have me believe."

As she spoke, she swiftly gestured over her virtual desktop, allowing the flicking of her fingers to be seen. A file promptly arrived through the local net, and an icon started blinking in Haruyuki's field of view. Clicking on it, a large image opened up in front of his eyes.

It was a picture of himself, curry spoon in mouth, exposing his idiotic, gaping face.

"Gaaah!" he shouted, seeing it and immediately throwing the file in the trash. "Wh-wh-wh-when did you take this camera screenshot?! Even speed has its limits!!"

"What? It was just to commemorate."

While they were having this back and forth, eyes seemingly capable of actual murder and maiming bore holes through Haruyuki. Too late, he pulled his shoulders in but couldn't completely hide himself in the shadow of Kuroyukihime's slim body.

"Stand up a little taller. Not that many boys in this school have blown me off. You are, in fact, the only one."

"But exactly when did I do that?!"

"You're so harsh. You'll hurt me all over again…Anyway."

With a single word, she put the issue on hold, and, recovering her center, she said in a low voice: "Once you leave the school gates, your Neurolinker will be connected globally. Which means that any Burst Linkers in Suginami area number three, which includes here, will be able to force you to fight. Before someone jumps you, accelerate, find Ash Roller in the matching list, and challenge him."

"A-area? Does that mean that there are limits on the range where you can fight?"

Kuroyukihime dipped her head slightly at his question. "There are. You might start a Duel with someone on the opposite side of Tokyo, but thirty minutes will pass before you can even meet them. At any rate, you might one day set foot on a group field where any number of people can connect without limits, but that won't be until you get past level four. Right now, focus on the battles in front of you." She brought the lecture to a close in a slightly sharper voice. "I'll just say this: If you lose, you can't ask for a rematch right then and there. You can only fight the same opponent once a day. I'll be in the Gallery, but unfortunately, I won't be able to help you... Don't look so disheartened. If you just fight like I outlined in the mail I sent you, you won't lose."

"O-okay." His throat issued a gulping sound, and he nodded. He copied and pasted the content of the text she had sent him during sixth period to his brain.

"This is your real debut battle, Silver Crow. Good luck."

She pushed his back lightly, and Haruyuki stepped out onto the road leading to the battlefield.

4

The battlefield was a Century End stage again, dotted with a nightscape of abandoned buildings lit up by fires. Haruyuki made his small avatar even smaller and concealed himself on the pedestrian bridge running over Kannana.

During the previous fight, he had been too freaked out, so he hadn't noticed that in addition to the remaining time and the health gauge, a small light blue triangle was displayed in his field of vision. It was a guide cursor roughly indicating the direction of the enemy.

The triangle merely wavered as it hovered due north Haruyuki's position along the wide road. Even so, Haruyuki knew his enemy, Ash Roller, was definitely not just twiddling his thumbs somewhere off over the horizon. He was most likely making a beeline right for him. The cursor didn't go so far as to tell him the distance.

In his head, he went over the walkthrough Kuroyukihime had sent.

After going over the information you gave me, I've determined that Ash Roller has two significant weak points. The first is that he makes a great deal of noise when he moves.

That was definitely true. If he had been paying proper attention to his surroundings last time, he would've been able to hear the enormous roar of the gasoline engine from a ways off. He couldn't make that mistake again. He held his breath and strained his ears.

There it was!

An overbearing, thunderous sound made its way into his head, although the cursor still didn't waver. Ash Roller sounded like he was racing down deserted Kannana Road with the engine open full throttle. No doubt he was enjoying himself. If he rode a bike in real life, too, it was probably a low-powered electric scooter that crawled forward in the usual heavy traffic on this road. And if his challenger happened to be the newb he had completely crushed that same morning, all the better.

But this time, you at least won't get a perfect win. Because the first attack is mine.

Haruyuki gritted his teeth and glared at the blue cursor.

As before, it was still pointing due south, but he could tell how close his enemy was by the sound of the engine. However, his opponent shouldn't have been able to do the same. Given that he was approaching at a high speed in a straight line, the direction of Haruyuki's cursor would only change the instant they were already entangled.

Flat on his stomach against the pedestrian bridge, Haruyuki stared intently at the hill leading down toward Koenji Station. The explosive noise gradually grew louder until he could feel it shaking his body.

And then Haruyuki saw him.

The bike's headlight was off, of course, but he was sure he saw the red reflection of the bonfire flames shimmer across the chrome. Fifteen—no, ten seconds until he made it to the intersection at the top of the hill.

Haruyuki would only have this one chance for a surprise attack. But the only weapons he had were his normal Punch and Kick attacks. Which meant he had no choice but to jump from the bridge and slam his entire body into the rider.

Too scary. I can't actually do that. Haruyuki cursed in his heart the version of himself who allowed this thought to flicker through his head. *Don't be stupid. The me right now isn't overweight, thirteen-year-old Haruyuki Arita; I'm the Burst Linker Silver Crow. And this isn't the real world, it's a virtual game field. I've given this world everything, all my time, my passion. To the point where this basically is reality for me. In which case, I can't lose. Better—this time, the easy win'll be mine, you stupid skullhead!*

"Aaaaaah!" Haruyuki screamed and yanked himself to his feet, taking the iron rail in one step to leap over the edge.

The task of jumping from high up and landing a kick on the rider of a motorbike flying along at more than a hundred kilometers an hour was next to impossible, probably even more impossible than Haruyuki thought.

But given that Haruyuki had spent so much time so focused on hitting a nearly invisible ball in virtual squash, Ash Roller's skull helmet was too big a target to miss. Thrusting his right leg out into the air and controlling his posture with his arms splayed, Haruyuki became a silver arrow, shooting forward.

"Ohwaa?!"

He thought he heard a faint voice beneath the helmet's visor, but at that moment, Haruyuki's silver-armored heel slammed into its mark, right in the center of the skull.

Crrrrrunch!! With an incredible detonation, cracks pierced the center of the visor shooting outward. The rider's head snapped back, and Haruyuki slid over his face before crashing into the asphalt and tumbling forward. His head spun momentarily, but he was quick to raise his eyes and check the damage behind him.

The motorbike careened off diagonally to the right, large sparks flying from the front and rear brake rotors, before finally crashing to a stop in a pile of rubble on the shoulder. The rider's body slammed into the tank, while the engine shut off with a pathetic clicking noise.

"…I—I did it," Haruyuki murmured, clenching his fist before checking their health gauges.

Silver Crow's was down about 5 percent, appropriate damage for a drop from high up. In contrast, Ash Roller was naturally seriously hurt; with both the flying kick and the crash, it looked like he had taken considerable damage. More than 20 percent had been shaved off his gauge, which was now slightly purple.

His first attack was basically a total success. But this wasn't the time to sit and bathe in the lingering sweetness of the critical hit.

Standing up, he set his sights on the five-story building on the left side of the road that he had scoped out in advance, and he started running. According to Kuroyukihime, since the road was the main field in the Century End stage, you couldn't enter the buildings. But that didn't mean you couldn't use a building's external stairs.

The half-ruined stairs seemed to have been attached to the wall as almost an afterthought. Leaping onto them, Haruyuki sped up to the roof in one go.

Ash Roller's second weak point. The majority of his avatar's potential is tied up in the bike. The rider's battle power should be essentially zero. Which is why, after you strike in your initial attack, you move to the roof of a building his bike can't climb.

This was the battle strategy Kuroyukihime had given Haruyuki.

If he climbed the stairs while ahead damage-wise, all he had to do was wait for the time to be up and he'd win. Even if the rider got off his bike and came up, he could easily beat him up with Punch and Kick. Depending on your point of view, this was perhaps a cowardly strategy. But the truth was, Haruyuki loved this style of winning, the clever assault at an opponent's weak points. In fact, he even thought that this path to victory was the true nature of gaming.

Haruyuki moved to the edge of the rooftop as he plotted and tried to pay back in spades the sneering laughter Ash Roller had dealt him that morning. Peering down, he saw that the rider had finally managed to restart the engine of the crashed bike. The machine, idling raspily as if out of breath, pulled itself out from the rubble.

As he wondered what sort of challenge he should issue, Haruyuki heard a voice whispering somewhere, "Wow, he can play after all, that little guy."

"Totally different from this morning, huh? Wonder who his 'parent' is."

Turning his eyes, he saw silhouettes sitting a little ways off on the roofs of buildings around him, on the edge of an enormous water tank, looking down at him. The Gallery.

Because Burst Linker fights lasted at most a mere one-point-eight seconds in the real world, you wouldn't make it in time if you accelerated once a fight had begun. So the game allowed you to register the names of friends and Burst Linkers you were interested in, so that when any of those people started to fight, you would also automatically accelerate and dive into the battlefield, where you could watch. In this case, none of your points were consumed.

Looking around, Haruyuki could make out figures who had come to loiter on rooftops and the road here and there while his attention had been on Ash Roller. Since there was no reason for them to have marked Haruyuki, they were likely Linkers who had registered his opponent's name. However, there should have been one person among them in the Gallery who had checked Silver Crow's name. Black Lotus, i.e., Kuroyukihime.

Whirling his head around, wondering where she was, Haruyuki saw one of the two sitting on the tank wave a hand lightly at him.

"If you win this Duel, I'll put you on my list, too. Good luck, kid!"

"Well, I don't think it's going to be as easy as all that."

To the other person, Haruyuki responded in his heart, *Sorry, but you're not going to get any more big-show stuff. We'll prob'ly just time out.* With that thought, he shrugged lightly and refocused his attention on the road.

And froze in astonishment.

In no time at all, Ash Roller's bike, which had been nothing more than a speck in the distance below him, had its front wheel up against the building wall.

Hey… what do you think you're doing?

The reply was a shrill cry of rage. "You really think you're something, huh, baldy!! I'll make you dance to the sound of my V-twin!!" The engine roared furiously, and puffs of exhaust rose from the chrome muffler. The enormous American bike then began to storm straight up the wall.

"Gah…"

Widening his eyes beneath his silver mask, Haruyuki pulled back a step. A scant two seconds. The bike flew past the iron rail, so close he could practically touch it if he reached out, bringing the roaring and the smell of burning with it. The engine raced, growling thunderously, and the bike, having flown up nearly two meters past the top of the roof, turned to aim at Haruyuki and started to drop.

"Aaaah!!" Panicking, he dashed a few more steps backward.

The rear tire hit the concrete roof with a tremendous *crash.* Cracks spread out radially from the impact, and several shards flew up and hit Haruyuki's armor. Instantly, his health gauge dropped, although by a mere dot, and Haruyuki was surprised again.

In an ordinary fighting game, damage could occur only in ways prescribed by the system. Brain Burst really wasn't any ordinary game. There was a degree of realism in the high-level graphics and sound, and the persistence of the effects, to the point where you couldn't really distinguish it from reality.

This had to be the key to winning fights in this world.

Burning this into his mind, Haruyuki looked up at his enemy, who had far more experience than he did.

Standing the bike up deftly, Ash Roller glanced down at Haruyuki and started to talk in a high-pitched, metallic voice. "Tell you what, kid, taking you down this morning finally pushed my awesomeness over three hundred points. Made it to level two."

The skull visor on the gunmetal helmet had been smashed in, revealing part of his bare face. Haruyuki had thought whatever face was under that skull would have to be terrifying, but it was more science-club style, the thin lines of a boy's face.

The duel avatar is a manifestation of your inferiority complex. Kuroyukihime's words flickered to life in the back of his mind.

Ash Roller, stiffening his thin lips into something approximating a smile, revved the engine once before continuing. "And I was having suuuuuch trouble deciding on my level-up bonus, you know? In the end, I ditched the bonuses to my special attack and my riding speed and went with the ability to drive up walls, get it? And damn, I was so right!" He took his hands off the handlebars and pointed both index fingers sharply at Haruyuki. "And yoooouuu are hella unlucky!"

Haruyuki cursed in his head, but he wasn't simply standing there listening quietly to his enemy. He was staring intently at his surroundings, remembering the mail Kuroyukihime had sent, and using every bit of knowledge he had to try and find some way out of this situation.

If your initial attack and escape fails, and you have to fight Ash Roller on his bike face-to-face, I'm sorry to say your chances of winning are quite small. Because—

Kuroyukihime had followed that with an explanation of duel avatar "compatibility."

The English names automatically given to the Burst Linkers always included a color word. This color offered a rough grasp of the features of the particular duel avatar.

Blues were short-distance direct attacks, reds were long-distance direct attacks, yellows were intermediate attacks. Intermediate colors like purple or green had characteristics straddling two color types. In addition to colors on the color wheel were the metallic colors, set aside with metal names, which excelled in defensive abilities rather than attacks.

The metallic colors, including your silver, are fairly rare, but are also a strong color line. They have the ability to endure amputation, piercing, fire, and poison attacks, and given their hard bodies, their abilities in terms of close-range attack are certainly not insignificant. But, of course, they have weak points. Corrosion attacks are their natural enemy, with another weakness being strike attacks.

Kuroyukihime, analyzing Silver Crow's attributes, also went on to list the characteristics of Ash Roller, who she had presumably never seen.

In contrast, the "ash" in Ash Roller is a color belonging more to blue than green on the color circle. The low saturation indicates the peculiarity of his attack. Since his tires are not an obvious weapon, it's hard to tell, but most likely, his attribute is a close-range strike type. In other words, your armor is very nearly useless against Ash Roller's charge. So there's just one response in the event you end up in a face-to-face battle.

Run for your life for the entire remaining time.

Easier said.

Despairingly, Haruyuki checked the size of the building. Both width- and height-wise, it was no more than twenty meters. Kuroyukihime's evasion strategy was based naturally enough on a battle on the wide, deserted Kannana and didn't take into account a scenario where the motorcycle climbed walls.

All of which meant that Haruyuki had inadvertently fled to a disadvantageous position all on his own.

Given the bike's thrust, running for the emergency stairs was pointless. Should he jump from the roof and just take the damage? But if his gauge dipped lower than Ash Roller's, everything up to now would have been for nothing.

A triumphant mounted knight, his opponent laughed ringingly at Haruyuki rooted in place, unable to think of a way out. "Ha-ha-ha-ha! No fight left in you, baldy boy? Well then, allow me!!"

The internal combustion machine screamed and blue smoke rose up from the racing rear tire. The front tire made contact with the ground with a *thud*, and the enormous bike charged, the rider's sights set on Haruyuki.

"Aaah!" he screamed, leaping to the right, but there was just too little distance between them. The tire grazed the tip of his foot, and his health gauge dropped abruptly. Simultaneous with the shock of the impact, an instant pain danced across Haruyuki's nerves.

But re-creating the sensation of pain in a virtual game had supposedly been prohibited by law ages ago. This really wasn't just a bit of fun. The battle was virtual, but real at the same time.

The bike turned on a dime about three meters away, screeching deafeningly, preparing to charge again.

Anything! There has to be something! Some secret trick to totally turn the tables, to come back from the dead—

Right, the special attack!

Even if it was called the prosaic *Head Butt*, it might have the power to crush rocks or something. Haruyuki allowed himself this sliver of hope and quickly crossed both arms in front of his body exactly like the silhouette in the instructions. Next, he opened his arms wide and threw his upper body back as hard as he could.

Along with a vaguely dull *vroom*ing sound effect, Haruyuki was conscious of the fact that his shiny head was starting to glow with a white radiance. Impressed murmurs rose up from the surrounding Gallery.

You can do this!!

Confident, Haruyuki glared at the enormous bike headed right for him. "Aaaaaah!!" Screaming, he aimed his shining head at the bike headlight and thrust.

Long before he could hit his mark, he was struck by the tough tire and knocked on his back, opening up a human-shaped hole in the concrete. The light effect on his head disappeared into space and his special-attack gauge alone dropped to empty.

A burst of laughter from the Gallery shook the stage. Amidst the laughter, the murmuring of one person reached his ears. "Too bad, looks like this is the end."

Haruyuki's entire being was wrapped tightly in the familiar warmth of humiliation.

Dammit. Damn. I'm supposed to be the hero in virtual games. My character's too weak. I mean, a special attack that's just some Head Butt that doesn't even hit the target! I'm done for.

He managed to stand but crumpled again abruptly. As he moved to sit down, he saw off in the distance, on the roof of a remarkably tall building, a silhouette standing tall and staring right at him. Hair in thick rolls swaying in the night wind. Soft dress. Almost-transparent butterfly wings.

He couldn't see the expression on this shadow's face, the size of a grain of rice. However, Haruyuki felt its fierce energy.

No. You can't give up. If you have to lose, then struggle, fight, make it ugly. If you can't do at least that much, you can't even be her pawn.

Brushing aside his humiliation, Haruyuki mobilized every bit of knowledge and experience he had and thought intently.

Virtual while real. That was Brain Burst's major feature. Overwhelming detail and reality. In which case, Ash Roller's bike wasn't just a bunch of polygons. There had to be a weak point in that meticulous reproduction.

The bike. The main bit, the gasoline engine from the last century—what's that about? Noisy. Stinks like gas. Those would be weak points before you actually ran into it, but they don't matter now.

It can't move when it runs out of gas. If I made a hole in the tank— No, I can't pull off that kind of pinpointed attack.

Isn't there anything else? Anything—

The bike, whirling around and leaving a trail of burnt rubber under the rear tire, turned its shining yellow eye on Haruyuki for the third time.

In that instant, Haruyuki swallowed sharply. *Got it. That's it. The main feature of an internal combustion engine bike and its weak point.*

"Yeaaaaah! Ha-ha-ha-ha!! Dance for me!!" Screaming, the iron horse began to run.

Just one time is enough. Move, Silver Crow. Faster than that guy. Haruyuki clenched his teeth and glared at the charging bike. *Right. No matter how fast he goes, it's not going to be so fast I can't see him. I'll make a show of trying to avoid him, just barely dodge him.*

Gathering his powers of concentration, Haruyuki slid a mere fifty centimeters to the right when he was on the verge of being sent flying again. The tip of the handlebar brushed against him, and Ash Roller passed in front of him.

Instantly, Haruyuki stretched out both hands and, bracing himself for damage, grabbed the edge of the black fender covering the bike's rear tire. The shock threatened to rip his fingers loose, while sparks flew from every joint in his arms, and his health gauge dipped lightly.

The bike slowed a little. Haruyuki didn't let the chance slip by, digging both legs into the floor, putting all his energy into throwing his body backward. His steel feet crunched as they shaved concrete off the ground, and his gauge continued to drop.

"Whoo-hoo!!" Looking over his shoulder, Ash Roller let loose with a loud laugh. "Stuuuuuupid!! As if an insect like you could stop my monster machine!!"

The rider's boots kicked the foot pedal hard. Black leather gloves twisted the throttle. The engine screamed and roared, and flames shot out of the muffler. The impressive torque of the American bike worked its magic, and the machine started to accelerate again, dragging Haruyuki along.

"Zoooooowwwwww!!" As he listened to the incredibly abrasive sound of the bottoms of his own feet screeching along, Haruyuki let out a scream, overcome with pain and heat almost like his feet were being shaved off with a rough file; no, it was exactly like that.

"Ha-ha-ha-ha! You don't let go soon, you're gonna be at zero in no time!!" Over Ash Roller's triumphant voice was a grating metallic noise. Both of Haruyuki's feet were completely red, overheating, and his health gauge was dropping so fast, it was scary.

But he didn't let go. Gritting his teeth under his silver mask and fighting to endure the painful heat, he continued to simply dangle from the tail of the bike.

If it were the surface of Kannana Road below them, Silver Crow's small body might have become scrap iron and turned to dust soon enough, just as Ash Roller said. But in the limited space of the abandoned building's roof, Ash Roller couldn't run in a straight line forever.

The low railing drew near before his eyes, and the skull rider leaned on the bike with a strange whoop before entering a spin turn. Sparks flew from the brake rotors, and white smoke rose up from the fat tires.

"Ngaaah!" Haruyuki tried desperately to hold on as he was nearly thrown in the centrifugal force.

Just a little more. In half a second, my first and last chance is going to come.

The engine rpm dropped, and the bike ended the spin and went to commence its mad dash anew. Immediately before it could, for the tiniest sliver of time, the soles of Silver Crow's feet gripped the ground solidly.

"Aaaaaaah!!" Haruyuki screamed. At the same time, he dug deep for every bit of strength he could muster and yanked the fender he was gripping with both hands straight up into the air. His knees, elbows, and shoulders all sparked, and his health gauge, which had dropped to about 20 percent, was eaten down to its last 10 percent, but his thin arms bore the enormous load, stretched out in front of him.

A tenth of a second later, the fat rear tire raced fiercely, but the kinetic energy could not be transformed into propulsive force. Because, although just barely, the tread had been separated from the ground.

"Uh...uh?!" Ash Roller cried, straddling the seat with his back to Haruyuki. Apparently flustered, he jerked his right arm two, then three times. Each time, the engine roared and the rear wheel raced frantically. But the steel machine didn't move a centimeter.

This was the weak point Haruyuki had picked up on. Unlike electric motorcycles, which were equipped with motors in the front and rear wheels, the internal combustion engine motorcycles of the previous era only drove the rear wheel using a chain connected to the engine. It would have been absolutely impossible for him to lift the entire bike, but stiffening his metallic robot avatar and just bringing up the rear a tiny bit was something he could do for at least an hour.

"Y-you! Come on!! Drop it, stupid!!"

Haruyuki looked up at Ash Roller, twisting his body and yelling over his shoulder. And then, even though his opponent likely couldn't see, he smiled complacently. "Nah. If you're really stuck, try making your front wheel turn."

Having returned to the unaccelerated world, Haruyuki inhaled deeply in the afternoon sun before exhaling slowly. Given that the fight had been decided with the counter still at 600, he calculated that no more than a second or so had gone by in the real world. But the palms of his hands were dripping with sweat and cold to the point of being numb.

As he pushed the button on his Neurolinker to disconnect from the global net with a stiff finger, he was suddenly hit sharply on his back.

"Hey! You did it, Silver Crow! To be honest, I thought you were done for."

Turning around, he found Kuroyukihime's pretty face, complete with a rare, bright smile. It was only natural, since they had accelerated standing next to each other outside the school gate, but in the stage, she had been watching the battle from the roof of a building in the distance, so he was slightly confused.

That was the real distance between us. Don't go getting any ideas, he told himself as he returned her smile awkwardly. "I—I thought I was done for, too."

"Don't be modest. That was an amazing win. I hadn't given any thought to the internal structure of Ash Roller's bike at all. That was probably the first time that weak point had been attacked, thanks to that burst of power from your avatar. In any case, you certainly did get your points back."

"I got more than that. Twenty points were added to my total; he was at level two."

Kuroyukihime blinked in surprise, the smile on her face quickly becoming even wider, and she hit Haruyuki on the shoulder again. "Ha-ha-ha! He was? So that's why he could ride up the wall like that."

"It's not funny. I was totally terrified."

"Hee-hee-hee, no, I'm sorry. But, well, that did allow you to win in an interesting, cool way, didn't it? I overheard members of the Gallery talking, and apparently, you're the first one to attack Ash Roller like that. It was a magnificent win."

"U-uh-huh."

After spending about five minutes stubbornly yelling and screaming from on top of his bike, drive wheel up in the air and going nowhere, Ash Roller finally climbed down.

Haruyuki leapt forward immediately, as if the chance might slip away, and shifted the conflict to an intimate hand-to-hand combat, swinging his fists, silver like his name, to win handily.

"Punch and Kick are starting to look better and better somehow. As for Head Butt, at any rate, with a more orthodox hand-to-hand-type opponent, you won't have to deal with that delay. But how long are we going to stand here talking?"

At Kuroyukihime's question, he looked around again and discovered students on their way home walking along or stopping and staring openly and curiously at the two of them in front of the school gates.

Shrinking his body with a start, as if to hide himself in his own shadow, Haruyuki saw Chiyuri's face in the circle of people and stopped breathing. Reflexively, he turned his face away abruptly. The memory of fleeing from Chiyuri and Takumu the day before was still fresh. After going and doing that, even though he still hadn't apologized for the sandwich thing, he didn't have the slightest idea how he was even supposed to start trying to fix things.

No. It's not my fault. It's Chiyuri's fault. I mean, I told her I don't know how many times to keep it quiet, and she went and told Takumu anyway. I didn't ask them to pity me or feel sorry for me.

"What should we do?" Kuroyukihime said somewhat doubtfully to Haruyuki as he cast his eyes downward obstinately. "If we're going to go somewhere else, there's that cafe over there. Hm? You—"

"What do you want with Haru?"

Haruyuki jumped at Chiyuri's voice, suddenly so close. Lifting his face with a start, his eyes flew to his childhood friend arching her small body fiercely and confronting Kuroyukihime. Thick eyebrows fixed at an angle that only Haruyuki knew indicated maximum competitiveness, Chiyuri continued argumentatively in a low voice, "The reason Haru got into that fight yesterday was because of your meddling, wasn't it? And yet here you are again, making a spectacle of him like this. What do you want? Is this fun for you?"

Eeep. What is this, what is going on, what am I supposed to do here?

His entire body paralyzed, the situation having surpassed his capacity to deal with it, Haruyuki tried to move his frozen mouth. "H-hey, Chiyu—"

"Shut up, Haru!!" She shot him a look that had been carved into his memory since infancy, and Haruyuki had no choice but to stand at attention and stay silent as her former subordinate.

Even faced with the superheated Chiyuri beam, Kuroyukihime showed her usual composure and tilted her head ever so slightly, cool smile on her lips. "Hmm. I don't quite understand. Are you saying that I am playing around, that I am doing something Arita is not happy with?"

"Aren't you? Haru hates this kind of thing, standing out so much, being stared at. He's been seriously bothered this whole time, although I suppose you can't tell."

"Hmm, I see. It's true that I may have placed Arita in a situation not entirely to his liking. However, I believe that choosing or not choosing is up to him. I wonder if you have any right to be saying anything here?"

"I do. I've been friends with Haru longer than anyone at this school."

"My! Friends...hm?" Hearing Chiyuri's proclamation, the chilliest Kuroyukihime smile rose up on her beautifully pale face. "In that case, I rank somewhat higher. You may have heard the rumors, but I confessed my crush to him and am currently awaiting a reply. We were just about to go on a short date."

Gaaaah. I can't can't, this is the end of the world, no choice but to change schools tomorrow.

Chiyuri and everyone around them froze almost like when he was accelerated. Haruyuki also froze in an unnatural position, just his sweat in motion, pouring off his face.

In the silence, Kuroyukihime pulled a snow-white handkerchief from her uniform pocket. "He's a strange one. Almost winter and yet..." After wiping away Haruyuki's sweat, she hooked her arm tightly through his right elbow. "Now then, farewell, Miss Friend."

And she began walking forward through the students to their left and right, almost as if walking a red carpet, dragging Haruyuki's large body with her.

Dragged along and facing backward, Haruyuki watched in terror as the face of his childhood companion changed from dumbfounded shock to the brink of detonation, anger gauge three times above capacity.

*　　*　　*

"I—I—I know I'm repeating myself, but…wh-what are you thinking?!" Haruyuki shouted and finally ripped his arm free of Kuroyukihime after they had left the main road and entered a brick-paved back lane. "L-l-l-let me just tell you, there are some things in this world that can't be fixed by acceleration!!"

"A-ha-ha-ha-ha!" Kuroyukihime laughed delightedly from her belly. "Ha-ha-ha! And you've already arrived at the very heart of the Burst Linker! Isn't that lovely?"

"It's not! Not at all! If I stop coming to school, it's all your fault!"

"Now, now, you didn't look entirely displeased, you know. I also managed to get the perfect screenshot this time, too. Want to see?"

"I do not! Please throw it away!!"

"Hee-hee-hee…" Kuroyukihime continued laughing for a while, shoulders shaking slightly, as the heels of her loafers hit the wear-resistant brick surface of the road with a biting sound. Finally, she recomposed her face, exhaling softly, and continued. "I'm a little concerned. Or rather, there's something I'd like to confirm."

"Huh? Concerned? You mean, about Chiyuri?"

"Oh? You're on a first-name basis?"

"Oh! Uh, no, it's Kurashima, Chiyuri Kurashima, grade seven, class one."

"I know. Although this is the first time I've heard about her being your best friend. What I really want to know, though, is… are you really just plain old friends?"

Bathed in her suspicious gaze, Haruyuki bounced his head fiercely up and down. "We are. Childhood friends, stuck-with-each-other kind of thing…I mean, she has a boyfriend."

"Oh? Even still…no…mm. Hmmmm."

"What's 'hmmmm'?"

"Oh, nothing. I just saw again the depths of the real world."

"Uh…uh-huh." Not understanding, he swallowed a sigh and

asked something that had been bugging him for a while. "Um...
before, did you say you already knew Chiyuri's name?"

"Yes, I did. Quite coincidentally, I've been paying attention to
her for different reasons than I have been you."

"Wh-what do you mean?"

"I can't explain it in just a few words. It's directly connected to
why I came to invite you to the accelerated world. Anyway, let's
discuss it at length over tea. It's my treat, a celebration of your
victory," Kuroyukihime said as she changed direction, stepping
toward the branch of a coffee-shop chain, which was apparently
the destination she'd had in mind right from the start.

Maybe because the afternoon was still young, fortunately, the
shop had only a smattering of customers. As soon as Kuroyukihime stepped through the door, though, Haruyuki felt those few
gazes locked onto them. It made him afraid to keep going.

Even at the best of times, Haruyuki had never done anything
even remotely close to having tea alone with a girl on his way
home from school. Indeed, he had never done anything like this
in his life, and his brain immediately overloaded. He ordered a
large, sweet drink almost automatically, quietly allowed himself
to let her pay, and staggered to a table in the back. As he inserted
the cable she produced, he thought, *Whoa! What's going on? This
is almost like a real date—*

*Prob'ly doesn't look like that, though. I mean, the two of us?
Older sister, little brother? No, mistress and flunky?*

"*I know what you're thinking, you know.*" She scowled
lightly, and he hurriedly sipped at his sweet, caramel-flavored
concoction.

"*N-no. It's nothing. Anyway, before... The reason you invited me
to the accelerated world—*"

"*Don't be in such a hurry. It's...a long story.*" After gracefully
raising her not-very-sweet-looking drink to her lips, Kuroyukihime rested her chin in her hand with a short sigh.

In the pale yellow light coming in through the window, she
looked like something out of some old foreign movie while

nevertheless remaining a uniformed junior high school student, and Haruyuki was unconsciously struck dumb. It was almost like he was sitting in front of an old projector screen with a direct cable stretching out from it. He'd been spacing out like this for who knew how long when Kuroyukihime suddenly rapped his right hand on the table, and he nearly flew out of his seat.

"Anyway, you really did great back there. Let me congratulate you on your victory once again, Haruyuki."

"Uh, thanks. Thank you. It's because of all your advice."

"No, it was your own resourcefulness. If you keep it up, you'll be level two in no time. You might even make it up to three before the end of the year."

"Uh…uh. Honestly, I can't even imagine that…" He had only just barely snatched up his first victory. The idea of having to win dozens more fights like that in the future made his mind go blank.

The smile disappeared abruptly from Kuroyukihime's face, and she nodded as if reading Haruyuki's thoughts. "Mm. In fact, the road ahead is unimaginably long. Of the estimated thousand Burst Linkers, the number of those who have been raised to level four is fairly limited. Getting to five or six is nearly impossible in solo play. And it's no mistake to assume that level-seven and -eight Burst Linkers are all commanders of enormous groups."

"G-groups?"

"Like the guilds or teams you often see in other online games. We are army corps. Called Legions. The current accelerated world is split into and ruled by six enormous Legions. And commanding these are the only six Burst Linkers who have reached level nine. Named Blue, Red, Yellow, Green, Purple, and White, they are the Six Kings of Pure Color!" Her voice, suddenly sharp like a knife, echoed in his brain, and Haruyuki opened his eyes wide. Conscious of his gaze, Kuroyukihime fluttered her eyelids briefly and gave a faintly bitter smile. "I'm sorry for yelling."

"It's fine…but, so, six people?" He was surprised there were even as many as a thousand Burst Linkers, but he could only be baffled that so few had made it to level nine. *"I've played a lot of different net games, but I've never heard of so few players reaching the level cap."*

"Must feel incredible," Haruyuki murmured jealously, and Kuroyukihime, listening to him, raised a single eyebrow and shook her head.

"I didn't say that level nine was the limit."

"Huh? Th-then there's a level ten, too? How many people...?"

Her response was another dismissive gesture. Kuroyukihime took another sip of coffee, her seat back making a faint noise as she turned her attention out to space. Pulling at her motion, the direct cable shook, shining silver between them.

"Brain Burst... Formally titled Brain Burst 2039, the program was released seven years ago by an unknown maker and has already been updated several times. However, despite the fact that so much time has passed, there is not a single Burst Linker who has reached level ten. The sole reason is... the severity of the dictated rules."

"Do you mean you have to win an incredible amount of fights? Like a thousand or... ten thousand?"

"No, just five is sufficient." A slightly dangerous smile flitted across the lips pronouncing this unexpected revelation. *"However, for this purpose, you may only fight another level nine Linker. And if you lose once in a level-nine battle, you instantly lose all your points, and Brain Burst is forcefully uninstalled."* Kuroyukihime turned her pitch-black eyes on her speechless companion. *"Haruyuki. Don't you think it's strange that Brain Burst, which makes possible the marvelous phenomenon of accelerated thought, has been able to stay hidden from the general public for the last seven years?"*

Haruyuki was bewildered by the sudden question, but now that she mentioned it, it was seriously weird. If there were a thousand Burst Linkers, the secret should have leaked out from somewhere long ago and amazed the world.

"It stays a secret because of how strict the requirements are for compatibility with Brain Burst."

"Requirements? Like being good at games or something?"

Kuroyukihime smiled bitterly at Haruyuki's question and replied, *"Nothing as ambiguous as that. The most serious requirement is having 'continuously worn a quantum connection Neurolinker terminal from shortly after birth.' The first-generation Neurolinkers went on the market fifteen years ago. Which means"*— Kuroyukihime paused before continuing slowly—*"there are no adult Burst Linkers. The oldest are a meager fifteen years old, mere children. And because they are children, while they are Burst Linkers, they will try to protect that privilege at all costs. And after the program is forcefully uninstalled, they wouldn't be believed even if they were to say anything to an adult."*

For a brief moment, an ironic smile crossed her glossy lips.

"And because they are children, they share the same sweet fantasies. In summer two years ago, the young kings all reached level nine at very nearly the same time. A system message then informed them of the brutal requirements to reach level ten. Did they, as a result, plunge into bloody dispute? No. What the kings chose was eternal stagnation. Rather than move forward, they prioritized maintaining their own tiny gardens. In other words . . . they decided to divide and rule over the accelerated world in Legions and concluded agreements to prevent the invasion of other territories. It's honestly a total farce. This, even though we had hunted countless Linkers to reach level nine."

Haruyuki swallowed hard. A pain raced down his dry throat, and after taking a large sip of his melted caramel frappe, he put forth his thoughts timidly. *"So you're saying your objective is to challenge these Six Kings of Pure Color . . . ?"*

Hearing this, Kuroyukihime allowed a mysterious smile onto her lips. *"No, I already did that."*

"Wha . . . ?!"

"The Six Kings . . . they used to be the Seven Kings of Pure Color.

Seven boys and girls, who, although rivals, were bound by strong ties. They fought one another countless times, winning and losing nearly the same amount but never holding even a shred of resentment. The Black King betrayed them all and tried to hunt them. Until that night two years ago."

Black...King.

*Which means that avatar name...ruled Black...*Haruyuki opened his eyes wide and gulped his breath back.

Kuroyukihime nodded slowly. *"Yes...It was me. The Black King, Black Lotus, was the only one of those who had reached level nine who spoke out against choosing peace. I threw away everything—ties, friendship, respect—and insisted that we should throw ourselves into fighting, wagering our accumulated points. And when they refused to listen, I dyed the round table of our meeting with fresh blood."*

"Wh-what did you do?"

"The last night the Seven Kings met in one building—although, of course, we have never met in the real world. Burst Linkers must do their utmost to hide their real names and faces."

Haruyuki was about to ask why, but he quickly deduced the reason. If other Burst Linkers found out your name or what you looked like, in the worst-case scenario, they could attack you in the real world. People pressed into a desperate situation, people who needed to earn points no matter what, would probably go to such lengths.

Kuroyukihime nodded slightly, as if reading Haruyuki's mind, and continued. *"The meeting that night took place in Battle Royale mode, connecting all seven of us as fighters on the same field. I... The Red King appeared before me, preaching friendship and insisting we stop fighting. He caught me off guard..."*

The pale face beneath her shining bangs collapsed. Fixing her empty eyes on a single point, Kuroyukihime recounted the rest mechanically. *"I cut his head off. A perfect critical hit...He instantly lost all the health in his gauge and, under the new rules, all his points as well, finally losing Brain Burst itself as a result.*

The current Red King is the second one. After that ... all hell broke loose. Ha-ha! Purple, who had been in love with Red, screamed and wept; Blue went crazy with rage; and we all began to try and kill one another—no honor, no respect. We knew it was our first and last chance, you see ... We struggled desperately to take the other five heads, we were so reckless."
Her lightly colored lips twisted and a laugh slipped out of her actual mouth. *"The ability to make rational judgments went out the window. Stirred up by madness, I fought, and although I couldn't take another king, I was also not defeated, and before I knew it, thirty minutes had passed and I was linked out. In the two years since, I've focused on running and hiding. Right now, I am the biggest traitor in the accelerated world, I have the largest bounty on my head, and I am the worst coward."*
"... Why ..." Haruyuki's thoughts were half paralyzed by the gruesomeness of this near-monologue, and even simple questions escaped his consciousness. *"Why would you ..."*
"Because I put it far above friendship, above honor ... becoming level ten. You could even say that alone is what I lived for. The system message also told us this. That Burst Linkers reaching level ten would have the chance to meet the program creator and would be told the true meaning behind the existence of Brain Burst, as well as its ultimate goal. I ... I want to know. Whatever it takes, I have to know." Propping her elbows up on the table and hiding her face in tightly clasped hands, Kuroyukihime whispered to Haruyuki, in neurospeak so leaden it was as if it were echoing up from an infinite abyss. *"Accelerating your thinking, you can get money, grades, fame. Is this really the meaning behind our Duels? Is this the compensation we seek, the limit we can reach? Isn't ... isn't there something beyond this? This ... shell called a human being ... outside ... something more ..."*
Aah.
A little, honestly just a tiny bit ... I get it. Like being on the ground, where it's hard to hold on, and looking up at the distant sky.

Almost as if even this fleeting thought had been communicated to her, Kuroyukihime slowly lifted her face and stared at Haruyuki with eyes glowing urgently.

But that, too, was fleeting, and the beautiful senior, both arms flopped down on the table, smiled dryly and murmured, *"So? Are you shocked? Or maybe you hate me, Haruyuki. Perhaps I'll sacrifice even you at some point for my objective. It's fine if you say you can't help me anymore. I won't try to stop you. I won't try to take your Brain Burst."*

After thinking for approximately two seconds, Haruyuki nervously reached his right hand out and stopped about a centimeter in front of Kuroyukihime's fingertips. *"Er, well...,"* he said. *"In any game, some people want to forget about seeing the ending, and they just roam around the map right before the end forever. They're obviously idiots. It's only natural to try for higher levels, if there are any. I mean, that's why Brain Burst exists, right?"*

This wasn't just a lie to suck up to Kuroyukihime. As a hardcore gamer from before he could remember, he sincerely believed this from the bottom of his heart.

Kuroyukihime's eyes widened in surprise, and then she laughed lightly and brilliantly a few seconds later. *"Pft, ha-ha-ha! How did this happen? You're already more of a Burst Linker than I am. I get it... Only natural to aim for it; that's where we are, is it..."*

"I-it's nothing to laugh at." Slightly hurt, Haruyuki pursed his lips, and then sat up straighter before continuing. *"A-anyway, that's why I'll keep helping you. I mean, I want to get there one day, too... to level ten."*

Kuroyukihime's left hand suddenly moved over the tabletop to grab Haruyuki's right hand. *"Thank you."* Her thought, free of the empty undertone it had held only recently, poured warmly into a flustered Haruyuki. *"Thank you, Haruyuki. I knew... I knew I made the right decision. I'm so glad from the bottom of my heart that I chose you."*

Here was where he should squeeze her hand back and meet her

eyes. But there was absolutely no way Haruyuki could do anything like that.

Instead, instinctively, he pulled his hand back, drew his shoulders in turtle-like, and mumbled in tight neurospeak, *"N-no, it's— You won't really be able to get a lot of use out of me…A-anyway, to get to the main part of it, you…What am I supposed to do?"*

In the short silence that followed, was it pity that floated up in those still eyes regarding him?

Finally, after a quiet sigh, Kuroyukihime uttered softly, *"Right. The introductory bit ended up going long. But let's get to the heart of it. I told you before I managed to survive these last two years, yes?"*

Haruyuki released the long breath he had been holding as he lifted his face and nodded with a gulp at Kuroyukihime, whose expression had returned to its normal complacency.

"That doesn't mean that I've won out in challenges from the blood-crazed kings themselves or assassins they've dispatched. Rather…these two years, I haven't once connected my Neuro-linker to the global net. If your name isn't on the matching list, you won't get any challenges, you see?"

"Guh…a-are you serious?" he groaned unconsciously. For Haruyuki, taking in information from the global net was as necessary as drinking water and breathing air. This wasn't just a metaphor; he had no doubt he would wither and die without it.

"Very serious. With the fixed-panel terminal, you can still view sites and read your mail. Although the 2-D screen does make my eyes tired. You can get used to anything. But even if I'm cut off from the global net, there is just one net I absolutely must connect with every day, because of my position in society."

"Y-your position…? You mean, a rich girl—I mean, a princess?"

"Idiot!"

Shot down by that cool voice, he finally started to realize the person before him was just a junior high student like him. *"O-oh, right. The Umesato Junior High local net. So, so, w-wait a minute. You can't mean…"*

"I do mean." Kuroyukihime drank down the last of her coffee and crushed the cup. *"Two months ago, the very day summer vacation ended, I was challenged to a Duel through the in-school local net. By someone at Umesato, just like us."*

The words that followed further baffled an already dumbfounded Haruyuki.

"Then the worst thing... Back then, I changed my original duel avatar to a dummy spectator avatar."

"Dummy... There's a function like that?"

"Mm. There are many times when it's preferable to hide who you really are and watch from the Gallery. Naturally, the dummy avatar has no battle capacity. However, that's not the problem... When I think about it now, I realize I was extremely careless. I used my avatar for the local school net as my dummy as well. I certainly didn't expect a Burst Linker to show up all of a sudden at our school."

After a moment's confusion, Haruyuki jumped up lightly, sending his chair clattering back. *"Huh? You mean that black swallowtail...?!"* The bewitching avatar that popping up in the back of Haruyuki's mind projected perfectly onto the graceful uniformed figure in front of him. *"Your enemy saw it... on the school net? Which means... Then that's..."*

"Good guess. That's right, this person knows"—Kuroyukihime released the cup onto the tray and pressed her right hand firmly against her chest—*"that the real me here is Black Lotus. A Burst Linker's greatest taboo: outed in the real world. I was afraid of real attacks by assassins sent by the Six Kings."*

Attacks... in the real world.

Haruyuki had already guessed at the terror hidden in those words. If you could pinpoint someone's identity in the real world, then at the extreme end of the spectrum, it was possible to kidnap, confine, beat, or threaten that person and steal every last point they had.

Of course, this would be a serious crime. But even in "normal games," problems between players had been known to develop into deadly incidents in the real world. And Brain Burst was not just a game.

Haruyuki held his breath and waited for Kuroyukihime to continue. But…

"That said, there haven't been any, not one. Not even a vague sense of contact, much less an attack."

"What…?"

"I was deeply perplexed, but— This is all I can think. My enemy… intends to monopolize me. With the good fortune of having discovered me, whoever it is wants to gradually run me down, big-game bounty that I am, and take every single one of my points for themselves, without telling the Legion they belong to."

"Run you down…?"

Staring intently at Haruyuki tilting his head, Kuroyukihime coughed and began making a list as if it were obvious. *"In the toilet. While I'm changing. In the shower. There are plenty of moments where I'm emotionally defenseless at school. If someone pinpointed these times and challenged me to a fight, I certainly wouldn't be able to respond at the top of my game."*

"In the… shower…" Unthinkingly, he imagined the whole scene, and betrayed by his voice, Haruyuki was once again the recipient of an icy glare. Fortunately, however, Kuroyukihime didn't press any further and continued with a sigh. *"The truth is, in these last two months, I've been attacked more than a dozen times. The timing has always been less than ideal, although I've managed to get away with draws so far."*

"I—I get it. So basically, this guy's, like, seriously greedy, then… but in a sense, that's the silver lining, I guess…"

"Well, better than an attack in the real world, anyway. But that being said, I can't exactly trade in my dummy avatar for my original duel avatar and beat him down. My enemy might end up thinking his plan isn't going to work and give up on my points, then strike a bargain to give my head to the Six Kings for some meager bounty."

"O-oh… right… uh-huh." Haruyuki nodded unconsciously.

This was basically the definition of *cornered*. "*Okay, but what are you going to do? You can't run, and you can't even get them before they get you.*"

"*This I know. There's only one way to break free. I find out the player's real identity. Just who is this unknown Burst Linker—what grade, what class?*"

Haruyuki was suddenly overcome with the urge to slap his knee. If they both knew the other's identity, they would naturally be forced to a cease-fire to protect their own Brain Burst. "*Right, of course. Then your enemy would be totally blocked. And, I mean, that's fairly simple, right? Like at morning assembly or something, when all the students are together in the auditorium, you just accelerate and challenge whoever it is to a fight. You can figure out their class and student number from where they appear.*"

"*Oh, aren't you something? It took me a full day to come up with that idea.*"

"*So . . . you've already tried that?*"

"*I have. And . . . I was shocked. It's been quite a while since I was that surprised.*"

"*Wh-who was it?*"

"*No one was there.*" Kuroyukihime's response was something Haruyuki had not expected. "*My name was the only one on the matching list. Listen, we both know Umesato students are not allowed to disconnect from the school net for even a second while they're at school, because attendance and the lessons themselves happen via the net. So if you were to disconnect, there would immediately be a school-wide warning broadcast. This is exactly the reason I can't avoid my enemy's attacks. And yet . . . whoever it is wasn't on the list!*"

"*M-maybe they were home sick or something.*"

Kuroyukihime stared at Haruyuki and sniffed lightly. "*I checked. Everyone came to school that day. And moreover, once, immediately after I was attacked and barely managed a draw before escaping, my opponent's name was not on the list. In other words . . . it's hard to believe, but this player can block, by some means or other. They can challenge people to all the fights they want, but not a single Burst Linker can trespass on them. A tremendous privilege, and one that erases the great underlying principle of the accelerated world. Someone able to do that... You'd have to be a super hacker, so much so that you could change the Brain Burst program itself, a program which is supposedly impregnable, or—someone with some connection with the program creator..."*

Her only purpose in life was to meet the creator and learn the meaning of Brain Burst. That's what she had said only moments ago. In which case, discovering the true identity of this mysterious opponent was for her more essential than protecting herself.

Having guessed this, Haruyuki felt an inexplicable throbbing in his chest as he murmured softly, *"So then... what you want me to do... You want me to help you find out the true identity of your enemy, right?"*

Not to protect the princess from evil.

Well, it's only natural. Don't think such stupid things. I'm just a hunting dog chasing prey, a pig sniffing out mushrooms in the earth.

"Hmm... well, that's about it, yes." Seemingly unaware of his momentary internal conflict, Kuroyukihime nodded slightly. *"To be honest, I've obtained a fair bit of information already. To list everything I know now, let's see... First, my enemy's name. The duel avatar is called Cyan Pile. Level four."*

"Cyan... Pile..."

That's kind of... cool. And sounds strong. No, but Kuroyukihime also said that level four is the first barrier. Which meant Cyan Pile was strong.

"Affiliation is a fairly pure close-range blue. I've seen this Linker punch right through the thin walls of the stage several times. Conversely, he or she doesn't seem to have any flying equipment. Which is why I've been able to escape somehow up to now, but... to be honest, I'm coming up against my limit. My powers of concentration are essentially shot."

They must have been. Not knowing when you would be attacked from the moment you came to school until the second you left. Haruyuki probably wouldn't have been able to make it three days. However, Kuroyukihime continued speaking in clear thoughts without a hint of exhaustion. *"And, this is at best a guess, but... it's not just me. Whoever it is, he or she is backed into a corner, too. I get that feeling somehow."*

"What? By what?"

"The fear of losing acceleration. Most likely, from being on the verge of running out of burst points. People with points to spare normally try to have more fun with the Duels as fights. Like that Ash Roller you fought."

"O-oh, yeah. He was definitely having a seriously great time."

"However, my assailant doesn't have a drop of wiggle room. Silent, not giving a thought to appearance, Cyan Pile comes at me half insane. That feeling, that's the sign of a Burst Linker afraid of losing everything. So afraid that the stingy prize the kings have put up for me isn't enough. All the points I've accumulated is the goal. But just understanding this desperation doesn't get me anywhere."

"I... guess not. I mean, we can't make all the students get a psychological checkup or anything. Is that all you know?" Haruyuki asked casually, but he got the impression that Kuroyukihime's thoughts abruptly froze.

Huh, he thought.

Before he could voice the question, Kuroyukihime shook her head and said, *"No. I have one other important piece of information... the guide cursor."*

"Huh? That blue arrow?"

"Exactly. It points in the direction of your enemy from the moment the Duel starts. So even if I can't see the exact moment when Cyan Pile appears, as long as I remember the direction the cursor is pointing when the fight starts, the real body of my enemy must be somewhere along that straight-line trajectory. That's my theory."

"Oh…oh! Right, of course. The stages are the real world land-scape as is, so you can at least see which direction in the school Cyan Pile is hiding!"

"Exactly. I've memorized the direction of the guide cursor each of the dozens of times I've been attacked up to now, made a list of the students in those parts of the real-world Umesato, and pulled out the duplicate names. As a result, I've reached a conclusion about which student is most likely to be Cyan Pile. But I have absolutely no solid proof. A single straight line in a place so densely packed with people is simply not enough. There are always dozens of students on any given trajectory. Haruyuki, I want you to watch the next attack on me and memorize the direction of the cursor pointing out Cyan Pile to the Gallery."

"If there are…two cursors, then…" Haruyuki mumbled, dazed, and Kuroyukihime nodded, the expression on her face hardening.

"Exactly. If we have two, then the intersection will give us a single point. And then, the student in that place…I can settle this once and for all. The true identity of Cyan Pile." Pursing her lips tightly, Kuroyukihime traced a nimble finger in the air, manip-ulating the virtual desktop only she could see. Just as she was about to slide the file she had called up toward Haruyuki, her finger stopped abruptly.

"What's wrong? Who is it, this suspect of yours?" Haruyuki leaned forward, swallowing hard to wet his throat, dry despite the fact that he had just finished drinking that enormous frappe, because he was worked up.

Kuroyukihime still seemed to be hesitating, but finally, mutter-ing as if making excuses, she flicked the file and sent it over. "Listen. I prepared this file a week before I found the third acceleration-compatible person I was looking for at Umesato—which is to say, you—in that game corner."

Not understanding at all why she would tack on such a disclaimer, Haruyuki accepted the file, brow knitted. He didn't hesitate to stab the icon displayed on his virtual desktop with the tip of his finger.

Which opened into a single image. A portrait from the neck up, probably taken from the school register.

"...Huh...? This...? Why...?"

The fiercely short hair. The blue hairpin. The big eyes, somehow catlike. It wasn't just a face he had seen before. It was the only face in this world he had seen more of than his mother's.

"Ch-Chiyuri? She's...a Burst Linker...?" After a full five seconds of muttering and wondering, Haruyuki turned toward Kuroyukihime again, perplexed. "No...that's not possible! She's super terrible at games and stuff. Doesn't matter what kind, she's just bad, bad...There's no way she'd be Burst Linker material. She's so slow...and everything shows up on her face...She can't be the person who's targeting you with such relentless focus."

"You know her pretty well, hm?" Kuroyukihime said without meeting his eyes, her voice the slightest bit harder.

"That's...I mean, we've been friends since we were kids..."

"When she came up to us at the gates before, inside, I was surprised. If she is Cyan Pile, she should obviously know I'm Black Lotus. I suspected it was some kind of strategy."

"Um, but that—she doesn't have that kind of skill; she's not that kind of person. I mean, she's super awkward. Everything she's thinking shows on her face and in her attitude."

The more Haruyuki protested, the sharper the angle Kuroyukihime's eyebrows formed, and she returned in an even chillier voice, "Don't you think in that case it's even more natural to think she is Cyan Pile? You saw the obvious hostility she—Kurashima— has toward me."

"No, that was just, it wasn't like that. It was just you and I are directing and stuff..."

"Why would she get mad about that? Kurashima has a proper boyfriend, doesn't she? In which case, she doesn't have any reason to complain if I direct or link arms with you, does she?"

"I...I...*That's true, but...*," Haruyuki stammered, wanting to hold his head in his hands and wondering how they had gotten to this point. *Chiyuri definitely has the perfect boyfriend in Takumu, but besides that, it's— I'm her— Subordinate? Possession? Under exclusive ownership?*

Several words he couldn't quite bring himself to say flitted through his mind, and as he struggled with the nuances, Kuroyukihime hit him with a merciless final blow. "*Isn't that exactly what her attitude says? Kurashima has been a Burst Linker for some time, and she was intending to make you her 'child.' And yet here I come out of the blue and snatch you up. Furious and unable to stand it, she then comes after me. Hmm?*"

He was completely unable to process Kuroyukihime's thinking, sounding so much like a petulant child, and her persuasive, impossible logic...and yet before he even realized it, he had given himself over to it, declaring, "*I—I understand! I'll check directly with her!*"

"*You will?*" Kuroyukihime's voice was hard as a lone eyebrow snapped up. "*But what do you intend to do exactly? I'm sure you understand that you can't simply go up to her and ask if she's a Burst Linker. And it's no use accelerating and trying to fight, to get a visual confirmation of Cyan Pile. Whoever it is has no problem blocking Duels. Which is exactly why I've been working so hard. I have no way of confirming any of this. Honestly, I need you to think things through.*"

"*I—I am thinking things through!*" Haruyuki returned sharply, his tit-for-tat reflex triggered. "*It's fine. I'll go and direct with her. She can block the Duels, but if I look in her memory directly through her Neurolinker, I should be able to check if she has the Brain Burst program or not. That should satisfy you, right?*"

5

Why? How?

His shoulders fell dejectedly, and Haruyuki repeated these two words over and over in his mind as he trudged along the twilit road home.

Why is this happening? I just wanted to be Kuroyukihime's faithful pawn, and now here I am, headed home after practically flying out of that café and away from that "discussion," which was really more like an argument.

Please! Just let me rewind the last thirty minutes! Haruyuki wished desperately, but even in Brain Burst, where you could basically stop real time, going back in time was not an option.

And even if he could reload the scene like in some adventure game, he was still going to have a hard time quietly agreeing with the idea that Chiyuri was Cyan Pile. He couldn't even believe it was possible for her to be a Burst Linker, much less that she'd kept it from him for such a long time.

No. It wasn't that he couldn't. It was that he didn't want to.

To be honest, he had no objective basis for being certain Chiyuri wasn't a Burst Linker. Things had been different when they were little, but this past year or two, he'd hardly ever had deep conversations with Chiyuri. She might not have been in the same league as Kuroyukihime, but the mere fact that Chiyuri was a girl almost made her too mysterious for Haruyuki.

And if he needed to refute the idea that she wouldn't hide things from him, he could do that, too. Despite the fact that Haruyuki had repeatedly asked her not to discuss the bullying with Takumu, she had clearly done it anyway, all the while covering up her indiscretion.

Now that Haruyuki thought about it, before asking Chiyuri some big favor like directing with him, he had to at least apologize for the sandwich-flipping thing. In order to do that, he had to accept the fact that Chiyuri and Takumu had been talking about him behind his back.

That would take at least a week. Or rather, he just didn't want to think about it. Maybe he should forget this whole investigation. But if he did, he'd basically be forced to accept the supposition that Chiyuri was Cyan Pile.

What exactly do I want? What do I want to happen with Chiyuri and Takumu, and with Kuroyukihime?

As heavy feet carried Haruyuki through the entrance of his building, his brain smoldered in plumes of smoke accompanied by a burning stench, overloaded as it was with thoughts that were too oppressive for him to handle. He glanced at the clock display at the edge of his vision: 5:30 PM.

Chiyuri was already home, but as Takumu had kendo practice, he was probably still at school. Which meant the two of them wouldn't be together at one of their apartments chatting privately or anything.

In the elevator, Haruyuki agonized long enough that a warning bell finally sounded. He then pressed the button for the twenty-third floor, where his own apartment was located.

Halfway to his destination, he pressed the button two floors below.

"Goodness! Haru, I haven't seen you in so long!" Chiyuri's mother cried the moment she opened the door, beaming, and Haruyuki muttered a vague apology for not stopping by more.

"You've gotten so big. How old are you again? Oh, thirteen, of course, just like Chiyuri. You haven't come to see us at all since you started junior high. I've missed you! You can stay awhile today, can't you? Stay for supper. That girl of mine barely eats anything at all these days, so it's hardly worth the trouble of making something. And I was just thinking I'd make curry rice, and I know it's your favorite, Haru. I'll whip up a whole pile of it, so you make sure and ask for seconds. I'm sure Chiyuri will be delighted, too. She's always moaning about how you never come over anymore."

Chiyuri's mother seemed like she could go on chattering forever, but a sharp voice echoing at the end of the hallway cut her off. "Mom!!"

Looking up, Haruyuki saw Chiyuri—or rather, just her head poking out from the living room—glaring in their direction, her face ablaze. "Quit blabbing!!"

"Yes, yes. This rebellious period, I just hate it. Haru, you make yourself at home."

Haruyuki watched Chiyuri's grinning mother wave as she disappeared through the kitchen door halfway down the hall, and then he smiled stiffly. "H-hey."

Chiyuri glanced at him and jerked her small chin up in a *come in* sort of way before disappearing back into the living room. Exhaling with a long sigh, Haruyuki took off his shoes and muttered quietly, "Okay, I'm coming in."

Up until he'd been in the third or fourth grade in elementary school, Haruyuki had just said, "I'm home!" as he stepped up into this foyer. The Kurashimas' was the first place he'd come home to, covered in sweat after playing outside with Chiyuri and Takumu until it got dark. He took a bath, had supper, and even stayed to watch TV before staggering back to his empty apartment two floors up. For Haruyuki, who was already being bullied at school even then, these evenings were the only time he could relax and have fun.

However, that all ended two years earlier. When Takumu told Chiyuri he liked her and Chiyuri talked to Haruyuki about it.

Haruyuki's blue bear-face slippers were still in the slipper stand in the entryway. He slipped on the faded footwear and timidly pulled open the living room door, but Chiyuri wasn't there. He wiped his sweaty palms on the pants of his uniform, passed through the apartment, the layout of which he was only too familiar with, and knocked quietly on the door farthest back. Chiyuri's.

After a brief pause, he heard her short response. "Come in."

Gulping, he turned the knob.

Stepping into Chiyuri's room for the first time in two years, he saw that it was still simply decorated, basically the same as it stood in his memory. The desk and the bed were adorned with black and white keynotes, and the curtains were also monotone. It looked a lot like Haruyuki's room.

However, there were a few changes. First off, something smelled amazing. Also different were the clothes Chiyuri was wearing as she sat on her bed making an ugly face. Naturally, she wasn't still in her uniform. However, despite the fact that she had always had a boyish look in elementary school, she now wore some kind of soft white sweater with a fluttering pink skirt.

That's gotta be...like when she goes on a date with Takumu, Haruyuki was thinking absentmindedly when he was unexpectedly, preemptively attacked.

"I called you a million times yesterday."

"Huh?" Haruyuki uttered idiotically as she glared up at him.

Yesterday? Oh, right. I ran away from Chiyuri and Takumu, and that was that. Whoa! Before I apologize for the sandwich thing, I better apologize for that.

"O-oh, sorry. I had my Neurolinker disconnected the whole day—"

"You could've at least e-mailed me. Thanks to you, I went to bed super late!"

"S-sorry..." Apologizing to Chiyuri as she puffed out her cheeks, Haruyuki muttered to himself, *I knew it couldn't be her.*

No matter how he looked at it, there was just no way. *Her? The*

Burst Linker Cyan Pile and a level-four warrior to boot? As if. And the icing on the cake, she's a super hacker who managed to change the Brain Burst program, something no one else has been able to do? No way! However, that said, it wasn't going to be easy getting proof. The only way would be to direct with her Neurolinker and search her memory, just like Kuroyukihime had insisted, but how was he supposed to ask her to do something like that with things between them the way they were?

No. Wait, hold up a sec. A thought fluttered through the back of his brain suddenly, and Haruyuki quickly seized on it.

Couldn't he ask her precisely *because* things between them were like this? It was a jerkish thing to do to Chiyuri, but it wasn't like he'd be tricking her. He'd be apologizing wholeheartedly and taking the opportunity to just poke around a little in her memory at the same time.

"Uh, uh, uh, um, Ch-Chiyuri!" Haruyuki shouted with an authentic, violent stutter.

"Wh-what?"

"Uh...I—I...There's all...The sandwiches and the thing at the gate...I came to apologize. B-b-but, it's, I have a hard time actually saying stuff like this, so...d-d-direct with me for a minute."

It wasn't an act. Beads of sweat formed on his forehead, and Chiyuri's mouth dropped open as she stared. The angle of her thick eyebrows passed from surprise to doubt and rose still higher.

No go? I was too pushy. Haruyuki braced himself for a reprimand, but a strange, challenging look came over the face of his childhood friend. This...It was the look he used to see way back when whenever Chiyuri fought with a boy, the look that said, *If you think you can take me, go on and try.*

"Did you bring a cable?" she asked abruptly, her voice hard, and Haruyuki said, *Crap!* to himself as he shook his head. "Hmm. Well, fine, all I have is this."

Bending over, Chiyuri opened the drawer under her bed and

pulled out an off-white XSB cable a mere thirty centimeters or so long.

"Th-that's short! You...So you and Taku always...?" he asked unthinkingly, and as soon as the words were out, she started yelling.

"Y-you jerk!! Taku has one that's a meter long. This is the one that came with my Neurolinker when I bought it, the one to connect to a computer!!"

"O-oh..."

Because the super-high-speed transfer protocol extra serial bus required a high-grade cable with serious shielding, the cables that came with the devices were, without exception, short. Even so, thirty centimeters was a bit much. This manufacturer was exceptionally stingy.

Thoughts of escape ran through his mind as Chiyuri pushed the cable, about as long as a cat's tail, at him.

She snorted lightly and rolled her small body over on the bed. "If you wanna do it, do it." She snapped her eyes shut and turned her face away.

The cable in his hand was like a live wire, and Haruyuki said nervously, "Uh, um...if it's okay, maybe you could sit on that chair and not turn around...?"

No answer. Sprawled on the sheets, Chiyuri didn't look like she planned on budging any time soon.

Again, he seriously considered just fleeing, but he had already done that with Kuroyukihime today. If he ran away again now, the situation would be irreparable.

"O-okay."

Haruyuki mustered his courage and shuffled over to the bed, where Chiyuri was stretched out, and then took off his slippers. Ever so gently, he rested a knee upon the white and gray striped sheets. The sturdy pipe frame squealed in protest at the extra weight, which was several times greater than its usual load.

On all fours, seventy centimeters to Chiyuri's right, Haruyuki first plugged one end of the cable into the external connection terminal on the back right-hand side of his own Neurolinker. Then, tilting his head at an unnatural angle, he grabbed the other end and stretched it out. However, the Neurolinker terminal on Chiyuri, lying there with her eyes closed, was still about a light-year away. *Aaaugh, crap. I should've come up from the left. Should I pull back and go around? No, I don't have that much left in me,* he told himself. But there was absolutely no way he could go over Chiyuri to get to the other side of her.

About to descend into full-blown panic mode, Haruyuki moved just his upper body into an extremely unbalanced position and tried to force their necks closer together. A smell like milk wafted up from Chiyuri's body, and his equilibrium became suspect.

His left knee slipped abruptly. On the verge of crushing Chiyuri's slim body with his enormous bulk, his left hand shot out and just barely broke his fall.

Now, however, he was on the brink of crisis. His left knee was in between Chiyuri's legs, which were sprawled out, his left hand had made contact right next to her cheek, and he was just barely holding himself up. *Whooaaaaaa! Whaaaaat!* The needle on his panic meter swung over into the red zone when Chiyuri's eyes popped open, too close, not more than ten centimeters away.

Haruyuki couldn't read the emotion in her large brown eyes. Of course, there was anger and annoyance. But it seemed more like something she had been holding back for a very long time than a consequence of Haruyuki's current rude conduct.

Unable to face those eyes any longer, Haruyuki moved his right hand and inserted the plug into her neck. The direct-connect warning that appeared hid her face momentarily, which gave him a mere second, but he managed somehow to compose his thoughts. He blinked several times, shifted his eyes from her face, and fixed his gaze on the thin collarbone peeking out from the neck of her white sweater.

"*Uh... I... I came because I have to apologize for the day before*

yesterday." Although there was some awkwardness in the words he put together in neurospeak, they were both able to hear his think speech without any problems. *"I ruined that lunch you went to the trouble of making me...I'm really sorry."* And while he was sincerely apologizing, Haruyuki moved a finger on his right hand outside Chiyuri's field of view and opened the storage icon. In the window that opened up, which covered nearly half of Chiyuri's actual face, there was a folder with Chiyuri's ID name on it, next to the folder showing the physical memory area of his own Neurolinker. At this point, he could say that the possibility that Chiyuri was Cyan Pile was essentially zero. If she was, then she would have already known that Haruyuki was Kuroyukihime's subordinate, Silver Crow, and she wouldn't have let him direct with her in the first place.

Or maybe she'd lain down on the bed like that on purpose, a strategy to get Haruyuki to give up on directing on his own? Maybe right now, Chiyuri was surprised and panicking inside.

Ashamed of himself for suspecting this girl he had been friends with for more than ten years, Haruyuki gently nudged his cursor to the physical memory folder in Chiyuri's Neurolinker.

"B-but I was just kinda shocked." The words came pouring out, perhaps to cover up his feelings of guilt. *"You and Takumu... When I imagine you talking about those guys, I can't even handle it. I know you're always thinking of stuff for me, but...but I—"*

I wanted at least you and Takumu to not pity me. Because we're friends. The three of us, at least...I wanted us to be in the same place.

Although it's probably already too late for that.

Haruyuki stiffened his finger and clicked the folder.

At the same time that a differently colored, semitransparent window popped open, Chiyuri's voice resonated in both his head and his ears. *"Haru...you're misunderstanding."*

Her speech was clumsy, like she hadn't used neurospeak before. The small lips in front of him moved, and she continued, *"I didn't say anything to Taku. How could I? I promised you I'd stay quiet about it. All Taku knew about the sandwiches was that I was talking about maybe making a lunch for you, too, when I went to his kendo tournament that time."*

"What..."

Haruyuki automatically turned eyes that were preoccupied with checking the new window to meet Chiyuri's. The fierceness there suddenly softened, and her eyelashes lowered almost as if somehow yearning for something long gone.

"How many years has it been since you shared this much about yourself, Haru...?" She turned her gaze away from Haruyuki, who was speechless, and murmured, *"I'm...I'm terrible, too. I'm a coward. You're...For a long time, such a long time, things have been so terrible for you, but the only thing I did was pretend I didn't see, even though I did. The truth is, if I had wanted to, there were so many things I could've done. I could've told the teacher, I could've written to the student council, I could've gone and asked Taku and he would've taken them all on. But I couldn't...I thought you would get mad at me and hate me...I was scared we'd stop being us."*

Haruyuki held his breath and stared as drops of clear water built up on the long eyelashes along the edges of her sharp, single-lined eyelids. Even though he had only two days earlier knocked her sandwiches away and made her cry—and they had fought and cried and made each other cry countless times up to that point—he felt like these tears were somehow different from all the others that he'd seen before.

"But Haru, you're terrible, too." Closing her eyes tightly, Chiyuri continued with trembling lips. *"You said nothing would ever change. That we would still be friends. Two years ago...when I talked to you about Taku...you said that if I said no, Taku wouldn't hang out with us anymore. But you promised that even if Taku and I were dating, you would always be our friend. I...I just didn't want anything to change. I wanted it always to be the three of us..."*

Me, too. Haruyuki very nearly gave voice to this thought but managed to hold it back.

But almost as if she had heard it anyway, Chiyuri popped her eyes open, and she looked directly at Haruyuki as she wiped away the droplets. *"That's it...so why?! Why are you leaning on her now?! You tell me not to do anything, so why are you fawning all over her and getting her to help you?! You're terrible...It's so frustrating. I spent all these years worrying about what to do, and she— In a single day, she goes and fixes everything. And almost like you're...like you're hers..."*

Her. Kuroyukihime.

Having her come up now so unexpectedly, Haruyuki practically forgot about peeking inside Chiyuri's memory and shook his head as if convulsing. *"N-no, that's not it. It's not like I asked her. She's the vice president of the student council, so she just took care of the bullying for me—"*

"Then why is she parading you around like you're her pet or something?! And why are you all small behind her like you're her servant?!"

"No...it's not like that!" Shaking his head fiercely once again, Haruyuki found himself wanting to ask what on earth he was trying to do here.

When Kuroyukihime had insisted Chiyuri was Cyan Pile, he'd stubbornly fought her, and now Chiyuri was blaming Kuroyukihime and he was earnestly denying that. The situation was like a jigsaw puzzle stirred up in a mixer, and he had no idea what piece to put where anymore. Lowering his voice, he repeated, *"It's not like that. I mean, I...I don't hate it or anything—"*

"Well, I do!!" Chiyuri interrupted, shouting so loudly she could probably be heard on the other side of her door. *"Ever since we started junior high, you've been so cold, Haru. You never walk home with me, you give me this annoyed look whenever I talk to you at school, and, I mean, you never come over anymore. That never happened when we were in elementary school."*

"That's...that's just how it is. You already—I mean, you have a boyfriend."

"And you're the one who told me to get him! You're the one who

said that that way, you and Taku and I could always be together!! Was that a lie?!"

"It wasn't a lie! It wasn't a lie, but…we can't be little kids forever!!" Haruyuki yelled, clutching the sheets on either side of Chiyuri's face. "Back then, it didn't bother me, walking together with you and Taku. Going to get a burger together was totally no big deal! But…I can't anymore. It's too hard! Taku gets cooler and cooler, and you…you're cute, and then standing there next to you guys is me looking like this! Just being in the same place as you guys makes me want to dig a hole and crawl right into it!"

He had never before confessed his own inferiority complex so honestly to Chiyuri—no, to *anyone*. Although he was certain he would regret it and the mere memory would make him squirm so hard, he'd bore a hole into the ground. Haruyuki couldn't manage to stop his thoughts.

If he were to try and say the same things using his mouth, the words would probably get stuck and never make it out. But they were directing and using neurospeak, and Haruyuki's thoughts were a raging stream pouring into Chiyuri's brain.

"I mean, it's the same for you! Taku gets to walk along holding hands with you, but I don't! Really, you're the one who chose Taku! What I said had nothing to do with that!!"

Twenty centimeters below Haruyuki, Chiyuri opened her eyes wide as she took in this monologue.

A film of saline once again covered her light eyes. Screwing up her face, lips trembling violently, a voice like a whisper slipped out of her. "Do you really think that? Do you really believe someone's value is totally decided by how they look? You always do this. You always just decide things on your own like this. Why do you hate yourself so much? Why do you have to be so critical of yourself?"

"Of course I hate myself," Haruyuki replied, almost groaning. "And if I were someone else, I'd definitely hate me, too. I'm fat, I sweat all the time, I'm spineless…There isn't a single thing

*about me a person could like. Being with me...just looking at me,
I hate it."*

"But there are things. I know so many things to like about you.
I know so many good things I can't even count them using both
hands!" Chiyuri continued, heaving with sobs just like when
they were kids. *"When it was snack time, you always gave me the
biggest one, and that time I lost the charm I had on my backpack,
you stayed out late looking for it for me, and you always fix my
Neurolinker for me right away whenever it does something weird,
and you have all these great things about you that no one else has.
It doesn't matter how you look. I-if that time two years ago, you
had..."* Chiyuri looked like she was swallowing something back
suddenly and then smiled sadly. *"I'm sorry. I shouldn't say that,
should I? I...I was afraid it wouldn't just be the kids at school you
pulled away from, it would be me and Taku, too. So I just did like
you said."*

Haruyuki felt the back of his throat close up tightly but managed somehow to squeeze out a thought. *"You didn't actually...
for me...? So that Taku and I could stay friends...?"*

"Because you always looked like you were having the most fun
when you were fooling around with Taku. And I used to have the
most fun watching the two of you. I didn't want that time together
to change. That's all I was thinking. But...I guess it's impossible,
huh? Everything changes; you can't stop people's feelings."* Chiyuri
suddenly lifted both arms and wrapped them around Haruyuki's
large body, squeezing tightly.

Frozen, Haruyuki was confronted with an extremely close,
tearstained, smiling face.

*"You're already somewhere I can't reach, aren't you? To be
honest, when I saw you and Kuroyukihime at the gates before, I
thought maybe...you were hers then. And I hated it. Because I
know that I know you a million times better than she does. But...
if she has the power to change you..."*

Caught up in a serious maelstrom of confusion, Haruyuki

could only listen to what Chiyuri was saying. Her body pressed up against his hadn't changed at all from those long, long ago days, still small and warm. *"But please, quit with the attitude. Quit acting like her follower. If you're going to do it, then do it. Be her boyfriend. And give everyone at school a heart attack."*

If I hugged Chiyuri back right now, what would happen?

For just a moment, Haruyuki seriously entertained the idea. Of course, he didn't actually move his body, but the fingers on his right hand twitched, betraying his thoughts.

The holo cursor moved in sync with this movement and happened to hit the icon for the installed applications folder in the window showing the contents of the internal memory in Chiyuri's Neurolinker. After the tiniest lag, a new window opened silently.

Unconsciously checking each of the apps shown one by one, Haruyuki murmured in his physical voice just as unconsciously, "I'm sorry...I'm sorry, Chiyu. I...I didn't even think that you would be worrying about stuff or struggling. Which is exactly why I'm no good."

"That's right. I do worry, and Taku has stuff he worries about, too, and probably...even her...She does, too. Everyone's the same; no one's any different from you, Haru." He felt the warmth of Chiyuri's voice and her small hands in his bones.

What is wrong with me? Haruyuki wondered in his head. *Suspecting for even an instant that she was a Burst Linker and hiding it from me.*

He saw at a glance that, in fact, there was no icon patterned after that flaming *B* in her application folder. Just in case, he went through each of her installed programs, but they were all things like off-the-shelf mail programs and media players, and simple games. He didn't find a single thing that came from anywhere suspicious.

So Chiyuri's not Cyan Pile or anything after all, he said to himself as he opened the properties on a few of her apps, when suddenly something felt off. The program wasn't the problem. It was— The reaction time as he clicked and moved around the screen was slightly slower than before.

If it were a wireless signal through their cheap home server, that'd be one thing, but he was directing with Chiyuri's Neurolinker through a high-grade (although short) cable. There shouldn't have been a response lag he could feel. The only reason for such a lag to occur would be if a large part of Chiyuri's Neurolinker transmission bandwidth was being monopolized by some other circuit.

Increasingly suspicious, Haruyuki opened a network status window.

Chiyuri's Neurolinker was currently connected to three routes: the global net, the Kurashimas' home net, and the direct link with Haruyuki. The only one of these that should have been having this kind of packet exchange was the one with Haruyuki.

But when he checked the routes, he very nearly cried out loud. A large quantity of packets was being sent on the global net. The local sender was an unknown program installed incredibly deep in the folder. The receiver on the global side was unknown. That would mean—

There's a back door!!

Someone had hacked Chiyuri's Neurolinker and was secretly connecting to the outside. And more than that, that someone was right now, this very instant, stealing information from Chiyuri's vision and hearing.

That bastard!!

Very close to screaming, Haruyuki moved his finger to try and delete the problem app. But he stopped on the verge of dropping the icon he had dragged over into the trash.

The someone connected through this back door right now was Cyan Pile. Whoever Cyan Pile was, he or she hadn't managed to change Brain Burst; using Chiyuri's Neurolinker as a stepladder would, without a doubt, make it possible to erase one's existence from the matching list.

In other words, if he identified where the packets were going, he could discover Cyan Pile's true identity. But to pursue whoever it was without making that player suspicious would be nearly impossible. The only time it would be even remotely doable was during a fight. In which case, he had to hide the fact that someone had noticed this back door until the next attack came.

Exhaling quietly, Haruyuki closed all the windows. "Thanks, Chiyu," he murmured, and he gently pulled his body away.

The quietly sobbing Chiyuri also lowered her arms and nodded, smiling.

Returning her smile awkwardly, Haruyuki reached out with his left hand and pulled the plug from Chiyuri's Neurolinker.

6

Friday.

Haruyuki trudged forlornly down the road to school alongside students whose shining faces were full of excitement at the thought of the approaching end of the long week's studies; soon they would be free for two whole days.

"I…A guy like me…," he groaned to himself, having been overtaken first thing that morning by the deepest self-hatred.

If the dream he had the night he installed Brain Burst was the worst of his life, then the one last night would have to be said to be the lowest low point in his life. If it had been only Kuroyukihime performing acts he knew only virtually, it might have instead been the best dream of his life. But in the space of a heartbeat, the one person had become two, and on top of that—

"Ah! Aaaaaah…" He desperately resisted the urge to run off with his head in his hands.

Currently, Neurolinker companies were in ruthless competition to develop an app to record dreams, an idea that was itself almost dreamlike. He was deeply relieved technology hadn't yet materialized. Well, a not-insignificant part of him had to admit that this was slightly regrettable, but—

"Oh! Good morning, boy!"

Haruyuki jumped at the sudden, chipper voice and corresponding pat on his shoulder. Turning and seeing the beautiful girl in black standing there, he jumped again. "Hyaho?!"

"Is that some kind of hip hello?"

Haruyuki shook his head back and forth at Kuroyukihime and the doubtful look on her face. "No! Uh! It's nothing!! Um, g-good morning!"

"Mm." Tilting her head even farther to the side, Kuroyukihime coughed lightly and continued. "Hmm. Oh. Yesterday...I apologize. That was childish of me."

"N-no, not at all. I'm sorry, too...I barely even said good-bye before I left."

On either side of the pair as they stood talking, students wearing the same uniform gradually came to a halt. Not only seventh graders, but eighth and ninth graders as well, looking on longingly and trying to say good morning to Kuroyukihime. Before they knew it, a line had formed behind them.

Seeing this, Kuroyukihime addressed the issue with a collective shout at the assemblage. "Oh! Morning, everyone!" She slapped Haruyuki on the back and started walking quickly. Haruyuki hurried after her, whispered conversations in hushed voices still reaching his ears.

"No. It's completely understandable that you would want to leave. After all, your close...friend was accused of being a cowardly assailant. And on top of that, I made you say there's no way you could direct with her to check it out. I am so sorry."

"Huh? Uh...um. I did, though...direct."

Kuroyukihime's profile stiffened. "What?" Faster than the warning bells telling him something was off again somehow: "Where?"

Pinioned by that sharp voice, Haruyuki had no choice but to answer her honestly. "W-well, at her house..."

"Where in her house?"

"H-her...bedroom."

"I see."

For some reason, Kuroyukihime's pace gradually started to

increase. Her stride already a fair bit longer than his own, Haruyuki chased after her, sweat popping up on his forehead. In a few seconds, he was walking alongside her again, attempting to resume their conversation.

"I peeked into her physical memory. And her Neurolinker, it's—"

"How long was the cable?" Kuroyukihime's aura was piercing as she cross-examined him.

"Th...irty centimeters," Haruyuki answered fearfully.

"Mm."

Tak tak tak tak tak tak tak tak.

Dumbfounded, Haruyuki watched Kuroyukihime's long hair swinging as she approached the school gates, now visible before them, at an incredible pace.

I don't get it. This world is nothing but stuff I don't get.

Haruyuki listened earnestly during morning classes, in an escapist kind of way, taking extensive notes, and when he heard the light chimes that signaled the lunch break, he had a hard time bringing himself to move.

If he'd thought about it rationally, he should have gone to see Kuroyukihime, who was likely in the lounge, to inform her immediately about the back door Cyan Pile had set up in Chiyuri's Neurolinker and to discuss a means to follow the packets. But unless he figured out the reason for Kuroyukihime's strangely foul mood before then, he wouldn't be able to concentrate on their conversation at all.

The truth was he often made people around him uncomfortable. Overweight guy, sweating like a greasy waterfall, talking nervously in a quiet voice; it was rare to find people who weren't annoyed by him. Then the looks on their faces would just prompt Haruyuki to shrink further, lower his voice to its bare minimum, making it even harder to hear anything he said.

Kuroyukihime must have secretly been putting up with him until now. Maybe she had finally reached her limit.

In which case, it might have been better to just give up entirely on having a face-to-face conversation with her in the real world. If he did a full dive and they talked as avatars, at least he wouldn't be sweating and the volume of his voice would be automatically adjusted. If everything would go more smoothly that way and proceed in a more businesslike fashion, then that should have been what he wanted.

Dejected, eyes on his desk, Haruyuki was in the middle of hashing out this debate with himself when suddenly he was loudly interrupted by an unfamiliar voice above him.

"Hello! You're Haruyuki Arita from grade seven's class C, right?"

Haruyuki lifted his head with a start. Standing before him were two female students he had never seen before. They wore eighth-grade ribbons, and both had holo tags displayed on their shoulders indicating that they were on club business. *Newspaper club.*

Throwing his head back with a grunt, Haruyuki saw a new icon flashing in his view: SREC. This was to let him know that the Neurolinker of the person with whom he was speaking was recording their conversation. Of course, this wasn't permitted for just any conversation, and within the school, it was only allowed in a handful of situations.

For instance, reporting for the school newspaper.

Without even noticing the students around them watching, ears perking with interest, Haruyuki got ready to run as fast as he could, not caring how it looked. However, he saw that his interlocutors clearly had experience in this type of situation, as one of them had slipped in behind him to block his retreat.

As he sat paralyzed in a half-standing position, a pair of hands popped out to rest atop a holo keyboard, and after a quick glance over at the recording icon flashing brightly, the newspaper club's hard-nosed investigative journalist let fly with a question that hit too close to the heart of things.

"We're working on the column 'Heart of the Rumor: Head

Shot' for the *Umesato Real Times*! Let's clear this up once and for all: Is the rumor that you and Kuroyukihime are dating actually true?!"

Haruyuki mustered all his mental strength and responded in a voice that could almost have been called calm. "It's a lie. It's a rumor. No basis in fact."

Ten fingers tapped away in front of him at the invisible keyboard while the owner of those fingers attacked again. "But according to the information we have obtained, you and Kuroyukihime have directed on two occasions in the lounge. Not only that, but the two of you even went on a direct date at a café within the school district!!"

"Wh..."

The girl looked down at Haruyuki, who was stunned they knew that, and the light caught the lens of her glasses, which appeared to be real.

This is bad. This is super bad. If I get the answer wrong now, there's no coming back.

In the back of his mind, several sensational headlines flashed past. He could hear somewhere the battle cries of the members of the Kuroyukihime fan club seeing them and calling for blood.

One cheek spasming and twitching, Haruyuki set his brain to work—three times more accelerated than when he'd been fighting Ash Roller—deriving a response that wasn't entirely inoffensive.

"Uh, th-th-that was...okay. I—I—I just know a bit about her Neurolinker OS, so uh, her Neurolinker was weird in this one place, and she asked me to fix it. That's all. The café thing was nothing more than her thanking me. That's it. Nothing more. Not in the slightest." With a tight smile on his face, he shook his head briskly.

The newspaper club girl stopped typing and knitted her eyebrows.

There shouldn't have been any way that she could check whether people directing were having a conversation in neuro-speak or whether they were just operating their Neurolinkers. As an excuse, it strained credulity, but she shouldn't have been able to find anything to disprove his story.

Relieved, Haruyuki added new bricks to further build on the wall he had created. "I—I mean, if you saw how she is when she's with me, you could tell. When we talk, she gets into a bad mood pretty quickly. So there's, like, no way we could be dating or anything."

And that should be the end of this interview.

Or so he thought, but the girl tilted her head and returned doubtfully, "Bad mood? It didn't look like that at all, though."

"I-it's true! I mean, this morning, she got mad and stormed off. She always gets like that when Chiyu, I mean Kurashima, comes up."

"Kurashima...? I'm sure she and Kuroyukihime talked about something in front of the school gates." After blinking rapidly several times behind her glasses, the theatrical journalist disappeared from the newspaper club girl's demeanor, and her fingers raced. The recording icon disappeared from Haruyuki's view.

"Is the interview over?"

"Oh. Yeah. Or rather...," she mumbled in a strange tone. After exchanging a glance with her partner behind Haruyuki, she started talking in a normal tone. "Okay, look. The truth is, we weren't actually buying into that rumor at all. To be blunt, we figured it was some kind of mistake, which is why we came to interview you."

"Huh?"

Bringing her face in close, the girl whispered so that only Haruyuki could hear. "Hey, Arita. I mean, it's kind of crazy, but... maybe Kuroyukihime and you are really...you know?"

"Huh?!"

"I mean, look. You're close with Kurashima, and whenever you talk about her with Kuroyukihime, she gets in a bad mood. That's, well...you know?"

The other club member, who had come around to the side again, picked up where her associate had left off. "Yeah. I mean, no matter how you look at it..."

Then they both whispered at Haruyuki like shrine maidens uttering an oracle. "She's jealous, right?"

When he came to, Haruyuki was in his usual stall in the boys' washroom. Which meant that he had run away again, but he didn't have a drop of energy to spend regretting his actions. *Jealous? How do you write that character? Ugh, too hard, I don't know.* In an attempt to allow his thoughts escape, too, he was already drawing possible characters, one line at a time, in stark red like a brand.

Kuroyukihime has that sour look every time we talk about Chiyuri because... she's jealous.

That's what they had said. Jealous. Envious. In other words, Kuroyukihime wasn't putting on a show or joking around, she really—

"No way," Haruyuki muttered, his thoughts racing ahead. *There's no way. Maybe that could happen to someone else, but it could never happen to me, not to Haruyuki Arita. Don't even think it. Don't hope. You're obviously just going to be squirming with double, no, triple the regret later.*

Hitting the back of his head against the water tank, Haruyuki spoke aloud again. "No way... No way." But the more he said it, the more the many things Kuroyukihime had said and done, the many faces she had shown him up to then broke into an infinite number of pieces and played back like a slide show in his mind.

That time... and that time, and that time, she was seriously—

"No way!!" He slammed his right hand against the stall wall and held his head.

Thinking about all this was just making him crazy; he needed to get even farther away. Just as he was about to give the command for a full dive, the insanely high score Kuroyukihime had managed jumped back at him from his memory.

He would never be able to beat that score. Which meant that he couldn't use the game as an escape from reality anymore.

"…Why?" In a slightly louder voice, he shouted again, "Why?! Why me?!"

You have everything. Looks, ability, popularity. And even the one thing I was proud of—reaction time in a virtual game. And me, I'm nothing but a loser with a dumb face and a squishy, sweaty body. I lose to you in every single possible way.

"And yet despite all that…how am I supposed to believe…"

It's true Haruyuki had the aptitude for Brain Burst that Kuroyukihime was looking for. But that didn't mean anything other than there were only three such people at their school.

And Haruyuki's Silver Crow was totally good for nothing, an enormous helmet head plopped onto a gangly wire body that could only punch, kick, and head butt. With a duel avatar like that, about the only thing he could do was help her unearth the true identity of her enemy, Cyan Pile. So he wished she would treat him that way. He wanted her to just give him cool, dispassionate orders, like she would any servant.

He didn't want anything more than that. He was absolutely not deluding himself into thinking he could have anything else. And yet…why did Kuroyukihime take that attitude, get that expression on her face, look at him with those eyes?

Finally, wanting only to ease his mind, Haruyuki latched on to a single conclusion. He couldn't come up with any other reason for her behavior.

Haruyuki missed lunch again even though he didn't have anyone taking his lunch money anymore, but he wasn't even aware of his empty stomach as he sat disinterestedly through afternoon classes.

In homeroom, their teacher had apparently said something to Araya and his gang, but he missed that, too, and when the last bell rang, he sluggishly stood, bag in hand, after his classmates had flown out of the classroom, full of anticipation for the weekend. He headed for the entrance slowly, changed to his outside shoes, and left the school.

Even though it was still only just after three, the late autumn sun was already fading and shone on the school gates at a steep angle. Seeing a black silhouette standing as if transformed into one of the pillars, Haruyuki dragged his feet as he approached.

"Hey."

Kuroyukihime's hands—which were busy typing on a holo keyboard—stopped, and she raised one hand slightly, a faint, hard smile on her face. She had probably deliberately come to stand out here in the cold even though what she was doing could've been taken care of in the student council office.

Haruyuki could only dip his head silently in response.

An awkward silence ensued. A chilly wind rustled the fallen leaves at their feet and then passed on.

He kept his head down, and Kuroyukihime started speaking after lightly clearing her throat. "Can we talk while we walk?"

"Yeah." Haruyuki accompanied this brief reply with a nod.

She started to walk silently, and he took a position to her left and a step behind as they passed through the gates.

They had been walking silently for a couple minutes when Kuroyukihime cleared her throat again and began speaking. "Look. I'm sorry about this morning. I was being weird."

"No, it's fine. I wasn't upset. I'm sorry I didn't come during lunch."

Kuroyukihime seemed to tilt her head slightly at this unusually smooth response but then nodded. "It's fine. But. Even I wonder what I'm doing, but...when it comes to Cyan Pile, I just can't seem to stay calm—"

Kuroyukihime sounded somewhat rushed, keeping her eyes forward as she spoke, and Haruyuki cut her off in a dry voice. "About that...I know the connection between Kurashima and Cyan Pile."

"What? Oh...r-right. Then let's talk about that over direct. It wouldn't do to have someone overhear the names," Kuroyukihime said quickly and reached into the bag hanging from her right hand instead of her pocket.

She pulled out a small paper bag stamped with the name of the Umesato student shop. After tearing the tape off sharply, she pulled a brand-new XSB cable out of the bag. "I accidentally burnt out the one we've been using so far. And...they didn't have much stock, so I had to buy this one." She sounded almost as if she was making excuses as she pulled out the one-meter cable—the shortest they sold in the student shop—and Haruyuki tried not to think about what was going on in her head.

Without meeting her eyes, he silently accepted one of the plug ends and inserted it into his Neurolinker.

Kuroyukihime looked like she was waiting for him to say something, but finally, she put the other plug into her own Neurolinker. The wired-connection warning appeared, and as it disappeared, Haruyuki sent dry thoughts at the girl on the other end of the wire.

"Kurashima isn't Cyan Pile. It looks like Cyan Pile actually set up a virus in her Neurolinker to make a back door. Which is why they show up from wherever Kurashima is in the school."

Kuroyukihime didn't immediately respond to Haruyuki's torrent of words, but when she finally did, the voice in his brain sounded doubtful. Or just a little scared.

"What...what's going on with you? Since before...you've been kind of weird."

"Nothing. Nothing's going on," Haruyuki responded, obstinately refusing to turn and look at Kuroyukihime walking next to him, a meter away.

"But...are you maybe mad? Because I was weird this morning. And yesterday."

"As if. There's no way I could be angry with you. Don't worry about me; we have more important things to talk about, don't we?"

Once again, only silence passed along the thin cable.

On the road as dusk approached, because of the group of buildings standing along the left side of the path, people passing along it sank into black shadows in the dim light. No eyes fell on Haruyuki and Kuroyukihime walking together and directing, making it seem almost as if the two of them alone had somehow wandered into a country of flat shadows. *"Do you have proof?"* Changing suddenly, the voice in his head was cold. *"Did you get proof that Kurashima is not Cyan Pile?"*

"No. If I reached out to the virus, Cyan Pile might have noticed, so I just looked."

"I see. A calm decision, but at the same time, not very persuasive. Even I have never heard anything about a virus that connects you to the Brain Burst matching server through a back door. How exactly am I supposed to believe what you're telling me?"

The sharpness in her thoughts seemed to swell with each word enunciated. Haruyuki clenched his teeth and sent an even flatter voice through the cable. *"So you're saying I made up the virus story. Are you actually trying to say I've gone over to Kurashima-slash-Cyan Pile's side? If that's the case, then proof or whatever doesn't matter. You're just going to have to decide what you believe."*

"I'm not saying that. You're leaping to conclusions."

Haruyuki stubbornly refused to respond to Kuroyukihime's slightly shaken words.

"Are you saying this because you really believe it?" Her legs stopped in place suddenly, and her voice, which had gotten even colder, sounded hard. Haruyuki stopped, too, before the cable went taut. *"The moment I conclude that you've aligned with Cyan Pile, I will hunt you. I will take your meager burst points, and I will press you toward a forceful uninstallation of Brain Burst. You will lose the ability to accelerate forever. Are you fully aware of this as you tell me this now?"*

"I understand. You're free to do what you will. I'm just a pawn, just a tool. Throw me away when you don't need me anymore."

"You." She lightly took hold of Haruyuki's left shoulder. When he lifted his eyes, Kuroyukihime's face, strained like carved ice, was very near. However, her pitch-black eyes alone reflected the feelings inside, burning almost white hot.

"I knew you were angry. And it's true, I'm to blame. I apologize.

But..." Lips trembling almost imperceptibly, she pushed out a voice that sounded like she was forcing it under control. "*It's not as if I can freely control all of my emotions. I get annoyed, I get uneasy. And when it comes to you and...Kurashima...*" Her gaze dropped momentarily, and, pale cheeks stiffening, Kuroyukihime continued. "*Look, if you want me to tell you why, I will. I—*"

Before that thought could travel down the cable, Haruyuki turned to the side and cut in. "*It's fine. Let's just forget it.*"

"*Ah. Wh-what?*"

"*Watching this is hard, too. It's just sad.*"

"*What are you talking about? What do you mean?*"

Fixing his gaze on a single paving stone to his lower right, Haruyuki finally gave voice to the "only conclusion" he was able to reach that afternoon. "*You...you hate yourself, don't you?*"

The sound of a sharp intake of air.

Haruyuki was suddenly self-conscious about the words he had loosed, words he couldn't take back. In the depths of his ears, the encouragement Chiyuri had given him the night before played like a refrain, but he could no longer stop the thoughts being uttered.

"*You hate yourself, the you who's too perfect in every single way. Which is why you're trying to lower yourself. That's it, isn't it?*"

Kuroyukihime's fingers, resting on his left shoulder, stiffened, turned to steel. Thinking that would likely be the last time she ever touched him, Haruyuki unleashed his final words, which were sure to destroy everything. "*You, me... Talking to me, a fat, clumsy loser, touching me, showing me something like...something like kindness—it's just you trying to dirty yourself. You don't need to do all that; I'll still do what you want. I don't want anything. I don't need any compensation. I'm just a sacrificial pawn, a tool to be ordered around. A guy like me, you should know exactly what the proper way to handle me is!!*"

The pale hand slipped slowly, slowly from his shoulder.

This was how it had to be.

Never touching him again, never meeting his eyes.

As long as you make me your tool, we don't even ever have to meet in the real world. Haruyuki didn't know if this thought reached her as neurospeak or not.

Good-bye.

As he went to murmur this final word, a sharp sensation snapped across his left cheek. Haruyuki lifted his face in shock, cheek burning.

"Idiot!" The voice burst forth with real sound from the light-colored lips.

Haruyuki stared baffled at the waterfall of tears flowing down that beautiful face, distorted to the point of violence.

Her right hand still high in the air, Kuroyukihime's entire demeanor crumpled like a child's, and tears streamed down her face.

"You idiot…idiot…" The word repeated now sounded almost entirely different from the *fool* paired with a wry grown-up smile that he had gotten from her so many times before.

Kuroyukihime cursed Haruyuki over and over and over, age-appropriately, like a fourteen-year-old girl.

And Haruyuki simply stood, eyes wide open, unable to think of a single one of the several reactions he should have had as a thirteen-year-old boy. With his words, he had deeply hurt the person before him. That much he understood.

But when it came to Kuroyukihime, when it came to this person who was so perfect in every way, who had an ability to think and reason greater than any adult, he thought she was just disgusted with Haruyuki. She had exhausted her social graces; her heart was just being pulled away.

But crying this much. And she looks so fragile. This—this isn't how it was supposed to…

Haruyuki opened his mouth as if to speak.

Kuroyukihime wiped away flowing tears with both hands.

For a moment, only the wind passed over them as they stood there stationary together on the road in the deepening twilight.

And then a terrible sound like metal scraping against metal hit Haruyuki's ears.

*   *   *

At first, he thought it was a quantum noise through his Neuro-linker, the sound was that strange. Baffled and heart pounding, he swiveled his head and torso around to the right.

And had a terrifying spectacle leap into his field of view.

A white passenger car was plunging straight at them, removing in the process the guardrail separating the sidewalk from the road with the right front fender.

An accident?! No! There's no brake noise. The series of ideas flashed through his mind in less than one tenth of a second.

His mouth moved basically on automatic, and a single phrase surged out. And at the same time, the exact same words echoed in the back of his brain in a different voice via the direct cable.

"Burst link!!"

With a cracking noise like lightning, the world stopped.

Blue.

The landscape frozen, clear and blue as far as the eye could see.

But Haruyuki quickly understood that this didn't mean everything had stopped completely.

The tires of the large sedan filling his view were turning bit by tiny bit as if fighting the freezing, biting into the road surface and closing the distance.

"Wha?!" Haruyuki cried out finally, and jumped out of the way. Instantly, the car disappeared. Hiding it was his own round back clad in the uniform of Umesato Junior High.

This blue world was just the real landscape, recreated as a polygonal pseudo-reality by the Brain Burst program hacking into the images from the social security cameras, placed in great numbers around the city. Dropping his gaze, he saw his body had changed into the pink pig. He moved the familiar virtual avatar to cut around his own real-world back and looked again at the white sedan.

The vehicle, charging diagonally from the lane and aiming for the gap in the guardrail, was not even three meters away from him. Roughly calculating the speed that allowed it to keep moving forward, however gradually, he realized they would come into contact in less than ten minutes, even in this accelerated world.

This is—Why?! Confused, Haruyuki tried desperately to think. Normally, a car could not leave its lane. The second an abnormal route was detected, the AI controlling the vehicle would take control from the driver and automatically correct the vehicle's course, decelerate, and stop.

Which meant either the control AI in this car was broken or that it had been temporarily turned off by the driver.

He quickly deduced that it was most likely the latter, because he had heard nothing like the screeching of tires skidding against the road surface during full braking. The driver wasn't stepping on the brakes. On the contrary, he was pushing forward with the accelerator all the way to the floor.

This was deliberate. It was the attack by a Burst Linker on the real side that Kuroyukihime had hinted at before.

Coming to these conclusions more or less instantaneously, Haruyuki took another few steps forward and tried to make out the face of the driver behind the windscreen. Was their assailant an unknown Burst Linker belonging to one of the king's Legions? Or Cyan Pile, possibly someone at Umesato?

The majority of the social cameras in the area were apparently not capturing images from inside the car as he couldn't really see through the window. Haruyuki changed his angle, strained his eyes, and finally found a position that allowed him to see inside. Stretching out his short pig avatar as far as possible to finally reach up over the hood, he saw the driver—

"Wha…?!" Haruyuki let slip another surprised, scream-like cry the moment he saw the driver. It was the face of a classmate he was utterly familiar with, a face he had hoped never to see again.

"A…Araya…?! Wh…why…"

Why is he here?

Hadn't he just been arrested—no question, no fight—after hurting us at school? And then they found out pretty quickly from his Neurolinker that he had the social camera evasion app installed, along with a bunch of illegally copied games and images, and then on top of that, digital drugs? He should've been tossed in juvie or reform school. For the time being, at least—he shouldn't be back at school while I'm still there!

Unable to believe his own eyes, Haruyuki blinked over and over, staring at the face of the icy blue driver. But the hair pointed straight up like the needles on a flower-arranging stand; the thin, arched eyebrows; the pinhole pupils; the lips twisted in cruel excitement; the feeling of terror these features elicited in Haruyuki whether he liked it or not, all these things told him that the boy in front of his eyes was Araya in the flesh.

"He was bailed out this morning," a grave voice noted beside him abruptly, and Haruyuki quickly whirled around.

Standing there was Kuroyukihime, wrapped in her black swallowtail, fairy-princess avatar, biting hard on her lip. "I heard he was sentenced in family court at the beginning of the week and that he'd be locked up for at least a year. So I thought there was no need to trouble myself about him anymore. But…I can't believe he'd…" Having murmured this much in a strangled voice, Kuroyukihime lowered her eyelashes and shook her head slowly. "No, I should've had an idea, been on guard. For one person to assault another, you don't need the power of acceleration, after all. I thought I knew that as long as you have a knife, a car, it's more than enough, but it seems that I hadn't truly understood."

As she related this information in her usual tone, Haruyuki could see no trace of the childlike weeping from moments ago. *No, that's just what I want to think*, Haruyuki immediately corrected himself. He could clearly see the keen regret and something like resolve in eyes that should have been nothing more than a creation of the avatar.

Kuroyukihime slowly closed those eyes, took a deep breath, and said in a near whisper, "This…this is payback, then. For me.

Not knowing how people might feel, not even trying to know, and yet, I play with those feelings however I want."

"Wh-what...what are you talking about?" Haruyuki finally managed.

Not responding immediately, Kuroyukihime turned to Haruyuki and had her avatar, nearly twice as tall as his, kneel down soundlessly. The black dress spread out, and the eyes, lowered to the same height as Haruyuki's, met his straight on. "Arita... Haruyuki."

This voice calling to him caressed his ears more gently, more calmly than any other sound in his memory.

"I'm sorry. I'm the one who brought this on. But I won't let you get hurt. I will do whatever it takes to protect you."

"Huh? Wh-what—" Dumbfounded, Haruyuki could only repeat himself.

There was nothing they could at this point do once the acceleration was released. The moment they returned to reality, the sedan in front of them would cover the remaining distance at an incredible speed and send first Haruyuki himself and then Kuroyukihime behind him flying.

He was glad it would be in that order. If he acted as a cushion, there was a chance, although slight, that Kuroyukihime would get out of this without major injuries. This thought had already occurred to Haruyuki earlier.

However, Kuroyukihime surprised him, declaring in a tone that hid a strong resolve, "I will save you at least. I still haven't told you about it: Brain Burst's...the best and final power of acceleration."

"Huh?!"

Save...? You, the hero; me, nothing more than a tool...?

Haruyuki swallowed hard and shook his head violently from side to side. "N-no!! You can't do that! If that kind of power exists, I should be the one to use it! And then I can protect you! I'm your servant, after all. I'm the one who has to protect you!!" he shouted desperately, stretching both of his short arms out. "Please tell me! What is this final power? What command do I need to use it?!"

"Impossible. You can't use the command unless you're at least level nine, and it uses ninety-nine percent of your accumulated points. And more importantly, I'm your 'parent.' And what would the world be like if parents didn't protect their children?"

"B-b-b-but!!"

"Don't make that face. I...In this situation, there's only one saving grace."

"S-saving grace?"

"Mm. Given that these are my last words to you, you'll believe me, won't you?"

Kuroyukihime raised both hands gently and placed her open palms against each other, bringing them to her chest. Her eyes closed, and a smile like flowers blooming appeared on her lips. "Haruyuki. I like you." From below the raised eyebrows, her black eyes stared at Haruyuki, concealing an infinite radiance. "This is the first time in my life I've felt like this. Unable to control it, totally confused. At school, at home in bed, I'm always thinking of you, and I'm happy and I'm sad. So this is love...It's wonderful. It's a miracle." She gripped her hands together tightly in front of her chest and grinned.

That smile was warm, gentle, good. But it pierced Haruyuki's chest as if ripping him apart. *I want to believe. I want to believe.*

I want to believe—

The effect of the tears welling up in his avatar's eyes was too strong, distorting Haruyuki's vision. Wiping them away roughly, he stared back at her eyes so close to his own and asked hoarsely, "Why...? Why me? Me...A guy like me, why?"

"Mm. The reason? I can't even count all the reasons. But, no, I don't think love needs a reason. So I'll just tell how it happened." Smiling, Kuroyukihime stretched out her hands and placed them on Haruyuki's shoulders. "Haruyuki. Do you remember the first time we met?"

"Yeah. Of course, of course I remember. On the local net... you said to me in the virtual squash room, 'Don't you want to go further?'"

"I did. The high score I got in that game..." Her smile changed into something slightly mischievous. "I used acceleration."

"Wh-what?!"

"I could never have gotten a score like that if I hadn't. I thought it would pique your interest and make it easier to persuade you; I felt like I had to beat your score. I—" Kuroyukihime cut herself off and turned her gaze up to the sky of the accelerated world. "I became a Burst Linker six years ago, when I was just eight. Ever since then, I've craved nothing but strength and speed, cutting down countless enemies to become level nine, and still not satisfied with that—these hands are stained with the blood of friends. Even someone like me couldn't possibly beat that high score you recorded."

She recomposed her expression and directed her strong eyes straight at Haruyuki before continuing. "Listen, Haruyuki. You're fast. You can become faster than anyone else. Faster even than me, faster than the other kings. And speed is a Burst Linker's greatest strength. One day, your name will be known far and wide as the fastest Linker in the accelerated world. You'll defeat the kings, beat the other levels, and reach the source of Brain Burst. Then you'll know. The ultimate potential hidden in a person's...in our brains and souls."

Nodding slowly, Kuroyukihime went on. "I...I shook when I saw you playing that game. I shivered in a way I never had before. I was moved. At the fact that a person could become that fast. In my heart, I shouted, 'Eureka! I finally found him, the true king to accelerate against a stagnant world.'"

Haruyuki was so dumbfounded all he could do was let her words wash over him. *Me, faster than anyone...?*

It was too incredible all of a sudden. But given the situation, Kuroyukihime's words did not permit even a shred of doubt. He could not doubt her; that was the one thing he couldn't do.

"But although you conceal such strength and potential, in reality, you are very fragile...so pitiful it's sad. It was like my heart was being ripped apart. I want to kneel before the future king.

But at the same time, I want to protect you, wrap you up and keep you safe. These conflicting feelings rapidly swelled up in me, and before I knew it, you were the only thing I could see. I fell in love with you. I finally realized it yesterday."

"Yesterday?"

"Mm. When you were talking about Kurashima. How can I say it? It was the first time in my life I had ever been jealous; I couldn't control myself. Which is why I took that attitude with you. And this morning as well. I was too slow to realize it... Well, I was slow, but not *too* slow, I suppose. Here, like this."

Tightening her grip on Haruyuki's shoulders ever so slightly, Kuroyukihime brought her face closer and smiled broadly. "I got to tell you everything. Although if I had had my way, I would've liked to have faced you properly and told you in the real world." Tears like jewels welled up in her sparkling jet-black eyes, forming drops and collecting in the corners of her eyes. "So... it's about time to say good-bye."

"Wh-what are you going to do? I don't— Good-bye, it's not..."

Facing Haruyuki, swallowing hard and shaking his head, Kuroyukihime spoke her final words like a warning. "Please. Become strong. And become fast. Defeat the kings on my behalf, climb to the top, and see for me what I wanted to see."

"No... no!!" Haruyuki shouted in a voice that resembled a wail. "That's not how it is! That's— You can't be the only one to go!! I'll protect you! And if I can't, we'll both go together! Please don't leave me... I—I still haven't... For you... I..."

A voice mixed with sobs surged out of Haruyuki's open mouth. Leaning in softly, Kuroyukihime's lips closed it.

Even though they were both virtual avatars, the sensation was softer than anything, warmer than anything, gentler than anything.

After a kiss lasting a few thousandths of a second in the real world, and essentially an eternity from Haruyuki's perspective, Kuroyukihime slowly pulled her lips away and whispered,

"Another time... We'll definitely meet again." Her tears falling joined together in a silver radiance following the lines of her body as she stood up.

There was an almost-terrifying purpose in Kuroyukihime's back as she faced the approaching car with her legs out resolutely, and Haruyuki couldn't even speak, much less move.

Spreading her arms out wide, she straightened her back with a snap and called out in a clear voice: "Physical Full Burst!!"

Kuroyukihime's avatar disappeared, enveloped in a blinding white light.

What the—? What happened?

Caught in an explosion of confusion and uneasiness and an emotion overwhelming both of these he couldn't put a name to, Haruyuki screamed at the top of his lungs. "Kuroyukihime!!" His tears spilled over onto his cheeks, distorting his vision, and he lost his sense of balance, staggering a few steps backward.

And then Haruyuki saw something incredible.

Kuroyukihime—the body of Kuroyukihime in the real world, transparent and blue—was moving.

Kuroyukihime, who should've been standing back, with Haruyuki wedged in between her and the passenger vehicle barreling down on them, was definitely moving in the real world, albeit at a speed about one-tenth that of the car, successively putting one foot in front of the other, kicking the ground and moving forward.

This can't— There's no way this can be happening!!

The Brain Burst program overclocked the quantum signal generated by the heart rate a thousand times and accelerated only the user's consciousness. In other words, the process had absolutely no effect on the physical body. Thus, even accelerated, the body was unable to even shift its gaze. That was why the program sent the user's consciousness into a full dive at the same time as it accelerated, cutting it off from the physical body and connecting it to a copy of reality produced by the social cameras.

And yet, right now, the real-life Kuroyukihime was moving her

physical body at a speed that accelerated Haruyuki could clearly see. Was the occasional blurring here and there on her ice-blue body because she was exceeding the filming speed of the social cameras? Which meant she was dashing around in the real world at the super speed of more than a hundred times that of a normal person!

Was this the best and final power of Brain Burst? A forbidden command to overclock not just the consciousness but the entire body?

There was no way the body could come out of something like that okay.

As she charged ahead, Kuroyukihime's expression was full of firm determination and something else, a stiffness like she was enduring something with every fiber of her being.

A something that was probably intense pain. She would no doubt have been unable to stop the screaming of muscles and joints being driven at a speed that was essentially impossible. But she herself did not stop. In one, two, three steps, she was standing to the left of the real-world Haruyuki.

The front bumper of the car Araya was driving was already a scant eighty centimeters from Haruyuki.

Kuroyukihime raised both hands and placed them gently on Haruyuki's body, as if she were about to embrace him. She applied the smallest amount of force onto his side, and his body began to move.

At the same time, he felt an incredible impact in every part of his body, and his vision faded to black.

Kuroyukihime had been gentle, but her push was equivalent to being slammed into at high speed in the real world. The impact activated the safety on his Neurolinker, which automatically canceled the full dive. As the center of his vision sank into darkness, the original colors of the real world stretched out radially.

Instantly, Haruyuki returned from his avatar to his flesh-and-blood body. He hit the pavement with his back and started choking. Forgetting to even breathe again, he opened his eyes and saw in front of him Kuroyukihime, both hands still stretched out, smiling somehow.

Immediately, the white car plunging savagely onto the sidewalk caught Kuroyukihime's slim body, lifting her up onto the hood, both legs flying up as if saved somehow by the bumper. She hit the front windscreen and flew even higher.

Her long black hair flowed through the air, tracing an arc.

Shining orange in the evening sun.

On one side, the disconnected direct cable danced whitely.

7

In Haruyuki's fragmented consciousness, his memories of the events that followed existed only as three-color images.

Black—the slender figure twisted unnaturally on the paving stones of the sidewalk.

Red—the terrifyingly large amount of blood spreading out underneath her.

White—closed eyelids, cheeks that had lost all color.

In the blink of an eye, his own hands and the necktie he used to stop the bleeding were also dyed red.

Araya's clothing was red too as he crawled, laughing loudly, out from the driver's seat of the white car, which had smashed into the wall of a shop.

Police cars rushed to the scene, red lights flashing, and someone shoved the still-laughing Araya into a backseat.

Then the white ambulance arrived, rotating light on top the same bright red, and the men in white who got out fixed Kuroyukihime to a stretcher. Haruyuki also got in the ambulance at their prompting, and the vehicle started moving at high speed.

And now, he was staring up at the ER's red surgery lamp in the corner of an entirely white hallway.

*   *   *

He had no room in his brain to think about what was going to happen now. He could only replay every single moment of the last four days since he'd met Kuroyukihime.

That time. And that time, that time, too...Haruyuki should've done something different. If he had, then they wouldn't be here now.

Why couldn't he just trust the hand Kuroyukihime offered him, the feelings she had for him? If he had just accepted it, if he hadn't fought it, if he hadn't so obstinately turned his face away, they wouldn't have had a quarrel like that on the road, and they would've noticed the car approaching.

Of all the many mistakes I've made in my life up to now, this is the biggest one of all, and I can't ever take it back.

In each and every one of the shards of his fragmented consciousness, Haruyuki went back to all of the branching points and tried to move forward into a different future, but even Brain Burst couldn't change the past.

How long had he been thinking like this and staring at that lamp?

It was still on, indicating that surgery was in progress, but the door slid open unexpectedly, and a single female nurse stepped out. Haruyuki simply stared at the white-clad figure approaching him.

She was young, as if she had only recently finished nursing school. The expression on the face under her neatly arranged bangs was strained as Haruyuki turned to her, words coming out of his mouth essentially on their own.

"How...how is she?"

"The doctors and everyone in there are doing absolutely everything they can." The nurse's voice was slightly husky and tense. "But...she suffered a lot of damage to her internal organs. To treat her injuries, we've done a full insertion of nanomachines, and we've managed to prevent her condition from worsening.

And...well, we'd like to contact her family, but she didn't have any emergency contact information in her Neurolinker."

"What..." Haruyuki didn't know what to say.

The nurse sat down next to him, crouched forward, and continued. "I was wondering if you knew her telephone number. You're...her...?"

She let the end trail off as if to ask a question, but Haruyuki didn't have any answers.

I'm her what? Pawn, servant. I don't want to use words like that anymore. But friend, classmate—that's not right, either.

Mumbling to himself, Haruyuki lifted his head involuntarily at the nurse's next words. "Her boyfriend, aren't you?"

"Uh! Wh-why?"

Just going by Kuroyukihime's beautiful face, miraculously unscathed, and Haruyuki's physical appearance, there should have been nothing to even suggest such an idea.

He shrank his body reflexively as she gently handed him a small notebook. It was an Umesato Junior High student agenda, the blue synthetic leather embossed with an emblem in gold.

"When I was checking her personal effects for a telephone number, I found this. I'm sorry." The slightest of smiles crossed her tense face, and the nurse opened the student notebook to the last page.

In the clear pocket on the left was Kuroyukihime's student ID with her picture. And on the right was a familiar round face.

Taking the notebook with trembling hands, Haruyuki gazed at the photo of himself wearing a stupid expression. That time, there was no doubt. The photo was a printout of the view capture she had taken when she first told him that she liked him in the lounge. A drop of water fell with a *plop* on the front of the notebook.

It took Haruyuki a while to realize it was overflow from his own eyes.

"She...Kuroyukihime." His hushed voice trembled with

emotion. It didn't take long for the tremble to explode into the heavy sobbing of a child. "Unh…aaah! Aaahaaaaah!!"

Clutching the notebook to his chest, bending over, Haruyuki cried.

The tears poured out of his eyes and slid over his cheeks, falling to the floor. In the pain hollowing out his chest, Haruyuki finally and for the first time understood what his own true feelings were.

The surgery took nearly five hours.

During the time the clock display in the corner of his vision moved from evening to the middle of the night, Haruyuki sent a single text message to his mother, saying that a friend had been in an accident, so he was going to be late that night or he might not come home at all. Then he simply continued to sit resolutely in his chair.

Apparently, the hospital had gotten in touch with Kuroyukihime's family through the school, but surprisingly, rather than anyone from her family, a man calling himself the family lawyer appeared on his own.

The middle-aged lawyer, equipped with a large Neurolinker and looking like a machine himself, simply took care of the paperwork in a businesslike fashion and departed a mere fifteen minutes later without even glancing at Haruyuki.

A long, long time passed, and it was approaching ten when the red lamp finally went off.

A young doctor emerged looking exhausted and seemed slightly confused at finding Haruyuki alone in the hallway but still sat down and carefully explained Kuroyukihime's condition.

Explained that they had succeeded in stopping the bleeding, but as there was extensive damage to her organs, she could drop into a state of shock at any time. That the synthetic protein nanomachines were doing everything they could to repair and assimilate the tissues, but in the end, it depended on the strength of the patient herself.

"All said and done, I have to tell you she's currently in serious condition. The next twelve hours are going to be the worst of it. Please keep that in mind." Finishing with a severe expression, the doctor headed off down the white hallway with the rest of the operating team.

The only person left was the female nurse from before. Glancing at the student agenda Haruyuki still clutched, the nurse spoke to him in a kind voice. "You, too. You should go home and get some rest. Someone from her family is supposed to come tomorrow."

"Tomorrow...that's too late," Haruyuki answered stubbornly. He had no desire to move even a step from this spot. "The doctor said the next twelve hours are going to be the worst. And no one here with her even though she's in there fighting...It's too awful."

"...Right. I guess you're right. Did you call home and let your family know where you are?"

"Yes. And anyway, my mom won't get home until one or so."

"All right. Well, I'll bring you a blanket, then. Just hold on a minute." She marched to the nurses' station at the end of the hallway and returned quickly, handing Haruyuki a thin blanket and nodding firmly. "It'll be fine. I'm sure she'll pull through. She's so pretty. And she has such a wonderful boyfriend. The two of you still have a lot of fun ahead, I'm sure."

We do. Much more than you think; everything's still ahead of us. We're going to defeat Cyan Pile, destroy the kings' Legions one by one, and get to where she's been working so hard to go. I'll be with her every step of the way.

Thoughts like these flitting through his mind, Haruyuki said, "Th-thank you. Um...when can I see her?"

"Not right now. The nanomachine operation room has an air seal. But you can see video of her at least, via the hospital net. Just right now, special for you."

The nurse smiled and made a finger dance in the air. At the same time she flicked at something, an access gate was displayed in Haruyuki's vision.

He was a bit surprised to be getting a wireless transmission from the nurse's Neurolinker, since he was disconnected from the global net, but he quickly realized that it must have come over the hospital's local net.

He clicked for access, and a video window opened. The image was dim and hazy, but when he strained his eyes, he saw a strangely shaped bed in the center.

It was like a capsule with only the top half open. The inside was filled with a semitransparent fluid, and he could make out the white body immersed in it to somewhere just below the shoulders. The tubes connected to both arms and her mouth were painful to look at. Her closed eyelids didn't even twitch.

"Kuroyukihime..." Haruyuki unconsciously murmured her name, calling out to her.

Right now inside that slender body, countless nanites were allying with her own will to live to battle her severe injuries. And in this battle alone, Haruyuki could offer no assistance. All he could do was pray.

"Don't worry. I'm sure she'll make it," the nurse repeated, patting Haruyuki's head before getting up. "We're monitoring her condition very closely. I'll come let you know if anything changes. You just try and get a little rest."

"Okay. Uh, um, thank you." Haruyuki thanked the nurse standing before him and bowed his head.

That was when he unexpectedly remembered something strange in the window displayed in the right of his field of view. His instincts, honed through his enormous experience with virtual games, whispered to him about things he should notice, things he should consider.

What? What did I see just now?

Kuroyukihime's naked body, exposed to the shoulders. But there was something on her. He couldn't really make it out, given that she was immersed in semitransparent fluid, but finally he saw it, a black thing around the back of her neck. Her Neurolinker. A single thin cable stretched out from the bed in line with the oxygen tube and connected it to a large machine beside her.

"O-oh, um, excuse me."

Stopped by his hurried call, the nurse turned, head tilted to the side. "Yes? "

"No, it's just... You left her Neurolinker on?"

"We did. It's monitoring her brain waves."

"Then, um, the machine the cable's connected to, it's not a stand-alone..."

"Oh no, it's connected to the hospital net."

What?!

Haruyuki swallowed hard, and watching him with a doubtful look, the nurse smiled reassuringly. "What's wrong? Are you worried about security? It's fine. The treatment level of the hospital net is behind a very thorough wall. There isn't a hacker out there who could hurt her."

Waving a hand in farewell, the nurse disappeared into the nurses' station, and Haruyuki replied in his head, almost groaning, *That's probably true normally. But this isn't normal. It can sneak into the social camera net and steal images in real time with zero trouble, and that net's supposed to have the nation's strongest walls.*

Brain Burst.

Alone in the hallway, Haruyuki set himself down on the bench with a *thud*, holding the blanket in his left hand.

Kuroyukihime's Neurolinker was completely disconnected from the global net. But it was connected to the hospital net via direct so she could be treated. Which meant...

Haruyuki murmured in a trembling voice, "Burst link."

Immediately, the world froze, accompanied by the usual thunder.

Haruyuki, in his pig avatar, staggered to his feet and, with a feeling akin to prayer, clicked on the flaring *B* mark among the icons lined up on the left side of his virtual desktop, launching the Brain Burst console. He opened the matching list.

After a moment of searching, the name Silver Crow was displayed at the top of the list.

And then, barely a beat later, "Black Lotus."

"N-no way," Haruyuki moaned.

If he clicked around in his Neurolinker and disconnected from the hospital net, he could make himself disappear from the matching list. But Kuroyukihime, currently having her brain waves monitored, could not.

Obviously she wasn't connected to the global net, so there wouldn't be endless trespassing from outside. But if there was a Burst Linker in this hospital, and if that person launched Brain Burst, and if they found Black Lotus and challenged her to a fight...

Unconscious, Kuroyukihime would simply be hunted.

No, that was too perfect. There was no way another Burst Linker would be in the same hospital at the same time. And this late at night, there really shouldn't have been anyone coming or going. If any Burst Linkers other than Haruyuki and Kuroyukihime connected to the hospital net, their names would have to show up on the list.

So there was no need to panic.

Haruyuki tried to calm himself. But the sensation of sweat soaking the round hands of his avatar didn't go anywhere.

That's not it. Not yet. I'm missing something.

What if... what if there's some Burst Linker in a position to find out that Black Lotus—the biggest bounty in the accelerated world—was seriously injured and in the hospital, and even which hospital she was in?

He tried to force his thoughts to conclude, *There's no way someone like that exists*, but his eyes widened with a fearful shudder.

There is, though. Just one person, one enemy like that. Cyan Pile.

The mysterious enemy who had gone so far as to infect Chiyuri's Neurolinker with a virus, whose real identity they hadn't been able to figure out. At this stage, all he could say was that it was someone at Umesato.

And the school had already been informed of Kuroyukihime's accident. Adding in the fact that the cause of the accident was Araya driving without a license and assaulting her with a car immediately after making bail, it was sure to be big news already. Right about now, it was no doubt spreading like wildfire through the students at Umesato.

The hospital itself probably hadn't been identified yet. If one of the girls who worshipped her in the lower grades or a member of her fan club had found out the name of the hospital, there would already have been hundreds of them pushing through the doors. But...the teachers would know already. In which case, it was only a matter of time before it got out to the students. Tons of visitors would show up, and if Cyan Pile happened to be among them, he or she would be nearly impossible to pick out.

So...that's that, then.

He slumped crestfallen and sat down next to his frozen, blue real-life self.

Kuroyukihime was fighting for her life. No matter how you looked at it, it was a fact that this was not the time for a Duel.

Fortunately, the same opponent could only challenge you to one Duel per day. Until Kuroyukihime's condition improved, she'd just have to get beaten by Cyan Pile a couple times and lose some points.

No! I'm an idiot!! What did Kuroyukihime say before the accident?! Haruyuki clenched both fists and stood up abruptly.

The final command she had used to save Haruyuki: physical full dive.

That the price for this transcendental effect of accelerating not just your consciousness but your physical body as well was losing 99 percent of your burst points.

Kuroyukihime's points were currently on the verge of being wiped out. So depleted, in fact, that if she were to lose even once to the much-lower-ranking Cyan Pile, her points would no doubt drop to zero quickly enough. And in that instant, her Brain Burst would forcefully uninstall.

For her, that would be…For Kuroyukihime, who had been fighting all this time to reach level ten, it would basically be the same as dying. That couldn't happen; that absolutely could not happen. He couldn't let Cyan Pile go up against Kuroyukihime even once.

Kuroyukihime risked her life to save me.

So now I have to save her. That half of her.

I will monitor the hospital entrance. I will not sleep a wink. I will be ready to spend every one of my points and accelerate each time a student from Umesato shows up. I will find and challenge Cyan Pile. And then I will defeat him or her. I will beat Cyan Pile over and over until my enemy's points are nearly exhausted and I will banish Cyan Pile from the accelerated world.

"I'll protect you. I'll do whatever it takes to protect you." Haruyuki spoke out loud, the sole inhabitant of the blue world around him. "Because…I—I have something I have to tell you. When I see you again. So I'll fight," he declared firmly, turning his eyes toward Kuroyukihime, supposedly lying down on the other side of the blue wall.

Returning to reality with the "burst out" command, Haruyuki wrapped his arms around his knees, faced sideways on the bench, wrapped the blanket around his body, and fixed his gaze on the entrance to the left down the hall.

There were other ways into the hospital, but to connect to the hospital net, you had to authenticate your Neurolinker at the entrance. So Cyan Pile would have to come in there.

The time was ten thirty.

It wasn't very likely that Cyan Pile would show up at this time of night when visiting hours were long over, but his enemy was also cornered. If Cyan Pile was going to target Kuroyukihime while she was known to be unconscious, it was possible he or she would come and attack after finding out the name of the hospital.

Haruyuki set the alarm in his Neurolinker to the loudest

volume. This way, if he got sleepy, a bell so noisy it would practically ring the life out of him would force him back awake.
Time had never in his life moved as slowly as it did that
night. However, he didn't feel bored, much less sleepy. For the
most part, he continued to face the dim entrance with eyes wide
open, once in a while glancing over at the minimized ER video
window.

Kuroyukihime's white body in the capsule bed didn't move in
the slightest, but Haruyuki felt keenly that a desperate battle was
currently playing out there.

Fight. Fight, he pleaded each time he looked at the video. They
were connected through their Neurolinkers and the hospital net,
and through the Brain Burst program. So these pleas of encouragement had to be getting to her. Haruyuki believed this firmly;
there was no room for doubt.

Around two in the morning, the worried-looking nurse came to
check on him, a paper cup of coffee in one hand. He refused the
milk and sugar, and his first-ever cup of black coffee tasted so bitter, it nearly pierced his tongue.

At five in the morning, the first light of dawn pushed faintly
through the entrance. After hesitating briefly, Haruyuki dashed
to the washroom and, taking care of business faster than he ever
had in his life, rushed back out to curl up on the bench again.

Six AM. The number of employees coming and going in twos
and threes started to increase, and Haruyuki pushed his vigi-
lance up a level.

Seven AM. The night staff, having finished their work, started
trickling out, the nurse along with them. She handed Haruyuki a
second cup of coffee and a sandwich and spoke to him encourag-
ingly before she, too, departed.

Eight thirty AM.

The automatic doors of the hospital's main entrance were
opened, taking over from the night reception. As if waiting for
that moment, several people, mostly older patients, came in.

Haruyuki, feeling even more alert, opened both eyes wide and stared intently at the flow of people.

Given that it had only been six months since he'd started at the school, there was no way he could actually remember the face of every student at Umesato Junior High, no matter how small the school might be, with just three classes for each grade. When he saw the face of a young person he wasn't sure about, he had to instantly accelerate and check the matching list.

He had strained his powers of concentration very close to their limit, but the digital clock display in the corner of his vision changed numbers slowly, so slowly it was as if the display were laughing at him.

Thirty-five minutes. Forty minutes.

Kuroyukihime probably still wasn't out of the woods yet. Of the twelve hours the doctor had cited, more than ten had already passed.

Hurry and wake up. And then cut off the brain monitoring, Haruyuki prayed with all his heart.

One more time. Once more. He wanted to meet her in the accelerated world, just the two of them.

And this time he would tell her how he felt. He would hold nothing back.

Eight forty-five.

Haruyuki finally saw the first familiar face appear in his alert eyes. He caught his breath for an instant, and then expelled it in a long sigh.

It wasn't just familiar. It was one of the two faces he knew best in this world. The tall, slender form was packaged in a grown-up velour jacket and chino pants. The airy hair shone brown, catching the morning light.

You came...

Haruyuki relaxed his shoulders, and his face split into a smile.

"Heeey, Taku! Over here!"

The moment Haruyuki's salutation, a little too loud for inside a hospital, reached the entrance from the hallway, Takumu—

Takumu Mayuzumi—froze in midstep. He didn't seem to have spotted Haruyuki. Scanning left to right, he finally turned straight toward the hallway farthest from the entrance, leading to the emergency room. Haruyuki got up from the bench and waved again. Meeting his eyes, Takumu tilted his head slightly and blinked rapidly several times before his usual relaxed and bright smile spread out across his face. After tossing his navy-blue-jacketed right arm up in a wave, he poked at his blue Neurolinker with a fingertip.

Haruyuki quickly understood that he had to wait until he was authenticated on the hospital net and smiled slightly wryly at Takumu's usual methodical style.

Regardless of whether you were at the hospital for a checkup or to visit someone, to go past the entrance, the common rule at all hospitals across the country was to either sign in to the hospital net with your Neurolinker or to show your ID at the reception desk to get a visitor's pass.

However, it didn't really matter if you stood and waited in the entrance for the mere thirty seconds it took for the strict authentication or moved while it was authenticating to save time. When Haruyuki had come last night, he'd run straight to the ER without stopping for even a second, so the authentication had finished after Kuroyukihime had disappeared onto the other side of those doors.

However, Takumu was apparently not interested in committing even this trivial violation of the rules. He turned his eyes toward Haruyuki, and with an irritated look on his face, he stood in the middle of the entrance hall and waited for the sign-in to be complete. Then, suddenly, as if noticing something, Takumu turned to the side. His eyes ran off in the direction of the automatic doors, and he brought his left hand to his mouth, the way you do when you call out to someone in a loud voice.

Haruyuki wondered if maybe Chiyuri had come and tried to see beyond the front entrance himself.

The moment his eyes left Takumu, it hit him: a faint sense of wrongness.

Would the irreproachable (unlike Haruyuki) Takumu shout in a hospital?

Cupping his mouth like a megaphone. Almost as if he were trying to hide from Haruyuki the words being uttered.

In an instant, his feeling of wrongness turned to shivers, and an arrow of ice pierced Haruyuki's spinal cord. Opening his eyes, standing stiff as a board, several thoughts flashed simultaneously through his brain.

I— Why did I assume Cyan Pile had to be someone at Umesato? Obviously because Chiyuri's Neurolinker was infected with that virus. Because someone was using Chiyuri as a stepping-stone to attack Kuroyukihime from somewhere in the school net like a ghost.

But. If that back door was made for access from the global net? In that case, the suspect didn't have to be at Umesato Junior High; he or she could be anywhere in the country.

As his brain worked in overdrive, his thoughts were overlaid with a new filter to narrow things down.

Why Chiyuri? Because she was easy to contact.

Someone outside school, closer to Chiyuri than anyone else. Someone with her, so close they could direct. Only one person met these conditions. And he was standing a mere twenty meters away from Haruyuki at this very moment.

The instant his thoughts reached this point, Haruyuki's mouth moved automatically and the command surged out.

"Burst link!!"

The boy who was Chiyuri's childhood friend and boyfriend. Takumu.

Boooom!

The cold, dry thunder froze the world. The Takumu before his eyes was frozen in blue, left hand still raised to his mouth.

But he wasn't frozen, in fact. Takumu had shouted the command into that hand at the same time. And his consciousness was accelerated in a different frozen space from Haruyuki's.

You. It was you. I can't believe it. No way. Why? Why?

Confused screams echoing in the back of Haruyuki's mind, the right arm of his avatar began flashing over his virtual desktop as fast as possible.

Right now, Takumu would be doing the exact same thing. Launching the Brain Burst console, waiting for the matching list to update. And then clicking on the name Black Lotus when it drops down in the results and requesting a Duel.

Haruyuki had to get Cyan Pile into a Duel before that.

He clenched his teeth, opened his eyes wide, and stared at the matching list search display.

Pop! His own name at the top of the list. Silver Crow.

Then the person he loved, the person he had to protect. Black Lotus.

And finally, the name of the enemy he had to defeat appeared before Haruyuki's eyes for the first time. Cyan Pile.

Be in time!!

Screaming with every fiber of his being, Haruyuki clicked on the name impossibly quickly and hit the "duel" command in the window that popped up.

8

Skree! Skree! Skree! Skree!

The world shook unnaturally for a moment, innumerable masses of metals grating against one another.

The fresh morning light that had been shining in from the entrance became an unsettling yellow. Rusty, metallic, slimy gills grew up like some monstrous creature from Haruyuki's feet to cover the floor and walls around him. The pillars twisted and became ridged like the stomach of an insect, while several protrusions resembling strange eyeballs popped out from the ceiling. In seconds, the interior of the cutting-edge hospital, which had been so clean, was enveloped in an organic, metallic pollution, the nightmare of an old Cyberpunk author.

As Haruyuki held his breath, standing stock-still, shining silver armor reached down from the tips of his limbs to encase his body, which stretched out and narrowed like wire. Hips to stomach, and then up to his chest, he was transformed into smooth silver, and then finally, his head was sealed in a rounded helmet.

Almost simultaneous with the change from pink pig to Silver Crow duel avatar, two health gauges snapped out to the sides in the top of his vision. Between the gauges, the number 1800. Finally, in the center, flames rose up, and the word FIGHT! appeared within the flames, flaring bright red before bursting and scattering.

*   *   *

Glancing at the counter as it started its countdown, Haruyuki breathed a sigh of relief; he had made it. He looked over to where Takumu had been at the end of the slimy hall. Incredibly, standing in the same place, facing the side, was the unexpected form of Takumu's duel avatar.

That's... Takumu?! That's Cyan Pile?!

Unconsciously, Haruyuki pulled his right leg back a half step in shock.

He was enormous. No, he wasn't as tall as that. The avatar was just another five centimeters taller than Takumu, who was already 175 centimeters in seventh grade. But from Silver Crow's perspective at barely 155 centimeters, it was enough for him to have to look up.

However, the most overwhelming thing was the sheer immense girth of Cyan Pile's body. Which wasn't to say he was fat. Four limbs and a trunk with muscles bulging like a pro wrestler's, wrapped in close-fitting, metallic blue, bodysuit-type armor. On his feet, rugged dark blue boots. On his left hand, an enormous glove in the same color. He looked like the macho hero from some American comic, a full one hundred eighty degrees from slim, lithe Takumu.

Awestruck, Haruyuki was rooted in place.

Cyan Pile slowly turned to the left and stared down at Haruyuki. His head was covered by a stylish teardrop mask. Several thin slit-shaped gaps opened up horizontally on his face, with a single brace piercing them vertically in the center. Depending on how you looked at it, it was almost reminiscent of a kendo mask.

Behind one of the slits, two bluish-white eyes sparkled in a sharp shape with a sudden snap. The left foot came up slowly and fell to the floor heavily. The slime that had built up there whizzed to both sides.

As Haruyuki pulled his left leg back to take another step, his eyes were drawn to Cyan Pile's bare right arm. What was that?!

Not a glove like on his left hand. A thick pipe connected at his elbow. The pipe was probably fifteen centimeters around and a meter long. The tip of the metal pole apparently equipped inside protruded from the opening and emitted a dangerous, dazzling radiance.

From the color of the armor covering his entire body, Cyan Pile's attribute was close-range blue. But it was infinitesimally close to the pure blue Kuroyukihime had told him about. In which case, that sharp pole shouldn't have been a flying weapon.

Even as he had this thought, Haruyuki felt compelled to take another step back.

As if to torment the slender, motionless Silver Crow, Cyan Pile took one slow step, then another, down the organic metal hallway. Then he stopped abruptly.

The mask with its lines of slits turned to survey the environment. Coming out of the mask was... It was twisted gloomily, but it was still definitely the clear voice of his good friend Takumu he had heard so much over so many years.

"Huh. So we got a Purgatory stage. It's been a long time since I've seen one of these. What were the attributes again?"

As the carefree voice spoke, Haruyuki unconsciously opened his mouth. "T-Taku..."

Skkkkrrrk!

Suddenly, the iron rod, driven by Cyan Pile's right arm, bit into the metal wall of the hallway, tearing it open horribly. Slime and pieces of steel were sent flying and tiny, crushed, peculiar insects he didn't know the names for dropped to the floor.

Haruyuki swallowed his words and flinched, cowering.

Glancing at him, Cyan Pile continued in an even more cheerful voice, "It's definitely solid. Might be a little hard to destroy this stage."

Thud. He started walking again, and the large blue frame drew near, as if bending over. "Haru... Haru. You always were fast on the virtual desktop. I was literally about to push the duel button, but right before I could, you sucked me in."

"Ta...kumu..."

Is it really you? Why? Since when?

Since when are you a Burst Linker?

Before Haruyuki could voice the questions swirling around in his heart, Cyan Pile made a further utterance. "Honestly, you being a Burst Linker...I have to say I'm surprised. You have no idea how hard it was to keep my calm yesterday. I mean, betrayed by my best friend like that, huh, Haru?"

"T-Takumu...It's not like that. It's..." The words Haruyuki blurted hoarsely were drowned out by the iron rod slamming into the wall again.

"How'd it feel, Haru? Directing on Chi's bed? How'd it feel to be held by her? Did you enjoy Chi's body, touching her while you thought about me?"

You're not Takumu! Haruyuki screamed voicelessly. *This isn't the Taku I know. Taku would never say things like that. He's always cheerful and bright and absolutely never negative. That's the real Takumu. Cyan Pile is someone else. He probably built a back door in Takumu's Neurolinker, too, and is connecting from someplace far off.*

Haruyuki tried desperately to make himself believe this.

But there was the aura he had felt then.

Haruyuki was keenly conscious of the fact that the exact same aura he had felt when he was directing with Chiyuri and discovered the virus in her Neurolinker—that shadow of someone hiding back there, eyes and ears wide open—was radiating off the blue duel avatar in front of him.

And maybe it was the same shadow he had felt since way back when, since the three of them were kids, when Takumu would sometimes turn glancingly at Haruyuki and Chiyuri when they were fooling around.

"Taku...is this you?" The words Haruyuki uttered from under his silver mask echoed so sharply and clearly that they surprised even himself. "You infected Chiyu's Neurolinker with that virus? You hid from Chiyu and connected to her, making her senses your own private peep show?!"

"I'd rather you didn't call it a virus."

The enormous avatar, stopping a mere five meters away, opened up its left hand nimbly, a smart gesture that alone was like Takumu. "Chi's my girlfriend. So of course I direct with her. And directing means offering up your Neurolinker to your partner. It means circumventing password authentication, laying bare the depths of your local memory, and accepting whatever happens, whether it's some file getting looked at or some program getting installed. Am I wrong? Haru, I mean, you…" Inside the slits cutting across Cyan Pile's mask, Haruyuki could feel a sneer sliding across the face he couldn't see. "You directed with Chi and dug through her memory without her knowing, right? And you're not even her boyfriend or anything. Aren't you the one who took advantage of Chi's kindness to do something dirty?"

"Th-that—"

"You've always been like that, Haru." As Cyan Pile spoke in a calm voice, a large, strangely shaped metal insect scuttled by on the wall to his right. He casually raised the enormous needle in his right hand and lightly pierced the insect's back. Pinned to the wall and squealing, the insect moved its countless legs frantically, trying to get away. "Ever since forever, with Chi, you've been all, *Poor me. Pathetic me. Be nice to sad little me. Hang out with me more.* That's all you've ever said to her. Not in words, but with your attitude, the look in your eyes—with your entire existence, actually."

The rod sank deeper into the insect's carapace, making a wet sound. Green liquid splashed out, and the virtual insect began to writhe even more frantically.

"Girls, they don't get it. Chi always looks like she had so much more fun dragging you along by the hand, complaining the whole time, than she does when I'm the one holding her hand. Ever since we were kids, she looks so happy watching out for you, taking care of you. Did you know? Wherever she goes, Chi always brings a big handkerchief. For sweaty you."

Clang!!
With a terrifying noise, the insect was pulverized, and the dark green shell and limbs shot out with the slime from the wall.

Half bewildered, Haruyuki asked Cyan Pile, insect fluids still dripping from the needle, "So that's why...? That's why you told Chiyu you liked her two years ago? Like that...like you were in a hurry?"

"Not *like* I was in a hurry. I *was* hurrying. I was sure if things kept up like that, Chi'd try to spend the rest of her life watching out for you. Like those ancient manga you keep an archive of. She'd end up all, *You can't live without me, so I'll marry you.* Ooh, or maybe your strategy was to lead Chi there? Ha-ha-ha!"

Cyan Pile laughed brightly, but with a distorted echo that made a shiver run down Haruyuki's spine.

No. No.

Takumu, you're wrong. Chiyuri definitely did not have fun looking after sad-sack me. She's been seriously worried. She doesn't know what to do about me.

But Haruyuki didn't know how to say these things so that they would reach Takumu. Because on a superficial level, there was a certain truth in what Takumu was saying.

Turning to Haruyuki still standing there, Cyan Pile took another step. "I was pretty happy two years ago when Chi picked me. I thought she finally understood that she was better off being happy with me than working so hard to look out for you. I suppose...it was a practical decision?"

"Practical?"

"'We can't be little kids forever,' right?"

The words Haruyuki had said to Chiyuri the day before.

Cyan Pile raised the tip of the metal needle, dyed green, up into the air as if seeking agreement. "I mean, Chi's a girl—well, a woman. She'll realize someday that she'll be way happier with a boyfriend she can brag to her friends about, a nice marriage, a satisfying life. So I tried my best. I studied so much it nearly killed me and got into the school I'm at now. I run every day to train my body while you play your dumb video games and sleep like a little baby, Haru."

"A-are you serious?" Haruyuki shouted almost mechanically, unable to collect his thoughts. "Do you really think Chiyu chose you because of some calculating self-interest?!"

"I don't like that phrase, *calculating self-interest*. It's just a fair way of looking at things." Cyan Pile laughed again. "Chi has the right to be happy. The right to date me—best student in my grade, kendo champion—and be happy."

Haruyuki inhaled sharply.

This isn't Takumu.

He couldn't believe that this was Takumu's true self. He didn't want to believe it. Something had warped Takumu.

Part of it was probably Haruyuki and Chiyuri's relationship. Chiyuri continued to care about Haruyuki while dating Takumu. He probably felt driven to the wall by that in a way. But more than that, what had changed Takumu was probably...

"This isn't you, Taku." Haruyuki raised his silver mask and stared directly into Cyan Pile's sharp eyes. "Being the best in your grade, the championship, that's not you. It's Brain Burst; it's the acceleration. When? When did you become a Burst Linker?"

For a moment, the Purgatory stage was shrouded in silence.

A group of small insects skittered past his feet, and occasionally vapor like a living creature spewed from the gills in the walls. Two hundred seconds had already passed on the counter, which had started at 1800. As the hundreds position on the counter clicked down to five, Cyan Pile spoke.

"It is me." The needle on his right hand pointed at Haruyuki. "Acceleration is me. I was the one with brain-training software crammed down my throat through my Neurolinker from the time I was just a baby until I was totally sick of it. I cultivated the aptitude! And it's only been a year since I became a Burst Linker. My kendo team captain is my parent, a close associate of the Blue

King. He's got high hopes for me. I'm a cadet in the royal guard. And yet—"

Ka-chaaaank!!

His right hand, gesturing broadly, ripped several enormous scars in the wall. "Now!! Now you're a Burst Linker?! And you think you're my equal, Haru?! The ability to accelerate's given you confidence, so you're trying to take Chi back?! Is that it?! It's no good, Haru. You can't beat me. In grades, in sports, in Chi's heart. And, naturally, not in the accelerated world. I'll help you understand. My power…I'll teach that pathetic duel avatar of yours." A brilliant light burst forth from Cyan Pile's eyes.

He's serious. Takumu is seriously planning to fight me.

Haruyuki still felt like he could make Takumu understand if he just found the right words. He wanted to explain Chiyuri's— and his own—true feelings. He didn't want to fight like this.

But if Haruyuki lost here…

Cyan Pile would try to fight Black Lotus again. And then he would hunt her while she was unconscious. In an instant, Kuroyukihime would lose all her points and, with them, the power of acceleration.

Just that. No matter what else happened, he had to prevent at least that.

"Taku. You really are amazing. You're good at school and sports; you're cool, too. You have everything I don't," Haruyuki murmured in a stifled voice, looking down. Then he jerked his face up at Cyan Pile and shouted sharply, "But you're an idiot. A super idiot!"

"What was that? I'm an idiot?"

"Yeah. Which is why you can't beat me! Did you forget? Have you ever in your life beaten me at any game?"

"…Haru. Haru." A voice mixed with laughter and echoes of violence. "In that case, you're about to lose the very last thing you can be proud of!!"

Cyan Pile's boots kicked hard against the floor, and the enormous body, nearly two meters tall, began to close the distance between them at an incredible speed belying his form.

But he was still slower than the charge of Ash Roller's bike.

Slip by him. Then move to a bigger area. The entrance hall—no, the roof.

Haruyuki focused on Cyan Pile's right hand. His opponent was a close-range fighter; as long as he didn't come within striking distance of that needle, he wouldn't take any damage.

After watching Cyan Pile move, right arm drawn back as far as it would go, Haruyuki dashed forward, intending to slip through on the opposite side.

Silver Crow's speed, essentially his only redeeming feature, appeared to take his opponent off guard. Seeming faintly surprised, Cyan Pile thrust his right arm forward, carving out an arc.

You can dodge this!

Predicting the trajectory of the attack, Haruyuki dropped down and tried to break through alongside Cyan Pile's left arm.

Krsshk!

An unexpected sound rang through the air.

Eyes open wide, Haruyuki saw in his periphery flames shooting from the end of the fat pipe that was Cyan Pile's right arm. The dazzling, thick iron rod shot out so fast he could hardly see it.

It may not have been a flying weapon, but it did stretch out to nearly double its length, and the range was more than sufficient to grab hold of Silver Crow. Haruyuki heard an unpleasant shrieking pass through his own body concurrent with the impact. And then a sharp, numbing pain.

The tip of the rod had pierced his left elbow, and Haruyuki watched as his arm separated in that spot. He remembered belatedly that *pile* could also mean *stake*.

The arm, carving out a trail of sparks as it fell to the floor, immediately smashed into a thousand tiny pieces and disappeared. The health gauge in the upper left of his vision dropped abruptly, nearly a third with just the one blow.

But Haruyuki didn't have the time to feel sorry about taking such serious damage right at the start of the fight. Even as he crumpled and his back scraped along the hallway wall, trying to regain his balance, he saw the evil iron rod in Cyan Pile's right arm, still extended—or rather, he saw it being pulled in again. It was clear that the instant the stake was reloaded, he would again have to face that terrifying attack.

The attack attribute was probably "piercing" and Silver Crow's metal color should have meant he was resistant to it. So his arm being torn off in one blow meant it hit him in exactly the wrong place. This was the difference three levels could make, or simply, Cyan Pile was really strong.

Considering this momentarily, Haruyuki picked himself up again and jumped hard, gaining some distance. Without looking back, he dashed for the entrance hall as fast as he could.

"Ha-ha-ha! What? Running away so soon, Haru?"

The sneering laughter echoed up from behind him almost as if urging him on, and Haruyuki ran his eyes quickly over his surroundings.

The long benches in the waiting area had been transformed into cast iron, spikes sprouting up everywhere like some torture device from the Middle Ages, and the reception counter to his right was entwined with rusted barbed wire. Naturally, there weren't any people. And on the other side of the counter was the thing he was looking for: the elevator doors.

In the Century End stage, the elevators were naturally not likely to have been functioning because entry into the buildings themselves was not permitted, but in this Purgatory stage, with the interior reconstructed in such detail, they just might be working.

Running over, Haruyuki smashed the skull-shaped button beside the door—now mesh like a cage—with a prayer in his heart. Sure enough, the mesh opened to the left and right, accompanied by a grinding, metallic noise. He clenched his right hand in victory.

From behind him, the sound of Cyan Pile's thudding footsteps grew closer moment by moment.

He leapt into the solitary-confinement cell of an elevator, and his right hand repeatedly punched the button with an *R* carved into it. *Hurry. Hurry up and move.*

The instant the lattice closed at a speed so sluggish it seemed designed to irritate, something slammed into the door. Poking its face through a gap of about five centimeters in the mesh was the iron rod's shining, dazzlingly sharp tip.

Haruyuki stifled the urge to shriek and jumped away, pressing his back against the wall.

Skreeeee!

The iron stake shot forward, bending the lattice slightly, before finally stopping mere millimeters from Silver Crow's thin abdomen. As its malignant radiance retracted, the elevator finally trembled and rattled, beginning its ascent.

"Ha-ha-ha! Ha-ha-ha-ha-ha!!"

Haruyuki stomped his right leg against the floor, banishing the sticky, sneering laughter chasing up from below him.

Tumbling out onto the roof, Haruyuki scanned his surroundings, breathing heavily. Involuntarily, his eyes grew wider.

The sky in the Purgatory stage was filled with an unsettling yellow light, and dark clouds wound through the sky like living creatures. The buildings around him, the heart of Suginami ward, had been changed into bizarre forms bearing a distant resemblance to something living and shone slimily with a reddish-black rusty color. He supposed the lancelike spires he could see in the distance were the Shinjuku Government Building and the surrounding skyscrapers.

Just as he started to wonder exactly how far the stage reached, Haruyuki noticed something with a start and gasped.

There was someone there.

Well, if by *someone*, he meant a strikingly eccentric silhouette.

From the roofs of buildings around him that were taller than the hospital, groups of twos and threes were looking down on Haruyuki. Unknown Burst Linkers. Spectators. Momentarily bewildered, Haruyuki finally hit on it.

He might have been cut off from the global net, but the other fighter, Takumu, probably connected globally right before the match started. Why he would have done that and taken the risk of someone else calling him out was unclear, but in any case, because he had, this stage was open to the outside, and the Burst Linkers registered for the automatic Gallery for Cyan Pile and Silver Crow had appeared. Although it made no real difference to his situation if there was a Gallery or not.

The light blue, arrow-shaped cursor displayed in his field of view slowly started to change direction, vibrating slightly. Cyan Pile had also gotten in an elevator and was headed for the roof.

After moving about ten meters across the expansive roof, Haruyuki turned and faced the elevator. Up here, he had plenty of space for evasive moves, unlike in the hallway.

And he now understood from firsthand experience the reach of Cyan Pile's metal stake. As long as he paid attention to the position of Cyan Pile's right arm, Haruyuki should be able to avoid it. *Don't be afraid. You have no choice but to do this.* As he told himself this, the elevator lurched to a stop in front of him and the doors slowly pulled open.

Cyan Pile's enormous body was stuffed into the elevator, taking up every bit of space. Scraping along the walls, he stepped out onto the roof, and the eyes in the depths of the slits lit up faintly. "Oh, I get it. Up here, you can dart in and hit and then dart back out again, huh, Haru—I mean, Silver Crow."

"It's just that down there, you looked cramped, like you were having a hard time."

"A-ha-ha! I can't believe you're saying something like that to me." Still chuckling, Cyan Pile started to advance mechanically.

Haruyuki crouched and measured the distance between them.

He shouldn't fully understand how fast Silver Crow is yet. That's my only chance of winning. Before he gets used to my speed, I have to do something and win.

A heavy-looking boot took its fourth step, and just as it was on the verge of making contact with the ground, Haruyuki kicked off as hard as he could.

The sky rang out shrilly, and the enormous blue body approached instantaneously. Haruyuki plunged forward in a straight line, and Cyan Pile's right arm followed, targeting him.

Right here!!

He abruptly took off on his left leg and started running to the right. With an enormous roar, the metal spike shot out at an extremely high speed. Reacting after seeing the spike launched was basically impossible, but if he could anticipate where it would go and make the right call, he could pull this off.

Haruyuki traced an arc over the surface of Cyan Pile's left arm and darted in, the tip of the metal spike stopping just in front of his left cheek. Feeling a scorching heat there, Haruyuki kicked his right leg at the floor with all his strength.

"Nngaaah!" He beat into the defenseless flank with his right fist. *Thunk.* Serious resistance. The big frame shuddered.

I can still do this!

As if chasing Cyan Pile's back as he tried to turn his body around, Haruyuki dashed forward another step and landed a right roundhouse kick on his enemy's left calf. As Cyan Pile lost his balance with a jolt, Haruyuki brought a final blow, a left knee strike toward the center of that enormous back.

Wham! Serious impact. The hulking body bent over into a sideways *V.*

Cyan Pile, staggering to put distance between them, roared hatefully, "Rrrgh! I—I guess you really are good at games, Haru. But little tricks like that are useless!!"

Haruyuki just barely managed to dodge the left fist thrown at him, used the inertia to spin his body around, and buried his right heel in the nape of the neck presenting itself defenselessly.

"Nnngaaaaah!"

Haruyuki closed his ears to the broken shrieking in Takumu's voice and continued his rush. Using not just both legs and his right fist, but even his severed left arm, he delivered combo after combo without a break. At some point, half-screamed shouts began to tumble from his mouth. "You...idiot! You stupid idiot! Chiyu! Chiyu isn't asking you to be number one in your grade or the kendo champion or anything!"

In desperation, he used a leg kicked out in front as a step ladder to jump up high, grab Cyan Pile's mask, and smash his own silver-armored helmet into it with everything he had. Part of the blue mask cracked loudly and caved in.

Cyan Pile lost his balance, falling back onto the floor, and Haruyuki jumped on his chest to continue battering him with his right fist. "Chiyu just wants you to be you! You're the one making her look back at the past, making her want to go back to when we were kids, Takumu! The only one of us who's changed is you!"

Mind blank, he simply screamed.

However, at the sound of Haruyuki's voice, Cyan Pile's eyes shone from beneath the cracked slits with a light strong and cold enough to send shivers down spines. "D...on't..." He crossed his thick arms abruptly as if to protect himself. "Don't get so carried awaaaaaaaay!!" He flung his arms out wide to reveal the sharp tips of at least ten stakes that rose up with a grinding noise from the chest to the stomach of his body suit.

What the—?! This is bad. Gotta dodge—

But the instant Haruyuki tried to kick down on the ground with both legs and send himself flying backward: "Splash Stingerrrrrrr!"

Thk thk thk thk thk thk!! Sounding like a heavy machine gun, the multitudinous stakes shot toward Haruyuki at point-blank range.

"Gaaaah!!"

Haruyuki somehow managed to avoid the stakes flying straight for his head and chest. But he then took serious hits to his left shoulder, his left flank, and his right knee, which sent him flying high in the air like a hunk of scrap, landing on his back against the roof.

"Nngaah!!" The breath knocked out of him mixed with a cry from deep in his throat. His vision flickered, and a sharp, intense pain ran through his entire body. He couldn't believe this was virtual damage from the Neurolinker.

What was that?!

Haruyuki braced his right arm and somehow managed to raise his upper body to watch Cyan Pile sluggishly get up a step ahead of him.

"Hnn…Heh-heh-heh-heh-heh!" Short bursts of laughter leaked out from beneath the blue mask as if a screw had come loose somewhere. "Heh-heh-heh-heh! You really…got a lot of energetic poking in there, huh? You surprised me a little. But in the end, you're just an annoying little bug. And you even went out of your way to build up my special-attack gauge."

"Special…attack…" Haruyuki muttered as he checked the gauges at the top of his vision.

Cyan Pile's thick health gauge stretching out on one side was at 60 percent. He had taken more damage in Haruyuki's rush than he was letting on. But Haruyuki, having been caught directly by the random stake shooting, only had about 30 percent health left.

And below each of the health bars, a thin green gauge stretched out. Cyan Pile's was glowing brightly at around 70 percent. In contrast, Haruyuki's was basically full.

"Now, now, don't talk like it's the first time you've heard the words, Silver Crow." Cackling, Cyan Pile started to advance slowly. "The give-and-take of special attacks is the best part of any Duel. That Splash Stinger before's my level-two special attack. Perfect for knocking down annoying insects, huh? Oh, that reminds me. Your gauge looks like it's full up already. Go ahead, come on. Use whatever you'd like."

Haruyuki clenched his teeth grindingly. The special attack given to Silver Crow was just Head Butt, which basically had no reach at all and could definitely not stand up against Cyan Pile's long range. And the motion was long and very obvious, so using it was basically like saying *Shoot me* while you were getting ready to act. *Dammit. I don't need a special attack or anything. I have my fists and my feet. And speed.* Once his shaky vision settled, Haruyuki quickly rose and focused his strength in his right leg.

But.

He heard a repulsive breaking noise, like a snap. And then the metallic sound of his own body collapsing to the ground again with a *crack*. Hurriedly turning his eyes downward, he saw that he had been pierced with one of the shotgun stakes, and his thin silver leg, smashed from the knee—

"A-ha! A-ha-ha-ha-ha-ha!!" Cyan Pile's piercing, loud laughter. "I got it! Your leg!! You're so brittle!! And you're supposed to be a metal color?!"

Haruyuki was oblivious to this sneering voice. *Crap. Crap!! I lost my leg, which means I can't run anymore. Forget avoiding him, forget running; I don't think I can even move.*

The sense of panic sneaking in chilled him to the depths of his bones.

This is bad. I can't, there's no way I can lose here. I have to protect her; I have to.

Crack.

The boot, stomping down uncomfortably close, smashed Haruyuki's severed leg as if it were glass.

The corners of the bluish-white eyes Haruyuki could see in the distance turned up sharply. "So this is how it ends, Haru." A faint whisper of a voice. "You here, like this: it suits you. And you even managed to get a lot of stuff off your chest back there, huh? Almost like you're the only person who understands Chi?"

"I do, you know. At least better than you do, anyway."

"Then what about me? Have you thought about me at all? Have you ever thought about how I feel when I'm alone with Chi and she gets this sad look on her face all of a sudden...and I know it's because she's thinking about you? Huh, Haru?" He cut himself off and brought his face in close. Cyan Pile—Takumu—gave voice to the decisive phrase. "It's because you're like this."

There was almost a gentleness somewhere in his tone, but his words dug a deep hole in Haruyuki's chest, an enormous iron stake.

"It's because you're like this that me and Chi and you are totally caught in this muddy swamp and can't get out. Just disappear already, Haru. Set me and Chi free."

Crack.

This step caught the bottom of Haruyuki's foot on his good leg.

Cyan Pile, drawing himself up abruptly, raising the launcher in his right arm high, drew a complicated trajectory with the tip in the air. As he did, the launcher was wrapped to his shoulder in a crisp blue light.

Suddenly, the launcher expanded to three times its size with a thick noise. From within, something akin to an enormous hammer popped its head out, front face flattened. The striking surface of the hammer turned sharply toward Haruyuki, who was unable to think, much less move.

"Now. Shall we put an end to this, Haru? All of it." *This Duel and the pretense of our friendship.* Cyan Pile's eyes communicated this message loud and clear.

The end of the hammer began to emit an intense light. "Spiral Gravity Driver!"

Skrrrrk!

Haruyuki tried desperately to avoid the hammer as it struck while still rotating, making a mechanical noise like countless gears catching. However, Cyan Pile had a firm hold on the bottom of his lone leg, and he couldn't escape. The massive hunk of steel came crushing down on Haruyuki's chest, followed by a duet between the high-pitched shriek of his silver armor being pulverized and the deep rumble of the floor beneath him being crushed.

Unable to even cry out, Haruyuki was beaten down a level along with the rooftop below him, slamming into the floor below in the hospital. But the hammer didn't stop there, smashing Haruyuki right through that floor as well.

Thump! Thud! Thump!!

The sound of destruction ringing in the air, Haruyuki plunged through all five levels of the hospital and finally stopped moving after becoming embedded in the ground floor.

Flash. Flash.

In the obscure darkness, something red was blinking in the top left of his vision. It took Haruyuki a few seconds to realize that it was his own health gauge reduced to just under 10 percent.

As if regretting the fact that it hadn't beaten his gauge down entirely, Cyan Pile's hammer stayed wedged in Haruyuki's chest for a while but eventually rose up, grindingly, rotating in the opposite direction.

Once the hammer had been lifted causing debris to rain down, all that was left in front of Haruyuki was a tiny hole leading up to the distant roof. Through it, he heard Cyan Pile's voice echoing weakly.

"Aaah, you still have a little health left. Well, whatever. We only have five or six minutes; it'll be time up before I can come find you and finish you off. And once I'm done here, I can get to my real mission, the boss battle. So!" His tone of voice changed, tinged with pride or perhaps fawning. "I hope you saw, all of you watching! Especially all of you in the Blue Legion!! I can still be of great use! I mean, I can definitely fight in the unlimited field above this! You must be regretting tossing me aside just because I used a few too many points? Right?!"

Taku...Takumu...You...

A broken doll at the bottom of a dark hole, Haruyuki felt hot fluid running along his cheeks. His tears. But he didn't quite know what he was crying about. He was probably shedding these tears for something that broke without him noticing it, something important he had completely lost.

But he couldn't afford to lose this Duel. He absolutely had to win—for himself, for Takumu, for Chiyuri. And for Kuroyuki-hime. And yet...

Carrying the pain of his tremendous regret, Haruyuki pulled himself up slowly. From all over his body, pieces of his cracked armor fell like rain and scattered. There was no more point in standing up anymore. He should just accept his decisive defeat and go back to the him before he knew Brain Burst. Haruyuki clutched his knees and decided to wait for the timer to reach zero.

Just before his eyes closed.

In the corner of a dim room.

She floated up like an illusion.

The bed was braided out of black wild roses. The slender figure lay as if enclosed by the inky black petals of countless flowers in full bloom.

A dress blacker than night. Silver edging. Parasol resting close by. And the shiny black hair fanning out over shining skin whiter than snow in the dim light. Her long eyelashes peacefully shut.

Am I hallucinating?

As he wondered this, Haruyuki approached the black rose bed slowly, very slowly, dragging what was left of the right leg he had lost. But no matter how close he got, Kuroyukihime's avatar showed no signs of disappearing.

Thrusting his right hand onto the edge of the bed as if to catch himself before he fell, Haruyuki finally understood. This, this place was the nanomachine room in the ER where the real Kuroyukihime was being treated. And Kuroyukihime's Neurolinker was connected to the hospital net. So the instant Haruyuki initiated the accelerated fight, her automatic spectator mode was activated, and she was also brought onto this stage.

"...Kuroyukihime," Haruyuki murmured hoarsely, stretching out his battered right arm to stroke her cheek softly. The words came tumbling out, one after another, as if the dam had broken. At the same time, more tears. "I—I couldn't save you. I couldn't protect your dream, your hopes. I couldn't live up to your expectations."

The tears trickling from the cracks in his half-shattered helmet fell in drops on Kuroyukihime's cheek, caught the minimal light, and shone before disappearing.

"I can change…That's what I thought. With your words, your kindness, your love, I could change…But I couldn't. It's not my avatar's fault…This avatar was probably created to reflect my 'resignation.' I'm the one who made him, who made Silver Crow like this. Me, never trying to look up, eyes always on the ground, living my life on my hands and knees." Haruyuki bent over slowly and clung to Kuroyukihime's shoulder. "I wanted to go there. Where you were…High up in the sky, where you were lightly flapping your wings. High up…far away…escaping the swamp of the real world…with you…"

With a sob, Haruyuki squeezed the last words out.

"I wanted to—fly."

Thump.

Almost as if in response to his voice, he heard a faint sound.

Thump. Thump.

The source was Kuroyukihime's chest against Haruyuki's cheek. A small, faint, but definite rhythm being carved out. Her heartbeat.

Here in the accelerated world, there was no way he should have been able to hear the sound of her heart beating in the real world. But it couldn't have been a hallucination. He strained his ears and listened, and suddenly, Haruyuki understood.

This was the echo of Kuroyukihime's will. Right now, Kuroyukihime was fighting desperately. On the border between life and death, she was fiercely fighting to hold her ground. Her strong will became a heartbeat, echoing in the virtual battleground.

"Right," Haruyuki murmured. At the same time, new tears spilled out and trickled down warmly. In his ears, something Kuroyukihime had once told him echoed faintly.

In the end, strength doesn't mean winning.

It's like I never knew the meaning of the word strong. *And not knowing, I was jealous, and I gave up.*

"Strength isn't just winning…"

Even if it was ugly. Even if it was funny. Even if you lost in the end, fell to the ground, and ended up covered in mud.

After surviving the death match of the kings, Kuroyukihime—Black Lotus had held her breath in a tiny net and stayed hidden for two years. But it wasn't because she was sneaky or cowardly. It was because she hadn't given up. It was because she refused to hang her head in shame.

"Just fighting itself. Falling down and still looking up at the sky…That's the proof of strength. That's right, isn't it… Kuroyukihime."

He got no answer.

But he felt a powerful heartbeat being born deep inside his own chest. The pulsing of his heart became a signal to drive his brain. And then his spirit, his will, and the nerve to face adversity, all of it accelerated.

As long as this sound echoed in his chest…

"I'm still standing…I can still fight!" he screamed to himself and to Kuroyukihime.

Gripping the edge of the bed with his right hand, he put his strength into his left leg and stood up, staggering. Tiny shards glittered as they fluttered down from all over his body. However, the heat generated from within his chest reached to the tips of his four battered limbs, and he shivered fiercely.

Suddenly.

Several rays of intense white light shot out from the cracks in his armor.

At the same time, the armor on his back cracked wide open, and he had the sensation of it being blown off. Haruyuki opened his eyes wide and threw his head back.

On the wall not far in front of him hung a large mirror. It was probably the two-way mirror leading to the monitoring room next door in the real world. Now it was an enormous full-length mirror edged in the same black cast-iron roses as the bed. Reflected in its center were the rose bed, Kuroyukihime lying in it, and Silver Crow standing there.

The armor all over his body was in a terrible state. His left arm and his right leg were half torn off, and deep cracks radiated outward across his chest. The fractures also wrapped around to his back, which was the source of the cracking sound. Each time a tiny spark flew up, a piece of his smashed armor scattered.

Haruyuki stared dumbfounded as something white and shining started to very slowly spread out on each side of his back. Thin, sharply triangular shards of metal. Swords?

The moment he had this thought, the two pieces of metal stopped crawling out and expanded into semicircles with a cold, clanging noise. Perhaps ten thin metal fins folded up on either side were deployed, the tips of those initial sword-shaped protrusions as fulcrums.

This...this isn't a weapon...

They're wings.

Haruyuki stood dazed for less than a second.

Hot!

At the intense heat running through his body from the center of his back, Haruyuki snapped to attention. Writhing in agony, he retreated a few steps on his knees and drew his body in, cradling his shoulders in his arms. More than the temperature, he felt as though a ball of pure energy was sealed up in his back and was whirling around like a vortex, seeking a way out.

I can't. I can't stand it anymore.

Arching his body back like a bow, Haruyuki turned to look straight up.

There he saw the enormous hole he'd torn through the building only seconds earlier. A small yellow light alone up there in the deep, black sky. A corridor leading to the distant heavens.

It was calling to him.

In an unconscious motion, Haruyuki raised his shattered left arm high and pressed his uninjured right arm to his side. He felt the raging energy at the tips of his shoulder blades increase in intensity suddenly and then contract.

Bringing his eyes back down for just a moment, he saw the figure of his beloved lying there.

He looked up again.

"Gooooooo!!" He thrust his right arm straight out with a cry.

Fwoomp!!

With a half crash, half explosion, a silver light ripped through the darkness. Instantly, Haruyuki's body shot up in a straight line like an arrow released from its bow.

The air roared in his ears each time he passed a floor of the hospital.

Piercing the dark path in mere seconds, his silver avatar flew out through the large hole drilled through the roof and soared higher, ever higher. The metal fins on his back shook at high speed. The energy accelerated his small body with an overwhelming power, and he easily cut his ties to any virtual gravity. Haruyuki pushed up, up, endlessly up.

Soon enough, a swirling black cloud drew near. The moment his raised right fist came into contact with the thick lump, the round cloud was shoved aside with a *thud*, shooting through the black tunnel and ascending even farther. Haruyuki's field of vision was filled with a blinding, pale yellow light.

After passing through the sea of clouds, Haruyuki spread out his arms and legs and eased his acceleration. The high-pitched shuddering noise dropped in pitch, and a soft sensation of floating came over him, like being in a plane after takeoff.

Hovering gently, Haruyuki rolled over. "Aaah...," he half sighed. An unimaginable scene spread out below him. From the breaks in the sea of clouds twisting as they flowed along, he could make out the sharp colors of the enormous city sprawling endlessly. The building on the other side of the city subcenter of

Shinjuku transformed into twisted spires, and the deep wood beyond was probably the Imperial Palace, looking like a soaring, magical castle.

In the opposite direction, the city extended off into the distance from Suginami to Mitaka and on into Hachioji, with the Okutama Mountains beyond that. The steep mountain peak piercing the sea of clouds and towering high above them was probably Mount Fuji.

Finally, turning his gaze to the south, Haruyuki caught sight of a gray, flat plane glittering. *The sea. That's Tokyo Bay. And, extending limitlessly, the Pacific Ocean.*

Infinity.

"This world... it's infinite..." Haruyuki gasped as he started to descend ever so slowly.

Sinking into the clouds on his back, he slipped through to the bottom and approached the earth's surface. When he had dropped to an altitude where he could once more see the details of the city, he made the fins vibrate fiercely to hover again.

Directly below him as he straightened out was the roof of the hospital, a mere thirty meters away. After seeing the immensity of the Duel field, the roof looked small enough to pick up in both hands. Standing stock-still on the edge of the large hole piercing the center of the roof, a large blue figure looked up at him.

Cyan Pile stared up at Haruyuki for a full three seconds as if his soul had been ripped out. He raised his left hand slightly and said hoarsely, "H-Haru—"

But his words were erased abruptly in a sudden roar.

Voices. The members of the Gallery watching the Duel between Silver Crow and Cyan Pile encamped on the roofs of the buildings surrounding the hospital shouted out all at once.

"He's not... he's not falling?! He's perfectly still!!"

"It's not a jump... He's flying?! No way!!"

"He has the ability to fly... It's finally showing up! Check out those wings!! It's a flying avatar!!"

Haruyuki didn't understand why the members of the Gallery

were making such a huge fuss. As he stared down in mute amazement, some of the several dozen duel avatars were moving, aiming for ground higher, while others were running their fingers along consoles.

"Isn't there any info on him?! Who the hell is this guy?! His Legion... Who's his guardian?!"

"Wh-whatever! We need to contact the head office! You, drop and tell them!!"

"You gotta be kidding! You think I'm gonna miss this?!"

Quelling the beehive-like commotion was an abrupt, fierce scream.

"Aaaaaaaaaah!!" Cyan Pile howled, spreading out his arms and legs. The vibrations of his scream ripped the atmosphere, reaching Haruyuki in the sky far above like an electric shock. "No! No no no no no nooooooooo!!"

With a mechanical *crack*, the launcher in his right arm turned toward Haruyuki. "You!! You!! On me!! You don't look down on meeeeeeee!!" A cry like vomiting blood.

At the same time, a jarring screech echoed through the air, and the loaded stake sent out several rays of light. As he adopted a posture with both legs spread out, hips dropped, and launcher readied in his left hand, the remaining 40 percent of Cyan Pile's special-attack gauge dropped abruptly all at once.

In the sights of what was most likely Cyan Pile's final attack, Haruyuki, still hovering in one spot, raised his right hand lightly and closed it tightly into a solid fist. He finally understood what the special attack he had been given was.

Punch. And then Kick. While these were his normal attacks, they were also his special super attacks.

He pulled his tight fist back and expanded all his fins as far as they would go to change direction. Toward Cyan Pile, directly below him.

"G-gooooooo! Lightning Twin Spikes!" As he screamed the name of the attack, a steel needle, transformed into a beam of light, shot forward from Cyan Pile's right arm.

Faced with this, Haruyuki simply readied his fist and released the propulsive power from both wings.

"Unh! Aaaaaaah!"

Silver Crow's body became a bullet of light, a rocket engine igniting, and charged.

In the left corner of his vision, his green special-attack gauge started to drop all at once. At the same time, the radiance of the white light enveloping his right fist increased endlessly.

"Haruuuuuuuuuu!" Takumu screamed.

"Taaaaaaaku!" Haruyuki cried.

Skreeeee!

A feeling of super acceleration, greater than the acceleration of Brain Burst, rushed over Haruyuki from his back, enveloping him.

The color of the world changed.

He saw Cyan Pile's blue lance rushing up from the ground, the glint of the tip. The line of fire he had anticipated rose up in his vision like a phantom. The blow, like the lightning bolt of its name, was far surpassed by the speed of Haruyuki's spirit. The power of one truly accelerated, who Kuroyukihime had found and believed in.

I can see it...I can see it, Kuroyukihime!! Haruyuki cried in his heart.

The lance slowed.

Before it, Silver Crow increased his speed limitlessly, as if his very existence had become light itself.

At the moment the two approached and blended, Haruyuki slid his charging trajectory slightly to the right.

Skrrrrk!

The lance scraped the left side of his helmet and passed by, releasing an intense shower of sparks.

Then...

Haruyuki's punch penetrated deeply, ever deeper into the center of Cyan Pile's chest. Carving out a gaping rut in the floor of the roof with a shrieking roar, the two bodies became one and went flying.

Crashing into and pulverizing the railing of iron lances, sending bits in every direction, Haruyuki sprang out into the sky. "Aaaaah!!" he howled, flapping his metal fins.

A powerful, dynamic lift enveloped his body with a start. His right arm still buried up to the shoulder in Cyan Pile, Haruyuki turned upward and ascended ever higher. In a few seconds, he had pierced the sea of clouds and sailed out into the yellow sky.

When he eased up on the acceleration and shifted to hovering, Cyan Pile, who had apparently lost consciousness in the collision, made a coughing sound from under the mask riding on Haruyuki's shoulder. "Keh...Hrk..." The enormous body twitched and shuddered, and he gradually lifted his face.

An action that was immediately followed by a faint cry that seemed almost unreal after the previous angry roars of deep resentment. "Wh-wha—?! I-I'm flying...?!" Mask shaking from side to side, he shouted again. "Stop! Haru! D-don't drop me!! If I fall now, I'll...I'll lose!!"

Both of their health gauges were dyed red and had dropped so that they were no more than a hair's width. Cyan Pile stiffened as if fearing he'd be dropped if he moved, and his tone changed to one of supplication.

"I-if I lose...if I lose to you, and you're level one, my points will drop to zero! Y-you'll be fine. I mean, you'll only lose four or five points! Please! Let me have this one, Haru! I can't lose Brain Burst now!!"

"Taku...Takumu..." Half groaning, half muttering the name, Haruyuki firmly clenched his right fist, still piercing Cyan Pile. *Now? Now?! You tried to take all of Kuroyukihime's points... You tried to erase her Brain Burst, her only desire!*

All he had to do was change the angle of his arm slightly, and Cyan Pile's enormous body would lose its support and go crashing into the ground far below. Takumu would lose forty points,

and Brain Burst would be forcefully uninstalled. And then...
he would never again be able to come after Kuroyukihime from
outside the local net.

Haruyuki gritted his teeth hard enough to break them. His
entire body shook, and a momentary impulse ran from head to
foot before disappearing. The voice he pushed out from between
his clenched teeth was so cracked, it didn't even sound like his
own. "Do you concede, Taku?"

"Wh-what?"

"That you totally cannot beat me in this accelerated world. Do
you concede, Taku?!"

A moment's silence.

The words returned through the body pressed against him
were quiet, deflated somehow. "...Yeah. I do...I guess I can't
beat you, after all. Just like way back when we used to play all
those games together..."

Haruyuki inhaled deeply and exhaled. And then he said in the
same quiet voice, "Then...we're equals."

"Huh?! What...?!"

"In the real world, there's not a single thing I can beat you at.
But in this world, you can't beat me. We're equals. So...so—"

Cutting himself off and staring at the bluish-white eyes under
Cyan Pile's mask, Haruyuki continued. "So you...be...be my
ally, Taku. My friend. Fight as her servant from now on, like me."

Speechless, Takumu gasped sharply. After a while, a hoarse
moan slipped out from the thin slits. "...Idiot. You have to know
this, too, Haru. I know you do. Your guardian...Black Lotus...I've
been hunting her in secret from my own Legion. She's the biggest
traitor in the accelerated world! I mean...to fight on her side..."

"You're right, she is. She took down the Six Kings of Pure Color.
You can say it. It's fine. And I'll tell you something really good...
Look, that's how games are supposed to be."

Takumu reacted to the words Haruyuki uttered with a long
silence.

His response a few seconds later was tinged somehow with a

masochistic laugh. "Haru, would you really trust me? Like, if I said yeah right now, what reason would you have at this point to trust what I say? After I broke my Legion's rules, broke the rules of Brain Burst, and even betrayed both of my friends?"

"We're going to go and tell Chiyu everything." The second Haruyuki came back with this, Takumu gasped in shock again for what seemed like the hundredth time.

"What?!"

"Brain Burst, us fighting, and…all the feelings you and I have been hiding. We tell her everything." Haruyuki turned his gaze off into the infinite sky and continued slowly. "We probably have to start there. The three of us have been hiding things we shouldn't have. We've been suspicious of stuff we didn't have to be. Somewhere…we have to start over."

"…Start over…You really think we can, Haru? I…Chi's Neurolinker…" Takumu's voice shook as he spoke, and Haruyuki lightly patted his back with the stub of his left arm.

"She'll probably be so mad, she'll kill us. She'll yell and get mad…but she'll forgive us in the end. That's how she is," Haruyuki said with a smile as he started to slowly descend.

Having returned to the hospital roof and been released from Silver Crow's right arm, Cyan Pile sank down to the ground with a *thud* after a few staggering steps.

Haruyuki glanced up to check the remaining time. In a little more than two minutes, the long fight would be over. Just in case, he checked his gauge, but the remaining health was exactly the same number for both of them. If they timed out like this, the result would be a draw, and no points would be transferred either way.

Haruyuki looked over again at Cyan Pile, motionless, head hanging between raised knees, and thought to himself, *I…Did I make a mistake? Should I have shown no mercy and dropped Takumu into the ground back there to make completely sure he couldn't break his promise after this fight and come after Kuroyukihime?*

No. No, I can't. Suspecting people, trusting people, it means suspecting yourself, trusting yourself.

I trust the me who Kuroyukihime told she likes.

I trust the me who decided to believe Takumu.

That's enough.

Immediately after he told himself this, the elevator doors opened behind him, and a heavy metallic noise reverberated through the air.

His whole body stiffened with a start, and in the instant before he spun around, Haruyuki guessed who he would see before him and was then certain of it.

It couldn't possibly be a new enemy. Because the only people who could attack and be attacked in this stage were Haruyuki and Takumu. And it wouldn't be an unfamiliar duel avatar. There was no reason for an unconnected spectator to appear from within the hospital.

However, the moment he actually confirmed his hunch with his own eyes, Haruyuki stopped breathing, his chest was full of something hot, and tears spilled out of both eyes.

A pure black, as if a distillation of the essence of darkness. Edges gilded in a dazzling silver. The cold wind blowing past made the long rolls of hair and the hem of the skirt flutter, and the bells decorating the parasol rang softly.

"Kuro…yukihime…" His wrung-out voice trembled faintly like a small child's.

Watching Haruyuki dragging his shattered leg, taking one step, then another, Kuroyukihime's face twisted up and broke into a grin at the same time.

"Kuroyukihime!!" Finally able to cry out in a proper voice, Haruyuki ran as fast as he could, making an irregular metallic noise.

Kuroyukihime also ran toward him, high heels ringing out sharply.

Both stretching arms out straight ahead, neither showed the

slightest hesitation or timidity in leaping into the open arms of the other.

Hugging her sweet, softly scented body with all his might, Haruyuki cried, almost groaning, "You...you're awake!! I'm so glad...I knew it, I knew it. I knew you'd make it...I'm so glad... so glad..."

Kuroyukihime, holding onto Haruyuki as if wrapping him up, snuggled against his cheek silently for a moment. "In the darkness, no heaven, no earth...All I heard was your voice. I...You saved me. And got hurt so badly..." The whispered voice that finally echoed in his ear was similarly wet.

Her right hand gently stroked Silver Crow's broken body. "You're shattered...Thank you. Thank you, Haruyuki."

"No...you're the one who saved me. Because you told me...to believe in myself, so...I could fly."

Nodding silently several times, Kuroyukihime stretched a hand out to trace the edge of a thin wing extending from Haruyuki's back. "They're beautiful...This is your power, the potential hiding in Silver Crow. Until now...there's never been a duel avatar realizing the ability of pure flight. I knew my prediction wasn't mistaken. You really are the one who's going to change this world."

Kuroyukihime gently brought Silver Crow's small body down to the ground with both hands. Tilting her head to the side and smiling, she looked down at him, and the ephemeral silhouette of the fairy princess spoke in a slightly forceful tone. "It seems the time has come...the time when I must also emerge from my safe cocoon and aim for the sky again."

She glanced behind her. Cyan Pile, seated a ways off, head still hanging, had raised his eyes only slightly to watch the two of them.

"You as well...I've wronged you, eh, Cyan Pile?" The words Kuroyukihime uttered were unexpected. "On more than one occasion, I sullied Duels with you, Duels that should have been full of honor. Shall I show you now? My true form. And if you wish it, I will engage you with all my might." She raised her right hand to quickly move her virtual cursor.

Suddenly, the fairy princess avatar was shrouded in repeated surges of black lightning.

Her silhouette, engulfed in a bluish-purple light before Haruyuki, who hurried to take a few steps back, began to change shape slowly, bit by bit. The skirt that reached nearly to the floor shortened all at once and split into sharp notches. Hands and feet snapped out into perfectly straight lines, tips converged into needles. The long hair dissolved and disappeared in the light, and in its place, a mask appeared in the shape of a bird of prey, wings stretching out to the back. Finally, one last, terrible bolt of lightning struck, and all the effects disappeared.

Standing before them was a beautiful—extraordinarily beautiful, as if carved out of a black crystal—duel avatar.

Her overall form resembled Silver Crow somehow. But she was much taller, more than 170 centimeters. Her body, encased in flowing, seemingly transparent black armor with a straight line at its core, was slender like a doll's and connected to an armor skirt resembling a black lotus around her hips.

More than anything else, the limbs were her main feature. Both arms and both legs were long, sharp swords, enough to send a chill up the spine. The bright, glittering edges that looked as though they could immediately bisect anything touching them rang out crisply in the slight wind of the stage. The front surface of the angular head, with a *V* reaching out behind it, was a pair of goggles like an inky black mirror. Inside, two bluish-purple eyes shone with a humming, vibrating sound.

Haruyuki just stood there for a moment as if the wind had been knocked out of him. Farther off, he sensed Cyan Pile, similarly speechless. Both were overwhelmed at the almost violent beauty of this figure and the boundless potential seeming to radiate from the slender, pitch-black body.

Haruyuki was convinced that if he found himself in a Duel with her, he wouldn't have to wait more than a second before he was sliced into thin pieces and eliminated. Finally, he pushed a voice somehow resembling a sigh from his chest. "You're beautiful...so beautiful...Before, you said you were ugly, but...you're not at all..."

"Mm. I wonder..." Only the voice was the original Kuroyukihime's. "I don't even have any hands to hold someone else's—" She didn't get to finish.

Cries of surprise filled the air all at once at an incredible volume from the surrounding buildings.

"Whoooaaa! Oooooh?!"

"That's...That duel avatar...!"

"Black Lotus!! The Black King!! She's alive!!"

The shouts from the Gallery were clearly several times louder than at the appearance of the flying Silver Crow.

Kuroyukihime glanced around and shrugged lightly before saying, "Well then...Silver Crow. Perhaps you could fly away with me?"

"Huh? Uh, sure."

No matter how great her potential, she didn't actually weigh any more than Cyan Pile. But however willing he was to fly off with her, there was still the question of how.

In front of Haruyuki in his confusion, Kuroyukihime hovered with a faint vibration noise and turned to her right casually before raising both arms and dropping her hips. Almost as if she was urging him to pick her up and carry her across an unknown threshold.

Although he wondered at this, he could definitely not run away here, not at this point. Sweat dripped across the surface of his silver helmet—or rather, he had that illusion as he awkwardly stuck out both arms and fastened them around Kuroyukihime's waist.

"Please and thank you," she said, sounding somehow excited, before leaning back into his arms with a slight *thump*.

As Takumu, seated, gave them a slightly teasing look that he could well have been imagining, Haruyuki readied himself and lifted the black crystal avatar. Fortunately, she turned out not to be so heavy, and he made the fins on his back vibrate fiercely before kicking off with one foot. Accelerating moderately, he aimed for the sky.

Against his chest, Kuroyukihime craned her neck to look out at the city below them and cried out in a subdued voice, "This is…amazing! I could get addicted to this…The next time we direct and have a Duel, I want to spend the whole thirty minutes flying…Oh, here's good."

"Okay." Nodding, Haruyuki switched to hovering.

They weren't so high up. Below them, they could clearly make out the countless duel avatars looking up at them from the roofs of the buildings, still yelling and shouting.

Kuroyukihime drew in a deep breath and shouted in a crisp voice that seemed to reach all the way to the distant horizon. "Hear me!!"

In an instant, the entire stage fell into silence.

"Hear me! You Burst Linkers before me, Legions of the Six Kings! My name is Black Lotus! I am the one who fought against the rule of the usurper kings!"

The twisting black clouds grew shorter and even the blowing wind held its breath. The only thing still moving in his field of view was the timer with ten seconds left on the clock. In the quiet, the ringing proclamation echoed endlessly.

"I and my Legion Nega Nebulus come forth from behind the veil of obscurity to destroy this false peace! Take out your swords! Call up your flames! The time to fight…has come!!"

9

Indian summer.

What month is that again? Haruyuki wondered as he walked along the road to the now–completely familiar hospital. The rhythm the soles of his shoes tapped out on the paving stones increased unconsciously. *If I keep speeding up, I'll be covered in sweat by the time I get there,* he thought, but even so, he couldn't hold back.

Today was the day Kuroyukihime would finally be moved from the ICU to a general ward.

Since visits were naturally not permitted in the ICU, it had in fact been three weeks since they'd actually seen each other face-to-face. So he really couldn't help it if he was a little lighter on his feet today.

The instant classes were over, he'd dashed out of school, so the sun was still high, and the light, warm for October, beat down on his back. At the school gates, the newspaper club shock troops who had somehow managed to get wind of the news were standing waiting, but he'd activated his now-rusty run-and-escape skill and had managed to break away beyond the reach of the local net.

The fact that he was so lighthearted was also partly because yesterday, Sunday, he had hung out with his oldest friends for the first time in a very long time.

Except for when they went up the new Tokyo Tower and Haruyuki accidentally connected to the sightseeing guide net and ended up getting challenged to a Duel (with the super-high-altitude local advantage, he just barely won), it was a very problem-free, fun day off.

The day of the fight three weeks earlier, Haruyuki and Takumu had gone together to Chiyuri's house and confessed everything in Chiyuri's bedroom, all of it: the reason Takumu told Chiyuri he liked her two years before, why Takumu had been gradually pressed against a wall since then, and why now, all of a sudden, Haruyuki and Takumu had pitted themselves against each other in battle.

Chiyuri had a hard time believing that Brain Burst actually existed. They finally managed to get her to accept it after they accelerated and took care of all the homework Chiyuri had been given that day in one-point-eight seconds, but the biggest hurdle was still ahead.

When Takumu told Chiyuri about the back-door virus he got from his guardian, the Blue Burst Linker who served as his kendo team captain, that he had used to infect her, Chiyuri exploded many times more fiercely than Haruyuki had predicted, chasing them both out of her apartment, screaming all the while that she hated them and they were through forever.

The following week, Chiyuri wouldn't talk to them, but over time, she made allowances in her own way for Takumu's feelings, and she forgave them—almost like she wondered if she was part of the reason Takumu felt forced to that extreme—on the condition that they treat her to all the finest parfaits she could eat.

The truth of the matter was that Chiyuri and Takumu were still somehow awkward together, even now. But Haruyuki believed that time would fix that, too.

Because it had taken ten years, but Haruyuki and Takumu finally had the relationship Chiyuri wanted. They really were best friends.

In fact, they were probably more than that.

Silver Crow and Cyan Pile were now a tag team fighting side by side in Kuroyukihime's Legion.

Smiling and saying hello to the female nurse whose face he had at this point memorized, Haruyuki signed into the hospital net and set his sights on the hospital's top floor at the limits of permissible speed. He got out of the elevator he had used in the Duel and arrived at the navigation line leading to the room number he had sent by mail.

In the middle of the bouquet of pink baby's breath and the tropical water lilies in his right hand was a bud that was as close to black as possible. Since it was out of season, it had cost more than he had expected, and he had ended up spending what little money he'd been saving up for a new game on it, but he had somehow lost the desire to buy new games anyway. No game in the world could possibly be as stimulating as Brain Burst.

After he had taken just a few steps, the navigation line abruptly disappeared from sight. In front of him was the sliding door of a private room in the southeast corner of the top floor.

"Ummmm." Haruyuki swallowed with a gulp and rehearsed in his mind what he should say. *Congratulations… That's good, right? No, wait, it's not like she's been discharged from the hospital yet. Maybe that's kinda weird. Good job… That's obviously wrong. It's been a while…Something like that? But we see each other every day on the net. Um, aah, I don't know.*

Shmp.

The door in front of him abruptly slid open, and Haruyuki, flustered, jumped back.

As he did, a scolding voice came from inside. "Look, you. Just how long do you intend to make me wait? Hurry up and get in here!"

"Uh, okay!" he cried in a pitiable voice, and, pulling his shoulders in as far as they would go, Haruyuki took an exaggerated step over the threshold. Once he heard the door close behind him, he timidly raised his face.

In that instant, the large room, the scene outside the window, even the large bed disappeared from view. Haruyuki's eyes took in only this girl he hadn't seen in three weeks, wearing a black cardigan over cute pink pajamas.

She was a little thinner, maybe. Her skin, already pale, had lost even more color so that it was almost translucent. The normally free-flowing, silky hair was tied up tightly in braids, and her right leg was completely covered in a large cast.

But...

Those eyes. Those large, pitch-black eyes alone shone exactly as they always had, as if they had stars locked up inside them, welcoming Haruyuki.

Kuroyukihime smiled like a flower opening up and said in a slightly hoarse voice, "Hey... it's been a while, Haruyuki."

"Uh... uh-huh."

All the lines he had thought up flew out of his head, and Haruyuki simply nodded sharply, blinking several times.

After they had stared at each other like this for nearly ten seconds, Haruyuki finally returned to his senses and took a few steps forward to offer up the modest bouquet. "Uh... um, here. It's small, but..."

"Thanks." Kuroyukihime grinned, taking them from him. She brought them to her face and inhaled their scent. "Black lotus, hm? I look forward to it blooming. There's a vase over there. Could you put them in water for me?"

"Okay!"

Haruyuki took the small vase from the sideboard, filled it with water in the sink in a corner of the room, put the flowers in it, and returned.

Once again, silence.

It was Kuroyukihime who untangled their eyes glancing past each other. The expression on her face became suddenly severe and, clearing her throat lightly, she said in an increasingly hard tone, "Now then... shall I hear you report on that matter? Sit in the chair there."

"Oh...O-okay."

Right, this is no time to be giddy. Feeling a tinge of sadness at the thought, Haruyuki gently lowered his body into the guest chair.

Flicking around on his virtual desktop, he slid the report he had put together over to Kuroyukihime. "Ummm...so, for the back-door program that Taku's guardian had several of his subordinates test in absolute secrecy, a patch for the matching server came out last week, and it's completely unusable now. This guardian was 'executed' within the Blue Legion. I mean, it looks like he had all of his points taken away from him. But he still didn't spill the beans about who the program's creator was."

"Hm, I see." Kuroyukihime exhaled shortly and rested her head on intertwined fingers. "Most likely, a yellow, expert at exploiting weaknesses, was the originator. Especially given that whoever it was had it tested out on the top brass of an enemy Legion. Well, one of these days, I'll yank that black curtain up." Muttering this dangerous line as she moved the tips of the fingers of her right hand like a sword, Kuroyukihime recomposed her expression and looked at Haruyuki. "So how is it? My Legion."

"Right...well, I have to say it's bit by bit, but we're slowly getting control of Suginami Area numbers three and four."

"Ha-ha-ha!" Kuroyukihime's shoulders shook lightly as she laughed. "A modest territory. But it's wonderful. Just right for a Legion made up of three people."

The Black Legion, Nega Nebulus, was once an enormous group, ranked alongside the Legions of the six kings, but with the events two years earlier, it had apparently gone the way of dissolution and disappearance. Her spectacular proclamation of the Legion's return was fine as far as it went, but as of now, the only three members were Kuroyukihime, Haruyuki, and Takumu. And Black Lotus, as the world's most powerful traitor, wouldn't be able to appear in any Duels for the time being. They had their hands full just protecting the field around Umesato Junior High.

As if reading Haruyuki's mind, Kuroyukihime said, smiling,

"Don't be so down. There's no need to hurry. We'll gain companions gradually and slowly expand our area."

"R-right." Haruyuki nodded.

When he went to wipe away the slight sweat beading on his face because of this first real-life meeting in some time, he stuck his hand in the pocket of his uniform, where his fingers struck something other than his handkerchief. He pulled the completely forgotten item out. The student agenda with the blue cover that had never been used for its original purpose. Kuroyukihime's.

"Oh…right. I was hanging on to this for you. Here." Not thinking too hard about what he said, he offered her the agenda.

Seeing it, Kuroyukihime blinked with surprise and opened her mouth slightly before her cheeks suddenly flushed bloodred. Snatching the agenda away from him, she pressed it to her chest and turned her face downward. "Did you look inside?" A question uttered in a voice that was almost disappearing.

Haruyuki finally grasped the reason for Kuroyukihime's reaction. "Oh! No! Yes! No, uh, well…I—I did…"

Silence.

Abruptly, a short phrase cut through the extremely dense, frozen air. "Forget it."

"…Huh?"

"Erase it from your memory and never speak of it again. And if you mention this in the future, you'll learn exactly what someone with level-nine special attacks can do."

Eeaah?!

Swallowing this cry, Haruyuki shook his head vehemently. "I won't say anything! I won't remember it! Oh, I've forgotten, I've already completely forgotten it!"

She glared sideways at Haruyuki dripping with sweat, standing at attention, and a chastising smile rose up on her face. "Honestly. Even though the name Silver Crow is known across the accelerated world at this point, you're still the same old you, aren't you, Haruyuki?"

Slightly releasing the tension in his shoulders, Haruyuki

returned, "A-and this scary part of you hasn't changed at all, either…Black Lotus."

"Well, that's unexpected. I'm always so kind…Anyway, Haruyuki." She cleared her throat with a cough and sat up straight again before continuing with a gentle smile, "Maybe it's time for you to get it together and just call me by my name, instead of my nickname."

"Oh!…R-right." Nodding sharply, Haruyuki realized with a start a single preposterous fact. "Uh…um."

"Hm?"

"I…I…Your real name…I don't…know it…"

Snap.

The world froze again almost like when he was accelerated—no, harder and thicker than that.

But Kuroyukihime's laughter mixed with a sigh melted it soon enough. "You…I thought you looked in my agenda?"

"Oh! I…I just glanced in it once, at the start…"

"Ha-ha. Of course. That's very you, Haruyuki. Well then, let's introduce ourselves anew, shall we? That said, it's not that different from my nickname."

A gentle breeze blew in through the slightly open window, gently diffusing the scent of the black lotus. Stretching her thin body up straight, she clasped both hands in front of her chest.

The beautiful older student and rebel black king said in a clear voice, "My name is…"

END

AFTERWORD

I'm not sure when it started exactly, but whenever I'm faced with something, I always end up preparing for disappointment and discouragement.

Always expecting and preparing for the worst is not such a great thing as all that. The only thing is that if you give up right from the start, you at least can get away with using less energy when you do really end up failing.

When I started writing this story in October 2007, I was pretty sure I wasn't actually going to finish it or anything. And when I did finish it, I was convinced I wouldn't get all the deletions and revisions done to meet the guidelines of the Dengeki Prize. I continued to tell myself, as a matter of course, even after I sent my submission in, that there was no way I was going to make it through all the stages of judging.

Thus, on the occasion of winning the prize and being published, I was obviously not prepared to do things like write an afterword like this, and as of this moment, I am still at a total loss. I want to write something rich with brilliant insight and style, along with a wafting of sad pathos in the midst of vital humor, but since not one of these things is popping into my head, I'll simply write down what I'm feeling at this point in time.

For me, it's already a miracle that I managed to write this story.

Because as I write this afterword for the pocket book edition, an extension of the writing of the story, I can't even guess at how minuscule the likelihood that it would have become a reality.

Haruyuki, the protagonist of *Accel World*, is also someone who tries not to hope for too much. But where he is decisively different from me is that Haruyuki will squeeze out every last drop of energy he has to keep running away. He's incredibly dedicated to his pessimism.

This is just my thinking, but whatever trajectory it might take, as long as you at least have the energy, something is bound to happen at some point. Haruyuki's dedication can't be beat, but if there is a reason I won this prize other than miracles and luck, I think it might be the meager energy I stored up being pessimistic.

For my rough manuscript submission to become a proper book like this, I was honored to have the invaluable assistance of so many people.

Minoru Kawakami, not only for taking time out of his busy schedule to write the commentary, but also for his many suggestions for important parts of the action scenes. The *Accel World: Kawakami Edition* he wrote for this book is one of my most cherished treasures.

Hima, who drew so wonderfully my protagonist whose visualization I had expected to be fraught with difficulty. The other characters, too, are so vibrant that I almost think that this is how they always were; my own image of them has changed.

My supervising editor, Kazuma Miki, who always gave me guidance with such patience and careful kindness when I definitely could not be said to be obedient, despite the fact that I was a newbie who didn't know left from right. If I can always have this fountain of editorial power with me, I will continue to tap away at these keys with everything I've got.

And the many people who have been supporting me these last

seven years on the global net. It was precisely because of all of your support that I am here now.

Finally, my greatest gratitude to you for reading this far. Thank you so much.

November 28, 2008
Reki Kawahara

COMMENTARY

NOTE

Below begins my own (Minoru Kawakami) version of an *Accel World* commentary, but please understand there's nothing official about it. Officially, it's Reki Kawahara and Hima. I ask for your understanding on this matter.

So there we have it and here we are. I'm Minoru Kawakami. I'll be your guide through the commentary for this book. Although, well, I was going to give you a commentary, but I got stuck-ish on how exactly to do that. Which is why, here, I'm doing something like summing up the things I imagined while reading in a short story, together with in-their-brain character profiles. I have seen absolutely none of the images by the artist or anything, so these images are entirely the product of my own brain. If I am able to expose the commonalities between and differences from your own impressions after having read the book, I'd like to make that in and of itself the commentary. Oh, I definitely plan to get permission from Reki Kawahara and Mr. Miki, the supervising editor for this work. Now then, please join me for a moment.

Well, hello there, ladies and gentlemen! My name is Kawakami; I'm a second-year junior high school student with a duel avatar called "White Turnip." I have an old-looking face, and there are times when I seem to be more than thirty, and a little girl who sat in front of me on the train uttered the terrible words, "Mama, it's a murderer," but I am, in fact, a junior high student.

Like all of you, I'm also just another Burst Linker, but I'm not anything close to a fight freak like you. Things like that, that's the realm of children— Eep, sorry. I said too much. Let's see, to go back to who I am; I'm a programmer working to create improvement mods for Burst Linking.

For the Brain Burst world, a programmer like me is only there to provide elements of abundance or of bad health. But as long as we don't put together various types of the latter or as long as these combinations don't leak if they are put together, programmers are basically protected from every faction as contributors to the Brain Burst world. Which is to say, we're exempt from Duels and protected from unfair Duels. And if we're taken in by a faction, we get the burst points of those punished, so we level up quickly.

I also work under the patronage of a certain faction, but I make programs that are shared by all Burst Linkers. With the programs I make, first of all, the faction I belong to buys it with burst points, and then the faction's Blocker sells it to people in the Duel Gallery, in effect making the program a faction asset. There's competition and the commotion of changing teams for programmers like myself, and life gets quite busy even though we essentially have an indoor job.

And now I'm making—you could almost call it my specialty at this point—a forwarder to send information from meatspace to an avatar in the Burst Link world. This forwarder will tell you what meatspace you is sensing and feeling while you are in the Brain Burst world, compressed a thousandfold.

…You say we don't really need something like that? That you're sped up over a thousand times, so even if you don't go back and check on your body, it's less than two seconds anyway?

I wonder. One: Let me first talk about something only the guys will understand.

Okay?

It takes point-three seconds for your mother to open the door behind you and come into your room.

Get it?

If you're watching porn videos or in the middle of playing an erotic game, and you end up wanting to Burst Link because that stuff is just not getting you hard enough and you need more, and this slight return time lag might leave a stain on the memory of your boyhood years…When you think of it like that, the alarm to warn you that your mother's in the room (abbreviated to "mother room") in the forwarder I'm making becomes an essential item.

Oh, I don't know about women. Hmm, that's one unknown set of unknowns to work out.

However, currently, we've moved past version seven, and we only take burst points at updates, but I suppose this, too, is the style of a long unbroken line of programmers. My grandfather was an erotic-game programmer from the eight-bit era; he apparently fired a barrage of empty dialogue into the empty sky even as he was dying. He really was a model man. Although it's a mystery as to how he ever got married.

And then the grandson of this remarkable man, me, also developed a taste for the X-rated games at the age of thirteen, and now I spend my days in the real world earning small change by unlocking the hardware on my friends' Neurolinkers and making them region free. Heh-heh-heh, you guys, the text in the erotic games you all are playing now is a remake of the hot text my grandpa came up with sixty years ago. But Grandpa had Beast attributes. Can't fight your blood. Oh, but I do wonder what kind of impressions he would've had if Grandpa had managed to live to the present day and age. No, forget it. I mean, Grandpa was a 2-D kind of guy, a world where polygons are useless. The one time I brought it up, we got into a fight in the bath. You can't push your values on a kid. You gotta leave it to genetics.

In any case, I'm now testing version eight of the current program, and I seem to be plunging into some incredible areas as I do. I've come to understand the Brain Burst system, and I'm finally able to not just raise an alarm with the information from meatspace, but to forward the actual experience itself.

It may be stretched out a thousand times, but you can bring your five senses from the real world over to this side. You probably think there's no point in this. Because when you stretch out sound or whatever a thousand times, it simply gets stretched out, and that's that.

But right now, the truth is, meatspace me is in the middle of dinner. And I'm testing version eight.

Do you get what I mean?

Exactly. In my meatspace mouth right now is curry on a spoon.

Right, you get it, don't you?

My mouth is already closed, and the heat of the curry is pressed up against the roof of my mouth; the soft grains of rice are spilling over onto my tongue; the spicy sweetness slipping up my nose is the very essence of the Vermont curry. Medium-spicy for a junior high student...!

Because this is prolonged a thousand times, the heat of this spoonful of curry and rice will continue to sit in my mouth and on my teeth for thirty minutes. For the next thirty minutes, whatever I do, whether I go for a walk, look up at the sky, look down, sit in the Gallery, get in a Duel, go to sleep, the curry will be with me the whole time!

How about that?

Even if you were to lose a Duel, if you had curry the whole thirty minutes, don't you think you'd be glad you leapt into this Burst world?!

However... when you return to meatspace, you eat the rest! That is the curry that is a thousand times plus one!

But! But it doesn't stop there. Human beings have more darkness in them than that.

Yes. If you get the timing right in meatspace, you can make every pleasure continue a thousand times longer in the Burst world.

Whoa.

Get it? Taking things simply in the erotic direction is a junior high–level reaction, isn't it? Oh, I'm a junior high student, so I already did that. No, i-it's a test, okay? A test! A test!! Well, I did give a midterm exam to my erotic-game partner in my house, but apparently, after crying out sharply in a strange voice for about five minutes on the floor of the other world, there was some kind of feedback in my flesh-and-blood body and meatspace me had a heart attack and nearly died. On the Burst side, too, you are utterly defenseless faced with your male destiny because you are completely impotent at fighting.

But that was a close one. I'd be in serious trouble if I died and the parent who found me at the scene misunderstood. Father, Mother, your son is not the kind of man who would die playing older-sister-type erotic games. That is precisely because he is one thousand times faster. If it was the blond, big-tit type, I'd probably die at five times.

Which is why that time the "winged one" that everyone's talking about who somehow managed to start up a Duel with me was apparently looking for me and loitering around outside, but he would never even dream I was in my house, tossing my head back, pounding away, happily crying out, "Eeeaaah! Kawakami sweat's comiiiiiiing!" throwing away my life and my caste. I don't want to think about it, either.

But the worst damage might be the problems of the life and future production plans for the prosperity of my descendants, but that's the forward on the visual side. My luck being bad, leaving me staring at my face for thirty minutes in that instant, reflected in the window, scarred psychologically, and it really is regrettable. The next time I do it, I'll close the curtains, but I'll also do it when I'm fed up with everything and I die. It's actually kind of a tough thing.

But all you young men thinking you can't use this program. If that's the case, please listen carefully. This thousand-times forward, there are other ways to use it than just for sex.

That's right. Peeing.

The idea popped into my head the other day when I was standing there letting loose in the bathroom at school, and I went ahead and Burst Linked, but to be honest, I couldn't handle thirty minutes of letting it go. Also, it would be amazing if you could use your senses and make the opening like an anti-warship beam! It's like that thing, you know: how many pop bottles you can fill. Let's see, to put it into words, it was something like *E-everything in me is coming out*... Unconsciously, I went pigeon-toed, and during the thirty minutes I spent shaking like a Burst coward, the "staker" everyone's been talking about lately was apparently running around the halls looking for me, but he would never dream that my main battleground was the bathroom. I didn't really want to dream it, either.

In any case, you might think that version eight, with its greater destructive power, would probably bring about a rapid reform in the Brain Burst world, but that won't happen, since those guys who got wind of it early on kept complaining. I'll look into it a little more, and let's see, th-this is a test? A test, well, that's what I'd like to do, but those guys targeting the top brass of my faction come along, trying to find fault, all *You planning to sell to other factions?* Honestly, all of them, every single one, are perverted junior high students, which is seriously problematic. These guys who Burst Link those times they find a porn magazine on the roadside and pretend to pass by while looking them over a thousand times faster noodle around and feint each other out in the Burst world—all I can think is *You guys, okay.* I feel sorry for them, so I decide to pick it up in meatspace and flip through every page at high speed to show these Bursted guys. I get a lot of thank-you mails for these godlike actions with my consciousness in both worlds, but you know, you should do good deeds. Although when I folded the magazine up halfway through and took it home, the number of Duel request appointments was greater than four digits.

I've gotten a little off topic, but in any case, with this forward, my boss is targeting me, and it's super annoying.

Like the other day, just when I was shooting off a huge one in my main battlefield, and I was testing the program with the thousandfold pleasure of getting it out into the world, that idiot comes riding along—No, I can't call my boss an idiot, but he's an idiot. However, this idiot—No, no, he's my boss, so (omitted). In any case, that time, I prolonged a thousand times the information on "the sensation of the moment you stick your finger in your nose" that I had previously saved, and forwarded that to his ass, earning a trip to the hospital, but there's a limit to how many times I'll be able to pull through that. I've been thinking it's getting to be about time I left the faction and struck out on my own, and today, I'm planning to go and take some temporary measures.

That's why I'm going to sell this forward, and, well, I'm deciding where to sell it. At the very least, it probably wouldn't be so great to let it be used for things like drawing out the pain of torture a thousand times or something.

I mean, Burst Linkers get hurt or sick in meatspace, too. Even if they can Burst Link in their hospital room, life in the hospital is pretty boring. However, if you have this program, you can stretch out the flavor of the snacks people bring you a thousand times. If you're limited to taste and smell, you don't just get the taste, you can also stop a flower or a moment in the season. Lately, there's also a faction of Burst Linkers who are taking care of hospital-related stuff and watching over people, so I have no doubt they'd pay big money for this thing.

But I'm also a heartless man. Yeah, I'll put this up for sale. As for payment, right. It'll be the price I feel like at the time, and you get to shake in your boots about when I'll come after you for some enormous sum after you've gotten your pleasure.

Now then, once I've eaten dinner, I guess I'll go and see those guys who've gotten some kind of clue. Oh, but I have to go to the bathroom first. It's nothing strange, gentlemen. It's the term-end test.

So something like that, I guess. The truth is this short story is something I sort of sent in after I accepted the job writing the commentary and dashed it off once my ideas solidified while chatting with Miki, the editor, immediately after I read the book. However, we did agree that this would be used as a bit of help in understanding the text; it really took it out of me, this job. Anyway, at the very least, all of you having finished reading the book no doubt had the sense of looking at the world outside and feeling that someone over there was fighting at a thousand times the speed. I think it's a novel that really has an appeal like a tool to stimulate the imaginations of a wide variety of readers... Oh, I didn't mean stimulates like Kawakami sweat or anything like that. On a larger scale, like (omitted).

On the next few pages are drawings of the characters and their avatars like I see them in my head and miscellaneous impressions. The artist's drawings are the official ones, so this is just me playing around, and I'd just be happy if they were a stimulation for you.

HARUYUKI

I remember
that the
boy looked
up at the
sky then.

commentary

Maybe he tilted his head back. With Haruyuki, I'm sort of
worried about the distance from his mom. Thinking about
the structure of his house in the text, his mom did give
Haruyuki the room with the windows and took the inner
room for herself. Just wondering how Haruyuki understands this parent-child relationship. There's a lot of fun
you can have with this protagonist.

Haruyuki and Silver Crow, my style. Wondering what it would be like if the drive system and armor programs and data were depicted in parts. For the enhancements, it would be easy to have stabilized external parts for a Cyan-like body type, and internal improvements for a Crow-like mechanical type, but stability would be tough, maybe. Just blue skying here.

Silver Crow/Haruyuki

KUROYUKIHIME

The refined taste of the boy who falls in love with the dashing girl and her unbeknownst bloodshed

◆◆ commentary

An upperclassman like me, Kuroyukihime… Get out of here, you! The most fun person in life for no reason at all.

If Kuroyukihime was in disguise, she'd be in a skirt or something and the whole thing would be a sword covered by swords, and the parasol would be made of swords on top of one another and you could make it into a super sword or something. Just by squeezing her lower arms and below her knees in a vise, she'd end up like one of those round Daruma dolls. The swords coming from her chest are a manifestation of her caution with her own self, but in front of someone with whom she can let down her guard, the front is left out and it's a throbbing blade or something.

commentary

Kuroyukihime/Upperclassman

ANOTHER

●● commentary

Y-You guys! You're all in the way!
Cyan Pile is fearless in Kawahara's conception, but I was
all it'd be great if he could be like a gorilla shape or something, and then you could add in some enhanced
parts and beef up that silhouette. Or something.
Like no matter from where you were looking, his
eyes would be staring down at you. Chiyuri's
purple cat is as if you made a human-
shape avatar like a cat.

Hot/Cold?
No.
Pile/Cold.

Purple Cat/Cyan Pile/Chiyuri

ENDING

commentary

And so the commentary (?) comes to an end. The background is (incredibly hard to make out, but) modeled after Hikawa Shrine in Koenji. The Linkers are students who go to school just like other kids, but battles and everything start on their own initiative. When they're not fighting, it's regular life; I mean, it's basically the same as throwing yourself into a fight you're not forced into, which is to say, just like taking on reading or a video game. You're hoping to become totally focused on your own. I think I'd like this world, which has increased the number of my interests, factoring in my irritation, to always be accelerated. I'm not sure what I should think, what I should do. If the impatience and desperation of your own desires could move the world, then the acceleration of the kings should bring about the results they want. However, a boy leaps into the fray. This is the story of him always desperately accelerating. The boy who is always, always desperately accelerating. He is a desperate boy. Personally, I want to support people who are desperate. I wonder how it is for you.

Minoru Kawakami

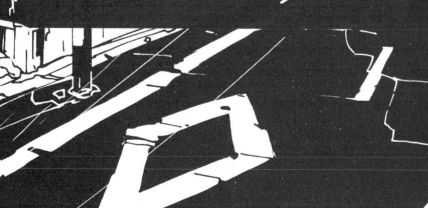

ACCEL WORLD, Volume 1
REKI KAWAHARA

Translation: Jocelyne Allen

ACCEL WORLD
© REKI KAWAHARA/KADOKAWA
CORPORATION ASCII MEDIA WORKS 2009
All rights reserved.
Edited by ASCII MEDIA WORKS
First published in Japan in 2009 by KADOKAWA
CORPORATION,Tokyo,
English translation rights arranged with KADOKAWA
CORPORATION,Tokyo,
through Tuttle-Mori Agency, Inc., Tokyo.

English translation © 2014 by Hachette Book Group, Inc.

Yen Press
Hachette Book Group
237 Park Avenue, New York, NY 10017

www.HachetteBookGroup.com
www.YenPress.com

Yen Press is an imprint of Hachette Book Group, Inc.
The Yen Press name and logo are trademarks of Hachette Book Group, Inc.

First Yen Press Edition: July 2014

ISBN: 978-0-316-37673-0

10 9 8 7 6 5 4 3 2 1

CW

Printed in the United States of America

What To Eat
When You're
Pregnant

PEARSON

At Pearson, we believe in learning – all kinds of learning for all kinds of people. Whether it's at home, in the classroom or in the workplace, learning is the key to improving our life chances.

That's why we're working with leading authors to bring you the latest thinking and the best practices, so you can get better at the things that are important to you. You can learn on the page or on the move, and with content that's always crafted to help you understand quickly and apply what you've learned.

If you want to upgrade your personal skills or accelerate your career, become a more effective leader or more powerful communicator, discover new opportunities or simply find more inspiration, we can help you make progress in your work and life.

Every day our work helps learning flourish, and wherever learning flourishes, so do people.

To learn more please visit us at: **www.pearson.com/uk**

What To Eat
When You're
Pregnant
Third edition

Including *the* A-Z of what's safe and what's not

Dr Rana Conway

PEARSON

Harlow, England • London • New York • Boston • San Francisco • Toronto • Sydney • Auckland • Singapore • Hong Kong
Tokyo • Seoul • Taipei • New Delhi • Cape Town • São Paulo • Mexico City • Madrid • Amsterdam • Munich • Paris • Milan

PEARSON EDUCATION LIMITED
Edinburgh Gate
Harlow CM20 2JE
United Kingdom
Tel: +44 (0)1279 623623
Web: www.pearson.com/uk

First published 2008 (print)
Second edition published 2012 (print and electronic)
Third edition published 2016 (print and electronic)

ISBN: 978-1-292-15510-4 (print)
978-1-292-15511-1 (PDF)
978-1-292-15512-8 (ePub)

British Library Cataloguing-in-Publication Data
A catalogue record for the print edition is available from the British Library

Library of Congress Cataloging-in-Publication Data
A catalog record for the print edition is available from the Library of Congress

10 9 8 7 6 5 4 3 2 1
20 19 18 17 16

Text design by Design Deluxe
Cover image © Britt Erlanson/Getty Images

Print edition typeset in 9.5/13pt NeoSansPro by iEnergizer Aptara®, Ltd
Print edition printed in Great Britain by Henry Ling Ltd, at the Dorset Press, Dorchester, Dorset

NOTE THAT ANY PAGE CROSS REFERENCES REFER TO THE PRINT EDITION

To my three beautiful babies –
Joseph, Daniel and Madeleine

Contents

About the author

Rana Conway is a registered nutritionist and a member of the Nutrition Society and the Association for Nutrition. Over the past 20 years she has established herself as an expert in nutrition for pregnancy and childhood. She has carried out research and lectured at leading universities and was awarded a PhD in 1997 for her research into the diets of pregnant women. She wrote the first edition of *What To Eat When You're Pregnant: Including the A-Z of What's Safe and What's Not* in 2008 and has also written *Meals Without Tears: How to Get Your Child to Eat Healthily and Happily* (Pearson, 2007), *Weaning Made Easy* (White Ladder, 2011), *What To Eat When You're Pregnant and Vegetarian* (Pearson, 2013), *Weaning Made Easy: Recipes* (White Ladder, 2014), *My Pregnancy Recipes and Meal Planner* (White Ladder, 2014). She lives in London with her husband and three children.

Acknowledgements

A big thank you to everyone who provided me with help, advice and encouragement in writing this book and earlier editions: Eloise Cook, Lisa Robinson, Rachael Stock, Emma Shackleton, Emma Devlin, Laura Blake, Joanna Pyke, Jane Graham Maw, Jennifer Christie, Patrick Bonham, Cherry Poussa, Deb Feuters, Dr Adrienne Cullum (NICE), Nadar Mazhar, Richard Laffar, Adam Hardgrave and Olu Adetokunbo (Food Standards Agency), Iain Gillespie (Health Protection Agency), Susan Furmage (Vegetarian Society), Jonathan Chapman and Kevin O'Hare (Sainsbury's), Rebecca Raynor (Prezzo), Conor Hughes (Bella Italia), Siobhan Rantanen (Tesco), Kirsten Michells (Tartex). Lastly, thank you to all the women who have told me about their food worries and to Olly Conway (editorial, computer and emotional support and husband).

Introduction

The food and drink you consume during pregnancy can have an enormous impact on the health and development of your baby. It also plays a crucial role in keeping you fit and well, at a time when your body is working especially hard. Eating regularly and having a well-balanced and varied diet is more important now than ever. But don't worry: this doesn't mean you have to follow a special strict diet or eat specific foods that you can't bear. You just have to think a bit more about your diet. Start by working out which healthier foods you actually enjoy and would eat regularly. It's important to be realistic when planning any changes to your diet, otherwise you will find it hard to stick to them. This book will show you how you can eat well without too much fuss. If the merest whiff of fish turns your stomach, or the thought of milk makes you grimace, it will point you towards alternative sources of omega 3s or calcium. Eating well should be enjoyable, not an ordeal.

As you read the chapters on healthy eating and essential nutrients, you will see that the best diet for pregnancy is not as complicated as you might think. This book identifies which foods are great for your growing baby and which ones you should try to avoid. It also explains how diet can be used to tackle common problems such as morning sickness, how to achieve a healthy weight gain and what to look out for if you are vegetarian. It should allay any fears you have and leave you feeling confident that you are doing the best for your baby. It also covers what to eat while breastfeeding, and the ideal diet to follow when you start thinking about your next baby. (If you are reading this book in anticipation of getting pregnant, then Chapter 11 is the best place to begin.)

Whatever stage you are at, once you know you are doing the very best for your baby and avoiding any problem foods, you will be better able to enjoy your pregnancy to the full.

Most women get plenty of general advice about healthy eating for pregnancy, but they can't always find answers to specific questions. If you are worrying about exactly which cheeses should be avoided or whether peanuts are OK, you'll find the answers here. The A–Z of foods means you can look up anything you're not sure about to discover whether it's safe to eat.

On the other hand, some women find they get too much conflicting advice, which can be overwhelming. To help anybody who is unsure about what to take seriously and what to ignore, we begin by looking at some common questions.

Common questions

Everyone disagrees about what you can eat. Who can I trust?

The advice provided by respected organisations is on the whole the same. This includes the Department of Health (DH), the National Health Service (NHS), the Food Standards Agency (FSA), Public Health England (PHE), the National Institute for Health and Care Excellence (NICE), the Royal College of Midwives (RCM) and the Royal College of Obstetricians and Gynaecologists (RCOG). The same advice is also given by GPs, midwives, health visitors and dietitians or registered nutritionists (who have the letters RD or RNutr after their name). Sometimes women are given advice by their doctor or midwife that goes against the latest guidelines but this is more likely to be because the doctor or midwife hasn't had enough time to investigate the latest recommendations, rather than a genuine difference of opinion.

The guidelines provided by these organisations and indi-viduals is based on scientific evidence and it is regularly updated. Unfortunately much of the dietary advice we now hear about comes from self-styled nutritionists and food bloggers, who may be beautiful and charismatic but lack a scientific understanding of nutrition. Alternative therapists may also come up with different suggestions. It is important to make sure that the advice you follow comes from suitably qualified organisations or individuals, that it is up to date and that it is relevant to the UK. Internet searching can bring up lots of conflicting recommendations and sometimes this is simply because it is out of date or relates to food risks in other countries, which may be different to those in the UK.

Internet chat rooms can be another source of conflicting advice: they may provide valuable support and a sense of camaraderie, but you should be careful about following sug-gestions that are not backed by experts. Frequently, women post messages such as 'I craved ripe Brie and ate it all the time I was expecting my son. He was a healthy 9lb baby, so soft cheese can't really be that bad!' or 'My homeopath told me to stop having dairy foods while I was breastfeeding and it cured my son's colic completely'. Such comments are, no doubt, well meant, but they don't prove anything. Many of us have heard about people who smoked 40 cigarettes a day and lived to 95, but we don't do it ourselves. Reports from individuals can be very compelling, but it is more sensible to follow advice based on research carried out with large numbers of women. Organisations such as the NHS, FSA and NICE offer such guidelines.

Occasionally there are genuine differences of opinion among experts, because clear evidence regarding the safety or health benefits of a particular food or drink is not available. There is a long-running debate about whether a small amount of alcohol is OK or if total abstinence is necessary. There are also disagreements over exactly how much oily fish pregnant women should eat, because of pollutants in the sea. When the findings of a new study are reported, it is crucial to consider them in the context of all the other available evidence and not simply rely on the media's interpretation.

The advice in this book is in agreement with the guidelines provided by the NHS at the time of publication (June, 2016). If you find differences this is probably because new evidence has been gathered and the NHS has changed its advice. It is best to follow the new NHS recommendations and the content of this text will be updated as soon as possible. You can also check my website www.ranaconway.com for updates.

How does the government decide what is safe?

When advising pregnant women about which foods are safe and healthy, expert groups take into account the best evidence available around the world. For example, when assessing how much oily fish you should eat, they will look at investigations into the relationship between fish consumption and birth weight. They will also use their knowledge of how the UK food industry works and look at data on food safety issues, such as surveys monitoring salmonella contamination in eggs sold in the UK.

Eating food, like crossing the road, or just about any other activity, carries some risk. Any food could be potentially dangerous. In the past, there have been cases of listeria and salmonella contamination in products as diverse as sandwiches and chocolate. Pregnant women are advised to avoid a particular food only if it has consistently been found to pose a risk to health and the consequences of eating it are thought to be significant. By taking into account all the evidence, it is possible to weigh up health benefits against potential risks for foods such as oily fish, blue cheese or pâté.

What should I do if I eat something I shouldn't have?

If you eat something and later find out it is on the 'avoid list', try to keep things in perspective. If you feel OK, then try not to worry. The chances of getting food poisoning on any single occasion are extremely small. Instead, remember that stress can have adverse effects on a developing baby, so try to relax and be glad you are not feeling sick.

If you do feel unwell, then it may be a coincidence or a result of something else, such as morning sickness, but go to your doctor as soon as possible. He or she will be able to assess whether you might have listeria, salmonella or any other form of food poisoning. If necessary, your doctor can arrange for you to be tested and, if the tests prove positive, for you to receive treatment to avoid the infection being passed to your baby.

I've never heard of anyone getting listeriosis or toxoplasmosis. Isn't the advice overcautious?

The chances of you getting any form of food poisoning are very small. However, you are more likely to get sick from something you eat when you are pregnant. This is because your immune system undergoes several changes so your body doesn't reject your growing baby. It is estimated that, during pregnancy, you are about 20 times more likely to get listeriosis.

Although you may not personally know anyone who has been affected by anything she ate during pregnancy, cases do occur every year. Around 50 babies are born with congenital toxoplasmosis because their mother was infected during pregnancy, and between 20 and 30 cases of listeriosis occur in pregnant women in the UK. The numbers are small, but given that infection could result in miscarriage or stillbirth, you can understand why women are advised to avoid particular foods during pregnancy. Ultimately it is up to the individual to assess whether any risk is worth taking.

Do I need to eat for two?

Yes, because what you eat and drink now will affect both you and your baby. However, if you mean 'do you need to eat twice as much as usual?', then this certainly isn't the case. Sorry to spoil any dreams you have of lying around eating chocolates. Current recommendations suggest that women don't need to eat any more than usual during the first six months of pregnancy; after that, they need only 200kcal (calories) extra a day. That is equivalent to an extra bowl of cereal, or a pot of yogurt and an apple, or a banana and a digestive biscuit, or one scoop of premium ice cream. It's best to follow your appetite, but also to stick to a healthy diet, and not use pregnancy as an excuse for getting fatter. If you do, you'll have the extra challenge of losing weight on top of looking after a baby.

How come French women are allowed to drink wine when they're pregnant and their babies are fine?

In France, as in the USA, Canada, Australia and New Zealand, pregnant women are advised not to drink any alcohol in pregnancy. The French, as a nation of wine drinkers, have traditionally been more relaxed about mums-to-be having the odd tipple, and we still have an image of sophisticated French women with a glass of red. However, in 2006 the French authorities brought in new guidelines recommending total abstinence, based on evidence that moderate levels of drinking were linked with permanent brain damage for the baby.

Some pregnant women in France still drink in moderation during pregnancy, but 'moderation' in France probably means less than here in the UK. A pregnant French woman would be very unlikely to drink spirits, and she would have only one small glass of wine with a meal – and then only occasionally. A British woman who drinks 'in moderation' is likely to have much more than this and she may also underestimate the number of units of alcohol she consumes (see page 50).

It seems like everything tasty is banned, so what can I actually eat?

We love to blame the 'Food Police' for spoiling our fun and making us eat nothing but vegetables. However, it is important to keep things in perspective. There is actually very little that is completely off-limits while you're pregnant.

The foods that make up the bulk of our everyday diets, such as bread, cereals and milk products, can still be enjoyed guilt-free, as can occasional treats like chocolate and chips. Most women find that only some of the advice about what to avoid is relevant to them. You might find, for example, that the guidance on pâté and oysters doesn't affect you because you never eat these anyway, but if your favourite cheese is Camembert you need to find something else, such as a mature Cheddar, to replace it. Or if you are craving Camembert and nothing else will do, have it hot.

In most cases, it is fairly easy to find an alternative for the foods and even the drinks that you enjoy. A decaf cappuccino can be a fairly good substitute for the real thing. Once you understand more about why pregnant women are advised to avoid certain foods, you will see that there are plenty of tasty things you can eat, or precautions you can take to make the foods you usually eat safer. If you are still feeling hard done by, remember that it's for a good cause, and it's not forever.

1 Healthy eating for two

Healthy eating is never more important than when you are pregnant. Your diet will affect you and your baby both now and for years to come. It may even influence your grand-children's health. In the immediate term, a healthy diet can help prevent gestational diabetes, constipation and other common pregnancy problems. It will also provide the energy and nutrients your baby needs to grow and develop in the coming months, so he or she has a healthy birthweight and is born at the right time. What you eat in pregnancy is also important for your child's long-term health. There is increasing evidence that a mother's diet during pregnancy affects whether her baby has allergies in childhood or develops heart disease in later life.

During pregnancy, your diet needs to supply all your normal energy and nutrient requirements, but it also has to:

- provide all the needs of your growing baby;
- fuel the growth of new tissue, including the breasts, uterus and placenta;
- lay down a store for the final weeks of pregnancy when your baby is growing rapidly, and for breastfeeding.

Enough calories for two

The total energy cost of pregnancy is estimated to be around 76,000kcal for a healthy woman gaining an average amount of weight. It sounds like a lot, but don't reach for the chocolate biscuits just yet. Changes to your metabolism, and a reduction in exercise and general activity, mean you don't actually need to consume many more calories during pregnancy than usual. In fact, for the first six months, women of a healthy pre-pregnancy weight don't need any extra calories at all. Then, during the final three months, they need only an extra 200kcal a day. This is the time when the baby is growing rapidly and laying down fat in preparation for birth.

Appetites vary greatly and some women find that they are incredibly hungry at the beginning of pregnancy, even though their baby is no bigger than a raisin. This is due to hormonal changes and the adaptations that the body is already making. Usually this settles down as pregnancy progresses. Energy requirements also vary from person to person according to a variety of factors, including weight and level of physical activity. If you are underweight you may need extra calories from the beginning. It is important to listen to your body but not to use pregnancy as an excuse for overeating.

Programming in the womb

What you eat now can affect your baby for life. We have known for some time that certain people have a predisposition to developing obesity, heart disease or other health problems as adults. We are now learning that this predisposition exists at birth and is due to both genes and the environment in the womb. Theoretically, two babies could have the same genes, but if one were born to a mother who smoked or was undernourished, he or she would be more likely to develop certain chronic diseases in later life. We don't know exactly why this happens, but it is believed that babies are somehow 'programmed' in the womb.

In the late 1980s, David Barker and colleagues started exploring the idea that the risk of developing certain adult diseases was associated with development in the womb. They found that in general babies whose birthweight was towards the lower end of the range were more likely to develop certain degenerative diseases in adult life, including obesity, coronary heart disease, stroke, type 2 diabetes and cancer. It seemed that if they were undernourished before birth, then their bodies adapted, ready for a life of food deprivation. When these babies then lived in an environment where food was actually abundant, their body couldn't cope. The real problem was the mismatch between the food supply in the womb and their later diet.

There has now been a considerable amount of research in the area and we know that it is not just undernourishment in the womb that is a problem. Babies with a mother who is obese or diabetic lay down extra fat and may even be programmed in the womb to have a bigger appetite, which therefore predisposes them to developing weight problems. A mother's intake of protein, omega 3s and certain vitamins and minerals can also affect the development of a baby's internal organs and metabolic systems. For example, her salt intake may affect the structure of her baby's kidneys which in turn affects how well that baby can cope with dietary salt in the future and his or her risk of developing high blood pressure.

It is only during the past five years or so that researchers have found out that what a woman eats during pregnancy actually affects her baby's DNA. These epigenetic changes, as they are known, affect the way the genes work although they don't actually change the underlying DNA sequence. One of the initial studies showed that eating a low-carbohydrate diet in early pregnancy could result in epigenetic changes that meant babies had more body fat as children. The researchers were surprised by how significant a difference early diet could make. The epigenetic changes due to a low-carbohydrate diet in early pregnancy explained a quarter of the difference in the children's levels of body fat six to nine years later. More recently it was found that women having a high-fat diet, and a high intake of saturated fat in particular, had babies with less muscle and more fat, which increased their risk of diabetes. In another study, epigenetic changes due to low B vitamin intakes were found to affect babies' growth in the first three years of life. This is a relatively new area of research and there is plenty more being uncovered.

Flavour-learning in the womb

The very first food your baby will taste is the amniotic fluid he or she is swimming around in. Flavour components from whatever you eat are transmitted to the amniotic fluid and swallowed by your baby so they start becoming accustomed to the foods you commonly eat. If you breastfeed, this transmission of flavours continues and starts preparing them for their first mouthfuls of solids.

You may wonder how we know this, but there are several pieces of evidence. Scientists have asked some women going for an amniocentesis to eat garlic beforehand and others not to. The amniotic fluid has then been smelt by several researchers, who have been able to identify the garlic eaters. We also know babies can detect flavours in the womb, as they appear to swallow more amniotic fluid when it's sweet and less when it's bitter. What's more, babies actually remember the flavours they first tasted in the womb and seem to like them. In a study where one group of women drank carrot juice during pregnancy their babies appeared to like it more when given it mixed with cereal. They actually ate twice as much as babies who hadn't tasted carrot juice in the womb. Early exposure to certain flavours before birth appears to prime babies, which makes perfect evolutionary sense, as it is a good idea for babies to eat the same safe food that their mothers would be likely to choose during pregnancy.

So you can start getting your baby used to a wide range of healthy foods before birth. However, this also means you have to be careful. Eating a lot of junk food in pregnancy may increase your baby's liking for the same high-calorie and low-nutrient foods. Animal research has shown that being exposed to junk food in the womb, and through breast milk, could desensitise the reward pathways in the baby's brain, so that he or she needs to eat more junk food than other individuals to experience the same feelings of pleasure.

Allergy-proofing your baby

In the past it was thought that by avoiding peanuts or other foods during pregnancy you could reduce your baby's chances of developing allergies. This theory has been tested in a number of well-conducted research studies, including trials in which some women have avoided certain foods during pregnancy and others have consumed them. It has now been concluded that avoiding foods such as peanuts, dairy foods, wheat or eggs during pregnancy is not beneficial. It does not appear to protect a baby from developing allergies, including food allergies, eczema, asthma or wheeze, and it can mean that both a mother and her baby miss out on essential nutrients. Some research suggests that restricting your diet could actually have the opposite effect. A study from Finland published in 2016 found that a high intake of milk products in pregnancy reduced the risks of having a baby with an allergy to cow's milk, especially in women who didn't suffer from any allergies themselves.

Although food avoidance isn't beneficial there are plenty of things you can do to reduce your baby's risk of developing allergies. Most of these boil down to avoiding junk food and eating a healthy well-balanced diet instead. For example, a Californian study of 1,200 pregnant women and their babies found that the more often mums-to-be ate fast food the higher their baby's risk of having asthma when they were three and a half years old. Having fast food 3–4 times a week doubled the asthma risk and indulging every day increased it by four and a half times. It could be something in the fast food itself or simply that these mothers are missing out on essential nutrients.

Several studies have looked at the protective effect of antioxidants. In one such Australian study it was found that higher vitamin C intakes in pregnancy were associated with a reduction in food allergies and wheeze in children. Another study, carried out in Scotland, found that vitamin E in pregnancy was linked to children being less wheezy. Among the Scottish mums who suffered eczema-type problems it was also found that higher vitamin E intakes protected their children from developing similar skin problems. The best way to ensure an adequate supply of antioxidants is to have a good intake of fruit and vegetables. Opting for supplements instead may not have the desired effect.

Iron has also been found to be protective, with several studies showing it reduced the risk of wheezing and eczema. Other studies have found that adequate vitamin D levels offered some protection against wheeze by affecting the way cells lining the airways respond to substances that could potentially cause a reaction. Fish oils have also been shown to help prevent allergic conditions. Australian researchers found that when pregnant women took fish oil supplements, their babies were three times less likely to show signs of egg allergy at one year of age. The researchers had hoped the supplements might also reduce the incidence of eczema, but this wasn't the case. However, babies whose mothers had taken fish oil did have significantly milder symptoms of eczema.

All this evidence suggests the best way to allergy-proof your baby is to follow the general healthy eating advice for pregnancy (see page 12). Some researchers, rather than looking at nutrient intake, have focused on the potential benefits of probiotics and prebiotics (see pages 156-157). One trial found that children exposed to a probiotic (given to their mother before birth and to them for six months) were much less likely to have eczema at the ages of two and four years than those receiving a placebo. Other studies have found that a combination of several probiotics along with a prebiotic offers similar protection. However, not all research has found an effect, so some probiotic strains may not offer any benefit. It seems more promising to focus on following healthy eating guidelines, and this will also benefit other aspects of health.

Don't let allergy warnings alarm you
There is no need to avoid foods just because they are labelled with 'Allergy information' or 'Allergy advice'. This simply highlights ingredients, such as milk and peanuts, that most commonly cause allergic reactions. This is so that people with allergies to these specific foods don't miss them in a long list of other ingredients.

Protecting yourself from pre-eclampsia

Pre-eclampsia is a serious health problem for some women in pregnancy and although the exact causes aren't clear we know some women are more likely to develop the problem (see page 99). Although there is nothing you can do about most factors, research suggests eating certain foods could be protective.

A Norwegian study involving more than 20,000 first-time mums found women who ate more fruit, vegetables and vegetable oil were less likely to develop pre-eclampsia than those eating more processed meat, sugary drinks and salty snacks. Exactly how a healthy diet helps isn't understood but other research has found that eating plenty of antioxidant-rich foods (including foods rich in vitamins C and E) is beneficial. An antioxidant-rich diet appears to be particularly beneficial for women at increased risk, but interestingly, taking these vitamins in the form of supplement pills doesn't have the same effect.

Research has also looked at whether garlic and chocolate might reduce the risks of pre-eclampsia. It would be nice if this were the case and theoretically it is possible, as they are both rich in flavenoids, but there isn't any good evidence at the moment.

Reducing your risks of gestational diabetes

Gestational diabetes increases the risks of your baby becoming very large and suffering from long-term health problems (see page 3). By eating healthily right from the start you can reduce your chances of developing the condition. Putting on an appropriate amount of weight is one way of protecting yourself (see page 22) and research has shown that gestational diabetes risk is reduced in women eating more fruit and vegetables and less processed foods, especially those high in fat and sugar, including sugary drinks.

The benefits for mum

As well as giving your baby a great start in life, healthy eating will improve your own health and wellbeing now and in the long term. This is something that can easily be forgotten but is just as important. Avoiding too many processed foods and eating a well-balanced low GI diet will help you avoid common problems such as morning sickness and constipation (page 33) as well as pre-eclampsia, which is potentially life-threatening for mums-to-be. Pregnancy is also a key time in women's lives when weight problems can start or become significantly worse but sensible eating can help avoid this and the long-term risks of type 2 diabetes and associated chronic conditions.

Depression and anxiety affect about one in 10 pregnant women and there is some evidence that what you eat may improve your mental health and wellbeing. A recent Australian study found women eating fruit, vegetables, fish and whole-grain cereals were less likely to suffer depression during pregnancy.

How to grow a baby

From conception to birth, a baby needs enormous quantities of nutrients to grow. The requirements include about 925g of protein and 20-30g of calcium, as well as a massive 680mg of iron, equivalent to the amount found in about 34kg of beef or 113 400g cans of baked beans. Fortunately, you don't actually need to consume all these extra nutrients. Just as your body becomes more efficient at using energy, so it gets better at extracting certain nutrients from the food you eat. As pregnancy progresses and you require more iron, so your body absorbs more. In the first three months of pregnancy, women have been found to absorb only 7% of dietary iron, but this increases to 36% around the middle of pregnancy and to 66% by the end. Because of these metabolic changes, your requirements for certain nutrients, including calcium and iron, are no greater than normal. However, many young women in the UK consume too little of these nutrients anyway, so it is important to ensure you have a good intake now. The requirements for certain other nutrients, including iodine, thiamine, riboflavin, folate and vitamins A, B_{12}, C and D, are higher during pregnancy.

Although it is essential you get enough of these nutrients, you don't need to worry about monitoring your intake of each vitamin and mineral every day. If you eat a healthy and varied diet, full of wholesome unprocessed foods, you should be getting all the nutrients you need. The healthy diet checklist (page 12) shows the different types of food you should be eating and the main nutrients they supply. You can see how a diet including all of these food groups contains all the essential nutrients. If you want to find out more about any particular nutrient, you can look it up in Chapter 5. To get a better idea of how much of your diet should be made up by different foods, look at the 'Eatwell Guide'. Some people are surprised at just how much of our diets should be made up of fruit, vegetables and carbohydrate-rich foods.

Eating an unbalanced diet, for example by avoiding carbs or having a high protein intake, isn't good for your baby's long-term health. Women eating a diet roughly in the proportions shown in the Eatwell Guide are most likely to have the right proportion of protein, carbohydrate and fat in their diet for optimal foetal growth. They are also more likely to consume enough of all the different vitamins, minerals and phytonutrients needed.

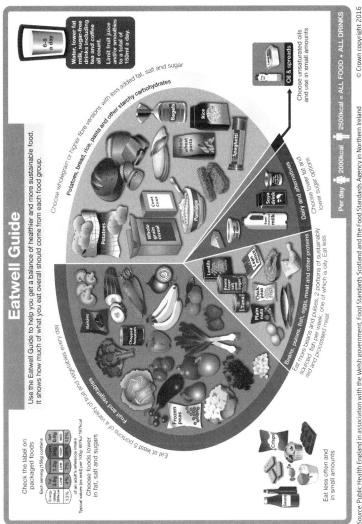

Eatwell Guide

Use the Eatwell Guide to help you get a balance of healthier and more sustainable food.
It shows how much of what you eat overall should come from each food group.

Water, lower fat milk, sugar-free drinks including tea and coffee all count.

Limit fruit juice and/or smoothies to a total of 150ml a day

6-8 a day

Choose wholegrain or higher fibre versions with less added fat, salt and sugar

Potatoes, bread, rice, pasta and other starchy carbohydrates

Bagels

Rice

Whole wheat pasta

Spaghetti

Cous Cous

Porridge

Whole grain cereal

Potatoes

Choose unsaturated oils and use in small amounts

Oil & spreads

Dairy and alternatives

Choose lower fat and lower sugar options

Soya drink

Semi skimmed milk

Lentils

Beans

Chick peas

Lean mince

Tuna

Plain nuts

Eat more beans and pulses, 2 portions of sustainably sourced fish per week, one of which is oily. Eat less red and processed meat

Beans, pulses, fish, eggs, meat and other proteins

Raisins

Chopped tomatoes

Frozen peas

Fruit and vegetables

Eat at least 5 portions of a variety of fruit and vegetables every day

Check the label on packaged foods

Each serving (150g) contains

Energy	Fat	Saturates	Sugars	Salt
1046kJ 250kcal	3.0g	1.3g	34g	0.9g
13%	LOW 4%	LOW 7%	MED 38%	HIGH 15%

of an adult's reference intake
Typical values (as sold) per 100g: 697kJ/167kcal

Choose foods lower in fat, salt and sugars

Eat less often and in small amounts

Crisps

Sauce

Per day   2000kcal   2500kcal = ALL FOOD + ALL DRINKS

© Crown copyright 2016

Source: Public Health England in association with the Welsh government, Food Standards Scotland and the Food Standards Agency in Northern Ireland

The healthy diet checklist

A healthy diet for two should include the following:

- A variety of **fruit and vegetables** (fresh, frozen, tinned or dried). Aim for at least five portions a day for a good supply of vitamins A, C and E, folic acid and iron. If you can manage seven or eight portions a day that's even better.

- Plenty of **starchy foods** such as breakfast cereals, bread, rice, pasta and potatoes for carbohydrates, B vitamins and zinc. Where possible choose wholegrain varieties, such as brown rice, as these provide fibre and extra micronutrients.

- **Protein foods** such as beans, lentils, lean meat, chicken, fish and eggs. These also supply iron and zinc.

- **Dairy foods** such as milk, cheese and yogurt to provide calcium, vitamin B_{12} and extra protein. Choose low-fat versions to avoid increasing your fat and calorie intake.

- **Iron-rich foods**, such as meat and fish, green vegetables and fortified breakfast cereals, to prevent anaemia.

- Good sources of **folic acid**, such as oranges, broccoli and fortified breakfast cereals.

- **Fish** at least twice a week, including one or two portions of oily fish to supply long-chain omega 3s for brain and eye development. Fish also provides protein, iodine, iron and vitamins B_6, B_{12} and D.

- At least six to eight cups or glasses of fluid.

Eating a balanced diet has been shown in numerous studies to improve your chances of having a baby with a healthy birthweight, not too low or too high, as both of these increase the risks of poor health. Healthy eating also plays a major role in preventing premature birth (birth before 37 weeks).

Although individual nutrients are important it is better to think about overall diet. A recent study of more than 60,000 women found they were less likely to deliver prematurely if their diet was mainly made up of fruit and vegetables, rice, wholegrain cereals, yogurt, chicken, fish, cooking oil and water. Also, it helped if their intake of white bread, pizza and processed meat products such as sausage rolls was low. Interestingly, this study found that what the women ate was more important than what they didn't eat. Completely cutting out junk or processed foods didn't have as much impact as increasing the proportion of healthy foods in their diet.

Brain food
Eating fish during pregnancy could help your baby reach his or her developmental milestones, according to researchers from the Danish National Birth Cohort study. More than 25,000 women in Denmark were asked about their fish intake during pregnancy and their babies' development at 6 and 18 months of age. Developmental scores for the babies of fish eaters were then compared with those of babies whose mothers ate little or no fish (less than one portion per week). Babies whose mothers ate about one and a half portions of fish each week were found to have 10% higher developmental scores. What's more, babies whose mothers ate about three and a half portions of fish a week scored 30% higher. Studies in the past have highlighted the benefits of fish and the importance of the nutrients in it, especially omega 3s, iodine and vitamin D but these results really add to the evidence showing early nutrition may affect later brain development.

During pregnancy, it's easy to focus on what you shouldn't eat, but this shows there's something positive you can do and something you can eat to really benefit your baby.

Ten ways to boost your fruit and vegetable intake

1   Mix some chopped fruit, such as banana or
    strawberries, with your breakfast cereal.
2   Have a piece of fruit ready for a mid-morning snack.
3   Keep some raisins, dried apricots, figs or prunes in your
    desk drawer or handbag ready for when hunger strikes.
4   Add plenty of salad (washed well) to sandwiches.
5   Buy some frozen vegetables. Then, even if you're too
    tired for peeling and chopping, you can microwave them
    to go with your evening meal.
6   Make a fruit pudding such as crumble, raspberry fool or
    fruit salad with mango, melon and fresh berries.
7   Swap your lunchtime sandwich for salad made with
    leftover wholemeal pasta, tuna and lots of vegetables.
8   Have some vegetable soup for lunch or make a really
    chunky soup for supper.
9   If you're baking, replace some of the sugar in the recipe
    with grated carrot, mashed banana or other fruit or
    vegetables.
10 Add extra vegetables when cooking dishes such as
    shepherd's pie, pasta, fish pie and pizza.

Time for a little something

During pregnancy you are more likely than usual to be rubbing your tummy and looking for a little snack. It may be that
you are suffering from morning sickness and can't face
proper meals, and so you are trying to eat small amounts
rather than nothing. Perhaps snacking seems the only way
to keep nausea at bay. Eating little and often can also be
helpful towards the end of pregnancy if you are suffering
from heartburn or if large meals just leave you feeling
uncomfortable.

When you eat snacks, try to make them as healthy as possible. Avoid always choosing chocolate, biscuits and crisps, as

these contain 'empty calories'. This means that they provide energy (calories) but not the essential nutrients, particularly the vitamins and minerals that you need. Instead go for something that will provide you with plenty of nutrients and slow-release energy.

Ten healthy snacks

1 A low-fat yogurt.
2 A piece of fresh fruit or a handful of dried fruit, nuts and seeds.
3 A bowl of breakfast cereal, preferably a high-fibre one with added vitamins and iron.
4 Oatcakes with some low-fat cheese and grapes.
5 Lentil and vegetable soup.
6 Wholemeal toast with yeast extract, low-fat cream cheese or mashed banana.
7 Houmous with vegetable sticks.
8 Wholemeal pitta bread filled with ham or chicken and salad.
9 A milkshake made by blending milk with a banana, strawberries, mango or peach.
10 A bowl of homemade popcorn.

Cravings and how to handle them

Cravings are quite common in pregnancy, especially during the early stages. They are usually seen as quite a fun part of being pregnant. When you eat whatever it is you have been longing for, you might be surprised at just how delicious it tastes - whether it's ice cream with gherkins or something more ordinary. You might find that nothing hits the spot quite like the cream crackers you've been dreaming of all day.

The most common cravings are for fruit, sweet or salty foods, and foods with a strong flavour, such as pickles. Nobody can explain exactly why cravings occur, but it is thought that changes in hormone levels, particularly oestrogen, are partly responsible. There is no evidence at all that cravings reflect what you or your baby need. Otherwise almost everyone would crave fruit and vegetables. Psychological factors also play a role. In some cultures, pregnant women do not experience cravings. Women sometimes admit that 'cravings' are a good excuse for eating things they always fancy. It's fine to eat the foods you crave if it's Granny Smith apples or tomato soup that you're after, or even if it's something without much nutritional value, such as ice cubes or pickled onions. However, if you're craving sugary foods and drinks or high-fat foods like burger and chips, then you need to be more careful. An occasional indulgence won't do any harm but eating foods like this every day will soon pile on the pounds, so you need to think about how to turn things around.

How to beat unhealthy cravings
- Eat breakfast every day. Skipping breakfast leads to low blood sugar levels mid-morning and can increase cravings for sugary snacks. Breakfasts made up of wholegrain cereals, fruit and low-fat milk have been found to be particularly good for appetite and glucose control.
- Have three meals and two or three snacks a day to avoid big dips in sugar and energy levels that can increase the likelihood of unhealthy cravings. Have healthy snack foods ready so that you don't have to grab the nearest biscuit or chocolate bar.
- Swap high GI foods and drinks like white bread, cookies and sugary drinks for low GI alternatives (pages 37–38). Refined carbs and sugary snacks may satisfy you initially but will soon leave you craving another hit (see page 33).

- Have some protein with every meal as this will keep you feeling fuller for longer.
- Get enough sleep. Being tired has been shown to increase your appetite, make you eat more and lead you to choosing the wrong types of food.
- Find a distraction – go for a walk, talk to a friend or rearrange a cupboard.

If you have a craving for something that wouldn't usually be considered a food or drink, it is called 'pica'. Studies of pica during pregnancy have found women craving (and consuming) items such as chalk, ice, raw potato, mud, clay, coal, baby powder and laundry starch. Although most of us have heard of pregnant women eating things like this, pica appears to be more of a myth than a reality in well-fed populations. One Danish study found the incidence to be just 0.02%. However, pica appears to be more common among certain ethnic groups, including African Americans and less affluent populations around the world. Several studies have found that pica among pregnant women is associated with lower iron levels. So if you do find yourself craving something unusual, talk to your midwife or doctor. If your iron levels haven't been tested yet, it may be a good idea to have blood tests done as soon as possible. Also, your doctor or midwife should be able to advise you about the safety or otherwise of eating particular substances.

As well as experiencing cravings, many women find they develop an aversion to particular foods or drinks during pregnancy. Even the smell of something such as wine that they previously enjoyed might make them feel nauseous. Again, hormonal changes that affect the sense of taste and smell are probably to blame. Aversions to tea, coffee, alcohol, fried or spicy food, and strong flavours and odours are all quite normal. For some women, these are the first signs of pregnancy. Aversions to certain items such as alcohol have an obvious role in protecting your baby from exposure to potentially harmful substances. However, it's not uncommon for women to develop an aversion to more healthy foods, such as meat, fish, eggs or vegetables. This sometimes happens during periods of morning sickness. You are likely to feel more normal when the sickness subsides. If you go off foods that you feel you should be eating, then it may help if someone else does the cooking or if you eat those foods cold. Then the smell isn't as strong, which can be part of the problem.

2 A healthy weight gain

The amount of weight women gain during pregnancy varies enormously. The extra weight isn't just the baby; it is also the placenta, amniotic fluid, increased blood volume and extra tissue in the breasts and uterus. It is also natural to lay down extra fat so that you have energy stores for breast-feeding. Some women have fluid retention during pregnancy, which contributes further to weight gain.

The general advice is that if you eat according to your appetite then you should gain a healthy amount of weight. Unfortunately, many women these days aren't used to eating in response to hunger and fullness. This is especially true of those who have been yo-yo dieters or particularly weight-conscious in the past. As a result, they can become worried about putting on weight and try to restrict their weight gain. Other women take the opposite view and see pregnancy as a time to relax their usual rules about avoiding fattening foods and instead eat whatever they fancy. Neither approach is good, as gaining too little or too much weight can both cause health problems.

How much weight should you gain?

The amount you should gain during pregnancy depends on your weight before you became pregnant. Women who are overweight need to gain much less than those who are underweight to produce a healthy baby. You can find out if your pre-pregnancy weight was appropriate by calculating your BMI using the online calculator (www.nhs.uk/tools/pages/healthyweightcalculator.aspx) or by following the steps in the box below.

Calculating your pre-pregnancy BMI

By working out your pre-pregnancy BMI, you can see whether you were a healthy weight for your height.

1 Measure your height in metres. To convert from feet and inches, multiply your height in inches by 0.0254. For example, if you are 5ft 2in, this is 62 inches (12 inches to a foot), so the calculation is 62 × 0.0254 = 1.57m.

2 Measure your weight in kilograms. To convert from stones and pounds, multiply your weight in pounds by 0.454. For example, if you weighed 10 stone, this is 140lb (14lb to a stone), so the calculation is 140 × 0.454 = 63.6kg.

3 Divide your weight by your height squared. For example:

$$\frac{63.6}{1.57 \times 1.57} = 25.8$$

Alternatively you can use the graph on the next page. If you find your height up the side and your pre-pregnancy weight along the top or bottom, depending on which units you prefer to use, you can see which weight category you belonged in. You can then use the guidelines in the table (page 22) to

Height/weight chart

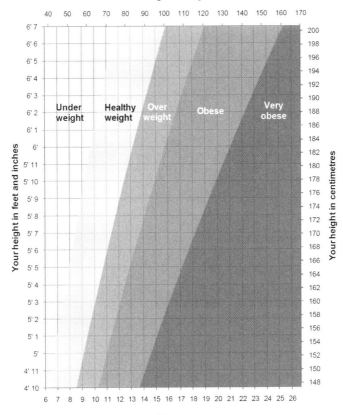

Source: NHS Choices © Crown copyright 2011

see roughly how much weight you should gain during pregnancy. The recommendations come from the Institute of Medicine in the USA and they have been calculated using data from thousands of women. Weight gains within the recommended ranges are associated with the lowest risk of complications during pregnancy and labour (including the need for a Caesarean) and the best chances of having a healthy baby whose weight is within the normal healthy range. Women with weight gains within the recommended range are also less likely to have lots of weight to lose after having their baby, and their baby is less likely to become overweight or obese.

BMI before pregnancy	Recommended weight gain
Underweight, less than 18.5	12.5-18kg (2st to 2st 12lb)
Healthy weight, 18.5-25	11.5-16kg (1st 11lb to 2st 7lb)
Overweight, 25-30	7-11.5kg (1st 1lb to 1st 11lb)
Obese, more than 30	5-9kg (11lb to 1st 6lb)

Source: Data from Institute of Medicine (2009) *Weight Gain During Pregnancy: Re-examining the Guidelines.* National Academies Press, Washington, DC.

The weight gain ranges in the table look fairly broad and at first glance you may think that they look easily achievable. However, the majority of women in the UK and the USA gain either too much or too little weight during pregnancy. Weighing yourself regularly may help you stay on track. You can use the grid on the next page to keep a record of your weight gain and see how it compares with the recommendations.

Some women find it easier if they think about their pregnancy in stages rather than as a whole. You might have read that you don't need to gain any weight during the first trimester (three months) of pregnancy, but in reality most women put on between 0.5 and 2.5kg (1-6lb). During the second and third trimesters, women in the 'underweight' or 'normal weight' category should gain about 0.5kg (1lb) per week and 'overweight' or 'obese' women should gain about 0.25kg (0.5lb) each week.

If you're concerned about gaining too much or too little weight, it is important to talk to your GP. Remember that there is not an exact amount of weight that you should be putting on, and women with a wide variety of weight gains

Weight gain chart

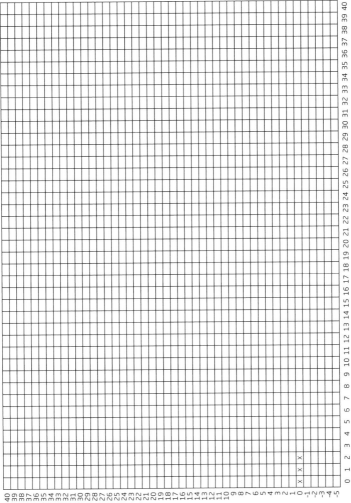

Weight gain (kg)

Week of pregnancy

Weight gain (pounds)

have good pregnancies and healthy babies. Your GP or mid-wife will be able to tell you whether or not you need to be doing anything about your weight gain, not only based on the number on the scales, but also taking into account how your baby appears to be growing and your general health.

Making sure you gain enough weight

There is a very strong association between weight gain during pregnancy and birthweight. The more weight you put on, the bigger your baby is likely to be. Your weight before pregnancy is also important, and if you start off lighter you need to gain more weight to have a baby that's a healthy weight. Some women feel that a small baby isn't such a problem, and that it should make labour easier anyway. However, low-birthweight babies are more likely to have problems at birth and in later life (see page 3).

If you've been particularly weight-conscious in the past or have had an eating disorder, such as anorexia nervosa or bulimia nervosa, you may feel particularly anxious about gaining weight during pregnancy. If this is the case it's good to talk to your GP or midwife. They may offer extra appointments to monitor your baby's growth and they should be able to help you deal with your concerns or refer you to someone who can.

Healthy diets, which are low in fat, high in fibre and contain lots of fruit and vegetables, can have a low energy density, which means you don't get a lot of calories per mouthful. This is generally considered a benefit, but if you're finding it difficult to eat enough calories then you could try some of the following:

• Include more energy-dense foods in your meals, such as cheese, nut butters, beans and lentils.

- Cook with a little more oil, such as olive oil or rapeseed oil.
- If you have a salad, add some avocado, a handful of seeds and some salad dressing.
- Have a mid-morning and mid-afternoon snack such as dried fruit and nuts, flapjack, oatcakes and cheese.
- Eat breakfast every day.
- Have a snack or milky drink before bed.

Making sure you don't gain too much weight

Gaining more weight than recommended increases your risk of complications during pregnancy, including gestational diabetes, high blood pressure and pre-eclampsia. It also raises the chances of your having a very large baby, which can increase the risks during delivery, including the need for a Caesarean. A large European study, known as the DORIAN project, has followed mothers and their babies for 60–70 years to monitor the long-term consequences of a mother's diet. It found that the likelihood of developing heart disease and type 2 diabetes was greater in those whose mothers were overweight in late pregnancy. What's more, the effects of being overweight before pregnancy, putting on too much weight during pregnancy and having poor blood glucose control in the last trimester were each individually important. Improvements in any one of these three factors mean better outcomes for babies. So if you are overweight before pregnancy, but don't put on too much weight during pregnancy, then your baby will benefit. Even if you put on more weight than you should during the first two trimesters, eating more carefully and watching your blood glucose levels by eating a low GI diet (see Chapter 3) in the last trimester will still help your baby's long-term health.

Putting on too much weight also increases your own risks of being obese in future, which in turn means that you are more likely to develop heart disease, diabetes and cancer. Some women take the attitude that they won't worry about their weight for now, they'll just eat what they like and enjoy being pregnant, then lose the weight afterwards. Unfortunately, losing weight after pregnancy isn't as easy as many celebrities would have you believe. A Swedish study found that women who gained more than 16kg (2.5st) during pregnancy were on average 5.5kg (12lb) heavier a year after their baby was born. For some women, the effects can still be seen many years after having a baby. Research involving more than 2,000 women in the UK found that those gaining more weight than recommended were three times more likely to be overweight 16 years later. Similar results were found in a group of Australian women 21 years after they had had their babies.

The O word
Nobody likes to be described as obese, but if your BMI is over 30 you are likely to hear doctors and midwives using the word. It's not meant to be judgemental or offensive; it's a clinical word used to make sure you get the care you need during pregnancy. This might mean extra monitoring or antenatal appointments, or special facilities may be needed during the birth of your baby.

We know that women who are overweight are more likely to have conditions such as high blood pressure, diabetes and problems during labour, but going on a strict diet now won't benefit you or your baby. Dieting to lose weight during pregnancy is associated with an increased risk of neural tube defects and other complications. However, if you weigh more than about 100kg or 16st, your GP or midwife may feel that a calorie-controlled diet is appropriate, with careful monitoring.

Although now is not the time for dieting, it is good to develop healthier eating habits. Women who avoid junk food, including sugary drinks, fast food and processed meat and chips, are much less likely to have a very large baby, whatever their weight was before they became pregnant. The best thing is to try to make a conscious effort every day to eat as healthily as possible and increase the amount of time spent walking or taking gentle exercise. These healthier habits will stand you in good stead for when your baby is born and then you can think seriously about achieving a healthy weight for the long term. You can still have the occasional treat, but factor these into the overall plan. For example, if you have a few chocolate biscuits or other treats one afternoon, don't think 'healthy eating is ruined for today'. Instead try to eat as healthily as possible later on. If you find you're constantly tempted by high-fat and high-sugar foods, such as crisps or chocolate, then have a look at the advice on page 16 about beating those cravings and look at the 'Ten healthy snacks' (page 15).

Recent studies have shown that monitoring your weight gain and having a plan really helps. As well as using the grid (page 23) you can set yourself small targets, such as taking fruit to work instead of biscuits. Or cut down from two sugars in tea to just one and a half, then in a couple of weeks you could cut down to one sugar. Set goals that you feel are achievable and can stick to in the long term. Also, don't let other people spoil your good intentions by telling you that you need an extra roast potato or biscuit because you're eating for two.

Low-carb eating

Low-carb diets can be dangerous during pregnancy. They can lead to your baby laying down extra fat, and the proportion of the diet made up of protein inevitably increases, which is also undesirable. Animal studies show protein-rich diets increase

▶

the risk of miscarriage and genetic abnormalities. Research in Scotland has also shown that a high protein intake during pregnancy makes babies more susceptible to raised blood pressure, insulin sensitivity and heart disease in later life.

How to gain a healthy amount of weight

NICE has identified the following strategies as really helping women to achieve a healthy weight gain:

- Eat breakfast.
- Watch your portion sizes (don't eat for two).
- Base meals around starchy foods such as potatoes and rice.
- Eat fibre-rich foods, such as oats, wholegrain products and vegetables.
- Make sure you get your five-a-day.
- Eat a low-fat diet.
- Avoid high-fat and high-sugar foods, such as fried food, fast food, fizzy drinks and cakes.

Keeping active

As well as thinking about what you eat, it's important to stay active to avoid putting on too much weight. Research in the Netherlands found reduced physical activity was the biggest predictor of excessive weight gains. Getting out and keeping physically active is also essential for your general sense of wellbeing and it is particularly important if you have gestational diabetes as it helps to stabilise blood sugar levels. This means avoiding spending long periods sitting and watching TV or using the computer, and instead making walking part of your daily life. Taking some exercise will help you feel healthier and more relaxed, and as a bonus you're likely to sleep better. If you are fit, you are also likely to have more stamina for labour and an easier birth. In addition, it'll help you recover more easily after the birth and make you feel more energetic and better able to look after your baby.

The NHS recommends at least 30 minutes of moderate exercise per day during pregnancy. This can include swimming or brisk walking. If you took little or no exercise before pregnancy, it is best to start with just 15 minutes per day and build up gradually. Most leisure centres hold classes that are specifically for pregnant women, such as prenatal aqua aerobics, or you could find out if there are antenatal yoga classes nearby. These are also a good way to meet other mums-to-be. If you feel you really don't have time to go to a class, then any exercise, even a 10-minute walk around the block, is better than nothing.

Diet or exercise?
This question has been tested in about 65 different experiments. In 2015 they were all considered together and the conclusion was that if you start eating more healthily or start taking more exercise, or use a combination of both, you're less likely to gain too much weight while you're pregnant. So it all helps. Other benefits of making these changes included a lower risk of raised blood pressure; having an unhealthily large baby; needing a Caesarean; and infant breathing problems.

Twins and more!

If you are expecting twins, triplets or even more babies, you are likely to gain more weight than a woman expecting just one baby. This is due to the weight of an extra baby as well as an extra placenta and more amniotic fluid. You are likely to feel particularly hungry in early pregnancy and gain more weight in the first few months.

The amount of weight that women expecting twins should gain during pregnancy has been calculated by the Institute of Medicine (IOM) in the USA. The recommendations are based on evidence of weight gains associated with the healthiest outcomes for mums and their babies. The IOM describes these guidelines as 'provisional' as there is not as much data available for twin pregnancies. However, since there are no other recommendations available, you might find them useful. If you were underweight before you became pregnant, you might notice that there is no recommendation in the table. This is because there simply was not enough data available for the IOM to base one on. However, you should aim to gain slightly more than is recommended for 'healthy weight' women.

BMI before pregnancy	Recommended weight gain
Healthy weight, 18.5–25	17–25kg (2st 9lb to 3st 12lb)
Overweight, 25–30	14–23kg (2st 3lb to 3st 8lb)
Obese, more than 30	11–19kg (1st 11lb to 3st)

Source: Data from Institute of Medicine (2009) *Weight Gain During Pregnancy: Re-examining the Guidelines.* National Academies Press, Washington, DC.

There are no official guidelines regarding additional energy and calorie requirements for multiple pregnancies. However, extra calories are needed, and these should come from nutrient-rich foods rather than extra sugary or fatty foods. The additional foods also need to supply extra vitamins and minerals, including iron and vitamin A, which are more likely to be lacking in multiple pregnancies.

3 Low GI eating

Low GI eating is beneficial for all pregnant women and their babies. If you are diabetic or have developed gestational diabetes since you've been pregnant you will probably have been told to eat more low GI foods (see page 112). If not, you may be wondering if low GI diets are just another fad and whether they are for you. Low GI diets are sometimes used for weight loss but those diets are low in calories as well as being low GI and they aren't suitable for pregnancy. Here we are not talking about reducing calories, although if you need to cut down then eating low GI foods can make it easier. Instead we're focusing on foods that help stabilise your blood sugar levels. Eating a low GI diet benefits you and your baby whether you are overweight, a healthy weight or underweight. People of any weight will suffer if they have too much sugar. Research suggests their baby will too.

What's so good about low GI eating?
Low GI eating will help you:

- Put on a healthy amount of weight and not too much.
- Avoid gestational diabetes, which affects nearly one in five women.
- Treat morning sickness and generally feel better.
- Combat cravings for unhealthy sugary and high-fat snacks.
- Avoid constipation.
- Eat a more balanced diet and get the vitamins and minerals you need.

The glycaemic index (GI) is a rating system for carbohydrate-rich foods that shows how the food affects your blood sugar (glucose) levels. When you eat high GI foods you get a quick hit and your blood sugar levels spike rapidly and then plummet. Low GI foods, by contrast, take longer to digest so your blood glucose levels increase and fall more slowly and gently. The effects of high and low GI foods can be seen more easily on the graph.

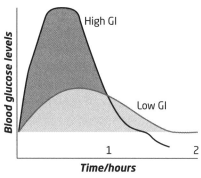

Source: The University of Sydney Glycemic Index Research Service

Low GI, weight gain and cravings

Women eating low GI diets have been found to be less likely to put on too much weight while they are pregnant and their babies are at lower risk of being very large, so there is less chance of problems during delivery. As low GI foods also spend more time in your stomach they make you feel fuller for longer. In addition, they cause blood sugar levels to fall less steeply so you don't get the same signal going to the brain to tell it you need to eat again. By reducing your appetite, it makes it much easier to gain a healthy amount of weight.

Researchers have compared the effects of eating high and low GI meals, containing the same number of calories. They found that four hours after eating, people who had a high GI meal had lower blood glucose levels, felt hungrier and brain scans showed greater activity in the region related to rewards and cravings. This could help explain why having a high GI snack, such as a mid-morning muffin, may satisfy you initially but can leave you feeling especially hungry and looking for another sugar fix. As pregnant women are especially prone to cravings, you don't want to make things worse by eating sugary snacks that may lead to more sugary snacks. A banana and a few nuts would be a much better option if you feel hunger and flagging energy levels between meals.

Low GI eating may also help with morning sickness, as we know that hunger can make women feel worse. Having more stable blood sugar levels may enable women to avoid the waves of nausea that can occur throughout the day. Research has shown that high-carbohydrate meals can increase feelings of nausea, while high-protein meals can help reduce symptoms. These studies didn't look at GI specifically but high-carbohydrate meals would inevitably have a higher GI than high-protein ones. If you're feeling sick you may not fancy a cooked meal but a chicken sandwich or even a protein bar would be a better option than a sugary biscuit.

Low GI and your baby's health

As well as being beneficial for you, low GI eating could be healthier for your baby. There is evidence that low GI eating in pregnancy may improve your baby's blood glucose and insulin control. It can also reduce your baby's chances of being born with a high birthweight and extra body fat. Some fat on a baby is desirable but babies born with too much fat are likely to become overweight children and then overweight adults and be at higher risk of developing certain illnesses. Children around five years old have been found to have more body fat if their mother ate a high-sugar or high GI diet in pregnancy. A 20-year study in Denmark found that as adults, people were more likely to have unhealthy levels of cholesterol if their mother ate a high GI diet when she was expecting. These young adults also had higher insulin and leptin levels, all of which would increase their risk of developing cardiovascular disease and type 2 diabetes in later life. This type of research is in the early days but it certainly appears to show the possible long-term consequences of allowing your blood sugar levels to soar and dip.

What GI really means

In general the more processed a food is the higher its GI, whereas the closer it is to its natural state the lower its GI. Glucose has a GI of 100 and other foods are rated in comparison to it, giving a GI score between 0 and 100. When grains such as wheat or oats are milled they become less coarse and their fibre is removed, which makes them easier to digest and for the carbohydrates they contain to be broken down and absorbed. Blood glucose levels then increase more quickly. For example, porridge made with coarse oats has a GI of 51, which makes it a low GI food, whereas instant oat cereal has a high GI of 83. Clearly coarse oats aren't as quick and easy for your body to digest as instant oat cereals sold as a fine powder. The GI of a food depends on its physical makeup, so the coarser and chunkier the oats you use, the lower the GI will be. Likewise, eating your potatoes with skins and not cooking your pasta until it goes really soft will make these harder to digest and reduce their GI.

Low GI foods

- Oats (but not instant oats)
- Beans and lentils
- Most fruit and vegetables
- Milk
- Most wholegrain cereals and bread

High GI foods

- White bread
- Biscuits
- Cakes
- Sweets
- Sugary drinks such as cola

Glycaemic load

Some very healthy foods, such as watermelon, have a high GI. This is because they contain lots of water and very little carbohydrate. For this reason it is sometimes more sensible to look at the glycaemic load (GL) of a food as this takes into account both the GI and the amount of carbohydrate in a food.

There are many books and apps available to look up the GI or GL of various foods, and these can be very useful, but GI shouldn't be the only criterion you use when judging the healthiness of a food. If you only ate low GI foods you could end up eating an unbalanced and unhealthy diet. GI can be helpful, for example when choosing between similar foods such as cornflakes or bran flakes, but it is also important to look at your overall diet and think about all the food groups and the need to include fruit and vegetables, dairy foods, fish and so on (see page 12). If you have diabetes then looking at the GI can also help show you which foods need to be cut out or only consumed in small amounts with meals.

Warning: not all low GI foods are healthy!
Some foods, such as chocolate, have a low GI because they contain lots of fat, which slows down the absorption of the sugar. However, chocolate is still high in calories, fat and sugar and should only be eaten as an occasional treat.

The GI of a food is measured when it is eaten on its own. However, we don't usually have just a single type of food, for example a slice of bread with nothing else. The combination of foods we eat together will affect the GI of the meal or snack. Both fat and protein slow down the absorption of sugar, so having these with your carbohydrate-rich foods will reduce the GI of a meal. If you eat a high GI food, such as a slice of white bread, with eggs rather than on its own or with jam, then the overall GI of the meal will be much less and the effect on your blood sugar levels will not be so dramatic. This means there are several ways to reduce the GI of a meal. For example, if you are having pasta then choose a wholemeal variety, don't have a large portion and have a sauce made with chicken or lentils and vegetables. Also, if you've got gestational diabetes but you really want a slice of cake, then having a small slice at the end of your low GI meal will be much better for you. The absorption of the sugar in the cake will be slowed down as it is being digested with lower GI foods.

Low GI swaps

It is often possible to make simple swaps in your diet to reduce the GI. As well as improving your blood sugar control, making these changes will improve the overall quality of your diet. A recent study found that the lower the overall GI of pregnant women's diet the higher their intake of key vitamins and minerals. This is because many low GI foods contain fewer calories but more essential micronutrients.

High GI foods	Lower GI alternatives
White bread, including French bread, ciabatta and panini	Granary, multigrain, seeded, rye bread
White pasta	Wholemeal pasta, egg pasta
	Have it al dente as less cooking means lower GI.
Easy-cook white rice	Basmati rice, brown rice
Potatoes	Sweet potatoes, yams, regular potatoes baked or boiled with skins
Cornflakes, rice krispies	Wholegrain cereal or muesli
Instant oats or quick oats with syrup	Homemade porridge topped with cinnamon and sliced banana.

▶

High GI foods	Lower GI alternatives
Breakfast cereal bar	Peanut butter sandwich and a banana
Fruit juice (e.g. pure apple juice or orange juice)	Whole apples or peeled oranges or satsumas
Fruit smoothie	Fruit salad
Sugary drink (e.g. cola, Lucozade)	Water, sugar-free drinks or fruit tea
Fruit yogurt	Raspberries or chopped strawberries with natural yogurt
Biscuits	Ryvita with seeds, spread with low-fat cream cheese
Jam	Mashed banana, peanut butter or yeast extract

Top tips for stabilising your blood sugar

- Avoid snacking on very high GI foods and drinks such as a packet of sweets or can of cola.
- Swap high GI carbs for low whenever possible (see table above).
- Eat potatoes with their skins on.
- Have high GI treats such as cake only at the end of a meal.
- Eat smaller portions of high GI foods such as pasta.
- Choose less ripe bananas as these have a lower GI than ones that are starting to turn brown.
- Have your carbs, like bread, with protein foods such as peanut butter or cream cheese.

4 Foods and drinks to avoid in pregnancy

When you are pregnant, you should avoid certain foods and drinks, and cut down on others. Some, such as raw eggs, pâté and blue cheese, can lead to food poisoning. Others, including liver products, certain fish and alcohol, contain substances that could be toxic in high doses to your developing baby. As mentioned previously, you should also try to avoid eating too many sugary and fatty foods such as take-aways, fizzy drinks, crisps, biscuits and sweets, which contribute to weight gain without providing essential nutrients.

This chapter provides a complete checklist of what to avoid and what to cut down on. It looks at particular food hazards to help explain why there are quite so many rules and shows how some foods can be made safe simply by freezing or cooking. To find out about the risks associated with particular foods, such as tuna or goats' cheese, you can look them up in the A–Z section (see Chapter 9).

What to avoid

The following all pose a risk to you or your baby:

- Soft mould-ripened cheeses, such as Brie and Camembert, and soft blue cheeses, such as Danish Blue and Roquefort. These can contain listeria (see page 45).

- Raw or partially cooked eggs. Any dishes containing egg should be cooked until the yolk and white are solid. Foods such as homemade mayonnaise and mousse should be avoided (see *eggs*, page 132).

- Unpasteurised milk, including goats' and sheep's milk, and products such as yogurt and cream made from these.

- Liver, liver products and any supplements containing high levels of vitamin A, such as cod liver oil.

- Raw or undercooked meat, including cured meats and salami. The main concern with these is toxoplasmosis, but they may also contain other types of food poisoning bacteria.

- Shark, swordfish and marlin. This is to avoid ingestion of mercury, which could harm the unborn baby's developing nervous system.

- Raw shellfish such as oysters, and cold dishes containing seafood such as prawns, unless freshly prepared.

- Pâté, including vegetable pâté, to avoid the risk of listeria.

- Alcohol. Drinking during pregnancy increases the risk of miscarriage and birth defects.

What to cut down on

There are certain foods and drinks that you don't need to avoid completely but should consume only in moderation:

- Tuna should be limited to no more than two fresh steaks or four 200g cans per week, as it contains small traces of mercury.
- You should limit your intake of oily fish and certain other types of fish to two portions per week, to avoid consuming harmful levels of pollutants (see page 150).
- Caffeine intake should be limited to no more than 200mg per day, which is equivalent to about two mugs of instant coffee or two cups of real coffee.

Peanuts

In the past, some women were advised to avoid peanuts during pregnancy, but this is no longer recommended. It was thought that if women with a family history of allergies (including asthma, eczema or hay fever) ate peanuts it might increase their babies' risk of developing a peanut allergy. However, in 2009 the government changed its advice based on new evidence. The current guidance is that if you want to eat peanuts during pregnancy or breastfeeding, you can do so as part of a healthy, balanced diet. The previous advice, issued in 1998, was based on a review of the scientific literature that existed at the time, which suggested a possible link between peanut consumption during pregnancy and peanut allergy in infants and children. The evidence was only weak, but there was concern that the number of children with an allergy to peanuts was rising, and that in severe cases it could be life-threatening. It was agreed that more research was needed, but as a precaution, mums with babies thought to be most at risk were advised to avoid peanuts. More recent studies found no evidence that eating peanuts in pregnancy affects a baby's chances of developing an allergy to peanuts.

Beware! Food hygiene hazards

During pregnancy, you are more susceptible to food poisoning. This is because your immune system undergoes certain changes to prevent your body reacting against your growing baby. To avoid getting food poisoning, it is important to pay special attention to food hygiene. Around 70% of people say they usually rely on smell to assess whether food is safe to eat, but while you're pregnant this really isn't good enough and it's important to strictly follow 'use by' dates.

Most forms of food poisoning are caused by bacteria. There is usually a delay between eating the contaminated food and the development of any symptoms. This is known as the incubation period and it can range from a few hours to several days, depending on the bacteria's method of attack. Some bacteria stick to the lining of the intestine and destroy cells directly. These cause symptoms such as nausea, vomiting, abdominal cramps and diarrhoea. Others produce a toxin that is absorbed and can produce symptoms elsewhere, such as headaches. In warm environments, bacteria multiply rapidly, for example at picnics and barbecues and on buffet tables. A single bacterium can become several million bacteria within eight hours.

You can reduce your risk of getting food poisoning considerably by taking some sensible precautions when you are preparing and storing food, and when you eat out or get a take-away.

Preparing food

• Always wash your hands before eating or preparing food.

• Wash all fruit and vegetables before eating, including bags of salad leaves labelled as 'washed and ready to eat'.

• Keep your kitchen clean and don't allow pets on tables and kitchen work surfaces.

- Before eating hot foods, make sure they are piping hot right the way through. This is particularly important for ready meals, pies and processed meat products such as burgers and sausages.

- When using a microwave, follow the instructions carefully, including stirring and standing times. Then check the food is cooked all the way through before eating.

- After handling raw eggs, meat and poultry, wash your hands and any utensils thoroughly with hot soapy water. Kitchen worktops should be washed well after any spills or splashes from these foods. If you don't wash and dry your hands thoroughly, bacteria can easily be spread to fridge handles, cutlery and other foods.

- Don't wash raw chicken as this can spread campylobacter and other bacteria to the surrounding area. Cooking will kill any bacteria on the chicken.

Storing food

- Make sure the temperature of your fridge is below 5°C and your freezer below −18°C.

- Check the use-by date and storage instructions on packaging, and stick to them.

- Store any raw meat at the bottom of the fridge, wrapped and separate from food that is ready to eat. Raw eggs should also be stored carefully.

- Cool and refrigerate any leftovers within an hour of cooking and eat them within 24 hours.

Take-aways and eating out

When someone else is preparing your food, it is impossible to be 100% sure about hygiene standards. It is best to eat only in places you trust, and it is generally safer to choose hot dishes rather than cold ones such as salads. If you get a take-away meal and it's not piping hot when it arrives, you could heat it in the microwave as an extra precaution.

Don't be afraid to ask about ingredients or information about how dishes have been cooked, for example whether mayonnaise is homemade or ice cream contains raw eggs. Most places will be happy to help, and a bit of embarrassment now is better than worrying about something later. Many restaurants also provide useful advice on a website or you could email in advance if you really don't want to ask when you're there.

Different types of food poisoning

Campylobacter

Campylobacter is the most common bacterial cause of food poisoning in the UK. It is responsible for more than 280,000 cases in the UK each year. It is thought chicken and other poultry are responsible for 80% of these cases. The rest are due to raw meat, unpasteurised milk and untreated water. Campylobacter is present in 73% of raw chickens in the UK, according to a 2015 report from the FSA. However, it is killed by thorough cooking. Campylobacter is also present on the packaging of 7% of raw chickens so it is best to place packaged chicken in an extra bag.

Infection with campylobacter doesn't usually result in vomiting, but symptoms can be severe and include fever, abdominal cramps and diarrhoea, which may contain blood. Infection during pregnancy can cross the placenta. It is very unlikely to affect your baby, but there is an increased risk of premature delivery or miscarriage, so it is important to see your doctor if you suspect infection. If campylobacter is detected then you may be given intravenous antibiotic treatment.

Listeria

Listeria (*Listeria monocytogenes*) is a type of bacteria found in some foods, soil, vegetation and sewage. It can cause an illness called listeriosis, which can have serious consequences during pregnancy. It is impossible to tell whether a food is contaminated with listeria as it will look, smell and taste normal. Listeria is found in small amounts in many foods, but some, such as pâté, may have much higher levels.

Although listeriosis is unlikely to be serious for the mother, it can result in miscarriage, premature delivery, stillbirth or severe illness in newborn babies. According to Public Health England's (PHE) 2015 figures, about 180 cases of listeriosis are reported each year, including 22 involving pregnant women. It is fairly rare, but if you are pregnant there are certain precautions you can take to reduce your risk of infection. It is important to follow the general food hygiene rules for storing and preparing foods, but there are also certain foods that are more likely to contain listeria and are therefore best avoided completely during pregnancy:

- Soft mould-ripened cheeses and soft blue cheeses (for a full list, see page 124).
- Pâté, including liver pâté and vegetable pâté (see page 154).
- Unpasteurised dairy products, including milk, cream, yogurt and ice cream.
- Pre-packaged salad leaves – these need to be rewashed thoroughly.
- Ready meals such as lasagne and curry – the manufacturer's reheating guidelines should be followed carefully, and you should also check that the food is piping hot all the way through.

Symptoms of listeriosis can take up to two or three months to appear after exposure and may include fever, a mild flu-like illness or diarrhoea. These symptoms can, of course, have other causes. If you are concerned, it is best to see your GP, who may ask for blood or urine tests. If you do have listeriosis, it can usually be treated successfully with antibiotics.

Toxoplasmosis

This is an infection caused by a microscopic parasite called *Toxoplasma gondii*, which is found in meat, soil and cat faeces. More than half of people with toxoplasmosis don't know they have it, but in others it can cause flu-like symptoms or more severe symptoms similar to those of glandular fever. If a woman becomes infected during pregnancy or in the two to three months before conception, it can cause miscarriage, stillbirth or a range of birth defects, including hydrocephalus (water on the brain), brain damage, epilepsy, deafness, blindness or growth problems.

There are around 350 cases of toxoplasmosis recorded with PHE each year but the NHS estimates that the actual number of infections could be as high as 350,000. The most common cause of toxoplasmosis is consumption of raw or undercooked meat, so you should only eat meat that has been thoroughly cooked and shows no traces of blood or pinkness. Raw cured meats such as pepperoni should either be cooked or frozen for four days before consumption to make them safe. Otherwise they should be avoided (see page 130). Toxoplasmosis is also caused by unpasteurised milk products, including unpasteurised goats' milk, and any food contaminated with soil. As well as making sure that fruit and vegetables are completely free of soil, women are advised to wear gloves when gardening and handling cat litter, and to wash their hands carefully afterwards.

If you think you may have toxoplasmosis, it is important to see your doctor. In about 40% of toxoplasmosis cases, the infection is passed from a mother to her baby. The baby then has congenital toxoplasmosis, which can have serious complications. However, if a mother is treated promptly with antibiotics, it can prevent the baby from becoming infected. If the baby is already infected, then different antibiotics can be given to reduce the severity of the infection.

Salmonella

This is one of the commonest causes of food poisoning. It differs from the listeria and toxoplasmosis bugs because it doesn't cross the placenta to the baby. However, salmonella can make you very ill, with a high temperature that could harm your unborn child. Symptoms include severe vomiting and diarrhoea, but the effects vary. There are 200 different strains of salmonella. High-risk foods include raw and partially cooked eggs, and poultry and meat that hasn't been thoroughly cooked.

Brucella

This is sometimes found in unpasteurised milk and dairy products, including cheese and yogurt. Infection can result in fever, illness and miscarriage. It is rare in the UK but more common in Middle Eastern countries and some Mediterranean countries, including Spain. If you are travelling abroad it is best to ensure that any dairy products are made from pasteurised milk. At home, avoid 'country' or 'locally made' cheeses from these countries.

E. coli

Most strains of *Escherichia coli* (E. coli) bacteria are harmless, but some can cause severe food poisoning. These produce verocytoxins and are known as verocytoxin-producing E. coli (VTECs). In the UK E0157 is the most common VTEC, but in other countries E0111 and E026 are more common.

The foods most likely to contain harmful strains of E. coli are undercooked minced beef (e.g. in burgers) and unpasteurised milk. E. coli can also be transmitted directly from infected animals, people and soil. If a pregnant woman contracts E. coli, it isn't transmitted to the foetus. However, symptoms can be serious and include bloody diarrhoea and abdominal cramps. The illness can also have serious complications, such as severe anaemia and problems with the nervous system and kidneys.

Mercury
This metal can have a toxic effect on the development of an unborn or very young baby's nervous system. The FSA recommends that pregnant women avoid eating shark, swordfish and marlin, as these fish have been found to contain high levels of mercury. Lower levels of mercury have been found in tuna, so consumption of this fish should be limited to no more than two fresh tuna steaks or four 200g cans a week.

Alcohol

Drinking alcohol during pregnancy can lead to long-term harm to your baby and the more you drink the greater the risk. New guidelines were issued by the Chief Medical Officer in 2016 recommending that for those who are pregnant or planning a pregnancy the safest approach is not to drink alcohol at all. This is because experts are unsure how much, if any, alcohol is safe to drink and it is now the advice of the Department of Health, NHS and Royal College of Midwives. Alcohol can also affect your baby while you are breastfeeding but the current advice is that the occasional drink while breastfeeding isn't harmful (see page 184).

Drinking alcohol before pregnancy can reduce your fertility and ability to conceive. During pregnancy it increases the risk of miscarriage, low birthweight (weighing less than 2.5kg) and premature delivery, especially if you drink in the first three months of pregnancy. Alcohol is known to cross the placenta to your baby and because a baby's liver is immature it can't process the alcohol in the same way as yours can and the baby's development can be affected.

The term Foetal Alcohol Syndrome Disorder (FASD) is used to describe a whole range of problems associated with alcohol consumption in pregnancy. Heavy alcohol consumption carries the highest risk and is associated with foetal alcohol syndrome (FAS). FAS is characterised by low birthweight and length, a variety of congenital abnormalities, facial malformations and also learning and behavioural problems that can be lifelong. Regularly drinking less than this or only drinking heavily occasionally (binge drinking) is also associated with FADS and similar but less severe problems, including physical, mental and behavioural conditions

In the past women were told that the occasional drink was probably OK. However, caution is now seen as the best option because it is known that alcohol passes through the placenta, and there really is no proven safe level of exposure for a foetus. The only way to ensure that your baby is not affected by alcohol is to stop drinking completely.

What if you drank before you knew you were pregnant?
If you drank alcohol before finding out you were pregnant, try to relax. You are certainly not the first woman to do this, and you won't be the last. Although drinking any amount of alcohol in pregnancy has the potential to cause problems, it in no way makes them a certainty. However, once you suspect you are pregnant, it is best to stop drinking completely. According to the Chief Medical Officer it is unlikely in most cases that your baby has been affected, but if you're worried about the amount you've drunk then speak to your GP or midwife.

If you do decide to drink while you're pregnant or breast-feeding it's important to know exactly how much alcohol you are consuming. Many women underestimate the number of units they consume.

		Units of alcohol
Wine	175ml glass (12% ABV)	2
	250ml glass (14% ABV)	3.5
Beer, lager or cider	Half pint (3.5%)	1
	330ml bottle (4.5%)	1.5
Spirits – e.g. vodka, gin, rum	Single 25ml measure (40% ABV)	1
	Single 35ml measure (40% ABV)	1.5

ABV is % alcohol by volume.

Caffeine

Caffeine is found in tea, coffee, cola, chocolate, energy drinks such as Red Bull, and some medication including cold and flu remedies, headache treatments and diuretics. It is a stimulant and diuretic (it makes you wee).

It is fine to have up to 200mg of caffeine per day during pregnancy, according to the FSA. This is equivalent to about two cups of instant coffee. Having more than this can increase the risk of having a low-birthweight baby or even a miscarriage. Caffeine crosses the placenta and affects your baby in the same way it affects you.

To help stay within the limit, use the table as a guide.

		Caffeine content (mg)
Chocolate	Plain (50g bar)	Up to 25
	Milk (50g bar)	10
Hot chocolate	Drinking chocolate (cup made with powder)	1-8
	Hot chocolate (mug/ take-away)	10-30
Coffee	Filter or percolator (cup)	100-115
	Filter or percolator (mug)	140
	Filter (Starbuck's Venti)	400
	Flat white (regular)	150
	Instant (cup)*	75
	Instant (mug)*	100
	Espresso (single)	75-100
	Cappuccino/latte (regular)	100-200
	Americano (regular)	150-225
	Decaffeinated (cup)	4
Cola	Regular or diet (330ml can)	40
Energy drink	Containing caffeine or guarana (can)	Up to 80
Tea	Regular/black tea (medium strength cup)	50
	Regular/black tea (medium strength mug)	Up to 75
	Green tea (mug)	Up to 75

The amount of caffeine varies with the blend of tea leaves or coffee beans, the strength of tea or coffee, and the serving size.

*Caffeine levels may be higher in instant coffee containing 5-15% ground coffee beans - e.g. Nescafé Azera, Carte Noire Wholebean Instant and Kenco Millicano.

5 Nutrients – what they do and how much you need

We all know nutrients are important, but what exactly are they? Basically any substances found in food or drink that are essential to health. There are two types. **Macronutrients** – protein, carbohydrate and fat. These provide energy (calories) and have specific roles in maintaining health. **Micronutrients** – vitamins and minerals (e.g. iron and calcium). They are equally important but are needed in smaller amounts.

Here we look at each nutrient in turn, giving a brief run-down on what it's for, how much you need[1] and where to find it.[2] However, if you just want to know about good meals that contain all these nutrients in the right amount, go to pages 77-78.

Protein

What it's for: Protein provides amino acids, one of the basic building blocks of human tissue. It is needed for the growth

---

[1] In Chapter 5 most of the figures for the 'Amount needed' for each nutrient are based on the UK recommendations. However, the UK recommendations for some nutrients haven't been updated since 1992, therefore figures quoted for omega 3s, vitamins B_{12}, C and E and fluorine come from the EFSA and the iodine figure is set by the WHO.

[2] Information for the nutrient content of foods is taken from various sources including *McCance and Widdowson's the Composition of Foods: Seventh Summary Edition*, 2014, Royal Society of Chemistry.

of the foetus and placenta and for changes in the mother's body that occur during pregnancy. Protein is also essential for the production of breast milk.

Amount needed: 51g per day while pregnant and breast-feeding. There is usually no need to increase your protein intake during pregnancy, since the average (non-pregnant) woman consumes about 60g of protein a day anyway. However, if you are vegetarian or eat little meat, fish and dairy produce it's important to think about how much protein you are getting. If you mainly eat vegetables and cereals you can easily increase your protein intake, for example by adding lentils to vegetable soup or a tin of chickpeas to vegetable curry or pasta sauce.

	Grams of protein per 100g	*Protein per portion*
Lean beef	30	30g per 100g portion
Chicken	27	27g per 100g portion
Salmon, cod	25	35g per 140g portion
Eggs	13	16g in two eggs
Milk	3	10g per half pint/300ml
Yogurt	6	8g per small pot
Baked beans	5	10g per half tin
Chickpeas, kidney beans, lentils	8	8g per half tin
Bread	9	7g per 2 slices
Muesli	10	5g per 50g bowl
Peanuts	25	8g per 30g handful
Brazil nuts, hazelnuts, walnuts	14	5g per 30g handful

Carbohydrates

What they're for: Carbohydrates are the main source of energy in our diets. They contain fewer calories per gram than fat, making carbohydrate-rich foods better than fatty ones for avoiding excess weight gain. Low-carbohydrate diets can negatively affect a baby's long-term health, including increasing the risk of high blood pressure (see pages 27–28).

Amount needed: There are no specific guidelines as to how much carbohydrate you should eat each day, as it depends on how many calories you need. It is estimated that about 50% of a person's calories should come from carbohydrates.

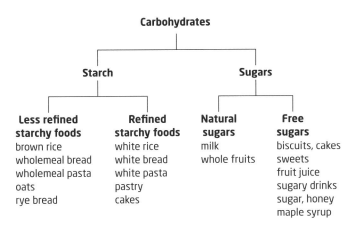

Where they're found: Carbohydrates come in the form of either starch or sugars (see diagram). Among the starchy foods, less refined are better than refined varieties as they have a lower GI (see page 35), provide extra fibre and more vitamins and minerals. Sugars are found in many foods, including fruit and milk, where they are accompanied by essential nutrients such as vitamin C and calcium. They are also found as free sugars in products such as cakes and sweets, which contain few or no useful nutrients. The advice of PHE is not to consume more than 30g of added sugar per day. The terms 'good carbs', 'smart carbs' or 'slow release carbs' are sometimes used for foods such as whole-grain cereals and 'bad carbs', 'dumb carbs' or 'quick release carbs' for more refined starchy foods and those containing free sugars.

Acrylamide

Acrylamide is a chemical that is produced naturally when starchy foods such as potatoes and bread are fried, baked or grilled at a high temperature. Generally the browner these foods become when they are cooked the more acrylamide will be formed. In 2015 the FSA looked at the evidence concerning acrylamide and concluded that at current levels of exposure, acrylamide could be increasing the risk of cancer. A large study being conducted across Europe has found that women with higher acrylamide intakes in pregnancy have smaller babies, which we know could increase risks to long-term health. This NewGeneris study is collecting data on childhood cancers, among other things, to see if the risks of these are increased, but so far we don't know.

To minimise your intake of acrylamide the FSA recommends:

- homemade chips should only be cooked until they are a light golden colour;
- toast should be as light a colour as possible;
- when frying or oven heating foods such as chips, follow the manufacturer's instructions carefully.

Fibre

What it's for: There are two types of dietary fibre. Insoluble fibre, generally known as roughage, helps food move through the digestive system so you don't get constipated. Soluble fibre, found in oats and lentils, helps to stabilise blood sugar and cholesterol levels.

Amount needed: 30g per day. This should come from foods that contain fibre naturally, such as wholegrains, fruit and vegetables, rather than fibre drinks or bran sprinkled on other foods (see page 120). It's a really good idea to have a high-fibre breakfast, otherwise it's difficult to meet the daily recommendation. There are plenty of suitable foods to choose from so it's fairly easy to do.

	Grams of fibre per 100g	Fibre per portion
Bran flakes	13	5g per 40g bowl
Muesli	9	5g per 50g bowl
Cornflakes	3	1g per 40g bowl
Wholemeal or granary bread	7	6g per two slices
White bread	3	2g per two slices
Brown rice	2	4g per 180g portion
White rice	1	2g per 180g portion
Wholemeal pasta	4	8g per 200g portion
White pasta	2	4g per 200g portion
Peas	6	5g per 80g portion
Carrots	3	2g per 80g portion
Apples, oranges	1	1g per fruit
Strawberries	4	3g per 80g bowl

Fats

What they're for: Fats get a bad press, but some fatty acids (the building blocks for fat) are essential for good health. There are three different types of fatty acid, which are found in varying amounts in foods. These are:

- **Saturated** – the type found in meat and dairy products such as cheese. These are not essential, and a high intake increases the risk of heart disease.
- **Monounsaturated** – found in olive oil and rapeseed oil, and also not essential to health.
- **Polyunsaturated** – some polyunsaturated fatty acids (PUFAs) are known as 'essential fatty acids'. They can't be produced by the body and must be supplied by the diet. There are two families of essential fatty acids:
  - **Omega 6** (n-6) – derived from linoleic acid (LA) and found in vegetable oils such as sunflower oil.
  - **Omega 3** (n-3) – there are two main types: short- and long-chain omega 3s. Alpha-linolenic acid (ALA) is a short-chain omega 3 found in flaxseeds (3.8g per tablespoon of ground seeds), flaxseed oil (8g per tablespoon), rapeseed oil (1.6g per tablespoon) and walnuts (2.5g per 25g handful). Longer-chain omega 3s, docosahexaenoic acid (DHA) and eicosapentaenoic acid (EPA), are found in oily fish (800–1,200mg per portion) and some fortified foods and supplements.

Simply looking at the total amount of fat in a food (see table on next page) can be misleading because not all fats are the same. Pizza and sausage rolls contain mainly saturated fat, salmon is rich in healthy long-chain omega 3s and nuts contain mainly mono- and polyunsaturated fats. As well as providing essential fatty acids, fat is needed for the absorption of the fat-soluble vitamins A, D, E and K.

Amount needed: Fat shouldn't make up more than 35% of your calorie intake. However, you do need about 30g of fat per day for the absorption of fat-soluble vitamins and 350-450mg of long-chain omega 3s (DHA plus EPA) are needed per day while pregnant or breastfeeding.

	Fat (g) per 100g	Fat per portion
Cooking oil - e.g. olive, rapeseed, sunflower	100	14g per tablespoon
Butter and margarine	80	8g per 10g portion
Cheddar	35	10g per 30g portion
Pizza	7-12	30g per half meat feast pizza
		20g per small margherita
Sausage roll	20-25	6-25g per sausage roll
Salmon	15	21g per 140g portion
Chocolate cake with icing	20-25	15-25g per slice
Chocolate	30-40	10-15g per single bar
Nuts	50-70	15-20g per 30g portion

The best source of long-chain omega 3s is oily fish and the body can also make them from short-chain omega 3s (found in flaxseeds). However, the body does not convert short-chain to long-chain omega 3s very efficiently and you are unlikely to get enough long-chain omega 3s just from eating foods rich in short-chain omega 3s. Part of the problem is that the conversion process is disrupted by high intakes of omega 6 fatty acids. Reducing the ratio of omega 6 to omega 3 fatty acids can help to some degree. This can be done by replacing sunflower oil or corn oil with rapeseed oil, flaxseed oil or olive oil, and eating more ALA-rich foods.

Conversion of short-chain omega 3s into beneficial long-chain omega 3s can also be limited by a lack of certain micronutrients, including iron, calcium, zinc and vitamin B_{12}. There is speculation that conversion is boosted during pregnancy, but the evidence suggests this isn't true. A study of pregnant Dutch women who were given short-chain omega 3s (via a fortified margarine) found no increase in the mothers' or babies' levels of long-chain DHA at birth compared with a control group. A similar American study found no change in DHA levels in breast milk when mothers were given 20g of flaxseed oil a day. The researchers in both cases concluded that the only efficient way of meeting a baby's DHA requirement is to increase the mother's intake of pre-formed DHA. So, if you don't eat oily fish or foods fortified with long-chain omega 3s, you might like to consider taking a supplement containing DHA (see page 84).

Omega 3s – what's all the fuss?
Research has shown that a good intake of long-chain omega 3s during pregnancy reduces the risk of having a low-birthweight or premature baby. A Danish study of nearly 8,000 pregnant women found low birthweight and premature birth were three times more common for mothers who did not eat any fish compared with those who had the highest intakes (just under two portions a week). The researchers also noted that risks were reduced significantly even for women consuming small amounts of fish (less than one portion a week).

As well as having a positive influence on the outcome of pregnancy, your DHA intake is important for your child's development. It is estimated that during pregnancy a baby accumulates at least 10g of DHA, and 6–7g of this is during the last trimester, mainly for brain development.

Consuming higher levels of DHA during pregnancy and after birth has been found to have beneficial effects on a baby's visual acuity, cognitive function, attention, maturity of sleep patterns and spontaneous motor activity. A high intake may also reduce a baby's sensitivity to common allergy triggers, including egg, and reduce the severity of eczema if it occurs.

Vitamins and minerals

There are two types of vitamins: water soluble and fat soluble. The water-soluble vitamins are the B vitamins and vitamin C. The fat-soluble vitamins are A, D and E. Water-soluble vitamins are easily lost if foods containing them are overcooked or boiled in lots of water that is then thrown away. Water-soluble vitamins are also lost more easily from the body. If you have a large intake of water-soluble vitamins, much of it will be lost in the urine. In contrast, there is a greater potential for problems if you have a large intake of fat-soluble vitamins as your body has to work harder to deal with them. You are extremely unlikely to have an excessively high intake of any vitamin or mineral (other than vitamin A) from diet alone. You only really need to be careful if you are taking a supplement.

Vitamin A

What it's for: This vitamin is needed for a strong immune system and the development of healthy skin and eyes. One of the first signs of deficiency is night blindness (an inability to see in dim light), but more severe deficiency can result in permanent eye damage. It is also important for the development and maturation of your baby's lungs.

Amount needed: 700µg of vitamin A (retinol equivalents) per day during pregnancy and 950µg per day while breastfeeding.

	Vitamin A (µg) per 100g	Vitamin A per portion
Liver (calf)	25,200	25,200µg per 100g portion
Liver pâté	7,300	1,825µg per 25g portion
Haggis	1,800	2,700µg per 150g portion
Milk	19	57µg per half pint/300ml
Eggs	126	
Carrots*	1,850	1,480
Mango*	116	93
Apricots*	84	68

*These foods don't contain retinol but their beta-carotene content has been multiplied by 6 to give a retinol-equivalent figure. This is to allow a comparison with the recommended amount.

There are two forms of vitamin A: retinol and beta-carotene. Retinol is found in foods derived from animals, including milk, and beta-carotene is found in fruit and vegetables, particularly orange-coloured ones.

High intakes: Although you need some vitamin A, be careful not to have too much, as levels in your body can build up. Because it is a fat-soluble vitamin, excess amounts aren't eliminated through the urine.

Vitamin A in the form of retinol is teratogenic. This means that a high intake (more than about 3,300µg per day) is associated with an increase in birth defects. For this reason, pregnant women and women trying for a baby are advised not to eat liver or liver products. They should also avoid supplements containing vitamin A, such as cod liver oil, unless advised by their doctor to take them. It is perfectly safe to consume other foods containing retinol, such as milk and cheese, as these have much lower levels. You can also eat foods containing high levels of beta-carotene during pregnancy; the worst effect this could have is to make your skin look slightly orange. Some experts believe that women need to increase their intake of beta-carotene during pregnancy, as vitamin A deficiency can be a real risk, particularly for women having twins and those having babies close together.

Folic acid

What it's for: It reduces the risk (by as much as 70%) of your baby developing a neural tube defect, such as spina bifida, if taken from before conception until week 12 of pregnancy. It also reduces the risk of cleft palate and harelip, and it works with vitamin B_{12} to form healthy red blood cells.

Amount needed: 300µg a day during pregnancy and 260µg a day while breastfeeding. In addition to this you should take a folic acid supplement before pregnancy and in the first 12 weeks of pregnancy (see page 82). Folic acid is easily destroyed by cooking, so it's important not to overcook vegetables. For example, if you boil peas in a pan of water you'll lose more than half the folate present.

	Folate (µg) per 100g	Folate per portion
Broccoli, steamed	72	58µg per 80g portion
Peas	50	40µg per 80g portion
Orange	33	50µg per medium orange
Milk	9	27µg per half pint/300ml
Yeast extract (e.g. Marmite)	2,620	100µg per 4g portion

▶

	Folate (µg) per 100g	Folate per portion
Fruit and fibre cereal	125-250	50-100µg per 40g bowl
Bran flakes	300-400	120-160µg per 40g bowl
Oats	32	16µg per 50g portion

Vitamin B$_2$ (riboflavin)

What it's for: You need this vitamin for the conversion of fats, protein and carbohydrates into energy. Deficiency results in cracked skin at the corners of the mouth and skin problems around the nose, eyes and tongue.

Amount needed: 1.4mg per day during pregnancy and 1.6mg per day while breastfeeding. If you consume too much, it will be excreted in your urine.

	Riboflavin (mg) per 100g	Riboflavin per portion
Milk	0.2	0.7mg per half pint/300ml
Cheddar	0.5	0.2mg per 30g portion
Mushrooms	0.3	0.2mg per 80g portion
Almonds	0.7	0.2mg per 30g handful
Yeast extract (e.g. Marmite)	11.9	0.3mg per 4g portion
Bran flakes, Weetabix and similar cereals	1.2	0.5mg per 40g bowl or two bisks

Vitamin B$_6$ (pyridoxine)

What it's for: Needed for the metabolism of protein and release of energy from foods. Vitamin B$_6$ is also required for the development of a healthy nervous system and red blood cells. Deficiency is rare, but there is some evidence that women with low levels are less likely to become pregnant and more likely to miscarry in early pregnancy.

Amount needed: 1.2mg per day during pregnancy and while breastfeeding.

	Vitamin B$_6$ (mg) per 100g	Vitamin B$_6$ per portion
Salmon	0.2	0.3mg per 140g portion
Tuna	0.3	0.4mg per tin
Hazelnuts, peanuts, almonds	0.6	0.2mg per 30g handful
Avocados, green peppers	0.3	0.3mg per 80g portion
Bananas	0.3	0.3mg per medium banana

See page 85 for information on vitamin B$_6$ supplements.

Vitamin B$_{12}$

What it's for: This vitamin is important for healthy red blood cells, the release of energy from food, and the development and normal functioning of the nervous system. It is also needed for the body to be able to process folic acid. Pregnant women with low vitamin B$_{12}$ levels appear to be at slightly greater risk of having a baby with spina bifida. However, the evidence for this is only limited, compared with the very strong evidence of an association between folic acid and spina bifida prevention.

Amount needed: 4.5µg per day during pregnancy and 5µg per day while breastfeeding.

	Vitamin B_{12} (µg) per 100g	Vitamin B_{12} per portion
Beef, pork, lamb	2	2µg per 100g portion
Salmon	3	4µg per 140g portion
Tuna	3	3.4µg per can
Milk	0.9	2.7µg per half pint/300ml
Yogurt	0.3	0.4µg per small pot
Eggs	2	1.0µg per egg
Marmite	15	0.6µg per 4g serving
Fortified breakfast cereals (unfortified cereals contain no vitamin B_{12})	2–4	1–2µg per 40g bowl

Vitamin B_{12} isn't found naturally in foods of plant origin, so vegetarians tend to have a lower intake. It is added to some vegetarian-friendly foods including marmite and some other brands of yeast extract, some breakfast cereals, soya products and milk alternatives. However, many of these products aren't fortified with vitamin B_{12} so it's important to read labels.

Choline
This is not by strict definition a vitamin, although it is some-times grouped with the B vitamins. Choline is important for

fat metabolism and the transmission of nerve impulses. There is also some evidence that choline plays a role in memory. The main sources of choline are milk, eggs and liver, but it is also found in meat and fish at lower levels. The body can make small amounts of choline, but not enough for optimal health. Individual requirements appear to vary and be dependent on genetic makeup. It is thought a varied diet should supply adequate amounts for pregnancy.

Vitamin C (ascorbic acid)

What it's for: This vitamin protects cells and keeps them healthy. Vitamin C is particularly important for wound healing. It also increases the absorption of iron from foods of plant origin such as breakfast cereals, bread, beans and vegetables (see page 73).

Amount needed: 105mg per day during pregnancy and 155mg per day while breastfeeding.

	Vitamin C (mg) per 100g	Vitamin C per portion
Oranges	52	85mg per medium orange
Strawberries	57	46mg per 80g portion
Kiwi fruit	59	35mg per kiwi
Potatoes	8-10	12-15mg per 150g portion
Broccoli, steamed	60	48mg per 80g portion
Cauliflower, boiled	30	24mg per 80g portion
Red pepper, raw	126	38mg per quarter pepper

If you boil vegetables such as broccoli, as much as a third of the vitamin C will be lost, whereas steaming will retain almost all of it, so whenever possible steam or lightly cook vegetables. If fruit is cut, it should be eaten as soon as possible.

Vitamin D

What it's for: This vitamin helps with absorption of calcium and building strong, healthy bones. It is particularly important during the later stages of pregnancy. If you don't get enough vitamin D during pregnancy or while breastfeeding, your baby may have low vitamin D and calcium levels. This can lead to the baby developing seizures in the first months of life. It also puts the baby at risk of the bone disease rickets, which results in a softening of the bones as they grow and is characterised by bowed legs. Other symptoms of deficiency in babies are poor teeth formation and general ill health. Poor vitamin D status during pregnancy is also associated with reduced bone mass in childhood and may increase the risk of osteoporosis in later life. Recent research suggests that a lack of vitamin D may also increase the risks of multiple sclerosis.

Amount needed: We get most of our vitamin D from normal exposure to the sun but all pregnant or breastfeeding women are advised to take a daily supplement containing vitamin D (see page 83). Ultraviolet B (UVB) radiation converts a vitamin D precursor in the skin to the active form of the vitamin. People with darker skins are at greater risk of deficiency, as they require longer exposure to sunlight to make the same amount of vitamin D. Women who have limited exposure to sunlight are also at greater risk of deficiency, for example those who remain covered for religious reasons when they go outside, and shift workers.

Supplements are particularly important in the winter months when there may not be enough sunlight of the appropriate wavelength to stimulate the production of sufficient vitamin D. During the summer months it is estimated that 15 minutes of sunlight on the arms, shoulders and head each day will supply enough vitamin D. During the winter months, people living at latitudes above 52 degrees (in the UK, people living north of Birmingham) are thought to receive no UV light of the appropriate wavelength to make vitamin D in their skin.

	Vitamin D (µg) per 100g	Vitamin D per portion
Sardines	5	5µg per small tin
Salmon	8	11µg per 140g portion
Eggs	3	2µg per egg
Margarine	8	0.8µg per 10g portion
Fortified breakfast cereals (unfortified cereals contain no vitamin D)	8	3µg per 40g portion

Vitamin E

What it's for: Vitamin E is an antioxidant. It helps protect cells, particularly those of the nervous system, from damage. There is some evidence to suggest that eating a diet high in vitamin E during pregnancy may protect your baby against developing asthma and other allergies in later life.

Amount needed: 11mg per day while pregnant and during breastfeeding.

	Vitamin E (mg) per 100g	Vitamin E per portion
Spinach	1.7	1.4mg per 80g portion
Broccoli	1.8	1.8mg per 80g portion
Tomatoes, canned	1.4	2.8mg per half can
Almonds, hazelnuts	25	8mg per 30g handful
Peanuts	10	3 per 30g handful
Rapeseed oil	22	3mg per tablespoon
Sunflower oil	49	6mg per tablespoon

Calcium

What it's for: Calcium helps build strong bones and teeth. It also regulates muscle contraction and is needed for normal blood clotting. Higher calcium intakes in pregnancy are also associated with lower blood pressure in childhood.

Amount needed: 700mg per day during pregnancy and 1,250mg per day while breastfeeding. To help your body absorb calcium, it's important to have enough vitamin D. You need to be especially careful about getting enough calcium if you are a vegan, or a teenager, or if you don't drink much milk or eat many dairy products as these are the main source of calcium for most people. Foods such as spinach, beans, seeds, nuts and dried fruit shouldn't be relied on as your main source of calcium because they contain oxalates and phytates, which reduce the amount of calcium your body can absorb.

If you consume little or no milk or milk products then a fortified milk substitute may be a good idea (see page 106). When having seeds and nuts it's best to have them crushed (e.g. almond butter or tahini), as this will mean you can absorb more of the calcium they contain. Bone broths are becoming increasingly popular and although it would seem feasible that they are rich in calcium this has not been found to be the case. Analysis shows that even when bones are cooked until soft, broths contain little, if any, calcium.

	Calcium (mg) per 100g	Calcium per portion
Milk (whole or low fat)	120	360mg per half pint/300ml
Yogurt (plain)	160	200mg per small pot
Soya milk or other milk substitute with added calcium	120	360mg per half pint/300ml
Organic soya milk or other organic milk substitute	13	40mg per half pint/300ml
Sardines (mashed with bones)	679	611mg per can
Almonds or almond butter	240	72mg per 30g handful or three teaspoons
Tofu	100-500	100-500mg per 100g portion depending on ingredients
Sesame seeds or tahini	675	68mg per teaspoon
Broccoli	44	35mg per 80g portion
Kale	150	120mg per 80g portion

Iron

What it's for: Iron is needed for healthy red blood cells, which carry oxygen around the body. During pregnancy, iron requirements are increased. It is needed both to supply the baby and placenta and also to produce extra red blood cells for your own circulation. Most pregnant women are routinely monitored for iron deficiency or anaemia. Women who are overweight or obese are more likely to have low iron levels. Studies have also shown that they may have impaired iron absorption. If your iron levels are low, you may feel especially tired and lethargic or even faint. It can also affect your baby - iron-deficiency anaemia is associated with lower birthweight and prematurity. In addition, a good iron intake may reduce the risk of your child developing asthma.

Amount needed: 14.8mg per day during pregnancy and while breastfeeding. Rather than relying on particular foods for iron it is best to eat a variety.

	Iron (mg) per 100g	*Iron per portion*
Beef	2.5	2.5mg per 100g portion
Chicken	0.4–0.8	0.4–0.8mg per 100g portion (darker meat has more iron)
Mackerel	1.3	1.8mg per 140g portion
Muesli	2.7	1.6mg per 50g bowl
Fortified breakfast cereal (unfortified cereals have less than 1mg iron per bowl)	10–13	4-5mg per 40g bowl
White pasta	0.6	1.2mg per 20g portion
Wholemeal pasta	1.5	3mg per 20g portion
White bread	1.5	1.2mg per two slices
Wholemeal bread	2.4	1.8mg per two slices
Red lentils, cooked	2.4	2.1mg per three tablespoons

Chickpeas (cooked)	1.5	1.8mg per half can
Peas	1.8	1.4mg per 80g portion
Dried fruit (e.g. apricots, sultanas)	3.5	1mg per tablespoon

See page 83 for information on iron supplements.

Easy ways to boost iron absorption
The iron in meat and fish is absorbed more easily than that in foods of plant origin. However, you can boost the amount your body absorbs from foods such as cereals, bread and lentils by having vitamin C at the same time. You could have strawberries with breakfast cereal or fruit salad after a sandwich. It also helps if you avoid tea or coffee at mealtimes and for about an hour afterwards, as they contain polyphenols, which bind to iron, making it more difficult to absorb.

Zinc

What it's for: Zinc is needed to make new cells and enzymes and to help with wound healing. The body also needs zinc to process the protein, carbohydrates and fats we eat.

Amount needed: 7mg per day during pregnancy. While breastfeeding, this increases to 13mg per day for the first four months and 9.5mg a day thereafter.

	Zinc (mg) per 100g	*Zinc per portion*
Chicken	1–2	1–2mg per 100g portion (dark meat has twice as much as light meat)

▶

	Zinc (mg) per 100g	Zinc per portion
Beef	5	5mg per 100g portion
Milk	0.4	1.2mg per half pint/300ml
Cheddar	4.1	1.2mg per 30g portion
Bran flakes	2.1	0.8mg per 40g bowl
Wholemeal bread	1.6	1.3mg per two slices
Muesli	1.7	0.9mg per 50g bowl

Iodine

What it's for: Iodine is important for the production of thyroid hormones and the development of the nervous system, particularly during the first three months of pregnancy. The most obvious sign of severe deficiency is a goitre, which is a large swelling on the neck, but this is extremely rare in European countries. However, recent research has shown the re-emergence of mild iodine deficiency in pregnant women in the UK. This is a concern, because even mild deficiency in pregnancy can lead to impaired brain development and have long-term implications, such as lower IQ.

Amount needed: 250µg per day during pregnancy and while breastfeeding.

If you eat two to three portions of dairy products (e.g. milk, cheese, yogurt) per day and one or two portions of fish per week you should get enough iodine. Most plant foods, including cereals, beans and vegetables, contain very little iodine, so if you consume little or no milk it is important that you have foods with added iodine or take a supplement (see page 85). Meeting your iodine requirements by eating seaweed is not recommended (see page 86).

	Iodine (μg) per 100g	Iodine per portion
Milk (conventional, not organic)	25–40	75–120μg per half pint/300ml
Milk (organic)	15–30	45–90μg per half pint/300ml
Cheddar	30	9μg per 30g portion
Nori (dried seaweed)	1,470	36μg per 2.5g sheet
Wakame (dried seaweed)	16,830	168μg per 1g
Kombu/Kelp (dried seaweed)	440,670	4,400μg per 1g
Haddock	421	589μg per 140g portion
Cod	200	280μg per 140g portion
Tuna, canned	26	29μg per tin
Meat or poultry	Less than 10	Less than 10μg per 100g

High intakes: Having too much iodine can interfere with thyroid function. The British Dietetic Association advises against consuming more than 600μg of iodine per day.

Selenium

What it's for: Selenium is an antioxidant and therefore protects against cell damage. Selenium also plays an important role in the immune system, thyroid hormone metabolism and reproduction. Research suggests that having a good intake of selenium during pregnancy may reduce the risk of your baby developing eczema and wheezing (an early warning sign for asthma).

Amount needed: 60μg of selenium per day during pregnancy and 75μg per day while breastfeeding.

	Selenium (μg) per 100g	Selenium per portion
Tuna	85	94μg per can
Cod	44	61μg per 140g portion
Brazil nuts	254	76μg per 30g handful
Cashew nuts	34	10μg per 30g handful
Eggs	25	15 per egg
Kidney beans	6	5μg per two tablespoons

Fluoride

What it's for: Fluoride is needed for strong tooth enamel and bone formation.

Amount needed: 0.5mg a day per kg of body weight. During pregnancy and breastfeeding this should be calculated based on weight before becoming pregnant.

Where it's found: Tea is the main source of fluoride in the UK. It is also found in water, milk and fish that are eaten with bones, such as sardines.

See page 86 for information on fluoride supplements.

From nutrients to meals – sample meal plans

Learning about the key nutrients for pregnancy can be helpful, but for you to benefit this information has to be translated into everyday eating. Below is a one-week meal planner to show you how you can get all the nutrients you need from meals and snacks. This isn't a menu plan for you to follow, but it should give you an idea of what a healthy, balanced diet really looks like.

DAY 1

Breakfast	Porridge and a handful of dried apricots.
Lunch	Tomato and lentil soup with a wholemeal roll, and a peach.
Dinner	Grilled salmon, a baked potato with cottage cheese, and some broccoli and carrots. Apple crumble and Greek yogurt.
Snacks	Oatcakes with cream cheese and grapes.

DAY 2

Breakfast	Bran flakes with a sliced banana.
Lunch	A tuna and sweetcorn sandwich with salad.
Dinner	Chickpea and sweet potato curry with chapatti. Fresh raspberries with natural yogurt.
Snacks	Mixed nut flapjack and an apple.

DAY 3

Breakfast	Muesli.
Lunch	Baked beans on granary toast, and fresh fruit salad.
Dinner	Stir-fried chicken with peppers, mange tout, baby corn, carrots and egg noodles.
Snacks	A slice of carrot cake and fresh strawberry milkshake.

DAY 4

Breakfast	A grapefruit, and wholemeal toast with Marmite.
Lunch	Cheese and tomato toasted sandwich with watercress and pine nut salad.
Dinner	Pasta with roast vegetables (e.g. peppers, tomatoes and courgette), and a pot of yogurt.

Snacks	A banana and chocolate brazil nuts.
	Houmous with carrot sticks and pitta bread.
DAY 5	
Breakfast	Scrambled eggs on granary toast with grilled mushrooms, tomatoes and sliced avocado.
Lunch	Mixed bean salad with tomatoes and avocado, and a slice of rye bread. Pot of yogurt.
Dinner	Roast chicken with potatoes, broccoli, red cabbage and carrots. Rice pudding.
Snacks	An apple and a bag of dried fruit and seeds.
DAY 6	
Breakfast	Weetabix with mixed berries.
Lunch	Vegetarian pizza, salad and an orange.
Dinner	Fish pie with peas.
Snacks	Date and walnut cookie and a decaf skinny cappuccino.
DAY 7	
Breakfast	Muesli and chopped strawberries.
Lunch	Leek and potato soup with bread and cream cheese. A pear.
Dinner	Chinese beef with mixed peppers, stir-fried kale and rice.
Snacks	Bowl of cereal and banana. Slice of chocolate cheesecake.

Healthy meal ideas

It's very easy to get in a food rut and keep eating the same things, but the more varied your diet the more likely you are to get all the nutrients you need. Breakfast and lunch are often rushed, if they're not forgotten completely, but there's no need to have the same breakfast cereal and sandwich every day. Most of these don't take long to prepare but they may take a bit of forward planning if you don't usually have the ingredients in your fridge or cupboard.

Ten healthy breakfasts

• Nutty muesli with sliced banana and yogurt.

• Homemade porridge made with oats, grated apple, milk and a large pinch of cinnamon.

• Scrambled egg on granary toast with a couple of tomatoes cut in half and grilled.

• Weetabix with mixed berries and chopped nuts.

• Seeded toast with peanut butter and sliced banana.

• French toast with blueberries.

• Wholemeal pancakes with plum compote.

• Slices of melon and grapefruit, baked beans on granary toast.

• Toasted rye bread with low-fat cream cheese, sliced strawberries and a drizzle of honey.

• Bircher muesli – oats soaked in milk overnight then mixed with dried fruit, nuts, seeds and yogurt.

Ten healthy lunches

• Rye bread or granary toast with mashed avocado, lemon juice and black pepper.

• Tuna niçoise salad with tuna, hard-boiled egg, new potatoes, green beans and olives.

• An egg mayo sandwich and salad.

• Chunky vegetable and lentil soup.

• Mashed sardines on toast.

• Houmous, grated carrot and salad wrap.

• Spanish omelette with potato and onion and a green salad.

• Baked sweet potato with chopped tomato, spring onion and cottage cheese.

- Couscous salad with roast vegetables and feta cheese.
- Granary roll with grilled chicken, avocado and salad.

Ten tasty suppers

- Vegetarian chilli and brown rice.
- Homemade vegetable and goats' cheese pizza with salad.
- Baked salmon, new potatoes, broccoli and carrots.
- Spinach and chickpea curry with wholemeal chapatti.
- Thai noodles with prawns, mushrooms, carrot, peppers and pak choi.
- Wholemeal pasta with tomato, tuna and black olive sauce.
- Butternut squash and red lentil stew with baked potato.
- Wholemeal spaghetti with meatballs and tomato and red pepper sauce.
- Roast chicken, sweet potato wedges, coleslaw and green salad.
- Shepherd's pie with potato and swede mash and peas.

6 Supplements – who needs what and why

For most people in good health, a well-balanced diet provides all the necessary nutrients. However, there is clear evidence that certain supplements are beneficial during pregnancy. Supplements containing folic acid and vitamin D are recommended for all pregnant women, irrespective of how well or badly they eat. Other supplements, such as iron tablets, should be taken during pregnancy only if blood tests show they are needed. Then there are multivitamin and mineral supplements and omega 3 capsules. The manufacturers would have you believe that every mum-to-be needs them, but it's important to think about your own diet and to look at the evidence before deciding whether they are really for you.

The government advises all pregnant women to take:

- 400µg of folic acid daily before conception and for the first 12 weeks of pregnancy;
- 10µg of vitamin D daily for the entire course of pregnancy.

Folic acid supplements

There is strong evidence that folic acid supplements reduce the risk of having a baby with a neural tube defect (NTD) such as spina bifida or anencephaly. In fact, trials with folic acid supplements had to be stopped early because the benefits were so clear that it was unethical to continue giving some women a placebo. These supplements are recommended even if you have a very healthy diet as it is almost impossible to get enough folic acid in a form that is easily absorbed from food alone.

Ideally you should start taking folic acid supplements two to three months before you become pregnant, but otherwise begin as soon as possible and continue until week 12 of pregnancy. It's safe to continue taking folic acid beyond 12 weeks, but there is generally no need if you are eating well. Supplements are available from chemists and most supermarkets quite cheaply, or you may be eligible for free ones (see page 88).

Supplements containing 400µg (sometimes written as 0.4mg, 400mcg or 400 micrograms) of folic acid are recommended for most women. However, some may benefit from higher doses of up to 5mg (5,000µg). Ask your doctor about taking a higher dose of folic acid if:

- you have had a previous pregnancy affected by a NTD;
- you or your partner has a family history of NTDs;
- you have diabetes;
- your body mass index (BMI) falls in the obese category.

Unless you have been advised to take more than the recommended 400µg per day, it is best not to take more than 1,000µg (1mg) per day.

Vitamin D supplements

The government advises women to take supplements containing 10µg (10mcg, 10 micrograms, 400 international units, 400 i.u.) of vitamin D throughout pregnancy and while breastfeeding. This is needed for the absorption of calcium. Low levels can be detrimental to both mother and baby (see page 68).

About a third of pregnant women have low levels of vitamin D in their blood. One in five is clinically deficient according to research published in 2016. Those most at risk are women who don't get much sunlight, women of South Asian, African, Caribbean or Middle Eastern descent, women who are obese, and women who are pregnant during the winter months. However, it is also important not to take too much vitamin D, as very high intakes can result in more calcium being absorbed than the body can cope with, leading to kidney damage. Taking supplements containing more than about 25µg (1,000 i.u.) is not advisable.

Iron supplements

You need to take iron supplements during pregnancy only if blood tests show you have low levels of iron, in which case your midwife or doctor will prescribe them. If your iron levels are normal, then you should be able to get all the iron you need from the foods you eat (see page 72) and it may actually be harmful to take high doses of iron (i.e. more than is found in pregnancy multivitamin and mineral supplements).

Some women find that the iron supplements they are prescribed (usually ferrous sulphate) cause unpleasant side effects, including nausea and constipation. Women with only borderline low iron levels sometimes decide to increase the amount of iron in their diet rather than taking supplements. Doing this, along with taking measures to improve absorption (see page 73) may be sufficient.

If you find iron supplements make you feel unwell it may help to take them with food. If this doesn't work, you could try switching to a different iron supplement. Your GP or midwife could prescribe iron gluconate instead of sulphate or you could buy a supplement such as Spatone. Any iron supplements you are prescribed while pregnant will be free, but you'll probably have to pay for alternatives – though if it makes you feel better, it's generally worth it. Some iron supplements have added vitamin C to increase absorption. If yours doesn't, you could just take it with a glass of orange juice. You should also avoid having tea or coffee for an hour after taking iron supplements as this reduces absorption.

Omega 3 supplements

There are several different types of omega 3 supplement available. Some contain ALA, which is one of the shorter-chain omega 3s found in various seed oils, including flaxseed, but it is better to take a supplement containing readymade DHA (see page 60).

Supplements containing long-chain omega 3s (including DHA and EPA) are derived either from oily fish or from algal sources (seaweed), which are suitable for vegetarians. Guidelines suggest taking between 200mg and 300mg of DHA per day, but fish oil supplements containing up to 1g (1,000mg) of DHA per day or 2.7g of long-chain omega 3s per day have been used in research studies without any adverse effects (apart from belching and a nasty taste). There has not been much research on DHA supplements made from algae. However, the studies that have been done, in non-pregnant individuals, suggest that they are effective in raising blood

DHA levels and that they appear to be safe and well tolerated.

Supplements containing cod liver oil, or other fish liver oils, are also high in beneficial omega 3s. However, they are not suitable for pregnancy because they contain high levels of vitamin A, which could be harmful to your baby.

Vitamin B$_6$ supplements

There is a small amount of evidence suggesting that taking vitamin B$_6$ supplements can relieve nausea and vomiting during pregnancy in some women. However, the FSA advises against taking more than 10mg of supplemental vitamin B$_6$ a day. Others suggest doses of up to 40mg should be considered safe, and some people say that taking around 100mg a day for a short period may be quite safe, but nobody really knows. Taking large doses (200mg a day) is associated with nerve damage and loss of feeling in the hands and feet, which may be irreversible. If you want to try supplements, it is best to talk to your doctor before starting.

Research in Thailand found that vitamin B$_6$ supplements weren't as effective as either ginger or acupressure at relieving nausea and vomiting, so you may like to get some wristbands and ginger before following this route.

Iodine supplements

If you don't consume milk, milk products such as cheese and yogurt or eat fish then it can be extremely difficult to get enough iodine from diet alone (see page 74) and a supplement may be a good idea. Iodine in supplements should be in the form of potassium iodide and it is best not to take more than 150µg per day from supplements without the advice of your doctor. Some but not all multivitamins and minerals for pregnancy include about this amount of iodine.

Supplements made from seaweed, including kelp, are not recommended as the amount of iodine they contain may be very different to that stated on the label, so you could end up having too much. This is because seaweed is natural and therefore the amount of iodine it contains can vary considerably depending on factors such as where it was harvested and how it has been processed.

Fluoride supplements

These are not recommended. There is some evidence that taking fluoride supplements during pregnancy reduces the risk of your child developing tooth decay. However, this research is controversial, as other studies have found no benefit. There is also some suggestion, although it has not been researched properly, that taking fluoride supplements in pregnancy could adversely affect foetal brain development.

Multivitamin and mineral supplements

If, for any reason, you think your nutrient intake is inadequate, then you may want to take a multivitamin and mineral supplement. A general supplement for pregnancy and breastfeeding provides a good safeguard for women with limited diets, for example vegans and those who don't eat dairy foods. Some others, such as diabetic women and teenagers, may also benefit. If you are concerned, ask for further advice from your doctor or midwife, or ask to be referred to a dietician.

The safest supplements are those available on the high street labelled as suitable for pregnancy and breastfeeding. It is not advisable to take a multivitamin and mineral supplement that is not specifically formulated for pregnancy, as it may not contain the right balance of nutrients. It may have too much vitamin A or not enough folic acid or vitamin D for pregnancy. Not all multivitamin and mineral supplements contain the same nutrients, so if you are choosing one, look at exactly what is in it. Some don't include iodine or selenium, and if you think you might not be getting enough of these minerals, for example if you don't include dairy produce in your diet, then it would be a good idea to choose one that does.

It is not good to take high doses of specific nutrients either, as some have unknown effects. A study with high doses of vitamins C and E found an increased number of babies with low birthweight but no preventive effect on pre-eclampsia, which these vitamins were thought to provide. Further research is being carried out, but because of these unwanted results, supplements containing large doses of vitamins C and E are no longer recommended. Pregnancy multivitamin supplements usually contain lower doses and shouldn't be a problem. In fact, another research trial found that pregnancy multivitamins might help in preventing pre-eclampsia.

For a healthy woman with a mixed diet (including meat, fish, dairy produce, fruit and vegetables) the benefits of taking a multivitamin and mineral supplement during pregnancy are unclear. On balance, the evidence suggests that they are either beneficial or have no effect. It is difficult to determine the impact because women who take them are less likely to smoke or drink alcohol and more likely to eat well and exercise compared to women who don't take supplements. It could be that any reported health benefits are the result of these factors rather than of the supplements themselves.

If you do decide to take a supplement, remember that it is not a substitute for a good diet. For one thing, real foods such as fruit and vegetables contain many beneficial phytochemicals, such as lycopene in tomatoes and anthocyanins in blackberries and aubergines, which are not found in most supplements. A good diet is also high in fibre and low in salt and contains the right balance of fatty acids. So, if you take a supplement, you should still try to eat as well as possible. It is best to take any supplements during or after a meal in order to maximise nutrient absorption.

Diabetic mums and supplements
If you have diabetes you may benefit from taking a general pregnancy multivitamin and mineral supplement as well as taking a higher dose of folic acid. A study conducted in the USA found that although diabetic women had an increased risk of having a baby with a birth defect such as hydrocephalus, a heart defect or cleft palate, those who took a multivitamin supplement before and during pregnancy had no greater risk than non-diabetic women.

Healthy Start

If you are on a low income or under 18, you may be eligible for free supplements through the Healthy Start scheme as well as vouchers for free fruit, vegetables and milk. See 'Resources and useful contacts' to find out more (page 208) or ask your doctor, midwife or health visitor.

7 Pregnancy problems and how to deal with them

It would be great if every woman could spend her pregnancy feeling radiant with health and vitality. However, few of us make it through the whole nine months without at least a bit of queasiness or constipation. Some women feel downright rotten for some or even most of their pregnancy, and the majority fall somewhere in between. But there are often things you can do to make yourself feel better. If you have morning sickness or any form of digestive problem, fairly simple dietary changes can make a big difference.

Morning sickness

Despite its name, 'morning sickness' can occur at any time of the day. Some women find that it gets worse if they are feeling tired, stressed or hungry. It can also be triggered by certain odours, such as cooking smells or strong aftershave.

Around 80% of women experience some feelings of nausea during pregnancy and about 30% are affected by severe nausea and vomiting. Symptoms tend to be worst at around

9-10 weeks and disappear by about the fourteenth week. The exact cause of morning sickness isn't known, but it is thought to be related to the sudden rise in blood levels of a hormone called human chorionic gonadotropin (hCG) in early pregnancy. Women carrying twins are more likely to suffer from morning sickness, as they have higher levels of this hormone in early pregnancy.

If you can't face eating anything at all or anything healthy, try not to worry. The good news is that, although you are feeling awful, your baby is very unlikely to be affected. Research shows that mothers who suffer from pregnancy sickness are less likely to have a miscarriage, a premature delivery or congenital malformations. However, this doesn't prove that if you're sick your baby will be OK or, equally, that if you're not feeling sick it's a bad sign.

If you are not eating very much or not keeping very much down, your baby will simply draw on your store of nutrients. If you can't face proper meals, then eating small snacks throughout the day will help to keep up your strength. Ideally you should make snacks as healthy as possible (see page 15), but if you can't face anything other than salty crisps or fruit pastilles, then have a few. Just try to eat more healthily as soon as you start feeling a bit better. There are lots of things you can do to help relieve your symptoms, and make yourself feel more normal, so why not give some of them a try.

Tried and tested remedies

There is no single treatment that works for all women, but different strategies can be helpful for different women. You could try the following:

- Eat little and often. By eating small, carbohydrate-rich meals or snacks every couple of hours, you can stop your blood sugar levels dropping too low, which can make you feel worse.

- Eat some dry crackers or biscuits in bed before getting up in the morning.
- Avoid foods that you find trigger nausea, such as fatty or spicy dishes or foods with a strong odour. It may be better to eat certain foods cold or, if you can, get someone else to do the cooking.
- Avoid other triggers. Some women find that the smell of petrol or perfume is a problem or that travelling in the back seat of a car makes them feel worse.
- Vitamin B_6 supplements may help (see page 85).
- Have plenty of fluids, but avoid caffeine and alcohol.
- Have ginger in any form, for example ginger tea or ginger biscuits (see page 138).
- Get more fresh air.
- Rest and sleep as much as possible.
- Get some seasickness wristbands from a chemist. These act on the acupressure point for nausea. Some trials, though not all, have found that they are effective for morning sickness.
- Complementary therapies such as aromatherapy, homeopathy and acupuncture work for some women.

Mums' tips

These may not stand up to scientific research but they all worked for someone. It just shows that one woman's poison really is another woman's cure.

- Eat pickled onion crisps first thing in the morning.
- Sip water with slices of lemon.
- Carry around a lemon to scratch and sniff.
- Sip cider vinegar in water (see page 125).
- Drink bitter lemon mixed with tap water.

- Have some chewing gum.
- Suck on a mini milk or fruity ice lolly.
- Chop an apple and eat it throughout the day.
- Snack on ice cold melon.
- Sip water with lime juice and salt.
- Eat meals very slowly – e.g. have a quarter of your sandwich every 15 minutes.
- Suck on mints – some women liked mild mints but for others only extra strong will do.
- Have a protein-rich snack at bedtime.
- Eat salty crisps or crackers with peanut butter.
- Keep some strong freezer bags in your handbag for the morning commute, just in case.

Ten meals for morning sickness

If you don't feel like cooking or eating you might find something here to inspire you:

1 Cheese and grated Granny Smith apple on toast.
2 Jacket potato with grated cheese.
3 Miso soup, maybe with chicken, tofu or vegetables.
4 Hot cross buns, preferably wholemeal.
5 Pitta bread filled with marmite, cream cheese and cucumber.
6 Stir-fried chicken or prawns with vegetables and ginger and plain rice.
7 Pasta, either plain or with grated cheese or a little ragu sauce.
8 Mashed potato and cooked chicken.
9 Chicken noodle soup.
10 A bowl of cereal with ice cold milk.

There is sometimes a feeling that sickness is a normal part of pregnancy and that you should just put up with it, but in some cases it can have serious consequences for both a mother and her baby. A small number of women, around 1%, suffer from Hyperemisis Gravidarum (HG) and experience severe vomiting, dehydration and weight loss. HG can increase the risk of premature delivery and low birthweight and it is associated with physical and mental problems for the mother, including malnutrition and depression. If you can't keep anything down for 24 hours, have very dark wee, a high temperature, severe weakness or tummy pains then contact your doctor straight away.

GPs in the UK have been criticised for not taking the condition more seriously, particularly as early treatment can help stop it becoming so bad that hospital care is needed. In the USA and Canada, severe morning sickness is treated with antihistamines and pyridoxine (vitamin B_6), but in the UK, GPs tend to be more reluctant to prescribe any drug treatment. This situation does seem to be changing slowly, partly thanks to publicity surrounding Kate Middleton's pregnancies. See your doctor to discuss treatment options.

Heartburn

Whereas morning sickness is most common at the beginning of pregnancy, heartburn is more likely to be a problem in the last three months. Of course individuals vary and some women suffer from heartburn throughout their pregnancy. The main symptom is a burning sensation in the chest, caused by acids going back up the food pipe from the stomach. A muscle valve usually prevents this from happening, but during pregnancy it becomes more relaxed because of hormonal changes. The pressure of your growing baby pushing on the stomach can make heartburn even worse towards the end of pregnancy. This may be particularly true for those expecting twins, as the uterus is inevitably larger and therefore presses on the stomach more.

Heartburn can be particularly bad after a large meal or during activities that involve bending over, such as cleaning the floor or even just picking something up. Some women find that symptoms lessen in the last few weeks of pregnancy when their baby's head becomes engaged and it moves further down into the pelvis ready for birth, as this reduces the pressure on the stomach. The good news is that when the baby is delivered, heartburn usually disappears almost instantly.

There are several things you can do to ease the symptoms of heartburn:

- Wear loose-fitting clothes to reduce extra pressure on your stomach.

- Avoid becoming too full, by eating little and often instead of having large meals. Also, don't drink too much at mealtimes.

- Try to identify trigger foods and avoid them, especially in the evening. Common culprits include spicy food, citrus fruits, rich and fatty foods, tea and coffee, and bananas. You might also find foods such as onions, garlic or pepper 'repeat' on you and make matters worse.

- When you eat, sit upright instead of slouching and try not to rush.

- Try to stay sitting upright for a while after meals. When you go to bed, prop yourself up with several pillows.

- Milk is good for neutralising the acid and easing symptoms, so try drinking a small glass before bed or have some ready to sip during the night.

- Homeopathy, aromatherapy and yoga may all help.

- If symptoms are severe, talk to your midwife, doctor or pharmacist and they will be able to provide you with a treatment. If you ask your pharmacist be sure to say you are pregnant as not all heartburn treatments are suitable.

Constipation

Constipation is more common than usual during pregnancy because of hormonal changes. Increasing progesterone levels cause all the muscles in your body, including intestinal muscles, to relax, so food moves through your intestines more slowly. This helps your body to absorb more nutrients from the food, but it can also lead to constipation. In addition, the pressure of your baby on your bowels can make going to the toilet more difficult. Iron tablets can also cause constipation (see page 83).

To treat constipation, try the following:

• Eat plenty of fibre-rich foods (e.g. wholemeal bread, wholegrain breakfast cereal) and lots of fruit and vegetables.

• Have some prunes or prune juice (see page 158).

• Drink plenty of water, but avoid having too much caffeine, as it can contribute to dehydration, which makes constipation worse.

• Take some gentle exercise, such as walking, swimming or yoga.

• When you go to the toilet, relax and take your time.

• Switch iron supplements if necessary (see page 84).

If this doesn't help, talk to your midwife or doctor; they may prescribe laxatives that are safe to take during pregnancy. Not all are.

Wind and bloating

As well as constipation, pregnant women often have more wind, bloating and general digestive discomfort than normal.

Because food spends longer in the intestine, it has more time to ferment and produce more gas or wind.

To relieve the symptoms of wind and bloating, try the following:

• Avoid foods that are particular triggers. Different foods seem to affect different people, but beans, cabbage and onions are common culprits. To prevent your diet becoming too limited, you may occasionally want to have individual trigger foods, but avoid having several at the same time.

• Don't eat large meals.

• Try to relax and sit up tall at mealtimes.

• When you eat, chew properly, and avoid gulping air by eating slowly and not talking too much.

• Avoid swallowing air when you drink by using a cup or glass rather than a bottle or straw.

• Take gentle exercise such as yoga or walking to help keep your digestive system working efficiently.

• Avoid fizzy drinks.

If you are feeling pain rather than just discomfort, talk to your doctor or midwife as soon as possible.

Haemorrhoids (piles)

Piles or haemorrhoids are varicose veins around the rectum and anus (back passage). They may develop for the first time during pregnancy, or existing piles may get worse. Piles are exacerbated by straining when you go to the toilet and by constipation. The best way to prevent piles from developing, and to treat them if you get them, is to follow the advice for dealing with constipation. You should also try not to strain on the toilet. If the piles are very inflamed and itchy, talk to your midwife or doctor about a suitable cream to ease your discomfort.

Sometimes piles become worse after the birth - particularly if it is a difficult vaginal delivery. However, the good news is that as you recover from the birth, piles become much less of a problem.

Diarrhoea

Although constipation is a much more common complaint during pregnancy, some women do find diarrhoea is a problem. This is nothing to worry about unless the diarrhoea is severe and continues for more than a few days. If this is the case, you should see your GP or midwife for further tests, such as a stool culture, to rule out salmonella and other infections.

Like so many pregnancy problems, diarrhoea can be caused by changing hormone levels. It is not a problem in itself, but it can cause dehydration. If you have diarrhoea, it is important to drink plenty of water or take a rehydration powder available from a pharmacy. Taking a probiotic yogurt or drink may also help.

If you find that diarrhoea is a problem towards the end of pregnancy, it can be one of the signs that labour is imminent.

Urinary tract infections (UTIs)

Some women are more prone to UTIs and while mild infections can occur at any time, during pregnancy you are more likely to develop a more severe UTI. This is because progesterone levels increase, which causes muscles to relax, including the muscles of the ureter; this means urine flows more slowly from the kidneys to the bladder so there is more time for an infection to take hold. The growing uterus also adds to the problem. A UTI can occur in the lower part of the urinary tract including the bladder, in which case it is called cystitis, or in the upper part of the urinary tract. If the upper part is infected it is potentially more dangerous as the kidneys can become damaged.

The symptoms of UTIs include:

- a need to wee more often;
- a burning sensation or pain when you wee;
- a pain in the lower abdomen (tummy);
- raised temperature.

To avoid developing a UTI:

- Drink plenty of fluids.
- Avoid constipation.
- Drink cranberry juice.
- Wipe from front to back when you go to the toilet.
- Go for a wee after sex.

If you develop a UTI while you are pregnant it is best to see your GP as soon as possible as having a UTI increases the risks of premature birth and growth restriction. You can then be tested and prescribed antibiotics if appropriate. After one UTI it is especially important to follow the preventative advice to avoid a recurrence.

Restless legs

Restless leg syndrome (RLS) involves a strong urge to move the legs and also sometimes the arms. Women generally find symptoms are worse when they settle down for a much-needed rest, particularly at night. RLS can occur at any stage of life, but it is two to three times more likely during pregnancy, particularly in the last trimester. Typically symptoms disappear after the baby is born.

It is not clear what causes RLS, but people with it have been found to have lower levels of dopamine in a region of the brain known as the substantia niagra. Iron is known to be important in the production of dopamine, and low iron levels may be part of the problem. Certainly RLS appears to be more common in pregnant women with low iron levels, and symptoms tend to reduce when iron supplements are given. In addition, folic acid supplements have been found to help alleviate symptoms, although the reason for this is less clear.

Pre-eclampsia

This is a serious pregnancy disorder characterised by high blood pressure and protein in the urine. Symptoms may include headaches, blurred vision, pain just below the ribs and swelling of the hands, feet or ankles. If you suffer from any of these problems you need to see a doctor immediately. It is estimated that about 6% of pregnant women develop high blood pressure and pre-eclampsia. You are more likely to get the condition if you are overweight, diabetic, aged over 40, expecting more than one baby, or if any of your close relatives has had it.

If pre-eclampsia isn't treated, it can progress to a more serious condition called eclampsia, which results in fitting and, very occasionally, death. However, drugs can usually be given to treat the symptoms of pre-eclampsia and, when necessary, the baby will be delivered early.

Past your due date

If your due date comes and goes and nothing seems to be happening, it can be very frustrating, particularly if friends and family start phoning to see how it all went. There are many myths and old wives' tales about what you can do to kick-start labour – some more pleasant than others. With food, there are several suggestions:

- raspberry leaf tea;
- pineapple;
- curry.

Unfortunately, none of these actually appears to be effective. Raspberry leaf tea may help during labour (see page 159), but there is no evidence that it gets labour started. Fresh pineapple could theoretically help, as it contains an enzyme called bromelain; however, you would need to eat between 7 and 10 whole pineapples to get enough to have any possible effect (see page 155).

The final strategy, eating curry, has the greatest potential for getting things moving, but only if it is so hot that it causes you considerable discomfort and acts as a strong laxative. Then it could have the same effect as a dose of castor oil, which has been used for centuries to kick-start labour. It is thought that when the gut is stimulated, it in turn stimulates the uterus to cramp or spasm, thereby bringing on labour. Castor oil contains ricinoleic acid, or ricinic acid, which irritates the small intestine and has a strong laxative effect. One American study found that after a 60ml dose, 58% of women started labour within 24 hours, compared with just 4% of untreated women. However, this was only a small study, and self-treatment is not recommended. Castor oil can result in severe nausea and cramps, persistent diarrhoea, dehydration and other complications. If you want to try castor oil or an extremely hot curry, it is important to talk to a doctor or midwife first. They will be able to advise you according to your medical history (e.g. irritable bowel syndrome or piles), the position of your baby and the condition of your cervix.

There are other non-food strategies that might help, which are less likely to have the unpleasant side effects of curry or castor oil. You could try nipple stimulation or having sex - although both these methods are thought to help only if labour is about to happen in the next few days anyway. Or you could try walking, bouncing on a birthing ball, watching a weepy movie or an alternative therapy such as homeopathy or acupuncture.

8 Special diets

If you exclude certain foods from your diet you will need to think more carefully about particular nutrients. Vegetarians, vegans and women following a dairy-free or gluten-free diet have to make sure they get an adequate intake of certain vitamins and minerals. Those who were diabetic before becoming pregnant or have developed gestational diabetes should receive dietary advice from their care team, but the information here should help you put this into action.

Clean eating

Food bloggers have popularised the idea of 'clean eating' and increasing numbers of women are avoiding dairy, wheat, gluten, sugar and additives. However, this approach should be treated with caution as it is often based on a lack of understanding about nutritional science. While the idea of eating more plant-based foods, fewer processed foods and drinking plenty of water is in line with general healthy eating advice, it is not wise to exclude foods that provide essential nutrients. ▶

The idea that certain foods such as wheat are 'bad' and that they should never pass your lips can be dangerous. Dietitians and registered nutritionists would not advise you to avoid foods such as dairy or wheat unless of course you have a specific health problem such as lactose intolerance or coeliac disease. This is because these foods provide essential nutrients. Sometimes individuals may promote an approach to eating that suits their own set of circumstances or health problems but that doesn't mean it will be suitable for others. As well as the risk of missing key nutrients there is a concern that these diets may lead to an overly obsessive way of eating and possibly even eating disorders.

Having a varied and balanced diet with a wide range of foods really is the best approach to eating, especially if you are planning a pregnancy, pregnant or breastfeeding (see page 12). There is no need to restrict your diet unless you are advised to by a professional such as a GP or midwife, a dietitian or a registered nutritionist.

Wheat-free and gluten-free diets

If you have coeliac disease or an allergy or sensitivity to wheat or gluten you should continue to follow your wheat- or gluten-free diet during pregnancy. However, if you don't have one of these problems, there is no evidence that eating a wheat- or gluten-free diet offers any benefits. In fact there is some suggestion that it could be harmful. An American study found that 10-year-old children had a 36% reduced risk of eczema if their mother had a higher intake of wheat during pregnancy and the NHS warns that these diets could damage friendly bacteria in the gut.

Coeliac disease affects about 1% of the population. It is an autoimmune disease rather than an allergy or intolerance. The immune system mistakenly reacts against substances in gluten and attacks them, damaging the intestines and interfering with nutrient absorption. The only way to treat the disease is to eat a completely gluten-free diet. This means no foods containing wheat, barley or rye, including pasta, bread, cakes and any products containing even a tiny amount of flour, such as some gravies and crisps. Women with poorly controlled coeliac disease may find it harder to become pregnant. Some have been found to have increased risk of complications such as miscarriage, premature birth and low birthweight. However, a review of research, published in 2016, found that these risks could be significantly reduced by strictly following a gluten-free diet. So if you have coeliac disease, it is especially important to read labels carefully and avoid all traces of gluten.

If you need a wheat-free or gluten-free diet it is still important to follow a balanced approach so you get all the nutrients you need. You should still eat plenty of fruit and vegetables, a variety of different protein-rich foods and dairy produce. You can replace starchy foods including bread, pasta and breakfast cereals with gluten-free versions made from other ingredients, such as rice, corn, tapioca or potatoes. You can also eat foods such as potatoes, rice and quinoa. However, some of these foods are lower in B vitamins, iron and fibre than wheat products so you may need to compensate. One option is to take a multivitamin and mineral supplement before becoming pregnant and throughout pregnancy and breastfeeding. Coping with wheat or gluten avoidance as well as following all the additional guidelines for pregnancy can be overwhelming. If you are finding it difficult, talk to your midwife and ask for a referral to a dietitian if you need more detailed advice.

Milk- and dairy-free diets

Dairy products such as milk, yogurt and cheese contain several important nutrients, so if you don't eat them you need to get these nutrients from other sources. Some people can't drink milk because they are allergic to it or have lactose intolerance. Others, including vegans, choose not to for ethical reasons. Unless you are allergic or intolerant to milk there are no known health benefits to a dairy-free diet. Two research studies have shown that the less milk and yogurt mothers consume, the smaller their babies tend to be. Lower dairy intakes during pregnancy are also associated with increased risks of asthma and eczema in children and an increased risk of milk allergy.

If you are lactose intolerant you don't produce enough of the enzyme lactase to digest the lactose sugar found in milk. This can result in stomach cramps, bloating and diarrhoea. People with lactose intolerance may be able to consume small amounts of milk without problems or eat cheese or other dairy foods. It is also now possible to buy lactose-free milk, yogurt and cheese in many supermarkets. These are a good alternative as they still contain the vitamins and minerals found in milk. One Canadian study found that women were able to tolerate slightly more lactose towards the end of their pregnancy than when they weren't pregnant.

If you don't consume dairy products, you can still have a healthy pregnancy and get all the nutrients needed, but you have to be more careful about what you eat and possibly take a supplement. Particular care is needed for calcium (see page 70), vitamin B_{12} (see page 65) and iodine (see page 74).

Milk alternatives made from soya, oats, rice, hemp or nuts are now readily available. These can be a valuable source of calcium and vitamins B_{12}, D and E if you get one fortified with these nutrients. Some milk alternatives aren't fortified, including all organic varieties. Some have calcium added but not vitamins, so it is important to read the labels carefully. Similarly you can also get dairy-free alternatives to cheese, yogurt and other desserts. Unfortunately these milk alternatives don't usually have iodine added, so it may be necessary to take a multivitamin and mineral supplement that includes iodine.

A healthy vegetarian pregnancy

Vegetarians sometimes come under pressure to start eating meat during pregnancy 'for the good of the baby'. But there really is no need. Babies born to vegetarians are usually just as big and healthy as those born to non-vegetarians. It is perfectly possible to have a healthy diet for pregnancy without eating meat or fish. You just need to avoid a few possible pitfalls. So you can reassure any well-meaning relatives and friends that there's no need for you to tuck into that steak any time soon.

In some ways, vegetarian diets are positively beneficial. They tend to be lower in saturated fat and higher in fibre, beta-carotene, folic acid, vitamins C and E and magnesium. However, they usually contain lower levels of some key nutrients too, such as protein, long-chain omega 3 fatty acids and vitamin B_{12}. When you know the potential problems, it is fairly simple to make sure you don't miss out on anything important. With a little bit of planning, you can have a vegetarian diet that is as good as, if not better than, any meat eater's. If you are not a strict vegetarian, but one of the growing number of women who eat very little meat, you still need to think about the same dietary issues.

One of the most basic nutrient requirements is for protein, and vegetarians tend to get less of it than meat eaters. However, protein intakes vary widely among different vegetarians. They are lower among those who live on vegetables and cereals, but vegetarians who eat dairy foods and eggs, along with a variety of soya products, pulses, seeds and nuts, consume plenty of protein. Vegetable sources of protein are sometimes described as being of low biological value, because they contain fewer essential amino acids. However, you can get all the amino acids you need by eating a mixture of different cereals, peas, beans, lentils, seeds and nuts. If you eat dairy foods and eggs too, then there is really no need to worry. If you tend not to have these different foods regularly, then start trying to include a source of protein in every meal.

Vegetarians have very low intakes of long-chain omega 3 fatty acids, as these are found mainly in oily fish. Consuming foods such as flaxseeds, flaxseed oil and walnuts will increase your intake of alpha-linolenic acid (ALA), a short-chain omega 3, but not the beneficial long-chain omega 3s (see page 60). Another problem is that vegetarians tend to have higher than average intakes of omega 6 fatty acids, including linoleic acid (LA), which inhibit the conversion of ALA to the long-chain omega 3s. To improve the fatty acid content of your diet and to optimise the amount of long-chain omega 3s your body produces, you could switch from sunflower oil or corn oil or margarine (which have high levels of LA) to soya bean or rapeseed oil. You may also like to take a DHA supplement (see page 84).

Anaemia is often thought of as a particular problem for vegetarians, but while this is something to watch out for, vegetarians don't appear to be at greater risk than other women. However, vegetarians often have low iron stores, so you need to make sure you include iron-rich foods in your diet and also try to increase iron absorption (see page 72). A lack of calcium is sometimes highlighted as a potential problem for vegetarians, but this is really only an issue if you don't have much milk or many dairy products in your diet (see 'Extra advice for vegans'). Vitamin B_{12} is another one to watch. Again, women who eat few dairy foods or don't eat eggs are most at risk of missing out (see page 66).

There has been some concern in recent years over high intakes of soya during pregnancy. Vegetarian mothers were found to be more likely than meat eaters to have babies with hypospadias, which may be linked to soya intake (see page 166). However, evidence from countries with a high intake of soya suggests that normal soya consumption is fine.

On a more positive note, vegetarians have been found to have higher levels of folic acid during pregnancy, because they eat more fruit and vegetables. But this doesn't mean that folic acid supplements aren't needed – these are recommended for all women. Vegetarians also have slightly higher intakes of magnesium than meat eaters and, possibly related to this, a lower incidence of leg cramps in the last trimester of pregnancy.

Your diet will generally be much better if it includes a variety of different beans, pulses, lentils, seeds and nuts, as well as yeast extract and other fortified foods. If you're not sure you're getting all the nutrients required it might be a good idea to take a pregnancy multivitamin and mineral supplement to be on the safe side (see page 86).

Meat cravings
Cravings for meat are fairly rare among pregnant vegetarians, although you'll probably be asked about them. Vegetarians tend to have similar cravings to other women, although they are more likely to crave pickles and salty or savoury foods such as yeast extract, and less likely to crave fruit and sweet foods.

Extra advice for vegans

Vegans, who consume only foods of plant origin, need to be aware of a few extra issues. Your diet can still be perfectly adequate while you are pregnant or breastfeeding, but you need to plan a bit more carefully and you are more likely to benefit from supplements. Vegans, just like vegetarians, tend to have lower intakes of protein, vitamin B_{12} and long-chain omega 3 fatty acids, and are more likely to have low iron levels. The advice for vegetarians above therefore applies to vegans too.

In addition, you need to ensure you don't miss out on the essential nutrients that vegetarians get from milk and eggs, particularly calcium, iodine and vitamins B_{12} and D. If you drink soya milk or another milk alternative, make sure you have one that is fortified (see page 106). Other fortified foods, including orange juice with added calcium, veggie burger mixes, breakfast cereals and puddings are also available. A vitamin D supplement is recommended for all pregnant and breastfeeding women, but it is particularly important for vegans. You may also choose to take a general multivitamin supplement (see page 86).

Gestational diabetes

Diabetes is a condition where there is too much sugar (glucose) in the blood. If you were not diabetic before, but developed the problem during pregnancy, it is called gestational diabetes.

Gestational diabetes is an increasingly common condition. The NHS estimates as many as 18% of women giving birth in England and Wales are affected. It usually develops in the second half of pregnancy and disappears when the baby is born. Gestational diabetes occurs when hormones from the placenta interfere with insulin, the hormone that regulates blood sugar levels. As a result, the levels of glucose in your blood can rise and dip steeply.

Risk factors for gestational diabetes
You're more likely to get gestational diabetes if:

- a close family member is diabetic or has had gestational diabetes;
- you have previously had a very large baby, more than about 4,500g or 9.5lb;
- your BMI was over 30 before pregnancy;
- you gain a lot of weight during pregnancy;
- your family history is South Asian, black Caribbean or Middle Eastern.

Gestational diabetes is usually detected between weeks 24 and 28 of pregnancy, but it may be found earlier. Symptoms include excessive thirst and urination, tiredness and infections such as thrush. However, these can be confused with just being pregnant. During pregnancy, urine samples are tested routinely for glucose, as this is usually the first sign of a problem. A single positive urine test is not usually a cause for concern, but if traces of glucose are found on several occasions, you may be given an oral glucose tolerance test (OGTT or GTT). This involves having a blood test before breakfast and another two hours later, after having a glucose drink.

Women who develop the condition, like those who have diabetes before pregnancy, are likely to have bigger-than-average babies. This is because the baby receives more glucose and therefore more calories than normal. In turn this increases the likelihood of problems during delivery, including the need for a Caesarean. If you develop gestational diabetes, your baby will also be more likely to have health problems and develop obesity and diabetes in later life. However, if the condition is controlled carefully, it should not harm you or your baby.

Controlling gestational diabetes is done by keeping blood sugar levels as stable as possible, so that the baby doesn't receive extra glucose. You will be shown how to monitor your blood sugar levels and told the levels you should be aiming for. This can usually be achieved by changing to a low glycaemic index (GI) diet, as described in Chapter 3. Taking regular exercise, such as walking every day, is also important (see page 28). If this doesn't work, then extra insulin may be needed. If you have gestational diabetes, you will be given antenatal appointments more frequently to check that you and your baby are both well.

Foods and drinks to avoid

• Fruit juice. Instead have a piece of fresh fruit as this has a lower GI.

• Sugary drinks such as cola or lemonade. Instead have water, diet cola or other low- or zero-calorie drinks.

• Sugar or honey in tea, coffee or other drinks and on food. It is best to leave these out altogether, otherwise use a sugar substitute.

• Too much fruit. Aim for two to three portions a day but only have one at a time and don't have more than three portions per day.

• Sweets, biscuits and cakes in between meals as the free sugars in these will increase your blood sugar levels considerably. It is better to have just a small amount of these foods with a meal, then they will be digested more slowly.

• There is no need to buy special diabetic foods.

What you should be eating and drinking

• Follow the healthy eating advice on page 12; there isn't really a special diet just for gestational diabetes.

• Start the day with a low GI breakfast (e.g. nutty muesli, scrambled eggs and granary toast or homemade porridge).

• Eat three meals a day and two snacks as well if you are hungry between meals. Don't skip meals as this will disrupt your blood sugar levels.

• Use skimmed or semi-skimmed milk, eat low-fat dairy products and lean meat to avoid putting on too much weight.

• Eat plenty of plant-based foods, especially vegetables, beans and lentils, as these have a low GI.

Gestational diabetes usually goes away completely after the baby is born, but your blood glucose levels will be checked and so will your baby's to make sure they are normal. Once you've had gestational diabetes you are at increased risk of going on to develop type 2 diabetes. Breastfeeding is particularly advantageous after you've had gestational diabetes as research shows it can reduce your own and your baby's risk of developing diabetes.

9 The A-Z of foods and ingredients

In this chapter, you can look up any food or ingredient to find out whether during pregnancy and while breastfeeding it is:

✔   Safe to eat in normal quantities

✘   Best avoided for safety

✔ ✘   OK in moderation or under certain circumstances

Some items don't have a symbol because the jury is still out. Instead, all the evidence is provided so that you can make up your own mind about whether or not you want to consume them. If you eat something and then notice later that you shouldn't have, try not to worry: the risks are generally small (see page xiv).

Additives The FSA considers all additives used in the UK to be safe for consumption during pregnancy. When considering the safety of any additive, the FSA looks at the reproductive toxicity of a chemical and its ability to alter genetic material. Although the safety of individual additives is tested, there is some concern about the possible effect of consuming a combination of many different additives at the same time – the so-called 'cocktail effect'. Another concern is that foods containing lots of additives are generally over-processed, high in fat, salt and sugar, and low in essential vitamins and minerals. Ideally you should keep foods containing additives to a minimum and instead eat plenty of unprocessed foods such as fruit, vegetables, beans and wholegrains. See also *artificial sweeteners*, *nitrites* and *sulphites*.

✔ **Almonds** A good source of protein, copper, niacin, riboflavin and vitamin E. There is no need to avoid almonds unless you are allergic to them.

✔ ✘ **Anchovies** These are an oily fish and a good source of omega 3 fatty acids, just like salmon or sardines. Cooked anchovies are fine to eat in pregnancy although you shouldn't eat more than two portions of oily fish a week. Tinned anchovies are also safe but tend to be very salty so high intakes aren't recommended. Marinated anchovies, bought in a sealed tub from a supermarket, should also be OK but if you are in a tapas bar, delicatessen or somewhere where you don't feel completely confident about food storage or hygiene, then they are best avoided. The same applies to anchovies on a pizza since, although these are tinned, they may have been open for too long or stored out of the fridge.

Artificial sweeteners These are widely used as low-calorie or zero-calorie alternatives to sugar. Some may be considered 'natural' as they are extracted from leaves or sugar. All the sweeteners listed here have been evaluated by the European Food Safety Authority (EFSA) and approved as safe for use in foods and drinks as part of a healthy diet. Some experts have raised concerns about the safety of using artificial sweeteners in general and in particular during pregnancy but there is no real evidence to support these claims. The EU safety assessment also checks that additives, including sweeteners, are not carcinogenic or toxic and do not pose a risk to pregnant women or children. Ideally it is better to eat unprocessed foods, and drink water rather than diet drinks, but if you are struggling to cut down on the amount of sugar you're consuming, then having artificially sweetened foods and drinks in moderation may help.

Sweetener	Where found	Other information
Acesulphame K (acesulphame potassium)	Sweetener granules and tablets (e.g. Canderel). Also chewing gum, diet drinks, yogurts, puddings and salad cream.	Some controversy over use in pregnancy but no proper evidence.
Aspartame	Diet drinks, chewing gum, fat-free yogurts, cold and flu medicines.	Some controversy over use in pregnancy but no proper evidence. It should be avoided by anyone with phenylketonuria (PKU).
Saccharin	Sweeteners such as Hermesetas and Sweetex, soft drinks, salad cream, toothpaste, vitamin supplements.	This is the most controversial of the sweeteners as it crosses the placenta into the baby's bloodstream and remains there for some time. It is banned in Canada.
Sorbitol	Diabetic jam, chewing gum, toothpaste.	Banned from soft drinks in the EU as it has a laxative effect when consumed in large amounts. ▶

Sweetener	Where found	Other information
Stevia (labelled as steviol glycosides or rebaudioside A)	Sweetener granules and tablets (e.g. Truvia and Green Canderel), soft drinks including Coca-Cola Life and reduced sugar baked beans.	
Sucralose	Splenda (granulated and tablets), chewing gum, salad dressing, fizzy drinks.	
Xylatol	Toothpaste, chewing gum.	Banned from soft drinks in the EU as it has a laxative effect when consumed in large amounts.

✓ **Bananas** A good healthy snack to have if energy levels drop when you're pregnant or breastfeeding. Some women find that bananas cause heartburn, but otherwise there's no need to avoid them.

✓✗ **Barbecued food** Make sure all meat, burgers, sausages, fish, etc. are cooked properly, otherwise there is a risk of food poisoning. Even if something looks cooked on the outside, check that it's piping hot in the centre. Also, try to avoid heavily charred food: the cooking process produces polycyclic aromatic hydrocarbons (PAHs) and heterocyclic amines (HAs), including some carcinogenic chemicals that could be harmful during pregnancy. It is best to keep your intake to a minimum, though no safe level has been established. At barbecues, it's also important to check that salads have been washed thoroughly and to steer clear of food that's been sitting outside for a long time, because food poisoning bugs multiply rapidly in warm weather.

Basil This is safe to eat in normal amounts. However, it is ✔ one of several herbs that act as a uterine stimulant when concentrated or used in very large amounts. Therefore you should avoid using basil oil (commonly used for aromatherapy) during pregnancy.

Bean sprouts You should avoid eating raw bean sprouts ✔ ✘ during pregnancy because of the risk of salmonella. If you want to eat them they should be heated thoroughly until piping hot. This includes those labelled as 'ready to eat'. The FSA issued this advice in 2010 after more than 100 cases of Salmonella Bareilly were found with possible links to raw bean sprouts.

Béarnaise sauce/Bernaise sauce This usually contains par- ✔ ✘ tially cooked egg yolk and so should be avoided as it carries a risk of salmonella poisoning. It is possible to make Béarnaise sauce with pasteurised egg instead, in which case it is safe.

Beer Once believed to be good for breastfeeding, but ✘ research has shown that this is a myth. For safety in pregnancy, see the information on alcohol on page 49.

Bitter lemon It is safe to drink bitter lemon while you are ✔ pregnant. Also see *quinine*.

Black pudding It is fine to eat black pudding while you are ✔ pregnant, providing it has been stored in the fridge and cooked properly all the way through. It is a good source of iron but also high in salt and saturated fat so it is not healthy to eat large amounts.

✖ **Bran** The outer layer of cereal grains, such as wheat and rice, is called bran. It's a concentrated form of dietary fibre. Sprinkling bran on your food may help to relieve constipation, but it will also reduce the absorption of some vitamins and minerals, including iron and zinc. It is much better to eat fibre-rich foods such as wholegrain cereals (e.g. wholemeal bread, brown rice), pulses (e.g. lentils, beans) and fruit and vegetables, as these contain higher levels of essential nutrients.

✔ **Breakfast cereal** It's good to start the day with breakfast cereal and it also makes a healthy snack. Try to eat a cereal that's fortified with vitamins and minerals, including folic acid and iron, as these are particularly important at this time. Organic cereals are not fortified in the UK, and neither are some budget-value ranges of cereals, so check the label. It is also a good idea to choose a high-fibre breakfast cereal to help prevent constipation.

✔ ✖ **Brie** Should be avoided because of the risk of listeria, which could harm your unborn baby. This includes Brie made with pasteurised or unpasteurised milk. However, dishes such as deep-fried Brie, where the cheese is piping hot, are safe, because any listeria is killed during cooking. See page 45 for more about listeria.

✔ ✖ **Caesar salad** The dressing on Caesar salad usually contains raw egg, which carries a risk of salmonella, so it is best avoided while pregnant. See page 47 for more about salmonella. However, bottles of Caesar salad dressing sold in supermarkets will be made with pasteurised egg and are therefore considered safe.

Calabash chalk This is a type of chalk (also known as ✖ Calabar stone, La Craie, Argile, Nzu and Mabele) used to alleviate morning sickness. It is traditionally used by women from West Africa and is imported from Africa to the UK. However, it is not recommended, as it has been found to contain high levels of lead, which could harm your baby's developing nervous system.

Camembert This is a soft cheese and should be avoided ✔ ✖ during pregnancy because of the risk of listeria. This includes Camembert made from pasteurised or unpasteurised milk. However, dishes such as deep-fried Camembert, where the cheese is piping hot, are safe, because any listeria will be killed during cooking. See page 45 for more about listeria.

Carbonara sauce Spaghetti or other pasta with home made ✔ ✖ carbonara sauce should be avoided during pregnancy as it is usually made with raw eggs. If you buy carbonara sauce from a supermarket, either refrigerated or in a jar, it is fine to eat, as it will contain pasteurised eggs or be made without eggs. Most restaurants, including Bella Italia and Prezzo, also make their sauce with pasteurised egg but in more expensive or traditional Italian restaurants it may be best to check.

Chalk White chalk is calcium carbonate, which the body can use just like the calcium in food. If you experience a craving for chalk, or anything else that isn't normally considered a food or drink, it is known as 'pica' (see page 17). Eating small amounts of white chalk is unlikely to do any harm. However, consuming large quantities could cause the calcium level in your blood to become too high, which might cause problems for you and your baby. It is not advisable to eat coloured chalk, as the colourings it contains may not be the same as those used for food and will not have been tested to see whether they can be safely consumed.

✓ **Cheddar cheese** This is a hard cheese and is safe to eat, whether made from pasteurised or unpasteurised milk.

✓✗ **Cheese** Some cheeses should not be eaten during pregnancy as they could be contaminated with listeria. This applies to soft, mould-ripened cheeses (e.g. Brie) and soft blue-veined cheeses (e.g. Danish Blue), whether they are made from pasteurised or unpasteurised milk. You should also avoid soft cheeses made from unpasteurised goats' and sheep's milk (e.g. Chèvre). However, thorough cooking kills listeria. Therefore, it should be safe to eat these cheeses if they are part of a hot dish (e.g. on a pizza or in a sauce) – you just need to make sure that they are properly cooked and piping hot all the way through.

Hard cheeses (e.g. Cheddar, Edam) are safer because they are more acidic and contain less moisture, so they're less likely to allow bacteria to grow. These are considered safe whether they are made from pasteurised or unpasteurised milk. The suitability of Stilton can vary (see page 166).

Feta cheese and soft cheeses that aren't mould-ripened (e.g. mozzarella, ricotta, cottage cheese) are considered safe if they are made from pasteurised milk. You are unlikely to come across cheeses, such as cottage cheese, made from unpasteurised milk but if you do they should be avoided. It is best to buy soft cheeses pre-packaged and eat them before the use-by date, and avoid buying them from delicatessen counters, where cross-contamination from other foods may occur.

CHEESES THAT ARE SAFE
Austrian smoked cheese
Babybel
Boursin
Caerphilly

Cheddar

Cheese spread, e.g. Dairylea, Laughing Cow, Primula

Cheestrings

Cheshire

Comté

Cottage cheese (provided it is made from pasteurised milk)

Cream cheese (provided it is made from pasteurised milk), e.g. Philadelphia,
or similar own-brand products described as 'soft cheese', are safe

Double Gloucester

Edam

Emmental

Feta (provided it is made from pasteurised milk)

Goats' cheese: hard goats' cheese (e.g. St Helen's Farm hard goats'
cheese) and soft goats' cheese described as full-fat or medium-fat
goats' milk cheese, which doesn't have a rind (provided it is made from
pasteurised milk)

Gouda

Gruyère

Halloumi (provided it is made from pasteurised milk)

Havarti

Jarlsberg

Lancashire

Leerdammer

Manchego

Mascarpone (provided it is made from pasteurised milk)

Mozzarella (provided it is made from pasteurised milk)

Paneer (provided it is made from pasteurised milk)

Parmesan/Parmigiano or similar Italian hard cheese (including those made
from unpasteurised milk)

Port Salut

Processed cheese

Quark

Red Leicester

Ricotta (provided it is made from pasteurised milk)

Roulé

Stilton (unless labelled as unsuitable for pregnancy)

Wensleydale

CHEESES TO AVOID
Blue d'Auvergn
Blue Shropshire
Blue Vinny
Brie
Cambozola/Cambozala/Cambozola blue Brie
Camembert
Castello blue
Castello white
Chaource
Chaumes
Cornish Yarg
Crème de Saint Agur
Danish Blue
Dolcelatte
Dovedale
Goats' cheese: Chèvre, Capricorn Somerset goats' cheese, any goats' cheese with a rind like Brie or described as being ripened or mould-ripened
Gorgonzola/blue Gorgonzola
Pont l'Évêque or Demi Pont l'Évêque
Roquefort
Saint Agur
Saint Agur Blue Crème

NB The rules for organic cheese are the same as those for non-organic cheese, both for cheeses that are safe and cheeses to avoid.

✓ ✗ **Cheesecake** It is fine to eat cheesecake that has been cooked (sometimes described as a baked cheesecake). You can also safely eat cheesecake sold in supermarkets and similar shops, as they should be made with pasteurised egg, which removes any risk of salmonella. Cheesecakes are sometimes made with ricotta or mascarpone cheese, both of which are safe to eat during pregnancy.

You should avoid eating homemade cheesecakes that are not cooked. These contain gelatine and are put in the fridge to set. They carry the risk of salmonella as they contain uncooked eggs. If you are unsure about how a homemade cheesecake or one in a restaurant has been made, it is best to ask.

Cheese spread Processed cheese spreads, such as Dairylea, Laughing Cow, Primula and similar own-brand products from supermarkets, are fine to eat. Also see *cream cheese*. ✔

Chicken Provides a good source of protein, iron and B vitamins. It is important to check that it is cooked thoroughly until the juices run clear before eating, otherwise it can cause salmonella food poisoning. See page 47 for more on salmonella. ✔ ✖

Chillies See *spicy food*.

Chocolate A study in Finland found that mothers who ate chocolate regularly when they were pregnant had babies who smiled and laughed more. The results of another study, from the USA, suggest that chocolate may reduce the risks of pre-eclampsia, though there is not enough evidence at the moment to know whether this is true. ✔ ✖

Despite these possible benefits, you should avoid eating too much chocolate, as it contains caffeine as well as sugar and fat, which can contribute to a high weight gain.

Chocolate mousse See *mousse*.

Chorizo See *cured meats*. ✔ ✖

Cider vinegar/apple cider vinegar To treat morning sickness, some people recommend putting a few drops or a teaspoonful of cider vinegar into a glass of cold or warm water. This remedy seems to be more popular in the USA ✔ ✖

than the UK. Advocates believe that sipping this with meals or throughout the day will help reduce nausea. A teaspoon of honey can be added to make it taste better. It is also thought to be effective for heartburn or acid reflux. There is no scientific evidence that it is effective, but some women believe it helps and there is certainly no harm in trying.

Some enthusiasts believe only unpasteurised apple cider vinegar is effective. However, this is best avoided because of the risk of food poisoning.

✓ **Cinnamon** It is fine to eat cinnamon while you are pregnant, including porridge or breakfast cereals flavoured with cinnamon and baked goods such as cinnamon swirls and other cakes and biscuits. Indeed, adding cinnamon to foods like porridge can be beneficial as it has a sweet flavour and therefore you don't need to add as much sugar. However, cinnamon supplements should be avoided and it is probably best not to eat very large amounts - e.g. more than one teaspoon of cinnamon per day.

Two different types of cinnamon are widely used. The first is Ceylon cinnamon (real name Cinnamomum zeylanicum and also known as 'True cinnamon' or 'Sri Lankan cinnamon'). The other type is cassia cinnamon (also known as Cinnamomum aromatium or Chinese cinnamon). Cassia cinnamon contains high levels of coumarin, which is associated with liver damage when eaten in large amounts. It is estimated that one teaspoon of cassia cinnamon would contain about 6–12mg of coumarin, which is more than the European Food Safety Authority (EFSA) considers safe to consume in a single day. Therefore if you use a lot of cinnamon it is best to choose Ceylon cinnamon. If you buy cinnamon sticks in the UK these will almost certainly be Ceylon cinnamon. However, if you buy ground cinnamon powder it may be either Ceylon or cassia cinnamon. At the time of writing Bart's and Tesco 'ground cinnamon' was Ceylon cinnamon but Schwartz 'ground cinnamon' was cassia cinnamon. Information about the type of cinnamon is sometimes provided in the small print on labels but otherwise you can contact the manufacturer.

There is some suggestion that cinnamon is good if you're feeling especially hungry as it acts as a natural appetite suppressant. There are also claims that it helps stabilise blood glucose levels, reduce blood pressure and blood cholesterol levels and that is has anti-microbial and anti-oxidant properties. The evidence to support these health benefits is weak at best and research has produced mixed results.

Clay Sometimes known as sikor or shikor mati. Baked clay ✖ is thought by some to be beneficial during pregnancy, but in 2011 the FSA warned women not to eat it. They found it contained high levels of lead, which could affect a baby's brain development, and arsenic, which increases the risk of lung, skin and bladder cancer.

Coffee It is safe to drink coffee during pregnancy and while ✔✖ breastfeeding, but you shouldn't have more than about two mugs of instant coffee or two cups of real coffee a day (see page 50).

Cola It is safe to drink cola before or during pregnancy, and ✔✖ while breastfeeding, but you shouldn't have too much. It contains about 40mg of caffeine per 330ml can, so you need to count it alongside tea and coffee (see page 50). Regular (not diet) varieties also contain about 140kcal per can, so if you drink large quantities you may gain excess weight without giving your baby the vitamins and minerals he or she needs. Diet, light and lite varieties contain the same amount of caffeine as regular colas, unless you specifically choose a caffeine-free product. They also contain artificial sweeteners.

Coleslaw It is fine to eat coleslaw that is freshly made with salad cream or mayonnaise from a jar. Once coleslaw has been prepared, it should be stored in the fridge. Readymade coleslaw sold in the UK is also considered safe by the FSA. In some other countries, including the USA and Australia, women are advised to avoid pre-prepared coleslaw, particularly when sold at deli counters, because of the risk of listeria.

Coleslaw prepared using homemade mayonnaise should be avoided as it contains raw eggs and could therefore result in salmonella poisoning.

Cookie dough ice cream It is fine to eat cookie dough flavoured ice cream, such as that made by Häagen-Dazs or Ben & Jerry's. Both the ice cream and the cookie dough pieces are made with pasteurised egg. However, as it is high in sugar, fat and saturated fat, it is best eaten in moderation.

Corned beef This is fine to eat while you are pregnant but make sure you follow the storage instructions on the packet or tin. In some countries pregnant women are advised to avoid pre-packed cold meats during pregnancy but this is not the case in the UK.

Cottage cheese It is fine to eat cottage cheese during pregnancy, provided it is made from pasteurised milk. However, avoid buying it from a delicatessen counter.

Crab It is OK to eat crab if it is cooked properly and eaten hot – for example, crab cakes or crab and sweetcorn soup.

You shouldn't have more than two portions of crab per week as it could be contaminated with similar levels of pollutants as oily fish. It is best to avoid any crab that is served cold if you are unsure about how recently it has been cooked and how it has been stored. It could be contaminated with listeria or other food poisoning bacteria.

Crab sticks See *seafood sticks.*

Cranberry juice It is safe to drink cranberry juice while you ✓ are pregnant. It contains proanthocyanidins and fructose, which seem to prevent bacteria sticking to the wall of the bladder. This helps reduce the risk of a urinary tract infection (UTI). However, these components aren't able to unstick bacteria that are already attached so if you have a UTI already, drinking cranberry juice is not an appropriate cure. Instead it is best to see your GP as antibiotics may be needed to relieve the symptoms and prevent pregnancy complications (see page 97).

Crayfish See *shellfish.*

Cream It is safe to eat all types of cream, including soured ✓ ✗ cream, clotted cream and crème fraiche, provided it is made from pasteurised milk. Raw or unpasteurised cream is not widely available but is sold at some farmers' markets and specialist farm shops. Cream, and products such as cream cakes that contain raw cream, are legally required to give a warning on the packaging.

Cream cheese This is safe to eat in pregnancy provided it ✓ ✗ is made from pasteurised milk. Products such as Philadelphia and similar own-brand soft cheese are therefore safe.

Crème anglaise See *custard.*

Crème brûlée It is generally safe to eat crème brûlée sold ✓ ✗ in supermarkets and other shops as it is made from pasteurised eggs.

Homemade crème brûlée contains partially cooked eggs and should be avoided. In a restaurant, it is best to ask how it has been made.

✔ ✘ **Crème caramel** It is safe to eat the kind of crème caramel sold in individual tubs in supermarkets, as it is made from pasteurised egg.

Homemade crème caramel contains partially cooked eggs and should be avoided. In a restaurant, it is best to ask how it has been made.

Crème fraiche See *cream.*

✔ ✘ **Cured meats** For example, Parma ham, salami, prosciutto crudo, chorizo, Serrano ham and pepperoni. These are not cooked but preserved by salting and smoking, or by treating with sodium nitrite and nitrate. This means there's a risk they could contain parasites that cause toxoplasmosis (see page 46). To reduce the risk of toxoplasmosis the NHS suggests freezing cured or fermented meats for four days before eating. This will kill most parasites and make the meat safer to eat. However, if you are going to cook it (e.g. pepperoni pizza or pasta with chorizo) then there is no need to freeze the meat, as cooking will also kill the parasites.

Some 'cured ham' or 'dry-cured ham' is roasted or baked after curing, in which case it is safe to eat. However, if there is no mention of cooking on the label, then you should assume that it is not cooked.

Curry See *spicy food.*

✔ ✘ **Custard** It is fine to eat custard from a tin, long-life UHT readymade custard sold in a carton, chilled custard sold in a supermarket described as 'fresh custard', and custard pre-pared by mixing custard powder with milk (providing it's pasteurised milk). All these products are made with pasteur-ised egg. It is also fine to eat egg custard tarts and custard slices sold in supermarkets.

Homemade custard prepared using fresh eggs should not be eaten, as the eggs are only partially cooked and therefore could contain salmonella. In restaurants this is sometimes called crème anglaise – if you see it on a menu, it is best to ask whether it has been made with pasteurised eggs, and if not, avoid it.

Deli foods The advice in the USA, Australia and New Zealand is not to eat food from delicatessen shops or coun-ters if you are pregnant. The UK has no specific guidelines. However, it would be sensible to choose pre-packaged food rather than deli products whenever possible. This is because unpackaged foods can become contaminated with listeria from other products. Low-risk foods such as ham may have been handled with the same utensils used on higher-risk foods such as salami. In addition, you have no way of know-ing whether deli foods are beyond their use-by date.

Diet drinks These are considered safe during pregnancy or while breastfeeding. However, no one knows whether a high intake of artificial sweeteners could have long-term effects, and so moderation is sensible. See also *artificial sweeteners*.

Dips Pre-packaged dips such as houmous, tzatziki, salsa and sour cream or yogurt-based products should be safe to eat during pregnancy.

Dips sold at a deli counter are best avoided because of the risk of cross-contamination and less certainty about the use-by date. Any dips containing blue cheese should be avoided.

✓ ✗ **Duck eggs** These are safe to eat during pregnancy provided both the yolk and the egg white are cooked until solid. Any dish containing duck eggs should be cooked until it is steaming hot all the way through. In 2010, the FSA issued an official warning to remind people to be careful about hygiene when cooking and handling duck eggs. This was prompted by an outbreak of *Salmonella Typhimurium* DT8, linked to duck eggs, which involved 63 cases and included one death.

✓ **Edam** It is fine to eat Edam cheese during pregnancy.

✗ **Eggnog** As well as alcohol, fresh eggnog contains uncooked egg, which could contain salmonella. Best avoided.

✓ ✗ **Eggs** The FSA currently advises pregnant women to avoid eggs that are raw or partially cooked, as they may contain salmonella bacteria. However, in February 2016 the FSA started a consultation process that could result in this advice being changed. New guidelines may suggest that eggs with the British Lion Quality stamp are OK to eat raw, but other raw or partially cooked eggs should be avoided. Under the British Lion Quality code hens are vaccinated against salmonella. Tests have shown their eggs are extremely unlikely to be infected with salmonella. The advice about eggs without the British Lion Quality stamp and eggs eaten outside the home would remain the same - they should be avoided unless pasteurised or cooked until solid. This would mean that making your own ice cream with British Lion Quality eggs would be considered safe, but eating homemade ice cream in a restaurant would not.

Foods likely to contain raw or only partially cooked eggs include:

- homemade mayonnaise;
- Béarnaise sauce and hollandaise sauce;

- Caesar salad dressing and similar salad dressings;
- homemade puddings such as ice cream, mousse, cheesecake, tiramisu and lemon meringue pie;
- homemade royal icing, e.g. on a Christmas or wedding cake;
- homemade custard.

Organic eggs are just as likely to contain salmonella as free-range, barn fresh or any other type of egg.

It is safe to eat eggs that are cooked until both the white and yolk are solid. This will destroy any salmonella that might be present. So, you can have boiled, fried or scrambled eggs if they are cooked thoroughly.

It is important to keep raw eggs away from other foods and to wash your hands and any utensils after handling raw eggs to avoid cross-contamination. Pasteurisation kills salmonella, and so it is generally safe to eat commercially produced foods containing egg, as it is almost always pasteurised. This includes foods such as mayonnaise, ice cream and mousse.

In restaurants, watch out for sauces and desserts that may contain eggs that are not completely cooked. If you are eating out and are unsure, it is best to ask.

Also see *omega 3 eggs*.

Eggs Benedict This dish contains poached eggs, which have ✖ a runny yolk, and hollandaise sauce, which is made with only partially cooked eggs. It should be avoided, as it could contain salmonella.

Energy drinks If you are feeling tired and in need of a pick- ✔ ✖ me-up, an energy drink may seem like the answer. However, most have added caffeine or guarana (which also contains caffeine). Just like coffee or cola, these drinks count towards your daily caffeine limit of 200mg per day during pregnancy (see page 50). Some energy drinks also contain herbs that could affect you or your baby. It is best to avoid them if you are unsure. Also see *Lucozade*.

✓ ✗ **Escargot** Snails that have been safely sourced, processed and cooked should be safe to eat in pregnancy. However, it is best not to eat snails that you have gathered yourself, as they aren't subject to the same hygiene laws and may be contaminated with harmful bacteria or chemicals.

✓ ✗ **Fennel tea** This is not recommended for pregnancy, as it is thought to have a mild hormonal action and to be a uterine stimulant. There is no official advice about consumption, but some people recommend avoiding fennel tea completely during pregnancy, and others suggest that up to two cups a day should be fine.

Some breastfeeding mothers drink tea made from fennel, sometimes combined with other ingredients, to improve their milk supply. There is no scientific evidence that it works, but some women believe that it does. It will not do any harm, so if you think your milk supply is low it may be worth trying fennel tea, as well as making sure that you are drinking plenty of fluids, resting and following the general advice for breastfeeding (see page 175). See *herbal teas* for information about other teas to boost breast milk supply.

✓ ✗ **Feta cheese** This is safe to eat during pregnancy provided it is made from pasteurised milk.

✓ ✗ **Fish** Women who are pregnant, breastfeeding or planning a pregnancy are advised to eat at least two portions of fish a week, including one portion of oily fish. A portion is about 140g of cooked fish, which is equivalent to about

170g before cooking. When you eat fish, make sure that it is cooked properly to avoid the risk of food poisoning.

You should avoid eating shark, swordfish or marlin if you are pregnant or planning a pregnancy. They have been found to contain traces of mercury, which could affect your unborn baby's developing nervous system. If you are breastfeeding, you shouldn't eat more than one portion of these a week. Tuna has also been found to contain mercury, but in much lower amounts. See *tuna*.

Oily fish such as anchovies, hake, herring, kipper, mackerel, pilchards, sprats, salmon, sardines, trout and whitebait are great for your baby's brain and eye development. However, oily fish may contain traces of pollutants, so you shouldn't eat more than two portions a week. See *oily fish* (page 150) and omega 3s (page 60).

Some other fish may have similar levels of pollutants as oily fish. You shouldn't have more than two portions a week of dogfish (rock salmon), sea bass, sea bream, turbot, halibut and crab.

There is no limit on the amount of other white fish you can eat during pregnancy - e.g. cod, coley, haddock, hake, flounder, gurnard, monkfish, mullet (red or grey), plaice, pollack, red snapper, skate, sole, tilapia. White fish is low in fat and provides protein, iodine, niacin and selenium.

Also see *sushi* and *smoked fish*.

Fizzy drinks It is safe to drink the odd fizzy drink during pregnancy, although they are not a healthy choice, particularly if you have sugary ones and have gestational diabetes. Some also contain artificial sweeteners, and both colas and energy drinks contain caffeine.

✔ ✘ **Flaxseeds** Also known as linseeds, these are a good source of alpha-linolenic acid (ALA), which is a short-chain omega 3 fatty acid (see page 58). However, there are a number of issues surrounding whole flaxseeds, and it may be better to choose flaxseed oil rather than the whole seeds.

Firstly, flaxseeds have a tough coating, so they need to be ground, or at least crushed if you are to benefit from the ALA-rich oil inside them. But, perhaps more importantly, flaxseeds also contain lignans, which have a hormone-like effect. For this reason, they can be used to help treat hot flushes during the menopause. But it may not be such a good idea to have a high intake of flaxseeds during pregnancy. The actual effect on pregnant women and their babies is unknown, but studies on animals have found that a high intake of flaxseeds during pregnancy can reduce litter size and birthweight. The Vegetarian Society and others warn pregnant women to avoid high intakes of flaxseeds because of the possible effect on their hormone balance.

Lignans are only found in the husk of flaxseeds, so you will only get them if you eat whole or crushed flaxseeds, not if you buy flaxseed oil (though do be careful, because some health food companies sell 'high lignan flaxseed oil', which has lignans added to it). If you want to include flaxseed oil in your diet, it is best eaten cold, for example in a salad dressing, or added at the end of cooking, otherwise the beneficial ALA may break down.

✔ ✘ **Fromage frais** It is safe to eat fromage frais during pregnancy, provided it is made from pasteurised milk.

✔ **Fruit** Fruit is an essential part of any healthy diet, but this is especially true if you are pregnant, breastfeeding or thinking about having a baby. Fruits are packed with vital vitamins, minerals and phytochemicals. You should aim to eat at least five portions of fruit and vegetables a day.

Some women find that acidic fruit, such as oranges, gives them heartburn, especially during the later stages of pregnancy. If this is a problem for you, then avoid acidic fruit late in the day or completely for a while. If you are eating out and you have concerns about hygiene levels, it may be a good idea to avoid fruit salad and other pre-prepared fruit.

Fruit juice Pure fruit juice counts as one of your five rec- ommended portions of fruit and vegetables a day – but no matter how much you drink, it can never count as more than one portion. This is because it doesn't contain as much fibre as whole fruits do, and it contains free sugars, which damage teeth and cause blood sugar levels to increase steeply. The general advice is not to drink more than 150ml of fruit juice or smoothie per day. It is always healthier to buy 100% pure fruit juice rather than a 'juice drink', as the latter contain only a small amount of fruit juice as well as sugar, artificial sweeteners and other additives.

Some women find that if they drink large quantities of orange juice while breastfeeding, their baby develops diarrhoea. If this happens, you should cut down on the amount of juice you drink.

During pregnancy, you should drink only pasteurised fruit juice or juice you have squeezed at home yourself. Unpasteurised juice can be a source of listeria or E. coli. Most juices bought in supermarkets are pasteurised, even those that are sold chilled and described as 'freshly squeezed'. However, freshly squeezed juice bought from street stalls, farmers' markets and farm shops may not be pasteurised.

Game You should avoid eating game that has been shot with lead pellets during pregnancy as it may contain unhealthy levels of lead, which could harm a baby's developing brain and nervous system. This includes grouse, duck, partridge and pheasant if they are lead-shot. Venison (deer meat) usually has a lower concentration of lead in the meat, compared to smaller game birds. Venison sold in supermarkets is considered safe as it should have been killed in a safe way. If in doubt it is best to ask. Eating more than 100g of lead-shot game each week is thought to be particularly dangerous. If game birds are cooked in an acidic liquid such as wine, vinegar or tomato juice they become more of a problem, as the lead can be dissolved, making it easier for the human intestine to absorb.

✔ **Garlic** Eating garlic or taking a garlic supplement during pregnancy is believed by some to help prevent high blood pressure and pre-eclampsia. However, there has not been enough research carried out to say whether or not it is effective. It is unlikely to do any harm and the only side effect reported has been 'odour'.

Eating garlic while breastfeeding has been shown to affect the flavour of breast milk. This isn't a problem and there is no need to avoid garlic unless your baby seems to dislike the flavour or has an adverse reaction such as an upset stomach (see page 180).

✔ ✘ **Ginger** Ginger is a traditional remedy for morning sickness and nausea during pregnancy. Its effectiveness has been tested in several research studies and these have shown that it significantly reduces feelings of nausea, compared to having a placebo. It doesn't seem to be quite as effective at stopping women from vomiting but it certainly helps some. In two trials, ginger was found to be more effective than vitamin B_6 capsules and in a third it was found to be equally effective. Trials have typically used syrups or capsules equivalent to doses of 1g (1,000mg) root ginger per day, generally split into two 500mg doses, three 350mg doses or four 250mg doses. Researchers have looked for possible risks, such as an increase in miscarriages, but this has not been found. Ginger doesn't seem to increase the risk of problems such as heartburn or drowsiness either. If you want to take ginger capsules or sweets choose carefully, as some contain very concentrated forms of ginger and the effects during pregnancy have not been tested. It is best to avoid having more than an equivalent to 1,500mg (1.5g) root ginger per day.

There are several ways to eat ginger: grated in stir-fries, soups and sauces, in biscuits and cakes, crystallised ginger, ginger marmalade, ginger beer and ginger ale (non-alcoholic). You can also make ginger tea by grating a little into a cup and adding boiling water. Some people find that adding lemon and honey makes this more palatable.

Goats' cheese There are several different types of goats' ✔ ✘ cheese available. When we think of goats' cheese, we usually mean Chèvre. This is a soft cheese with a white rind, similar to Brie. Like other mould-ripened cheeses, it should be avoided in pregnancy because of the risk of listeria. However, if it is cooked thoroughly and eaten hot, any listeria will be destroyed.

It is fine to eat hard Cheddar-type cheeses made from goats' milk. It is also OK to eat soft goats' cheese if it is made from pasteurised milk and doesn't have a rind, as this means it is not mould-ripened.

Gravlax Also called gravad lax (Swedish) and gravlaks (Norwegian). This is raw salmon that has been pickled or marinated, usually with salt and dill. It looks similar to smoked salmon, but it is not actually smoked. In Scandinavian countries, where it is more commonly consumed, pregnant women are advised that smoked salmon is safe to eat but cured fish, such as gravlax, shouldn't be eaten. There is no official advice regarding the safety of eating gravlax during pregnancy in the UK.

✓ ✗ **Green tea** There is not enough information available to know whether drinking green tea during pregnancy is safe so the NHS advices pregnant women to drink no more than four cups per day. Green tea contains caffeine, just like regular black tea, therefore you should include it when estimating your daily caffeine intake and make sure you don't go over the daily limit of 200mg per day. The amount of caffeine will depend on how strong you make it. One mug of green tea will contain up to 75mg. It is often regarded as a healthy option as it is rich in antioxidants, which are protective against heart disease and certain cancers, although there is no evidence that green tea actually protects against cancer.

There is some suggestion that drinking large amounts of green tea around the time of conception may increase the risk of neural tube defects. This is because the anti-cancer compound epigallocatechin gallate (EPCG) found in it lowers folic acid levels. Although the evidence for this isn't strong you may want to limit your intake to just two cups a day while you are trying to get pregnant.

Researchers in Canada found that pregnant women who drank green tea had higher levels of lead and cadmium in their blood than those who didn't drink it. These metals are considered environmental pollutants and are associated with poor foetal growth and brain development. Levels were within the range considered normal for the population but the fact that they were higher than for women who didn't drink green tea suggests caution is needed.

✓ **Gruyère cheese** It is fine to eat Gruyère cheese during pregnancy.

Guarana This is a seed extract originally found in the Amazon. ✖
It contains caffeine and related compounds and is added to
some energy drinks, herbal drinks and chewing gum. It is not
advisable to take it during pregnancy or while breastfeeding
as it is a stimulant and the effects on your baby are unknown.

Guinness Along with other kinds of stout, Guinness was ✖
once thought to be good for pregnancy because it had lots
of iron and would 'build you up'. However, Guinness contains only about 0.01mg of iron per 100ml, or 0.3mg per half
pint, compared with 3.0–7.0mg in a typical bowl of breakfast
cereal. It also contains alcohol of course and so is not good
for pregnancy or breastfeeding.

Haggis One of the ingredients of haggis is liver, and there- ✔✖
fore it should be avoided due to its high vitamin A content.
See *liver*.

Vegetarian haggis is safe to eat in pregnancy.

Halloumi cheese It is fine to eat halloumi cheese during ✔✖
pregnancy, provided it is made from pasteurised milk.

Ham It is fine to eat pre-packaged cooked ham during ✔✖
pregnancy. This is often described as baked, boiled or honey-
roasted ham.

Parma ham and other cured meats should be avoided because
of the risk of toxoplasmosis. It may also be wise to avoid ham
bought from deli counters, as there is an increased risk of listeria due to cross-contamination from other, higher-risk foods.

Herbal teas These include any tea made from roots, ber- ✔✖
ries, flowers, seeds or leaves other than tea leaves. Women
may choose to take them during pregnancy and while

breastfeeding to reduce their caffeine intake but the NHS recommends drinking no more than four cups of herbal or green tea per day during pregnancy. Some herbal teas, including peppermint and ginger teas, are recommended for pregnancy-related symptoms such as nausea. Others are thought to increase milk supply, for example fennel, fenugreek, aniseed, raspberry leaf and nettle. If you buy a herbal tea, make sure it is from a reputable source. It should contain a full list of all ingredients and be labelled with the manufacturer's and distributor's details and a best-before date.

Fruit teas containing ingredients that you might normally eat (e.g. blackcurrant, lemon, orange) are considered safe but it is sensible to avoid drinking any teas made from unfamiliar ingredients, such as black cohosh, ginseng and pennyroyal. These should be treated as drugs or medicines rather than foods, as many contain active ingredients that pass through the placenta to your baby or into breast milk, in the same way that medicines do. It is best to seek professional advice regarding their safety.

If you are pregnant, you shouldn't drink raspberry leaf tea before about 32 weeks of pregnancy.

If you are breastfeeding, you should avoid sage tea.

Also see *green tea, raspberry leaf tea* and *sage.*

✔ ✘ **Hollandaise sauce** This generally contains partially cooked egg yolk, so it should be avoided in pregnancy because of the risk of salmonella. However, if you buy a packet mix or a jar of Hollandaise sauce from a supermarket it is safe to eat in pregnancy.

✔ **Honey** It is fine to eat honey during pregnancy and while breastfeeding. Honey very occasionally contains the

Clostridium botulinum spores, which babies' intestines may be unable to cope with, resulting in infant botulism. For this reason, babies under 12 months shouldn't have honey. However, the intestines of adults, including pregnant women, are able to stop any botulinum bacteria from growing and causing any problems.

Horlicks This is safe to drink during pregnancy. See *malted* ✔ *hot drinks*.

Houmous It is fine to eat houmous during pregnancy. ✔

Ice cream It is fine to eat ice cream sold pre-packaged in ✔ ✖ tubs or individually from supermarkets or similar shops.

Homemade ice cream generally contains raw or partially cooked eggs (just like custard). It should therefore be avoided in pregnancy, as it may contain salmonella (see *eggs*). If you are making your own ice cream, either follow a recipe that doesn't include egg or use pasteurised eggs.

You should only eat soft (Mr Whippy type) ice cream from a kiosk or ice cream van if you feel confident about the level of hygiene, as there is a risk of listeria if the soft ice cream machine isn't kept scrupulously clean.

Icing Most types of icing are safe to eat during pregnancy. ✔ ✖ Icing on foods bought from supermarkets and bakers should be fine. This includes soft buttercream icing, icing made with cream cheese (e.g. on a carrot cake) and royal icing.

However, homemade royal icing is made with raw egg white and should therefore be avoided because of the risk of salmonella. Royal icing is often found on Christmas cakes and wedding cakes. If it has been made and stored carefully, the risk is very small, but if you are at all worried it is best avoided.

✓ **Jarlsberg** It is safe to eat Jarlsberg cheese during pregnancy.

Juice See *fruit juice*.

Kelp See *seaweed*.

✓ ✗ **Lemon curd** Commercially prepared lemon curd bought from a supermarket is fine to eat during pregnancy.

Homemade lemon curd contains partially cooked eggs and should be avoided in pregnancy because of the risk of salmonella.

✓ **Lemon juice** Some women report that a tablespoon of lemon juice is an effective natural remedy for heartburn. There is no scientific evidence to support this, but it's perfectly safe and worth a try.

✓ ✗ **Lettuce** It is safe to eat lettuce during pregnancy, provided that you wash it thoroughly. You should even wash pre-washed salad leaves bought in bags, in order to avoid the risk of listeria and salmonella.

✓ ✗ **Liquorice** It is fine to eat liquorice in pregnancy, according to the NHS. However, moderation is advisable as consuming more than about 250g a week is associated with an increased risk of premature delivery (birth before 37 weeks). This was discovered in Finland, where liquorice is very popular among young women. It is not understood why liquorice has this effect, but it is probably related to its glycyrrhizin content.

✗ **Liver** Liver and foods made from liver, such as liver pâté, liver sausage and haggis should be avoided during pregnancy. They contain high levels of vitamin A in the form of retinol, which can harm your baby's development (see page 62). Previous generations of women were encouraged to eat liver during pregnancy because of its high iron content, and this may have been good advice at the time. However, animals now consume feeds with a high vitamin A content, leading to increased levels of the vitamin in their liver, so this advice is no longer appropriate.

It is fine to eat liver while you are breastfeeding.

Liver sausage This should be avoided in pregnancy as it is very high in vitamin A in the form of retinol. See *liver*.

Lucozade Lucozade is considered safe to drink during preg- nancy but some varieties contain caffeine and some are extremely high in sugar.

A 500ml bottle of 'Lucozade Energy' contains 62g sugar and a 500ml bottle of 'Reduced sugar Lucozade Energy' has 40g sugar, which is more than the recommended daily maximum of 30g. Lucozade Sport has less sugar than Lucozade Energy but still contains 18g per 500ml bottle. Lucozade Energy also contains 60mg caffeine per 500ml bottle, which should be counted against your daily limit of 200mg.

Mackerel This is an oily fish and a good source of long-chain omega 3 fatty acids. However, you shouldn't have more than two portions a week (140g each). See also *fish* and *smoked mackerel.*

Malted hot drinks Horlicks and Ovaltine are both safe to drink during pregnancy. They have vitamins and minerals added, including vitamin A, but the amount of vitamin A is in line with recommendations for pregnancy. A cup of Horlicks or Ovaltine contains less than 300µg vitamin A, which is little more than you'd find in two eggs and only 2% of the amount you would get if you ate a 100g portion of liver.

Marzipan Homemade marzipan usually contains raw eggs and it should therefore be avoided during pregnancy because of the risk of salmonella. However, if the marzipan is left to dry out on the cake for between one and three days, before the cake is iced, then the risk of bacteria growing is very small.

It is safer to use cooked marzipan, as it doesn't include eggs. Similarly, marzipan bought from supermarkets does not usually contain any egg. This includes marzipan on cakes and marzipan sold in a block.

Mascarpone cheese It is fine to eat mascarpone cheese during pregnancy, provided it is made from pasteurised milk.

Mayonnaise It is safe to eat mayonnaise bought in a jar from a supermarket or similar shop during pregnancy. Mayonnaises sold at room temperature (rather than chilled) are made with pasteurised egg.

During pregnancy, you should avoid homemade mayonnaise as it contains raw unpasteurised egg and could potentially contain salmonella (see *eggs*). Occasionally, fresh mayonnaise containing unpasteurised eggs is sold in shops and at markets. You can usually recognise this, because it's sold chilled and has a relatively soon use-by date.

Meat Most meat and poultry is fine, as long as it's cooked properly so that there is no pinkness. Meat joints and steaks that are cooked rare should also be avoided. Similarly, if you're eating a ready meal, it's important to make sure it is heated properly so that it is piping hot all the way through.

You shouldn't eat raw or undercooked meat, as it may contain salmonella, campylobacter, toxoplasmosis or E. coli. This means cured meats such as Parma ham and salami are out unless they have been frozen beforehand (see page 130).

To avoid cross-contamination from raw to cooked meat, store them separately and covered, use different knives, chopping boards and other utensils, and wash your hands carefully after handling raw meat.

Meringue Meringues sold in supermarkets and similar shops should be safe to eat during pregnancy, as they are generally made using pasteurised eggs. It is also safe to eat homemade meringues that are hard, for example a Pavlova or meringue nest, if it has been cooked properly and is no longer sticky in the middle. The core temperature should reach 70°C for two minutes to ensure that any salmonella that might be present are killed. If normal cooking instructions are followed and the meringue is cooked for two to three hours at about 110°C, this shouldn't be a problem.

Soft meringue that has only been browned in the oven should be avoided, as the egg white isn't cooked properly and there is a potential risk of salmonella (see *eggs*). This means that puddings such as homemade lemon meringue pie and baked Alaska should be avoided. Otherwise you can use pasteurised egg white, which you can buy as a powder or in a refrigerated carton from many supermarkets.

Milk During pregnancy, it is safe to drink milk provided it has been heat-treated to kill any harmful bacteria. This means that you can have pasteurised, UHT, sterilised and dried milk. It is safe to drink whole milk, semi-skimmed, 1% fat and skimmed milk provided it has been heat-treated in one of these ways. Likewise, you could drink goats' or ewes' milk instead of cows' milk if it has been heat-treated. It is also safe to drink evaporated milk and condensed milk.

Whenever possible choose lower-fat options, such as skimmed or semi-skimmed milk.

It is best to avoid drinking unpasteurised milk (including goats' milk and sheep's milk) and using it in cooking as it may contain listeria and other bacteria, such as E. coli and brucella, which can cause food poisoning.

Also see *organic milk*.

Monkey nuts See *peanuts*.

✓ ✗ **Mousse** It is safe to eat mousse bought from a supermarket or large retailer while you are pregnant. Any egg it contains should be pasteurised.

Homemade mousse usually contains raw egg and should be avoided in pregnancy because of the risk of salmonella (see *eggs*).

✓ ✗ **Mozzarella** It is safe to eat mozzarella cheese during pregnancy, provided it is made from pasteurised milk. Cooked mozzarella on a pizza or other hot dish is fine whether it is made from pasteurised or unpasteurised milk.

✗ **Mud** If you have a craving for mud or earth, this is one that you shouldn't satisfy. By eating bits of mud, even if it's just very muddy potatoes, you risk toxoplasmosis, listeriosis and other forms of food poisoning. See the section on cravings on page 16.

✓ ✗ **Mussels** It is OK to eat mussels if they are cooked properly and served as part of a piping hot dish, such as moules marinière, seafood soup or fish pie. Canned mussels are also OK.

It is best to avoid mussels served cold, unless you are sure they have been freshly cooked and chilled.

✓ **Nettle tea** Nettle leaves contain several vitamins and minerals, including folic acid, iron and calcium. However, nettle tea has been found to contain little, if any, of these nutrients. Some herbalists recommend nettle tea for pregnancy, claiming it provides a variety of benefits: strengthening the kidneys, reducing leg cramps and labour pains and preventing haemorrhoids. There is no evidence to support this, but drinking nettle tea during pregnancy is generally considered safe.

Nitrites Nitrates and nitrites are added to cured meats ✓ ✗ and meat products as a preservative (to prevent bacterial growth) and to produce their characteristic pink or red colour. They are generally added to ham, salami, bacon, corned beef, and hot dogs. To identify foods containing nitrites, look on the food label for potassium nitrate, potassium nitrite, sodium nitrate, sodium nitrite and saltpetre, or the E numbers for these additives (E249 to E252).

Concern has been raised about these preservatives because they are converted to nitroso compounds in the body. These have been shown to cause cancer when given in large doses to animals, and it is suspected that they could have the same effect in humans. One study found that women with a high intake of cured meat (more than 100g per day throughout pregnancy) were more likely to have children who developed childhood brain tumours. Other, similar studies have not found the same effect, but it seems sensible to consume cured meats and similar products containing nitrites only in moderation during pregnancy. It is not known whether nitrites pass into breast milk, so moderation is advisable while breastfeeding as well.

Nutmeg It is fine to eat nutmeg in normal cooking, for ✓ ✗ example in cakes, biscuits and rice pudding.

Large quantities of ground nutmeg and nutmeg oil, which is sometimes used in aromatherapy, should be avoided during pregnancy. These can result in hallucinations and palpitations in pregnant women and increased foetal heart rate.

✓ **Nuts** It is OK to eat almonds, Brazil nuts, hazelnuts, peanuts, pecans, walnuts and other kinds of nuts while you are pregnant, unless you are allergic to them. This applies whether you are pregnant, trying for a baby or breastfeeding.

✓✗ **Oily fish** Women who are pregnant, breastfeeding or trying for a baby should have one or two portions of oily fish a week, according to the FSA. Oily fish, such as salmon and sardines, are rich in beneficial omega 3 fatty acids and provide protein and essential vitamins and minerals. However, you shouldn't eat too much, as oily fish can contain high levels of dioxins and polychlorinated biphenols (PCBs). These are pollutants found widely in the environment but in higher concentrations in oily fish. Neither has an immediate effect on health, but high levels may cause problems in the long term.

You shouldn't let this put you off eating moderate amounts of oily fish. Dioxins and PCBs are impossible to avoid entirely as they are present in many other foods and are widespread in the environment. Exposure from dietary sources has fallen by about 75% in the past 20 years because of tighter controls on industrial pollution. Furthermore, scientists have found that the benefits of eating oily fish far outweigh the possible risks if you consume one or two portions a week. Some experts believe that the limits should be raised. A study of more than 5,000 women in the Bristol area found that children's development (including scores for social development and dexterity in skills such as drawing at age three years and verbal IQ scores at age eight years) benefited most when their mothers consumed more than 340g of seafood per week during pregnancy (which is nearly two and a half portions a week).

See *fish*, *tuna*, and page 60 for more on the benefits of omega 3s.

✓ **Olives** It is OK to eat black and green olives during pregnancy, but they tend to be very salty so it isn't a good idea to have too many. When you are buying olives, it may be better to get those in a jar or other sealed container, rather than from a deli counter, where cross-contamination of bacteria from other food items may occur. If you share a bowl of olives with friends, the food poisoning risk depends on the level of hygiene of the other people.

Omega 3 eggs These contain more of the beneficial long-chain ✓ ✗ omega 3 fatty acids than regular eggs as they are laid by chickens that eat a diet of flaxseeds or other feed rich in short-chain omega 3s. Omega 3 eggs aren't available in every supermarket but you can get them from Sainsbury's, Waitrose or Ocado. Two eggs provide about 350mg long-chain omega 3s (DHA and EPA). They are safe to eat during pregnancy and a good way of boosting your intake of long-chain omega 3s provided they are cooked until the yolk and white are solid. Also see *eggs*.

Omelette It is fine to eat omelettes during pregnancy provid- ✓ ✗ ing you ensure that the egg is cooked until completely set. Check in particular that it is not runny in the centre (see *eggs*).

Oregano It is safe to use oregano in cooking while you are ✓ pregnant. However, when oregano is added to a meal, it reduces the amount of iron your body absorbs, so it is best not to use it regularly, particularly if you have low or borderline iron levels.

Oregano oil (used in aromatherapy) is considered a uterine stimulant and should be avoided in pregnancy.

Organic food Eating organic food reduces your consump- ✓ ✗ tion of fertiliser and pesticide residues. Organic food is also free from genetically modified (GM) ingredients and contains a much smaller range of food additives. It may also have higher levels of certain nutrients and flavonoids, but this hasn't been established firmly.

Nobody knows whether eating organic food during pregnancy or while breastfeeding is really better for your baby. Some people claim that going organic could reduce the risks of childhood cancer and early puberty, or benefit cognitive development, but there just isn't the scientific evidence to back this up. All chemicals used in food, including pesticides sprayed on crops and colourings added to processed foods, are tested for safety, and there is nothing to suggest that these are harmful to babies' development. However, hundreds of new chemicals have been introduced to the food system in the past 60 to 100 years and no one knows what long-term effects may be uncovered in the years to come. Many women choose to eat organic food as a precaution to reduce the amount of chemicals they, and therefore their baby, are exposed to.

If you eat organic food, you need to be just as careful about washing all fruit and vegetables before eating, in order to avoid exposure to harmful bacteria. You should also remember that just because something is organic, it isn't necessarily healthy. Organic cola is still sugary water containing caffeine and a few other additives, and organic carrot cake and chocolate still, unfortunately, contain lots of calories. Also, organic food products are not fortified with extra vitamins and minerals. Therefore, if you eat foods such as organic breakfast cereals, you may have a lower intake of certain nutrients, such as iron and B vitamins.

✓ ✗ **Organic milk** Pasteurised organic milk is safe to drink when you are pregnant or breastfeeding (see *milk* for further information). Unpasteurised organic milk is sometimes sold in farm shops, but this should be avoided because of the risk of listeriosis and other forms of food poisoning. In 2016 a review of several different studies was published which concluded that overall the levels of omega 3 fatty acids in organic milk were higher than those in conventional milk.

However, milk contains short-chain omega 3s, not the beneficial long-chain omega 3s found in oily fish.

Another issue to consider is that organic milk has around 40% less iodine than conventional milk, reflecting the lower iodine intake of the cows. As iodine levels are low in some women (see page 74), and milk and milk products are the main source of iodine, this is an important issue. If you consume organic milk and milk products it is particularly important to ensure you have alternative sources of iodine in your diet.

Ovaltine It is safe to drink Ovaltine during pregnancy. See ✔ *malted hot drinks.*

Oysters Oysters are usually eaten raw and should be avoided ✖ because of the risk of food poisoning. Like other raw shellfish, they can, very occasionally, contain hepatitis A (see *shellfish*). They can also contain a virus called the norovirus, which can result in nausea, diarrhoea, abdominal pain, headache and fever.

Papaya (pawpaw) Papaya is a good source of vitamin A (as ✔ beta-carotene) and vitamin C, and there is no need to avoid it while you are pregnant or breastfeeding. In the past, particularly in parts of Asia, it was believed that eating papaya during pregnancy could cause miscarriage. Papaya contains an enzyme called papain, which breaks down proteins and helps to tenderise meat. This may have something to do with the traditional beliefs, but there is no evidence that normal consumption presents any cause for concern.

Parma ham (prosciutto di Parma, prosciutto crudo) See ✖ *cured meats.*

Parmesan cheese This is considered safe to eat during ✔ pregnancy, whether it is made from pasteurised or unpasteurised milk. This is because it is acidic and has a low moisture content, so it isn't a suitable environment for bacteria such as listeria to grow.

✔ **Parsley** This is safe to eat in normal cooking.

Consuming extremely large quantities of parsley should be avoided as this could have a uterine stimulant effect.

✔✘ **Pâté** Any pâté containing liver should be avoided during pregnancy, as it contains high levels of vitamin A (see *liver*). Other types of fresh or chilled pâté, including vegetable pâté, should also be avoided as they may contain listeria.

It is safe to eat pâté that comes in a tin or tube, such as Tartex or GranoVita, while you are pregnant, provided it does not contain liver. Storage instructions should be followed carefully.

Pâté (all types) is considered safe while breastfeeding.

✔ **Pavlova** It is OK to eat Pavlova during pregnancy, provided the meringue is cooked until solid right through to the centre. See also *meringue*.

✔ **Peanut butter** This is considered safe to eat during pregnancy, unless you are allergic to peanuts. See *peanuts*.

✔ **Peanuts** Also known as groundnuts and monkey nuts. The current government advice is that if you want to eat peanuts while pregnant or breastfeeding, you can do so as part of a healthy, balanced diet (see page 41).

✔✘ **Peppermint tea** It is safe to drink peppermint tea during pregnancy. Some women find that it helps to relieve indigestion, heartburn, nausea and morning sickness.

There is some suggestion, although no firm evidence, that drinking large quantities could cause miscarriage. As a precaution, it is probably best not to drink several very strong cups of peppermint tea close together.

Pepperoni See *cured meats*.

Philadelphia cheese During pregnancy, it is OK to eat Philadelphia cheese and other brands of cream cheese.

Pineapple You may have heard that pineapple should be avoided during pregnancy because it can cause miscarriage, or that you should eat it at the end of pregnancy to kick-start labour. The truth is that normal pineapple consumption is highly unlikely to have any effect at any stage of pregnancy.

Fresh pineapple contains an enzyme called bromelain, which breaks down proteins. In a highly concentrated tablet form, bromelain is used to treat inflammation. Taking bromelain tablets or capsules during pregnancy is not advised, as it may cause abnormal bleeding. However, some alternative therapists may recommend them for the end of pregnancy, to help the cervix soften and dilate more readily, although no evidence has been found that this is effective. To get enough bromelain from fresh pineapple to have any possible effect, you would need to eat between 7 and 10 fresh pineapples at one sitting. Tinned pineapple and pineapple juice contain little or no bromelain.

Pine nuts (pine kernels) Pine nuts are safe to eat unless you have a specific allergy to them. There is no evidence that avoidance during pregnancy or while breastfeeding will reduce the risk of your child developing a nut allergy or any other form of allergy.

✔ ✘ **Pizza** It is generally safe to eat any kind of pizza where all of the topping is cooked properly. This includes pizzas made with goats' cheese, Stilton, Gorgonzola and any other kind of cheese, provided that it is cooked until piping hot. These cheeses could contain listeria, but it would be killed by proper cooking.

Pizzas topped with Parma ham should be avoided as the ham is added after cooking and there is a risk of food poisoning (see *cured meats*).

✔ **Port Salut cheese** It is fine to eat Port Salut while you are pregnant.

✔ ✘ **Potato salad** It is safe to eat homemade potato salad during pregnancy provided it is made with mayonnaise from a jar. It is also safe to eat commercially prepared potato salad sold in supermarkets and similar shops.

Potato salad made with homemade mayonnaise should be avoided during pregnancy, as it contains raw eggs and could be contaminated with salmonella. Potato salad from delicatessens and any that is left out for several hours at a barbecue or on a buffet table is best avoided because of the risk of listeria.

✔ ✘ **Prawns** It is safe to eat prawns that are cooked properly and served as part of a hot meal, for example in a curry or stir-fry. Cold prawns in a salad or sandwich should be safe if they have been cooked and then chilled and kept cold until they are eaten.

If you have any doubts about how cold prawns have been cooked or stored, they are best avoided because of the risk of food poisoning (see *shellfish*).

✔ **Prebiotics** These are food ingredients that aren't digested directly but are consumed by so-called 'friendly bacteria' in the large intestine. They help the beneficial bacteria in the gut to multiply at the expense of potentially harmful bacteria. There is nothing to suggest that prebiotics, such as galacto-oligosaccharides, shouldn't be consumed while you are pregnant or breastfeeding. There is little research so far, but they may be beneficial.

Probiotics These are live micro-organisms that are bene- ficial to health. It is safe to drink products containing probiotics during pregnancy and while breastfeeding. If a food or drink containing probiotics is not safe for pregnancy, then it should carry a warning saying so. If you are thinking of taking a probiotic supplement, rather than a food or drink containing probiotics, check carefully what other ingredients it contains. Some probiotic supplements include vitamins and minerals, as well as probiotics, and these may be at levels that are not suitable for pregnancy.

There is some evidence that exposure to particular probiotics around the time of birth is protective against allergies (see page 7). In addition, it appears that taking probiotics during pregnancy may help with constipation and in the treatment of vaginal infections, which are sometimes associated with premature labour.

Profiteroles Profiteroles or chocolate éclairs are considered safe to eat during pregnancy if they are bought from a supermarket, high street bakery or similar shop, or a restaurant. They contain egg but this is cooked in the choux pastry, and the cream will be pasteurised, unless bought from a farm shop licensed to sell its own unpasteurised milk and milk products.

Prosciutto This is the Italian word for ham, but in English it usually means smoked spiced Italian ham. Prosciutto is cured but not cooked so should be considered in the same way as other cured meats. See *cured meats*.

✓ ✗ **Protein shakes** The long-term effects of drinking protein shakes during pregnancy have not been tested, therefore it is unclear whether they are safe. There are different types of protein shakes. Some say on the label that they are not suitable for pregnancy and these should be avoided completely. Other protein shake may be fine to have as a snack, as part of a varied healthy diet, but it is not a good idea to use them as a meal replacement. Most women consume more than enough protein already and it is much better to meet your protein requirements by eating real foods and having a balanced diet (see page 12). That way you will also get all the vitamins, minerals and phytonutrients that you need as well as the right balance of protein, carbohydrates and fats. Having too much protein or an imbalance of protein relative to other nutrients isn't good for your baby (see pages 27–28).

✓ ✗ **Prunes** Prunes and prune juice are age-old remedies for constipation. Their laxative effect cannot be explained completely by fibre – prunes contain similar amounts of fibre to other dried fruits, and prune juice contains no fibre at all, as it is filtered before bottling. The unique effect is more likely to be due to the high levels of sorbitol that prunes contain, which is a type of sugar that is absorbed very slowly and can pass into the large intestine like fibre. Prunes also contain large amounts of phenolic compounds, which can also have a natural laxative effect.

Pu-erh tea This is the tea reported to have helped Victoria Beckham regain her pre-pregnancy figure. Among the health benefits attributed to it are an ability to melt fat and reduce blood cholesterol levels. There is no evidence to back up these claims or other beliefs that it raises metabolism and aids weight loss. The best way to lose weight after having a baby is sensible eating and regular exercise (see page 182). Also, drinking tea with meals is not recommended, as it reduces your absorption of much needed micronutrients, particularly iron.

Quiche Commercially prepared quiche should be safe to eat ✓ during pregnancy. If you are in any doubt, rather than eating it cold heat it according to the manufacturer's guidelines and ensure that it is hot all the way through. Homemade quiche should also be cooked carefully to ensure the egg becomes solid (see *eggs*).

Quinine Tonic water and bitter lemon contain quinine ✓ and are fine to drink in pregnancy in moderation. Quinine is a drug used to treat malaria and there is some debate as to whether it should be used in pregnancy. However, the amount present in tonic water is tiny compared to that used for malaria treatment, so unless you were to drink several bottles every day there is no need to worry. There is some suggestion that quinine helps relieve night-time leg cramps. However, if you are suffering from these it is best not to self-treat but instead talk to your midwife or GP.

Quorn All Quorn products contain mycoprotein, which is ✓ suitable for vegetarians. Unlike tofu, which is derived from soya, mycoprotein is part of the fungi family, like mushrooms. Quorn products are a good source of vegetable protein, are low in fat and also provide fibre. There is nothing to suggest that Quorn products are not suitable during pregnancy or while breastfeeding.

Raspberry leaf tea Taking raspberry leaf tea in the later ✓ ✗ stages of pregnancy is thought to help prepare the womb for labour. Raspberry leaf is available as a tea and in tablet form from most health food shops. Raspberry leaf is a uterine stimulant and is thought to strengthen the muscles of the womb, so that when you have contractions they are more effective and labour is easier. In an Australian study, women were given two raspberry leaf supplements per day (1.2g each) from 32 weeks of pregnancy. The second stage of labour (pushing the baby out) was 10 minutes shorter on average for these women than for those receiving a placebo. They also had a lower rate of forceps delivery (19% versus 30%). There is no evidence that raspberry leaf tea will bring on labour, even if your baby is overdue.

It is not advisable to take raspberry leaf tea before 32 weeks of pregnancy, as you don't want to stimulate the uterine muscles before the baby is ready to be born.

Red Bull See *energy drinks*.

✓ **Red wine sauce** It is fine to have red wine gravy and foods such as pears poached in red wine while pregnant or breast-feeding. A single serving will contain so little alcohol that it's not worth worrying about. Most recipes use very little wine anyway, and much of the alcohol is cooked off. It is estimated that after 15 minutes of cooking, 60% of the alcohol is lost; after an hour, 75% is lost.

✓ ✖ **Rice** It is generally safe to eat rice, but take care with rice salads and dishes containing reheated rice, such as kedgeree, biriyani and egg-fried rice. Rice can contain spores of *Bacillus cereus* bacteria, which can germinate if the dish is left standing at room temperature. The longer rice is left, the more these bacteria will multiply. The bacteria produce toxins that can cause food poisoning (vomiting and diarrhoea). It is not known whether *Bacillus cereus* has any other effects during pregnancy.

It is best to eat rice that has just been cooked. Alternatively, it should be cooled down within an hour, stored in the fridge and eaten within 24 hours. When reheating rice, make sure it is piping hot all the way through.

✓ ✖ **Ricotta** It is fine to eat ricotta cheese in pregnancy, provided it is made with pasteurised milk.

Roquefort cheese This is a soft blue cheese and should be avoided during pregnancy because of the risk of listeria.

It is fine to eat a dish such as steak with Roquefort sauce, if it is cooked until bubbling hot, as this will kill any listeria present.

Saccharin See *artificial sweeteners*.

Sage It is fine to eat foods containing sage while you are pregnant or breastfeeding. Sage is thought to have an oes-trogen-like effect and may stimulate the uterus when taken in large quantities, so sage oil (used in aromatherapy) should be avoided during pregnancy. If you are breastfeeding, avoid sage tea, as it may interfere with milk production. However, if you want to stop breastfeeding, drinking sage tea may help to reduce the amount of milk you are producing and therefore ease any discomfort.

Salad Salads are a healthy option, but it is important that all ingredients are washed well to reduce the risk of food poi-soning. Pre-packaged salad bought in bags should also be washed, even if it is labelled as washed and ready to eat. This is because such bags have very occasionally been found to be contaminated with listeria or salmonella.

If you are eating out, particularly if you are travelling abroad, it is best to avoid salads unless you are completely confident about the levels of hygiene.

See also *coleslaw* and *potato salad*.

Salami See *cured meats*.

Salmon Salmon provides protein, iron, vitamins B_6, B_{12} and D, and long-chain omega 3s, which are beneficial for your baby. However, as all oily fish contain traces of pollutants, you are advised not to eat more than two portions a week. There has been some speculation about whether farmed or wild salmon is better, but the FSA has concluded that there is no significant difference between the two. Wild salmon has been found to contain higher levels of omega 3s, but also higher levels of pollutants, than farmed salmon.

See also smoked *salmon*, *gravlax* and *oily fish*.

✔ ✖ **Sandwiches** When you are making sandwiches at home, remember to wash any salad ingredients. If you are buying a sandwich, go to a shop or restaurant where you trust the level of hygiene. It may be better to choose a pre-packaged sandwich than one prepared at a deli counter, where cross-contamination is more likely.

The following sandwiches should all be safe to eat: cheese and pickle, ploughman's, egg mayonnaise, ham salad, tuna and sweetcorn, chicken, houmous, poached salmon. If you have any doubts about how sandwiches have been stored, for example whether they have been chilled from the time of preparation, it may be better to avoid sandwiches filled with prawn mayonnaise, crab or crayfish.

Sandwiches filled with Brie or goats' cheese (Chèvre) should be avoided.

✔ ✖ **Sardines** These are an oily fish and a good source of long-chain omega 3s, iron, zinc and vitamin B_{12}. One tin of sardines contains about two-thirds of a portion of oily fish. Therefore, you can eat up to three tins of sardines a week if you don't have any other oily fish.

✔ **Satay (saté)** Dishes such as satay pork, lamb or chicken are prepared with a peanut sauce. There is no need to avoid satay dishes or any other foods containing peanuts unless you have a peanut allergy. See *peanuts*.

Scallops While you are pregnant it is safe to have cooked scallops but they should not be eaten raw.

Scrambled egg It is fine to eat scrambled egg while you are pregnant. However, make sure you cook the eggs well. If they are slightly runny, there is a risk of salmonella. See *eggs*.

Seafood See *shellfish*.

Seafood sticks These are sometimes referred to as crab sticks or fish sticks. They are usually made from processed white fish with crab flavouring, among other additives. They should be safe to eat, provided they are kept chilled.

Seaweed Nori, wakame, kombu, kelp and other types of seaweed are extremely rich in iodine. You need to be careful about the type and amount of seaweed you eat otherwise you could easily have too much iodine, which could interfere with thyroid function (see page 75). The British Dietetic Association advises pregnant women not to eat seaweed more than once a week and not to take supplements made from seaweed or seaweed extract (see page 86).

Shellfish It is OK to have shellfish (including prawns, clams, scallops, mussels, crayfish, winkles and shrimp) when you are pregnant, providing it is cooked thoroughly and eaten as part of a hot meal. For example, you could have shellfish in a fish pie, curry or stir-fry.

It is also safe to eat shellfish such as prawns or crab that has been freshly cooked and chilled. This means that products such as prawn sandwiches are OK if they are bought from a reputable shop and you are confident that they have been kept chilled.

Shellfish, such as oysters, whelks and cockles, that is usually eaten raw should be avoided as it can be contaminated with harmful bacteria and viruses, including hepatitis A, which affects the liver. Symptoms include nausea, abdominal pain, tiredness, fever, dark urine and jaundice.

It is also best to avoid shellfish that is cooked but served cold, for example prawn sandwiches and crab or lobster salad, if you have any doubts about the way it has been prepared or stored.

Also see *crab*.

✓ ✗ **Smoked fish** In the UK smoked fish is considered safe to eat in pregnancy, including smoked salmon, smoked mackerel and smoked trout. In the USA and Australia, pregnant women are advised not to eat smoked fish, unless it is hot, because of the potential danger of listeria. However, in the UK the risk is low compared with foods such as Brie and pâté. That said, in 2013 and 2014 batches of smoked salmon were recalled by the FSA because they were found to contain listeria, and in 2015 a batch was recalled because of concerns over Clostridium botulinum.

Another issue that concerns some women is the polycyclic aromatic hydrocarbon (PAH) content of smoked fish. PAHs are present due to both sea pollution and the smoking process. Most PAHs are safe to consume, but some are believed to be carcinogenic. Levels of the carcinogenic PAHs benzo(a) pyrene have been found to be higher in fish smoked in traditional kilns than in fish smoked in larger commercial kilns. The level of salt in smoked salmon and other smoked fish is also usually high, and much higher than that in ordinary fish. These issues do not mean that smoked fish is completely out, because the risk is not really known. However, it is best to consume smoked fish in moderation (see *oily fish* for portion limits), and satisfying a daily craving for smoked salmon bagels probably isn't a good idea.

Smoked mackerel In the UK, it is considered safe to eat ✓ ✗ smoked mackerel during pregnancy (see *oily fish* for portion limits). See also *smoked fish.*

Smoked salmon In the UK, it is considered safe to eat ✓ ✗ smoked salmon during pregnancy (see *oily fish* for portion limits). See also *gravlax* and *smoked fish.*

Snails See *escargot.*

Soft cheese See *cheese.*

Sour cream It is OK to consume sour cream during preg- ✓ ✗ nancy, provided it is made from pasteurised milk. Sour cream made from unpasteurised milk is only available direct from farms, and should be avoided.

Soya There are no problems associated with eating soya ✓ beans or products such as tofu and soya milk, as part of a normal healthy diet. Concern has been raised about possible adverse effects that soya may have on foetal development, but these are not well founded. Soya contains a phyto-estrogen called genistein, which can have a similar, but much weaker, effect to the hormone oestrogen. Research has shown that when pregnant rats consume a diet rich in genistein, it can affect the future fertility of their babies. It has been speculated that a diet rich in soya could have a similar effect in humans, but there is no evidence for this.

One study found that the incidence of hypospadias (a defect of the penis) was more common among babies of vegetarian mothers, and it was suggested that this could be related to a higher phyto-estrogen intake. However, countries with a high intake of soya, such as China and Japan, do not appear to have such problems. Therefore, the balance of evidence suggests normal consumption is fine.

✓ **Spicy food** It's fine to eat spicy foods such as curry and chilli while you are pregnant, as long as you feel OK when you eat them. If you eat food that is too spicy, it can irritate the lining of the intestine and have a laxative effect. This is very unlikely to have a serious effect on your baby, but it will be unpleasant for you and will also leave you dehydrated.

It is sometimes suggested that eating a hot curry will bring on labour but this is not proven (see page 100).

✓ **Spinach** This is safe to eat and is a good source of beta-carotene, folate and vitamin C. However, it is a myth that spinach is a good source of iron: spinach contains oxalic acid, which binds tightly to the iron, making much of it unavailable for absorption.

Splenda See *artificial sweeteners*.

✗ **Steak tartar (steak Americaine)** This is a definite no-no during pregnancy. It contains raw meat, which could be infected with toxoplasmosis, and raw egg, so there is also a risk of salmonella.

Stevia See *artificial sweeteners*.

✓✗ **Stilton** This is a blue-veined cheese but the FSA considers it safe to eat during pregnancy because it is hard. This means it doesn't contain as much water as soft cheeses so it is difficult for bacteria to grow in it. However, it is best to check on the packaging as Stiltons vary in the amount of time they are left to mature, which affects their salt and water content and in turn their safety. So despite the general advice, you shouldn't eat cheeses carrying a warning that they should be avoided by expectant mothers as this will be based on the specific formulation of the manufacturer.

Sucralose See *artificial sweeteners.*

Sulphites If you usually consume foods and drinks containing sulphites, there is no reason to avoid them during pregnancy. Sulphites are additives (numbers E220 to E228) used to preserve food and prevent discoloration or browning in products such as dried apricots and sun-dried tomatoes. They are also found in sausages, burgers, soft drinks and wine. Some people are sensitive to sulphites and may have an asthmatic attack when exposed to them. Therefore, any food or drink containing sulphites carries a warning to alert these individuals. There is no evidence to suggest they should be avoided unless you are allergic to them or have asthma.

Sunflower seeds These are a good source of iron, zinc and vitamin A and they can safely be eaten during pregnancy. While it is fine to consume sunflower seeds in moderation, it is probably not a good idea to have very large amounts. This is because they are rich in linoleic acid (LA), which is an omega 6 fatty acid. High intakes of omega 6 fatty acids can interfere with the metabolism of omega 3 fatty acids, which are particularly beneficial during pregnancy (see page 59).

Sushi Raw farmed fish is considered safe to eat in pregnancy but raw wild fish must be frozen before it is eaten.

Freezing kills off any tiny parasitic worms that may be present in wild fish, which could otherwise make you ill. Readymade sushi brought into shops or restaurants should be safe, since food safety regulations state that it must have been frozen to −20°C for 24 hours. Restaurants that prepare their own fresh sushi may not have done this, so check with the staff. If you make sushi at home, freeze the fish for at least four days before using it.

✖ **Swordfish** High levels of mercury have been found in swordfish, and women who are pregnant are advised not to consume it at all. If you are breastfeeding, the advice is that it is OK to consume one portion a week but no more.

✔ **Taramasalata** The FSA considers commercially prepared taramasalata safe to eat during pregnancy.

✔✖ **Tartar sauce** It is safe to eat tartar sauce from a jar or sachet, as this is made with pasteurised egg.

Homemade tartar sauce is often prepared in the same way as homemade mayonnaise, in which case it will contain raw eggs and carry a risk of salmonella. However, it can also be made with hard-boiled egg yolks, which are safe, so it is best to ask.

✔✖ **Tea** It is fine to drink normal black tea in moderation. However, each cup contains about 50mg of caffeine, so during pregnancy you shouldn't drink more than about four cups a day. If you like your tea strong, and drink large mugs, then the caffeine content will be higher. Also, if you drink coffee and cola as well, then you should have even fewer cups of tea (see page 50). You could try alternatives such as decaffeinated tea, peppermint tea or fruit teas.

Try to avoid drinking tea (regular or decaffeinated) with meals or just after, as it can dramatically reduce iron absorption. The polyphenols in tea, known as tannins, bind tightly to the iron in foods such as breakfast cereal and bread, so the iron passes through your digestive system unabsorbed. Likewise, if you are taking iron supplements or multivitamins with iron, avoid drinking tea for about an hour after taking them.

See also *green tea, herbal teas, peppermint tea, Pu-erh tea* and *raspberry leaf tea.*

Thyme It is fine to use thyme in ordinary cooking. ✓

Strong medicinal doses of thyme and thyme essential oil should be avoided during pregnancy, as it is thought to be a uterine stimulant.

Tiramisu It is fine to eat tiramisu bought from a supermar- ✓ ✗ ket or similar shop while you are pregnant. Any egg and cream it contains will be pasteurised and if it contains alcohol and coffee these will be in such tiny amounts that they are not a concern.

Homemade tiramisu may contain raw eggs in the creamy topping, so it should be avoided because of the risk of salmonella. It may also contain a considerable amount of alcohol and strong coffee, which need to be taken into account.

Tofu It is fine to eat tofu during pregnancy and while ✓ breastfeeding. See also *soya.*

Tonic water It is safe to drink tonic water while you are ✓ pregnant. See *quinine.*

Tuna It is safe to eat tuna in moderation. It is recommended ✓ ✗ that while pregnant you have no more than two portions of fresh tuna (140g a portion) or four 200g cans per week. If you do have four cans of tuna in a week, you can still have two portions of oily fish, such as salmon or mackerel, but not fresh tuna.

Fresh tuna is an oily fish and provides long-chain omega 3s, which are good for your baby's development. However, it can also contain pollutants (dioxins and PCBs). Tinned tuna is not considered an oily fish, since during the canning process much of the oil is separated and lost. As a result, tinned tuna has a similar fatty acid composition to white fish. This means that tinned tuna isn't a good source of long-chain omega 3s, and it is not a problem as far as PCBs are concerned. However, because both fresh and canned tuna have been found to contain mercury, they should be consumed only in moderation.

There is no limit on the amount of tuna you can eat while breastfeeding.

Venison See *game*.

✔️ **Water** All adults need to drink at least six to eight glasses of fluid a day. While you are pregnant, you may notice that you become thirstier. Breastfeeding is definitely very thirsty work. If it's hot or you're exercising, you will need more fluids. Since it is not advisable to drink alcohol while pregnant, and your caffeine intake should be limited, water is an important part of your diet. Tap water is just as good as bottled water and its quality is closely monitored.

✖️ **Wine** It is not advisable to drink wine during pregnancy. See the information on alcohol on page 49.

✔️✖️ **Yogurt** It is safe to eat yogurt while you are pregnant. This includes products described as 'bio-yogurts' or containing 'live bacteria'. The bacteria they contain are probiotics or 'healthy bacteria', so they will not cause food poisoning.

Yogurt made from unpasteurised milk should not be eaten during pregnancy, as it may contain listeria or other bacteria, which could cause food poisoning. In the UK this is only available from farm shops.

10 Breastfeeding – the best diet for you and your baby

Just because your baby has been born, it doesn't mean you can stop thinking about healthy eating. If you've chosen not to breastfeed or if it hasn't been possible, a balanced diet is important to help your body recover from all the work it's been doing and to replenish the nutrient stores lost during pregnancy. If you are breastfeeding, it is even more important, as the food you eat now will affect the growth and development of your baby. Also, before you know it, your little one will be eating proper food, and if you have good eating habits there's a much better chance that he or she will follow suit.

If you found it hard to resist the temptations of ripe Brie or fried eggs while you were pregnant, the good news is that these can go back on the menu. However, small amounts of what you eat will pass into your breast milk, so caffeine and alcohol should still be limited.

Breastfeeding your baby gives the best possible start in life. The list below highlights the many benefits. By paying a little extra attention to your diet, you can improve your baby's chances of a healthy future even more. For example, you can boost brain and eye development and reduce the risk of allergies and asthma.

Breastfeeding gives your baby:

* protection against diarrhoea and vomiting;
* protection against middle ear and respiratory tract infections;
* a reduced risk of obesity;
* a reduced risk of diabetes;
* a reduced risk of heart disease in adulthood.

What's in breast milk?

The composition of breast milk changes in the first few days after birth from colostrum, which is rich in protein and protective factors, to mature milk. It also changes during each feed from foremilk, which is more watery, to hindmilk, which contains more calories and nutrients. It even varies with the weather, so that your baby gets more fluids when it's hot, and with the time of day. So your baby really does get just what he or she needs.

On average, breast milk contains about 70kcal per 100ml. It is 1.3% protein, 4.1% fat and 7.2% carbohydrate. It also contains omega 3 fatty acids, more than 100 different oligosaccharides and a range of vitamins and minerals, including B vitamins, vitamins A and E, calcium, iron, iodine and zinc. It also has growth factors, hormones and other special proteins, antibodies, white blood cells and nucleotides, which help protect against infection.

It is estimated that if every baby in the UK were exclusively breastfed for six months, it would halve the number of babies hospitalised for diarrhoea, and cut by a quarter the number hospitalised for respiratory infections.

A healthy diet for breastfeeding

A healthy diet while you breastfeed is similar to that for any stage of life. However, there are some things you need to pay closer attention to. When you've just had a baby, it can be nice to have things laid down as simply as possible, so the guidelines below should help:

- At least **five portions of a variety of fruit and vegetables** every day. Fruit such as bananas and raisins are especially handy for snacks when you're busy with a new baby.

- **Protein foods,** such as meat, fish, eggs, cheese, beans and lentils.

- **Starchy foods,** like bread, pasta, rice and potatoes. The extra energy you need for breastfeeding should come from these foods rather than from snacks that are high in sugar or fat.

- **High-fibre foods,** such as wholemeal bread, high-fibre breakfast cereals and pulses. These are particularly important in the early days after having your baby, when constipation is a common problem.

- **Fish** at least twice a week, including one or two portions of oily fish to provide your baby with a good supply of long-chain omega 3s.

- **Dairy foods** such as milk and yogurt to supply calcium for your own milk production. This is important for your health too, as you will have less calcium in your body than normal, no matter how well you ate during pregnancy.

- **Plenty of fluids**. The general advice for people who are not breastfeeding is to drink at least six to eight glasses of fluid a day (approximately 1.2 litres). Since you are likely to be producing about 800ml of milk a day, you obviously need more than this. However, you shouldn't force yourself to drink more than you want. The best drinks are water or milk (skimmed, 1% fat or semi-skimmed).

- **Iron-rich foods**. During the last trimester of pregnancy, your baby accumulates most of the iron he or she needs, at the expense of your iron requirements. Your iron levels may therefore be depleted after birth. You will also lose some blood during labour, so it is important to have a good supply of iron after your baby is born. This will replenish your stores and ensure you have sufficient iron for breastfeeding.

Ten tips for eating well with a new baby

When you have a baby to look after, it can be difficult to think about your diet. However, it is important to make healthy eating and regular meals a priority. This will benefit both you and your baby.

1 Always have healthy snacks at hand so that you don't have to rely on biscuits and buns when you are busy.

2 Don't get into the habit of eating unhealthy take-aways and ready meals to save time. Instead, keep meals simple – you can buy ready-chopped vegetables for a stir-fry, or try one of the almost instant meals listed.

3 Have a big glass of water next to you every time you sit down to feed your baby. When you have a cup of tea or coffee, try to match it with a glass of water.

4 If your baby sleeps in the morning, make yourself a big sandwich with plenty of salad and put it in the fridge for later.

5 When things are going well and you have time to cook, try making extra to go in the freezer.

6 Shop online. If your baby is not a fan of supermarket shopping then getting deliveries can make life much easier.

7 Remember that eating well is more important than how tidy your home is.

8 Try not to graze. Regular eating is important, but it is easy to get into bad habits when you are at home all day. This can result in putting on excess pounds.

9 When someone asks how they can help, ask them to cook a healthy meal, or suggest that visitors bring fruit instead of chocolates sometimes.

10 Think about whether you are turning to food when what you really need is more sleep, fresh air, exercise or emotional support. If you need help, ask for it (see 'Resources and useful contacts' on pages 207–210).

Ten almost instant meals for busy mums

1 A baked potato filled with tuna, low-fat mayonnaise and some salad.
2 Baked beans on toast, and a couple of satsumas.
3 Vegetable soup and a wholemeal roll.
4 A bowl of cereal with chopped banana or strawberries.
5 Mashed sardines on toast.
6 Peanut butter (or almond butter) and grated carrot sandwich.
7 Low-fat cheese on toast with sliced tomato.
8 Grilled chicken or salmon, couscous and vegetables.
9 Greek salad in wholemeal pitta bread.
10 Pan-fried steak and tomato sandwich.

Do you still need supplements?

Women who are breastfeeding are advised to take a supplement containing 10μg of vitamin D every day. This is because rickets, which is caused by vitamin D deficiency, appears to be re-emerging in the UK, and women with low vitamin D levels produce breast milk with a lower content. You may have started taking vitamin D supplements during pregnancy, but if not, it is a good idea to begin now. If you are eating a well-balanced diet, then you should not need any other supplements. However, if you needed iron supplements during pregnancy it would be a good idea to continue taking them for the first six weeks after your baby is born. If you're unsure your diet is supplying all the other nutrients you need, you may want to take a multivitamin and mineral supplement too and possibly a DHA supplement if you don't eat oily fish.

How your diet affects your milk

Some components of breast milk are affected by the food you eat. The protein and carbohydrate content doesn't seem to vary much with a mother's diet, but some studies have found that the fat content can be altered. If you have a low-fat diet and low fat stores, the amount of fat in your breast milk is reduced.

The levels of different fatty acids in your diet also affect the amounts of fatty acids in your breast milk. Women who eat more butter have been found to have increased levels of saturated fat in their breast milk, and women on macrobiotic diets have lower-than-expected levels of saturated fat. In addition, women who never eat fish have much lower levels of EPA and DHA (long-chain omega 3s). A study of more than 300 women in the Netherlands found that those consuming organic dairy products and meat had higher levels of conjugated linoleic acid (CLA) in their breast milk. CLA is thought to have many health benefits, including boosting the immune system and providing anti-inflammatory protection.

By eating one or two portions of oily fish a week, you can boost the levels of omega 3s in your breast milk. This can have benefits for your baby's brain and eye development. Breastfed babies of mothers with higher intakes of long-chain omega 3s have been found to score better on developmental tests, including those for hand and eye coordination.

The amount of some other nutrients in your breast milk also depends on how much you consume yourself. For example, if you eat more vitamin C-rich fruit and vegetables then your breast milk will contain more vitamin C. The amount of vitamin B_{12} in your breast milk will also depend on how much you consume yourself, and there have been cases of severe vitamin B_{12} deficiency reported in babies being breast-fed by unsupplemented vegan mothers. If you are vegan or consume little meat and dairy produce it is a good idea to ensure you are having an adequate vitamin B_{12} intake (see page 65). Calcium is another nutrient that breastfeeding mums sometimes go short of and, although it won't affect the amount of calcium in your milk, having a low intake can put your own bone health at risk.

The myth of poor-quality milk
Women sometimes believe that their milk isn't very good. They may even be told they have 'poor-quality milk'. In reality, the composition of breast milk is unlikely to vary so much that it affects your baby's feeding pattern or immediate growth, unless you are severely malnourished. It is much more likely that your baby's positioning and attachment while feeding need attention.

If you are concerned about your milk supply and are thinking about giving your baby the odd bottle or switching to formula completely, don't rush into it. Make sure you first talk to your midwife or health visitor or call one of the breastfeeding helplines (see 'Resources and useful contacts' on pages 207–210). They should be able to offer you plenty of advice on establishing good breastfeeding.

Yummy – garlic milk

The foods, spices and drinks you consume while breastfeeding directly affect the flavour and odour of the milk you produce. Your baby has already been exposed to a variety of flavours before he or she was born, via the large quantities of amniotic fluid he or she swallowed in the womb. Now your baby is continuing to learn about the great variety of flavours available.

You might think that garlic milk would put a baby off feeding, but this doesn't seem to be the case. It is known that garlic transfers into breast milk – the odour has been detected by scientists, who report that it is at its strongest two hours after garlic is eaten – but babies seem to like it. In fact, babies have been found to stay at the breast longer, suck more often and consume more milk when their mother has eaten garlic.

Another great advantage of flavoured breast milk is that it prepares babies for weaning and enjoying a varied diet in later life. Breastfed babies are less likely to become fussy eaters. A greater acceptance of different flavours is apparent right from the beginning. A number of studies have found that babies exposed to particular flavours, including carrot juice, aniseed and garlic, while breastfeeding are more likely to enjoy the taste later when they are weaned.

Weight loss

It is important to take a balanced and sensible approach to losing weight after you've had a baby. It is not a good idea to lose 5 stone in just a few months as some celebrity mums do. Equally, you can't expect breastfeeding to make the pounds melt away if you eat chocolate biscuits by the packet.

Many new mums feel enormous pressure to lose weight after seeing pictures of super-slim famous mums. If you have a nanny, a personal trainer and your own chef, you may be able to follow in their footsteps; however, this isn't a recipe for successful breastfeeding or bonding with and enjoying your new baby. Trying to lose weight rapidly will also leave you feeling drained of energy and could mean both you and your baby miss out on some of the essential nutrients you need. It is particularly important that you don't go on any kind of restrictive diet, such as dairy-free or low-carb, without talking to your doctor. It is much better for you and your baby if you breastfeed, eat a healthy, balanced diet and aim to lose the extra pounds or stones slowly.

It is estimated that if you are exclusively breastfeeding you will need an extra 330kcal per day. You may read that an extra 500kcal are needed each day but research suggests this is an overestimate and in 2011 the official advice was updated. If you are exclusively breastfeeding twins then you'll probably need an extra 600–700kcal per day. During pregnancy, fat stores are laid down to supply some extra energy and the number of additional calories you need will depend on the amount of milk your baby is having and on how much fat you have stored. If you are thin, it's important to make sure you consume plenty of extra calories. You should make regular meals and snacks a priority, to ensure that you and your baby are getting all the calories and nutrients you need. However, if you are overweight, then additional calories may not be needed. Instead, it is important to concentrate on eating nutrient-rich foods, as recommended on page 175, while limiting your intake of high-sugar and high-fat foods.

If you have a very low-calorie diet, your milk supply will be affected. However, if you do have extra pounds to lose, then slow weight loss won't adversely affect your milk. Research has shown that when women lose 1–2lb a week through healthy eating and regular exercise, the amount and quality of their breast milk is not affected, and nor is their baby's weight gain. Eating more high-fibre and low GI foods can help you lose baby weight at a healthy rate, without feeling so hungry (see page 33).

Although breastfeeding can help you lose weight, not every woman who breastfeeds sheds the pounds effortlessly. Breastfeeding certainly uses up energy, but many breastfeeding women are hungrier and eat more than non-breastfeeding mothers. One study found that weight loss in the six months after birth was related more to a desire to lose weight than to breastfeeding or bottle-feeding. So, if you want to lose weight, don't think that breastfeeding is the solution no matter what you eat. Research into losing weight after giving birth has found that using both diet and exercise together is more effective than either dieting or exercise alone.

Tips for successful weight loss

• Rather than short bursts of physical activity, like a workout once a week, aim for regular exercise such as walking every day.

• Try to establish regular eating habits. It is all too easy to snack if you're overtired and spending more time at home.

• Try getting some support by joining a slimming club that is suitable for breastfeeding mums, or just meet other mums for a long walk.

• Do exercise that fits into your new lifestyle. It may be easier to go walking with your baby, or get an exercise DVD to do at home, rather than finding someone to look after your baby while you go to the gym or an exercise class.

• Try not to eat on the run. It is much more satisfying to have a sit-down meal and eat slowly; you will then be less likely to overeat.

- If you are having trouble shifting the pounds, make a note of everything you eat for a few days. This may reveal that you are eating more than you thought, and it will show you where you can make some changes.

Foods to avoid when you're breastfeeding

There aren't any foods you need to avoid completely when breastfeeding, but the following should be consumed in limited amounts:

- Don't have more than two portions (140g each) of **oily fish** each week. This is because oily fish, such as salmon and sardines, contain traces of pollutants, which can pass into your breast milk (see page 150).

- Avoid having more than one portion of **shark**, **swordfish** or **marlin** a week.

- Try not to have too much **caffeine**. You may feel in need of a strong cup of coffee, especially if you haven't slept well, but bear in mind that caffeine passes into breast milk, so it won't just be you who enjoys the stimulant effect. Also, babies can't metabolise caffeine as easily as adults, and so caffeine can build up in your baby's system. The FSA advises women to limit caffeine intake to 200mg per day, the same as for pregnancy (see page 50). Caffeine also makes you dehydrated, so it is important to have plenty of drinks without caffeine as well in order to keep your fluid levels up.

- **Alcohol** should be drunk only occasionally as, like caffeine, it passes into breast milk. It is recommended that you don't have more than 1–2 units once or twice a week.

- Some **herbs** are traditionally thought to dry up a woman's milk supply. These haven't been tested scientifically, but it might be sensible to avoid taking large doses of sage, mint or parsley while breastfeeding. Use in normal cooking is fine.

In the past, women with a family history of allergies were advised to avoid eating peanuts during pregnancy, but this is no longer considered necessary. It was thought that small amounts of peanut could pass into the breast milk and increase a baby's risk of developing allergies. However, recent studies have shown this is not the case and there is some evidence that early exposure to peanuts may even be beneficial.

You may have heard that alcohol, particularly beer, is good for breastfeeding, but I'm afraid that this has been tested and shown to be a myth. Research has shown that drinking even small quantities of alcohol reduces the amount of milk women produce and affects breastfeeding. An experiment found that when women consumed orange juice containing 1–2 units of alcohol, they produced significantly less milk than when they had plain orange juice. Research into the amount of milk babies consume after their mother has had a drink have also produced significant results. One study looked at the number of sucks the baby made in the first minute of breastfeeding. It was found that the suck rate was 15% greater when mothers had consumed 1–2 units of alcohol; however, the babies were found to consume 30% less milk. It seems that the babies had to work much harder to get milk when their mother had been drinking. It could be that alcohol affects the mother's milk letdown (release of milk to the nipple area). Curiously, babies don't seem to be put off by the smell or flavour of alcohol in the milk, which seems to be strongest 30 minutes to an hour after drinking. Babies given expressed milk from a bottle consume just as much when it contains alcohol as when it doesn't.

In the long term, having the odd drink is not likely to affect the amount of milk your baby takes. Although babies consume less in the four hours after alcohol is drunk, they appear to compensate to some extent 8-16 hours later by consuming more milk. However, drinking alcohol while breastfeeding can have other effects. The NHS recommends caution, because drinking more than a couple of units at a time can reduce your milk supply and affect your baby's development. Although alcohol may make mothers feel sleepy, it actually makes babies more restless and they spend less time in 'active sleep'. Also, in the long term, it can affect a baby's wellbeing. Regular drinking (one drink or more per day) has been found to adversely affect a baby's motor development.

Planning a night out

If you are going out and will be having a drink, it is best to plan your feeding beforehand. Alcohol clears from your breast milk at about the same rate as from your blood (just over two hours per unit). However, it varies slightly according to your weight. For example, if a 9-stone woman drank 6 units of alcohol, it would take about 14 hours to clear from her milk, whereas an 11-stone woman would clear the same amount in about 13 hours.

The level of alcohol in your milk isn't affected by feeding, so 'pumping and dumping' is unnecessary. It is best to express enough milk before you start drinking to last your baby until the alcohol has completely left your system.

Women are sometimes advised to avoid orange juice, garlic, spicy meals or other foods while breastfeeding. Although it may be sensible to skip a very hot curry when you've just had a baby, generally there is no need to limit your diet 'just in case'. You can eat as normal and just keep an eye on your baby for any adverse effects. Possible reactions to food include general upset or restlessness, a rash, runny nose, wind, diarrhoea and explosive nappies.

If your baby has green bits in the nappy, it is probably not because he or she has consumed something they shouldn't have. More likely, your baby has not been getting enough of the nutrient-rich hindmilk that comes later during a feed after the watery foremilk. This sometimes happens because the baby is switched from one breast to the other before he or she has a chance to get the good stuff. If you are worried about the appearance of your baby's poo, talk to your midwife or health visitor.

Sometimes your baby may be upset by something you have eaten, but it is hard to identify the food responsible or determine whether it was something completely unrelated. The section below on colic lists some of the foods most commonly thought to upset babies. Sometimes they are allergic to specific proteins in the food you are eating. This is not common but is worth considering. An allergy to dairy foods is the most frequently talked about problem, and women may be advised by alternative and complementary therapists to cut out milk and dairy foods from their diet – sometimes without good reason. Only 0.5% of exclusively breastfed infants have allergies to cows' milk protein, and there are many other reasons why babies suffer from problems such as eczema, diarrhoea and discomfort.

If you have eaten something that you suspect doesn't agree with your baby, then you could try avoiding the food for a week, before having it again. If the same thing happens, you might be better steering clear of it for a while. However, it is important that you don't cut out whole food groups, such as dairy foods or foods containing wheat, without talking to your midwife, health visitor or doctor. If you do, both you and your baby could be missing out on essential nutrients.

Colic

It can be very distressing if your baby has colic, and you are probably willing to give anything a go. However, before you start avoiding dairy foods, wheat, soya, eggs or any other food, it is important to learn as much as you can about colic. Sometimes improving your baby's position when feeding can make a real difference. If not, try not to worry unduly. Although feeding is unlikely to be enjoyable and relaxed for either of you, babies with colic generally take just as much milk as others and gain weight normally.

What is colic?
Colic is thought to affect about one in five babies. It is charac-terised by periods of frantic crying at roughly the same time every day, typically in the early evening. A baby with colic is also likely to draw their knees up to their chest, pass wind and become red in the face. Colic generally appears in the first few weeks and disappears by the time a baby is three or four months old. If you are unsure whether your baby has colic, it is best to talk to your doctor to rule out other possible causes of distress.

Colic and cows' milk

In some babies, colic may be the result of lactose intolerance or an allergy to cows' milk. These may sound very similar, but they have quite different causes and should be treated differently.

Lactose intolerance

This is a sensitivity to the sugar (lactose) found in milk, includ-ing formula and breast milk. If a baby doesn't produce enough of the enzyme lactase, he or she is unable to break down the lactose sugar in the small intestine. The lactose therefore passes into the large intestine, where it is fermented, producing hydrogen and methane gases and discomfort. If your baby is receiving formula, your health visitor may suggest switching to a lactose-free or low-lactose formula. Breast milk contains lactose irrespective of what you eat, so cutting out milk and dairy foods from your diet won't help: your body will still produce lactose. What you can do, however, is give your baby lactase, for example Colief. This shouldn't be given to your baby directly but should be added to a small amount of expressed milk. Your baby can then be given it from a spoon or cup, before being put to the breast as normal for a feed. The problem is often called 'transient lactose intolerance', because babies generally grow out of it. Once your baby is three to four months old, he or she should be producing sufficient lactase to digest the lactose so you won't need to supply any extra.

Allergy to cows' milk

This is an immunological response to the proteins that the milk contains. These are found in most formula milks, as these are based on cows' milk. The proteins are also present in breast milk if the mother consumes cows' milk or any dairy products such as yogurt and cheese. If your baby is receiving any formula, then switch to a hypo-allergenic variety. The only way to ensure that your baby does not receive cows' milk proteins from your breast milk is to remove all cows' milk products from your diet. Your doctor or health visitor will be able to advise you on how to do this, and how and when to try reintroduction, possibly in a clinic.

Other causes and cures

In reality, there is usually no cure for colic but it generally gets better on its own as your baby gets older. In the meantime several strategies may help to ease the symptoms of colic. No one really knows the cause of most cases of colic, but some research suggests that the baby's immature digestive tract could have difficulty coping with milk; as a result, the baby suffers from cramps. Colic may also be due to the baby swallowing air bubbles when he or she feeds or cries. To help minimise this, try to sit your baby as upright as possible during feeding rather than lying him or her flat on their back, and burp your baby well. The drug simeticone may also help; this is an anti-flatulent, which changes small bubbles of air in your baby's intestine into larger bubbles that are easier to burp up. Simeticone has been used for years and is readily available from pharmacists, for example as Infacol. It may also help if you breastfeed your baby on the same side until he or she has definitely had enough milk; switching from one breast to the other before your baby's got enough of the high-fat hindmilk may mean that he or she feeds more to compensate, so your baby has a larger volume of milk and more lactose than he or she can handle comfortably.

Sometimes women find breastfeeding so stressful with a colicky baby that they are tempted to stop. You may even wonder whether your baby would do better with a bottle of formula. However, research has shown that formula-fed babies are much more likely to get colic than those that are breastfed. Unfortunately if you're breastfeeding you can't leave it for someone else to do, but if someone else takes care of your baby so you can have a break for a while, it can help.

Adapting your diet may relieve your baby's colic symptoms. Different things seem to affect different babies, but it may be worth cutting out certain foods to see whether the colic is reduced. It is best to try just one dietary change at a time, otherwise you could end up eating a very limited diet and missing out on some nutrients. If, after a week, there is no improvement, go back to your normal diet. If your baby's symptoms get better, then it might be worth skipping the food for a while, if it is something you can live without, such as tea or onions. However, if it is a key food, like fish or dairy products, then you should try gradual reintroduction or look for alternative sources of the nutrients that you will be missing. It may be that you just need to eat less of the trigger food, or to eat it in a different form. For example, if milk is the problem, you may find that if you have a smaller amount of milk, or eat cheese, then it is OK.

Here are the foods most commonly suspected of causing or aggravating colic:

- tea and coffee;
- alcohol;
- cruciferous vegetables such as broccoli, cauliflower and cabbage: these may encourage the production of wind;
- cows' milk and milk products, such as cheese and yogurt;
- wheat and corn;
- fish;
- eggs;
- onions;
- chocolate;
- citrus fruit.

The whole area of diet causing adverse effects in breast-fed babies is quite complicated, and guidelines are still evolving. Whether it is colic or some other unwanted symptoms, it really is best to get professional help from your GP, health visitor or state-registered dietician.

What about me?

Most of this chapter has focused on how breastfeeding affects your baby, but breastfeeding also benefits you:

- It stimulates the uterus to contract back to its pre-pregnancy size.

- It reduces the risk of breast and ovarian cancers.
- It reduces the risk of heart disease.
- It increases the chances of losing weight and returning to your pre-pregnancy weight.
- It gives you some protection against osteoporosis.

Eating well while you are breastfeeding is important not only for your baby but also for your own health and wellbeing. If your diet is less than ideal, you could suffer, even if your baby is fine. Research has shown that mothers can have signs of malnutrition, including bone demineralisation, B vitamin deficiencies and multiple infections, even while their breastfed babies appear healthy, show no signs of malnutrition and have a normal or low-normal weight. So, by all means congratulate yourself if your baby is thriving, but don't forget that how you are doing is important too. As well as improving your physical health, eating well can make you feel better. It will boost your energy levels and could even help with postnatal depression.

There is growing awareness of mental health problems in the postnatal period. According to NICE, 15–20% of women suffer from depression or anxiety in the first year after childbirth. Old work colleagues may picture you meeting friends for coffee or watching daytime telly with a sleeping baby in your arms but the reality can be quite different. Postnatal depression affects 10–15% of women and for a small number this can be severe. Talk to your GP or health visitor and also have a look at the information provided by the mental health charity MIND. Although there is not much research into diet and postnatal depression, having a good intake of zinc and vitamin B_6 could be important. In addition, intake of DHA and EPA is thought to affect mental health. Several studies have looked at whether higher intakes of these long-chain omega 3s can prevent or treat postnatal depression and although the results are inconclusive some studies have shown a benefit.

11 Preparing for a new pregnancy

If you are starting to think about having another baby, or planning for your first, then this is the ideal time to get your diet and general lifestyle in order. A healthy, balanced diet is important before as well as during pregnancy. What you eat now can have an enormous impact on your chances of getting pregnant and of having a healthy baby. Research shows women with healthier diets before pregnancy are less likely to deliver their babies prematurely or to develop gestational diabetes. Eating a Mediterranean style diet pre-pregnancy has also been found to reduce the chances of high blood pressure in pregnancy

If you can make dietary improvements before you become pregnant, they will have a much bigger effect. So, rather than burning the candle at both ends while you still have the chance, use this time to get into shape and give your baby the best possible start in life. Taking even just a few steps in the right direction can help. And as your family grows, you will all reap the health benefits.

You are unlikely to know you are pregnant for about two weeks after you conceive, so it is worth erring on the side of caution when it comes to food safety. That means avoiding excess alcohol and caffeine and thinking more about food hygiene. If this is your first pregnancy, or you need reminding about just what to eat for pregnancy, then the following pre-pregnancy checklist will help, but you may also find Chapter 1 useful. Then, when you get a positive pregnancy test, you can celebrate without worrying and feeling guilty about what you have eaten or drunk over the past few weeks. Also, you can ensure that your body has a good store of nutrients in case you suffer from morning sickness and don't feel like eating much in early pregnancy.

The pre-pregnancy checklist

Do

- Try to reach a healthy weight.
- Take a supplement containing 400µg of folic acid or higher if needed (see page 82). If possible start two to three months before trying for a baby. This is important in the very early days after conception before you know you are pregnant and will reduce your risk of having a baby with spina bifida or a neural tube defect.
- Eat a healthy, balanced diet (see page 12).
- Be careful about general food hygiene (see page 42).
- Exercise to keep fit and relieve stress, but avoid rigorous exercise programmes as these can reduce fertility.
- Talk to your doctor if you are taking any prescription drugs or herbal medicines.
- Relax and make the most of life. You may get pregnant straightaway, but it could take some time. Stress reduces fertility and there won't be much time for relaxing once your new baby arrives.

Don't

- Drink alcohol. It can cause birth defects and increase the risk of miscarriage. Your partner should cut down too: not only for moral support, but because even moderate drinking can lower his sperm count.

- Eat liver or take supplements such as cod liver oil, which contain high levels of vitamin A.

- Eat shark, swordfish or marlin, and don't have more than two tuna steaks or four 200g cans of tuna a week.

- Drink too much coffee, tea and other drinks containing caffeine.

- Smoke or take recreational drugs such as cannabis.

Why weight matters

Your weight before you get pregnant can affect your fertility and your baby's health. If you are unsure whether your weight is appropriate for your height, you can find out by using the graph on page 21 or working out your BMI (page 20). Being underweight can make it more difficult to conceive and increases the risk of miscarriage in the first trimester of pregnancy. It can also increase the risk of your baby having a low birthweight and being unwell.

Being overweight can also reduce your fertility. A study in Denmark found that obese couples were three times more likely to have trouble conceiving compared with couples of a normal weight. Being overweight also increases the risk of complications during pregnancy, including infections, high blood pressure, pre-eclampsia and diabetes, and the risk of birth defects, including heart and limb deformities. Another problem is that being overweight makes it more difficult for your midwife to monitor your baby during pregnancy and labour, and there is a greater chance of problems arising during the birth.

However, don't be unduly concerned if you are overweight or underweight. These are risks, not certainties, and they are intended to show why it is important to try to reach a healthy weight. At the same time, you are in an ideal position now to do something about it and to increase the chances of everything going well.

Still carrying weight from your last pregnancy?
Mothers who don't manage to lose the weight they gained in their first pregnancy increase the risk of complications when they become pregnant again. A Swedish study of more than 150,000 women found that even small weight gains could be a problem. Women who gained just 1 or 2 BMI units following their first pregnancy (around 6–12lb) were 20–40% more likely to go on to suffer from high blood pressure or gestational diabetes than those who retained less weight. Gaining more than 3 BMI units presented further problems, increasing the risk of stillbirth by 60% and the risk of pre-eclampsia by more than 70%.

The risks weren't only increased in women who became classified as overweight or obese following their first pregnancy. They also applied to women who were still classified as normal weight but who had gained weight. If you are one of the many mums affected by lingering baby fat, then you may want to try to make some long-term changes to your diet and physical activity. To start with, work out how you can build some physical activity, such as walking, swimming or ball games in the park, into your everyday life.

How do you measure up?

If your BMI is under 18.5, you are underweight. To increase your BMI, you should eat larger quantities but still try to have a healthy diet. If you have only a small appetite, then choose more energy-dense foods such as full-fat dairy products, nuts, seeds and avocados. You could also use more vegetable oils in cooking or salad dressing. If you find large meals daunting, then don't worry – just eat small snacks throughout the day. If you do a lot of exercise, it might also help to reduce your workouts. In order to have a regular menstrual cycle and normal ovulation, women need to have a reasonable amount of body fat (at least 22%). Yours may be below this if you have a heavy exercise schedule. If you find it difficult to increase your body weight, then talk to your GP about getting some help, particularly if you have a history of eating disorders.

If your BMI is between 18.5 and 25, you are a healthy weight for your height. However, if you are right at the very bottom or very top of the range, you should keep an eye on your weight, and likewise if you gained weight following your last pregnancy (see page 196). Otherwise, you don't need to worry, and you certainly shouldn't think about losing weight in anticipation of putting it on when you get pregnant: research has shown that women who do this could be putting themselves at increased risk of premature delivery. Instead, you should make sure that you eat a healthy diet in order to get all the nutrients your body needs.

If your BMI is over 25, you are overweight. You should try to make some changes to your diet and increase the amount of physical activity that you do. You may be keen to get on with the business of baby-making, but don't try losing weight too quickly. Strict dieting will deprive your body of the essential nutrients it needs and can actually reduce rather than increase your fertility. Restrictive diets such as a low-carb diet may seem like a good idea - some people certainly achieve phenomenal weight loss with this kind of eating. However, research suggests that low-carb diets reduce your chances of becoming pregnant. Diets involving intermittent fasting, such as the 5:2 diet, can also help with weight loss but they too are not recommended if you are trying to become pregnant. Although the effect of this kind of diet on human fertility hasn't been tested, intermittent fasting has been found to interfere with hormone levels and reduce fertility in animals.

It is best to make long-term changes to your eating habits so that you can achieve a slow but steady weight loss of 1-2lb a week. This can be done by cutting down on fatty and sugary foods and increasing your intake of fruit and vege-tables, low GI foods, high-fibre foods and water. At the same time, you should take more exercise. Trying to incorporate more walking into your everyday life and using the stairs more often will also help. Eating a low GI diet can also help your chances of conceiving. A study involving 26 overweight and obese women attending a fertility clinic found that when half were put on a low GI diet their chances of weight loss and pregnancy improved. Three of the thirteen women on the low GI diet became pregnant before starting fertility treat-ment, and among those undergoing treatment 85% more eggs were retrieved from those in the low GI group than the control group.

Dad's weight matters too
A child with an overweight father is more than twice as likely to become overweight so dads-to-be need to make just as much effort as their partners. Researchers are only just beginning to understand how weight problems are passed on

from fathers but it appears that being overweight affects sperm DNA. One small study found that the sperm DNA of obese men differed from that of healthy weight men. Some of the differences in DNA related to brain function, possibly appetite control. Another study found that when obese men lost weight their sperm DNA changed quickly to become more like other men's.

Of course, losing weight is easier said than done, but what better incentive is there? By shedding the pounds now, you should feel better, increase your fertility, have an easier pregnancy and birth, and have a healthier baby. If you find weight loss difficult, particularly if you have a lot of weight to lose, then talk to your GP or join a reputable slimming club that doesn't promise instant success but encourages healthy eating and long-term results.

If you are very overweight, it is worth holding off trying to get pregnant until after you have managed to lose some of the extra pounds. Then you will have a better chance of everything going well. If you are less overweight, there shouldn't be any problem with you trying for a baby while you lose up to 2lb a week, providing you do it through sensible healthy eating and exercise.

What is a healthy diet?

A healthy diet when trying for a baby is basically the same as at any other time. It includes at least five portions of fruit and vegetables every day, plenty of starchy foods such as bread and rice, and some good sources of protein and calcium, like meat, fish, pulses, milk and dairy foods (see page 12). Folic acid is another key nutrient for pregnancy. As well as taking a supplement, try to increase your intake of folate-rich foods such as oranges and broccoli.

If it isn't long since your last pregnancy or you have recently stopped breastfeeding, then healthy eating now is especially important, as your stores of key nutrients, including vitamins A and D and omega 3s, may be low. In addition, up to half of young women have a low iron store, which puts them at risk of anaemia in pregnancy. By building up your iron stores now, you can prevent this happening (see page 72).

Fertility foods

Adopting a 'fertility diet' could boost your chances of getting pregnant, according to researchers at Harvard University. In a study of more than 17,000 women trying for a baby, they found that those with certain dietary habits and lifestyles were less likely to suffer fertility problems.

The 'fertility diet' pattern they identified was characterised by:

- a high consumption of monounsaturated fats rather than trans fats, e.g. consuming olive oil, nuts and seeds and avoiding processed foods such as cakes and biscuits;

- eating more vegetable protein than animal protein, e.g. avoiding large amounts of meat and eating beans and lentils instead;

- having plenty of low GI (glycaemic index) carbohydrates rather than high GI ones, e.g. wholegrain cereals and oats instead of white bread and cakes;

- eating a moderate amount of full-fat dairy produce rather than only low-fat versions of products such as milk and yogurt;

- consuming plenty of vitamins and iron from plant foods and supplements.

They also found that cutting down on alcohol and caffeine was important, as were controlling weight and having a reasonable level of physical activity. When they looked at infertility due to ovulatory disturbances, which is one of the most common problems, they found a 70% lower risk among women following the diet most closely.

Time to reduce your risk of gestational diabetes

Increasing numbers of women are developing gestational diabetes during pregnancy, which increases the risk of having a miscarriage, stillbirth and health problems in the newborn (see page 110). Some of the factors that increase your risk of developing the condition are out of your hands, for example having a family history of diabetes. But it is possible to modify your lifestyle before pregnancy to greatly reduce your gestational diabetes risk.

An American study following more than 20,000 nurses before and throughout pregnancy looked at four factors that affected the women's risks. Those without the risk factors before becoming pregnant had an 83% lower chance of developing gestational diabetes. The women at lowest risk had a BMI of less than 25, they didn't smoke, they did at least 150 minutes per week of moderate to vigorous physical activity and they ate a relatively healthy diet. It's important to note that a 'healthy diet' here wasn't an exceptional one. All the women received a score for their diet and those with scores in the top 40% were considered to have a healthy diet. Getting a good score meant eating more vegetables, fruit, nuts, whole grains, polyunsaturated fats, long-chain omega 3s and less red and processed meat, sugary drinks, trans fats and salt.

Another interesting finding from the American nurses' study was that women who ate more potatoes before pregnancy were at increased risk of developing gestational diabetes. This may be partly because potatoes have a high GI but women who eat them most days of the week, particularly in the form of chips, probably don't have the best diets in other respects. It was estimated that swapping two portions of potatoes each week for vegetables, legumes or wholegrain foods reduced the risk of gestational diabetes by 10%.

Slugs and snails or sugar and spice

If you already have a boy or two, and think that a little girl would be the icing on the family cake, is there anything you can do to achieve your ambition? There are certainly plenty of suggestions out there about what to eat to get the girl or boy you want, but can what you eat really determine the sex of your baby?

It is not guaranteed, but it may be possible to sway the odds slightly. One theory holds that eating certain foods alters the pH of the vaginal environment, making it more hospitable to X (female) or Y (male) sperm. It seems that X sperm prefer more acidic conditions, while Y sperm fare better in alkaline conditions. Some believe that the crucial factor is the ratio of sodium and potassium to calcium and magnesium in your diet. If you want a boy, then you need to consume more sodium and potassium, so foods such as meat, sausages and other salty meat products, bananas, rice and pasta are recommended. At the same time, you need to cut down on calcium- and magnesium-rich foods such as milk and dairy products, ice cream, nuts, pulses, chocolate, spinach and wholemeal bread. If you're dreaming of all things pink, however, you should do the opposite – consume less salt and more milk and chocolate.

Another theory, based on animal experiments, suggests that fat intake is crucial to sex selection. For years, scientists observed that animals in the wild were more likely to have male offspring if they were eating well. So researchers altered the fat intake of laboratory mice to see how their offspring were affected. They found that mice with diets high in saturated fat were twice as likely to produce male babies as female babies. Mice on a low-fat, high-carbohydrate diet, by contrast, were more likely to have female babies.

The most recent research with pregnant women found that a high-calorie diet and eating breakfast cereal regularly increased the chances of having a boy. Scientists from the University of Exeter divided women into three groups according to their calorie intake, and found that 56% of those in the high-calorie group had boys compared to 45% of those in the low-calorie group. The idea that eating more calories, like eating a higher-fat diet, increases the chances of having a boy makes evolutionary sense, as boy babies are usually bigger. So female bodies may have evolved mechanisms that favour the conception of boy babies when food is plentiful. Interestingly, what was eaten for breakfast seemed to have the biggest impact. Among women who had breakfast cereal daily, 59% had a boy, compared to 43% of those who ate cereal less than once a week. The reason for this isn't known, but it could have something to do with higher mineral intakes among cereal eaters.

On the whole, when it comes to diet and sex selection, it is probably wiser to leave it to fate. The suggested dietary manipulations are not particularly good for you or your baby, whatever sex they turn out to be. Consuming lots of salt or saturated fat or restricting your intake of certain minerals is unhealthy and certainly not ideal when trying for a baby. In any case, at best the diet can only slightly alter your chances of conceiving a child that is the 'right' sex. Some experts put the success rate at about 50% – i.e. the same as doing nothing. Alternatively, you could look at methods that don't involve manipulating your diet, such as only having sex at certain stages of your menstrual cycle or changing sexual positions. These are based more firmly on scientific principle and have a better chance of success. To conceive a girl, it may help to have frequent sex after menstruation but to abstain for two or three days before and after ovulation. For a boy, avoiding sex in the days before ovulation, and ejaculation deep into the vagina is advised.

A little extra – should you take supplements?

If you are healthy and eating a balanced diet, there should be no need to take supplements, apart from folic acid, which all women are advised to take when trying to conceive. However, if you have been trying for a baby for some time without success, evidence suggests that a multivitamin and mineral supplement may help. Vitamin D deficiency has been found to be particularly common among women finding it hard to become pregnant. One study found that women with healthy vitamin D levels when they went for IVF treatment were more likely to become pregnant. Make sure you choose a supplement that is specifically formulated for pre-conception and pregnancy. Also, think of it as an extra boost not a substitute for healthy eating.

Having trouble conceiving?

If you haven't become pregnant as quickly as you had hoped, try to relax. Some couples find that they conceive their first baby very easily, but second time around it takes longer than expected. This is called secondary infertility and appears to be a growing problem. It may be because women are delaying motherhood until fertility levels are starting to drop anyway, and they are then that little bit older when they try for number two. Also, having already had a baby, women may be more relaxed and less worried about eating 'fertility foods' or having sex at the right time of the month.

If you are trying to get pregnant either for the first time or to expand your family, don't get frustrated. This may be easier said than done, but the statistics may comfort you: 84% of couples conceive within the first year of trying, and even if you're not in this group you could be among the 92% who manage it within two years. Before suspecting more complex problems, make sure you address simpler issues such as your weight. Research has shown that both underweight and overweight women increase their chances of conception when they gain or lose weight, respectively. You may feel happy with your current weight, but making the necessary changes, so that your BMI is within the 18.5–25 range, could save you going through difficult, possibly expensive, fertility treatment.

An unhealthy lifestyle may not seem to harm some women's chances of getting pregnant. But for others, it can be enough to tip the balance. So, as well as addressing any weight issues, look carefully at every aspect of your diet, including your intake of alcohol and caffeine. As mentioned above, supplements may also help. In addition, you might like to look at your intake of vitamin B_6, which is found in fish and certain nuts and vegetables. A study of Chinese textile workers found that low intakes of vitamin B_6 reduced the chances of conception.

Of course, diet isn't everything. Don't overlook the obvious issues, such as having regular sex around the time of ovulation. Your partner can optimise his fertility too by improving his general health. If you both need to make lifestyle changes, then you can support each other. If you are still worried or have been trying to get pregnant for more than a year without success then talk to your GP. If you're over 35 or already know you may have fertility problems then see your GP sooner.

Resources and useful contacts

Allergy UK

Charity providing support and information for those with allergies and intolerances.

www.allergyuk.org
Helpline: 01322 619 898

Association of Breastfeeding Mothers

National breastfeeding helpline and online support.

www.abm.me.uk
Helpline: 0300 330 5453

Breastfeeding Network (BfN)

Drop-in clinics plus help and support by phone and online.

www.breastfeedingnetwork.org.uk
Helpline: 0300 100 0212
Drugline: 0844 412 4665 (for information about taking prescription drugs while breastfeeding)

Cry-sis

Support for families coping with excessively crying, sleepless and demanding babies.

www.cry-sis.org.uk
Helpline: 08451 228 669 (9 a.m. to 10 p.m. every day)

Diabetes UK

Information, advice, support groups, apps for diabetics and those with gestational diabetes.

www.diabetes.org.uk
Careline: 0345 123 2399 (9 a.m. to 7 p.m. Monday to Friday)

Healthy Start

Government scheme providing free supplements and food vouchers for pregnant women and mothers of young children on a low income.

www.healthystart.nhs.uk

La Leche League

Local support groups and helpline with calls being taken by mothers in their own homes.

www.laleche.org.uk
Breastfeeding helpline: 0845 120 2918 (any time)

MIND

Metal health charity providing information, support and details about help available locally. Includes information about anxiety in pregnancy and postnatal depression.

www.mind.org.uk
Tel: 0300 123 3393

NCT (formerly the National Childbirth Trust)

Organises antenatal classes and provides advice and local support for pregnancy and early childhood.

www.nct.org.uk
General enquiries: 0300 330 0770

NHS 111

Free NHS non-emergency help at any time.
Enquiries: 111

www.nhs.uk
Information about medical conditions, nutrients and healthy eating.

Samaritans

Confidential emotional support for yourself or someone else by phone or online.

www.samaritans.org
Tel: 116 123 (free at any time)

Tamba (Twins and Multiple Births Association)

Information and support network for parents of multiples.

www.tamba.org.uk
Twinline: freephone 0800 138 0509 (10 a.m. to 1 p.m. and 7 p.m. to 10 p.m. every day)

Tommy's

Website providing information about pre-pregnancy and pregnancy and advice on particular problems such as pre-eclampsia and toxoplasmosis.

www.tommys.org

Vegan Society

Provides information for vegans.

www.vegansociety.com

Tel: 0121 523 1730 (9.00 a.m. to 5 p.m. Monday to Friday)

Vegetarian Society

Charity providing information and advice, including lots of recipes. Calls welcome about any aspect of vegetarianism.

www.vegsoc.org

Tel: 0161 925 2000 (9 a.m. to 5 p.m. Monday to Friday)

Index